Sikh History and Religion
in the Twentieth Century

South Asian Studies Papers

South Asian Studies Papers, no. 3

Sikh History and Religion in the Twentieth Century

edited in Toronto by
Joseph T. O'Connell
Milton Israel
Willard G. Oxtoby

with visiting editors
W.H. McLeod
J.S. Grewal

University of Toronto
Centre for South Asian Studies
1988

Published by the Centre for South Asian Studies, University of Toronto, Room 2057, 100 St. George Street, Toronto, Ontario M5S 1A1, Canada

Copyright © 1988 by the Centre for South Asian Studies
Printed in Canada

ISBN 0-9692907-4-8 (hard cover)
ISBN 0-9692907-5-6 (soft cover)

SECOND PRINTING

Canadian Cataloguing in Publication Data

Main entry under title:

Sikh history and religion in the twentieth century

(South Asian Studies papers; no. 3)

Bibliography: pp. 457-486
ISBN 0-9692907-4-8 (bound) – ISBN 0-9692907-5-6 (pbk.)

1. Sikhism – 20th century. 2. Sikhs – History – 20th century.
I. O'Connell, Joseph Thomas. II. Israel, Milton. III. Oxtoby, Willard Gurdon.
IV. University of Toronto. Centre for South Asian Studies. V. Series.

BL2018.S54 1988   294.6′09′04   C88-094788-8

Frontispiece and jacket illustration: the Golden Temple, Amritsar
Photographed early morning, January 17, 1982, by Willard G. Oxtoby

Contents

Part 1. Religion and Culture

Part 2. History and Politics: India

Part 3. History and Society: Diaspora

Part 4. Comments on Recent Events

Acknowledgments

Generous financial support for both the 1987 conference on which this book was based, and for the publication itself, has been provided by the following government agencies and private foundations: Department of the Secretary of State of Canada (Multiculturalism Sector), Ottawa; Social Sciences and Humanities Research Council of Canada, Ottawa; Asia Pacific Foundation, Vancouver; Donner Canadian Foundation, Toronto; Smithsonian Institution, Washington.

Financial and moral support for the conference and for other aspects of Sikh-related scholarship in the University of Toronto has been given by a number of private individuals, mainly Sikh men and women, who are listed separately at the end of this volume. Suresh Pal Singh Bhalla, Gurdass (Gary) Singh and Amrik Singh of Toronto deserve special acknowledgment for co-ordinating this initiative in community support. We are pleased to cite those individuals whose generosity qualifies them to be listed as Patrons within the Presidents' Committee of the University of Toronto (with its federated universities): Guremez S. Bains, Savinder Singh Bhasin, Suresh Pal Singh Bhalla, Baljit Singh Chadha, and Brigadier D.S. Jind. We are especially appreciative of the very substantial contribution of Harbanse (Herb) S. Doman, which places him in the rank of Benefactor within the Presidents' Committee.

The Centre for South and Southeast Asia Studies, University of California, Berkeley (especially Jane Singh and Mark Juergensmeyer) co-operated in many ways, especially in securing Smithsonian Institution support for travel of scholars to the Toronto conference enroute to one immediately thereafter in Berkeley. Several universities—notably Rabindra Bharati University, Calcutta—and other institutions assisted individual scholars to travel to Toronto. Many scholars invited as respondents came to Toronto at their own expense. To all of these we are most grateful.

The University of Toronto, together with St. Michael's College and University College, provided helpful institutional support for both the conference and the volume. The Administrative Assistant of the Centre for South Asian Studies, University of Toronto, Shirley Uldall, has been unfailingly competent, gracious and generous in facilitating all phases of our work. Assisting her were Janet Rubinoff, Arlene Koteff, Jennifer Motha and Sarah Uldall. A number of students and former students have assisted in various ways, notably Pashaura Singh, Louis Fenech, Harpreet Singh Dhariwal, Jasject Kaur Dhariwal, Navneet Singh Arora, Gurbinder Singh Gill and Sonya Dhillon.

Brian Longstaff and the London [Ontario] Actors Showcase Theatre, through arrangements made by T. Sher Singh, presented a moving rendition of Sharon Pollock's drama "The Komagata Maru Incident." They all remain in our debt. Bhupinder (Laly) Singh Marwah and Marlène Marwah provided a display of Sikh memorabilia for the conference. Participants were grateful for the gracious hospitality of Beverly Israel. The editors appreciate the many ways in which Kathleen O'Connell helped with the conference and the preparation of the volume.

Page design and extensive file checking, stylistic editing and preparation of the text for camera-ready copy were the work of Willard G. Oxtoby. The contribution that Will has made in in the final six months of the project, in editorial stylistic revision, computer coaxing, and checking and proofreading has been truly herculean. Without his skills and stamina and the support of his spouse, Julia Ching, it would have taken many months longer to bring out the book. Page preparation was done using the word-processing program FinalWord II™, and PostScript® for laser printing. The support and facilities of the University of Toronto Computing Services, especially John Bradley, and of the Centre for Computing in the Humanities at the University of Toronto, are gratefully acknowledged. Offset printing of the book was done at the Coach House Press, Toronto, with the co-operation of Stan Bevington. The standards established by Narendra K. Wagle as series editor, and his advice for this volume, are much appreciated.

The most enthusiastic acknowledgment must be reserved for Margaret McLeod. Her constant support has been crucial to her husband's dramatic recovery from the stroke that laid him low on the eve of 1987 conference. In scarcely a year and a half Hew has resumed writing, editing, teaching, chairing his department at Otago, and in September 1988 returns to Toronto as visiting professor of Sikh history and religion. To Margaret go the thanks of the entire editorial panel and the cordial good wishes of all the conference participants.

Introduction

The Editors

This volume grows out of a conference, also entitled "Sikh History and Religion in the Twentieth Century," held at the University of Toronto, February 13-15, 1987. The conference itself was a significant event. It was the first academic gathering of its kind in Canada on Sikh scholarship, and probably the largest gathering ever, anywhere, of scholars expert on twentieth-century Sikh experience worldwide. It also provided a unique opportunity for a number of individuals beyond the university, especially Sikh men and women, to observe scholars proposing and debating their analyses of modern Sikh history and religion. Nearly a century of historical background leads up to the present situations in which Sikhs in Canada, in India, and elsewhere in the world find themselves.

The conference and the volume have eventuated as the result of a range of converging influences. There is, for instance, the mandate of the University of Toronto's Centre for South Asian Studies to teach and advance research on all aspects of the history and cultures of South Asia, notably of India with its plurality of regions and cultures. There is also the significant presence of a large "diaspora" concentration of Canadian Sikhs living in the province of Ontario, especially in the immediate environment of Toronto; many of these are keen to encourage study of Sikh history and religion. A third feature in the planning of the conference, a kind of "catalyst" for it, was the presence of the New Zealand scholar W.H. ("Hew") McLeod in Toronto. Hew, a senior scholar of Sikh religious history, was a visiting Commonwealth Fellow in the University's Centre for Religious Studies in the months of planning preceding the conference, though he was prevented by illness from actually attending. A final factor influencing the occasion was the current crisis in Sikh life, stemming from the tensions between certain political interests in Punjab and other interests in India, especially those concentrated at the political Centre, in Delhi.

If all these influences have made serious study of Sikh history and religion possible at this particular time and place, the last, regrettably, makes such study all the more urgent. Fast-breaking events in the ongoing conflict in India require that analysis be updated constantly. Indeed, we would like to have brought out this volume sooner, but the very size, complexity and importance of the undertaking have forced us to give care and quality higher priorities than haste. We hope that the result will be informative for all who read it and refer back to it, and that it may encourage and help focus further study and research. We dare to hope also that the book may to some degree foster more accurately informed and constructive relationships between Sikhs and non-Sikhs, both in South Asia and overseas, but especially in Canada.

Overview of the Volume

This volume, *Sikh History and Religion in the Twentieth Century*, follows the sequence of papers presented at the February 1987 Conference in Toronto, though enlarged by six papers (two in Part One, four in Part Three), by this introduction, a postscript, a glossary and a bibliography. We organize the papers under the broad categories "Religion and Culture" (Part One), "History and Politics: India" (Part Two), "History and Society: Diaspora" (Part Three) and "Comments on Recent Events" (Part Four). We have tried to represent most of the salient aspects of Sikh experience in the present century. In all cases authors have been asked to write on topics in which they are known to be expert. Most have supplied substantial notes, which may serve as reference points for further study. We have added a bibliography on the Sikh experience both in the Punjab and overseas, and a glossary (with brief definitions and alternative acceptable spellings).

This volume will serve, we hope, as an authoritative account of the topics covered and as a reference volume for at least a few years' time in this volatile period. By choosing the twentieth century as our period we have sought to address very recent events, but with enough historical (as well as religio-cultural) background to allow us to begin to make some sense out of recent events and current crises. At the very least, we want to challenge current stereo-types—simplistic, sensationalist and violence-inducing—by presenting a richer, sounder panorama of who Sikhs are, whence they have come and what has been their experience in the twentieth century.

Part One begins with J.S. Grewal's background chapter, a magisterial survey of the pre-twentieth century legacy of the Sikh past—stressing as salient points "Holy Granth, the doctrine of *Guru-Panth*, *raj karega khalsa*, social differentiation and ideological differentiation within the Sikh Panth."[1]   W.H. McLeod's chapter follows. It consists of a tentative outline of topics needing to be treated in any systematic treatment of Sikh theology in modern times. The perennial question in the background of this discussion regards the translatability of religious concepts: can someone brought up in one cultural heritage understand the individual ideas of another culture? Wisdom suggests, of course, that we do understand by working out analogically from the conceptual framework we already possess. Thus, as with all analogies, it is as important to

---

1. "Panth" is a widely used Punjabi term referring to the Sikh community. For this, as for other technical terms, see the glossary at the end of this volume.

specify differences (aspects of the analogy that do not hold) as well as similarities (the aspects that do). McLeod addresses the matter at the level of terminology and vocabulary, holding out for a recognition of the difference and specificity of key Sikh religious terms when one renders them into English. Amarjit S. Sethi complements McLeod's "outsider's" essay with his own "insider's" reflections on one specific focus of Sikh theology, *nam-simaran*, in its ethical and spiritual aspects. Mark Juergensmeyer combines theological sensitivity and empirical religio-historical scholarship to examine a movement closely related to the Sikh tradition and yet dissimiliar in crucial respects, the Radhasoami movement. He thus provides an occasion for considering the meaning of orthodoxy and heterodoxy as pertaining to the Sikhs.

The next two chapters explore "secular" dimensions of Sikh values. Surjit Hans, social and literary historian, carries out a twentieth-century reappropriation of the message of *gurbani* and *bhagatbani* of the Adi Granth in ways supportive of social justice and the "secular" values of India's pluralistic system. Darshan Singh Maini, critic of English and Punjabi literatures, explores the creative tension of "religious" and "secular" strains in twentieth-century Punjabi poetry. The evolution of Punjabi language itself, even within the short span of the present century, is the focus of the chapter by Christopher Shackle, scholar of Punjabi and Urdu languages and literatures. Himadri Banerjee, Calcutta-based socio-cultural historian, concludes Part One with an extensively documented account of how scholars and creative writers using the Bengali language have perceived Sikhs from the latter part of the nineteenth century to the present. His contribution is a model inviting comparable studies of how over time and in diverse parts of the subcontinent Sikhs have been perceived by others.

Beginning Part Two ("History and Politics: India"), Harjot S. Oberoi, anthropologically attuned historian, demonstrates the depth and extent of shared Hindu and Sikh patterns of social, cultural and religious life—especially as expressed in rituals marking the life-cycle—prior to the extensive alterations effected by the Singh Sabha movement in the late nineteenth and early twentieth centuries. The Singh Sabha movement itself, in particular the Chief Khalsa Diwan as prime agent of co-ordination within the Panth and for a generation or more the Panth's chief voice *vis-à-vis* the government and diverse non-Sikh interests and institutions, is the subject of Punjab historian N. Gerald Barrier's thoroughly documented chapter. Mohinder Singh, also a historian, takes up the next major institutional articulation of the Sikh Panth, the Akali Dal, analyzing especially its effective non-violent movement for gurdwara reform, its strenuous but unsuccessful attempts to head off partition of the Punjab, and its problematic efforts to secure and govern a unilingual Punjabi state since the independence of India.

Historian Ian Kerr assesses the theoretical achievements and empirical problems of anthropologist Richard Fox's book, *Lions of the Punjab*, and urges scholars of matters Sikh to emulate Fox by situating research on the Punjab and on Sikhs within more universal discipline-wide theoretical frameworks and debates, rather than confining it to an academic enclave of Sikh/Punjabi studies. Attar Singh departs—upon request—from his usual forte of Punjabi literature to provide a brief but incisive analysis of the Shiromani Gurdwara Prabandhak Committee, an institution that since the 1920's has steadily extended the scope of its influence to become a quasi-church with theocratic tendencies, challenging the secular state that initially sanctioned it and still provides its legal standing. Historian Indu Banga meticulously reviews Sikh (especially Akali) leaders' attempts to prevent partition of the Punjab and to secure the interests of the Sikhs by a variety of options (including the Azad Punjab scheme) within a united India and briefly, as a last resort, by countering the Pakistan proposal with the proposal of an autonomous Sikh state. Political scientist Paul Wallace concludes Part Two with a chapter in which he argues that Sikh anxiety as a threatened minority has been exacerbated by excessive insistence by the Congress Party, usually dominant at the federal level, to be dominant even at the Punjab state level; he recommends a less centralized, more accommodating revision of Indian federalism.

Part Three deals with the recent history of the Sikhs in the diaspora overseas, in Canada, the United States and England. Norman Buchignani, anthropologist and ethnic historian, begins with a chapter on method and theory pertaining to Sikh diaspora research. He argues for giving greater attention to cultural factors, and not simply to utilitarian ones, and urges greater co-ordination and methodological awareness in research in this field. Historian Hugh Johnston then sifts through the data on early Sikh and other Indian immigration into Canada and the United States and finds that it was almost entirely male, motivated largely by economic interests, in many cases not intended initially to be permanent, and was severely checked by xenophobic and racist restrictions to Asian immigration in force until the late 1940's. Next anthropologist Karen Leonard depicts in a disciplined but humane fashion the poignant experience of Sikh men in California, their Mexican-American wives and their offspring, the so-called "Mexican-Hindus." She reports on their problematic status once relaxation of immigration laws facilitated marriage with women from the Punjab and led to an influx of new Sikh immigration that overwhelmed numerically the small Mexican-American Sikh community. Verne A. Dusenbery, also an anthropologist specializing in diaspora Sikh communities, examines a case of reciprocal ambivalences and misunderstandings among Sikhs in the North American diaspora, i.e., between *gora* (white) Sikh converts (in particular, followers of Harbhajan Singh, "Yogi Bhajan," in the Healthy, Happy, Holy Organization, 3HO) and immigrant Punjabi Sikhs.

Arthur W. Helweg, migration historian, chronicles the rapidly changing conditions of life in the "receiving community" (in Gravesend, England) as well as in the "sending community" (in Jandiali, Punjab) and the significant mutual influences between the two, especially the deep repercussions in the "sending community," which may well be a microcosm typical of rural Punjab in the period of the Green Revolution. Eleanor Nesbitt, scholar of ethnic relations, contributes a bibliographic survey with content analysis showing how Sikhs have been portrayed in Britain in recent books of fiction and non-fiction intended for school-age children. Religious historian Owen Cole concludes Part Three with a broad conspectus of issues and developments (including the loss of Punjabi language and corresponding concern for the use of English in Sikh worship) facing Sikhs in England and applicable elsewhere in the diaspora. He observes that some of these issues and developments may well have impact upon Sikh institutions in the Punjab.

Two chapters in Part Four, "Comments on Recent Events," are by distinguished Sikh thinkers resident in Delhi. They include well-informed description and analysis, to be sure, but they go beyond this. The authors attempt to interpret and evaluate events and trends that are current, complex and controversial. They offer criticism, make recommendations, and hazard guesses as to the future. It is hardly possible to be definitive in one's views of current and controversial events and next to impossible not to be affected by emotions and loyalties, least of all if one is a Sikh and living in Delhi or Punjab. Yet we, as editors, think that we have chosen well in asking Amrik Singh and Patwant Singh to provide these articulate comments on recent events. While we do not necessarily endorse all of their respective statements, we consider them reasonable and responsible readings of the evidence of recent events as arising out of their historical background.

Patwant Singh, writer and editor, vigorously challenges what he considers false and destructive stereotypes (spread, he alleges, by government and private communications media), namely, that Sikhs as such are, or have been, opposed to participation in a united India and that Sikhs as such are responsible for or condone recent violence in Punjab, Delhi, and elsewhere. He is sharply critical of the custodians of the Harmandir Sahib (Golden Temple) for repeatedly allowing the most sacred sanctuary of Sikhs to be used by armed militants and thus exposed to desecration. He is severely critical of the present government at the Centre in India for its alleged role in communalizing Centre-Punjab politics and for failing to prosecute those responsible for the massacre of Sikhs in Delhi in 1984.

Amrik Singh, senior educationist and editor, paints a final panorama of trends affecting Sikhs in this century and on into the next. He charts the implications of demographics (e.g., concentration of Jat Sikhs in a single Indian state since 1956, emigration of many Sikhs to other parts of India and overseas) on recent Sikh history. He urges a return to constructive economic development-based politics, in place of the emotion-laden preoccupation with "national integrity" issues and the attendant downward spiralling pattern of repression-terrorism that has gained momentum in the 1980's. He notes the widespread influence of organized crime and corruption in the current malaise affecting Punjab and Punjab-Centre relationships. He calls upon Sikhs to revitalize their gurdwaras as centres of religious advancement and to commit themselves to secular education as well.

The final statement in Part Four is a brief postscript, "The View from Toronto," by Joseph T. O'Connell, a Toronto religious-studies scholar. He addresses several issues bearing on Sikh experience in the context of contemporary Canadian efforts to define and implement what is emerging as multiculturalism. While the incidents and developments noted are for the most part contentious and controversial—the Air India disaster and its investigation, proposed tightening of refugee immigration procedures, dress code restrictions in Canada—he sees the experience of "being locked in argument" as confirming an underlying civility that is being strengthened through the very process of confrontation, negotiation and debate.

References and Usage

We have included a glossary of terms in Punjabi that occur within the book or are of importance for an understanding of matters Sikh. We give the terms in the order of the Latin alphabet according to the simplified spelling we have favoured in the book. This spelling approximates pronunciation, but does not claim a rigorous matching (if that be possible) between spelling and (variable) pronunciation of Indian vernacular language words.

For simplicity, in the main body of the book we restrict the use of diacritical marks to terms and names in European languages. In the glossary, however, we do offer more systematic transliterations with diacritical marks for Punjabi. We provide, also, spellings in the Gurmukhi script. We then add a brief definition or comment. Credit for the glossary goes in large measure to Pashaura Singh, currently a Ph.D. candidate in the Centre for Religious Studies, University of Toronto.

Authors of the respective chapters are not responsible for the spellings and transliterations we have inflicted upon their texts in the interests of simplicity and in an attempt at consistency. One particular case, the first vowel of "Punjab" and "Punjabi" (which we have preferred to "Panjab" and "Panjabi"), deserves brief mention. We have opted for "u" against the technically more appropriate "a," both for its greater frequency in what we have found in past and current writing and for its suggesting the "un" sound, as in "pun" and "fun" in contrast with the "an" sound, as in "pan" and "fan." Also, we have tended, perhaps old-fashionedly, to call the general region of the five rivers "the Punjab." We have tried to restrict use of "Punjab" without the article to the (smaller) Indian state currently, since 1966, so named and constituted.

In matters of form and style, a more substantial decision was to permit international variation in spelling while striving for uniformity in punctuation. In spelling, our authors are divisible into three groups: 1) those located in Britain, India and elsewhere in the Commonwealth, excluding Canada; 2) those located in the United States; and 3) those located in Canada. We have tried to maintain spelling conventions appropriate to the area of the author's residence.

In the process, we have become more conscious of the recurring differences among these regions' orthographies.

British and Indian usage prefers a "u" in words like "colour," "behaviour" and "mould",[2] whereas in United States usage the corresponding spellings are "color," "behavior" and "mold." Also, as a rule, British and Indian usage prefers to double the final consonant of an unaccented syllable before adding the past or passive suffix "-ed," as in "worshipped," "benefitted," "focussed," whereas in the United States such doubling generally does not occur. Another salient class of contrasts is represented by British and Indian "organise," "modernisation," "realising" compared with the United States usage "organize," "modernization," "realizing." Canadian usage, interestingly enough, turns out to be systematically hybrid, drawing no doubt both on its historical links with Britain and on its geographical proximity to the United States. The style we adhere to for our contributors from Canada thus prefers British usage in the first two categories in the examples just given ("colour" and "worshipped") but North American usage in the third ("organize").

To counter the centrifugal effects of the diversity of spelling, our editorial policy has been to impose a degree of uniformity across the various chapters in matters of capitalization, punctuation, and the use of italics. Terms from languages other than English are italicized, unless in our judgment they have become domesticated in nonspecialist English vocabulary. Thus "yogi" is now an English word, and so, in our judgment and for this book, is "gurdwara." Terms that function in the text as proper names, such as "Khalsa" and "Panth," are capitalized without italics. Only the titles of published volumes, as a rule, receive both capitalization and italicization. But the names of religious scriptures, and of the portions thereof, are as a rule not italicized. Usage thus forces authors and editors in the field of religion to discriminate between those works that they hold to be scriptures and those they do not. Fortunately for the study of the Sikh tradition, scriptural status is comparatively clearly delineated by doctrine, with the result that the Adi Granth (or Guru Granth Sahib) and Dasam Granth appear in roman type but the *janam-sakhis*, *rahit-namas* and other literature in italics.

The common format we have imposed on notes and references, to the extent that available information has permitted it, is probably more familiar to scholars in North America than in Britain and India. Scholars in historical and literary fields, moreover, will likely find themselves somewhat more at home in our citation format than social scientists will. Given the ease of placing notes at the foot of the page in the word-processing technology we have used, we have tried to improve the readability of the text by moving most references out to

---

2. The "u" is retained before English suffixes of non-Latin function, as in "moulding," "neighbourhood" and "honourable." On the other hand, the "u" is generally dropped before suffixes of Latin type, as in "honorary" and "behavioral," and before any suffixes whatever that contain "u," as in "colorful" and "humorous."

footnotes, even when these are only the author-and-year references characteristic of writing in the social sciences.

For the spellings of authors' names and use of initials, we have tried to use the authors' own preferences.

In order that this volume may have a wider usefulness as a reference for further study, we have included a bibliography of works in English. The core of this has been supplied by J.S. Grewal. That core has been supplemented especially in two respects. A number of citations on the diaspora Sikh experience have been added. And, by way of introduction, a bibliographical essay is furnished discussing basic books and articles in English on Sikh history and religion, which would be of principal interest and relevance to the beginning student or general reader.

In the bibliography and other lists, the element of a name following "Singh" or "Kaur," if one is present, such as "Maini," is used for alphabetization. Names that end in "Singh" or "Kaur" will be found alphabetized under the element preceding, such as "Khushwant." In one instance, however, namely, the list of manuals on ritual at the end of Harjot S. Oberoi's chapter, we have retained the chronological sequence he provided, rather than attempting alphabetization.

Academic Perspectives: Contemporary Relevance

Academics are, or should be, theorists. But "the proof of the pudding is in the eating," as it is said, and the test of any theoretically formulated academic analysis is how well it actually facilitates grappling with the material at hand. Now though academics may adopt a clinical-looking air of detachment, they cannot long escape touching on two volatile topic areas: politics and religion. These two areas, tabooed as conversation topics in some circles precisely because of the passionate individual commitments they can often display, put the serious scholar on his or her mettle. The writer may well need to identify as a commitment his or her own position, and yet establish credibility by dealing "at arm's length," as it were, with the very substance of that commitment, in a way such that others who do not share it can recognize the description as valid and the analysis as responsible.

In this section and the one following, the editorial panel is indebted in particular to a draft by one of our number, Hew McLeod. Here we treat the relevance of Sikh studies to the current highly inflamed political context. We subsequently go on to reflect on the stance of the academic analyst who is an observer of religion. Discussing religion is like sailing between Scylla and Charybdis. On the one hand, we wish to steer a course that avoids the reductionistic stance of those who dismiss   religion out of hand. On the other, it would be inappropriate in an academic context to surrender uncritically to the faith-claims or the particularist identity of whatever community is under discussion.

First, then, to the reflections on the dilemmas posed by the political context of the scholar's work.

The current crisis in the Punjab is a tragedy, one that has added alienation and deepening hostility to suffering and death. Nothing that we may say should ever conceal this fact or imply that it is anything less than a disaster. As in all such situations, however, there are consolations to be acknowledged. These can be recognized without suggesting that they compensate for the misery or justify the damage that has been done. One such consolation concerns those of us who endeavour to develop an intellectual understanding of the Sikh tradition. As a result of recent events, there now exists an interest in Sikh matters and a prospect for advancing understanding seldom, if ever, experienced in the past. There also exist problems, some deriving from present circumstances and others of a more chronic nature.

For the Sikh people there is value to be derived from the significantly heightened awareness of Sikh identity that the crisis has produced. Some will perceive a related gain in the attention that Sikh history, religion and society are receiving from the world at large. The need for a deeper study of the tradition has been recognized by individuals within the Sikh community, as well as by others, prompting an interest and an activity that would have been inconceivable as late as four years ago. It is, needless to say, a long-overdue concern, and attempts to supply background material for analyses of the crisis have shown just how unprepared we are to meet the need.

Journalists and commentators quite rightly appreciate that some explaining is needed if their readers or listeners are to understand the nature of the crisis and the various Sikh responses to it. Their efforts dramatically demonstrate the extent to which scholars have failed them. Invariably, it seems, one can expect a brief reference to Sikhism as "a syncretistic derivative of Hinduism and Islam," which later developed into a "militant sect"—a far cry from a Sikh self-understanding as an independent and autonomous tradition with a devotional and peace-seeking spirituality. Normally one will find little more. Whatever the reasons, the usual rule has been one of inadequate research and persistent misunderstanding. It is true that the years since the mid-sixties have produced a flow of books and periodicals unequalled since the heady days of the Singh Sabha revival. It should also be acknowledged, however, that relatively little of this material represents sound, critical, documented research. Much of the output is based on dated assumptions inherited from the Singh Sabha period, and a certain amount should really be regarded as apologetic defense of the tradition rather than as detached analysis. The effect is certainly not limited to works produced within the Sikh community, the Panth. Interpretations developed by Singh Sabha scholars extend their influence well beyond the Punjab, and if one should seek the truly superficial, the best place to look will be in Western works that specialize in summary statements of the tradition.

Needless to say, comments of this kind betray an obvious bias, one that will certainly be contested by many of the writers who have contributed to the recent and continuing flow of literature. Critical scholarship of the Western variety has been vigorously attacked, whether as the vehicle for a misconceived, patronizing "Orientalism" or as an arid discipline that chokes the well-springs of spirit and experience. No excuse is offered for this bias, nor is there any present intention of abandoning it. The bias is one that readily acknowledges that apologetic is a perfectly legitimate activity and that words spoken from the heart should be heard with profound respect. Both make essential contributions to the total task of understanding any culture. A serious problem arises only when either acts as a substitute for detached analysis. If it be contended that detached analysis is an ideal impossible to realize fully, this rejoinder can be accepted without conceding that the ideal should be abandoned. Emphatically, it should not be abandoned. If critical scholarship be the choice, detached analysis must remain the ideal.

Since this is our choice and since future directions are our immediate concern, a first priority must surely be to identify the problems that currently inhibit progress and those that we should anticipate in the near future. Some of these problems can be attributed directly to the present political crisis in India, one which so obviously and so directly affects the Panth. Although these constraints may be serious at present, we can reasonably expect that if political solutions are found their influence will gradually diminish. Other issues must be regarded as permanent, or at least as long-term or recurrent. Some can be identified as general problems of the kind which are endemic in all areas of social-science research. Others are peculiar to Sikh studies.

Among the difficulties created by recent events in India, one stands out: the arousing of exceedingly strong feelings. Under present circumstances, it can be extremely difficult to preserve scholarly detachment as a practical ideal. Although a reasonable approximation to the ideal may be sustained, there can nevertheless be strong pressures inhibiting the publication of facts or interpretations.

Circumstances such as those created by the present turmoil can also serve to distract careful, balanced scholarship by reinforcing a cluster of common stereotypes. Some of these are merely misleading. Others are more damaging, and a few are positively dangerous. The influence of stereotypes is, of course, a problem all social science research encounters. As such, it can be treated as one of the general issues Sikh studies share with other areas of inquiry. Stereotypes are a particularly serious problem when the topic of research concerns a living religious tradition.

Academic Perspectives: "Outsiders" and "Insiders"

Research that relates to a living religious tradition necessarily requires sensitivity and a considerable delicacy of approach. Mere courtesy is not enough, though it is a first essential. The ideal approach is one that combines empathy with academic detachment. If that combination should seem to be a contradiction, it will serve to illustrate the complexity of this particular problem.

Each of us must make his or her own choices, recognizing that there will be wide differences of opinion concerning the manner in which we should proceed.

We who are editing this volume indicate our own choice when we affirm a combination of empathy and academic detachment. In so doing, we contest any claim that these two objectives are contradictory in theory or inconsistent in practice. This claim will probably seem much more relevant to the situation of the outsider than to the Sikh scholar working on his or her own tradition. Yet it can reasonably be maintained that the twin ideals of detachment and empathy are as appropriate for the scholar who stands inside the tradition as for the inquirer who looks in from outside. Each, in his or her own way, must recognize the need for a balance and articulate the criteria of reasonableness, if not of that elusive goal, "objectivity."

No one who is not himself or herself an adherent (or "insider") can pretend to study a living tradition adequately without maintaining regular contact with those who actually represent it. A certain kind of historian may make such claims, but for us at least they are impossible to sustain except in terms of the narrowest agendas of antiquarian inquiry. History is essentially meaningless if it does not relate to the contemporary present, and the present is arguably inaccessible to those who insulate themselves from the living tradition.

But while we do seek to communicate with the tradition and its believers, it is not with them alone. Those of us who affirm academic analysis as a worthy ideal and are concerned for the sensitivities of the believer share the arena with others who are distinctly skeptical about faith-affirmations of any sort. Our reaction to such skepticism should not be to dismiss it out of hand. It should be heard and considered with the same conscientious respect as the criticisms made by the believer. Neither should be ignored, for only by heeding both critics can the dual ideal of empathetic detachment be sustained. The problem, then, of how to deal with two distinct and radically different constituencies, with "true believers" on the one hand and "true disbelievers" on the other, is one that students of the Sikh tradition have in common with those who examine other religious traditions.

Two other problem areas in the study of contemporary religion may be briefly noted.

The first concerns the quantity and character of source materials. For the historian this may mean a shortage of sources for all but the modern period, a situation one certainly encounters in study of Sikhs. Those who focus their attention on present circumstances, nonetheless, encounter problems of interpretation. The outward forms of the tradition may be easily inspected, but the beliefs and conventions that lie behind the visible forms may be exceedingly complex. This, needless to say, is a challenge that the Western observer finds much more difficult to meet than does the scholar who has been nurtured within the tradition.

In the second problem area, language, we again find the outsider at a distinct disadvantage compared with many of the tradition's participants. It is axiomatic that in order to penetrate a culture one must master its principal language or languages.   In this regard the Sikh tradition is certainly no exception, and the need for a firm grasp of Punjabi is unlikely to be disputed. But while native speakers of Punjabi have an obvious advantage, if none also masters Persian or Braj they too will be evading a primary responsibility, for the literature of the Sikhs is not in Punjabi only. A casualty of limitation to Punjabi will be the history of the Panth during the eighteenth and early nineteenth centuries. The long-standing neglect of the Dasam Granth will also continue for as long as we assume that Punjabi is a sufficient means of access to the Sikh tradition.

One problem we can identify as specific to Sikh studies grows out of British influence in the Punjab from the second half of the nineteenth century. While, on the one hand, access to sources of information becomes easier for many outsiders because of the introduction of the English language, on the other hand, certain views that have gained currency in English have tended to monopolize modern interpretations of the Sikh tradition. It would be difficult to contest the claim that the rise of the Singh Sabha movement was unrelated to the recent arrival of the British in the Punjab. And no one is likely to question the transforming importance of the Singh Sabha movement.   It is, however, responsible for a major obstacle to our understanding of the Sikh tradition, one which is rendered all the more serious by virtue of its being so difficult to recognize.

The problem in this case is not the obvious one of inadequate research into Singh Sabha origins and strategies. That is indeed a serious issue, but at least it has been recognized as such, and some distinctly promising research is now under way. The problem derives from the remarkable measure of intellectual success achieved by a small group of Singh Sabha writers in formulating a distinctive interpretation of the Sikh tradition and in promulgating it as the only acceptable version of the tradition. Men such as Dit Singh, Vir Singh, Kahan Singh of Nabha, and M.A. Macauliffe are rightly regarded as writers of very substantial influence.

Singh Sabha scholars and writers were so successful in their attempt to reformulate the Sikh tradition that their general interpretation of the tradition acquired the status of implicit truth. That status it continues to hold to the present day. What this means is that most Punjabi scholars and virtually all Western students of Sikhism are nurtured on the Singh Sabha interpretation without any necessary or normal awareness of the actual nature of the process.

It is essential that we recognize the actual nature and extent of this influence and conditioning, if we are to comprehend the historical development of the Sikh tradition. This is not to suggest that outsiders are required to endorse or condemn it, declaring it to be true or false as a perception of reality. If any such task be undertaken, that must be reserved to those who are committed to the faith, not those who seek an academic understanding of the Panth's development and present circumstances. But those of us, Sikhs as well as non-Sikhs, who seek an academic understanding are confronted by the daunting task of separating ourselves from the Singh Sabha interpretation in order to scrutinize it anew.

The most conspicuous of the issues that will be raised by any such scrutiny will be that most basic of questions, the question of who is (and who is not) a Sikh. The general Sikh constituency seldom, if ever, hears about the Singh Sabha movement, yet it bears the marks of the movement's continuing influence. Those who are familiar with its history may also find the question of who is a Sikh to be superfluous. If so, the reason will almost certainly be the authoritative status of the Singh Sabha answer, an answer which demonstrates its strength by being so largely taken for granted. This does not deprive intellectual understanding of its importance, nor does it free students of the tradition from the obligation to be students.

This extended comment on the influence of the Singh Sabha should not distract us from other areas where significant scholarly work is being done—though rarely with as many able scholars as one might hope for—or should be done. One such area probably should not cause us very much anxiety, as there are by now many inquirers, professionally trained and casual, at work, namely the experience of Sikhs in the diaspora. There is a problem even here, however, and that problem is the weakness of background understanding among all but a few of the researchers. Attentions will inevitably tend to be focussed on the local context and will not necessarily be supported by a firm grasp of inherited Sikh tradition or its Punjabi setting. There are also problems of lack of co-ordination, unnecessary duplication and theoretical naïveté, which one expects will sooner or later be addressed as diaspora research develops.

It is the inherited tradition that presents the more worrying prospects, particularly those aspects of it that concern the earlier period of the tradition's development. The issue is serious enough to be addressed here, though the focus of this volume is the twentieth century. We should, we suggest, be genuinely concerned about the continuing neglect of the Gurus and their period, a two-hundred-year span of critically important history for which still very little has been offered in the way of detailed research or credible analysis. Where, for example, is a scholarly treatment of the life and work of Guru Arjan? And when were we ever offered a thorough examination of the contribution of Guru Hargobind? Are the policy changes of the early seventeenth century regarding the concept of *miri-piri* really so unimportant that we can entrust them to unscrutinized tradition?

Perhaps the most serious gap of all concerns the lifetime of Guru Gobind Singh and its immediate eighteenth-century aftermath. Some work has indeed been done in this area, the beginnings for a much larger task. However, we are still deprived of an essential range of understanding. A conspicuous deficiency, already mentioned, is the general reluctance to grapple effectively with the Dasam Granth. The period whence it comes is absolutely crucial, and until it is adequately treated we shall continue to grope in our efforts to trace the course of Sikh history or the development of the Sikh tradition.

Although the need is particularly acute in the case of the Panth's early centuries, it is by no means limited to them. The period of Partition is a modern example of the same kind of problem. It also serves as an example of another kind of problem. The events which precede and follow Partition plainly concern a far larger area than the Panth or the Punjab, yet the hesitant treatment which the Partition period has so far received within the context of Sikh history and politics has tended to treat it in isolation from the larger context. This particular example serves as a paradigm for a much more general approach. Sikh scholarship in general has remained out of touch with other scholarship, in terms both of methodology and also of shared or overlapping topics. Attention has already been drawn to the benefits which arguably can be derived from an awareness of the methods used in the scholarly study of religion. Another prominent example is supplied by the question of caste observance within the Panth. If we fail to maintain close contacts with anthropologists and sociologists who work on caste in other contexts we shall do more than deprive ourselves of valuable information and insights. We shall also invite justifiable accusations of limited understanding and weak analysis.

Close contact with anthropologists and sociologists should serve to raise issues many of us might otherwise ignore, or at least misconstrue. Scholarship relating to Sikhs has been heavily biassed in favour of historical analysis, and we have already acknowledged some of the problems created by the standard approach to such analysis. Other issues emerge when we expose the analysis to sociological and religious-studies scrutiny, an excellent example being the cluster of questions which our use of the word "religion" itself raises. It is far from being clearly defined, and if it is to be applied to the Sikh tradition some very careful explaining will be needed. We may also add political scientists to the list of useful allies, quite properly maintaining that the development of the Sikh tradition cannot be isolated from general issues of state and administration.

In pursuing such contacts we should heed yet another problem. From one point of view we should be grateful for any competent scholarship, regardless of its source. It is, however, possible for foreigners to exercise an excessive influence on the content and direction of scholarship, and it might well be claimed that this particular danger is looming ever larger on the Sikh-studies scene. The problem is not so much an increase in foreign participation as an apparent decline in Sikh numbers at precisely the time when those numbers should be increasing. If this claim seems exaggerated it can easily be tested by listing those Sikh scholars of distinction whose ages are less than sixty years and comparing this with the names of those who have passed the sixty-year mark. The result can be disquieting. Whatever the reasons may be, the results must cause increasing concern if the trend continues. "Outside" scholars do have a useful contribution to make, even if it should consist of asking questions rather than of delivering definitive answers. In the domain of social science, however, their credentials must always betray some major limitations. A significant range of understanding is bred in the bone, and no amount of interest or diligence will ever confer it on the foreigner.

Building for the Future

The preferred situation should, of course, be one that enables Sikhs and foreigners to work together. It is also possible that the partnership will secure some of its best results in Western universities. We have already noted the fact that the current crisis in the Punjab has created an unprecedented interest in the Sikhs, and this interest has prompted a willingness in some Western universities to take Sikh studies seriously. Newly established courses in Sikh religion have attracted a reasonable response from students, and if the University of Toronto experience is any indication it is a response that comes from both Sikh and non-Sikh students. Tentative plans to institute Sikh and Punjabi programs in a few North American universities may need to mature slowly, but eventually they should offer positions for academic staff specializing in various aspects of the field. This is a very promising development, one which could produce real progress.

A complement of training young scholars in programs that are explicitly and exclusively Sikh- or Punjabi-focussed is having them trained in the respective social science and humanities disciplines, but with adequate provision for language training and under the tutelage of a senior scholar who is well versed in Sikh matters. This alternative promises a wider permeation of Western scholarship by scholars knowledgeable in Sikh subject matter, though its impact may be less concentrated than that emanating from centres of Sikh and Punjabi scholarship *per se*. Discipline-based training may open up a wider range of academic appointment options as well, a significant consideration for the young man or woman contemplating commitment to a lifetime of scholarship in the field. Time alone will tell whether such opportunities will attract Sikh or non-Sikh candidates. Ideally they will attract both, thus sustaining and progressively extending a rewarding joint venture.

The immediate need is for the tentative proposals—and initiatives already under way—to develop Sikh and Punjabi scholarship at certain Canadian and United States universities to gain financial support. That will make it possible to train a generation of promising young scholars, provide some long-term faculty appointments and thus assure measurable and lasting results. In part such support will be a matter of money; in part, a matter of commitment and will. In both respects it will require the involvement of Sikhs as well as non-Sikhs. Universities—despite the chronic under-funding that inhibits many—must do their part, and governmental support must be secured. There will remain, however, the crucial area of private financial support where the generosity of Sikhs able to do so (supplemented by non-Sikhs who share a conviction of the need and value of scholarship related to the Sikhs) will make or break such initiatives. Rarely in North America have quality programs and institutions for scholarship in Christian, Jewish or other religious traditions taken root and flourished without substantial private support. Things are not likely to be different in the case of the Sikhs.

Bringing these initiatives in Sikh-related teaching and research to maturity will call for trust and understanding as well as tact and responsible commitment. Prospective donors will be expected to respect the Western university tradition of freedom of academic inquiry. This implies that within the broad guidelines of the purposes for which donations are made and accepted, universities will retain complete control over all aspects of their programs. For their part, scholars and institutions will be bound to abide by their professional norms of truth-seeking through critical inquiry, analysis and interpretation of evidence. But "critical" does not mean "hostile," and analysis does not imply insensitivity; nor does theoretically rigorous interpretation provide a warrant for arbitrary whim. There is, in fact, no reason why either scholars or prospective donors should fear the consequences of such a venture or decline to give it their strongest support. It is a unique opportunity that now confronts those of us who believe that Sikh-related scholarship deserves markedly greater commitment of energies and resources as well as wider formal recognition. If we fail at this juncture, we may have to wait a very long time for another such opportunity to build solidly for the future.

And we may hope that as political solutions belatedly lead to resolution of the current Delhi-Punjab crisis, universities and other academic bodies in the Punjab and throughout India will realize all the more clearly the importance of maintaining and enhancing high-quality scholarship on the Sikh tradition.

Part One
Religion and Culture

Legacies of the Sikh Past
for the Twentieth Century

J.S. Grewal

The "twentieth century" for our present purpose does not start with the year 1901 but about half a century earlier with the British colonial rule in the Punjab, and by "legacies" we mean simply the inheritance left by the pre-colonial generations of Sikhs to the succeeding generations. Much has been written on the precolonial history of the Sikhs but not specifically with reference to the major legacies of this period.[1]

The closest we come to a consideration of this question is in W.H. McLeod's essays published in 1975 as *The Evolution of the Sikh Community*,[2] in which he has discussed the Sikh scriptures, the cohesive ideals and institutions of the Sikh Panth and the problem of caste in the Sikh social order, besides an essay each on the *janam-sakhis* and "the evolution of the Sikh community." In fact, it is possible to adapt these essays for our present purpose with only a mild disagreement here and a minor modification there. However, McLeod has not posed the problem directly, and we can outline the significant developments of the pre-colonial period of Sikh history in slightly different terms. The major themes for discussion can be the Holy Granth, the doctrine of *Guru-Panth, raj karega khalsa*, social differentiation and ideological differentiation within the Sikh Panth.

The legacies of the Sikh past were related to the historical situations in which they evolved after the enunciation of a new religious ideology by Guru Nanak as the basis of a new social order. The peaceful evolution of the Sikh Panth into a distinctive socio-religious order under his first four successors during the sixteenth century took place in a politico-administrative framework marked by relative peace and prosperity. The response of Guru Nanak's successors and their followers to interference by an intolerant administration

---

1. For bibliography on the pre-twentieth-century legacies of the Sikhs we refer readers to the appropriate sections of the "Selected Bibliography" at the end of this volume. ...Editors' note.

2. W.H. McLeod, *The Evolution of the Sikh Community* (Delhi: Oxford University Press, 1975; Oxford: Clarendon Press, 1976).

[Joseph T. O'Connell, Milton Israel, Willard G. Oxtoby, eds., with W.H. McLeod and J.S. Grewal, visiting eds., *Sikh History and Religion in the Twentieth Century* (S. Asian Studies Papers, 3) (Toronto: S. Asian Studies, Univ. of Toronto, 1988)]

during the seventeenth century transformed the Sikh Panth into a potential instrument of socio-political change. The synchronisation of the emergence of the Khalsa with the decline of the Mughal empire in the early eighteenth century enabled them to carve out a large number of principalities, which were unified under one monarch in the early nineteenth century to become the most powerful state known to the Punjab in its entire history, with serious socio-economic and cultural consequences for the Sikh community.

The historical situation for the Sikh community changed radically with the annexation of the Punjab to a modern colonial empire. In this new context, the Punjab, like the rest of the country, witnessed socio-economic change on an unprecedented scale, affecting all aspects of the life of the people. The Sikhs responded to this change in diverse ways, in closer contact with the rest of their countrymen.

In the democratic Republic of India, with its ideal of socialism, the pace of change has become more rapid and the scope of change more comprehensive. The members of the Sikh community have witnessed and contributed to a great many changes, trying to find a place and to pursue wealth and power in the changing world of the twentieth century. To what extent and in what ways the legacies of the past have been relevant for the Sikhs in the twentieth century are surely important questions. They will find at least partial answers in this volume.

I

For an appreciation of the importance of the Holy Granth, we have to start with Guru Nanak's conception of the word *shabad*. God has neither form, colour, nor material sign, but is "revealed through the true Word." Without the Word one is condemned to the cycle of death and rebirth. The term *shabad* often occurs as *Guru ka shabad* or simply *Guru-shabad*. In fact the *shabad* is sometimes equated with Guru. "The Word is the Guru." At the same time "the Guru is God"; "the true Guru is *Niranjan* [unblemished]"; "the eternal and incarnate one is the Guru." Furthermore, Guru Nanak refers to himself as God's minstrel (*dhadi*) to proclaim "the glory of the Word."

From this to the equation of the Word with the utterances of Guru Nanak was only a short step. His first successor, Guru Angad, uses the term *Guru* as much for Guru Nanak as for God, and *Guru ka shabad* becomes the *amrit-bani* of Guru Nanak. It is understandable, therefore, that Guru Angad evolved the Gurmukhi script for recording the *bani* of Guru Nanak. His successor, Guru Amardas, refers to the *bani* of his predecessors as the only true *bani*, and at a few places, he refers to *bani* as God (*Nirankar, Brahman*). Guru Amardas had by his side not only a musician who used to sing the *bani*, but also a scribe who used to write it down. Two volumes (*pothis*) prepared by Guru Amardas served as the basis for an enlarged recension by Guru Arjan in the first decade of the seventeenth century, a recension generally known as the Adi Granth, to distinguish it from the Dasam Granth, a later compilation containing compositions of the tenth Guru, Gobind Singh. For Guru Arjan the Granth was "the abode of God."

The contents of the Adi Granth were systematically arranged according to a complex but generally consistent pattern of division and sub-division, so that structural consistency becomes a distinct feature of the Adi Granth. Another of its remarkable features is the inclusion of the compositions of several persons other than the Gurus, like Kabir, Farid, Namdev, Ravidas, Jaidev, Surdas and Ramanand. Many of them belonged to the low castes. The inclusion of their *bani* may be seen as an attempt to assimilate a growing popular tradition. They belonged to different places in the Indian subcontinent and their inclusion also suggests a pan-Indian stance on the part of Guru Arjan, who in any case was conscious of the increasing number of Sikhs in many cities of the Mughal empire outside the Punjab. There is a strong affinity between the ideas and attitudes of the Gurus and those of the *sants* and the *bhaktas* included in the Adi Granth. The fact that decisions regarding content were taken by the Gurus makes all the contents equally sacred.

Before his death in 1708, Guru Gobind Singh declared "the eternal Word" to be the true Guru of the Khalsa. Since the *shabad-bani* was contained in the Granth compiled by Guru Arjan, guruship was deemed to be vested in the Granth. During the early eighteenth century, however, the *Dasam Granth* also was compiled, and in the eyes of some of the Sikhs, guruship was vested in both the Granths. Around 1770, we find Kesar Singh Chhibber still maintaining that the two Granths were like "real brothers" and that the Adi Granth, being the older, was entitled to greater respect and veneration. Nevertheless, Chhibber clearly equates the Adi Granth with the Guru. By the mid-nineteenth century the doctrine of *Guru-Granth* was well established. The unity and continuity of guruship was built into this doctrine. Indeed, it was generally believed that the divine spirit which had inhabited the bodies of the ten Gurus dwelt now in the Granth.

The doctrine of *Guru-Granth* has been reinforced in the twentieth century, and without any ambiguity: the Granth prepared by Guru Arjan is clearly the "Adi Sri Guru Granth Sahib." The printed version is of one of the early recensions containing the *bani* of the ninth Guru, Tegh Bahadur; its compilation is attributed to Guru Gobind Singh. As W.H. McLeod remarks, the centrality of the Holy Granth in Sikh custom and the manifold uses to which it is put "leave no room for doubt concerning its enormous importance to the Panth." According to McLeod, the message of the Adi Granth is simply this: "Salvation is obtained by means of regular, persistent, disciplined meditation on the manifold expressions of the divine presence in the physical world and in human experience." This does take care of the major thrust of the message.

It may be added, however, that social and even political concerns are not outside the scope of the Adi Granth. Social inequality based on the caste system, for example, is denounced in explicit terms. Political injustice in the form of oppression by the rulers and discrimination based on differences of faith are similarly denounced in clear terms. Furthermore, even in the *bani* of Guru Nanak, we come upon the familiar Indian idea that God protects his devotees and destroys the wicked. In the *bani* of Guru Amardas, this idea comes to have a bearing on the situation of his followers, who are reassured that he whose Master is all-powerful can not come to any harm at the hands of a mortal. Guru Ramdas refers to his faction (*dhara*) as God's faction. God protects his own devotees and degrades their detractors and enemies. The emperors and kings, the *rajas*, the *khans*, the *umara* and the *shiqdars* are under his command. The Sikhs of the Guru do not have to fear the earthly *diwans* because their *Diwan* is God himself.

II

The term *Guru-Panth* was, and can still be, used in two senses: one, the Panth of the Guru, which is only a way of referring to the distinctive Sikh Panth; the other, the Panth as the Guru, which refers to the doctrine of *Guru-Panth*. The nucleus of the Sikh Panth came into existence with Guru Nanak's followers worshipping in congregation and maintaining a community kitchen (*langar*). The number of congregations (*sangat*) with places (*dharmsala*) for worship and community meal multiplied during the sixteenth century. One contemporary reference to a *sangat* at worship in a *dharmsala* on *ekadasi* festival (*mela*) underlines the centrality of congregational singing (*kirtan*). The seasonal gatherings were generally larger than the monthly gatherings, particularly at the time of Baisakhi and Diwali.

The places like Goindwal and Ramdaspur, where the Gurus resided, became centres of Sikh pilgrimage. Guru Ramdas specifically refers to the great merit of bathing in the "pool of nectar" (*amritsar*) at Ramdaspur. The elevation of Amritsar to the first rank of the Sikh centres of pilgrimage during the eighteenth century had its justification in the foundation of the town deliberately as a centre of pilgrimage. Coming to these centres, the Sikhs felt conscious of their larger fraternity. This consciousness was reinforced by the adoption of distinctively Sikh ceremonies for birth, marriage and death. Bhai Gurdas, a contemporary of Guru Arjan and Guru Hargobind, gives emphatic expression to the distinctive character of the Sikh Panth. Even at the popular level of the *janam-sakhis* there is a consciousness of distinction. In one version, Guru Nanak is told by God that his Panth will flourish, his followers will be called Nanak-Panthis and their distinctive salutation will be "in the name of the true Guru I fall at your feet." Indeed, as the Vaishnavas have their temples, the yogis their *asans*, and the Muslims their mosques, "so your followers shall have their *dharmsala*."

The individual Sikh and the *sangat* were both given an increasing importance by the Gurus during the sixteenth century. Guru Amardas says that a devotee of God is like God Himself (*Har ki murit*). The congregation of the Sikhs (*sangat*) is the only true congregation. In the *bani* of Guru Ramdas, the devotees of God (*Har log*) are the best people (*uttam*); the true Guru is among the Sikhs; and the *sangat* is dear to God. In an early *janam-sakhi* also, there is the statement that "the Guru is present in the congregation." It was generally believed that the prayers offered by a Sikh congregation found a sure response from God. Bhai Gurdas, in whose *Vars* many of the pre-Khalsa ideas crystallise, talks of the interchangeable position of the Guru and the Sikh, of the presence of the Guru in the *sangat* and in fact of the presence of God in the *sangat*. Thus well before the death of Guru Gobind Singh, in the literature of the seventeenth century we can perceive indications of a developing doctrine of the *Guru-Panth* which affirmed that "in the absence of the personal Guru, the local *sangat*, or congregation, within any area possesses the mystical power to make decisions on his behalf."

When Guru Gobind Singh decided not to nominate any single person as his successor, he could logically think of the entire body of the Khalsa as his successor. Senapat, a contemporary of Guru Gobind Singh, refers to the Khalsa as the visible form of the Guru. In the eighteenth century, we find the second Bhai Gurdas singing praises of Guru Gobind Singh with the refrain that he was at once the Guru and the disciple (*gur-chela*). The "codes" of Khalsa belief and conduct emphasised the injunction to consider the Khalsa as the Guru, "as the very embodiment of the Guru." The doctrine of *Guru-Panth* was based on an uncompromising equality of all members, and it implied democratic functioning. During the eighteenth century, this doctrine played a vital role in the affairs of the Sikh Panth. It did not contradict the idea of *Guru-Granth*. In fact these ideas appeared to be mutually complementary, and in combination they remained relevant as much for the social and political life of the Sikhs as for their religious life.

In the twentieth century the idea of *Guru-Panth* has been partially resuscitated. The demand for the management of the gurdwaras by the representatives of the Sikh Panth was in the last resort logically based on the assumption that the Sikh Panth collectively had the right to manage their religious affairs. The constitutional recognition of the collective entity of the Sikh Panth in the Gurdwara Act, which provided for the constitution of the Shiromani Gurdwara Prabandhak Committee, can be seen as both a culmination and a containment of the doctrine of *Guru-Panth*. It is interesting to note that the S.G.P.C was a more democratic institution in the 1920's than the state that gave it legal recognition.

Since Independence, the Akali Party has participated in the democratic processes of the country like other political parties. Its membership is open to non-Sikhs, but its President generally refers to himself as *Guru panth ka das*, a phrase suggestive at once of both the Panth of the Guru and the Panth as the Guru. Not all the Sikhs belong to the Akali Party; and among those who do not, many tend to think of themselves as secular in public life, either ignoring the past legacy or interpreting it in secular terms. The role assumed by the "cherished five" (*panj piare*) in different situations and meetings of the entire body of the Sikhs (*sarbat khalsa*) for different purposes suggests, however, that for certain sections of the Sikh community the doctrine of *Guru-Panth* has not exhausted its appeal.

III

By the time of Guru Arjan's martyrdom in 1606, the Sikh Panth had become a state within the Mughal empire. The far-flung local congregations, their link with the Guru through the *masands*, and the financial autonomy of the whole organization were important features of the Panth. Equally important was the local autonomy of Ramdaspur, which was not merely a place of pilgrimage but also a self-governing town without any financial or administrative link with the Mughal empire. The common allegiance of the Sikhs to the Guru was even more important. Furthermore, the Sikh Panth had its opponents and enemies among those who reacted negatively to the socially radical teachings of the Gurus and among the rival claimants to their position. Their disputes in fact brought in the administrators, and the Sikh Panth was already an irritant for the Mughal emperor Jahangir before he ordered the execution of Guru Arjan for his alleged blessings to the rebel prince Khusrau.

During the century following the death of Guru Arjan, the Sikh Panth underwent a considerable degree of transformation, due largely to external interference in the affairs of the Gurus and their followers. Bhai Gurdas refers to the martial response of Guru Hargobind to the martyrdom of his predecessor as hedging the orchard of the Sikh faith with the hardy and thorny *kikar* tree. As a spokesman of the devoted Sikhs, Bhai Gurdas approves of the new measures, which included the construction of a fort in Ramdaspur and of the Akal Takht facing the Harmandir. The anti-establishment stance of Guru Hargobind was kept up by his successors. Virtually forced to choose between their allegiance to the Guru and their allegiance to the Mughal state, some of the Sikhs chose to follow the dissidents like Prithi Chand, Dhir Mal and Ram Rai, who were all patronized by the state. External interference thus introduced a strong element of disunity in the Sikh Panth.

The institution of the Khalsa by Guru Gobind Singh in 1699 was meant to solve the problem of both external interference and internal disunity. To extend the metaphor of Bhai Gurdas, the Khalsa was at once the orchard and the hedge. Paradoxically, the institution of the Khalsa invited the external interference it was meant to obviate, and the implicit conflict between the Sikh Panth and the Mughal state was transformed into an open political struggle. At the time of Guru Gobind Singh's death in 1708, the issue was still unresolved, but Sikh rule was established in a large part of the Punjab within a few years by Banda Bahadur whom Guru Gobind Singh had commissioned to lead the Khalsa. This success was short-lived, but it left behind a legacy of sovereign rule outside the framework of the Mughal empire. "The Khalsa shall rule" (*raj karega khalsa*) became henceforth the aspiration of the followers of Guru Gobind Singh. In the seals used by Banda Bahadur, the victory was attributed to the grace of the Gurus. Thus, the political ambition of the Khalsa was sanctified.

The doctrine of *Guru-Panth* provided the principle of cohesion for their political struggle. It took a tangible form at three levels. For a limited purpose, only five members of the Khalsa (*panj piare*) could act on behalf of a congregation. For a larger but immediate purpose, all the Singhs present could resolve issues. As military and political issues began to command increasing attention, the doctrine of *Guru-Panth* began to cover the meetings of the entire body of the Singhs (*sarbat khalsa*) for decisions on issues of common interest. In all such meetings, the resolutions adopted (*gurmatas*) were in theory the decisions of the Guru deemed to be present in the Khalsa. Consequently, these resolutions were morally binding even on those who might be absent but who subscribed to the doctrine. The combination of the Khalsa hordes (*dal khalsa*) for a concerted action was a direct result of the common resolutions. Whereas the combination called *misl* was based on personal, kinship or local ties, the action of the Dal Khalsa was invariably based on a *gurmata*.

The doctrine of *Guru-Panth* served as the basis of consensus in several ways. The equality of the individual member built into the doctrine gave him the right to fight and conquer. Even if a single horseman occupied a village upon conquest, his right was recognized by others. This accounts for the emergence of a large number of Sikh "rulers" in the late eighteenth century. This recognition also implied the right of passage through the territories of other "rulers," made necessary by the occupation of small pockets of territory not always contiguous. Once the conquest was made, consensus was extended to the maintenance of the *status quo*. The "anarchy" associated with the *misl* period ignores the fact that by far the largest majority of the Sikh principalities and small *pattidaris* (shareholders in conquered territory) survived into the nineteenth century. The consensus was reflected also in the use of a common coin in the majority of the Sikh principalities.

The democratic consensus in certain areas of operation did not negate the rights of the individual in others. Every Sikh chief was free to enter into political relations with others. That was how a number of Sikh chiefs in the late eighteenth century established their suzerain claims over non-Sikh rulers. The autonomy of the individual Sikh ruler is more conspicuous in the exercise of power in relation to his government and administration. Significantly the term *khalsaji* came to be used for an individual too. Exercising autonomous power, nearly all the Sikh chiefs associated non-Sikhs with their government and administration from the very beginning of Sikh rule. That is how we come upon a considerable number of Hindu and Muslim *diwans*, *kardars* and *thanadars* in the territories of the Sikh chiefs during the late eighteenth century. Many of the Sikh chiefs kept up the *qazi's* court, which for certain purposes was open to Muslims and non-Muslims alike. A certain degree of liberalization in polity and administration was clearly in evidence in the territories of the late eighteenth-century Sikh chiefs.

The process of unification and expansion under Maharaja Ranjit Singh during the early nineteenth century was made possible partly by the late eighteenth-century background, in which co-operation between the members of different religious communities in secular matters was an important feature. The ruling class under Maharaja Ranjit Singh did not belong to any particular caste or community. Not all its members in fact belonged to the Punjab. The state patronage throughout the period of Sikh rule was extended to Sikhs, Hindus and Muslims. The Punjabis came to have the largest share in the political power of the state and consequently in the economic advantages of that power. Significantly, in the Punjabi literature of the period, there is a clear note of regional articulation. The Sikh *raj* was obviously of the Sikhs at the top, but it was administered neither by nor for the Sikhs alone. It is equally important to underline, however, that the largest measure of power and patronage was enjoyed by Sikhs.

"*Raj karega khalsa*" has remained a part of the prayer-anthem of the Sikhs to the present day even when Sikh rule in itself has not carried much significance. During colonial rule, individual Sikhs increasingly associated themselves with revolutionary and left-socialist movements. The largest number among the Sikhs supported the anti-British Gurdwara Reform movement and the national movement for freedom. Only in 1946 for a short time the proposal of a separate Sikh state was made by a few Sikh leaders in the context of the general proposition for the creation of two sovereign states in the Indian subcontinent. Like the rest of their countrymen, the Sikhs started participating in the democratic processes gradually introduced under British rule. The participation of Sikhs in the democratic processes of the Indian republic under the banner of different political parties on secular bases has reinforced the idea of sharing power in a constitutional democracy. The Akali Dal is the only political party with an overwhelming majority of Sikh members. Like some other political parties in the country, the Akali Dal supports the idea of greater autonomy for the states, but in their case the demand is looked upon by their opponents as a sort of prelude for *raj karega khalsa*. The really important aspect of the demand is its constitutional character. Recently, however, a few Sikhs have given expression to the idea of sovereign rule. This may be taken as symptomatic of dissatisfaction with the existing order of things, whether due to genuine frustration over deprivation of economic opportunities, or perceived discrimination against the Punjab state, or the rising aspirations of a privileged section of the Sikhs, or their ouster into the political wilderness, or all of these put together.

IV

The British administrators of the Punjab in the early 1850's gathered the impression that "Sikhism" was on the decline. This is stated by Denzil Ibbetson in the census report of 1881. In the first census, in 1855, there had in fact been no separate enumeration of Sikhs. Even in 1881, only those Sikhs were counted who were non-smoking *keshdharis*; in other words, only the Khalsa or the Singhs, and not all the Sikhs, were enumerated. Therefore, the number of Sikhs enumerated for the first time in 1868 at less than 12 *lakhs* (1,200,000) is misleading. However, the composition of the Sikh community could not have changed radically within a few decades, and the figures for 1881 and 1921 surely indicate that it was changing only gradually.

The figures of 1881 and 1921 clearly demonstrate that the bulk of the Sikh community, over 70%, consisted of agriculturists, and of these nearly 90% were Jats. About 8% of the Sikhs consisted of "outcastes" like the Chamars and the Churahs. Among the artisans and craftsmen there was a preponderance of carpenters (Tarkhans), who represented more than 7% of the community. The Aroras and Khatris together formed less than 7%. More than twenty-five castes were represented in the Sikh community, including the highest as well as the lowest of the low. It is interesting to note that Brahmans, Rajputs, Khatris, Jats, artisans, service-performing individuals and outcastes had found representation in the Sikh Panth already in the sixteenth century. What is important to know, however, is not merely the representation of certain castes in the Sikh Panth but also the proportion of the members representing a particular social background.

It is not possible to form a precise idea of the proportion of different sections of the population accepting the Sikh faith during the sixteenth century, but the general impression we get from contemporary and near-contemporary evidence on the point suggests that the trading castes, particularly the Khatris, formed the dominant part of the Sikh Panth in terms of leadership, if not also in numbers. From the evidence of Bhai Gurdas, writing in the early seventeenth century, it appears that the Khatris formed the most important constituency of the Sikh community. Over a score of well-known Khatri subcastes are mentioned in connection with the eminent followers of the Gurus. However, there were prominent Sikhs belonging to other castes and subcastes. There were some Randhawa, Khaira, Dhillon and Pannu Jats. Among the Brahmans, there were Tiwari and Bhardwaj. There were Suds and Aroras. Then there were Lohars, Nais, Chamars, Mistris, Sunars, Machhis, Dhobis, Kumhars, Telis, and even Chandals. In terms not only of social background but also of the economic means of its members, the Sikh Panth of the early seventeenth century was far from being homogeneous.

In the early eighteenth century, members with rural background appear to have dominated the Sikh Panth in terms of leadership and perhaps also numbers. Even in the early seventeenth century, Jat *masands* were noticed by the author of the *Dabistan-i-mazahib*. The institution of the Khalsa first, and then the political struggle with the Mughal state under the leadership of Banda Bahadur, brought in people from the countryside on a large scale. This development was accentuated during the long political struggle of the Khalsa, when the cities and towns were not safe for the activists and there was no permanent base. Dominant among the Khalsa who established their rule in the Punjab during the 1760's were Jats. However, there were a few non-Jat chiefs also, like Jassa Singh Ahluwalia (a Kalal) and Jassa Singh Ramgarhia (a carpenter). They too had risen from the countryside. Among those who were associated with the Sikh government and administration were not only Jats but also Khatris, Jhiwars, Nais and Ranghretas. A considerable number of people joined the Sikh fold after the establishment of Sikh rule. This process continued during the early nineteenth century. Cunningham's estimate of about 1.5 million Sikhs in the entire Punjab in the 1840's was not far off the mark. The political and numerical dominance of Jat Sikhs was beyond any doubt, but the composition of the Sikh community was marked by much diversity.

The Sikh social order was meant to be an egalitarian order and not a caste order. Guru Nanak perceived the light of God in all men: "Do not ask a man's caste, for in the hereafter there is no caste." "Worthless is caste and worthless an exalted name; for all mankind there is but a single refuge." These, and some other utterances of Guru Nanak and his successors, indicate that the distinctions of caste were disregarded. The idea of ritual purity and ritual status was discarded with scorn. The idea of equality was given a tangible shape in congregational worship and the community meal, the central features of Sikh *dharmsalas*. Bhai Gurdas insists that the social background of the Sikhs did not matter. Guru Nanak addressed himself to all the four *varnas* and persons coming from all the *varnas* accepted his path. Just as the betel leaf, *arica*-nut and lime produced one colour, the individuals coming from different backgrounds acquired a common colour when they joined the Sikh Panth. All the four *varnas* become one and acquire the *gotra* of *gurmukh*. The guru transmutes eight metals into one.

However, the increasing number of Sikhs and the diversity of their social background did present a problem. The occupation of a person did not change upon his joining the Sikh Panth, and his economic means did not necessarily change. There was no injunction against following the old patterns of matrimonial relations, and no need was felt to change them. Therefore, a horizontal link continued among the Sikhs coming from particular caste and occupation groups. As socially committed householders, the Sikhs were expected to earn an honest living and not live on doles; they contributed to the common pool in cash and kind. If the new ethos improved their economic condition, it was regarded as the grace of the Guru and the grace of God. In the *bani* of Guru Ramdas, for instance, the wealth and riches of the Sikh are sanctified. Indeed, of those who earn merit by following the path shown by the true Guru, their houses, their mansions and caparisoned horses are sanctified. Thus, in the single *varna* to which the Sikhs of Bhai Gurdas theoretically belonged, there were rich magnates as well as paupers, and the difference between them appeared to be part of the Divine Order.

The ideal equality was reasserted with the institution of the Khalsa. In fact, the idea was extended to the realm of politics. Paradoxically, the equal right to fight and conquer, which led to acquisition of power, also led to acquisition of material means and therefore to social differentiation. During the late eighteenth and early nineteenth centuries social differentiation among the Sikhs went on Increasing, due to the operation of government and administration. If the difference had ranged from a bondservant to a rich magnate during the early seventeenth century, in the early nineteenth century it ranged from a day labourer to a king. The gradations in between also became more numerous. Among the Jats, for example, there was all the difference between a member of the ruling class and a peasant, while there were other grades of Jats in between. Similarly, one Jhiwar could be a *jagirdar* commanding a hundred horsemen and enjoying revenues worth a hundred thousand rupees, while another was still performing the customary service in a village under the *jajmani* system. Caste solidarities and caste distinctions were weakened or broken in some ways, while social differentiation based upon the difference of economic means and social prestige was increasing. It should not come to us as a surprise that the doctrine of *Guru-Panth* now lost much ground and the doctrine of *Guru-Granth* came to the fore. The latter reconciled the ideal norm of equality to the existing social and economic inequalities in the Sikh social order. The Sikh monarchy extended its political umbrella over all, and yet the dream of *raj karega khalsa* appeared to have come true.

Under colonial rule the ideal of equality was revived with partial success by social reformers among the Sikhs, particularly in its bearing on socio-religious matters. Economic egalitarianism was not a part of the egalitarian legacy of the Sikh past, and no conscious thought has been directed towards the lessening of economic inequalities within the Sikh social order. In fact, the ideas of secular democracy and socialism appear to have overtaken the limited egalitarianism coming down from the Sikh past. If socio-economic inequalities are increasing or decreasing within the Sikh community due to state policies, the process is looked upon with indifference. Possibly, the gain of the few is equated with the gain of the community.

V

J.D. Cunningham noticed nearly a score of "Sikh sects or denominations" during the early 1840's. Some of these, however, were merely certain privileged groups like the Bedi descendants of Lakhmidas, the younger son of Guru Nanak, and the Trehan, Bhalla and Sodhi descendants of Guru Angad, Guru Amardas and Guru Ramdas. They all enjoyed generous patronage from the Sikh rulers, and their wealth added to the prestige of their descent. Cunningham's list included also Bhais and Gianis, Akalis and Nihangs, Ranghretas and Ramdasias, Banda Panthis and Masandis. Though interesting in the social configuration of the Sikh community, they did not constitute sects or religious denominations. However, Cunningham also refers to Udasis and Ramraiyas, who could certainly be regarded as belonging to different denominations. In any case, the question of ideological differentiation within the Sikh community, raised by Cunningham, remains important.

Dissent in early Sikhism can be understood with reference to the principle of nomination, on which was based the cardinal doctrine of the unity and continuity of guruship. Guru Angad, who used the epithet Nanak in his compositions, declared that the gift of guruship could be received only from the master and not by nominating oneself. Similarly, Guru Amardas appears to underline the principle of nomination when he states that there is no guru but the True Guru, or that there is only one True Bani and only one True Guru. In these utterances we can feel the presence of "other gurus." For Bhai Gurdas, succession through nomination was no ordinary succession. When Angad became the Guru, Nanak became his Sikh; the Guru became the Sikh and Sikh became the Guru. The Guru-disciple-Guru syndrome raised the principle of nomination into a doctrine at a time when dissent was becoming rather obtrusive.

Guru Angad's insistence on the principle of nomination was directed against Sri Chand, the elder son of Guru Nanak, who claimed to be a successor of Guru Nanak. Supported by custom and the state law, the sons of Guru Angad in turn claimed his establishment at Khadur, and the nominated Guru, Amardas, had to move to Goindwal. Before he nominated his son-in-law, Ramdas, as the successor-Guru, Guru Amardas started building a new centre for him, and the sons of Guru Amardas succeeded to his headquarters at Goindwal. Guru Arjan was the first nominated Guru who did not leave the headquarters of his predecessor. However, his elder brother Prithi Chand did not hesitate to seek help from the state functionaries in support of his own claims. Bhai Gurdas's denunciation of his followers, the "dissembling scoundrels" (*mina*), becomes loud and harsh.

Prithi Chand's son Mihrban occupied Ramdaspur after Guru Hargobind's departure from the town around 1630. Mihrban wrote his own compositions using the epithet Nanak of himself, with the implication that he was in the true line of succession from Guru Nanak. He wrote a *janam-sakhi* also to reinforce his claims. His son, Harji, succeeded him at Ramdaspur as the seventh successor of Guru Nanak. Thus, the "dissembling scoundrels" became rather formidable rivals of the successors of Guru Hargobind at Kiratpur. By the early eighteenth century, however, the *minas* were ousted from Ramdaspur. Under Sikh rule, the descendants of Harji received revenue-free lands at Guru Har Sahai in the present Ferozepur district. The descendants of his two brothers also received revenue-free lands in Batala and near Sarhind. By this time, the dissent of the *minas* had become a thing of the past.

Guru Hargobind's elder grandson, Dhir Mal, established his centre at Kartarpur in the Jullundur Doab, not recognising the nomination of his younger brother, Har Rai. Dhir Mal, too, had a considerable following. His fourth successor, Sadhu Singh, approached Jassa Singh Ahluwalia to intercede with the Khalsa for admitting him to their fold. Sadhu Singh henceforth received large *jagirs* from the Sikh rulers, and remained in a rather low key as a "Guru." The descendants of Suraj Mal, son of Guru Hargobind, were enjoying large *jagirs* in the early nineteenth century, holding in fact the Anandpur-Makhowal area virtually as minor chiefs. They were also laying their claims to guruship. Guru Har Rai's son, Ram Rai, did not recognise the nomination of his younger brother

Guru Har Krishan. He was patronised by Aurangzeb and received a considerable *jagir* at the present Dehra Dun. His centre was taken over by Udasis after his death in the early eighteenth century.

The Udasis set aside the principle of nomination by adopting parallel lines of succession from Guru Nanak through Sri Chand, Baba Gurditta and the four Ad-Udasis. They were patronised by the Mughal administrators in the early eighteenth and by the Sikh rulers in the late eighteenth century. They were more lavishly patronised by Ranjit Singh in the early nineteenth century, and they established a large number of centres in the countryside as well as in towns and cities. The rejection of the principle of nomination in their case was accompanied by some other differences of belief and practice.

From the viewpoint of ideological differentiation an important change was introduced by the institution of the Khalsa. Initiation through the baptism of the double-edged sword and the wearing of *kesh* and turban made the Singhs quite distinct from the earlier Sikhs. Furthermore, since only those of the Sikhs who became the Khalsa of Guru Gobind Singh were to be regarded as Sikhs, the Singhs were forbidden to have any kind of relation with the *minas* and the followers of Dhir Mal, Ram Rai and the *masands*. Henceforth dissent became easily identifiable and the dissenters stood excommunicated from the Khalsa Panth.

However, not all the Sikhs of the time of Guru Gobind Singh became his Khalsa. The non-Khalsa Sikhs survived into the eighteenth century, and their number, like that of the Khalsa, appears to have increased subsequently. Nevertheless, a basic difference was introduced by the Khalsa. The primary division now was between the *keshdhari* Singhs and the *sahajdhari* Sikhs. Even the latter status was accorded to only those Sikhs who were sympathisers of the Khalsa, or who at least were not openly opposed to them. Through this compromise, ideological differentiation was legitimized, and even the old dissidents were recognized as a part of the Sikh Panth. The minimum that was expected from the *sahajdhari* Sikhs was a belief in the guruship of Nanak and the acceptance of the scriptural authority of the Holy Granth; they were also expected to refrain from smoking.

In the early nineteenth century, there were further differences of belief and practice among the *sahajdhari* Sikhs. The Udasis were renunciants and their reverence for Guru Nanak was rather notional; their interpretation of the Holy Granth was clearly Vedantic. Their religious practices were not uniform but in all their establishments some Hindu practices were observed. At the other end, the Nirankaris in the 1840's had a deep respect for all the ten Gurus, recognized the exclusive authority of the Holy Granth for religious belief and practice, rejected all gods and goddesses except the Formless One (*Nirankar*), and adopted Sikh ceremonies for birth, marriage and death in accordance with their understanding of the Holy Granth.

Among the *keshdhari* Singhs, there were a small number of Akalis and Nihangs. They had survived the period of intense political struggle but without any territories or administrative positions. They had their own establishments (*deras*) and they were associated with some of the important gurdwaras. They upheld the primacy of the doctrine of *Guru-Panth* and paid equal veneration to the Dasam Granth as the sacred scripture. They prided themselves on observing the Khalsa code of conduct, which in their belief was enunciated by Guru Gobind Singh himself. The ordinary Singh also observed some items of the Khalsa code of conduct, besides wearing *kesh* and turban and refraining from smoking. Because of the increasing number of the Singhs during the late eighteenth and early nineteenth centuries, a need was felt for propagating the Khalsa code of conduct, and several *rahit-namas* became current during the period. Cunningham's extracts from two of such *rahit-namas* clearly indicate, among other things, that the doctrines of *Guru-Panth* and *Guru-Granth* and the idea of Sikh sovereignty were well established by this time.

The policy of Maharaja Ranjit Singh was to tolerate ideological differentiation. The Golden Temple and the Akal Takht, which had become the most important institutions for the Khalsa during the eighteenth century, were imperceptibly taken over by the Maharaja on behalf of the Singhs. The transition was rather smooth because Jassa Singh Ahluwalia had been managing the affairs of the Golden Temple by common consent. Maharaja Ranjit Singh entrusted the management of the Golden Temple to one of his *jagirdars*. He placated the Akalis and the Nihangs by enlisting them in the army or by giving them revenue-free lands. Individual Akalis, like Phula Singh, were allowed to proclaim that the authority of the collective body of the Khalsa was supreme in the Panth, but none was allowed to interfere in the affairs of the state. In fact, much greater patronage was extended to the most "unorthodox" of the Sikhs, that is, the Udasis, than to the most "orthodox" of the Khalsa, that is, the Akalis and the Nihangs. All Singhs believed in the end of personal guruship after death of Guru Gobind Singh and in the unity of guruship. This belief combined with the wearing of *kesh* and turban and refraining from smoking provided the common ground for the bulk of the Singhs during the early nineteenth century.

The Singh component of the Sikh community increased appreciably under colonial rule. Nevertheless, the *sahajdhari* component still forms an integral part of the community. The secularisation of life and thought which has taken place in the world during the recent centuries has influenced the members of the Sikh community as well. However, there is also a reaction. Secularisation involving indifference to religious belief and practice is regarded by many as a serious threat to the cherished legacies of the past. This is true not only of the Sikhs but also of other religious communities in the country. That may be the major reason why no effort has been made to translate the legacy of religious ideologies into secular goals. At any rate, religiosity and secularisation have developed side by side. What is referred to as fundamentalism, whether Sikh or Hindu or Muslim, has to be placed in this broad context.

A Sikh Theology for Modern Times

W.H. McLeod

During the early decades of the twentieth century, scholars associated with the Singh Sabha movement devoted considerable attention to the analysis and presentation of the Sikh tradition. Some major works were produced during this period, studies which expressed a distinctive interpretation and which have ever since exercised a determinative influence on the intellectual understanding of Sikhism. Notable examples are the various Adi Granth commentaries, Kahn Singh Nabha's *Gurushabad Ratanakar Mahan Kosh*, Teja Singh's *Sikhism: Its Ideals and Institutions*, and the diverse works of Vir Singh.[1] These and other such publications have conferred an enduring legacy on all later students of the Sikh tradition, and no one could possibly deny either the dedication of these scholars or the quality of their work.

There remains, however, a significant gap. The Singh Sabha approach to scholarship was particularly strong in some areas, stressing with great effect the importance of scriptural commentary and the historical traditions of the Panth. Theology, however, was largely neglected.[2] The one major work of theology produced by a Singh Sabha scholar is Jodh Singh's *Guramati Niranay*, yet even this justly popular work stands at the edge of the discipline rather than within it. *Guramati Niranay* is a brief work consisting largely of quotations from

---

1. The first of the vernacular commentaries was *Adi Sri Guru Granth Sahibji Satik*, commissioned by the Raja of Faridkot and published in four volumes under his patronage in 1905. The best commentary is arguably the four-volume *Shabadarath Sri Guru Granth Sahib Ji* (n.p., 1936-41), largely the work of the late Principal Teja Singh but published anonymously. Much fuller but still incomplete is Vir Singh's *Santhya Sri Guru Granth Sahib* (Amritsar, 1958-62). The latest in the line is Professor Sahib Singh's *Sri Guru Granth Sahib Darapan*, published in ten volumes (Jullundur, 1962-64). Kahn Singh Nabha's *Gurushabad Ratanakar Mahan Kosh* was first published from Patiala in four volumes in 1931. A revised edition with addendum has been issued in one volume from Patiala in 1960 with subsequent reprints. Teja Singh's *Sikhism* was first published in 1938, with a new and revised edition from Bombay in 1951. The works of Vir Singh are too numerous to mention (apart from his *Santhya*, already noted).

2. In its narrow sense theology concentrates on discourse and commentary about God. In its broader sense it concerns a systematic expression of beliefs flowing from that fundamental doctrine and integrally expressed. It is in this wider sense that the word is here used. There is no distinction between natural and revealed theology as in Christian usage. In Nanak's thought at least all theology is natural.

[Joseph T. O'Connell, Milton Israel, Willard G. Oxtoby, eds., with W.H. McLeod and J.S. Grewal, visiting eds., *Sikh History and Religion in the Twentieth Century* (S. Asian Studies Papers, 3) (Toronto: S. Asian Studies, Univ. of Toronto, 1988)]

scripture, and it presents a series of isolated concepts rather than a closely reasoned statement of the Sikh tradition. Arguably, it should be regarded as an addition to the several commentaries of the period rather than as a contribution to Sikh theology.

The example set by *Guramati niranay* has been followed ever since, with the result that the theological analysis of Sikhism remains undeveloped. Brief studies of individual concepts occasionally appear, but the effort is seldom made to build these blocks into a single integrated structure. Even when several concepts are treated in sequence, the result typically remains a series of discrete items, with little evidence of a developing pattern or a unified result. A theology of Sikhism, integrated and comprehensive, has yet to be written. Instead, attention has been largely focussed on the Panth's history. The teachings of the Gurus and the development of later traditions certainly receive attention, but it is a treatment which typically adopts an exclusively historical perspective. Such work is certainly needed. Alone it is not enough.

There is, of course, an obvious objection to this claim and to the procedure which it implies. Theology, it may be protested, is a Western discipline, one that has been developed to serve the distinctive needs of a Western tradition. As such it is inappropriate for an Indian tradition of the kind taught by the Gurus.

This objection can be rebutted, yet not to the extent of ignoring the important warning which it sounds. It can be contested on the grounds that we are dealing with Sikhism as an evolved tradition and that the doctrinal development which we owe to the Singh Sabha movement renders it eminently suited to theological treatment. Singh Sabha scholars put considerable effort into identifying and defining specific features of the tradition. The problem arises from the fact that they generally stopped at that point, leaving the integrated analysis to a later generation.

Having thus contested the objection, we must now acknowledge its substantial value. A simple transposition of concepts and structures drawn from Western Christian theology will certainly frustrate our purpose. Sikhism must be approached from within the tradition itself, and that tradition alone can deliver the basic components of an authentically Sikh theology. This need not mean that the scholar who attempts the task should necessarily be a Sikh, though the truly authoritative statement may well require that qualification. What it certainly does mean is that the analysis must concentrate on understanding and expounding the tradition in its own terms, and that it must be exceedingly wary of concepts introduced from alien sources. In particular, it should avoid the temptation to work from English translations. This axiom, long recognised in biblical studies, must surely be applied with equal emphasis to the treatment of Sikh doctrine.

If, therefore, we concede that a systematic analysis of doctrine is appropriate in the case of the Sikh tradition, we are faced by three general questions. The first concerns the material with which we should work. What doctrines and doctrinal issues should be included in any such analysis, and what should be excluded? Secondly, how should each doctrine be related to others and how is it to be incorporated within the system as a whole? Third, what is the appropriate method of conducting the analysis and presenting its results if English is to be the language which we use for that purpose?

It now becomes clear that we are actually begging two questions, not just the one already noted. We have already assumed that systematic theology is an appropriate discipline in the case of the Sikh tradition. To this we are adding the assumption that the language of analysis and presentation will be English. Is this a valid assumption?

If there is any suggestion that English should be the only language used for this purpose, the response must obviously be instant rejection. Such a proposition would be manifestly absurd. Much of the scholarship relating to Sikh Studies will continue to be conducted in Punjabi, and it is essential that this should be so. If the traditional language is abandoned as a vehicle for description and analysis, the tradition itself will eventually change.

This may be acknowledged, yet not to the extent of maintaining that all such scholarship must necessarily be confined to Punjabi. English has long since become the second language of the Sikh academic tradition, and this trend is bound to continue as Sikhs of the diaspora assert an increasing influence within the Panth. It is, moreover, necessary to communicate an understanding of the tradition to others, and for this purpose English is obviously the appropriate vehicle. For those who work in Punjabi there are only the first two general questions to be considered. Others will work in English, and for those who choose this latter route there are the three questions listed above.

In this paper an attempt will be made to indicate rudimentary answers to all three questions. The primary emphasis will have to be upon the third, and the intention will be to demonstrate the truth of the axiom already enunciated. If we choose to deal with a tradition in a foreign language, we must concentrate a substantial measure of our attention on analysing the terms and concepts which give expression to the tradition in its original form. The attempt to deal with this third issue should indicate the kind of answers which can be expected to issue from the first and second questions. Needless to say, such answers here will be brief, elementary and loosely structured. It would obviously be impossible to present within the space of a single paper either a detailed analysis of individual doctrines or the closely integrated sequence which an ideal theology of Sikhism should eventually deliver.

The paramount need for working from the tradition's own concepts and terminology can be illustrated by a brief examination of that most obvious of examples. We have all heard reasons why the word "God" is inappropriate as a translation when we move beyond the Christian or the Middle Eastern monotheistic traditions, and some readers will find those reasons very cogent indeed. The Sikh example must surely offer strong support for the claim. The term which is traditionally used to express Guru Nanak's concept is *Akal Purakh*, literally "the Timeless Being." Akal Purakh is a very different concept from the range of meaning covered by the English word "God"; if we persist in using the latter term we shall find it difficult indeed to avoid its distinctive connotations. *Kartar* is another of Guru Nanak's terms for the Supreme Being in which the translation "Creator" communicates a range of meaning different from the Western sense. I am well aware that some claim the ability to be able to make the necessary adjustments and thus to invest the old word with new meaning. Personally, I am exceedingly skeptical of this claim.

If this is correct, it necessarily follows that when we are endeavouring to communicate a Sikh understanding we should always speak of Akal Purakh and Kartar, never of God or Creator. If anyone should draw my attention to a repeated use of the latter words in my own books, I can only reply, lamely, that some of us take a long time to learn.

This particular issue is a complicated one as far as the Sikh tradition is concerned. Complications arise partly because Nanak's own meaning is necessarily elusive and partly because the Akal Purakh usage is accompanied by the more recent compound *Vahiguru* (often written *Wahguru*), which in modern usage also means God. This, however, is the kind of problem that belongs to a later stage in the analysis. Any survey of the tradition must start with Guru Nanak, and the word *Vahiguru* has no place in his teachings.

Nanak actually uses many different words in giving expression to the ultimate ultimate reality which Sikh tradition calls Akal Purakh. Some of these terms are traditional names, such as Hari and Ram. Many more are words that designate his attributes, commonly as negatives that attempt in the traditional style to define reality in terms of what it is not. Indeed, the word *a-kal* or "timeless" is a conspicuous example. Nanak's meaning is necessarily elusive because his belief and practice were essentially mystical, and in the last resort only those who comprehend Akal Purakh in their own mystical experience can truly grasp the meaning that human words endeavour to communicate. The final and all-embracing term is *alakh*: Akal Purakh is ineffable.

This does not mean, however, that Akal Purakh is altogether unknowable. On the contrary, the essential being of Akal Purakh is revealed for all to see if they will but open their eyes. We are brought to the word that can be regarded as the most important of all the many terms used by Nanak in order to communicate his understanding of Akal Purakh and of the way to liberation. And let us note in passing that we have just used a particular English word instead of another more common usage. The word was "liberation," and not "salvation"—a choice based on the conviction that the latter term is altogether inappropriate in the Sikh context.

The word to which we are brought is *nam*, frequently linked with *sati* to give the compound form *satinam* (often written *satnam*). The literal translation of *nam*, is, of course, "name," and for once we have an English rendering that corresponds closely to the original. The problem is knowing what *nam* or "the name" means in Nanak's repeated usage. A brief definition offered almost twenty years ago was "the total expression of all that God is."[3] Substitute "Akal Purakh" for "God" and you have, I believe, a reasonable summary. The definition adds that the same reality can also be called the Truth, thus indicating the sense of the "Satinam" form.

The *nam* is everywhere around us and within us, yet man is rendered congenitally blind by *haumai*, self-centredness. This is another compound, one which comprises two forms of the first person singular pronoun. As such it signifies the powerful impulse to succumb to personal gratification, thus earning the kind of *karam* (*karma*) which holds a person firmly within the cycle of *sansar* (*samsara*). Birth follows death and suffering infuses all. Akal Purakh, however, looks graciously upon the suffering of mankind and through the *Guru* utters the *shabad*, which communicates a sufficient understanding of the *nam* to those who are able to "hear" it. The Guru is thus the "voice" of Akal Purakh, mystically "speaking" within the *man* (heart-mind-spirit) of the devotee. The *shabad* or "Word" is the actual "utterance" and in "hearing" it a person awakens to the reality of the divine Name, immanent in all that lies around and within him.

The nature of the divine Name is itself determined by the *hukam* of Akal Purakh. This designates the divine order of the entire universe, an order which is synonymous with harmony. Liberation is achieved by means of bringing oneself within this harmony, an objective which is progressively attained by the strictly interior discipline of *nam-simaran* or "remembering the Name." This discipline ranges from the simple repetition of an appropriate word or *mantra* (*nam japan*) through the devout singing of hymns (*kirtan*) to sophisticated meditation. All are designed to bring the individual into accord with the *nam*, thus earning for him or her the kind of *karam* which provides release. The ultimate condition of blissful *sahaj* is achieved when the spirit ascends to *sac khand* (the "realm of truth"), a goal which may be reached before the physical death that is its final seal.

As the one responsible for communicating this truth, Nanak became the embodiment of the eternal *Guru*, and those who succeeded him in the lineage which he established assumed the same role. Although the line included ten individuals, there remained but one *Guru*, passing successively from one to the next as a single flame ignites a series of torches. Their compositions are known as *bani* or *gurbani* and the sum total of their teachings as *gurmat* (what we call "Sikhism"). The fifth in the succession, Guru Arjan, had the *bani* of the first five Gurus recorded in a book (*granth*) in 1603-04, adding to it approved works by earlier representatives of the *sant* tradition such as Namdev and Kabir. Upon the book was conferred the respect due to its authors and it was accordingly known as the Granth Sahib. Later, as the system of doctrine developed, it was to receive a further dignity.

3. W.H. McLeod, *Guru Nanak and the Sikh Religion* (Oxford: Clarendon Press, 1968), p. 196.

The establishment of a spiritual lineage followed the first forming of a group of disciples. These were the original *sikhs* or "learners." As a group of devotees with a common loyalty and tradition they constituted a *panth* ("path" or "way"), and because the first loyalty had been to Nanak they were known as the Nanak-panth. *Panth* is another of the key terms that refuse to yield a simple translation. This, however, is an analysis that is better postponed until we reach *Khalsa*, for the two terms overlap to a considerable extent. We note it at this point because we must necessarily refer to the following which the Gurus attracted, and for this group of disciples the appropriate term is either Nanak-panth or simply "the Panth."

Before we reach *Khalsa* there is an intermediate term to be introduced. During the period of Guru Arjan (as Guru, 1581-1606) the Nanak-panth became the object of Mughal suspicion, and the Guru himself died in Mughal custody. According to tradition he responded to the developing threat of Mughal hostility by instructing his son, the future Guru Hargobind (as Guru, 1606-44), to sit fully armed on his throne. In obedience to this command Hargobind, having succeeded his father, symbolically donned two swords. One sword designated a newly-assumed temporal role (*miri*) while the other represented the spiritual authority he had inherited from his five predecessors (*piri*).

The doctrine of *miri-piri* signals the Panth's immensely important shift towards militancy. This did not mean that the spiritual concerns of the earlier Nanak-panth had been renounced. On the contrary, these were explicitly affirmed throughout the remainder of the Gurus' period, and the same emphasis continues to the present day. The change should not be understood, however, as the mere defending by military means of an unchanging theory of spirituality. It was a change that significantly affected the subsequent understanding and promulgation of Sikh doctrine. It is during the time of the tenth Guru, Gobind Singh, that the change emerges to full view. Akal Purakh is characteristically called *Sarab Loh*, "All-Steel," and the sword assumes a central significance in the doctrine and ritual of the Panth.

> Thee I invoke, All-conquering Sword, Destroyer of evil, Ornament of
>   the brave.
> Powerful your arm and radiant your glory, your splendour as dazzling
>   as the brightness of the sun.
> Joy of the devout and scourge of the wicked, Vanquisher of sin, I
>   seek your protection.
> Hail to the world's Creator and Sustainer, my invincible Protector the
>   Sword.[4]

It is Akal Purakh who is here addressed, divinity made manifest in the burnished steel of the unsheathed sword. The intervening history of the Panth explains the change, and appropriate terminology reflects it.

The sword thus introduced into Sikh doctrine and tradition figures prominently in *amrit sanskar*, the initiation ceremony marking entry into the

---

4. *Bachitar Natak 2*, Dasam Granth, p. 39.

recreated Panth of Guru Gobind Singh. The recreated Panth is, of course, the Khalsa. Although the term is correctly traced to the word *khalis*, from Arabic by way of Persian, the immediate etymology seems not to be the common adjectival meaning of "pure." The Persian *khalis* had produced the form *khalsa*, used as a noun to designate lands under the direct administration of the crown or central authority. As the early Panth grew and expanded, the supervision of individual *sangats* (congregations) or small clusters of *sangats* was entrusted by the Gurus to vicars called *masands*. Some *sangats*, however, remained under the continuing supervision of the Guru as his *khalsa*. By the time of Guru Gobind Singh many of the *masands* had become arrogant or corrupt, and in commanding all Sikhs to abandon the *masands* the Guru simultaneously summoned them to join his *khalsa*.

All who heeded the Guru's summons and accepted initiation were required to observe the *rahit* (also written *rehit* or *rehat*), another of our key terms. The *rahit* comprises the outward symbols, the very specific rules of conduct, and the distinctive rituals which a Sikh of the Khalsa is expected to observe. As such it is a very important word indeed, one which should certainly be much better known. In its developed form it includes such celebrated features as the *panj kakke* or *panj kakkar*), the "five k's" (five items, each of whose names begins with the letter "k," that a Khalsa Sikh should wear) and a rigorous ban on smoking.

We return now to the word *panth*. Are *panth* and *khalsa* synonyms? For some Khalsa Sikhs the answer is a firm "yes." Others, however, are obviously unwilling to adopt such a hard line, for in so doing they necessarily imply that many who call themselves Sikhs have no right to do so. The more obvious of these allegedly deregistered claimants are the so-called *sahajdhari* Sikhs, men and women who affirm allegiance to the teachings of Nanak and his successors (particularly to the doctrine and practice of *nam-simaran*) but who decline to accept Khalsa initiation or the full rigours of the *rahit*. Less obvious because they so closely resemble the Khalsa model are those who observe the outward forms required by the *rahit* (particularly the *kesh* or uncut hair) but who nevertheless fail to "take *amrit*," viz., to undergo initiation. Such people are certainly not members of the Khalsa. Are they thereby disqualified from membership of the Panth also?

The ambiguity of this situation reflects a real ambivalence. As far as the definition of the Khalsa is concerned there is no ambiguity, nor is there likely to be a problem in the minds of most of the uninitiated. For the latter the simple answer is that the Panth is a large entity, which contains Sikhs of the Khalsa together with many who for various reasons do not accept the full Khalsa discipline. The Khalsa may be regarded as an elite or as the "orthodox" version of the Sikh identity, but the *rahit* need not be regarded as a definition which automatically excludes all who do not meet its strict requirements. But what is the loyal Khalsa Sikh to think? If Guru Gobind Singh envisaged a purpose for the Khalsa, surely that intention must apply to all who claim to be his disciples.

Calling oneself a follower of Guru Nanak is certainly unacceptable if it implies a rejection of later developments within the Panth. The Guru is one, and instructions issued by the tenth Guru are as binding on Sikhs as is guidance given by the first.

The problem is a real one and at times of crisis (such as is currently experienced) it can become serious. It is further complicated by the widespread existence of multiple identities in Punjabi society, with individuals moving freely from one to another or, more commonly, maintaining multiple identities without any sense of incongruity. The question is one that the outsider is unable to answer except in strictly pragmatic terms. We may observe that many people claim to be Sikhs without taking *amrit* and that a substantial proportion of these people actually observe the more obvious requirements of the *rahit*. If their precise status is a matter for concern, outsiders are certainly not entitled to offer answers. The debate continues, advancing and receding as circumstances dictate. It has sometimes involved the terms *sikhi* and *singhi*, with the former used to describe the larger identity and the latter to designate the specific identity of the Khalsa.

The demarcation issue is not the only problem associated with this richly complex word *panth*. Another difficulty is signalled by attempts to supply single-word English translations, attempts that should serve to reinforce the point I am attempting to make with regard to the translating of basic terminology. We can easily dispense with one such suggestion, namely, the word "church." This still appears from time to time, but it is so patently inappropriate that it quickly creates uneasiness and is soon abandoned. Two other attempted renderings have achieved a wider popularity and deserve a little more attention. One is "sect," and the other is "nation."

"Sect" has had a long history, having acquired a firm hold on an early generation of European observers. It is, however, an inappropriate usage to describe the Panth, for the term implies the existence of an orthodoxy from which the body deviates. For most users of this particular "translation" the orthodoxy from which Sikhism diverged was presumably "Hinduism." The latter term is itself unacceptable (particularly as a word designating an agreed orthodoxy), and even if it were viable the suggestion that the modern Sikh Panth can be described as a "sect" of it would be absurd. Such a usage is also regarded as highly offensive by many Sikhs. The word "sect" has run its misguided course, and mercifully we seldom hear it nowadays except as a feature of the language of polemic.

For some people, of course, the use of "sect" derives from a cursory interpretation of the nature of the Panth rather than from any acquaintance with the semantics of the word. The same applies, in an even more complex way, to the word "nation" as a rendering of *panth*. British authors who, during the first half of the nineteenth century, referred to the Sikhs as a "nation" are most unlikely to have had the word *panth* in mind. Their usage obviously reflected the existence of the very visible kingdom of Maharaja Ranjit Singh. The description, having slumped with Sikh political fortunes in the later nineteenth century, has since revived. During recent years it has been ardently promoted by advocates of a larger political autonomy for the Sikhs. This modern usage, though specifically associated with the Panth, involves some crucial shades of meaning. Hovering in the background is the word *qaum*, an Arabic term that, having entered Punjabi via Persian, has long since been thoroughly naturalised in India. If one employs this vocabulary, it might be argued, the Panth constitutes a "nation" because the Sikhs are a *qaum*.

But does *qaum* really yield "nation" as an appropriate translation? The issue is an exceedingly controversial one, and great tact is required if we are to pre-empt an overwrought response. In its original sense *qaum* means "a people who stand together," and the substance of this meaning has carried over to Punjabi usage. Arguably the word can best be translated today as "ethnic identity." What it certainly involves is a conflict of attitudes that continues to ramify through Sikh society. In a very real sense we are dealing with a problem of translation which, having emerged in English usage, has now returned to create confusion in Punjabi. This is not to suggest that the fundamental problem derives from linguistic misunderstanding. What it does suggest is that the linguistic issue accurately reflects a basic problem concerning corporate Sikh identity, and that the basic problem has been seriously aggravated by linguistic misunderstanding.

Other terms that have figured prominently in the recent crisis will bring us back to clarity and firm definition. The founding of the Khalsa order, and the decades of warfare that followed immediately thereafter, remoulded the traditions of the Panth, creating an heroic ideal which endures to the present day. The ideal is commonly perceived to be the *sant-sipahi*, he who combines the spirituality of the devout believer (*sant*) with the bravery and obedience of the true soldier (*sipahi*). The supreme exemplar is Guru Gobind Singh, and to this ideal the loyal Sikh of the Khalsa must aspire.

Sant is an interesting term in that it has been required to do service for a succession of meanings. It is also interesting because it provides another example of a word that has been skewed by its standard English translation. The temptation to insert an "i" has proved irresistible, and *sant* has typically emerged as "saint." This is a misleading translation regardless of which meaning may be indicated by the actual Punjabi usage.

The word *sant* derives from *sat* and thus designates in its basic sense one who knows the truth or comprehends reality. As such it came to be applied to a particular devotional tradition, the one with which Guru Nanak himself was affiliated. The word passed into standard Sikh usage through the works of Nanak and his successors, bearing a strong sense of devotion and intimately associated with the concept of the *sadh-sangat* or *satsang* (the congregation of true believers). Increasingly it came to designate an elite within the *sangat* and thus acquired the status of an actual title. Those who have followed recent events in the Punjab will appreciate how influential some *sants* have now become. Such men are preceptors whose primary function is to give instruction in the beliefs and traditions of the Panth. These traditions stress worldly involvement as well as spiritual devotion, and it should thus come as no surprise to discover that men bearing the title of Sant are to be found amongst the political leaders of the modern Panth.

Such men teach the *miri-piri* tradition, and those who personally match the ideal will be regarded as *sant-sipahi*. Other terms used in current Sikh politics also recall the militant traditions of the Panth. The dominant political party is the Akali Dal or Akali Army. Each territorial unit of the party is designated a *jatha* (military detachment), and an organised political campaign is a *morcha* (facing the enemy). A particularly important and lengthy political struggle may be called a *dharam yudh*, "a war fought in defence of *dharam*."

This leads us to another of the words that defy translation, an instance that will have a familiar ring. *Dharam* is the Punjabi version of *dharma*, but one should not assume that the two are identical in terms of meaning and connotation. Although the Panth preserves the caste structure of society, it is non-caste in theory; and it thus rejects the specific definition of *dharma* as the obligations associated with a particular caste identity. In Sikh usage the stress moves away from the individual to the Panth or to society as a whole, and the sense connoted by *dharam* involves the moral order, which alone provides a sure foundation for harmony and social stability. An attack on *dharam* is an attack on justice, on righteousness, and on the moral order generally. It must be defended at all costs, and when other means have all failed the defenders of *dharam* must resort to the sword.

None of this should suggest that the Panth exists only to breathe fire or wield naked swords. The use of force is certainly sanctioned in a famous couplet attributed to Guru Gobind Singh[5] but is authorised only in defence of *dharam* and only as a last resort. In times of disturbance or crisis one is likely to forget that the *gurdwaras*, though legitimately used for political purposes, are primarily places of worship.

We have come to yet another of the key terms. The word *gurduara* (anglicised as "gurdwara") can be translated as either "the Guru's door" or "by means of the Guru's [grace]." Since earliest days, members of the Panth have gathered together in *satsangs* to sing *kirtan* (sacred songs, specifically those composed by the Gurus and other religious figures, eventually recorded in the Granth Sahib). The building in which a devotional gathering was held was originally known as a *dharamsala*, but during the course of the eighteenth century this term was progressively supplanted by *gurduara*.

The change presumably occurred because of the increasingly common presence within these buildings of the Guru himself in the form of the sacred scripture. Following the death of Guru Gobind Singh the mystical Guru remained present within the scripture, which Guru Arjan had compiled a century

---

5. *Zafar-nama 22*, Dasam Granth, p. 1390.

earlier. The Granth Sahib thus became the Guru Granth Sahib, sharing this dignity with the gathered Panth, which likewise incorporated the mystical presence of the eternal Guru. In practice the scripture has proved to be the effective vehicle and its mere presence constitutes any room or building a gurdwara.

Within a gurdwara most activity focusses on the sacred volume or its contents. The standard pattern of worship consists largely of the singing of *kirtan*, led by qualified members of the *sangat* or by professional hymn-singers called *ragis*. At appropriate times *karah prasad* (sanctified food) is distributed to all who are present, and *katha* may be delivered. This consists of an exposition of the scriptures, or perhaps the narrating of an incident form the lives of the Gurus or from later Sikh history. *Katha* is normally the responsibility of the gurdwara's *granthi*.

We come to yet another term that has been misunderstood during the course of the recent political crisis. A *granthi* is a person who serves as the custodian of a gurdwara, with responsibility for the maintenance of the shrine and the conduct of its routine rituals. Most are humble men serving small gurdwaras, but the few who are appointed to prominent shrines acquire a large dignity. Most prominent of all is the chief *granthi* of the Darbar Sahib in Amritsar (known to foreigners as the Golden Temple).

In recent times the chief *granthi* of the Golden Temple has come to be regarded as one of the seven "high priests" of the Panth. Five of the other "high priests" are the *jathedars* (or "commanders") of the five *takhats* (also written *takhts*) or "thrones," gurdwaras with a unique role and dignity. Special decisions affecting the temporal welfare and politics of the Panth are taken before the Akal Takht, the building that faces the Golden Temple and was so seriously damaged during the army assault in June 1984. Akal Takht is thus the principal focus of the Panth's worldly concerns, supported by similar institutions in Anandpur, Damdama, Patna, and Nander. The *takhats* are highly revered as institutions, and their custodians are accorded a certain measure of dignity and respect. Each *takhat* is also served by *granthis*; in the case of Akal Takht, as we have said, the chief *granthi* has been recognised as one of the "high priests."

It is, however, wholly incorrect to describe these two *granthis* and five *jathedars* as "high priests." The Panth recognises no priesthood, and by no stretch of the popular imagination can these seven men be legitimately regarded as priests. Moreover, they are not particularly high. All receive their appointments by committee decisions and each can be removed by the same process. It has been convenient in some circles to treat them as "high" during the recent crisis in order to lend weight to policy statements and claims that have been routed through them. Five of the seven are appointed by the Sikh organisation that controls the main gurdwaras in the Punjab, the Shiromani Gurdwara Prabandhak Committee. The remaining two have been vulnerable to central government pressure because their seats in Patna and Nander are well beyond the borders of Punjab. The media have picked up the term "high priests" and in persistently using it have distorted our understanding of both the nature of the Panth and the mechanics of the recent crisis.

If one is seeking genuine authority in the Panth, one should examine the term *panj piare*, "the Cherished Five." When inaugurating the Khalsa, Guru Gobind Singh chose five Sikhs of proven loyalty to receive the first baptism, and then to administer it to the Guru himself and to others. All initiation ceremonies have since been conducted by groups of *panj piare*, and important decisions within a *sangat* may likewise be entrusted to them.

One last word that deserves to be mentioned is *seva*; it is yet another example of a term that undergoes a shift in meaning when we introduce its standard English translation. The translation usually given is "service," designating service which is intended to assist a community or alleviate individual suffering. *Seva* certainly embraces these purposes, at least within the modern understanding of the term, but its primary meaning designates service to a gurdwara. It is another of the words which, in the full richness of its meaning and connotation, defies easy translation. As such, it reinforces yet again the claim that only through careful analysis of such terminology can we effectively penetrate the inner meaning of a culture or a tradition.

If we are able to achieve this purpose, if we can conduct a careful analysis of Sikh terminology, we fulfill a major need with regard to the shaping of a Sikh theology. It is merely a preliminary step, yet for those who choose to work in English it is an essential one, a prerequisite for any acceptable analysis of individual doctrines or of Sikh belief as a whole. In pursuing it we shall be identifying and initially analyzing those elements in the tradition which together constitute the rudiments of Sikh theology. A Sikh theology for modern times is now long overdue; and although we may never produce one for the twentieth century, we can surely do something for the twenty-first.

Ethical and Spiritual Aspects of Nam-simaran

Amarjit Singh Sethi

Introduction

The practice and philosophy of *Nam-simaran* meditation are drawn from Sikhism, which originated with Guru Nanak (A.D. 1469-1539) and was nurtured and developed by the succeeding nine Gurus up to 1708. Since then it has grown into a religion of over ten million people. This article is intended to examine the various ethical and spiritual dimensions of *Nam-simaran*. *Nam-simaran* refers to a way of life that encompasses both spiritual and ethical conduct in accordance with guidance as laid down in the Sikh scripture, Guru Granth Sahib.[1]

Sikh Spiritual Consciousness

Spiritually, Sikhism implies faith in one Omnipotent Being, Ekonkar Satnam Karta Purakh, and acceptance of and surrender to His will. This means a constant awareness and remembrance of the one Being who is beyond concepts, time and space, yet merciful, compassionate and ever-present in the universe. Avtar Singh explains Satnam Karta Purakh as follows:

> The Absolute is thus conceived in Sikhism as dynamic and is viewed functionally. This attribute of the creative activity has considerably influenced the ideal of self-realization...it is declared to be *karta*, the Creative energy, activity. Coming back to the use of *sat* we may see that the only appropriate course is to understand it in terms of its usage in Sanskrit (from where it is adopted) as "Real, existent, good" and when it refers to the ideals or self it, likewise, would mean "as any one or anything ought to be." But these meanings will have to be conjoined with *Sat Nam Karta Purukh* when a reference is made to the Absolute. The Gurus, however, do not always use the full *Sat Nam Karta Purukh* to refer to the Absolute but many a time simply use the symbol *sat* or *nam* for the same. Therefore, even when *sat* or *nam* is used singly it ought to be understood in the sense of *Sat Nam Karta Purukh* unless it is specified in some other manner in some particular

---

1. The basic Sikh *rahit* (code of conduct) is incorporated in Guru Granth Sahib, Dasam Granth, *Rahit Maryada* and *Vars Bhai Gurdas.*

[Joseph T. O'Connell, Milton Israel, Willard G. Oxtoby, eds., with W.H. McLeod and J.S. Grewal, visiting eds., *Sikh History and Religion in the Twentieth Century* (S. Asian Studies Papers, 3) (Toronto: S. Asian Studies, Univ. of Toronto, 1988)]

context, for example, when *sach* is used in the sense of truthful. And here we may refer to the earlier interpretations of *sat* by the scholars of Sikhism as truth, against which Macauliffe raised some doubt...The use of the term truth here may be objected to on two grounds. First, that it may cause it to be confused with truthful. It is in this sense that Macauliffe seems to have objected to its use. Second,...that it may fail to convey the dynamic aspect, which...is an important keynote of the Sikh ethics. It is perhaps due to this inability of mere *sat* as truth to convey this dynamic creativity that Guru Nanak prefers to use *Sat Nam Karta Purukh*. It would, therefore, be better not to fall into the error of calling it as true or truth. And if it is absolutely necessary to use the term Truth to convey the idealistic groundings of the Absolute it would be necessary to make it clear that it is being understood in the sense of this dynamic existence which, from the moral angle, is held to be the highest good or the absolutely perfect. It is this Absolute that is declared to be fearless (*nirbhau*) and without enmity (*nirvair*) by Guru Nanak.[2]

In order to attain enlightenment and appreciate the ever-abiding presence of Satnam Karta Purakh, a Sikh is urged to surrender his or her ego (or will) to the Guru's teaching as embodied in Guru Granth. No personal Guru is needed—in fact, a concept of personal Guru is rejected. There is a path of discipleship that entails both moral and spiritual obligations. This path provides an opportunity for spiritual growth and enlightenment. The Guru's teachings help the disciple to engage in *Nam-simaran*—a mental and spiritual culture.

It should be stressed here that spiritual consciousness and ethical conduct in Sikhism are the two elements that are so integrated and complementary to each other that one without the other is a sham. Guru Nanak says: "Truth is higher than everything else, but true conduct is higher even than Truth."

Some Features of Sikh Spiritual Consciousness

Sikh consciousness is basically a process of transformation—from ego consciousness to *wah* consciousness. The word *wah* literally means "wonder." When combined with *guru*, i.e., *Wahguru*, it refers to Ekonkar Satnam Karta Purakh.[3] The key principles involved in this process are listed in Guru Nanak's *mulmantra*, incorporated at the beginning of the Guru Granth. These are acceptance of and surrender to Ekonkar; recognition of *Satnam* as Reality, recognition of Ekonkar as Creator, Controller and Enjoyer, who is Timeless yet embodied in finite forms, under no discipline or restraint, free from generation and cessation, and does not require anyone else to bring Him into existence. The Sikh de-identifies from ego through Guru's grace, leading to selfless service, enlightenment, and freedom. Spiritually these values refer to the inevitable presence of Ekonkar Satnam; socially they entail selfless activity; psychologically they help one to de-identify from narrow egoistic consciousness. The result is the emergence of *wah* consciousness—creative, free and enlightened, also termed by the Gurus as *sahaj* consciousness.

---

2. We owe this analysis to Avtar Singh, *Ethics of the Sikhs* (Patiala: Punjabi University, 1970, pp. 44-45); also see A.S. Sethi, *Universal Sikhism* (New Delhi: Hemkunt Press, 1972).

3. The process is described in detail in A.S. Sethi, *Universal Sikhism.*

Sikh Meditation or *Nam-simaran*

To get beyond ego (*haumai*) is a task that can be handled through *Nam-simaran*—by recognizing the fact that *haumai* or ego-identification is nothing but a phantom. *Nam-simaran* means constant remembrance and awareness of Ekonkar, implying that the practice of *simaran* embraces an evolutionary process. This process may be visualized in eight interactive stages. These include: 1) the ego, or *manmukhta*, stage, a stage of false identification in which one seeks worldly objects, possessiveness and achievement; 2) realization that the life of *manmukhta* is futile (one further realizes that life in ego leads to a widening gulf of separation between oneself and one's divine essence; this realization is made possible by Guru's grace); 3) kindling of the desire for Karta Purakh; 4) intensification of the desire into yearning, *bairag*; 5) *liv*, or constant remembrance; 6) *samana*, or union in which one is egoless and spontaneously becomes one with Him; 7) *vismad*, or a response of wonder to omnipotent Reality; 8) *sahaj*, or equipoise, the ultimate realization, in which one lives as His instrument in social life. A *manumukh* is thus completely metamorphized into a *gurmukh*.[4] This framework is based on numerous *shabads* in Guru Granth Sahib, in particular the hymns of Guru Ramdas, contained in his work entitled *Lavan*. An alternate framework is provided by Guru Nanak in *Japji* (four *khands*), but the above framework is in accord with Guru Nanak's philosophy.

The initiation of *Nam-simaran* begins by realizing the futility of the life of *manmukhta*. A *manmukh* (unenlightened person) is living under the influence of ego; a *gurmukh* (enlightened person) lives in God's Will, with a constant awareness that God is the only one who has created the whole universe and is the cause of all causes. The whole creation is sustained by His divine spirit called *Nam*. The recognition of *Satnam* as a pervading spiritual reality helps the Sikh to view his social relationships in a spiritual context. Sikh conduct is thus rooted in a metaphysical realization of union with God.

Nam-simaran is a very significant topic contained in Guru Granth. The vision of *Nam* and the basic technique of *simaran* are depicted in the *shabads* of the Sikh Gurus and *banis* of the *bhaktas* included in the Guru Granth. In this section we will explain the soundness and value of *Nam-simaran* as an essential component of the Sikh's path to enlightenment.[5] We have mainly relied upon

---

4. Avtar Singh, *Ethics of the Sikhs*. The list of ethical values is not given any hierarchical importance. Also see A.S. Sethi and R. Pummer, eds., *Comparative Religion* (New Delhi: Vikas, 1979); and A.S. Sethi, J. Singh and Gurcharan Singh, "Nam-Simaran (Contemplation) in the Transformation of Consciousness," *Journal of Comparative Sociology and Religion*, 6-7 (1979-1980), pp. 211-21.

5. Various scholars have explained *Nam-simaran*. In the Punjabi language see: various works of Bhai Vir Singh published by the Bhai Vir Singh Sahitya Sadan, New Delhi; also Vir Singh, *Santhyas Guru Granth Sahib*, v. 3; Randhir Singh, *Gurmat Nam*; and Jodh Singh, *Gurmat Nirnay*. In the English language see: M.A. Macauliffe, *The Sikh Religion* (Oxford, 1909); A.S. Sethi, "Sikh Meditation," in Jarnail Singh, John W. Spellman and Har Dev Singh, eds., *Proceedings of the Sikh Conference* (Willowdale [Toronto]: Sikh Social and Educational Society, 1979); A.S. Sethi, Joginder Singh and G. Singh, "Nam Simran," *Journal of Comparative Sociology and Religion*, op. cit.; A.S. Sethi, *Universal Sikhism*, op. cit.

the *shabads* of Guru Granth as a base, supplemented by personal and group reflections to provide an explanation of *Nam-simaran*.[6]

Characteristics of *Nam-simaran*

Nam refers to the expressions of the Divine which pervade the universe; as Guru Nanak says, "Whatever God has made is an expression of His *Nam*. There is no place in creation where His *Nam* does not pervade." And, as Guru Arjan says, "Thy *Nam* is the Support of all Thy beings, O Lord! The *Nam* is the Support of the world and all the universes."[7] *Nam* is not a "conjunct of *nam* and *rup*, i.e., name and form,"[8] as understood in Indian philosophy. As "universal Being cannot be identified with any particular form He is simply the Name (i.e., the Spirit)."[9] *Nam* is universal, "it is something which is in everything (*jeta qita teta nao*—all that is created is the Name). It can be anything, therefore, not as its form, since that has been precluded, but as its spirit. The Name is, therefore, the Universal Spirit."[10] *Nam*, according to Guru Nanak, is absolute reality, and is the precondition of all beings and universes.

The *Nam* system of Guru Nanak did not incorporate the various views of the existing traditions—Hindu or Muslim—because in his system all views are rejected *per se*, all views and concepts are transcended in *Nam*. Both positive and negative views are subordinated to a position of Ekonkar Satnam which does not affirm one concept or the other, but rejects all concepts and philosophies. As the Guru says in *Japji*, the Real cannot be known through conceptualization, because in *Nam* there is no relativity. *Nam* is unconditioned, conflictless, without restraint, unhindered and above relative categories. Yet it also pervades the relative empirical world.

In the *Mulmantra* of Guru Nanak, *Nam* is not "non-existent," a state of void or *shunya*. It exists and can be realized inwardly through Guru's grace. For the Sikh the total absorption of intellect in His remembrance is enlightenment. This process is also termed *simaran*.

Simaran means living in His will and order (*hukam*) with a constant awareness of God's presence. *Simaran* is not a method among various methods, and it is not an alternative to thought. Undeniably we cannot use thought to realize enlightenment (*gurmukhta*); on the other hand, thought by using its analytic mode may obstruct enlightenment. We have to transform thought (*buddhi*) into pure thought (*nirmal buddhi*) to arrive at *Nam*. *Simaran*, as Vir Singh says, is the experience of *Nam*, the constant remembrance of who we are.[11]

---

6. Personal and group reflections have taken place for several years (commencing in 1978) in weekly "Simaran Sessions" of the Ottawa Sikh Study Circle, Ottawa, Canada.
7. Guru Granth Sahib, p. 284.
8. Sohan Singh, "Seekers' Path," p. 4.
9. Ibid., p. 5.
10. Ibid.
11. Bhai Vir Singh, *Shatabdi Granth* (1972), p. 284.

The Sikh practises *simaran* to remove false identification of *haumai* and to sing the songs of love in praise of the Ekonkar.

Vir Singh explains:

> I always think of Him.
> Deeper than Thought, Unseen and
> Unknown in me lives this unending Simaran.
> A thousand quivering melodies shake my depth.
> This Simaran is celestial music,
> My soul is now the heaven of song.[12]

The Sikh rejects speculation about *Nam*, God or Immortality, not because there is no Real that is transcendent, but because the Sikh knows that Ekonkar Satnam (Transcendent Reality) cannot be known through empirical methods. The conditioned *buddhi* cannot know the unconditioned Ekonkar. The Sikh is spiritual to the core because *Nam* is not void or *shunya*, but devoid of imperfections and impurities. It is nothing but the spirit of Ekonkar.

The goal of *simaran* is spiritual, that is, to free the mind of all *vikalpas* (mental constructions) by dissolving *haumai* (ego). By means of this, freedom from *vikaras* (passions and attachments) also is achieved, for the *vikaras* arise from *haumai*. *Simaran* is the state of consciousness which is free from *vikaras* and the influence of ego.

Simaran consummates the moral and the spiritual ideals. It is a state of undivided personality, of the person who has no conflicts and is not tied to his ego or *haumai*. The *gurmukh* abolishes all egocentric attitudes, as contrasted with the *manmukh*, who is caught in his own narrow ego-bound attitudes and habits. In the *gurmukh* the ego has been renounced. *Haumai* and *Nam* cannot co-exist: *simaran* is the process of negating *haumai* so that spiritual *Nam* can reside. All doctrines and standpoints are abolished, as Guru Arjan in the *Sukhmani* critically refutes all devices to arrive at *Nam*.

When we say that *Nam* is only spiritual, it does not imply that the Sikh does not recognize social reality. The Sikh does not deny the utility of thought, rational method of science and empirical activity. What needs to be understood is that relativity is not applicable to the Ultimate Real.

Sikh Ethics in *Nam-simaran*

The key thesis of this paper is that Sikh spiritual values developed through *Nam-simaran* are uppermost, and that a Sikh derives his or her ethical values from the spiritual core and not the other way around.

The first basic value is one's realization that ethics flow from one's faith in Supreme Identity. This implies an awareness of the omnipresence of Ekonkar, as we have indicated. In practice, this means that the Sikh does not identify himself or herself with his or her ego, but realizes the Supreme Identity within himself or herself, who is beyond time and showers grace on all. Based upon this faith, a Sikh practises his or her ethics in real life. In other words, a Sikh

---

12. Ibid., p. 285.

sacrifices *manmat*, or instruction based on his ego, with *gurmat*, or Guru's teachings.

If we accept that a Sikh ought to shed his *manmat* (through Guru's grace, let it be stressed), then an interesting implication follows. The Sikh accepts certain spiritual and moral obligations: for example, keeping of the five *kakars*. You become a Sikh with Guru's grace when you surrender to the Guru, which is a result of grace.

The Five *Kakars* and Their Importance in Sikh Ethics

There are five basic *kakars* that form the fundamental expression of Sikh ethics: *kesh* (uncut hair), *kara* (a steel bracelet), *kangha* (a comb), *kach* (short breeches) and *kirpan* (a sword). The word *kakar* has been translated as "symbol," but this translation is not precise. In Sikhism it is believed that *kesh* is not an outward symbol but an integral part of the natural state of human beings. *Kesh* represents the spiritual core of Sikhism because it implies surrender of one's ego to Guru. Surrender is the foundation on which spiritual growth is to occur. It is an essential step for all persons who aspire to become the Guru's own, i.e., *khalsa*. Metaphysically, *kesh* signifies that the person has given up his or her ego, and that one will fashion one's conduct in accordance with the Guru's teaching or *gurmat*; it thus serves as a linking pin with inner enlightenment. For a Sikh *kesh* represents one's declaration that one accepts the one and only Ekonkar. One becomes aware, through Guru's grace, that acceptance of Ekonkar is inescapable. Moreover *kesh* is a gift of the Guru, and thus it is a person's declaration that one leads one's life according to *gurmat*. Non-cutting of hair is thus a spiritual act for a Sikh, and its significance can be understood in light of its metaphysical interpretation.

Kara, a steel bracelet, is a reminder to the Sikh that one ought to shed falsehood and practice universal love.

Kangha, a comb, is not only meant to keep *kesh* clean, but also refers to the notion that one should comb one's mind inwardly and keep it free of impurities. This refers to the ethical values of humility, temperance and contentment.

Kirpan is the sword of knowledge (*gian*), which has cut the root of ego. It also refers to practical use when violence has overreached its limits. This refers to the ethical values of courage and justice. The sword reminds the Sikh to succour the helpless and fight the oppressor.[13]

Kach refers to sexual fidelity and the ethical value of overcoming *kam* or lust.[14]

A Sikh gradually prepares himself by keeping this *rahit*, and when he or she is ready baptism, or *amrit*, is administered by five Singhs (i.e., five *amritdhari* Sikhs, known as five *piare*) who have the spiritual authority to represent the Guru and thus pass on enlightenment. Sikh men and women have

---

13. Harbans Singh, *Guru Gobind Singh* (New Delhi: Sterling Publishers, 1979).
14. Gopal Singh, *A History of the Sikh People* (New Delhi: World Sikh University Press, 1979), pp. 290-91.

equal status, and all caste distinctions are dissolved in the Sikh system. The Sikh code (*Rahit Maryada*)[15] clearly gives importance to baptism in its definition of a Sikh. The code defines a Sikh as he or she who has faith in the teachings of the Gurus, in the baptism prescribed by the Tenth Guru and in the Guru Granth.

According to Sikh *Rahit*, a Sikh is instructed in the following four prohibitions: a) non-cutting of hair, b) non-smoking, c) non-adultery, and d) not eating *kutha*—meat prepared by the process of a gradual and painful slaughter of the animal (by contrast, *jhatka* meat is slaughtered quickly to minimize pain).

It is our intention to point out that a Sikh's *rahit* is basically spiritual and that he or she demonstrates this by his or her resolve to realize the utter futility of ego. *Kakars* are the demonstration of a Sikh's resolve that he or she accepts the Guru's guidance. Thus it is from the context of spiritually that Sikh ethics flow, namely, truthfulness, temperance, contentment, courage and universal love.

A Sikh's identity is such that he or she is aligned with the Supreme Identity and dedicates his or her life to the metaphysical realization of Ekonkar. That means the practical appreciation of the wonders of the universal Ekonkar—a living appreciation of cosmic consciousness (*sahaj* stage). On the foundation of the Guru's grace, a Sikh grows spiritually and ethically in daily life.

In summary, Sikh ethics refer to the overcoming of certain negative propensities and cultivation of certain positive attributes in line with our hypothesis that *Nam-simaran* begins by surrendering one's will to the Guru so that one's ethics stem from the Guru's grace and include positive attributes such as *seva* (selfless service) and *vivek* (discriminative awareness). *Vivek* in turn refers to values such as truth, courage, temperance, contentment and wisdom. This basic Sikh ethic is embodied in the five *kakars*.

Grace

Sikh ethical conduct in itself is a result of the Guru's grace. We cannot force ourselves to attain enlightenment or live in His will or remove *vikaras*. In Sikhism there is great emphasis on grace (*gurprasad*), which helps the Sikh to realize *Nam* or enlightenment.

Simaran, which is proposed as a means for enlightenment, is in itself an act of grace. Conceptualization and mental constructions (*vikalpas*) are

---

15. The *Sikh Rahit Maryada* (Amritsar: Shiromani Gurdwara Prabandhak Committee, 1950). Avtar Singh traces the history of *Rahit Maryada* as follows: "A sub-committee of Sikh conduct conventions...was set up with its terms of reference prescribed to consolidate the rules for the individual Sikh and the Sikhs' *Gurdwara*...the report was approved in 1945,...and was subsequently published by Shiromani Gurdwara Prabandhak Committee...The principle of having such a convention...is provided for, in addition to other sources, in the *Rahit-namas* by Daya Singh, who envisages deliberation by the Sikhs themselves about codes of conduct (*rahit bibek*). The *Sikh Rahit Maryada*, which is the result of the deliberations by the Sikhs themselves, by virtue of the above principle, occupies a highly respected place and validity in Sikhism. This formulary, however, does not attempt to lay down all the detailed principles of the Sikh ethics for the obvious reason that its role is mostly explanatory and in the ultimate analysis the *Adi Granth* is the final and complete guide." Avtar Singh, *Ethics of the Sikhs*, pp. 139-40.

removed in *simaran* through Guru's grace. As ego is abolished, the knowing intellect becomes transparent (*anbhav prakash*), free from attachment. *Nam* is no longer looked at through thought; the intellect is purified in the light of the real Ekonkar, and hence in Sikhism it is called *nirmal buddhi*. That is the state of mind of a *gurmukh*, who has non-dual knowledge free from all dualities (*dubidha*) because he lives in His will. The essence of the Sikh method is to acquire *Nam*, not through building merit, yoga, or any effort for that matter, but by understanding that the only way in which enlightenment can dawn is through the grace of Ekonkar. The moment one understands this, there is surrender. All devices are abandoned. Effort plays a part—but only to convince the devotee that effort alone cannot attain *Nam*. Realization depends upon grace. The devotee can seek, ask, pray, but it is the inner Guru who grants—it is a gift.

Conclusion

Nam-simaran can play a vital part in one's spiritual and ethical development. It is the central meta-technique of transforming consciousness and it brings freedom (*nirbhaita*) and happiness (*sukh*) and paves the way for inner change.[16]

The nature of the human condition is such that one is caught in one's narrow ego; the Guru's teachings help a Sikh to renounce his or her ego and live in accordance with those teachings. Five *kakars* are essential components of a Sikh's code of ethical and spiritual conduct in carrying out the practice of *Nam-simaran*.[17]

---

16. For an analysis of the relationship between stress and meditation (including *Nam-simaran*), see A.S. Sethi, *Meditation as Intervention in Stress Reactivity* (New York: AMS Press, in press).

17. Thanks are due to Dr. Jogindar Singh, Research Scientist, Government of Canada, Ottawa, who assisted me in the preparation of this article.

Patterns of Pluralism:
Sikh Relations with Radhasoami

Mark Juergensmeyer

Scarcely thirty miles from the Darbar Sahib, the Golden Temple that marks the spiritual center of Sikhism in Amritsar, stands another striking example of religious architecture. It is the massive brick Satsang Ghar that rises in the midst of the Radhasoami colony located on the banks of the Beas river, just off the Grand Trunk Road midway between the cities of Amritsar and Jullundur. The Radhasoami building is every bit as much the center of its community as the Darbar Sahib is of the Sikhs', although, of course, the Radhasoami community is much smaller. There are a million or so initiates into the Radhasoami faith throughout the world—half of them in Delhi and the Punjab—compared with at least twelve million Sikhs. Despite the difference in size, there is a closeness between Sikh and Radhasoami traditions that is well symbolized by the geographic contiguity of their centers. Closeness does not necessarily lead to friendliness, however, and perhaps no other religious tradition illustrates the complexity of the Sikh attitude towards religious pluralism, or tests its tolerance, as does Radhasoami.

The Radhasoami movement was founded in Agra in 1861 by Swami Shiv Dayal and through a series of schisms and branches now has some thirty separate lineages of spiritual masters. Four of them—Dayalbagh and Soamibagh at Agra, the Ruhani Satsang in Delhi, and Dera Baba Jaimal Singh at Beas—have garnered sizable numbers of followers.[1] The movement revives an

---

1. Most of my information on Radhasoami comes from its own voluminous publications (especially those of the Dayalbagh and Soamibagh centers at Agra, the Beas center and the Ruhani Satsang centers at Delhi) and from my many interviews with leaders of the movement. The major secondary works on Radhasoami are J.N. Farquhar, *Modern Religious Movements in India* (New York: Macmillan, 1924); Philip Ashby, *Modern Trends in Hinduism* (New York: Columbia University Press, 1969); Agam Prasad Mathur, *The Radhasoami Faith: A Historical Study* (Delhi: Vikas, 1974); and Lawrence A. Babb, *Redemptive Encounters: Three Modern Styles in the Hindu Tradition* (Berkeley: University of California Press, 1987). See also my articles: "Radhasoami as a Trans-National Movement," in Jacob Needleman and George Baker, eds., *Understanding the New Religions* (New York: Seabury, 1979); "The Radhasoami Revival of the Sant Tradition," in Karine Schomer and W.H. McLeod, eds., *The Sants: A Devotional Tradition of India* (Berkeley: Berkeley

[Joseph T. O'Connell, Milton Israel, Willard G. Oxtoby, eds., with W.H. McLeod and J.S. Grewal, visiting eds., *Sikh History and Religion in the Twentieth Century* (S. Asian Studies Papers, 3) (Toronto: S. Asian Studies, Univ. of Toronto, 1988)]

esoteric interpretation of the teachings of India's medieval *sants*, especially Nanak and Kabir, and adopts a strict adherence to a *nirguna bhakti* concept of a formless but loving God. The true fellowship (*satsang*) of believers is said to take shape around spiritual masters (*sat gurus*) who assist followers in practices aimed at merging their souls with the divine sound current (*surat shabd yoga*).

Many of the Radhasoami teachings are similar to those of Sikhs, and their concepts may be traced to the same *nirguna bhakti* roots that lie at the basis of Sikhism. Radhasoami's ideas and its social characteristics are also similar to those of a small religious community in North India that has come into confrontation with Sikhism—the Nirankaris—and this similarity gives a good many Radhasoami members cause for concern. Could the fate that befell Gurbachan Singh and his branch of Nirankaris also descend upon them?

Charan Singh, the present master at Beas, does not think so. For one thing, the Nirankaris brought many of their troubles on themselves.[2] They were aggressively and publicly anti-Sikh, whereas Radhasoamis have expressed nothing but respect towards their neighbors. Furthermore, Gurbachan Singh was touted as being a new Nanak, an appellation never given to Charan Singh, and the Radhasoamis have never claimed to be a revival of Sikhism in a new form. Quite the opposite, Charan Singh explains: "We are not in any way in competition with Sikhism; we do not threaten them and they do not threaten us."[3]

Yet in 1985, in the turmoil that followed the Indian Government's invasion of the Golden Temple, there were threats against Charan Singh's life, and his public appearances became rare. Even when he did appear he was surrounded by bodyguards, and for the first time in the history of the Radhasoami colony at Beas foreign devotees were not allowed to visit. For two years Charan Singh stayed at Beas, not travelling to Delhi and Bombay or receiving foreign visitors until the last months of 1985.[4] When Sant Jarnail Singh Bhindranwale made unkind remarks about the Radhasoami masters, the leaders of the Beas community, taking note of the tragic results of the Nirankari confrontation,

---

Religious Studies Series, and Delhi: Motilal Banarsidass, 1987); and Chap. 19, "Radhasoami and the Return of Religion," in my book *Religion as Social Vision: The Movement Against Untouchability in 20th Century Punjab* (Berkeley: University of California Press, 1982). I also have a book in progress, tentatively titled *Radhasoami Reality: The Logic of a Modern Faith.*
I would like to thank the leaders of the Radhasoami movement for their assistance in the research for this article, and Prof. John Stratton Hawley for his editorial suggestions and comments on an earlier draft.
    2. An account of the anti-Nirankari movement in Sikhism and its role in the development of Sikh militancy in the 1980's may be found in Kuldip Nayar and Khushwant Singh, *Tragedy of Punjab* (New Delhi: Vision Books, 1984).
    3. Interview with Charan Singh, master of the Radhasoami Satsang, Beas, at Dera Baba Jaimal Singh, Beas, August 4, 1978.
    4. According to some members of the Radhasoami community, Charan Singh stayed in Beas "not for safety reasons but because his presence there was essential for the community's support" (interview with Dalat Ram, office manager of the Delhi *satsang*, in Delhi, August 15, 1985). During the period of unrest in the Punjab the *bhandara* festivals continued as usual and the crowds were said to have been bigger than ever (interview with R.N. Mehta, head of the Delhi branch of Radhasoami Satsang, Beas, in Delhi, August 15, 1985).

urged their followers not to respond in kind. One Radhasoami member did rebut Bhindranwale in a letter to the editor of a Delhi newspaper, and was reprimanded by Beas leaders for having done so.[5]

Despite the tensions of the moment, is Charan Singh right in regarding Radhasoami-Sikh relations as basically sound? The answer to that question depends in part on how one understands Sikhism and its relation to other faiths and in part on how one views Radhasoami as a religion. In this paper I will look at both of these issues, and attempt to come to some general conclusions about Sikhs and Radhasoamis and about inter-faith relations in religiously pluralistic societies in general. I want to try to understand which sorts of relationships lead to confrontation and which do not.

Sikhism among the World Religions

Much has been written about the tolerance of Sikhs towards members of other faiths. "The Sikhs religiously believe in the freedom of all religions," writes one Sikh author.[6] To illustrate her point, she notes that both Hindu and Muslim poets are represented in the Guru Granth Sahib; that Guru Gobind Singh regarded all holy places and forms of worship, including those of Hindus and Muslims, as being of equal benefit; and that Guru Tegh Bahadur was martyred not only on behalf of Sikhs but also for Hindus who were being forcibly converted to Islam.[7] The writings of Guru Nanak also express an open attitude towards religious diversity. They show his respect for the best in all religions—an essential unity of spiritual truth—and his disdain for the worst: the superficiality of meaningless rituals and the pompousness that too often appears in the behavior of religious specialists, whatever their affiliation.

In an especially moving section of the *Japji*, the morning prayer of Guru Nanak, the Guru advocates listening for the divine name, and promises that those who hear will "flower forever."[8] Among those mentioned as having the ability to hear are Muslims: Sheikh, Pir, and Badshah. At other places he is critical of religious leaders from a variety of faiths: he chastises yogis for their conceits, Brahmans for their empty ceremonies and Muslims for reading the Qur'an but missing the real truth within. Guru Nanak was not so much condemning these religious traditions as he was excoriating the hypocrisy in all religions. What he was after was an experience of the truth that ran as a deep current through all traditions and was the sole possession of none.[9]

---

5. Interview with R.N. Mehta, August 15, 1985. One example of Bhindranwale's remarks about Radhasoamis is found in his "Address to the Sikh Congregation, November, 1983," trans. by Ranbir Singh Sandhu, distributed by the Sikh Religious and Educational Trust, Columbus, Ohio, April, 1985: "He who is a Sikh of the spinning wheel and the goat, or Radhaswamis or Nirankaris [is not worthy to be a Sikh]," p. 11.

6. Rajinder Kaur, *Why Social Boycott of Nirankaris? vis-a-vis Hukamnama* (Delhi: Delhi Sikh Gurdwara Management Committee, n.d. [ca. 1979-80]), p. 1.

7. Ibid.

8. This translation is from J.S. Hawley and Mark Juergensmeyer, *Songs of the Saints of India* (New York: Oxford University Press, forthcoming in 1988).

9. I discuss the various Sikh attitudes towards other religions historically in "The Future of Sikhism as a World Religion," *Sikh Times* (Vancouver), July, 1982.

Not all religions have regarded Sikhism with the same generosity as that with which Guru Nanak regarded them. But despite the brutality of some Muslim rulers and the attempts of Christian missionaries and others to convert them, the Sikhs have been remarkably hospitable to Muslims, Christians and adherents of other faiths with whom they have lived as neighbors. For that reason the recent hostility against the Nirankaris may appear to be something of an anomaly. In a booklet written at the time that the official notice of censure, or *hukumnama*, was issued against the Nirankaris, a Sikh Member of Parliament, Dr. Rajinder Kaur, explained that the Nirankari situation had to be seen against the background of its historical precedents. Sikhs, she said, have always been prepared to defend their faith—militantly, if necessary—against enemies within and without who wished to destroy it. They perceived the Nirankaris as just such attackers, and were therefore forced to deny them the rights of free speech they would normally have honored. The concept of freedom of religion, she explained, does not grant one the right to "abuse other religions or their religious practices."[10] In particular, she held the Nirankaris responsible for five serious failings. According to her:

1. The Nirankaris deceitfully deny being a religion and allege instead that they are a "society or club of all religions";
2. They deceitfully claim to be Sikhs "when certain benefits are to be drawn" from adopting that identity and then deny it at other times;
3. They use the Sikh scriptures for their own purposes and "distort the hymns of Guru Granth Sahib";
4. They make "offending and derogatory remarks against the basic tenets of Sikhism"; and
5. Most important, the Nirankari master, Gurbachan Singh, poses as the "living embodiment of Guru Nanak Dev."[11]

Perhaps the Nirankaris are indeed unique in these respects, for I can think of no other religious group against which such accusations could be made. The Radhasoamis, certainly, are innocent of almost all of these charges. They do not allege that their master is the "living embodiment of Guru Nanak Dev," nor have they made "offending and derogatory remarks" against Sikhism, nor have they distorted the Sikh scriptures or claimed that their community is a branch of Sikhism in order to receive government benefits allocated to Sikh groups. It is true that they are undecided as to whether their tradition should be regarded as a "religion" or as something else, but the reason for this uncertainty has nothing to do with any attempt to claim members of all other religious traditions as their own.

Even so, there are enough similarities between Radhasoami and Sikhism to make them seem competitive in some people's eyes, and Radhasoami has a

---

10. Rajinder Kaur, *Why Social Boycott of Nirankaris?* p. 2.
11. Ibid., p. 9.

sufficiently broad appeal to make such perceived competition seem a threat to some Sikhs. There is plenty of reason to ask, then, whether Radhasoami really is separate from Sikhism. To answer this question, we have to look at the history of Radhasoami and see how its teaching and organization evolved.

The *Nirguna Bhakti* Origins of Radhasoami

Sikhs and Radhasoamis both regard the medieval *nirguna bhakti* tradition as the fountainhead of their faiths. The leading figures of this tradition, the poet-saints known as *sants*, include Guru Nanak, the first Guru in the Sikh lineage, as well as many of the authors of the verses in the Guru Granth Sahib, such as Ravidas and Kabir. Radhasoami also regards the medieval *sants* of India—especially Kabir—as having preceded their founder, Swami Shiv Dayal, in providing conduits of spiritual power to the world.[12]   The main branches of Radhasoami—the two at Agra and the two at Beas and Delhi—differ, however, in their opinions about the nature of the links between Dayal and the earlier *sants*.   The Beas-Delhi view is that there was an unbroken connection that linked Dayal with the *sants*, a master-to-pupil succession of spiritual initiation.   The Agra position is that each luminary in the group was a separate manifestation of divine energy, which is a single source that has struck the earth like lightning at different times.   But all branches of Radhasoami agree that the medieval *sants* were in some way a part of the Radhasoami ancestry.   In fact, those within the Radhasoami tradition often characterize their faith not as Radhasoami but as *sant mat*—the way of the *sants*.[13]

The *sants* are not the private property of any one religious group in India, however.   They are revered by Indians of almost all religious stripes as innovators and religious radicals, rebels against whatever orthodoxies of belief and social structure they faced.[14]   Although it is difficult to identify a definite

---

12. Swami Shiv Dayal lists his predecessors as "Kabir Sahab, Tulsi Sahab, Jagjiwan Sahab, Garib Dasji, Paltu Sahab, Guru Nanak, Daduji, Tulsi Dasji, Nabhaji, Swami Hari Dasji, Sur Dasji, and Raidasji; and among Mohammedans, Shams-i-Tabriz, Maulana Rumi, Hafiz, Sarmad and Mujaddid Alifsani" (Swami Shiv Dayal, *Sar bachan* [prose], Radhasoami Satsang Sabha, Dayalbagh, 1959, verse 39, pp. 29-30).   According to the third master in the Agra line, Brahm Sankar Misra, Kabir was the first of the saints and was a manifestation of the highest regions of Radhasoami Dham; others after him were "Guru Nanak, Jagjivan Sahab, Paltu Das, Tulsi Das of Hathras" and, of course, Swami Shiv Dayal.   Misra places on a somewhat lower level other spiritual adepts, including "Garib Das, Dalam Das, Charan Das, Nabhaji, Darya Saheb, Raidas, Surdas, Shums Tabrez, Mansur, Sarmad, Moinuddin Chisti" (Brahm Sankar Misra, *Discourses on Radhasoami Faith*, Radhasoami Satsang Sabha, Dayalbagh, pp. 114-15; the spelling of the names follows the form in the English translation).   One of the present masters of Radhasoami, A.P. Mathur, leader of the Peepalmandi branch in Agra, told me that the *sants* emanating from Radhasoami Dham prior to Swami Shiv Dayal included the following, in this order: first Kabir, then Nanak, Dadu and Jagjivan (interview with A.P. Mathur, December 6, 1980).

13. The phrase *sant mat* is occasionally used in the *Sar bachan* (poetry) (cf. p. 184, Soamibagh translation) in a general sort of way and is used by Rai Shaligram in his Preface to refer to Radhasoami teachings in particular (p. 18).   According to Janak Raj Puri, the phrase was an invention of Tulsi Sahib (Introduction to *Tulsi Sahib: Saint of Hathras*, Beas: Radhasoami Satsang, Beas, 1978, p. 17).

14. For a general introduction to *sant* literature see Karine Schomer and W.H. McLeod, eds., *The Sants: Studies in a Devotional Tradition of India* (Berkeley: Berkeley Religious Studies Series and Delhi: Motilal Banarsidass, 1987); see also a forthcoming book of *sant* poetry which I have co-translated with J.S. Hawley, *Songs of the Saints of India* (New York: Oxford University Press,

core of motifs that can be found in the writings of all the *sants*, the following themes are widely shared: the concept of the absolute as beyond human attributes (*nirguna*, formless), and by implication the judgment that the entire Hindu pantheon is insufficient if taken in its own terms; the persuasion that all forms of religious leadership and accomplishment—whether claimed by Brahmans, yogis or Muslim *qazis*—are ultimately invalid, save one, that of the devoted follower of the Lord, whose own achievements in spiritual matters enable him or her to serve as a model for others; the conviction that such spirituality is essentially interior rather than bound up with external forms of piety and religiosity; and the belief that those who follow the path of spiritual growth enjoy a spiritual fellowship (*satsang*) with one another.[15]

Specific groups that trace their origins to *sant* teachings include Kabirpanthis, Ravidasis, Dadupanthis, Nanakpanthis and, of course, the Sikhs and Radhasoamis themselves. The Radhasoami allegiance to each of these tenets is refracted through a lens peculiar to itself.[16] In Radhasoami teachings, the nameless God beyond the gods is given a name—at least one that can be spoken in this world. This name is Radhasoami, according to those who follow the Agra branches of the movement; the Beas branch and its offshoots reveal five other names of God to their adherents at the time of initiation. The significance accorded to these names is initially the same. It is believed that their repetition enables the seeker to channel the energy contained within them and lift his or her own internal energy currents to the realms of ethereal light and sound that constitute the higher levels of God-consciousness. Beas teaching takes matters a step farther, claiming that believers also have access to an unspoken name that takes the seeker ultimately to the highest region of truth. That realm is itself an aspect of God, a level of being that has no connection with external practice. The medieval *sants* had said true religion should be divorced from outward observance in just this way, but the Radhasoami conception of this interior realm of faith is articulated in considerably greater detail than that envisaged by the *sants*: it has multiple tiers, the discovery of which involves a journey through increasingly rarefied strata of consciousness, all precisely and colorfully described.

1988). In it Hawley gives introductions to each of the *sants* and to the *sant* tradition in general. Selections from our translations appear in the section on *bhakti* literature in William T. de Bary, ed., *Sources of Indian Tradition*, revised edition (New York: Columbia University Press, 1987).

Besides Kabir and Nanak, other *sants* from the medieval period who are known throughout India are Ravidas, Namdev and Dadu. Other *bhakti* poets who are often linked with these figures are Mirabai, Surdas and Tulsidas; their poetry is usually addressed to particular gods rather than to a formless divinity, which is the usual criterion for demarcating those poets known as *sants* from writers of sacred devotional poetry in general. For an attempt to provide a defining set of criteria for *sant* ideas, see Pitambar Datta Barthwal, *The Nirguna School of Hindi Poetry: An Exposition of Medieval Indian Santa Mysticism* (Benares: Indian Book Shop, 1936).

15. I have based this summary of *sant* teachings on Barthwal, *The Nirguna School of Hindi Poetry*, pp. 32-56.

16. I develop this point further in "The Radhasoami Revival of the Sant Tradition," in Schomer and McLeod, *The Sants*.

Radhasoami conceptions of their spiritual masters and of the fellowship that binds together the community of believers are also permutations of familiar *sant* concepts. Seen through Radhasoami eyes, however, the *sants*, the "devoted followers of the Lord," are more than just models of spirituality: they are guides to spiritual progress, and the Radhasoami community sees them—including especially the recent representatives of the *sants*, the living masters—as incarnate forms of the absolute. And the "fellowship of the *sants*" (*satsang*), originally an idea that had nothing directly to do with formal initiation, is conceived by the Radhasoami tradition as primarily the gathering of those who have been properly selected and initiated by a Radhasoami guru. The *satsang* into which a new member of Radhasoami is ushered is a highly structured and well-organized association.

All aspects of Radhasoami, then, bear a family resemblance to elements of the early *sant* tradition, but they also have a distinctively Radhasoami stamp. To make it clear that when we are talking about the Radhasoami view of *sant* teachings we are talking about a distinctive interpretation, I have called this version of *sant* teachings "esoteric santism." It is santism because the concepts are roughly comparable to those taught by the medieval *sants*, yet it is in an esoteric, private form. The Sikh interpretation of *sant* teachings is not the same as that offered by Radhasoami, and to understand the divergency it may be helpful to understand how this esoteric form of santism arose.

In our search for the roots of esoteric santism, we are fortunate in possessing the extant writings of the putative founder of Radhasoami, Swami Shiv Dayal Singh. The most important of these writings is a two-volume work, *Sar Bachan* (*Essential Teachings*); one volume is a composition in versified Hindi and the other is a collection of sermons.[17] A reading of the *Sar Bachan* reveals two matters of interest regarding the origins of Radhasoami ideas. The first is the Swami's apparent reluctance to claim for himself any status as a *sant* or living master. It is certainly possible that others may have regarded him as such in his own lifetime, even with his approval, but his own claims are more modest. The other matter of interest is that, in espousing the major concepts of esoteric santism, he refers to the whole of the earlier *sant* tradition as his antecedent—not just the well-known medieval *sants* but many who were closer to his own era. In particular, he refers to one otherwise obscure spiritual master who lived during his own time in the nearby town of Hathras, a *sant* named Tulsi Sahib.[18]

---

17. English translations of the *Sar Bachan* volumes have been published by each of the major branches of the tradition. The Soami Bagh translation is by S.D. Maheshwari, published in 1970 (poetry) and 1958 (prose). Dayalbagh has published both poetry and prose volumes in Hindi, but has translated only the prose volume into English; that translation, unattributed, was published in 1955.

18. The question of whether or not Tulsi Sahib was Swami Shiv Dayal's guru is debated in Radhasoami circles: the Agra branches say "no," the Beas-Delhi branches say "yes." See Janak Raj Puri, "Introduction" to *Tulsi Sahib: Saint of Hathras* (Beas: Radhasoami Satsang, Beas, 1978); and Sant Das Maheshwari, *Param Sant Tulsi Saheb* (Agra: Radhasoami Satsang, Soami Bagh, 1979).

The teachings of Tulsi Sahib, it turns out, are remarkably similar to those of Swami Shiv Dayal. Both men depicted life as a series of struggles against *kal*—mortality, the negative force in life—and both held that the major means of avoiding the ravages of *kal* was to adhere to an even greater positive force, which is present in the words of the *satguru*, hidden deep within each person as a remarkable interior sound. The seeker is admonished to find that sound, fix on it, and follow its path as it makes its transit beyond the individual self through the third eye to level after level of increasingly higher realms of sound and light.

This sort of esoteric teaching was central to Tulsi Sahib, but it was not unique to him. There are, it seems, some interesting antecedents. Tulsi Sahib's best-known work, *Ghat Ramayana* (which could be translated either as the essence, or *ghat*, of the great Hindu epic, the *Ramayana*, or as the epic of the bodily vessel), is a dialogue between Tulsi Sahib and one Phuldas, a Dharamdasi—a follower of Dharamdas, who is believed to have been a favorite disciple of Kabir.[19] In it, references are made to an earlier dialogue, one between Kabir and Dharamdas. This dialogue is contained in a work entitled *Anurag Sagar* (*The Sea of Love*), which is perhaps a century older than the *Ghat Ramayana*. The *Ghat Ramayana* resembles it so strongly in style and content that the one may be regarded as the precursor of the other.[20] Several Radhasoami masters have acknowledged the relevance of the *Anurag Sagar* to Radhasoami teachings and have urged their followers to read it.

The main ideas of the *Anurag Sagar* are those we have described as esoteric santism, but particular attention is paid to the remarkable power of a salvific sound that can be transmitted only to appropriate persons, and only through initiation. Behind the *Anurag Sagar* lies an elaborate mythology about a cosmic conflict between the forces of darkness and the forces of good. As in Tulsi Sahib's writing, the former is called *kal*, and Kabir himself is given the role of embodying the latter. A particularly dramatic scene has Kabir meeting *kal* in combat at the top of the causal plane. According to the *Anurag Sagar*, the public, historical Kabir was only a momentary revelation, a brief glimpse of a much more important reality: a sort of cosmic Kabir-force that originated before creation, has entered into human history as Kabir, and is still accessible in the form of pure sound. This divine force is meant to liberate a fortunate few from the evil grip of time and mortality.

Although few of these mythological details survive as such within Radhasoami teachings, the grand role that Kabir plays within Radhasoami thought and its view of history is indisputable. One of the Radhasoami masters, for instance, claimed to have recognized the sights of Benares on seeing them for the first time because of having lived there as Kabir in a previous birth.[21]

---

19. Tulsi Sahib, *Ghat Ramayana* (Allahabad: Belvedere Press, 1911). I appreciate the help of John S. Hawley in translating this and the *Anurag Sagar* mentioned below.
20. *The Ocean of Love: The Anurag Sagar of Kabir*, trans. Raj Kumar Bagga and ed. Russell Perkins (Sanbornton, New Hampshire: Sant Bani Ashram, 1982).
21. Cited in *Souvenir in Commemoration of the First Centenary of the Radhasoami Satsang* (Agra: Radhasoami Satsang Sabha, Dayalbagh, 1962), p. 170. Kabir is highly regarded at all

And the general framework of the myth propounded in the *Anurag Sagar* is carried over in Radhasoami teachings. Like the *Anurag Sagar*, Radhasoami masters teach that time (*kal*) is evil, that religion has been created by *kal* as an opiate to deceive innocent people, and that a cosmic guru, incarnate in a living spiritual master, penetrates *kal*'s kingdom by a force of light and sound, rescues souls who are trapped there, and sends them on a journey of ascent that affords them vistas of an increasingly colorful and artful reality.[22]

It would seem, then, that the *Anurag Sagar* is the primary source of esoteric santism, and it, in turn, points to Kabir—or at least a certain branch of the Kabirpanth. For, although the *Anurag Sagar* is said to have been written by Kabir, its style and content suggest that it was written some time in the late eighteenth or early nineteenth century, several centuries after Kabir's death.[23] Its notions of esoteric santism are a bit extreme for most followers of Kabir, but in one branch of the Kabirpanth they are regarded as normative. This branch is the one that traces itself back to Dharamdas, and for Dharmadasis the *Anurag Sagar* is a primary scripture. Historically, the Dharamdasi Panth seems to have been the closest older relative of the Radhasoami Satsang.

Sikh and Radhasoami Connections

It would seem, then, that the origins of Radhasoami relate only tangentially to the Sikh tradition, since it is Kabir rather than Nanak who is held up as exemplary in the *Anurag Sagar*. But there are other aspects of Radhasoami doctrine that are more closely connected to Sikhism, and indeed the influence of the teachings of Guru Nanak has been considerable from the very beginning of the movement.

Although the founder of Radhasoami, Swami Shiv Dayal Singh, was born in Agra, his family originally came from the Punjab.[24] His father, Seth Dilwali

---

branches of Radhasoami. At Soamibagh, for instance, S.D. Maheshwari has called Kabir "the first harbinger of the message of Dayal Desh" (*Holy Epistles*, Agra: Radhasoami Satsang, Soamibagh, 1964, v. 1, p. 389); A.P. Mathur, leader of the Peepalmandi branch, calls him "a great force" (interview with Mathur, August 13, 1985); and B.L. Gupta, leader of one of the branches at Gwalior, calls Kabir "the first true *sant*" (interview with Gupta, Gwalior, August 21, 1985); and followers of Kirpal Singh have called him "the founder of the tradition of Sant Mat" (Russell Perkins, "Introduction" to *The Ocean of Love: The Anurag Sagar of Kabir*, p. xx).

22. For echoes of the *Anurag Sagar* account see *Sar Bachan* (prose), Soamibagh version, p. 31.

23. It is impossible to date the *Anurag Sagar* precisely, but since it makes reference to disputes over the lines of succession within the Dharamdasi branch of the Kabir panth it is unlikely that it was written before that branch was firmly established in the eighteenth century. J.S. Hawley believes that the literary style of the piece also would locate it no earlier than that century. Charlotte Vaudeville makes no attempt to date it, but simply lists it among "apocryphal works attributed to Kabir" (*Kabir*, p. 338). When I first encountered the *Anurag Sagar* it was available only in Hindi (ed. by Swami Sri Nanhelal Murlidhar, Narsinghpur: Sarasvati Vilas Press, n.d.), but it has recently been translated into English, accompanied by color plates of illustrations, and published in paperback in the United States by followers of one of the successors of Kirpal Singh under the title *The Ocean of Love: The Anurag Sagar of Kabir*, trans. Raj Kumar Bagga and ed. Russell Perkins (Sanbornton, New Hampshire: Sant Bani Ashram, 1982). In his introduction to the English translation, Perkins vehemently denies Vaudeville's description of the work as "apocryphal" and argues for its authenticity "on linguistic and doctrinal grounds" (p. xxxi).

24. In Radhasoami publications, the convention is to transliterate the term *swami* as "Soami," and to add the honorific syllable *ji* and the title "Maharaj." I have chosen to use the non-inflected

Singh, was a Punjabi Khatri who is said to have revered Guru Nanak. It is possible that he and his family were Sikhs, or at least Nanakpanthis, a term that sometimes designates those who venerate especially the first Sikh master, Guru Nanak. Kirpal Singh, leader of Radhasoami's Delhi-based Ruhani Satsang, marshals several pieces of evidence to indicate that Shiv Dayal Singh's family were Nanakpanthi Sikhs: the Swami's father was devoted to the Sikh scriptures, a copy of which was transcribed by his grandfather and is located in the archives of the Soamibagh branch; he is reported to have recited *gurbani* (prayers of the Gurus) at the time of his father's death; he gave discourses on Guru Nanak's morning prayer, *Japji* (one of which is published as *Elucidation of Japji* by the Soamibagh branch) and he is said to have been a frequent speaker at the Sikh shrine of Mai Than in Agra.[25] During Swami Shiv Dayal's childhood, the family turned in a different direction, towards the spiritual tutelage of a local holy man, Tulsi Sahib of Hathras, by whom the Swami was introduced to the esoteric writings of the Kabirpanth. But he continued to preach from the Sikh scriptures throughout his life.

Tulsi Sahib was almost certainly under the influence of the Dharamdasi branch of the Kabirpanth, but Kirpal Singh once theorized that he had ties to Sikhism as well. He claimed that there is a hidden but genuinely historical link between Tulsi Sahib and Guru Gobind Singh, the tenth of the Sikh Gurus in the lineage established by Guru Nanak.[26] According to his theory Gobind Singh is said to have visited a ruling family of Peshwas in Maharashtra on one of his travels. While there, he initiated one of the members of the family into "the inner science," and he in turn initiated one of the princes, young Sham Rao Peshwa, who in time left Maharashtra and settled in Hathras, near Agra, where he came to be known as Tulsi Sahib. Since some Radhasoami writers regard Tulsi Sahib as the guru of Swami Shiv Dayal, this story would imply an unbroken guru-disciple linkage from the last of the Sikh Gurus to the present-day Radhasoami masters. But even in Radhasoami circles, each step of the story is disputed. The link between Swami Shiv Dayal and Tulsi Sahib is debated, the Maharashtrian background of Tulsi Sahib is discredited, and the initiation of the Peshwas by Guru Gobind Singh is regarded as a fantasy of the story's author. In fact, the story embarrasses many members of the Radhasoami community, who would rather affirm the opposite of what the story implies: that their tradition is separate from the Sikhs' and not an appendage of it.

----

version of his title and name. The earliest reference to Swami Shiv Dayal in writings other than those from within the movement itself is a brief comment in an article in a Vedantic journal, *Prabuddha Bharata*, in May, 1898, to which Max Müller refers in *Ramakrishna: His Life and Sayings* (New York: Charles Scribner's Sons, 1899). Other early reports (these by missionary scholars) are found in H.D. Griswold, *Radha Swami Sect* (Kanpur: Cawnpore Mission Press, 1907) and J.N. Farquhar, *Modern Religious Movements in India* (Delhi: Munshiram Manoharlal, 1977; first printed in 1914). Farquhar gives a Vaishnava cast to Swami Dayal's teachings, claiming that on occasion he would pretend to be Krishna.

25. Kirpal Singh, *A Great Saint, Baba Jaimal Singh: His Life and Teachings* (Delhi: Ruhani Satsang, 1973), pp. 12-14.

26. Kirpal Singh, *A Great Saint*, pp. 9-10.

Although the historical connections with Sikhism are not direct, there is no denying that Sikhism is part of the background against which the Radhasoami tradition was shaped. For the movement was spawned and has been nurtured in the culture of western Uttar Pradesh and the Punjab, where Sikhism touches the lives of most everyone. The Agra branches tend to be less influenced by Sikhism than those headquartered at Delhi or in the Punjab, but even there it is worth noting that the founding master of the Dayalbagh branch, Anand Swarup, came from a family who had been Nanakpanthis (and later Arya Samajis). The Beas branch is noticeably influenced by Sikhism, not only because its base is in the Punjab, but also because Jaimal Singh, the master responsible for establishing the Beas community as a distinct branch of Radhasoami, was a *keshdhari* Sikh. So, in fact, have been all masters who followed in his line.

Jaimal Singh was virtually the only Sikh among Swami Shiv Dayal's small circle of disciples in Agra, and it is something of a coincidence that he was there at all. He was a soldier, a member of the 24th Sikh Regiment, which happened for a time to be encamped in Agra. Jaimal Singh was interested in spiritual matters, so when he heard that Swami Shiv Dayal was discoursing on the science of the soul, he came to listen to him. Before long he took initiation and became one of the Swami's favorite disciples. After Swami Shiv Dayal's death in 1878, Jaimal Singh returned to the Punjab with his regiment, and after retiring from the army in 1889 he found a lonely spot along the banks of the Beas that was favored by wandering *sadhus*. He picked out a cave for his shelter and settled down to serious meditation. It was one of his disciples, a fellow soldier named Sawan Singh, who developed that lonely spot into the flourishing city named for his master, the meditating soldier: Dera Baba Jaimal Singh. Unofficially the colony is simply called "Beas," since it is situated on the river and near the village of that name.

The current master of Beas, Charan Singh, is the grandson of Sawan Singh. He and his family are Jat Sikhs of the Grewal clan, and perhaps half of his followers wear Sikh insignia as well. Most of the leadership of the movement is drawn from Khatri castes, both Hindu and Sikh, and the rest are from varied social backgrounds, many of them from lower castes. The style of worship is congenial to those who are used to Sikh worship, but it is sufficiently simple and universal to appeal to all. Members of the movement who come from Hindu and Christian backgrounds feel comfortable in Radhasoami services, and there is no implication that they have to become like Sikhs to be adherents of Radhasoami. In fact, one's religious background—Sikh, Hindu, Christian, or whatever—is regarded as largely a matter of custom and clothing; it has little relevance to Radhasoami teachings and practice.

The Point of Contention: The Radhasoami Guru

What does have relevance in the Radhasoami community is the Radhasoami spiritual master and what he has to teach. It is this emphasis on a living spiritual master—a guru—that is the problem for many Sikhs, since it seems to be an imitation of the reverence for the ten Sikh Gurus. In fact, however, the veneration of gurus in Radhasoami is not an imitation of Sikh practice but a phenomenon parallel to it, for the Radhasoami concept of guruship has its origins in the same radical *bhakti* tradition in which Sikhism began.

As we have seen, many Radhasoami ideas are elaborations of themes found in the medieval *sant* tradition, and the rudiments of the Radhasoami concept of the master may be found there as well. One of the most prominent themes in *sant* writings is the importance of devotion to the divine guru, the *satguru*. It is perhaps natural that a tradition that places great emphasis on teaching should think of God as a master teacher, but there is another reason why the *sant* tradition conceived of God as Guru, and the guru as God: it helps to resolve a paradox that lies at the heart of *sant* religiosity.

The medieval *sants* held two central but potentially contradictory truths: that the Absolute has no true form—it is "without quality" (*nirguna*)—and that the appropriate response to the Absolute is loving devotion (*bhakti*). These two truths are potentially at odds, for if the Absolute has no personal qualities, toward whom or what is this love to be directed? The answer that is often given is that *nirguna bhakti* is love for the sake of love; yet most devotees desire to have an object for their affection, or at least a direction in which it may be channeled. That is where the guru becomes important. He is a visible symbol of what is ultimate and unseen. Because of his devotion to his own guru, the master is a paradigm of love; yet at the same time he functions as a revealer and a revelation of the love itself. In the figure of the guru the *sant* tradition recognizes an aspect of divinity toward which the devotee can express his or her devotion. The guru gives form to the formless and *nirguna bhakti* becomes in effect *guru-bhakti*: devotion to God as guru.

The Radhasoami concept of guru represents a continuation of this way of thinking about the Absolute; it rejects the traditional gods of Hinduism and claims that the guru is the only worthy object of one's love for God.[27] But there is a difference between the Radhasoami interpretation and that of others who revere *sant* teachings. For many who hold these teachings dear, the guru is not immediately accessible. In some cases the guru is perceived to be an historical entity at some remove from present experience; in other cases he is trans-historical in nature, an abstract guru within one's own soul, the "voice of God mystically uttered within," as one scholar describes it.[28]

The Sikh community, the largest religious group to have developed from the medieval *sant* tradition, views its Gurus in both these ways. Guru Nanak and the other nine Gurus in the Sikh lineage are historical personages, but Sikhs regard them as bearers of a divine, super-physical existence. Because the Sikh Gurus were, to Sikh perception, more than historical entities, it was possible for the tenth in their line, Guru Gobind Singh, to proclaim that the spiritual energy

---

27. One of the Radhasoami masters at Dayalbagh, Anand Swarup, is said to have even rejected Lord Krishna himself when he manifested himself before him. *Souvenir*, pp. 163-64).
28. W.H. McLeod, *Guru Nanak and the Sikh Religion* (Oxford: Clarendon Press, 1968), p. 150.

of the Gurus would be transferred after their lifetimes to the sacred book (the Guru Granth Sahib) and become manifest in the community of followers (the *Guru-Panth*). In the Radhasoami community the notion of guruship is in a sense less well developed, for, except in two branches of the movement where there is an "interregnum" and no living guru is present, the Radhasoamis still insist on the physical presence of the guru and not a symbolic or transferred form.[29] This fact more than anything else marks Radhasoami as distinctly different from the Sikhs and other communities that venerate the medieval *sants*, and it is a source of some tension between them.

This tension has led to a number of differing responses. It is said, for example, that in the early years of the Beas colony, Jaimal Singh removed the word *hukka*, meaning "water pipe," from the verse portion of the *Sar Bachan*, together with any reference to Swami Shiv Dayal's ever having used it. He was apprehensive that these references would offend Sikhs, to whom the use of tobacco is anathema.[30] In the 1930's, during the time of Sawan Singh, the great master at Beas, a group of Sikhs did indeed express their aversion to Radhasoami teachings by blocking the entrance to the Beas *dera*; the police had to be called to the colony to restore order.[31] And from time to time in the 1960's and 1970's such disruptions recurred. On one occasion a group of Sikhs erected loudspeakers outside the Beas colony walls and attempted to summon their fallen brethren back to the faith. With the rise of Sikh militancy in the 1980's, tensions surfaced again.

Is Radhasoami a Competing Religion?

There are two ways in which Sikhs might view Radhasoami, and there are positive and negative sides to both. The first option is for Sikhs to view Radhasoami as part of their own tradition, either as a benign sect like the Udasis or as a heretical movement like the Nirankaris. In the latter case, Sikhs would be regarding Radhasoamis as some Muslims view Ahmadiyyas and Baha'is, and as some Christians view Mormons. Because their tradition developed separately from Sikhism, however, most Radhasoamis reject this comparison. They resist being described as any kind of Sikh sect at all, whether heretical or benign.

This brings us to the second way of viewing Radhasoamis in relation to Sikhism: to regard them as two separate traditions. Adherents of Radhasoami find this option much more congenial. But the question remains as to what kind of tradition Radhasoami is and whether it competes in any way with Sikhism, even if it is fundamentally distinct.

These questions are sometimes debated within Radhasoami circles and sometimes outside as well, especially in the charged religious and political

---

29. The two branches of Radhasoami where there is at present no living guru are Soamibagh in Agra and Dhara Sindhu Pratap Ashram in Gwalior.
30. S.D. Maheshwari, *Truth Unvarnished*, part 1 (Agra: Radhasoami Satsang, Soamibagh, 1963), p. 110.
31. Julian Johnson, *With a Great Master in India*, 6th ed. (Beas: Radhasoami Satsang, Beas, 1975; originally published in 1933), p. 44.

atmosphere of the Punjab in the mid-1980's. But they have more than a political import; they are interesting from a sociological perspective as well. Sociologically, the issue is whether Radhasoami should be considered a reform movement—that is, a breakaway Hindu or Sikh sect—or a separate religious community of its own. According to one sociologist, Neil Smelser, movements may be classified according to whether they attempt to change the norms and values of society or verify them.[32]   To a large extent, Radhasoami has to be regarded as the former: it provides an alternative to the dharmic social order of Hindu society. But "value-oriented movements" such as Radhasoami should, according to Smelser's theories, be schismatic or revolutionary, and Radhasoami is neither.

The social situation of Radhasoami is complicated by the fact that its fellowships exist as islands within several religious cultures: Hindu, Sikh and Christian. Perhaps "island" is too static a term, for Radhasoami interacts in a certain way with each, and in each case Radhasoami may be regarded simultaneously as a revival of elements of the culture that it is in—the *sant* elements of Hinduism, the guru fellowship of Sikhism, and the messianic and mystical elements of Christianity—and as a special culture of its own. Its own culture is trans-national in character, for it attempts to avoid being too closely identified with the parochial customs of any particular national group.[33]

It would appear, then, that Radhasoami society has two dimensions. On one hand, it is intimately linked with the societies around it. Radhasoami masters are fond of demonstrating how their teachings are found in the religious traditions of the majority cultures where Radhasoami fellowships are located, and they urge their followers to participate in the customs of those traditions. When one of his American initiates asked Charan Singh whether he should leave Christianity behind, the Beas master assured him that Radhasoami was itself the truest form of Christianity, so he could embrace the church with a new enthusiasm.[34]   On the other hand, Radhasoami retains a certain suspicion of these traditional cultures, so the master cautioned him not to take seriously all the "dogmas, rituals and ceremonies" of the church. The "priestly class," he said, was out to "exploit" the unwary with rituals and such.[35]   Charan Singh explained his own case as well. He said that he kept the identifying marks of a Sikh—his long hair, turban and wrist bangle—but did so mostly out of social convention. Intrinsically, they held "no significance."[36]

Most Radhasoami devotees seem to have no difficulty with the notion that they can be good Christians, Hindus and Sikhs and at the same time be good

---

32. Neil Smelser, *A Theory of Collective Behavior* (New York: Free Press, 1962).
33. I develop this notion further in an article, "Radhasoami as a Trans-national Movement," in Jacob Needleman and George Baker, eds., *Understanding the New Religions* (New York: Seabury Press, 1979).
34. Charan Singh, *Spiritual Heritage* (Beas: Radhasoami Satsang, Beas, 1983), p. 213.
35. Ibid.
36. Charan Singh, *The Master Answers to Audiences in America* (Beas: Radhasoami Satsang, Beas, 1966), p. 499.

members of the Radhasoami fellowship, but for that reason they display some uncertainty over whether Radhasoami should be regarded as a separate religion. In a survey questionnaire I administered to a hundred residents of a Punjabi village, a number that included both Radhasoami *satsangis* and non-*satsangis*, I found that the adherents of Radhasoami consistently identified with the social aspects of their religion more strongly than did those who were not members of the movement. For example, the Radhasoami villagers said that in times of trouble they would look towards their *satsangi* comrades whereas the others would turn to the government or their caste associations.[37]

At the same time, Radhasoami leaders take great pains not to insult the sensitivities of those in the wider society around them. Inter-caste marriages, for instance, which go against the Hindu grain, are discouraged by Radhasoami leaders. Although such marriages would be consistent with the Radhasoami ideal of a non-stratified society, they might also be regarded as an affront to Hindu sensibilities. "We are not here to transform society," one of the Radhasoami masters told his followers, "but to transcend it."[38] When this statement was made at a gathering of liberal, politically-minded Western followers, a good number of them were displeased. Others who were more sensitive to the Indian situation felt it reflected a realistically cautious attitude toward Indian society, where religious and social issues are easily mixed and often inflammatory. Still others simply accepted his statement as an accurate reflection of what they regarded as fact: that social issues are essentially irrelevant to religion.

By holding a deep loyalty to the Radhasoami fellowship while maintaining a solid commitment to the wider culture, Radhasoami devotees seem to defy the expectation of sociologists such as Smelser that they should choose one or the other. In the complicated religious culture of North India, however, this is no anomaly, for one's religious identity is not a single, monolithic thing. As I have argued elsewhere, there are three different levels of religious identity in North India. One level is *dharma*, the social institution that embraces widely-held social values and caste networks; another is *panth*, the fellowships of *satsang* that cluster around certain spiritual teachers; and the third is *qaum*, the term for a unified people such as one might find in a religious nation.[39] It is possible—even common—in traditional Indian society for persons to subscribe to three different entities at the same time: they might adhere to the Hindu notion of caste, revere the Sikh gurus as saints, and wear the identifying marks of a Muslim. Traditionally, Hinduism has largely been a matter of *dharma*, Sikhism

---

37. The results of this poll and an explanation of how it was conducted are to be found in an appendix to my dissertation, "Political Hope: Scheduled Caste Social Movements in the Punjab, 1900-1970," Political Science, University of California, Berkeley, 1974. It should be noted that this survey was taken long before the current rise of Sikh militarism and the polarization of religious sentiments in the Punjab.

38. Charan Singh, discourse to foreign guests, Beas, November 12, 1980.

39. For further discussion of this way of looking at the social aspects of religion in the Punjab, see my *Religion as Social Vision*, pp. 2-3.

was primarily a *panth*, and Islam had the characteristics of being a *qaum*. But these matters have never been clear-cut, and they change over time. There have always been panthic movements in Hinduism and Islam, and the recent politicization of Hinduism has been leading many Sikhs to think of their community as a *qaum* of its own.

Radhasoami is a *panth*, of course—at least it was in its early stages—but it has come to challenge Hinduism on a dharmic level as well. It has no pretensions of being a *qaum* of its own, and it avoids the qaumic tendencies of Sikhism and other militantly political religious movements of today. It is a somewhat more elaborate version of some of the panthic movements that were established in veneration of the medieval *sants*, including the Kabir Panth and the Ravidasis, but is less extensively developed than the best-known of the medieval panthic movements, the Sikhs. Sikhism is now the dominant religious tradition of the Punjab, but Radhasoami continues to be what most panthic movements have always been, a counter-structure that exists in symbiotic relationship to the religious culture of the dominant societies around it.[40]

Patterns of Pluralism: A Schematic Outline

The relationship between Sikhism and Radhasoami depends on how one views Sikhism and how one views Radhasoami. If one views them both as panthic movements that stem from the same origins, then they can be seen as standing in a sort of competitive relationship with each other. If one sees Radhasoami as a *panth*, however, and Sikhism as something more, the competition vanishes—assuming, of course, that Radhasoami teachings are seen as separate from Sikhism and not as a heretical offshoot from it.

It appears that there are two significant variables in gauging the relationship between the Sikhism and Radhasoami: the degree of similarity in teachings between the two, and the degree of similarity in social form. I suspect that these variables have much to do with determining the relationship between many religious traditions and constitute an important element in the patterns of inter-faith relations in religiously plural societies. The interaction of the variables can be described by the table on the next page.

When two religious groups are dissimilar in both teachings and social type, they have little to fear from each other, and are likely to co-exist with little difficulty. There is no reason for Sikhs and members of the Ramakrishna Mission, for example, to perceive one another as a threat: the former constitute the *qaum* of the Punjab and the latter comprise a largely urban Hindu *panth*. When the teachings are dissimilar but the social forms of the groups are similar, there is a greater potential for tension. At one point Christianity, for instance, was perceived by Arya Samajis and some Sikhs in the Punjab as having the

---

40. I explore further the notion of social movements as counter-structures in *Religion as Social Vision*, pp. 278-82.

**Types of Inter-faith Tensions According to
Similarities and Dissimilarities of Teachings and Social Type**

| | | Teachings | |
		DISSIMILAR	SIMILAR
Social	DISSIMILAR	Mutual co-existence	Absorption of weaker group
Type	SIMILAR	Attempts at conversion	Tension between synthesis and competition

potential to replace dharmic Hinduism and *qaumic* Sikhism. The attempts at Christian conversion were then countered with *shuddhi* (Arya Samaj efforts at "repurifying" fallen Hindus) and by rebaptism into Sikhism as well.

It is when the teachings of the two groups are similar that some of the greatest problems of compatibility occur. When one group is perceived as being of a different social type from the other—as the Radhasoami community perceives itself as a *panth* compared with the *qaum* of the Sikhs—the larger community has little to fear from the smaller group, even if it is regarded as heretical. In fact, the Radhasoamis have more to fear from Sikhism, for the common fate of a small group within a larger but similar culture is that it will be absorbed into it and disappear. For some generations this has been the nightmare of Sikhs who find themselves overwhelmed by Hindu culture, and it might rightly be the fear of Radhasoamis who perceive themselves to be an island within a sea of Sikhism. Perhaps for this reason the Radhasoamis are adamant about being separate from Sikhism and have evolved some separate forms of cultural identity.

When two groups are alike in teachings and are also alike in social type, the tensions are most severe and the outcome most unpredictable; extremes of synthesis and confrontation are both possible. The relations between Roman Catholic and Protestant Christians, for instance, and between Shi'i and Sunni Muslims have all the ingredients of a family feud: the intimacy and competition that breeds extremes of love and hate. There are no large divisions within Sikhism, but there are smaller ones, and these have produced some of the same results. The Nirankaris, for example, were regarded by many Sikhs not as a separate *panth* but as renegade Sikhs who compounded their insult to the normative doctrines of the faith by pretending to be potentially as strong as the Sikh *qaum*. Their creation of a Nirankari militia was seen as evidence of a move in this direction.

There is no militia in Radhasoami and no need for it, for its relations with its neighbors are respectful and, for the most part, calm. Although it shares with Sikhism some ideas that grow out of their common *sant* origins, Radhasoami is not widely perceived by those within or without the community as being anything like a Sikh sect and it has expressed no interest whatsoever in competing with Sikhism on a social scale. For this reason the future of Sikh-Radhasoami relations bodes well and the traditional Sikh attitude of tolerance and good will to people of other religious persuasions will most likely continue to apply to Radhasoami for some time to come.

The Secular Heritage of the Sikhs

Surjit Hans

The secular heritage of the Sikhs is a subject of interest on several levels: academic, utilitarian and national-ideological. Sikhs and non-Sikhs may share academic interest in the changing history of Sikh values and world-view. Understanding the secular heritage of the Sikhs can be of utilitarian significance for Sikhs and Hindus because it could help in moving toward a solution of the Punjab problem. Indeed, my recent book in Punjabi, whose title could be rendered in English as *What Should the Sikhs Do? The Secular Heritage of the Sikhs*, is a product of that contemporary political crisis.[1] This paper presents the gist of the argument of that book. Finally, the secular heritage of the Sikhs is of national ideological interest in the sense that it advances a somewhat different argument in support of "secularism," the core of the national ideology of modern India. This paper develops at some length the academic issue of tracing secular elements through the religious literature and collective history of the Sikhs. It takes up more briefly the issues of contemporary utilitarian and national ideological application of the secular heritage of the Sikhs.

Thus far in human history secularism and secularisation seem to have been developments peculiarly related to the Christian-influenced West. The argument has been made that secularism is possible only under the influence of Christian religion, and it has been suggested that it may be logically fallacious to generalise from a particular case. Such views call for serious and critical attention.[2] One is surprised to find how much the modern world in its secular garb seems to owe to Christian influences. The philosophic problem of determinism may be seen as a transfiguration of the Christian problem of free will in relation to divine omnipotence. Similarly, the problem of body-mind relationship in psychology seems to have been inherited from Christian concern[3]

---

1. Surjit Hans, *Sikh Ki Karn? Sikh Dharma da Laukik Virsa* (Amritsar: Balraj Sahni Yadgar Parkashan, 1986).

2. David Martin, *A General Theory of Secularization* (New York: Harper & Row, 1979), pp. 1-2.

3. Gilbert Ryle, *The Concept of Mind* (Harmondsworth: Penguin, 1963), p. 20; Boring, Langfeld and Weld, eds., *Foundations of Psychology* (Bombay: Asia Publishing House, Indian reprint, 1963), p. 7.

[Joseph T. O'Connell, Milton Israel, Willard G. Oxtoby, eds., with W.H. McLeod and J.S. Grewal, visiting eds., *Sikh History and Religion in the Twentieth Century* (S. Asian Studies Papers, 3) (Toronto: S. Asian Studies, Univ. of Toronto, 1988)]

over the connection of body and soul. The standard periodisation of history as ancient, medieval and modern may be patterned on the incarnation and the second coming of Christ. The Judeo-Christian idea of the kingdom of God or heaven on earth has influenced world history in secular ways.[4] Assuming that the Sikh way of life, too, is being secularised, what aspects of the Sikh way of life are going to survive into the future in secular form, even though not apprehended as such at present? Here is a modest attempt to respond to that question.

The daily Sikh prayer (ardas) all the world over speaks of the Guru, or Wahguru, God conceived of as the Guru, as the "power of the powerless, the honour of the dishonoured, and the refuge of ones without shelter." The theological character of the Sikh is that he or she is a person without "power, honour and shelter." Sociologically, ardas is an institution that instills into the Sikhs their basic characterisation, reminds them of their history of persecutions and incorporates contemporary events into that history so that the sacred and the secular are inextricably fused. The traumatic events of 1984 (e.g., the attack on the Golden Temple and the Delhi massacre) have produced a high degree of inter-class and inter-caste solidarity among the Sikhs probably not witnessed before, at least not in the twentieth century. Coupled with the fact of their being a beleaguered minority community, the theological characterisation of the Sikhs has helped them forge such a solidarity.

The above characterisation of the Sikhs was literally true of the followers of Guru Nanak and the Sikhs of the sixteenth century.[5] The early Sikhs were petty traders, artisans, itinerant merchants (vanjaras) and slaves with a sprinkling of peasant cultivators. In fact, much of the Sikh theological imagery comes from the social groups embracing Sikhism. For instance, the term vanjara, itinerant merchant, itself serves as a symbol of soul, (wo)man and God in Sikhism. The Sikh religion is the religion of "the humble and the meek." Guru Nanak (1469-1539) says:

> I am the lowest of the low-castes
> Beyond the pitch of lowliness.
> I belong to them; I do not imitate the high.
> The place where the low are looked after
> Is the locus of grace and divine largesse.[6]
> M 1, Sri 3 (p. 15)[7]

---

4. R.G. Collingwood, *The Idea of History* (Delhi: Oxford University Press, 1976), pp. 50, 52-54, 328.

5. Surjit Hans, "Social Transformation and the Creative Imagination in Sikh Literature," in Sudhir Chandra, ed., *Social Transformation and Creative Imagination* (New Delhi: Allied Publishers, for Nehru Memorial Museum and Library, 1984).

6. All references are to the standard 1430-page edition of the *Adi Granth*. Translations given are by the author, with minor editorial adjustments. Compare *Sri Guru Granth Sahib* (Punjabi and English translation), tr. Manmohan Singh (Amritsar: Shiromani Gurdwara Prabandhak Committee, 1962); *Sri Guru Granth Sahib* (English version), tr. Gopal Singh (Delhi: Gur Das Kapur & Sons, 1960); *Sri Guru Granth Sahib* (in English) tr. G.S. Talib (Patiala: Punjabi University, 1984).

7. M followed by 1 indicates the first Guru; Sri is the musical *raga*; three indicates the number of the composition in the set of hymns in that *raga*; the final number refers to the page of the standard 1430-page Adi Granth.
Similar references are made in M 1, Maru 10 (992); M 1, Gujari Asht 4 (p. 504); M 4, Gauri 22 (p. 171); Kabir Gauri 7 (p. 324); Kabir Gujari 2 (p. 524); Ravidas Sorathi 6 (p. 659); Kabir

Guru Ramdas has a hymn which is a portraiture of contemporary Sikhs: "We were buffeted about, our cry unheard. The company of the Guru lifted the insects of manhood."[8] Kabir devotes a hymn to the social irony of men making yarn and weaving but not permitted to wear the sacred thread.[9] Kabir contrasts the spirituality of the "wretched of the earth" with the moral hollowness of the ruling class: "We are the humble and the meek, you love to rule."[10] Sadhna (according to Sikh tradition, a contemporary of Namdev)[11] expresses an "ideal type" of the Sikh:

> I am not, my being is nothingness,
> I own nothing.
>
> Sadhna, Bilawalu 1 (p. 858)

The medieval Namdev (according to Sikh tradition, born in 1271, though non-Sikh scholars place him in later times)[12] has a contemporary ring when he makes a hymn of his "expulsion from the temple for being low-caste."[13]

It is because of the sociological composition of the early Sikhs and their theological characterisation that we find a charter of material demands transmuted into divine revelation. The yoga-inclined mystic Kabir says:

> The hungry man knows no devotion.
> Take back your rosary!
> I hanker after dust at the feet of saints,
> But I do not owe anybody anything.
> God, how can we pull together?
> If you do not give, I am constrained to ask
> Four pounds of flour,
> Half a pound of fat along with salt,
> A pound of lentils
> To put life into me morning and evening.
> I want a cot
> With a pillow and a mattress,
> A quilt for a cover
> To make me attend to your devotion.
> I have not been greedy;
> Only repeating your name becomes me.
> Kabir, I have persuaded my mind;
> Self-suasion of mind leads to God.
>
> Kabir, Sorathi 11 (p. 656)

A similar demand for goods, dress, milch cattle, mare and wife is made in Dhanna, Dhanasri 1 (p. 695).

Bilawalu 4 (p. 856); Ravidas Bilawalu 1 (p. 858); Namdev Mali Gaura 2 (p. 988); Ravidas Malar 1 (p. 1293); Kabir Shlok 2, 51 (p. 1364, 1367); Shaikh Farid Shlok 17, 35, 44, 93 (pp. 1378, 1379, 1380, 1382).

8. M 4, Gauri 11 (p. 167).

9. Kabir, Asa 26 (p. 482).

10. Kabir, Asa 17 (p. 480).

11. Kahan Singh Nabha, ed., *Mahan Kosh* (Encyclopaedia of Sikh literature) (in Punjabi; Patiala: Bhasha Vibhag, 1960).

12. Majumdar, Ray, Chaudhuri, and Datta, eds., *An Advanced History of India* (Delhi: Macmillan, 1981), p. 398.

13. Namdev, Malar 2 (pp. 1292-93).

The disprivileged Sikhs have conceived of God in their own image. He is neither an introspective reality nor an idealistic principle. Despite His transcendence and immanence, what is important is that to the Sikh God is a toiler. There can be no greater glorification of work than if God Himself toils.

> The wise never forget
> God is a peasant.
> After preparing well one's land
> Truth and name are sown,
> One name produces nine treasures
> With His grace.
> > M 1, Sri 13 (p. 19)

Guru Ramdas calls creation the field of God, and men, his peasants.[14] The hymn Kabir, Asa 36 (p. 484) works on two levels. Creation is homologous to weaving. At one level, the weaver is God; at another, he is Kabir. The ambiguity of a present participle makes the second line of the hymn convey, first, that the world brings yarn to Kabir to weave and, second, that God has brought the world as His warp and woof. Similarly the loom of Kabir works like the earth and the sky, which in turn constitute the divine loom. "House" stands for the place of Kabir and the work of God, the weaver. Namdev pictures God as a carpenter.[15] Toiling for spirituality is equivalent to craft work. Ravidas expresses the quest for spirit on the model of shoe-making.[16] Namdev makes the job of a washerwoman a pattern of spirituality;[17] and the art of sewing, a model of devotion:

> My mind is a measuring rod,
> My tongue the scissors.
> What can I do about my [low] caste and family?
> I am remembering God day and night.
> I dye the cloth and sew it.
> I cannot live without God for a moment.
> I devote myself to Him and sing His praises
> Throughout the day.
> The needle is made of gold and the thread of silver.
> Nama's heart has gone to God.
> > Namdev, Asa 3 (p. 485)

Those who have nothing have rejected everything in favour of spirit.

> The heaven of Indra can be had with empty ascetic practices,
> Wherefrom a man is turned out after the draining of his merit.
> I keep God's name in my heart.
> Glory, rule, wealth, greatness
> Accompany none.
> Sons, wife, money
> Have brought happiness to few.
> Kabir has nothing to do with these things,
> Only the treasure of the name of God in his heart.
> > Kabir, Dhanasri 4 (p. 692)

---

14. M 4, Var Gauri Shalok 1, Pauri 9 (p. 304).
15. Namdev, Sorathi 2 (p. 657).
16. Ravidas, Sorathi 7 (p. 659).
17. Namdev, Basant 3 (p. 1196).

It is not surprising that the toiler God has his symbolic "beggars," "slaves" and "dogs" as his devotees.[18]

The Sikhs do not hope to improve their human worth through social and economic means. Such an outlook is beyond the mental horizon of the sixteenth century. Spirit is the only means of uplifting them from their humble status.

> I sacrifice myself a hundred times a day to the Guru
> Who did not take a second to change men into gods.
>   M 1, Asa Var, Shlok 1, Pauri 1 (pp. 462-63)

Devotion is a species of domestic service which comes naturally to the lower orders of society. Service and devotion are two aspects of the same thing, which holds true in Sikh practice today.

> The Master and the servant are joined together like warp and woof.
> The Lord nurtures the servant
> Who fetches water, waves a fan and grinds corn.
> He is busy in the service of the Master.
> The Master snapped my noose of death to make me serve.
> The servant loves the dispensation of the Master,
> He works on what is liked by Him.
> The servant is like the Master from inside and outside;
> The Lord is wise, knows all things.
> The servant lovingly accepts the ways of the Lord.
> That which is the Lord's also belongs to the servant.
> The servant exists in the Master.
> The Master gave the servant the robe of honour
> So that he is not called to account again.
> Nanak sacrifices himself to the servant
> Who is so wise and deep.
>   M 5, Majh 18 (pp. 101-2)

Kabir points out that spirit can make a person royal.

> No earthly king can equal God;
> The potentates last a few days sounding false trumpets.
> His servant remains unshaken
> To extend his influence over the three worlds.
> Who can lift a finger against the servant of God?
> Or make an estimate of his worth?
> Remember Him, O my foolish mind,
> To listen to the unstruck melody.
> Kabir, when the illusion is gone
> One joins the company of legendary Prahlad and Dhruv.
>   Kabir, Bilawalu 5 (p. 856)

From the point of view of the workaday world, the effort to appropriate spirit is ruinous:

> The river was spoiled on meeting the Ganges;
> The river became the Ganges.
> Kabir cries at the top of his house:
> I am spoiled by holding on to truth, and my mind has stopped
>   wandering.
> The tree was spoiled in the sandalwood forest,

---

18. "Beggars," M 3, Dhanasri 9 (p. 666); "slaves," M 1, Maru 6 (p. 991); and "dogs," Kabir, Ramkali 4 (pp. 969-70).

And the tree became sandalwood.
Copper was spoiled by a touch of the philosopher's stone,
And copper was turned to gold.
Kabir was spoiled in the company of saints
So as to exist in God.

Kabir, Bhairo 5 (p. 1158)

Yet at the end of the spiritual adventure one can be in a position to overrule God.

The saint who is attached only to the divine is my living image.
His sight cures men of three fevers,
And his touch lifts a person out of the well of worldly living.
What I do can be undone by the saints,
But the doing of a saint cannot be set aside by Me.
When the saint ties Me down to a thing
I am helpless.
I am the foundation of all life; (yet)
My life depends on My saints.
Namdev, one with such a mind
Propagates the light of love in this manner.

Namdev, Sarang 3 (pp. 1252-53)

Spiritual training makes the lowly artisan proclaim that the servant of God has more merit than the place of pilgrimage.[19] It can reasonably be assumed that a kind of spiritual strength was of some help to the Sikhs in surviving persecution. Its importance remains undiminished today, if the Sikhs want to see themselves come out at the end of the dark tunnel they have permitted themselves to enter. Throughout the world the quality of man behind the machine or the institution makes all the difference.

Despite their denominational garb, the Sikhs appeal to the universal man. Sikhism is a religion of inner spirituality. Inner spirituality is a common denominator of man. It may be conceded that Sikhism could ideationally transcend religious and caste divisions of Indian society, though it may have failed sociologically to embody the transcending principle because of the historical circumstances.

Yama has turned into Rama.
Pain has been wiped out for comfort to take its place.
Enemies have turned friends.
God-denying senses have changed into comrades.
Now I happily accept everything.
Peace has descended on me with the knowledge of God.
A body is heir to a thousand illnesses.
Things have been changed in my vision of contemplation.
One recognises one's self through Him.
The illnesses of body, mind, and spirit are gone.
My mind has returned to the original ways.
I knew it when I took myself to be dead.
Kabir exists in the happiness of contemplative vision;
Neither do I fear nor frighten others.

Kabir, Gauri 17 (pp. 326-27)

The doctrine of inner spirituality is eminently expressed by Ravidas.

---

19. Kabir Gauri 42 (p. 331).

> My noose of love
> Binds You as well.
> As I try myself to get loose from it
> I remember You.
> God, I know
> I cannot be tricked with excuses.
> A fish is cut to pieces,
> Cooked in many ways.
> The morsels of fish in one's stomach
> Cry loud for water.
> God is nobody's family member
> To love.
> The world is stricken with the illusion of attachment,
> But not His devotees.
> Ravidas, my devotion has increased so much!
> Whom should I tell? The reason why I remember You
> Is my pain that persists.
>
> Ravidas, Sorathi 2 (p. 658)

The Sikh scripture repeatedly criticises the religion of rituals in Hinduism and of external conformism in Islam. The Sikh appeal to universal man is the culmination of Sikh efforts to transcend Hinduism and Islam. Sikhism is not only a delayed response of the Hindu society to the advent of Islam in India, but it constitutes as well a societal epistemology of the Hindu-Muslim social reality of the time. Indeed, Guru Nanak may be seen as having devoted himself to the task of "the religious construction of society," rather in the sense of the French sociologist of religion Emile Durkheim.[20]

The Sikh religion takes over and makes its own the impulse in Kabir to speak for man beyond Hinduism and Islam. "Do not call the Vedas or the Qur'an false / The false are those who do not think."[21] "If God lives in a mosque / How about the rest of the country?"[22] "The Vedas and the Qur'an are exaggerations, / They do not rid one of existential anxiety."[23] "Where have the Hindus and the Muslims come from? / Who invented their different ways?"[24] These are hymns wholly devoted to this theme, and there are other references to it also.[25] The Namdev of the Adi Granth says:

> The Hindus are blind; the Muslims, one-eyed.
>
> Namdev, Gond 7 (p. 875)

In Ramkali, Ashtpadi 1 (pp. 902-3) Guru Nanak discusses the nature of Kaliyuga, the Turkish conquest of Hindustan and the way out of these

---

20. "Religious thought is something very different from a system of fictions, still the realities to which it corresponds express themselves religiously only when religion transfigures them. Between society as it is objectively and the sacred things which it expresses symbolically, the distance is considerable." As to the symbols with which a new faith will express itself, "whether they will resemble those of the past or not, and whether or not they will be more adequate for the reality which they seek to translate, that is something which surpasses the human faculty of foresight." Emile Durkheim, *The Elementary forms of the Religious Life* (London: Allen & Unwin, reprinted 1971), pp. 381, 428.
21. Kabir, Parbhati 4 (p. 1350).
22. Kabir, Parbhati 2 (p. 1349).
23. Kabir, Telang 1 (p. 727).
24. Kabir, Asa 8 (p. 477).
25. Kabir, Asa 13 (p. 479) and Asa 29 (p. 483); and Kabir, Bhairo 7 (pp. 1158-59).

difficulties through the religion of *nam*, i.e., of inner spirituality. In Basant 8 (pp. 1190-91) the social and religious impact of the Muslim conquest is taken up again. Guru Nanak writes:

> The times have changed,
> There is no union with God,
> Nor the way of truth;
> The religious places have been polluted.
> That is how the world is sinking.
> The *nam* of God is the remedy of Kaliyuga.
> To close one's eyes holding one's nose in the posture of yogic breath control
> Is to cheat the world.
> The yogic sitter claims to know the three worlds,
> But he cannot see what is in front or behind,
> So strange is the exercise.
> The Kshatriyas have abandoned their religion
> To learn a foreign tongue.
> Creation has been reduced to one caste,
> The state of religion is gone.
> They look to the eight sciences to know of the Puranas,
> To understand the Vedas.
> Redemption there is not without the *nam* of God,
> Says Nanak, the servant.
> > M 1, Dhanasri 8 (pp. 662-63)

Thus the Adi Granth hammers home the idea that spirituality should be relevant to the age. The third guru, Guru Amardas (reigned 1552-74) literally starts his hymn with the line,

> Learn the religion of the age, brothers,
> From the perfect Guru.
> > M 3, Gauri 3 (p. 230)

The idea is repeated in M 3, Asa 13 (p. 365). Guru Amardas proclaims that "every age has a religious norm peculiar to it."[26] Ravidas points out:

> Truth in Satyuga, rituals in Treta,
> Worship in Dwapar,
> The three *yugas* held to their respective norms
> Only *nam* holds in the Kaliyuga.
> > Ravidas, Gauri 1 (p. 346)

The question of "modern spirituality" is explicitly raised and institutionally answered by Sikhism. Sikhism may or may not provide the contemporary world with relevant spirituality, but the question posed by Sikhism cries for an answer.

The social group constituting the Sikhs of the sixteenth century could make their material needs a part of divine revelation. It was probably low, disprivileged, existential experience of the state which could make Ravidas express a political utopia—the city without grief, a society without oppression.

> It is called the city without grief,
> Without pain or anxiety,
> Without tax or worries or tributes,
> Without fear, crime or downfall.

---

26. M 3, Bilawalu 4 (pp. 797-98).

> Now I hold my native property
> In constant peace;
> The rule is lasting, strong,
> There are no grades of men, but all are equal.
> There is a famous, populous city
> With rich inhabitants.
> Men can go about where they like
> And the palace officials do not stop them.
> Ravidas, the "free" shoemaker, proclaims—
> "The fellow citizen, God, is my friend."
>
> Ravidas, Gauri 2 (p. 345)

The hymn is simple but unsettling. It describes a kingdom of God on earth in which God is not a king but a citizen. All the inhabitants, with their varied social activities, have turned godly. The city embraces the political, economic and existential life of its inhabitants.

After about a hundred years of its existence, Sikhism faced a crisis. The Mughal state was turning hostile. There were complaints against and attacks upon Guru Arjan long before his martyrdom in 1606. He responded to the crisis by compiling the Sikh scripture in 1604, and characteristically gave a more radical turn to the Sikh Panth (community) by including in its scripture hymns by low-caste saints from all over India and a Muslim, too, Shaikh Farid. Also, in the scripture compiled by Guru Arjan falling back on the "spiritual resource" is emphasised. The earlier appeal to "universal man," transcending Islam and Hinduism, is given a wider sociological base along with a deeper fathoming of the inner spirit. The saints included in the Sikh scripture are Kabir (Benares), Namdev (Satara), Ravidas (Benares), Trilochan (Sholapur), Farid (Pakpattan), Beni, Dhanna (Tonk), Jaidev (Bengal), Bhikhan (Lucknow), Surdas (Oudh), Parmanand (Sholapur), Sen (Rewa), Pipa (Gagraun-Quetta), Sadhna (Sindh), Ramanand (Prayag). They include a weaver, a tailor, a skin-worker, a trader, a Sufi, a Jat, a *sadhu*, a butcher and Brahmins, thus making Sikhism subsume the regional and caste diversity of saints of the *bhakti* and *sant* movements.

This response of Guru Arjan (reigned 1581-1606) in the critical years before his martyrdom is directly relevant to the contemporary crisis of Sikh identity and politics. The echoes of contempt for the disprivileged are still surviving in a hymn of Guru Arjan.

> Attaching himself to God,
> Namdev grasped Him in his heart;
> The tailor worth half a nickel
> Became a millionaire.
> Leaving aside his weaving,
> Kabir loved the feet of God;
> The low caste weaver
> Became chock-full of quality.
> Ravidas carried carcasses,
> But he bade good-bye to attachment
> To have a reputation among the saints,
> And had the sight of God.
> The barber Sen, going on errands,
> Was bruited about in every home

To have God in his heart,
To have joined the ranks of the saints.
Having come to know this,
The Jat hastened to practise devotion;
To see the manifest God
Was the good luck of Dhanna.

M 5, Gauri (pp. 487-88)

Guru Arjan's remedy against persecution is falling back on "inner spiritual resource." Historically, it did lead to militancy under Guru Gobind Singh without being supplanted by it.

If I forget You, everybody is my enemy.
I serve when I remember You.
I see none but
The True, the Invisible, the Mysterious.
When I think of You, You are kind.
People do not count,
None is good or bad.
All men belong to You.
You are the support,
You stretch your protective hand.
The recipient of Your kindness
Cannot be called helpless.
Comfort and greatness are
What are liked by God.
You are wise and kind
To make me enjoy *nam*.
We pray to You,
All men belong to You.
Nanak says, Only Your glory lasts;
None knows me.

M 5, Asa 49 (p. 383)

The egalitarian instinct of the Sikhs in particular and of the Punjabis in general springs from their native religion, a religion of small property owners. Sikh industriousness, initiative and business enterprise are a windfall from their conception of a toiler God. Sikh religion made a valiant effort to transcend denominations, regions and castes in search of universal man. Though it failed to become the universal church of India, it may yet contribute its secular heritage to the universal outlook of nationalism in India. Recourse to spirit in times of crisis is an abiding truth. The utopian "city without grief" calls for an organised, institutional, collective endeavour to make it a reality.

In addition to Sikh scripture, Sikh history too has a valuable secular aspect. After the death of Guru Gobind Singh in 1708, the line of succession came to an end. The guruship was vested in the scripture and the collectivity of the Sikhs, i.e., in *Guru-Granth* and *Guru-Panth*. Theologically the Guru is homologous to God and the word, i.e., the hymn. Thus it leads to the doctrine of *Guru-Granth*. In accordance with Sikh theology the Guru could become the Sikh; and the Sikh, his Guru. Paradigmatically, Guru Angad was invested with guruship in the lifetime of Guru Nanak, who bowed at his feet. After the death of Guru Gobind Singh, not a Sikh individual but the entire Sikh community was invested with guruship. Thus, inspired by the scripture, the Sikh community is divine. The biblically inclined theologian could term it a sin of human pride, but the divine is not supposed to be proud. This is the idea that fuels the Sikhs' *morchas*, i.e., agitations in which they are confident of success.

The rise of the Sikh monarchy was hugely helped by an apocryphal prophecy of Guru Gobind Singh that the Sikhs shall rule. It was a revised, sectarian version of the rule of "the humble and the meek." The prophecy changed into a slogan, *hane hane miri*, i.e., "a king on every saddle." Despite the fact that the idea made territorial conquests by the Sikhs a religious duty and spurred them in their efforts to rule over the Punjab, it can now be seen that the idea embodied an inherent contradiction. Not all the Sikhs can be kings; a country can accommodate only one king. The rise of Maharaja Ranjit Singh killed the doctrine of *Guru-Panth*. In its place the idea of *Guru-Granth* pointed to individual piety as an aspect of personal efforts to improve one's material prospects in life. Moreover, the theological idea of the "divinity of the Panth" was sociologically unviable with the Sikhs thinly spread over the land. The Sikhs were too busy in leading campaigns and managing the country to constitute a disproportionate part of the ruling class relative to their numbers.[27]

The idea of *Guru-Granth*, understood as a principle of individual piety, could work in the manner of a "Protestant ethic" for the Sikhs. It is remarkable that the idea of the "divinity of the Granth" helped the upper-crust Sikhs to take the lead in making the Sikhs adjust to the British conquest. The question of collective response by the Sikhs to the British domination became inadmissible because: 1) the Sikhs had abandoned its practice for about two generations, and 2) Sikh communalism began to be nurtured on the idea that the advancement of the community lies in the rise of Sikh individuals, howsoever small or large their number. The contradiction remains unresolved in the Akali politics of today. They do not want a specifically Sikh rule that could religiously accommodate the Hindus. The very mechanism of their politics, i.e., making appeal to the community in the interest of individuals, enjoins "bad faith" on the leadership.

It may be of interest to remark on an early critic of Sikh rule, Chaupa Singh.[28] The most extensive work on Sikh observances, i.e., *Rahit-nama*, probably a late eighteenth-century work, is by Chaupa Singh.[29] Reacting to the nascent class divisions in the Sikh community—which had brought the ingrained egalitarian instinct of the Sikhs under so intolerable a strain as to make an impossibility of a life-style based on social equality, the author declared the "Sikh rule" to be so un-Sikh that it was adding to the denizens of hell. Sikh thinkers, unfortunately, have not systematically gone into the question of specifically Sikh rule. Though Chaupa Singh is universally accepted among the Sikhs as an orthodox authority on Sikh observances, his misgivings on the

27. Surjit Hans, "Historically Changing Modes of Thought in Sikhism in the Over-all Social Context," *New Quest* (Pune), July-August, 1985, p. 52.
28. Surjit Hans, "An Early Critic of Sikh Rule," paper for Maharaja Ranjit Singh Seminar, Guru Nanak Dev University, Amritsar, 1986.
29. *Rehatnama* (Panjabi; Patiala: P.S. Padam, 1974).

politics of Sikh rule have not so far been removed. The dilemma of Akali politics is how to square individual interests with benefits to the community, which is all the more difficult in a period of economic stress. The exclusion of the Hindus makes the contours of the political constituency of the Sikhs sharper without in any way helping them in the solution of the dilemma, though it may appear to do so to the Sikh in the street in the heat of politics. The process of elimination continues with sects, unorthodox Sikhs and the atheists, being added to those who are not supposed to benefit from Akali rule, which proclaims itself the Sikh Raj.

The Punjab crisis was the immediate cause of my Punjabi book *Sikh Ki Karn* (*What Should the Sikhs Do?*). Briefly, the argument is that the Sikhs and the Hindus can have a common platform on the basis of the secular heritage of the Sikhs. The Sikhs stand by it because it is a Sikh heritage; the Hindus lend their support as it is a secular programme. Sikh politics, if faithful to this heritage, cannot but be the politics of uplifting the downtrodden. It can do so by championing the universal man. To work for a society without oppression must be a constant endeavour. The vision has to be translated into social and economic policies, to be realised with the help of institutions appropriately forged for the purpose.

Furthermore, Sikhs are a minority; they are not very rich, either. They are spread over a small state. Sikhs are a minority even in the cities of the Punjab. The working class in the state comes from outside. The scheduled castes are not very keen on Sikhism. Yet Sikh identity can be maintained with the help of politics based on honesty, integrity and vision. The situation demands that Sikh politics be of a higher order than the politics of the majority group. If the Sikh politics is as rotten as that of its competitors it is bound to lose. Sikhs' recent politics could well turn out to be a case of collective suicide, drugged by peasant populism.

The Sikhs can make others understand their politics of cultural identity in the idiom of a qualitatively better politics. The Anandpur Sahib resolution, demanding greater autonomy for the states, can be explicated in simple language: the state administration is clean; the central government departments in the state are corrupt. We want to stop these departments from robbing the people. So we demand greater powers for the states..."Khalistan is not a territory; it is superior politics."

Lastly, the argument of secular heritage is relevant to the making of Indian national consciousness. Before the British conquest Indian society was a congeries of caste and kinship groups. No caste, howsoever rich or high, could accept the ideological, educational and political challenge of British rule. Functionally, it was the religious reform movements that fused the caste groups into communalisms. Only communal groupings could run schools, contest elections, jockey for a greater share of administrative jobs and proclaim the superiority of the East over the West, not as individual eccentrics but as organised societies. The universalising impulse of the West stopped short at the communal fusion of the castes; the religious identities were not melted down in the crucible of nationalism.

The Western liberal strand of Indian nationalism lasted as long as the Moderates. The Extremists were revivalists as well. Mahatma Gandhi yoked the different communalisms of the Khilafat, the gurdwara reform, Ram Raj and Harijan uplift to the chariot of nationalism. The India of 1947 could not but be secular in the sense of equal validity of all religions. The founding fathers could not visualise the gradual atrophying of planted institutions, unsupported by native ideologies, and the inherent communalism of the electoral mechanism that has been getting worse over time. From the beginning of the eighties the Indian state itself has been communal. The massacre of Sikhs in Delhi in 1984 is the most blatant example; one can not be sure whether it is the last. The prospects of secularism on the basis of a Western liberal outlook are bleak in India. If the nation wants to survive in the form it has today we must move from the negative definition of secularism, i.e., the equal validity of all religions, to the positive realisation of the secular heritage of all the religions in India. We may fail; nothing in the world has a guarantee of success. An honourable failure would be far more humane than a hypocritical "success."

Religious and Secular Strains in Twentieth-century Punjabi Poetry

Darshan Singh Maini

I

At the outset it may be affirmed that there is hardly a poetry of note anywhere in the world which does not, in great measure, subsume both religious and secular themes as a matter of experience, vision and values. Since the human reality ultimately is indivisible, there is always a common grid underneath and a coalescence at the apex. To put it differently, there is a symbiotic nexus between these two strains, and even the purest form of religious poetry such as we encounter in the Bible, the Qur'an, the Gita or the Guru Granth is linked to secular themes from which it draws its language, analogies and energies. Thus, an inner dialectic informs both such forms of poetry, though understandably it is the *raison d'être* of such verses that ultimately determines their taxonomy. So, when we talk of religious poetry or of secular poetry, we broadly know the difference, and we also know that these two strains do not cancel out each other.

It is important here to state how I propose to use these two key words, "religious" and "secular," in the argument of this essay. The religious sense in man is that innate urge which would not let him rest with the mere form of things, and which always sought a meaning beyond meaning. Call it spiritual reality, or ultimate concern, or a hunt for some order of transcendence, the fact remains that such a concern—and God, in Paul Tillich's[1] view is the name of the content of such an ultimate concern—alone validates religious experience, and its nature is mysterious and universal. The secular concern, on the other hand, stipulates man's sense of engagement with the world of the senses, with the phenomenological aspects of reality, and with the awesome ambiguities of creature life—of sex, money, power, and the like. Ultimately, it is a question of man's concern with the affairs of societies, cultures and civilisations. However,

---

1. Paul Tillich, *Dynamics of Faith* (New York: Harper & Row, Torchbook edition, 1958), p. 45.

[Joseph T. O'Connell, Milton Israel, Willard G. Oxtoby, eds., with W.H. McLeod and J.S. Grewal, visiting eds., *Sikh History and Religion in the Twentieth Century* (S. Asian Studies Papers, 3) (Toronto: S. Asian Studies, Univ. of Toronto, 1988)]

as I have hinted above, there is a whole dialectic of correspondences and complementarities that binds these two strains in poetry so that in the end they constitute an aesthetic of being and becoming.

The larger meaning I seek to attach to these terms, then, is so germane to the business of Punjabi poetry as to constitute its rationale, its history and its health. For, as we shall see, this poetry uniquely celebrates both the spirit's voyage into the heavens imagined and perceived, and the physical side of ordinary things. The "affair with God" and the "affair" with the world of actualities, contingencies and imponderables only authenticate each other, and, in the end, constitute a paradigm of visionary possibilities. The unicity envisaged here belongs to the order of human experience where, at the base, things, persons and places reveal aspects of the sacred not in the theological religious sense as much as in the sense of inducing Wordsworthian wonder, awe and admiration or the sense in which for Walt Whitman, "a mouse is miracle enough to stagger sextillions of infidels," or, for a Theodore Roethke, the swarming soil of ants and worms and newts, and so on. In Punjabi poetry this meaning of "the sacred" permeates song after song, particularly in the verses of the Sikh Gurus. That is to say, the quest for the inner essence of things continues till "the matter becomes the spirit's willing bride"[2] in the memorable words of the modern Indian sage, Aurobindo Ghose. As I hope to show briefly, Punjabi poetry was continually and energetically pushing towards such a vision from the very beginning. The sacredness of all sentient life, and of all material goods and things, constitutes the sap and pith of this poetry, which, originating before the Sikh Gurus, had already achieved such a consummation in the poetry of Shaikh Farid and others.

In order, therefore, to isolate and identify these two dominant strains in twentieth-century Punjabi poetry, and to see how they intersect each other at various levels in some of the representative poets of the period, and how they tend, at times, to move toward a common visionary centre, it is important to know that a very strong and enduring tradition of some seven hundred years of verse is there to lend weight and verve and authenticity to this phenomenon in Punjabi poetry.

The great Muslim Sufi poet, Shaikh Farid (1173-1265), who elected to use his mother tongue, Punjabi, with its unique trick of inflection to sing of the spirit's urgencies and immediacies and ecstasies in the midst of so much terror and tragedy, is the first poet in the language to merge the secular with the mystical in his search for God. Undoubtedly, his nuclear impulse is religious, but if we examine his songs (there are 112 of his *shalokas* and 4 hymns in the Guru Granth) and the rich imagery of nature, of hearth and home, of business and commerce, and so on, we realise that a muted, iconographic admiration for God's earth is present. We realise this even more so when in song after song,

---

2. Sisirkumar Ghose, *The Poetry of Sri Aurobindo: A Short Survey* (Calcutta: Chutuskone Private Ltd., 1969), p. 42.

the themes of death and the transitoriness of life become an abiding concern, heightening the nostalgia for creature beauties and felicities. Indeed, the ravishing power of the "many-splendour'd" world and man's alienation constitute the dialectic of Farid's utterances. The secular strain, to be sure, is not as potent to begin with, but its latency and imbeddedness may not be doubted.

Similarly, in the poetry of Guru Nanak, particularly in the *Japji* and in the *Bara Maha*, there is a loud and clear affirmation of faith in the opulence and energy of life. A whole grammar of the relationship between the supernatural and the commonplace, between the sacred and the profane, between the religious and the erotic, is set up in the process. The bridal and spousal imagery, in particular, authenticates Guru Nanak's reverence for the secular aspects of life even when the metaphors are mystical in meaning and suggestion. Thus, the unique marriage of the numinous and the known, of the ineffable and the concrete, is effected out of a great humanist vision. This great legacy of Guru Nanak later is richly made use of by the later Sikh Gurus, particularly by the Tenth Master, Guru Gobind Singh. A truly religious personality is, as Nicholas Berdyaev[3] argues, "creative" in essence, and it cannot come into being without a discipline of moral insights. No Nirvana can, thus, be achieved without a commitment to the idea of human responsibility. A Nirvana of renunciation and asceticism is wholly foreign to Sikh thought. It is finally in the poetry of Guru Gobind Singh that the two sovereignties of *miri* (temporal sovereignty) and *piri* (spiritual sovereignty) as conceived by Guru Hargobind find their richest and profoundest expression. The world of the spirit may not, then, be dissociated from the spirit of the sword, for the unitary vision of the Guru demands a dialectic of thought and action, of *dharma* or righteousness, and *karma* or purposive deed. Guru Gobind Singh exemplifies in poetry and in life—and his life is *poetic* in the highest degree, involving both the play of the personality to its uttermost and the principle of sacrifice—the paradox of pity and power. And such a unitary vision is vouchsafed only to those select spirits who combine in themselves what the ancient Hindu scriptures call *karma-yoga* (the yoga of action) and *jnana-yoga* (the yoga of knowledge).[4] Here, in Guru Gobind Singh, knowledge has become power in the service of both God and man; it has assumed a God-like authority. The Tenth Master's poetry in the Dasam Granth fully vindicates his stereoscopic view of the human situation. The religious and the secular aspects, which appear as antinomies to most thinkers are, in his view, only sliding and overlapping panels of reality. Only a slight shift in perspective is needed to see how the two may not be viewed separately at the experiential level. With the finalisation of the Guru Granth and its consecration as Guru, a living master, the convergence of the two strains, religious and secular, in Punjabi poetry becomes an article of faith.

---

3. Nicholas Berdyaev, *The Destiny of Man* (New York: Harper & Row, Torchbook edition, 1960), pp. 55-57.
4. See John B. Alphonso Karkala, ed., *An Anthology of Indian Literature* (Harmondsworth: Penguin Books, 1971), p. 360.

II

Punjabi poetry in the twentieth century is often divided into three periods. The verse written between 1900 and 1930, best represented by Bhai Vir Singh, Puran Singh and Dhani Ram Chatrik, is at once modern and traditional both in thought and style. It hearkens back continually to the great Sikh poetry of the past, though it is beginning to move out of religious confines into secular themes in response to the political and societal compulsions of the day. Still, by and large, it is a poetry untouched by Western thought, which was then on the upswing in India. And, though certain new forms of verse and certain new poetic measures are adopted to dispel the influence of congregational and *kavi-samailan* verse, there is no evidence of modernity as such. If the English poets are remembered at all, it is the Romantics who still hold the ground. A T.S. Eliot is yet a far cry. Puran Singh's Whitmanian volumes certainly induct *vers libre* (free verse) into Punjabi poetry, and thus open up a whole new territory, but they otherwise resist contemporary thought. Thus, the poets of the transitional period still keep a happy balance between religious themes and secular subjects.

The second period, 1930-1947, witnesses the birth of socialist and proletarian verse under the impact of Marxian thought. At the same time, Freudian ideas are beginning to affect love poetry and give it a freedom, an openness and an authenticity wholly out of character with the culture of the period. Clearly, the quantum of the secular sentiment now outweighs the religious sentiment, and, in the end, becomes a more representative strain demanding coercive attention in such poets as Mohan Singh, Bawa Balwant and Amrita Pritam. One notable exception is Pritam Singh Safeer, who carves out a separate path of development while imbibing the modern spirit of freedom.

The third period, beginning with the poetry of the Partition and the post-Independence days is actually an extension of the poetry of pain and protest and revolt that the Marxian poets had made fashionable, and the poets of the Pink Decade and of the War period govern the ethos of the fifties and the sixties. The experiential base of this poetry is now widened, and many a new voice is heard. Of the new poets, Jaswant Singh Neki and Shiv Batalvi are examples of the talent overtopping the movement. Scores of younger poets move on from Marxian to existential and confessional verse, though they do not forswear radicalism as such. On the contrary, they emerge as psychic revolutionaries.

It is interesting to note that in the work of most of the new and younger poets, the values close to Sikh thought and religious sentiment are, by and large, subsumed in secular themes and images. Though religion *qua* religion is questioned and indicted for its reactionary role in human history, its hold on the imagination keeps the secular motifs anchored in the "Sikh unconscious"— which is, in effect, to say that Sikh religious thought has now mellowed into a sentiment and become a part of the collective consciousness of the community. Even the Marxist writers and their like among the Sikhs have imbibed the humanist dream of Sikhism as a matter of inheritance and nutriment. In such poets as Mohan Singh and Bawa Balwant, for instance, the Sikh metaphysic and ethic filter through the sieves of the imagination and add a new dimension to their radical perceptions. In other words, religious thought has been domesticated in a secular context and has become a partner in the proceedings.

To revert, then, to the first generation of twentieth-century poets, it may be reaffirmed that it is a transitional period of revaluations, of new orientations and formulations. The nuclear heart of Indian experience and values is preserved jealously, but there is also a realisation that centuries of spiritual subversion and moral erosion have created an air of collective inertia, and that the Indian imagination, thus pawned to the past, has to be recovered. On the whole, the emphasis is on recognitions and readjustments, and their modernity has not yet become a conscious, intellectual effort. In breaking away from the homiletic and conventional verse of the earlier period, these poets preserved the best of the past and made it an instrument of a progressive and regenerative vision.

The poet who gave modern Punjabi poetry its content and culture, its form and style, is clearly Bhai Vir Singh (1872-1957). No Punjabi poet since the Sikh Gurus has so powerfully and reverentially engaged the Punjabi imagination as this seer and savant who, rising out of the Sikh twilight following the destruction of the Sikh Raj, became the organ voice of Punjab. In him the Sikh tradition of spiritual life in keeping with the ethical core of the holy scriptures found its sweetest and comeliest expression. All his poetry, then, is a luminous commentary on those great and abiding strains in Sikh thought that continue to sustain the humanist dream. Briefly, there were three impulses at work in his poetry from the start, and these may be summed up as his visionary and unfailing faith in the words and values of the *gurbani*, his soulful concern for the human race, and his lover's passion for and devotion to the Punjabi language. And he sought transcendence through involvement, *moksha* (redemption) through immersion—not through retreat, estrangement or alienation, as in many ancient Hindu edicts.

Such an immersion in "the destructive element," however, did not mean for him any kind of aggrandisement of the self as in the Nietzschean reaches of Iqbal's poetry. On the contrary, Bhai Vir Singh is a picture of serenity, disarming humility and earned insights. In poem after poem, he longs for a life of obscurity, simplicity, restraint and sacrifice. Thus, the *kikar* tree becomes in his verse a recurring symbol of solitary and ascetic existence in the midst of life's endless beauties and amplitudes. Indeed, Bhai Vir Singh's life and verse were in complete unison and in utter accord with his poetics. He sang in the name of the Guru; he was himself but a humble vessel, a singing reed. Such an anonymity is not, however, raised to the position of a doctrine of impersonality, as in T.S. Eliot, for Bhai Vir Singh's genius was essentially lyrical, not dramatic. His desire to eliminate the ego has spiritual and moral, rather than aesthetic, connotations.

An early example of his mystic quest and deep religious sentiment is *Rana Surat Singh* (1905-1919), an epical poem of great metaphysical reach and spread, encompassing problems of self, identity, faith and salvation. Written in the form of a medieval dream allegory, its thirty-five cantos of varying length comprising 14,396 lines of blank verse make it the single greatest poem of its kind in the Punjabi language. To what extent Bhai Vir Singh was aware of Western models such as *The Romance of the Rose, The Divine Comedy* and *The Faerie Queene*, is difficult to tell, though certain conventions, motifs and forms of narration are common enough to suggest correspondences. Though universal in human import, this *magnum opus* is securely tethered in Sikh thought and theology. To that extent, it is as conscious a poetic exposition of the Sikh vision of life as Dante's poem is of the ways and values of Italian Christendom. Launching the story *in medias res*, the poem reconstructs the earlier and formative events as it proceeds full sail to describe the spiritual voyage of a young Sikh widow left in utter desolation of heart and soul, following the martyrdom of her princely consort. Symbolising the eternal yearning of the human soul for the reunion with the Lord, she traverses several planes of reality as a winged spirit, surveying the world below from ethereal heights:

> I felt as though I had dropped
> My bodily vestures, and risen
> Skyward in a flight hence
> Like a kite that
> Scours the skies beyond!

Written as something of a Sikh *Pilgrim's Progress*, *Rana Surat Singh* makes a consistent and continual use of apposite verses from the *Gurbani* by way of a structural-thematic device. There is a water-colour quality about most of the opening scenes in different cantos. The touch is impressionistic as though the vision on the other side of life were to be revealed fitfully through the onion-peels of reality.

In the volumes that followed, *Lehran de Har, Matak Hularay, Bijlian de Har, Preet Veena* and finally *Mere Sayyan Jeo*, the themes range from the love of nature, beauty and music to the love of freedom, values and humanity. A worshipful attitude envelops them all, binding bird and beast, man and God in one great community of continuities and affirmations. Though the secular strain appears subordinated to the religious-mystic vision, it breaks through the granite of reality, again and again, to register its presence in the unlikeliest places. This is particularly true of the songs written in the evening of his life.

As for Puran Singh, whom Bhai Vir Singh brought back from Vedanta to the soulful secularism of the Sikh faith, no poet in the twentieth century brings out so resoundingly the divinity of God and the divinity of man as a dialectical idea in action as he does. For his poetry, though singularly Sikh in inspiration and impulse, particularly towards the end, is yet so irrepressibly linked to the largesse of life as to make it secular in root and branch. The world of toil and labour, of love and sex, of war and peace, has its own blessedness in his scheme of things.   It is the celebration in Whitmanian measures of those multiple divinities that constitutes the quiddity of his verse.   Anyone who has savoured the unstoppered riches of Puran Singh's inebriated muses would see how the man and the song irradiate each other.   And when an aesthetic duplicates a life, as it does in his case, it acquires another dimension altogether.   And if ever a Punjabi poet came close to the Wordsworthian view of poetry as the "impassioned expression which is in the countenance of all Science"[5] it was the sugar technologist from Punjab.   The spiritual link between poetry and science was as clear to him as to that twentieth-century French thinker, Pierre Teilhard de Chardin, who affirms that all energy is psychic in nature and that there is incontestable interdependence of energy "between the 'within' and the 'without' of things."[6]

At the outset, Puran Singh felt a deep primordial calling within his body that tied him to all animate things and sentient beings.   Fish, fowl and flesh: all throbbed and pulsed to the music of life, and all carried within themselves the mystery and divinity of creation.   And this rage for life, and for its suns and moons and stars, found its happiest fulfilment when this nineteen-year-old Sikh under training in Japan as a technologist around the turn of the century chanced upon a copy of Whitman's *Leaves of Grass*.   It was a spiritual encounter, for Puran Singh instantly realised the epiphanic nature of that experience.   The American poet led him by the hand, as it were, into a mystic commune of kindred spirits.   He was "simmering, simmering," and Whitman brought him "to the boil," to recall Whitman's own words spoken in the context of his brush with Emerson.

And when the free-verse franchise, the Whitmanian catalogues and the vistas of a life of the spirit and of the good life begin to gather into a symphony of words (and the words, too, have a "divinity" in Whitmanian aesthetic), an ethic of affirmations is born.   Even the titles of his volumes of verse, *Khule Maidan*, *Khule Ghund* and *Khule Asmani Rung*, suggest the place of openness and amplitude in Puran Singh's poetics.

> I like open and wide life,
> My soul takes after vastnesses.
> Like the skies and the seas,
> I seek infinity!

In short, Puran Singh, more than any other Punjabi poet since the legendary Waris Shah, has so soulfully orchestrated the wash and swing, the quick and plume of Punjabi life as to become the literary barometer of modern Punjab.

But all this celebration of the phenomenal world or the world of the senses is rooted in Puran Singh's view of the *gurbani*.   As he advances in years, he is drawn more and more into the dynamics of Sikh scriptures.   The highest point in

---

5. See David Daiches, *Critical Approaches to Literature* (London: Longmans, Green & Co., 1963), p. 93.
6. Pierre Teilhard de Chardin, *The Phenomenon of Man* (New York: Harper & Row, Torchbook edition, 1965), p. 64.

the journey is reached when the poet's consciousness merges into what he calls "Guru-Consciousness," and then the Guru's word is all, and the word abides. The secular pleasures and business of life are seen as duties of a soul in labour and worship. The religious heritage and "tradition" impinging upon an "individual talent" now produce a poetry of what he termed *sadha vigas*[7] or "spiritual gaiety." It is not surprising that he called Walt Whitman "the Guru's Sikh born in America."

Of course, poetry is finally a question of the energies of language, and no poet may achieve power without realising fully the genius of a given tongue. And it is here that Puran Singh's verse affords us its richest aesthetic and secular pleasures. For a passionate love of the language is in itself an aspect of the secular imagination, though in his poetry, this aspect still remains a spiritual tender in the manner of the *shabad* or the word. Further, he catches superbly the unique sounds and inflections of the Punjabi language—its lilt and lyric flow, its sinewy and rugged strength, its resilience and plasticity. Again, its proneness to humour, ribaldry and extravagance, to wit and pun and innuendo, makes it so warm and earthy, giving off an aroma of grass and soil and seed. No word is too profane to be refused entry into the high *sanctum* of art. It is the widest commonality of verse whose democratic and secular vistas are subtended by peripheries and marginalities.

Similarly, the body-soul relationship, a recurrent motif in Whitman's poetry, finds a distinct echo in Puran Singh. No dichotomy is envisaged or tolerated here. While in the American poet the astonishing fecundity and force of his verse are linked to his unappeased sexuality, in Puran Singh there is a refined Keatsian sensuousness and a more controlled eroticism as in his little poem, *Ik Jungli Phul* ("A Wild Flower"), in the more ambitious *Puran Bhagat* and in *Heer te Ranjha*, or in his English rendering of the *Gita Govinda*.[8] His poetic *masti* or "joyful madness" reaches a point of transcendence where all coverings and raiment are naught; only the "naked" truth abides.

> Naked is the lotus,
> Naked all sunshine;
> Naked is the water,
> And naked am I;
> Naked the blue skies,
> And naked is God!

---

7. Puran Singh, *Spirit of the Sikh*, Part II, v. 2 (Patiala: Punjabi University, 1981), p. 158.

8. Puran Singh wrote with felicity and elegance in both Punjabi and English. He published several volumes of verse and prose in English, including *The Sisters of the Spinning Wheel*, *The Spirit-Born People*, *Spirit of the Sikh*, *The Temple Tulips* and a prose romance called *Prakasina*. He also brought out an English version of Bhai Vir Singh's *Nargas*. Some of these volumes first appeared in England during his lifetime, and all of them were subsequently published by Punjabi University in a uniform edition. He also left behind a large number of manuscripts in English. Of these, two volumes, *Guru Gobind Singh: Reflections and Offerings* with introductory essays by Darshan Singh Maini (San Francisco: The Sikh Centre of the Bay Area, 1967) and *Walt Whitman and the Sikh Inspiration* with an introductory note (Punjabi University Publication Bureau, 1982), also by Darshan Singh Maini, have seen the light of day. Some unpublished short stories in English were later edited and published in *Puran Singh Studies*, a Punjabi University journal edited (English Section) by Darshan Singh Maini.

Thus, Puran Singh remains triumphantly an example of the union of secular and religious energies on a heroic scale.   Kierkegaard's three "spheres"[9]—"the aesthetic" (primary, sensuous, phenomenological and contingent), "the ethical," and "the religious" constitute a hierarchy of the states of existence, "the religious" being at the top of the table and "the aesthetic" at the base.   In most religious poets, the first two spheres get lost *en route*, or get thrown out of focus.   In Puran Singh, as in Whitman, on the other hand, each sphere merges into the next to form in the end a complete paradigm of vision and values.   The sensuous is then vindicated in the religious through the interstices of what Lionel Trilling in a happy and expressive phrase calls "moral lyricism."

The third poet in the transitional period, Dhani Ram Chatrik (1876-1954), seems to combine at a somewhat reduced and lower level the virtues of Bhai Vir Singh and Puran Singh.   His "singing master" no doubt, was Bhai Vir Singh, under whose watchful and benign eye he came of poetic age, but this does not belittle his achievement.   On the other hand, it suggests a compact of kindred spirits.   In one respect, however, Chatrik's interests seem to overtop the master's, for the kind of secular vision we encounter in him has wider parameters.   In Bhai Vir Singh, secularism runs as a sub-stream, replenished quietly and invisibly by his Sikh worldview; in Chatrik, it is strong and central enough to have a sovereign image for the most part.   Even in his later verse, starting with *Chandanwari* (1931), where the mystic impulse is on the upswing, the secular vision never falters, but retains its earlier energy.

Chatrik also constitutes a bridge between tradition and modernity, moving felicitously between the poetic conventions of the earlier age and the new, freer poetic experiments.   His own poetic development exemplifies this.   Whereas his earlier verse is formal and dainty, the poetry of the later years shows a certain ruggedness of form and a certain engagement with the harsher aspects of reality. The religious motifs then yield place to experiential pain, nationalist and patriotic sentiment, societal miseries and anguish, nature, and the like, though where the mystic impulse erupts still, as in the following lines, strongly reminiscent of Bhai Vir Singh's famous lyric, "*Kambadi Kalai*," it shows the presence of an overarching vision of life.

O Great Light!
What message did Thou flash upon my eyes?
I stretch'd and strain'd my arms
To catch Thee; I ran breathless
To hold Thy hem in hand,
And in despair I sat down
To nurse a wailing heart.
All my pleas were naught,
And my eyes were lost
In tears of salt!
                    "Chananji" ("O Great Light!")

---

9. A.G. George, *The First Sphere: A Study of Kierkegaardian Aesthetics* (Bombay: Asia Publishing House, 1965), pp. 2-5.

While the volume called *Chandanwari* initiates a new secular strain in Punjabi poetry, and *Kesar Kiari* (1940) perpetuates the imbedded mystic strain in Chatrik, the volume entitled *Nawan Jahan* (1945) turns vigorously to the themes of social injustice, political slavery, religious fanaticism, corrupting myths and magic, ruinous superstitions, etc. Clearly, the socialist winds then sweeping India bring his muses home, so to speak. It is not a Marxian phase as such, for Chatrik was much too religious a person to accept Marxism as a complete philosophy of life. However, latent socialism in Sikh thought, which Chatrik had come to regard with reverence under Bhai Vir Singh's influence, now finds a congenial and receptive ground. And he advocates a life of action as opposed to the traditional Hindu-Buddhist view of Nirvana through contemplation, isolation and retreat.

III

The second generation of poets in the twentieth century constituted a new order of verse altogether, and there is a new note of authenticity and urgency in their compositions. Modernity in thought and style is beginning to mould this new verse. The Marxian sirens are now luring home many a radical and idealistic talent. The beauty and holiness of experience, and sexual candour, are increasingly surfacing in volume after volume. The British Raj ignites the political imagination into an outburst of radical and revolutionary verse. It may, then, be easily asserted that it is these poets—Mohan Singh, Bawa Balwant, Pritam Singh Safeer and Amrita Pritam, among others—who gave modern Punjab poetry its distinctive form, style and character. They have remained its leading lights till today.

Mohan Singh (1905-1978) came of age at a time when Punjabi poetry had not yet been fully liberated from what Northrop Frye calls "inorganic convention"[10] in letters. Though Bhai Vir Singh had lifted the poetry of convention to spectacular heights by the sheer weight of his genius, and Puran Singh had introduced free verse, there still lingered a culture of platitudes and pieties. Much of the poetry around that time was not a poetry of felt experience, but of induced religious sentiment and nostalgia. It lacked the power to surprise, to hurt or to ignite the mind. In Mohan Singh emerged a poetic talent that transformed a poetry of convention and clichés into a poetry of romantic agony, sexual experience and political protest. The new idiom was a fine blend of classical graces and regional energies. His native Pothohari dialect with its inflectional sweetness added a colour to it.

The poetic career of Mohan Singh spans nearly half a century. During this period he published eight volumes of verse and an epic, *Nanakayan* (1971), besides a verse translation of Arnold's *Light of Asia*. *Saway Pattar* (*The Green Leaves*, 1936), which is a work of seminal importance and which is still the most popular volume of modern Punjabi poetry, sets into motion a talent of rare

---

10. Northrop Frye, *The Anatomy of Criticism* (New York: Atheneum paperback, 1969), p. 104.

refinements. And, though since then his poetry has witnessed profound dialectical changes, he keeps returning compulsively to the dreams and urges of that period. Indeed, the hold of the unrequited romantic imagination is so strong as to unleash in him the archetypal conflict between body and soul, between blood and judgment, between dream and reality. These dichotomies, instead of weakening his vision, constitute the kinetics of his verse.

In *Saway Pattar* Bhai Vir Singh's serene and gentle influence is there in the wings, and a poem like "Sikhi" ("Sikhism") shows Mohan Singh's awareness of his radical heritage, but even then it is difficult to talk of religious consciousness in relation to his earlier verse. The poem in question is more an assertion of identity than a statement of faith or belief. The organic metaphor of the tree which the poet employs in this little poem is meant to bring out the dynamic nature of this creed. Sikhism, says Mohan Singh, is a "great-rooted blossomer," which spreads ever more when its branches are lopped and pruned. The language, for once, explodes like muskets when the tempestuous chronicles of the Sikhs are evoked. This poem, however, is a piece apart, for the dominant themes of this volume are love and beauty, nature and universe, time and flux, death and eternity, freedom and patriotism.

In his next collection, *Kasumbra* (1939), symbolically named after a beautiful wild red flower that yields no sweet odour, the imagination of romance is still not appeased. The rich and fruitful ambiguity of these poems gives this volume a troubled air. Social consciousness, where roused, is still linked to romantic urges. The most memorable poem of *Kasumbra*, of course, is "Kuri Pothohar Di" ("The Belle of Pothohar"), which has often been compared to "The Solitary Reaper" by Wordsworth. In some other lyrics, such as "Koi Tore Wey Koi Tore" ("Someone Ravishes Me Still"), the sexual strain is too naked to seek sublimation. After a long time in Punjabi poetry we see woman treated openly as an object of desire as well as a creature of carnal impulses seeking ravishment. The beauty of her sensuality is celebrated and adored. There are also signs of political disquiet, and a poem like "Suphne" ("Dreams") recalls not the poet's dream-pedlary and the gazelle-eyed girls, but the ordeals of freedom. Truly, for Mohan Singh, as for W.B. Yeats, dreams begin in "responsibilities."

From the volume called *Adhwate* (1944), which shows the poet torn between the two poles of romance and reality, to *Kach Sach (Illusion and Reality*, 1950), a poet struggling with uncertainties at last achieves a revolutionary breakthrough. The title may well reflect the Marxian concept of poetry as elaborated in Christopher Caudwell's well-known classic, *Illusion and Reality*, whose first Indian edition appeared in October, 1947. Now the imagination of indignation is fully engaged even as his romantic muses continue to seek radical remedies to problems of love and passion. All these poems of *Kach Sach* are inspired by a desire for a just, happy and beautiful world. Political titles are now on the increase, but most of them are not really a product of a truly political imagination. For it appears to me that Mohan Singh did not have a great sense of history or a philosophical temper. His radicalism remains subordinated to the poetry of passion, though in several *ghazals* the theme of meaningful and committed action in the service of secular ideals finds a felicitous expression.

> We've seen the drama
> Of the waves from the shores of life;
> Now's the time to plunge
> Into the thick of the fray.

However, in the volume entitled *Jandrey* (1964) politics and polemics seem to have yielded to para-mystical concerns and to the affairs of the heart. There is a new kind of verbal density in his style. Mohan Singh's poetic development may thus be seen as a movement from "feathers to iron," to use one of Keats's memorable phrases, though the reality of romance is never denied. While the sense of reality now dominates his verse, the romantic impulse is not spent. What one remembers about these poems is their unique lyric charm, which issues, as it were, from the smoking chimneys of the human heart.

Of the poets who came directly and forcefully under the influence of the tidal wave of socialist and secular thought after the Russian Revolution of 1917 and who fashioned their art as a visible instrument of protest and as a weapon of war, Bawa Balwant (1915-72) remains pre-eminently a voice of the age. No other contemporary poet represents so purely the radical temper as he does. A person with little formal education, he appropriated the Marxian idiom and dialectic as a matter of will, spirit and imagination. To be sure, in some of his poems, the hortatory aspect is weakened because of its shrillness and thus the aesthetic balance is upset. That is to say, the images and the symbols do not seem to evolve out of the heat and pressure of experience. However, where and when the imagination of protest and combat is fully engaged, as in poems like "Jawana" ("O Youth!") and "Dunia" ("The World"), the result is often both pleasing and moving. It is then a rhetoric of realisation and their sonorous and fast-stepping rhythm is a true index of the proletarian energies in action.

At the start of his poetic journey Bawa Balwant announces his manifesto, proclaiming himself a revolutionary poet whose sole purpose in putting pen to paper is to challenge reactionary forces and entrenched interests and values. Iqbal's philosophy of the sovereign and triumphant self, which had a profound effect on his youthful imagination, is now yoked to Marxian insights in an effort to unite the force of personality and the force of socialist thought.

> How should my embittered youth
> Find solace in verse alone?
> This sapling's but longing
> For a date with the sword!

Revolt and action constitute the matrix of his verse. The philosophy of purposive and committed action enunciated in the first volume called *Maha Nach* (1941) and in *Jawalamukhi* (1942) finds its richest expression in *Bandargah* (1951), which most Punjabi critics regard as a statement of his credo in the fittest measures. It becomes such a dominant theme that the poet would convert even defeated and unrequited love into an instrument for man's regeneration. All holiness lies in action, not in the textbook pieties of the Vedas and the other scriptures. And he sums up his credo thus:

> Action alone's the reality and the truth,
> All power issues from action...

A poem like "Inqilabi Amal" ("The Revolutionary Action") celebrates the idea of will as action. And in the poem called "Kalakar" ("The Artist") he avers that art can equip man with a vision that is transcendent in a revolutionary sense.

Bawa Balwant does not quite repudiate his religious heritage, and is prepared to distil its humanist potential into his verse, but he is also aware of the false gods man has set up to perpetuate exploitation and tyranny. For him, finally, man alone is the measure of man, and only a secular humanism can be the "religion" of an artist.

> Man alone's man's salvation,
> All gods are an illusion

As opposed to Bawa Balwant, Pritam Singh Safeer (1916-   ) remains stubbornly beyond the Marxian appeal of the day. He defends religion as a creative force of life in human history, and seems to reject the view that it is an "opium of the people," whatever its insufficiencies in actual life. No wonder the very first volume of his verse, *Katik Koonjan* (1941), which abounds in contemporary themes and attitudes, serves a notice that the young poet is not going to surrender his muses to any philosophy of life that does not accept the uniqueness of individual vision. Even as he endorses the humanist dream of egalitarianism, he does not equate that dream with a political vision of things. For this reason, above all, Safeer has generally been regarded as a *sui generis* phenomenon in Punjabi poetry.

As he moves from volume to volume, the more important being *Rakat Boondan* (1946), *Aad-Jughaadh* (1958) and *Sarab Kala* (1965), he sets out on his "God-hunt," in which the "bird-soul" of man alone becomes in the end the object of interest and analysis. It is not surprising, then, to see Safeer subordinating the social themes (which do erupt at times powerfully to stretch his muses) to his interest in the life of the mind and the imagination. It is states of mind and psychological complexities that lend his poems an air of intellection. The analogy with Robert Browning is strictly limited, for Safeer's verse has not a great variety to offer and he is not a dramatic poet. His penetration is not all that acute and absorbing. The obscurity we encounter is, therefore, not constitutive, as a rule, though in some of his later poems it does suggest visionary possibilities.

In this quest a streak of romanticism, Shelleyan in origin, persists, and Safeer's disappointments in love and his disputations add a note of urgency to his sexually starved overtures. Woman's "revolutionary" role in the business and meaning of life is recognised, though when his love comes to grief, he is not, like the Marxian poets of the day, prepared to put the blame on an unjust society. In any case, his lover's pride prevents him from turning his failure into a diet of feckless dreams.

In the end, Safeer's poetry moves not toward "the still centre" but toward an unresolved conflict. The Sikh religious heritage remains a recurring context in language, image and thought, but the double vision is not dispelled. On the contrary, it seems to provide that tension which poetry *per se* seeks as a condition of being. Here the conflict between God and Love is thus dramatised:

> Where should I go?
> On one side's the Light of God,
> A rare gift attained
> Over aeons of life and death;
> On the other side is
> The empire of love,
> And all its sweet delights;
> Which of the two's the truth,
> And which a mere mirage,
> Who can tell?

To turn to Amrita Pritam (1919-) is to realise the degree of experiential truth Punjabi poetry has attained since her advent. Virtually the first woman to sing openly and passionately of sexual love in the long history of this poetry, she has acquired the image of a rebel. And she has carefully and jealously tended that image and, at times, given it a wanton and wilful twist. There is, however, no doubt about the authenticity of her defiance and about the quality of her verse. She, therefore, remains till today a force and an influence, inveigling the younger poets into a poetics of protest. A psychological radical, Amrita Pritam has led the way to a confrontation with the Sikh religious establishment.

Starting with genteel, homiletic verse based on textbook virtues, she soon graduates to a new passional awareness of her womanliness, of her pain and suffering in a male-dominated world. The poetry of protest born in the process becomes in her case a hieroglyphic of the heart, a cry and a lament. The poetry of her "blood-sodden heart" erupts forcefully when the girl turns into a woman, and comes face to face with the dark desires of her body and flesh. What really urged Amrita to scaffold a beautiful house of poetry and to fill it with inviolate voices was surely the wrong done to her when she was driven at an early age into an unwanted, distasteful marriage. In *Kala Gulab* (*The Black Rose*, 1968), an autobiographical allegory in prose spun out of her dreams, memories and snatches of verse, she says that "the birth of a poem is the birth of a state of mind." All her poems, then, are happenings and incidents transmuted into art. "I have," she avers, "never turned away from any experience." Her poetry, thus, is a poetry of felt reality and earned insights.

The first two volumes, *Amrit Lehran* and *Jeondan Jiwan* (1939), are today something of an embarrassment. With *Lok Peer* (1944), Amrita is already in the swim of things, and the poetry of personal pieties is being eased out by urgent public and political issues. The Marxian impress is not deep, but it does induce her muses toward a confrontation with society. In all her subsequent verse, a vague socialist sentiment is encountered, but she imbibes the Marxian philosophy more at the level of feeling and emotion than at the level of thought and dialectic. In her best poems, this influence is like a breeze in the face, soft and psychological. The harsher and shriller aspects do not show, as they do in Bawa Balwant, for instance. Still, the Marxian interlude helps open the sluices of her sensibility, though it does not become a complete way of life and poetry.

And then in *Pathar Geetay* (1946) and *Lamian Vatan* (1948), Amrita Pritam returns to her inner fever and furies. The plight of woman *qua* woman now becomes her most persistent and agonising concern. The idiom now is ripe enough to orchestrate womanly pain and ache and grief, and is drawn from the wells and reservoirs of private experience. Several poems such as "Un-Datta" ("The Bread-Giver") and "Gau Shala" ("The Cow Ashram") voice the boundless agony of the bonded woman, a slave to man's hungers and lusts, a victim of societal duplicities and depravities—a plaything, a convenience and a commodity. The crowning achievement of her poetry of violated womanhood is that remarkable poem, "Waris Shah," which she writes in the wake of the Partition riots and bloodshed. It is a poem that remains, excepting Guru Nanak's famed *Babarbani*, the single greatest poem of its kind in the Punjabi language. "The poetry is in the pity," wrote Wilfred Owen when he was face to face with the horrors of the First World War. Amrita Pritam's poetry is one long lament, invoking pity and protest at the same time.

It is then to the sovereignty of love that she turns for a vindication of her lacerated psyche. Since love is woman's whole universe, she explores all its forms and formulations, all its states and conditions, all its blandishments and overtures. A love achieved in the teeth of opposition, or a love plucked from confusion and absurdity and terror seems to have had a special attraction for Amrita Pritam. And she also affirms the uniqueness of each individual love, for it is a singular statement of a virgin heart.

With *Sunehray* (1953), *Ashoka Cheti* (1956), and *Kasturi* (1958), there begins a period in Amrita Pritam's poetry that is characterised by a complexity of thought and expression, and by a certain richness and density of idiom. In the middle years of her life, the pressure of the heart's wildnesses increases, and the verse is at once more extravagant and more controlled. In *Nagmani* (1964) there are some very effective and moving poems such as "Janam Jali" ("The Wretched-Born"), "Chup" ("Silence") and "Galan" ("Let's Talk"), poems that with their Donne-like conceits show a taut structure of emotion and thought.

The secular strains in Amrita Pritam's poetry—in her political musings, in her sociological thought—have still a distinct feminine colour and flavour. The engagement with the human reality and the answers to its assaults stem from her creature state as woman, as lover and as wife. Her imagery and diction are typically feminine, centring round the hearth and the home, the fire and the flame. In a little poem called "Amrita Pritam" she writes:

> The pain that possessed me
> Was the cigarette I drew
> In silent rage;

And the gathered ashes
Were the poems I flicked off
One by one.

Of the poets who represent the third generation of Punjabi poets in the twentieth century, I propose to take up two outstanding talents to highlight the trends since the Partition. They do not, of course, encompass all new thought and all new styles, but, I trust, the achievement of Jaswant Singh Neki and Shiv Batalvi would suffice to show the manner in which the poetic tradition of their immediate predecessors, such as Mohan Singh, Pritam Singh Safeer and Amrita Pritam, has been owned and consolidated. Other notable poets—Prabhjot Kaur, S.S. Misha, Sukhpalvir Singh Hasrat, Ravinder Ravi, Harbhajan Singh, Balbir Singh Dil—do suggest continuities as well as departures, but most of them carry their modernity like a rose in a buttonhole.

Jaswant Singh Neki (1925-), a doctor and psychiatrist who has held prestigious positions in India and abroad, represents, like Safeer, a highly sophisticated form of verse both in thought and style. As a student activist in Sikh politics, he imbibed a great deal of Sikh lore, history and culture, though even then his approach was basically intellectual rather than emotional. All this is clear when one peruses his earlier verse in such volumes as *Asley Te Auhley* and *Eh Meray Sansay, Eh Meray Geet*. The element of ratiocination increases with each new volume so that when he comes to write *Smriti De Kiran Ton Pehlan* and his *tour de force*, *Karuna Di Chho Magron*, which won him the Sahitya Akademi Award for 1980, his verse begins to shine like a polished diamond, and his luminous intellect as an instrument of rare lapidary skill.

Thus, as Neki gets drawn into the multiplying ironies and ambiguities of life, and the deeper urges and visions begin to entice his imagination toward the territories of the spirit, in proportion do his poems become complex, tortured and involuted. Their authenticity lies in the intellectual tensions they tend to create. Though the lyric impulse is strong, his verse increasingly seeks a dramatic form in figures and ensembles of thought. Also, because he is a psychologist with a philosophic orientation, he seeks to render certain inner states of mind and to reach out toward the mysterious and the unknown. Historical, sociological and cultural overtones are not absent, but they are, on the whole, in a muted key. His drift in the direction of epiphanies, transcendences and mystic longings is clear enough in his more recent work. Neki's poetry, then, may be described as a journey of the spirit in search of breakthroughs and certitudes. It is still a poetry of affirmations in the midst of so much personal suffering and existential angst.

A late volume, *Karuna Di Chho Magron*, is, again, something utterly unique in Punjabi poetry. A symbolic dramatisation of a traumatic event in his life that brought him face to face with death, it is a poem of great metaphysical reach and penetration. The theme of death receives a pondered and agonised treatment. A harrowing vision after a smash-up in an accident turns finally into a vision of love and compassion. His return from "the brink" begins thus:

Tarry, o friend, for a moment,
And hear out the wondrous experience
I had last night!
And see how my bones and flesh,
My feelings and faith,
My thought and mind—
All, all were stretch'd on a rack!

In Shiv Batalvi (1936-73), Punjabi poetry at last produced a cult figure much in the manner of Sylvia Plath, though Shiv did not commit suicide to terminate the fever raging in his blood and bones. Nevertheless, an early death linked up with jilted love, drink and dissolution has invested him with an aura of glamorous fatality and poetic destiny, and a whole myth has come to stay.

What a tragic end
Has my story of songs!
As they come of age,
They seek the shroud!

Shiv was essentially writing in the romantic-radical tradition of Mohan Singh and Amrita Pritam. The luxury of romantic grief is strong at the start, and, in a manner, his muses courted suffering. It is as if he had willed such a fate as overtook him in the end. The overtures to Eros and Thanatos ("Love" and "Death") become eventually the warp and woof of his verse. The Keatsian analogy often cited by the Punjabi critics is valid only up to a point, for Shiv did not have anything of the English poet's larger artistic and philosophical concerns. His was a pure lyric voice of intense force and beauty, with an aching and a yearning for a free, uncomplicated, uncovenanted world.

From his first volume, *Peeran Da Paraga* (1960), it becomes clear that the clues to his fevers may well lie in the Freudian subconscious and in the Rankian trauma of birth. His alienation is, it appears, both congenital and cultivated. Nevertheless, it reflects a genuine state of a mind in disarray and distress. To be more precise, he evolves an aesthetic of agony. It is within such a wilderness that he could draw his ebbing breath with some ease. The very title of this volume, *A Lapful of Pains*, suggests the long struggle with fate ahead. Images of thorns, bleeding birds, black nights, trapped pawns, lacerated flesh, smoking bones, and the like, begin to multiply at an alarming rate. It is again typical of Shiv to have adopted the female *persona* to render the anguish of his heart. In poem after poem, the lyric voice of pain is the disembodied cry of the eternal woman in woe.

In his second volume, *Lajwanti* (1961), as in his later collections, a tormented psyche keeps spinning on the axis of pain, and there is no real ethical or socio-political or spiritual breakthrough. A few *avant-garde* images or even announcements do not, in effect, proclaim a radical awareness of reality. The new socialist ethos and Marxian thought have not affected him in any profound manner. His rebellion against bourgeois values makes him a romantic revolutionary in spirit, but the vigour and discipline of radical thought are missing. In *Attey Dian Chirian*, Shiv's sexual imagination takes an overtly erotic turn. Sexuality, he tells us, is primordial and sublime. It preceded the Word, and has its own eternal sanction. He recognises the primacy of life over love, but such is the urgency of sex and such its beauty and compulsions that Shiv, like Whitman and D.H. Lawrence, invests it with a touch of divinity. Perhaps the most powerful poem of this collection is "Shikra" ("The Hawk") which he used to recite in an excruciatingly painful and haunting voice at poetic symposia.

If there are any traces of religious sentiment in Shiv, they are too muted and too attenuated to claim attention. Shiv, undoubtedly, is one of our purest secular poets, though his range of subjects is severely circumscribed. In his epic, *Loona*, which is a long and sustained paean to sexual love, he seems in the end to suggest a religion of love whose intensity, however, has no mystic overtones.

Some Observations on the Evolution of Modern Standard Punjabi

Christopher Shackle

One of the most striking features of contemporary South Asia is the degree to which religion on the one hand, and language on the other, have come to determine social, political and cultural identities with ever sharper emphasis. Even now, of course, there is seldom a perfect congruence between these two factors, given the inherent complexity and variety of South Asian societies. Nevertheless, when there is a considerable measure of overlap between religious and linguistic boundaries, the results are liable to escape the full control of central governments, all committed to more or less open pursuit of the centralising ideals of the former imperial regimes. The most obvious current instances of this rule are provided by the civil war in Sri Lanka between Buddhist Sinhalas and Hindu Tamils, the long-running tension in Assam between Assamese-speaking Hindus and Bengali-speaking Muslims, and of course the seemingly insoluble crisis in Punjab, the state brought into being in 1966 as the result of the long Sikh campaign for the creation of a state in which Punjabi would have undisputed official status.

These and similar conflicts involve so many complex and inter-linked factors that they are hardly easier to analyse fully than they have been to resolve satisfactorily. It is, moreover, a striking common feature of the analyses of all these situations and of their historical antecedents in the colonial period that they tend to concentrate primarily upon political, social and economic factors, and only secondarily upon identifiably religious phenomena, with language issues tending to receive only cursory reference. There thus results a rather curious imbalance between the situations on the ground, where issues of religion and language are so prominently articulated, and the emphases of the analytical literature upon other factors presumed to underlie these rallying cries.

This imbalance is to be attributed to several factors. On the one hand, relatively greater prominence has come to be given to social-science-based studies of South Asia in Western universities, as compared with the meagre funding generally available for those based on language and literature. In South

[Joseph T. O'Connell, Milton Israel, Willard G. Oxtoby, eds., with W.H. McLeod and J.S. Grewal, visiting eds., *Sikh History and Religion in the Twentieth Century* (S. Asian Studies Papers, 3) (Toronto: S. Asian Studies, Univ. of Toronto, 1988)]

Asia, too, there is a comparable imbalance, if for rather different reasons, notably the greater pressure upon academics in departments of language and literature to conform to or, still better, to enhance local linguistic chauvinisms in their published work, rather than to analyse them. And finally, it is simply rather difficult to give a meaningful picture of what is going on in one or other South Asian language through the medium of English.

Since the emphasis of the majority of the papers included in this collection conforms to the characteristic pattern outlined above, it has been thought worthwhile to offer some reflections here on the development of modern standard Punjabi (MSP), from the point of view of a linguist. The creation of this literary language as the prime vehicle for Sikh thought and culture is after all one of the most striking achievements of the Sikh community in the twentieth century. It is hoped that the preliminary observations offered here, which in no way aspire to the status of the substantial paper the subject deserves, may serve to stimulate the development of long-overdue research in this branch of Sikh studies, still very much the Cinderella in the descriptive literature available in English.

The crude tripartite division of South Asian history into its ancient, mediaeval and modern periods is open to many sensible objections; but it serves well enough to establish rough parameters within which to outline characteristic changes in the currency of written languages in northern India, historically peopled by largely illiterate speakers of the endless varieties of the closely related group of Indo-Aryan languages.

The need for an unlocalised standard language to record administrative, religious and secular materials was met during the ancient period by the prolonged use of Sanskrit, carefully preserved for some 1500 years in the archaic mould established by Panini. The Muslim conquests resulted in the establishment of Persian in the place of Sanskrit, except in a restricted religious-intellectual sphere. During the Mughal period, many local Indo-Aryan languages began to be used for limited types of writing, typically religious poetry: but only Braj, jointly fostered by the huge spread of the Krishna cult and the casual patronage of the Agra court, was seriously to emerge as a widely used extra-local standard *bhasha*.

The imposition of British colonial rule gradually resulted, by the later nineteenth century, in major changes to this previous pattern of written-language use. English replaced Persian as an imperially imposed standard, but both the more meticulously applied administration of the new rulers and their related encouragement of "vernacular education" demanded the development of selected varieties of Indo-Aryan as standardised written languages. That segment of the role previously played by Persian which was not annexed by English was accorded to Urdu, the Persianised form of the *lingua franca* based on the Khari Boli dialect of Delhi, spoken to the immediate north of Braj; and thus it was that Urdu replaced Persian in the Punjab after the Anglo-Sikh wars of the 1840's. The great spread of Urdu over northern India, though generally welcome to the Muslim population, came under increasing challenge, however, from its Sanskritised variant, Hindi, promoted by the enthusiasts for this newly-formed medium from Benares and Allahabad in increasingly successful measure against the Urdu norms of Lucknow and Delhi. As the two great religious communities of northern India came into increasing conflict during the later years of the Raj, the Urdu-Hindi controversy—hardly affected by Gandhi's muddled flotation of that elusive middle ground, "Hindustani"—was eventually to be enshrined in the constitutions of the successor states, with Hindi ensconced as the *rashtra-bhasha* (national language) of India, and Urdu pushed back to the west as the *qaumi zaban* (national language) of Pakistan.

Although the outlines of this process are generally familiar, it is important to remember that the evolution of both Urdu and Hindi towards their present status as "national languages" has been accompanied and indeed effected throughout by a whole series of often hotly debated creative decisions by writers of those languages as to standards of correct usage, the account to be taken of the norms of everyday speech *vis-à-vis* those of formal niceties, and the extent to which the rival classical exemplars of Perso-Arabic on the one hand or of Sanskrit on the other should be more or less carefully followed.[1] While the continuing role of English as the carefully fostered language of the *élite* in both India and Pakistan has encouraged committed protagonists of both Hindi and Urdu to push for the excision of obvious anglicisms from correct usage in either language, both have been equally oblivious of the insidious influence of the world's currently dominant international language. This influence appears not simply in the coinage of neologisms at the familiar level of *dur-darshan* for "television" in Hindi or *havai jahaz* for "aeroplane" in Urdu, but in so many apparently unperceived syntactic patterns in everyday usage, e.g., *saval/prashn uthta hai*, "the question arises."

Thus it is that much formal writing in contemporary Urdu or Hindi gives the impression to the objective reader that it is composed in a sort of elaborately Persianised or Sanskritised translationese calqued on the same underlying English patterns, which is only remotely indebted to the classic styles of earlier writers. By the same token, modern formal Urdu and Hindi are often rather remote in syntax and style of expression, as well as in their mutually divergent vocabulary, from the natural patterns of everyday speech. But it is of course precisely this remoteness that has helped to ensure their establishment as standard languages over such a vast speech-area.

The Indo-Aryan languages outside this huge Hindi-Urdu zone, e.g., Bengali, Marathi or Gujarati, underwent a broadly similar process of standardisation during the nineteenth century, as they were transformed to meet the requirements of contemporary expression by the efforts of grammarians and lexicographers continually enticed by the inexhaustible capacity of Sanskrit to

---

1. The process is both surveyed in general and examined in detail in C. Shackle and R. Snell, *Hindi and Urdu since 1800: A Common Reader* (London: School of Oriental and African Studies [SOAS], University of London, forthcoming 1988).

produce all manner of neologisms. In each case, the process was aided by the prior existence of substantial quantities of pre-modern literature, usually recorded in a distinctive regional script.

The strong regional identification of these languages did, however, entail a much livelier debate as to the proper adjustment to be reached in written styles between classical standards and colloquial usage than was required in the evolution of Hindi and Urdu as non-local standards of a different type. Immediately related to this issue was the question of the most appropriate choice of dialect upon which the regional standard should be based, a choice inevitably determined as much by the location of major urban centres in the region as by cultural tradition. Obvious examples of both these issues are provided by the historic Bengali differentiation of the everyday *chalit bhasha* style from the Sanskritised *sadhu bhasha*, and by the modern replacement of Calcutta-based norms in favour of those of Dhaka in the contemporary Bengali of Bangladesh.[2]

What makes the evolution of modern Sikh Punjabi so strikingly interesting is that it represents the creation of a standard regional language not on the periphery of the Hindi-Urdu area, but one ensconced in its very heart. The map of contemporary official-language use would vividly show Indian Punjab as a small Punjabi zone between the Urdu territory of Pakistan and Jammu and Kashmir to its west and north, and the vast bloc of Hindi states to the south and east in India.

Since the institutional process by which this intrinsically rather remarkable situation was brought about, culminating in the success of the long Sikh campaign for a "Punjabi Suba," has been amply dealt with elsewhere,[3] the following observations relate to more strictly linguistic and cultural aspects of the language's evolution.

The conscious forging of modern standard Punjabi as the distinctive vehicle for the expression of a revitalised Sikhism was the achievement of a quite small number of outstandingly industrious and talented literary figures associated with the Singh Sabha movement around the turn of the century. The magnitude of their achievement is best appreciated against the background of the essentially quite unpromising linguistic and cultural situation that they faced. The intrinsic contrasts, with Urdu and Hindi on the one hand and with the regional languages of the Bengali type on the other, are worth underlining.

The transfer of the imperial crown from the Mughals to the British had permitted Urdu to enjoy an unbroken pattern of evolution as a literary language, and this firmly established heritage provided a solid linguistic base for the Sanskritising proponents of the new Hindi to work from, to such effect as soon to be able to claim the very different literary idioms used by Kabir, Tulsidas and

---

2. Cf. J.V. Boulton, "Bengali," besides the short surveys of other languages presented in C. Shackle, ed., *South Asian Languages: A Handbook* (London: SOAS External Services Division, 1985).
3. Most notably in part 3 of Paul R. Brass, *Language, Religion and Politics in North India* (Cambridge: Cambridge University Press, 1974).

Surdas as mediaeval Hindi. On any objective criterion, Punjabi is quite as close to the Khari Boli dialect, which underlies both Urdu and Hindi, as Surdas's Braj, and is indeed far closer to it than the eastern Avadhi of the *Ramcharitmanas*.[4]

Then, again as compared with the independent peripheral Indo-Aryan languages, Punjabi lacked the intrinsic advantages not only of recognisably sharp distinction from the norms of Hindi-Urdu grammar and vocabulary, but also the institutional patronage provided by the provincial governments in Calcutta or Bombay. Lahore was, after all, the seat of an administration which conducted its business in English and in Urdu until Partition (as it indeed still remains, although without direct impact on the Sikhs).

Finally, the pre-existent literary heritage in Punjabi was more than usually ambiguous in identifiable linguistic character. Although some form of Punjabi had always been the spoken language of the vast majority of the Sikh community, and although the distinctive Gurmukhi script had always been used to record the vast bulk of its sacred and other literary heritage, the triple Punjabi-Gurmukhi-Sikh equation that has come to be taken for granted by so many Sikhs in India and abroad today hardly existed before the creation of modern standard Punjabi (MSP) in the period around 1900.

The idiom which Guru Nanak, as a poet of utterly superb originality and power, evolved for the matchless expression of his universal message certainly owed much to his native Sheikhupuri speech. But the very requirements of the universality of his teachings, not to speak of then pre-existent norms of literary expression and his own wide travels, involved his drawing upon a far wider range of available linguistic resources. The composite idiom he thus created was expanded by his successors, most notably by the prolific and linguistically versatile Guru Arjan, and was also transferred to prose by the humbler compilers of the *janam-sakhis*. This scriptural language, which I have termed the "sacred language of the Sikhs," is certainly not "Old Punjabi," though many of its elements are drawn from that local source.[5]

Although modernised versions of this composite Punjabi-based sacred language of the Sikhs survived in some post-scriptural Sikh texts, it was Braj and Persian, the great North Indian literary languages of the later Mughal period, that came to dominate Sikh writing after the time of Guru Arjan. Those parts of the Dasam Granth that can plausibly be attributed to the pen of Guru Gobind Singh himself indicate that, while he was equally at home in Persian, his preferred medium was Braj, as it had been his father's. And Braj, written in the Gurmukhi script, was thereafter to be the prevalent medium for the production of

---

4. Although the traditional taxonomy of the Indo-Aryan languages effected by Grierson in the classic *Linguistic Survey of India* is open to all sorts of objections, these are hardly to be levelled against his alignment of Punjabi with Western Hindi and assignment of Eastern Hindi to a separate volume.

5. The picture given in my teaching manual, *An Introduction to the Sacred Language of the Sikhs* (London: SOAS, 1983), should be supplemented by reference to the preface of my earlier *A Guru Nanak Glossary* (London: SOAS; and Vancouver: University of British Columbia, 1981), and the listings of more specialist treatments of the sacred language of the Sikhs appended thereto.

most later Sikh writings throughout the heroic *gurbilas* period down to the colossally effective final synthesis of pre-modern Sikh tradition composed by Bhai Santokh Singh.

By one of those paradoxes with which the linguistic and cultural history of South Asia so abounds, it was precisely during this period of the eighteenth and early nineteenth centuries, when the Sikhs were writing in Braj, a now discarded language claimed by Hindu enthusiasts as one of the major "ancestors" of modern Hindi, that Punjabi was being developed as a literary medium for the creation of superb verse by Muslim poets. Drawing extensively upon their Persian heritage, and writing in the Persian script, such masters of the Sufi *kafi* as Bullhe Shah (1680-1758) were joined by such glorious exponents of the narrative *kissa* as Varis Shah, whose *Hir* (1766) is the universally acknowledged masterpiece of Punjabi literature,[6] and the later Hasham Shah (1753-1823). The universal appeal of this literature, generated from within the Muslim community, which has for so long constituted the majority of Punjabi-speakers, is attested to by the number of nineteenth-century manuscripts recording its compositions in Gurmukhi.[7]

Although literary histories and bibliographic listings record the names of many Sikh authors of *kissa*-narratives, they were latecomers to this well-established poetic tradition and are hardly to be resurrected as major contributors to it, except within the context of a careful examination from the linguistic viewpoint of that heterogeneous mass of Punjabi books put out by the publishers of Lahore and lesser centres during the formative years of the period ca. 1870-1914.[8] A necessary prerequisite of this urgently needed examination would be a carefully judged distancing from that prevalent Sikh-Punjabi chauvinist perspective which would view almost anything written in Punjabi as a part of the "Sikh literary heritage," however imperfectly understood.

As the preceding remarks should have served to show, "Punjabi" is one thing and "Sikkhi" is quite another, and the contemporary perception of a virtually complete overlap between the two is quite something else again. The following observations are offered in a deliberately disjointed fashion, in the hope of suggesting that the contemporary Sikh identification with the Punjabi language is quite as much in need of sympathetic but rigorous academic investigation as are rather more generously covered aspects of contemporary Sikhism.

---

6. A treatment of the poem, with rather full references to sources in English for the related Muslim literature, has been attempted in my paper "Transitions and Transformations in Varis Shah's *Hir*," to appear in C. Shackle and R. Snell, eds., *Studies in Indian Narrative* (London: Lokamaya, forthcoming).

7. Cf. the summary suggestions made in my "Some Observations on the London Collections of Panjabi and Gurmukhi Manuscripts," *IAVRI Bulletin* 13 (1986), 5-8.

8. E.g., the listings provided in the invaluable specialist bibliography of N.G. Barrier, *The Sikhs and Their Literature: A Guide to Tracts, Books and Periodicals 1849-1919* (New Delhi: Manohar Book Service, 1970), as well as the more general, also more casual, coverage of the catalogues of Punjabi holdings in the British (Museum) Library and the India Office Library.

These observations are loosely presented in ascending order of complexity of the phenomena involved. Their collective purpose is less to offer definitive answers than to raise questions which may some day receive an adequate explanation.

At the simplest visual level, the equation between script and separate linguistic identity is one inevitably seized upon by linguistic protagonists in the amazingly multi-alphabetic environment of South Asia. The early proponents of MSP had the Gurmukhi script to hand as an immediate weapon to support their cause. But the contemporary spelling norms of MSP are rather different from those of the sacred language of the Sikhs (although continuing to reflect these in the orthography of many words). When was it, for instance, that the modern conventions of the use of dotted letters to distinguish *sh, z, f* from *s, j, ph* became established? Here the prior influence of Hindi norms seems to be indicated; but on the other hand, the modern convention of indicating the doubled consonants so intrinsic to Punjabi by the use of the symbol *addhik* is hardly to be explained without reference to the convenient *tashdid* of the Perso-Urdu script. But how? And when?

These may seem very drily technical questions, but a much greater range of linguistic issues was involved in the successful creation of MSP. This, after all, had on the one hand to be created in explicit rivalry with the well-established norms of Urdu, the officially established medium of provincial administration and education, and its Hindi variant increasingly employed by the anti-Sikh Arya Samaji polemicists. On the other hand the very imperfectly established norms for the appropriately selected use of one or other of the many spoken dialects of Punjabi provided at best a shifting base from which to confront these major challenges to the carving out of the sort of linguistically-based community identity the Singh Sabha activists and the wider circle of associated Sikh writers so actively pursued.

Three broad stages may be distinguished in the evolution of MSP as an increasingly standardised medium of formal expression, and in the range of uses to which it has been put. Both these aspects, i.e., the linguistic and the literary,[9] naturally correspond in turn to the contemporary evolution of the Sikh community itself and to wider changes in its South Asian social and political environment.

In the formative first stage, the dominance of specifically religious concerns is symbolised by the enormously copious and influential output of Bhai Vir Singh (1872-1957). Linguistically, this stage is characterised by the strong influence of the earlier sacred language of the scriptures which provided the reformers with their spiritual inspiration. The location of Guru Nanak's birth and upbringing had given the sacred language of the Sikhs an equal heritage,

---

9. Neither aspect is very adequately treated in English, but some possibilities are suggested in my "Problems of Classification in Pakistan Punjab," *Transactions of the Philological Society* (London, 1979), pp. 191-210, or from a quite different perspective in M.P. Kohli, *The Influence of the West on Panjabi Literature* (Ludhiana, 1969).

deriving both from the Majhi dialect of the central Punjab, many of whose features are rather close to Hindi-Urdu norms, and from the so-called "Lahndi" dialects of the western Punjab, which are much more distinctive in linguistic character (e.g., the formation of the future tense as in *jasi* "he will go" or the use of suffixed pronouns as in *akhius* "he said"). This distinctive Lahndi component was sustained in much post-scriptural writing in the sacred language of the Sikhs originating from the non-Jat Sikh communities of the north-west. Drawing upon this heritage, the early creators of MSP preserved this Lahndi colouring in their writings, even if they themselves came from further east, as in the case of Bhai Vir Singh himself, born and bred in Amritsar.

The overlapping second stage may be dated from soon after the First World War and is characterised by the extension of MSP from an overwhelmingly religious emphasis to its use for the creation of a secular literature by Sikh authors. The exposure of most of these writers to Urdu and to English brought a new sophistication and suppleness to the language, and it is from this period that the classics of modern Punjabi date. Many of the most prominent authors of the period themselves came from the western regions, thus encouraging the continuance of the Lahndi influence on dominantly Majhi-based norms. This classic mix is to be seen, in varying degrees, in the elegant essays of Teja Singh (1894-1958), the immensely popular novels of Nanak Singh (b. 1897), the poems of Mohan Singh (b. 1905), or the short stories of Kartar Singh Duggal (b. 1917) and Kulvant Singh Virk (b. 1921).

Although many of these writers, of course, developed their careers in India after 1947, the post-Independence third phase in the evolution of MSP has been dominated by other factors. The wholesale eastward shift of the Sikh population was soon accompanied by a massively increased emphasis on the development and use of MSP as a medium of education and administration, thus extending it far beyond its already established functions as a medium for religious debate and literary expression. With the establishment of the Language Department in Patiala, MSP had for the first time something approaching an official academy, whose influence on the standardisation of the language was soon to be augmented by the proliferation of Punjabi departments in universities and colleges and the recognition of Punjabi as the state language of Punjab in 1966.

This great enhancement of the status of MSP has been accompanied by very noticeable changes in the character of its linguistic elements. The drawing of the Radcliffe line right through central Punjab left the Lahndi areas in Pakistan and split the Majhi area in two. Contemporary standard Punjabi has therefore tended to incorporate a greater colouring from the eastern dialects of Doabi and Malwai, which are intrinsically often closer to Hindi. At the same time, the abrupt termination of the previous official dominance of Urdu on the eastern side of the Partition line has resulted in a rapid loss of awareness of the historically influential Perso-Urdu component in the vocabulary of MSP, which is naturally still very prominent in the much less altered Punjabi of Pakistan.[10] It is true that some attempt has been made to preserve the distinctiveness of MSP by looking to indigenous sources to express new concepts: thus, while the English "researcher" is expressed in Urdu by the Arabic *muhaqqiq* or in Hindi by the Sanskritic *shodh-karta*, MSP has developed a new sense for the homely Punjabi word *khoji*, originally "tracker." But the intrinsic preference of all Indo-Aryan languages for coining neologisms from classical languages has usually proved too strong to resist, and the most formal registers of MSP are becoming quite as Sanskritised as Hindi.

As is so often the case when the attempt is made to examine the linguistic underpinnings of religious and cultural identities in South Asia, there are therefore a number of apparent paradoxes suggested by the modern evolution of Punjabi. It is, after all, somewhat extraordinary that while so much emphasis should be laid on the separate identity of the Sikhs and on the closeness of their identification with the Punjabi heritage, the formal expression of this position should increasingly be couched in a Sanskritised MSP divorced from the vital idiom of spoken Punjabi,[11] which is far less intelligible to educated Punjabi speakers from Pakistan than it is to the Hindi protagonists so often viewed as the bitterest critics of the Sikhs and their language. But then no one involved with the scholarly investigation of Sikh religion and history in the twentieth century is going to expect simple answers to any serious issue in the field. These preliminary observations will have served their purpose if they suggest that this general rule is quite as true of language as of any other area.

---

10. My earliest personal observations of the Punjabi scene in Pakistan are recorded in "Punjabi in Lahore," *Modern Asian Studies* 4:3 (1970), 239-69; my most recent ones, in "Language, Dialect and Local Identity in Northern Pakistan" in W.P. Zingel and S. Lallemant, eds., *Pakistan in Its Fourth Decade* (Hamburg: Deutsches Orient-Institut, 1983), pp. 175-87.

11. Although it is precisely to his exploitation of the vigorous resources of the spoken idiom that Bhindranwale's message has owed so much of its appeal, it is important to remember that this was primarily disseminated by cassettes, not by the printed page, where formalised MSP dominates.

Bengali Perceptions of the Sikhs: The Nineteenth and Twentieth Centuries

Himadri Banerjee

I

Nowadays the "study of history from below" is receiving serious attention of scholars in the subcontinent. Against this background, this chapter may not evoke much enthusiasm, for it is apparently based on a "horizontal approach" to history. To a casual observer it may also convey an impression of an exclusive middle-class literary endeavour, catering merely to its middle-class needs. But beyond this narrow limit, the chapter tries to trace the efforts of a community to understand one of its distant neighbours over the years.[1] Of these efforts, nineteenth- and twentieth-century Bengali writing dealing with Sikhs has been a meaningful index.

Bengali interest in understanding the Sikhs is reflected in a number of nineteenth-century works, and it continues to the present. A good number of Bengali writers were associated with this endeavour, and different factors brought them together on a common platform. They came from different walks of life: they were poets, historians, essayists, journalists, religious reformers, political leaders and dramatists. A few of them spent long years in the Punjab, where they had gone following the British annexation (1849) in response to the growing administrative needs of the colonial government. They often tried to communicate their local experience and knowledge of the Sikhs to their own people at home.

The majority of these writers were, however, of the city of Calcutta, then witnessing a growing upsurge of militant nationalist opposition to British rule. It brought in its train a greater appreciation of and interest in the Indian tradition of fighting against royal tyranny, foreign invasion and exploitation by the ruling class. Prose writers and poets were encouraged to incorporate this in their

---

1. I am deeply indebted to my friend Sri Tirthankar Mukherjee, Assistant Editor, *Amrita Bazar Patrika*, for his comments and editorial help. Dr. Nikhilesh Guha, Sri Chidananda Bhattacharjee and Sri Asoke Upadhyay also helped me in the preparation of the article.

[Joseph T. O'Connell, Milton Israel, Willard G. Oxtoby, eds., with W.H. McLeod and J.S. Grewal, visiting eds., *Sikh History and Religion in the Twentieth Century* (S. Asian Studies Papers, 3) (Toronto: S. Asian Studies, Univ. of Toronto, 1988)]

writing, thereby providing an added stimulus to the contemporary militant politics of Bengal. To many of them the birth of Sikhism, rise of the Khalsa, martyrdom of the Gurus, the "saga of Sikh resistance" to the Mughals and Afghans, the remarkable success of Maharaja Ranjit Singh in building up a powerful Sikh monarchy when the other Indian rulers were "meekly submitting to the British" and, finally, the "valour" of the Sikh army during the days of the Anglo-Sikh wars carried the message of patriotism. It kindled the imagination of many Bengali authors of this period. A few others tried to seek out any similarities between Sikhism and Hinduism, while others sought to evaluate the significance of the message of the Gurus in the wider Indian religious context.

The development of Sikh studies was again closely associated with the Brahmo search in the nineteenth century for a religious identity separate from that of orthodox Hinduism. The Panth perhaps first drew the attention of modern Bengali authors in the second decade of the last century when Raja Rammohan Roy referred to it in his writings.[2] Even after the demise of the Raja, Sikh monotheism continued to draw the attention and respect of leading nineteenth-century Brahmo reformers like Debendranath Tagore,[3] Akshaykumar Datta,[4] Keshabchandra Sen[5] and Krishnakumar Mitra.[6] According to many of them, the practice of social equality and rejection of caste hierarchy generated a spirit of confidence among the Sikhs and made them a community of martyrs.[7]

This Brahmo inquiry into the Panth was subsequently reinforced by a few Hindu nationalist and Sanatanist (i.e., orthodox Brahmanical) authors who

---

2. Rammohan Roy referred to the message of Guru Nanak on at least two occasions. See *Rammohan Rachanavali* (Calcutta: Haraf Prakashani, 1973), pp. 8, 262.

3. Debendranath Tagore was the father of Rabindranath Tagore. In his autobiography Tagore noted with reverence the significance of the message of the *Japji*. Debendranath Tagore, *Atmajibani* (Calcutta: Visva-Bharati, 1962), pp. 113, 182-87, 212, 233.

4. Akshaykumar Datta's pioneering contribution on the history of the Sikhs as well as his analytical exposition of the Sikh philosophy were serialised in the *Tattvabodhini Patrika*, the official organ of the Brahmo faith. Based on English sources, he emphasised the distinctive features of Sikhism in the Indian religious system. *Tattvabodhini Patrika*, Chaitra 1772 Shaka, 176-83; ibid., Ashar 1773 Shaka, 48-52; ibid., Kartik 1773 Shaka, 99-102; ibid., Magh 1773 Shaka, 135-37; ibid., Phalgun 1773 Shaka, 154-56. Add 78/79 to Shaka dates for C.E. equivalents.

5. Keshabchandra Sen was the leader of the Nababidhan group of the Brahmo movement. His admiration of Sikh monotheism paved the way for the publication of the *Nanak Prakash*, still regarded as an outstanding biography of Guru Nanak in Bengali. His interest in Sikhism was evinced in the naming of one of his books *Sangat*, published by the Brahmo Tract Society in 1916. Incidentally, the Brahmos had a small informal group for free discussion of different religious and moral problems of their own community. This was named the Sangat Sabha by Debendranath Tagore.

6. Mitra started writing on the history of the Sikhs in the 1880's. But the manuscript was lost while he was on his way to his native village, now in Bangladesh. He decided to start afresh as soon as he was back in Calcutta. When he had nearly completed it, he was arrested by the police for his association with Bengal militant politics. The police took away the manuscript, never to return it. Finally, when he was put in the Agra jail in 1908, he began the work with renewed confidence. He even managed to procure a copy of the *Bala Janam-sakhi* from the jail authorities and sat down to writing as soon as he had finished the text. His autobiography gives us a regular record of the progress of his writing. Unfortunately, Mitra mentioned nothing about the fate of the manuscript. For details, see Krishnakumar Mitra, *Atmacharit* (Calcutta: Prabasi Press, 1937), pp. 316, 319-20, 332.

7. For a further discussion on this point, see the author's article "Sikh History in Bengali Literature," *Studies in Sikhism and Comparative Religion* (October 1984), pp. 113-14.

provided a newer dimension to Bengali understanding of the Sikhs in the last quarter of the nineteenth century. The latter often portrayed Guru Nanak as one of the leading exponents of the fifteenth- and sixteenth-century *bhakti* movement, and declined to accord Sikhism any religious status distinct from that of Hinduism. A few of them were deeply impressed by Bankimchandra Chatterjee's Hindu revivalist sentiment and wanted to glorify the ancient Indian Hindu fighting tradition. In their opinion, this would offer an answer to India's enslavement to British rule. Rajanikanta Gupta,[8] for example, made no secret of the fact that the "heroic self-sacrifice of the Sikhs against the Mughals and Afghans was not an isolated chapter of Indian history." He emphasised the point that Rana Pratap, Shivaji and Ranjit Singh, like Guru Gobind Singh, preached the same message of resistance to royal tyranny and fought for political freedom in the pre-British days. Gupta was also of the opinion that the Sikhs inherited this "militant tradition" from the Hindus, and viewed the Panth in this light in the nineteenth century.[9]

Another point that may be noted in this connection was the ready response of Bengali authors to some significant developments affecting the Sikhs in the Punjab during the period under review. The process may be said to have started during Maharaja Ranjit Singh's reign in the early 1830's.[10] Similarly, with the signing of the treaty of Bhyrowal (1846), a monograph entitled *Punjabaitihas*, dealing with the history of the Sikhs from the days of Nanak till the cessation of the First Anglo-Sikh War, was brought out in 1847. The book was warmly received by the people because "the fate of the Sikh Kingdom was then deeply interesting to them."[11] There were three quick editions of this volume, an achievement matched by only a handful of famous authors in the mid-nineteenth century. Again in 1893, shortly after the death of Maharaja Duleep Singh, a detailed biography highlighting his career along with an account of the Second Sikh War was published.[12] This nineteenth-century interest persisted in the

---

8. Gupta was convinced that with the exception of Hunter and Cunningham, English historians were not favourably disposed towards the history of the Sikhs. Bengali authors, therefore, should do something for redressing the grievances of the Sikh people. See Rajanikanta Gupta, "Jhindan," *Bharat Kahini* (Calcutta: Bengal Medical Library, 1292 B.S.), pp. 70-85. Add 593/94 to B.S. for C.E. equivalents. See also his *Sikh* (Calcutta: Bengal Medical Library, 1883), p. 25.

9. In this context the Singh Sabha leaders' bid for redefining Sikhism raised newer questions in the minds of Bengali authors. They stimulated a long-term debate and furthered the case of Sikh studies in Bengal in the present century.

10. *Jnanannesan*, a bilingual Calcutta journal, reviewed the likely impact of Maharaja Ranjit Singh's death on the British policy towards the Punjab in an editorial published on March 27, 1834. Sureshchandra Moitra, ed., *Selections from Jnanannesan* (Calcutta: Prajna, 1979), pp. 155-58.

11. J. Long, "A Descriptive Catalogue of Bengali Works," quoted in Dineshchandra Sen, *Bangabhasha o Sahitya* (Calcutta: Dasgupta & Co. Ltd., 1356 B.S.), p. 425.

12. Barodakanta Mitra's *Sikh Juddher Itihas o Maharaja Duleep Singha* (Calcutta: the author, 1893), is still regarded as an important landmark in the development of Bengali historiography of the nineteenth century. The monograph is based mainly on official and other primary sources. It also heavily relies on a number of secondary works of authorities like Cunningham, Bell, Smyth and Steinbach. Mitra frequently quoted from them in defence of his arguments and cited them in his footnotes. He was also aware of the significance of chronology in the writing of history. Mitra may be credited with laying the foundation of the historiography on the Sikhs in Bengali. See also the author's contribution in the *Encyclopaedia of Sikhism* (forthcoming). A.R. Mallick, "Writings in the

twentieth-century Bengali press. Thus the Jallianwala Bagh massacre, Dyerism, the struggle for control of Sikh shrines, the religious atmosphere in and around the Golden Temple, the sufferings of the Akali *jathas* and the martyrdom of Bhagat Singh deeply agitated the Bengali mind. They generated a sense of solidarity between the militant nationalists of Bengal and the Punjab.[13]

But this is not to suggest that the Sikhs were always the "hot favourites" of nineteenth-century Bengali intellectuals. On the contrary, if we are allowed to apply an order of preference, they perhaps came third, after the Rajputs and the Marathas. For example, the two great contemporary novelists of Bengal, namely Bankimchandra Chatterjee and Rameshchandra Dutt, wrote novels depicting the chivalry and valour of the Rajputs and the Marathas against the "oppressive" rule of the Mughals in the seventeenth and eighteenth centuries. The Sikhs never figured prominently in their writings.[14] Of course, Rabindranath Tagore, somewhat later, was an exception. But in addition to these great masters, there are still many others who enthusiastically wrote about the Sikhs. Since they are too numerous to consider as a whole, we shall be dealing with the works of a few of them. They may be divided under the following heads:

i) biographical sketches and other works highlighting the lives of the Gurus and crowned heads;

ii) monographs on Sikh sacred literature; and

iii) other miscellaneous works.

II

In this paper we deal primarily with the first two categories of works, because they not only comprise the largest number of contributions in Bengali but also indicate some of the major trends in twentieth-century Bengali perceptions of the Sikhs. In this regard, a reference to a few nineteenth-century works on the lives of Sikh Gurus will help us better understand the problem. A modest beginning was made during the second half of the nineteenth century, with the serialisation of the history of the Panth with a special emphasis on the biographies of the Gurus and their writings, in such leading journals as the *Tattvabodhini   Patrika*,[15]   *Dharmatattva*,[16]   *Vividhartha   Samgraha*,[17]

Indigenous Languages: Modern Historical Writing in Bengali," in C.H. Philips, ed., *Historians of India, Pakistan and Ceylon* (London: Oxford University Press, 1961), pp. 451-52.

13. For example, Dyerism was reflected in Praphulla Kumar Basu's *Panjab Kahini* (Dhaka: Jnanchandra Mitra, 1328 B.S.).

14. Bankimchandra Chatterjee and Rameshchandra Dutt referred to the history of the Sikhs only on one occasion in their respective writings. For them, see Bankimchandra Chatterjee, "Bharat Kalanka," *Bankim Rachanavali* (Calcutta: Bangiya Sahitya Parishad, 1346 B.S.), p. 144; Rameshchandra Dutt, "Svamamandir," *Mukul*, Ashar 1302 B.S., pp. 10-11.

Bangadarshan[18] and *Balak.*[19] In spite of the conflicting commitments of these journals regarding the various politico-social problems of the times, their published articles generally provide an admiring view of the Panth and Gurus. Another important, if not the most significant, publication of this period was the *Nanak Prakash* by Bhai Mahendranath Bose of the Nababidhan group. Based on *janam-sakhi* sources, it is the most detailed biography of the founder of the Panth in Bengali and seeks to highlight the Guru as a man of saintly temperament fighting against superstition, ritualism and caste hierarchy. Unlike other Bengali biographers, Bose portrayed the Guru in a formal prose style and his interpretations of some of the major episodes of his life were marked by a scientific perspective.[20]

Although in the present century no biography of the standard of *Nanak Prakash* has been published, there are two separate monographs on the life of the founder of the Sikh faith, each displaying a distinctive style and form. The first one is a biography in verse entitled *Nanak* by Kshitishchandra Chakravarti, a lawyer at Midnapur in West Bengal.[21] In his private life he was a man of religious temperament with a definite bias towards the cult of *bhakti*. This largely explains his interest in the life and message of Guru Nanak. He was of the opinion that Nanak played a pivotal role in the sixteenth-century *bhakti* movement, spreading the gospel of love and devotion among the different religious communities of the Indian subcontinent. In his preface to the poem, he noted that this biography would not satisfy those who portray the Guru minus the various hagiographic tales inseparably associated with his life and mission. His work was an attempt, writes Chakravarti, to review Nanak's life with all its legends and miracles, though they may appear of dubious credibility in the eyes

15. It was the chief organ of the Brahmo Samaj; it first came out in August 1843. The journal carried articles on the different aspects of the Sikh faith in the following numbers: Shaka 1825, pp. 88-96; Shaka 1833, pp. 65-66; Shaka 1835, pp. 165, 175. See also note 4.

16. It was the chief spokesman of the Nababidhan group headed by Keshabchandra Sen. Bhai Mahendranath Bose's *Nanak Prakash* was originally serialised in it till July 1883.

17. With the financial assistance of the Vernacular Literary Society, Raja Rajendralal Mitra started *Vividhartha Samgraha*, the first penny magazine in India. It was a "copiously illustrated" monthly publication. In the very first issue of this journal, Mitra wrote a brief but critical life-sketch of Guru Nanak. He narrated the history of the Sikhs till the end of the Second Sikh War in the subsequent issues of the journal.

18. *Bangadarshan* is a monthly periodical founded by Bankimchandra Chatterjee in July-August 1872. The biographies of the Gurus were published in Ashar and Magh 1285 B.S.

19. *Balak* was run primarily by the Tagores in Calcutta. It was a literary magazine meant for the young boys and girls.

20. Bhai Mahendranath Bose tried to explain quite a few sixteenth-century "miracles" associated with the Guru's life in the context of nineteenth-century Indian socio-religious experience. In this connection one may refer to the story of Bhai Mardana's sufferings at the hands of demons. Bose suggests that this was "a myth contemplated by some medieval authors explaining Bhai Mardana's greedy character." While admitting their historical significance, he was the first Bengali author to point out that it is extremely difficult to reconstruct any meaningful biography of Guru Nanak exclusively on the basis of the *sakhi* sources. Throughout the book, he has tried to maintain a sane balance between myth and reality in the midst of a bewildering mass of contradictions. It attests to his great and healthy historical interest. It is for all these reasons that the *Nanak Prakash* still is regarded as a first-rate biography of Guru Nanak in Bengali.

21. Kshitishchandra Chakravarti, *Nanak* (Calcutta: Jnanendranath Halder, 1323 B.S.). The book was reprinted by the Sikh Cultural Centre, Calcutta, in 1983.

of an atheist or other nonbeliever. These episodes, according to him, were essential for a better understanding of some of the basic tenets of Sikhism and therefore should be presented without a critical approach on the part of the author.

Chakravarti's *Nanak* is the lone Bengali poetical work on the life of the Guru. His account is marked by certain distinctive features. For example, the poet presented a few interesting developments of Guru Nanak's life with significant Bengali overtone and colour. Chakravarti's Nanak, like Subramania Bharati's Guru Gobind Singh, often comes out of his provincial social milieu and moves freely within a different regional social and value system. The Guru does not always figure as a sixteenth-century religious reformer fighting against social maladies, religious obscurantism and economic inequality. He is often depicted as the son of a typical middle-class family torn between his family status and the broader social commitment of his times. Mother Tripta's frequent lamentations over the Guru's otherworldliness are reminiscent of the woes of Sri Chaitanya's mother, and the village of Kartarpur is set against a background remarkably like the rural Bengal of the early twentieth century. The poem is also imbued with an informal and popular touch, quite unlike the style of Mahendranath Bose's *Nanak Prakash*.

Perhaps the last Bengali monograph on Guru Nanak came from Rakhaldas Kavyananda in the late 1920's. Unfortunately very little is known about his life and other literary works. It seems likely that the author undertook the task as a result of politico-religious considerations.[22] He saw Nanak as a messiah propagating the cause of Hindu-Muslim co-operation in an age of religious persecution and communal hatred. He was of the opinion that a proper evaluation of the teachings of the Guru would help strengthen the bonds of inter-communal co-operation and good will.

Regrettably, Kavyananda's book can hardly be regarded a dependable biography of Nanak. It suffers from chronological lapses[23] and misrepresentation of the significance of the *sakhi* sources. The volume is also full of digressions from the central theme of the Guru's life; and a pronounced Hindu bias also dominates his style of writing.

III

During these years the life and teachings of Guru Nanak continued to be reviewed either in connection with the study of the religious history of ancient or medieval India or with reference to the general history of the Sikhs fighting against the declining Mughal authority in the later middle ages. The writers came from Brahmo and non-Brahmo ranks and their works are too numerous to permit individual attention to all. Here we take note of three categories of them

---

22. Rakhaldas Kavyananda said he wrote *Guru Nanak* to cement the ties of religion among Indians, irrespective of their caste and regional commitment. For this, see *Guru Nanak* (Calcutta: Barendra Library, n.d.), p. i.

23. For example, Kavyananda wrote that Guru Nanak was born in 1496; ibid., p. 55.

because they have some special characteristics of their own, viz., those presenting Guru Nanak as protesting against oppression, or as preaching Hindu-Muslim solidarity or as articulating a form of orthodox Hindu faith.

The first is represented by Debendranath Mitra of Chandernagore. While reviewing the history of the evolution of Sikh militarism of the later medieval days, Mitra sought to assess Guru Nanak's role in it. He argued that it was very much indebted to Guru Nanak's mission of protest against political oppression, social injustice and economic inequality of the times. The author argues that Nanak's inspired leadership made Sikhs "a bold, assertive and dominant race ever ready to defend the case of religion."[24] Like Debendranath Mitra, Kumudini Mitra also traced the history of Sikh militarism partially to the first Guru's message during the days of the *bhakti* movement.[25]

Another group of writers viewed Guru Nanak in the light of his preaching the message of Hindu-Muslim solidarity in the subcontinent. They pointed out that Nanak's commitment to a unitary God and his attempts at communal harmony were not radically different form the Indian cultural tradition. The Vedas, and later Lord Buddha in the sixth century B.C., had propagated a similar philosophy. During the middle ages the tradition continued uninterrupted through the preachings of Tukaram, Namdev, Ramananda, Kabir and Mirabai. The Guru inherited this religious legacy and made Hindus and Muslims aware of their common cultural heritage. This peculiar Indianness of the Guru's teachings explains his general acceptance among the people of the Punjab. It was this tradition that gave them the resilience to survive foreign invasion, internal strife and anarchy throughout the sixteenth and seventeenth centuries. Leading Brahmo authorities, like Kshitimohan Sen and Sharatkumar Roy, also argued that this cultural synthesis continued even after Nanak and asserted that Raja Rammohan Roy was one of its exponents in the early nineteenth century.[26]

Interestingly enough, the Sanatanists also projected a closer religious bond between orthodox Hinduism and the teachings of Guru Nanak. Following the lead of Rajanikanta Gupta, they argued in the present century that Guru Nanak was a Hindu and they advised Bengalis to read the history of the Sikhs, for they fought for the "defence" of Hinduism in the northwest of India. While analyzing the message of the Guru, they pointed out that Sikhism was, in fact, one of the innumerable forms of Hinduism; and had, in fact, rescued sixteenth-century Hinduism from the "clutches of superstitious priests." In their opinion, the founder of Sikhism preached nothing contrary to the message of the sacred Vedas, nor was he opposed to idol worship and the practice of *sati* (voluntary

---

24. Debendranath Mitra, *Sikh Parichay* (Chandernagore: B. Pra. Press, n.d.), p. 4.
25. Kumudini Mitra, *Sikher Balidan* (Calcutta: Sanjibani Office, 1919), pp. 1-3. But the earlier editions of this monograph did not contain any such reference to Guru Nanak.
26. Kshitimohan Sen, *Bharatiya Madhyayuge Sadhanar Dhara* (Calcutta: Kalikata Vishvavidyalay, 1930), pp. 73-74; Saratkumar Roy, *Bharatiya Sadhak* (Calcutta: Indian Press, 1914), pp. 24-33; Shashibhushan Bose, *Bhakticharitmala*, v. 1 (Calcutta: Indian Press, 1918), pp. 310-27; Binaykumar Sarkar, "Itihase Sikhjati," *Aitihasik Prabandha* (Calcutta: Students Library, 1914), p. 49.

self-immolation by widows). The Guru's reformist zeal also never discouraged Sikhs from coming closer to Hindus, for the two communities continued to share some common festivals, customs and religious symbols. This continued overlapping of these two communities, these writers concluded, reflected their common origin. Hence the attempts of some English authorities to project Sikhs as a community different from Hindus was nothing but an irrational and fallacious historical hypothesis.[27]

IV

Guru Gobind Singh's life and teachings and his fight against the Mughals leading to the birth of the Khalsa also figured in Bengali writing. Rajnarayan Bhattacharya was perhaps the first to refer to him in his *Punjabaitihas*. The author briefly recorded the exploits of the tenth Master against the Hill Rajas and Mughals while reviewing the rise of the Sikhs under their different Gurus. Like Bhattacharya, Swami Vivekananda dwelt on the importance of the Guru's mission in his speeches delivered in Lahore in the late 1890's.[28] Incidentally, these years also witnessed the publication of a brief sketch on the Guru by Rajanikanta Gupta. He painted the Guru as the father of Sikh militarism, ceaselessly defending the cause of the weak Hindus against the Mughals. The tenth Master, Gupta argues, preached the message of political unity and national consciousness and sought to salvage the Indians from the political anarchy of the seventeenth century.[29] It is obvious that a definite Hindu bias was the hallmark of Gupta's pen.

Tinkari Banerjee's *Guru Gobinda Singha* was another important work in this field. The author is accredited as one of the most widely known biographers of the Guru in Bengali. After years of labour in close co-operation with the Bhais of the Barabazar Gurdwara, Calcutta, the monograph came out in 1896. But it turned out to be an incomplete work, with an abrupt end. The author was aware of these limitations, and he assured his readers that he would overcome them should there be a second edition. Generally speaking, he did try to fulfill his promise when a revised and enlarged edition was brought out in 1918. This edition devoted about 350 out of 462 pages to the life and attainments of the tenth Guru, a theme which had covered hardly 60 out of 250 pages in the earlier edition. There are two other noteworthy features in the new edition. It included pictures of all the ten Gurus, which are not generally available in other Bengali books. It was further enriched by the incorporation of two maps, one of which shows the major political centres and religious places associated with the life of the last Guru. The author divided his study of the Guru into five broad sections,

---

27. This view found its most detailed exposition in Tinkari Banerjee's *Guru Gobinda Singha* (Calcutta: Sanskrit Press Depository, 1918). A similar view was recorded in Matilal Roy's *Yuga Guru* (Calcutta: Prabartak Publishing House, 1340 B.S.), pp. 211-12.
28. Swami Ranganathananda, *Swami Vivekananda on Guru Gobind Singh* (Bombay: Bharatiya Vidya Bhavan, 1985), pp. 4-5. See also *Swami Vivekanander Bani o Rachana*, v. 5 (Calcutta: Udbodhan, 1369 B.S.), p. 449; ibid., v. 9, p. 84.
29. Rajanikanta Gupta, *Birmahima* (Calcutta: Bengal Medical Library, 1292 B.S.), pp. 29-45.

each devoted to a specific phase, beginning with his birth at Patna and continuing till his death at Nanded in 1708.

During the years between the two editions, there was hardly any significant change in the attitude and commitment of the author to the Guru. Banerjee wholeheartedly admired and revered him as a messenger of God. *Guru Gobinda Singha* also merits our special attention for the richness of its source materials. Like Mahendranath Bose, Banerjee almost wholly depended on Punjabi sources. In his search for a biography of the tenth Guru from the point of view of the Sikhs, he drew heavily on the *Suraj Prakash* and *Daswan Padshah ki Granth* in addition to the Adi Granth.[30] He was equally conversant with the writings of authorities like Malcolm, McGregor, Cunningham, Cave-Browne and Cust, though he made little use of them in his work. And in cases when there were significant differences of opinion among the authorities, he almost invariably relied on the opinion of Bhai Santokh Singh, author of *Suraj Prakash*. His uncritical reliance on Punjabi sources, especially on the *Suraj Prakash*, does not speak highly about his scholarship.[31] Perhaps his conservative Hindu commitment constrained his ability to achieve a proper understanding of some of the fundamental distinguishing marks of Sikhism under Guru Gobind. His views on Sikhism often came closer to Bawa Narain Singh's monograph *Sikh Hindu hain* (i.e., *Sikhs are Hindus*). There are also a few historical inaccuracies in the biography, two of which merit our special attention: (i) Banerjee was of the opinion that the Guru and Aurangzeb went over to Mecca for a possible religious settlement between Hindus and Muslims;[32] and (ii) the Sisganj Gurdwara in Delhi was founded by the Guru after his meeting with Emperor Bahadur Shah.[33]

In spite of these shortcomings, Banerjee's *Guru Gobinda Singha* still remains a significant contribution in the field of Bengali understanding of the history of the Sikhs.[34] It surpassed the works of Rajanikanta Gupta both in historical detail and in the use of source materials in different Indian languages. Though he failed to establish any clear line of demarcation between Hindus and Sikhs, the author never faulted the Guru for the growing "radicalisation" among

30. Like Malcolm, Banerjee also relied whenever possible on Sikh sources in preference to non-Sikh ones and perhaps believed that "in every research...it is of the essential importance to hear what a nation has to say of itself." John Malcolm, *Sketch of the Sikhs* (London: John Murray & Co., 1812), p. 5.

31. Bhai Santokh Singh's testimony is often questioned by scholars. Macauliffe thus wrote: "It is, however, doubtful whether Bhai Santokh Singh had access to any trustworthy authority. From his early education and environment he was largely tinctured with Hinduism.... His statements accordingly cannot often be accepted as even an approach to history." *The Sikh Religion*, v. 1 (New Delhi: S. Chand & Co., 1978 reprint), p. lxxvii. Macauliffe was again criticised for not always being "fair to Hinduism and the Hindus." For it, see Indubhusan Banerjee, *Evolution of the Khalsa*, v. 1 (Calcutta: A. Mukherjee & Co., 1963), p. 290.

32. Ibid., p. 365.

33. Ibid., p. 388.

34. It was later on described as "a very valuable ornament of Bengali language." For it, see Anurupa Devi, *Bhudev Charit*, v. 2 (Calcutta: Bhudev Publishing House, 1330 B.S.), p. 52. For other scholarly observations on this volume, see Kartikchandra Mitra, *Sikh Guru* (Calcutta: Sulabh Granthamala Karyalay, 1329 B.S.), p. ii; Sunitikumar Chatterjee, *Guru Gobind Singh* (Chandigarh: Panjab University, 1967), p. 38.

the Sikhs. In this sense it even surpassed Sir Jadunath Sarkar's assessment of the Sikhs.[35] Based on the materials this book offered, nearly half a dozen Bengali monographs on the Sikhs were published in the present century and this is a great tribute to this historian's craft.

V

During the first quarter of the present century, four separate works were published which tried to focus upon Guru Gobind Singh's exploits from different standpoints. Haranath Bose's *Guru Gobinda*[36] is one of two historical plays written in appreciation of the tenth Master's role in the development of Hindu-Muslim communal unity in the later middle ages. The play is presented in the true colloquial Bengali literary tradition. In its five acts, twenty-two major characters appear, of which at least nine come from the pages of history. The drama was brought out during the anti-partition agitation,[37] and Bose sought to convey in his drama the cause of communal amity and good will. Aurangzib's "intolerant religious policy," according to Bose, sealed the fate of the Mughal Empire built up by Akbar on the basis of Hindu-Muslim co-operation. The Guru aimed at restoring the constructive Hindu-Muslim relationship.

The Guru was not alone in his war with the "oppressive Mughal state power." Bose emphasised that the Emperor's sister Jahanara, along with many liberal Muslim *fakirs*, was in full sympathy with the Guru's plan of bringing Hindus and Muslims closer together. In spite of his pronounced Hindu bias, however, Bose did not portray the war with Aurangzib as one emanating from a narrow Hindu-Muslim antagonistic relationship. On the contrary, he bitterly denounced the communalists of both camps. In the long run, the Guru's military success, argued Bose, brought the Emperor back to his senses. The latter realised the ill effects of his policy as well as the greatness of the Guru. The drama ended on an optimistic note of uniting Hindus and Muslims for fighting the disturbers of Mughal peace in India. His emotional appeal, cutting across religious barriers and political differences, was quite in tune with the aspirations of the Bengali middle class in the days of the Swadeshi movement, when the book came out. Bose's *Guru Gobinda* differs from Tinkari Banerjee's *Guru Gobinda Singha* in the sense that the latter viewed the Guru as a Hindu messiah fighting for the protection of Hindus. Banerjee's Guru had nothing to do with the problem of inter-communal co-operation and good will. Bose's Guru Gobind was more concerned with the contemporary political problems, while Banerjee's hero showed a greater keenness in defending Hindu religion and his wars with the Mughals provided an effective umbrella to all who accepted his leadership in times of crisis.

35. For Jadunath Sarkar's comments, see note 44 in Section VI.
36. Haranath Bose, *Guru Gobinda* (Calcutta: Bhattacharya & Sons, 1315 B.S.).
37. The partition of Bengal by Lord Curzon, begun in 1905 and rescinded in 1911. —Editors' note.

In the contemporary Bengali press, *Guru Gobinda* has sometimes been criticised as a caricature of history. It is even accused of introducing a few late-nineteenth-century politico-religious problems into the history of later medieval India. But the drama is especially worth considering on one count: Bose did not blame Guru Gobind Singh for "radicalising" Sikh politics—a theme that elicits bitter observations from Rabindranath Tagore and Jatindranath Samaddar.[38]

Within a year another important biography of the tenth Guru entitled *Guru Gobinda Singha* was brought out by Basantakumar Banerjee.[39] It seeks to highlight some of the constructive qualities of the tenth Master leading to the birth of the Khalsa and its impact on the Panth. The study begins with a general review of the politico-religious conditions of the Punjab on the eve of the birth of Sikhism. Its first three chapters, however, have no direct bearing on the life of the Guru except for a brief reference to his birth at Patna. This is followed by an account of the development of Sikhism under Tegh Bahadur and his martyrdom at Delhi. It is really from the sixth chapter, with Guru Gobind's installation on his father's seat, that he becomes the key figure. The birth of the Khalsa forms the subject of the next chapter. In the opinion of Banerjee, it "paved the way for the foundation of a new state for the Sikhs and provided them a decisive rallying point to protect their home and religion in the face of a determined Mughal persecution." Seven chapters are devoted to a detailed analysis of different aspects of the Mughal-Sikh hostility under the leadership of the Guru. The study is brought to an end by an elaborate exposition of the Guru's character and influence on the history of India during the later middle ages. "The Guru was not merely a religious reformer," concludes Banerjee; "he attempted to build up a new martial nation imbued with a religious spirit. In this sense he was a unique political personality of the country. He gave a distinct shape to the destiny of the Sikhs."

Unlike Banerjee's *Guru Gobinda Singha*, Jogendranath Gupta's volume[40] was a popular life sketch written in a simple style aiming at educating school children about the Guru's attempts to unite the Sikhs under the banner of the Khalsa. The contemporary press was favourably disposed to Gupta's efforts to bring the message of the fighting tradition of the Sikhs within easy reach of Bengali youngsters. A systematic perusal of this monograph also reveals his close association with the pioneering works of Rajanikanta Gupta and Tinkari Banerjee.

---

38. Jatindranath Samaddar in his *Sikher Katha* (Howrah: Dhirendranath Lahiri, 1319 B.S.) records nothing encouraging about the tenth Guru. He accused him of waging many futile wars throughout his life. Curiously enough, Sammadar offered no valid argument in his defence, and it seems likely that he was disillusioned with the contemporary militant Bengal politics, often guided by communal considerations, of the post-partition years. For Tagore's views on the tenth Guru, see Section VI.

39. Basantakumar Banerjee, *Guru Gobinda Singha* (Calcutta: the author, 1316 B.S.). There were three editions of this book, the last one appearing in 1926. The book was translated into Hindi in the 1920's while its English rendering appeared in 1950 from Chandernagore. It was promptly reviewed in the two leading monthly journals, viz., *Bharati*, Kartik 1316 B.S., p. 403, and *Prabashi*, Ashvin 1316 B.S., p. 448.

40. Jogendranath Gupta, *Guru Gobinda Singha* (Calcutta: Asutosh Library, 1330 B.S.).

A significant aspect of Gupta's writings was his detailed exposition of the Sikh code of conduct. He referred to a long list of the Guru's instructions relating to the Sikh view of God, good habits, value system and relationship with the different dissenting sects like Dhirmalis and Ramrais. As in Tinkari Banerjee's work, Gupta's Guru Gobind Singh was not a Hindu messiah born in India for fighting the Turks. Rather, he was a man of flesh and blood with natural human feelings and endowed with a penetrating understanding of human character. But the monograph is, however, not an original work in a class with that of Tinkari Banerjee. Its merit chiefly lies in the fact that he conveyed the message of the tenth Guru in a language easily understandable to Bengali school children of his times.

VI

Rabindranath Tagore produced some of the finest pieces of Bengali creative writing on Guru Gobind Singh, over a period of nearly twenty-five years (1885-1909). With the exception of one, these are all devoted to extolling Guru Gobind Singh's moments of joy and sorrow, his triumphs and anguish, and his deep commitment to the cause of Sikh cultural heritage. Tagore wrote his first essay, entitled "Bir Guru," when he was in his early twenties, and it was generally marked by a spirit of youthful exuberance regarding the Guru. Published in *Balak*, the essay primarily aimed at educating Bengali youngsters about the Guru's life and mission. He repeatedly sought to impress upon the mind of his young readers that Guru Gobind fought for "oppressed humanity" and laid down his life for bringing an end to Mughal authority in the Punjab.[41]

It was followed by three poems,[42] written over a period of nearly twelve years (June 1888 to October 1899): "Guru Gobinda," "Nishphal Upahar" ("A Futile Gift") and "Shesh Shikha" ("The Last Lesson"). These concern three phases of the Guru's life, commencing with his twenty years' commitment to a strict self-disciplined life and leading to the birth of the Khalsa in 1699 and his end at Nanded in 1708. The seeds of these poems were evident in his "Bir Guru" and they were included in *Manasi* and *Katha o Kahini*, generally regarded as his two major anthologies of the early period. Of these poems, "Guru Gobinda," a lyrical ballad, is the first. It was written when Tagore was disillusioned with the "degrading mendicancy policy" of the Indian National Congress in the late 1880's. Tagore's frustration is reflected in a number of poems, songs and essays. On the other hand, he set forth his view of an ideal Indian leader in various prose writings. Here he made no secret of his admiration for Guru Gobind Singh, who had spent twenty years of his life in obscurity before ascending himself to the leadership of his community. During

---

41. Rabindranath Tagore, "Bir Guru," *Rabindra Rachanavali*, v. 13 (Calcutta: Government of West Bengal, 1368 B.S.), pp. 457-61. This was originally published in *Balak*, Shraban 1292 B.S. It was also included in *Itihas* (Calcutta: Visva-Bharati, 1362 B.S.).

42. Rabindranath Tagore, *Rabindra Rachanavali*, v. 1 (Calcutta: Government of West Bengal, 1368 B.S.), pp. 653-60, 685-86.

these years of self-exile, wrote Tagore, the Guru wholly devoted himself to the study of sacred literature and introspection—hardly parallelled in contemporary politics. Tagore visualised that his ideal leader, like Guru Gobind Singh, would pay very little attention to any short-term gain, fame and publicity. Instead, he would keep himself away from the vortex of mundane politics so that he could develop his sense of deep commitment to the service of the community.[43]

Tagore portrayed Guru Gobind's years of self-imposed exile in "Guru Gobinda." In this poem, when the Guru was requested by his close disciples to come out of obscurity and take up the leadership of the Panth, he promptly turned them down. For providing the right type of leadership, the Guru argued, he still had much to learn, and this was the reason for his continued dissociation from the main current of national politics. Until completion of his training, the Guru concluded, he would remain in the woods trying to acquire as much inspiration as possible for serving the community better in the near future.

A similar reflection of the dedication of the tenth Guru to the national cause and his scant attention to any worldly possession characterises Tagore's "Nishphal Upahar." Taking his cue from McGregor's account of the Guru's contempt for wealth,[44] the poet projects the last Guru as his ideal Indian leader. Tagore's third and last poem on Guru Gobind Singh is "Shesh Shikha." It provides us an intimate picture of how the tenth Guru cut short his life by inviting the end at the hands of a Pathan assassin at Nanded. Here again the poet took the main theme from McGregor's *History of the Sikhs* and infuses an ethical message into the whole story of the assassination.

In the present century Tagore wrote a long essay entitled "Shivaji o Guru Gobinda Singha," which is, incidentally, the longest essay ever written by him on the Panth. Here we come across a significant change in the attitude of Rabindranath towards the Guru. While praising Guru Nanak for his saintliness and religious liberalism, he bitterly denounced Guru Gobind for "radicalising" the Sikh movement.[45] Instead of uniting the Sikhs on the basis of mutual love and co-operation, Tagore wrote, the tenth Guru sowed the seeds of hatred and revenge among them. This left a very unfortunate legacy for the history of the Sikhs. They were seen, concluded Rabindranath, fighting in the different parts

---

43. Tagore's view on the Guru may also be seen in his other prose writings. For these, see ibid., v. 11, p. 95; ibid., v. 12, pp. 361, 941.

44. W.L. McGregor, *The History of the Sikhs*, v. 1 (Patiala: Languages Department, 1970), pp. 79-80.

45. Rabindranath thus wrote: "Guru Govind organised the Sikhs to suit a special purpose. He called in the human energy of the Sikhs from all other sides and made it flow in one particular channel only; they ceased to be full, free men. He...dwarfed the unity of a religious sect into an instrument of political advancement. Hence the Sikhs, who had been advancing for centuries to be true men, suddenly stopped short and became mere soldiers." "Shivaji o Guru Gobinda Singha," *Rabindra Rachanavali*, v. 13, pp. 443-50. This was translated by Sir Jadunath Sarkar and quoted in *History of Aurangzib*, v. 3 (Calcutta: M.C. Sarkar & Co., 1928), pp. 302-3. For a similar opinion, see Jatindranath Samaddar, *Sikher katha*, pp. 142-44. Tagore's essay was originally published as an introduction to Saratkumar Roy's *Sikh Guru o Sikh Jati* (Calcutta: Indian Publishing House, 1317 B.S.).

of the globe and failed to build up any permanent state on the ruins of the Mughals.

This significant change in the writing of Tagore merits special attention. During the years of Swadeshi and boycott agitation, Tagore's attitude towards militant politics underwent a gradual but definite change. It "took place in the background of the rise of political extremism and the communal virus during 1906-07." Rabindranath was convinced that Hindu-Muslim riots frequently flared up in Bengal due to the failure of contemporary national leaders to win over the support of the Muslims. He became increasingly bitter towards both boycott and terrorism because they not only "accentuated communal tension" but also at times involved considerable hardship for the weaker section of the community. Rabindranath broached the plan of "building of a *Mahajati* in India on the basis of a broad humanism." This would envisage "a decisive rejection of sectarian barriers" and a "wholesale breaking down of walls of communal separatism." It would involve the discarding of "much of traditional Hinduism." This anti-traditionalism, in fact, was to pervade virtually all of Tagore's post-1907 writings.[46]

In this context, Rabindranath argued that Guru Gobind Singh's Khalsa could not offer any effective answer to contemporary national questions. In the later middle ages, he noted, the birth of the Khalsa had frustrated the plan of bringing Hindus and Muslims together on a common national platform. It diverted the liberal message of the founder of the Sikh faith in order to achieve short-term political gains, sharpened communal antagonism and generated an endless hatred and disunity in the rank and file of the community. Tagore attacked the last Guru for creating the Khalsa because it perpetuated sectarian politics at the point of the sword. Thus Tagore made a complete *volte-face* in his view of Guru Gobind Singh.

Tagore's critical observations on the Guru's policy sparked a lengthy debate. He was immediately criticised by Binaykumar Sarkar,[47] a noted sociologist and historian of the present century. In his view, the transformation of Sikhism was dictated by the contemporary pressing needs of the society. In the changed condition of the seventeenth century something more was needed, in Sarkar's view, than what had originally been preached by Guru Nanak. The Khalsa symbolised this change. It would therefore be wrong to regard the new development as a negation of Guru Nanak's teachings and to blame Guru Gobind for accomplishing it. Another important rejoinder came from Kartikchandra Mitra, author of *Sikh Guru*. He emphasised that "radicalisation" of Sikh politics provided a new lease on life to the Panth. The Mughal persecution would have crushed the Sikhs, had there been no Khalsa in the

46. This paragraph is based on Sumit Sarkar's *Swadeshi Movement: 1903-1908* (New Delhi: People's Publishing House, 1973), pp. 82-85, 90-91, 326, 449.
47. Binaykumar Sarkar, "Itihase Sikhjati," pp. 50-53.

eighteenth century.[48]   Similarly, Indubhusan Banerjee bitterly criticised Tagore's views. Rameshchandra Majumdar and Anilchandra Banerjee were generally of the opinion that Rabindranath misunderstood the spirit of the Khalsa and based his observations about the Guru's "militarisation of the community" on a complete misreading of the contemporary politics. The Khalsa saved the Sikhs during the critical years when their existence was in jeopardy, and offered them a symbol of unity throughout their wars with the Mughals.[49]

VII

The achievements and failures of Ranjit Singh were also a subject of considerable interest for nineteenth-century Bengali authors. They admired the Maharaja's superior military genius and diplomatic skill in uniting the Sikhs under his political authority, though a few of them were critical of his moral lapses.[50]   Writers in the present century were not much concerned with the Maharaja's moral lapses, but concentrated on his political success and organising ability. Of these works, Saratkumar Roy's *Sikh Guru o Sikh Jati* deserves special attention. It is a well-integrated history of the Sikhs from the birth of Guru Nanak till the collapse of Ranjit Singh's monarchy after the Second Sikh War. Roy's study provides us an account of the Maharaja's ancestry as well as his frequent wars with the *misl* leaders. In Roy's view, Ranjit's military success was partly due to his equal treatment of the Hindus and Muslims, which provided a definite source of strength to his royal authority. The writer was, however, of the opinion that Ranjit Singh's secularism was dictated by his narrow political considerations. There was also an interesting chapter on Ranjit Singh's relations with the East India Company.

Another important biographical sketch of the Maharaja was written by Jogendranath Gupta. His *Ranjit Singha*, published in 1923, was the seventh title in the "Three Anna National Biography" series.[51]   Like his *Guru Gobinda Singha*, the book under study aimed at educating school children (in this case about the Sikh monarch's attempt to build up the Khalsa Raj in the Punjab). The author devoted almost one-third of the book to the history of the Panth till the accession of Ranjit Singh. In his opinion, the martyrdom of Guru Tegh Bahadur, the stories of the lifelong struggle of the tenth Guru and the fierce resistance of Banda Bahadur inspired the Sikh ruler to rally the Panth under his political umbrella. In this grand design, argued Gupta, he not only crushed the *misl* leaders but defeated the Pathans at the Battle of Nowshera. The author

---

48. Kartikchandra Mitra, *Sikh Guru*, pp. 89-90. Saratkumar Roy also did not wholly share Tagore's views on Guru Gobind Singh. See Roy, *Bharatiya Sadhak*, p. 52.

49. For their views, see Indubhusan Banerjee, *Evolution of the Khalsa*, v. 2 (Calcutta: A. Mukherjee, 1962), pp. 122-25; R.C. Majumdar, "Rabindranath and Guru Gobind Singh," *The Sikh Review*, January 1967, pp. 219-22; A.C. Banerjee, *Guru Nanak to Guru Gobind Singh* (New Delhi: Rajesh Publications, 1978), pp. 185-97.

50. In this regard Brahmamohan Mallick's view on the Sikh monarch deserves our special attention. For it, see the author's contribution in the *Encyclopaedia of Sikhism* (forthcoming) on *Ranjit Singher Jiban Vrittanta*.

51. Jogendranath Gupta, *Ranjit Singha* (Calcutta: Asutosh Library, 1330 B.S.).

noted, however, that Ranjit Singh could not establish any permanent peace in northwestern Punjab with frequent revolts of the Pathans requiring an immense drainage of the Sikh treasury. Gupta had a high regard for Ranjit Singh's decision to modernise the Sikh army along European lines and for the Sikh monarch's administrative ability and common sense.

These years also witnessed the performance of a historical play entitled *Punjabkeshari Ranjit Singha* on the Calcutta professional stage (1940).[52] It was written and directed by Mahendranath Gupta, a well-known playwright. It idealised the Maharaja's reign as the last effective barrier between anarchy and order in the Punjab. The Maharaja was portrayed as the symbol of Indian unity, persistently fighting against the forces of anarchy and disorder.

VIII

In their search for the history of the Panth, Bengali writers often turned to the Sikh sacred literature. In this sphere they were primarily concerned with the message of the *Japji* and *Sukhmani*, though they were not unmindful of the significance of the *Vachitar Natak* and other literary works of the tenth Guru. Raja Rammohan Roy's quest for the unitary idea of God among different Indian creeds in the early nineteenth century brought him in touch with the Adi Granth. Debendranath Tagore continued this Brahmo tradition. His profound respect and love for these hymns found reflections in his autobiography, where he quoted a few lines from different *pauris* so suitably that they add a new taste and significance to his writing.[53] It was Shashibhushan Mukherjee who first published, in three installments, a full-length translation of the *Japji* in the *Nabajiban Patrika*.[54] But one had to wait till the beginning of the present century before another edition of the *Japji* would be published for the benefit of the Nanakpanthi Sikhs of Bengal and Assam, who had very little access to the *Japji* in the Gurmukhi script.[55] The *Japji* was rendered for the first into Bengali verse by an anonymous poet under the title *Upasanasar*. The translator was of the opinion that it was a non-communal text that might be read by members of different faiths. This was followed by a prose edition published in 1918, undertaken by Abinashchandra Majumdar, a member of the Lahore Brahmo Samaj.[56] His Bengali rendering, writes Majumdar in its preface, was not meant for highly educated and sophisticated people; he presented it, instead, to those "who had a genuine respect and love for the Sikhs and their literature."[57]

---

52. Mahendranath Gupta, *Punjabkeshari Ranjit Singha* (Calcutta: Sriguru Library, n.d.).

53. He referred to *pauris* 2, 5, 6, 7, 28 and 29. See also note 2.

54. Shashibhushan Mukherjee, "Japji," *Nabajiban Patrika*, Magh 1295 B.S., pp. 267-72; ibid., Phalgun 1295 B.S., pp. 328-43; ibid., Chaitra 1295 B.S., pp. 397-414.

55. Lalbehari Singh Khatri, *Japji Sahib* (Baharampur: the author, 1307 B.S.).

56. For his life, see Shibnath Shastri, *History of the Brahmo Samaj* (Calcutta: Ramananda Chatterjee, 1912), pp. 404, 409; *Prabashi*, Magh 1332 B.S., p. 575; Jnanendramohan Das, *Banger Bahire Bangali: Uttar Bharat Khanda* (Calcutta: Anathnath Mukherjee, 1322 B.S.), pp. 416-17.

57. Abinashchandra Majumdar, *Guru Nanakkrita Japji* (Calcutta: Calcutta Brahmo Mission, n.d.). It seems likely the monograph was published before October-November 1918, because it was reviewed in the *Prabashi*, Agrahayan 1325 B.S. Dhirendramohan Sen, another member of the

The process of translating the message of the *Japji* for the Bengali literary world was particularly enriched by the contributions of the disciples of Sri Bijaykrishna Goswami[58] in the present century. The first volume came out in 1921 under the editorship of Kiranchand Darvesh, a poet of considerable eminence. He rendered the text into poetry. The second was completed by Jnanendramohan Datta, a Muzaffarpur-based lawyer, and was published in 1925. Its text was in prose and there were annotations of some important Punjabi terms. The most important volume in the series was the work of Haranchandra Chakladar of the University of Calcutta. He carried on his work on the Adi Granth for nearly forty-five years. Based on the *Faridkot Tika*, his translation of the Adi Granth continued till his death in 1958. During his lifetime only a volume of his work was printed, under the title *Srisrigurugrantha Sahibji* (1958). It included the *Japji*, *Rahiras* and *Sohila* sections of the Adi Granth.

Generally speaking, Chakladar's translation of the *Japji* is still considered to be the most authentic, as well as the most extensive, edition of this text in Bengali. In translating it, he tried to maintain the spirit of the original and followed the written text of the *Japji*, which is sometimes slightly different form the way it is read. His translation also succeeded in communicating the deep emotional feeling and the grand poetic exuberance that are associated with the Sikh morning prayer. These hymns of Guru Nanak, according to him, were part of the Indian religious tradition handed down to us through the centuries. In this sense they are worthy of being respected and read along with the *Chaitanya Charitamrita* of Krishnadas Kaviraj and *Ramcharitmanas* of Tulsidas.

Incidentally, his explanatory note on the *Mulmantra*, running over more than ten pages (nearly one-fourth of the book), still remains an unsurpassed piece of Bengali literary work on the *Japji*. In this connection one may also refer to his long editorial comments on *Ekonkar*, which bear eloquent testimony to his scholarship. In addition, his writings were enriched by numerous cross references from the Adi Granth, which one does not find in any other Bengali edition of the *Japji*. He was also the first Bengali translator to draw our attention to a few points of resemblance between *pauri* 27 and the *Sodoru (I) Rag Asa Mahala I* in the *Rahiras*. Translators who came after him have so far failed to add any additional information on this piece of historical inquiry.

This scholarly effort has, however, a few minor limitations. To begin with, Chakladar was silent about his source materials. Secondly, the number of editorial notes as well as their scholarly quality strikingly declined as he moved from the *Mulmantra* to the *Solaku*. Finally, his observations about the role of the yogis in relation to *pauri* 27 seem to be of doubtful validity. Also he did not offer any logical defence of his hypothesis about the factors leading to the birth of this *pauri* vis-à-vis the criticism of the yogis in the Punjab. Chakladar's

Lahore Brahmo Samaj, also contributed to the *Prabashi* on the *Japji*. For it, see *Prabashi*, Kartik 1319 B.S., pp. 78-79; ibid., Magh 1319 B.S., pp. 376-78.
    58. For Sri Bijaykrishna Goswami, see the author's "Guru Nanak in Bengali Literature," *Journal of Sikh Studies*, October 1985, p. 62.

scholarship was taken up by the Sri Guru Singh Sabha, Rashbehari Avenue, Calcutta and the Sikh Association of Bengal. They partly financed the reprinting of the volume, which included the *Japji*, *Rahiras* and *Sohila*. It came out in 1977, but the task of editing was performed perfunctorily.

There are four more editions of the *Japji*, but none of them surpassed the scholarly achievement of Chakladar. One was translated by Jatindramohan Chatterjee, an enthusiastic admirer of Sikhism in Bengal.[59] It sought to project the *Japji* as one of the finest manifestations of Indian devotional literature.[60] The edition of Sudhir Gupta (perhaps partially financed by the Sri Guru Singh Sabha, Rashbehari Avenue), generally reiterated the message of love and surrender as preached by the founder of the Sikh faith.[61] It was followed by Jogeshchandra Bhattacharya's translation of a few *pauris* of the *Japji* in the *Shrigurubani* magazine.[62] Finally, in the early 1980's we find a verse edition of the *Japji* by Amar Chakravarti. The translator had no direct access to the *Japji* in Punjabi, and this perhaps largely explains his failure to give a coherent representation of Sikh philosophy of the mid-sixteenth century.[63]

During these years the message of the *Sukhmani* was not altogether unknown to the Bengali literary world. The followers of Sri Bijaykrishna Goswami played an encouraging role in this regard. There were at least three separate editions, all translated and published during the last seventy years. The first one was brought out by Jnanendramohan Datta in 1916. He presented the text of the *Sukhmani* in the way it is read and did the translation in prose. His translation was favourably received and there were three reprints of it during his lifetime, while the fourth one came out long after his death.[64] Another edition of the *Sukhmani* was produced by Kiranchand Darvesh. As early as 1917 he started translating it, though it took thirty years to complete. In his opinion these verses represent one of the finest expositions of the Indian quest for spiritual attainment and hence the Adi Granth must have been greatly enriched by their inclusion. Like Datta, Darvesh reproduced the *Sukhmani* in the way it is read in Punjabi and provided a brief history of the Panth under the fifth Guru. Chakladar's edition is so far the last and perhaps the most detailed analysis of the *Sukhmani* in Bengali.[65] It is a posthumous publication based on his scattered notes and commentaries, written in association with Prabhatchandra Das, a

---

59. Jatindramohan Chatterjee, *Japji athaba Nanak Gita* (Calcutta: D.M. Library, 1353 B.S.).

60. Jatindramohan Chatterjee wrote another book on the hymns of Guru Nanak: *Guru Nanak Gatha* (New Delhi: Guru Nanak Foundation, 1969). See also, R.K. Dasgupta, "Bangla Japji," *Ananda Bazar Patrika*, October 17, 1954; J.S. Grewal, *A Bibliography of References in Bengali to Guru Gobind Singh* (Patiala: Guru Gobind Singh Foundation, 1967.).

61. Sudhir Gupta, *Japji* (Calcutta: Punthighar Pvt. Ltd., 1374 B.S.).

62. According to Jogeshchandra Bhattacharjee, fifteen *pauris* were translated under the title "Shrishrijapji" during the period January 1975 to October 1985. He kindly gave me a few back issues of the *Shrigurubani* for necessary consultation.

63. Amar Chakravarti, *Japji* (Michaelnagar: Amar Prakashani, 1380 B.S.). Recently Sri Guru Singh Sabha, Siliguri, has brought out an edition of the *Japji* edited by Haren Ghosh.

64. It was reprinted by the *Bangiya Sikh Sangha* in 1982.

65. Haranchandra Chakladar: *Shrishrigurugrantha Sahibji Gauri Sukhmani Sahib* (Berhampur: Vedic Research Institute, n.d.).

resident of Benares. His translation is in elegant Bengali prose while the text is represented in the way Punjabi is written. This is the lone Bengali translation of the *Sukhmani* that has made extensive use of different Punjabi sources in the notes and commentaries.

The literary genius of Guru Gobind Singh also figured in the different Brahmo magazines of the last century. In the present century, Tinkari Banerjee undertook the task of introducing briefly the central theme of some of the tenth Guru's writing. He was also of the opinion that the *Chaupayan Chaubis Avatarn Kian, Mihdi Mir, Shasti Nam Mala* and *Istri Chariti* were not the compositions of the Guru, though he did not fail to bring out the historical significance of the *Vachitar Natak.* In this regard he closely followed Cunningham.[66]

The *Daswan Padshah ki Granth* (i.e., Dasam Granth) was partially reviewed by Debendranath Mitra and Kartikchandra Mitra in the present century, but we do not have any monograph exclusively on the tenth Guru's writing till Jatindramohan Chatterjee published *Japji athaba Guru Gobinda Singher Amar Bani* in 1949.[67] This was primarily a selection of the different compositions of the Guru. It was divided into three parts. The first gives us a long introduction (69 pages) emphasising the salient aspects of Sikhism under the tenth Guru. Part Two contains excerpts from his *Daswan Padshah ki Granth* (72 pages) divided into nineteen sections, their bulk coming from the *Jap, Akal Ustad, Vachitar Natak, Gianprabodh, Chandi Charitra* and *Shabad Hazare.* Part Three furnishes their prose translations along with explanatory notes and commentaries.

There is, however, very little order in the selection of these couplets. Further, Chatterjee often followed the rules of Bengali grammar when recording the Guru's Punjabi writing. The book includes only thirteen distiches from the *Jap* though it is named after it. Finally, a section of Part Three is devoted to the writings of Gian Singh (*Panth Prakash*) and Bhai Santokh Singh (*Suraj Prakash*), which, of course, do not constitute parts of the *Daswan Padshah ki Granth.*

IX

Bengali *littérateurs* also dealt with a few other aspects of the history of the Sikhs, three of which merit our special attention. The history of the Sikh Wars, Sikh religious institutions, and character sketches of later Sikh heroes evoked their deep interest after the commencement of hostilities between the East India Company and the Lahore *darbar* in 1845. There were, as we have already seen, two significant publications dealing with the two Sikh Wars in the nineteenth century, namely, *Punjabaitihas* and *Sikh Juddher Itihas o Maharaja Duleep Singha.* The former deals with the history of the First Sikh War in two out of its

---

66. Banerjee, *Guru Gobinda Singha*, pp. 216-22.
67. Jatindramohan Chatterjee, *Japji athaba Guru Gobind Singher Amar Bani* (Calcutta: D.M. Library, 1356 B.S.).

four chapters, while the latter reviews the Second Sikh War in the first part of the book. In the present century, in the wake of the partition of Bengal, a connected account of the Sikh Wars was published. It was a combined edition of Cunningham's *History of the Sikhs* in Bengali together with a supplement which carried the history to the Second Sikh War and sought to update Cunningham. This was entitled *Sikh-Itihas* and was edited by Durgadas Lahiri,[68] a noted Bengali historian of the first quarter of the present century.[69] He was a close associated of Pramathanath Sanyal, the translator of Cunningham's volume, and wrote the supplement. The entire book ran to 740 pages, of which Lahiri's contribution was 61 pages. Lahiri divided the supplement into five chapters, all more or less of equal size. The first chapter reviews the causes of the Second Sikh War, and the author blames the English administration in the Punjab for the Multan uprisings under Diwan Mulraj (1848). The second chapter carries the story of the war to the Battle of Suddosum. The Battle of Multan forms the central theme of the next chapter. Lahiri concentrates on the Battle of Chillianwalla in the fourth chapter, which is one of the two briefest chapters in the supplement. Finally, in the fifth and last chapter, he studies the Anglo-Sikh encounter at Gujrat. In his estimation this was the bloodiest battle the British ever fought in India.

Lahiri, like his predecessor, Barodakanta Mitra, seems to have depended primarily on English sources and to have blamed the policy of the British Resident at Lahore for the Multan uprising of March 1848. Mitra and Lahiri, however, stood poles apart in regard to their observations on Cunningham's *History of the Sikhs*. In spite of his deep regard for the English author, Mitra was of the opinion that Cunningham's volume did not furnish "a detailed and complete record of the First Sikh War." Lahiri had no such reservations and, indeed, an all-round admiration for Cunningham's *History of the Sikhs* was the hallmark of Lahiri's historiography. He made no secret of this in his editorial notes.

Another significant field of Bengali literary activity concerned Sikh religious institutions. It was Debendranath Tagore who first referred to the Harmandir Sahib in his memoirs (1857). His description of the serene religio-cultural atmosphere of the Golden Temple complex is an excellent piece of literary craftsmanship. There is an element of poetic exuberance in his observations which even today appears fresh. Rabindranath drew our attention to the place in his autobiography (*Jibansmriti*) and in an early novel (*Chokherbali*). The Golden Temple also figured in the writings of Krishnakumar Mitra and Rameshchandra Dutt. The former was not, however, happy with the presence of Hindu idols in the precincts of the Svarnamandir (Golden Temple) when he first visited the place in the late 1870's.[70] The latter

---

68. Durgadas Lahiri, ed., *Sikh-Itihas* (Calcutta: Bangabhashi, 1314 B.S.).
69. For a further discussion on this point, see the author's "*Sikh Itihas*: A Supplement to Cunningham's *History of the Sikhs* in Bengali," *Panjab Past and Present*, April 1986, pp. 186-96.
70. Krishnakumar Mitra, *Atmacharit*, pp. 130-31.

referred to the contributions of Maharaja Ranjit Singh in the development of this premier Sikh religious institution.[71] In the present century, the Jaito tragedy and its significance in contemporary politics found frequent references in the Bengali press.[72]

Bengali writing on the Sikhs was also greatly enriched by a few character sketches of those who had fought in defence of the Panth in the course of the last three centuries. In this connection one may refer to Kumudini Mitra's widely acclaimed monograph *Sikher Balidan* which brought her immediate fame.[73] Her writing is permeated with unbounded admiration for the Sikhs who suffered at the hands of the Mughals. The book was published on the eve of the partition of Bengal. Mitra preached the cause of militant nationalism, resulting in a rapid selling out of its first three editions within a few years of its publication. Bhai Taru Singh also figured in the writing of Basantakumar Banerjee, who had already made his mark as a biographer of the tenth Guru. Perhaps taking his cue from Rabindranath's writing on Bhai Taru Singh, Banerjee depicted him as a fighter for individual freedom "against the oppression of the Mughal state." The sketch concluded with a perceptive reference to the "unhealthy consequences of the loss of political liberty in a modern state"—a theme which we do not come across in the pages of the *Sikher Balidan*. The author also highlighted the chivalry and self-sacrifice of eighteenth-century Sikh women in *Sikh Ramani*. These women, the author pointed out, refused to yield to any Mughal pressure, even though they had to undergo immense hardship in the imperial jail.[74]

X

These works represent a fair index of Bengali interest in the history and culture, religion and literature of the Sikhs. They illustrate the pioneering role of the Brahmos in popularising the message of Sikhism in the eastern part of India. Later on, the Brahmo search was reinforced by a few Hindu nationalist and Sanatanist authors, who provided a new perspective to Bengali understanding of the Sikhs. Again the development of a militant nationalist movement led to a new quest for the Panth. Actually, the Bengali literary world was so enthralled by the spirit of martyrdom and self-sacrifice of the Sikhs that monographs like *Sikher Balidan* (1904), *Sikh-Itihas* (1907), *Sikher Jagaran* (1929) and *Sikher Atmahuti* (1932?) not only highlighted this tradition but provided an added stimulus to India's fight for freedom. A few of them made a direct appeal to the militant nationalists of Bengal to bring an end to the British Raj following the path of the Sikh martyrs. Consequently, it led to the imposition of a ban on

---

71. Rameshchandra Dutt, "Svarnamandir," pp. 10-11. .
72. Anonymous, "Jaito Gurudwar," *Prabartak*, Phalgun 1330 B.S. Incidentally, the gurdwara of the Ramrais at Dehra Dun was once portrayed by Jaladhar Sen in *Sahitya*, Shraban 1301 B.S., pp. 275-87. See also Saratkumar Roy, "Amritasarer Guru Darbar," *Prabashi*, Magh 1316 B.S., pp. 793-96.
73. For a further discussion of Kumudini Mitra's *Sikher Balidan*, see the author's contribution in the *Encyclopaedia of Sikhism* (forthcoming).
74. Basantakumar Banerjee, "Taru Singha," *Bharati*, Phalgun 1315 B.S., pp. 505-8; idem, "Sikh Ramani." *Prabartak*, Agrahayan 1330 B.S., pp. 698-701.

some of them. *Sikher Atmahuti*, for example, was so effectively proscribed by the British Government that not even a single copy of it can be found in any leading library of India.[75]

But Bengali appreciation was not always characterised by a spirit of universal admiration for the Panth. For example, Guru Gobind Singh was accused of "radicalising" the Sikh movement. Similarly, Maharaja Ranjit Singh was criticised for his failure in the field of administration. Tagore's criticism of the tenth Guru, as we have already seen, gave rise to a debate and it evoked a chain of criticism from scholars like Binaykumar Sarkar, Indubhusan Banerjee, Rameshchandra Majumdar and Anilchandra Banerjee. The attitude towards the Maharaja, however, underwent a significant change after the publication of Brahmamohan Mallick's monograph in the early 1860's. Unlike some of the nineteenth-century English and Bengali critics, all three Guptas (viz., Rajanikanta Gupta, Jogendranath Gupta and Mahendranath Gupta) portrayed the Maharaja as a symbol of Indian national unity, fighting against the forces of disintegration and disruption. These authors were often more enthusiastic about the Sikh monarch's success and tried to refute emotionally the charges of the English and Bengali historians against the Khalsa Raj.

These works represent an important landmark in the development of historical writing in Bengali. Though many of them did not have any professional training, the authors were not wholly unaware of the scope and significance of history in contemporary national life and social relationships. Their motives as well as styles of recording the past differed so strikingly from one another that Sikh studies in Bengal can hardly be regarded as a homogeneous school of historical inquiry. Thus, historians like Rajanikanta Gupta and Durgadas Lahiri took up the study of the history of the Sikhs with a note of sympathy and Hindu nationalistic pride, and concluded their writing with an open political tirade against British domination in India. On the other hand, Brahmo authors like Bhai Mahendranath Bose and Akshaykumar Datta had no such obvious political end and presented the history of the Sikhs in a formal, analytical style. In spite of these differences in style and commitment, the authors generally had an exaggerated notion of the role of the individual in history. They were not wholly aware of the significance of economic forces in the evolution of the history of the Sikhs in the sixteenth and seventeenth centuries.

The writers also differed in selection of their historical sources. Most of them were acquainted with the works of European authorities like Malcolm,

---

75. *Sikher Atmahuti* deals with the tradition of martyrdom and self-sacrifice among the Sikhs since the days of the fifth Guru. In the opinion of the author the history of the sixteenth century is the story of Sikh resistance to Mughal rule. The monograph is divided into four parts, two of which are devoted to the life and mission of Guru Gobind Singh. For it, see Dineshchandra Barman, *Sikher Atmahuti* (Calcutta: Arya Publishing Company, 1332? B.S.). A copy of it is available in the India Office Library, London. I am indebted to Captain Bhag Singh, Editor, *The Sikh Review*, for extending the necessary financial assistance for obtaining its photocopy from the India Office Library.

Cust, McGregor, Cunningham, Griffin, Macauliffe, Gordon and Trumpp. Of these works, Cunningham's volume was the most widely read and used by Bengali writers of our period, and it was even translated into Bengali at the threshold of the century. There are, however, a few works based on Punjabi primary sources. Again, we have a few works often accused of caricaturing Sikh history.

Sikh studies in Bengali spreading over a hundred and seventy years have had a salutary impact on teaching and research concerning the history of the Sikhs in this part of India. It was quite in keeping with this tradition that the University of Calcutta played a pioneering role in this field of historical enquiry. With the introduction of Sikh studies at the post-graduate level in the College Street campus in the present century, a new school of historical research based on archival materials gradually developed in the city of Calcutta. One of the earliest works was Narendrakrishna Sinha's *Ranjit Singh* in English, first published in 1933. It was followed by Indubhusan Banerjee's *Evolution of the Khalsa* (in two volumes), Narendrakrishna Sinha's *Rise of the Sikh Power*, Niharranjan Ray's *The Sikh Gurus and Sikh Society* and Anilchandra Banerjee's works on the history, religion and philosophy of the Sikhs[76]—all of them widely read and quoted in the 1980's. Perhaps this Bengali interest partially explains the uninterrupted publication of *The Sikh Review* over a period of thirty years from Calcutta, as well as an active participation of different Sikh cultural organisations of Bengal in the publication and reprinting of different Bengali works on the history of the Sikhs over the years.

The works mentioned here were all written by Bengali Hindus. They do not reflect the sentiment of Bengali Muslims on the Panth. Generally speaking, the latter did not always hold a sympathetic attitude toward the Sikhs who fought against the Mughal imperial authority, and they sharply reacted against those who had tried to destroy it. A rapid survey of the native newspaper reports would point out that the Sikhs, like the Marathas, were frequently viewed as an enemy of the Mughal Empire and hence received bitter denunciations from those sympathetic to Mughal rule. Many Muslim writers were quite apprehensive of some Hindu authors' attempts to project Guru Gobind Singh as the "sword arm of Hinduism," and questioned the relationship of this notion to the Hindu *swarajya*. Similarly, they were critical of Banda Bahadur's conflict with the Mughal revenue officials and denounced Maharaja Ranjit Singh for waging a war with the "freedom-loving Pathans" and for "destroying their independence." Instead of the Sikh Gurus, they often looked towards some of the medieval Islamic heroes for redressing the sufferings of the Indian Muslims. Conversely, it seems likely that the Singh Sabha leaders' bid for redefining Sikhism, their

---

76. Anilchandra Banerjee has so far contributed five major titles to this field of historical enquiry: *Anglo-Sikh Relations* (Calcutta: A. Mukherjee & Co., 1946), *Guru Nanak and His Times* (Patiala: Punjabi University, 1971), *Guru Nanak to Guru Gobind Singh* (New Delhi: Rajesh Publications, 1978), *The Sikh Gurus and the Sikh Religion* (New Delhi: Munshiram Manoharlal, 1983), and *The Khalsa Raj* (New Delhi: Abhinav Publications, 1985).

bitter pamphlet duel with the Arya Samajists, purging the Golden Temple and other gurdwaras of Hindu idols and priestly rituals and, finally, the emergence of a new Sikh identity in the present century have received a warm reception in the Muslim press. This point, however, requires detailed and separate research.

The present study confirms that numerous Bengali authors have taken a lively interest in the history of the Sikhs and Sikhism. They adopted different literary forms, communicating their appreciation and admiration of the Panth. These authors also made no secret of the fact that their goal was to reach the common people. They often used popular religious and cultural symbols to be easily understood by them. They respected the martial tradition of the Sikhs and praised their spirit of self-sacrifice. They admired the Sikhs' monotheism and often tried to share their joys and sorrows. They communicated their feeling through their mother tongue, thereby enriching their own culture and adding a new dimension and colour to their cosmopolitan social milieu. They brought the extreme northwest of India closer to Bengal, and thus indirectly participated in the process of integrating India in the post-Independence decades.

Part Two
History and Politics:
India

From Ritual to Counter-Ritual: Rethinking the Hindu-Sikh Question, 1884-1915

Harjot S. Oberoi

> Notwithstanding the Sikh Gurus' powerful denunciation of Brahmans, secular Sikhs now rarely do anything without their assistance. Brahmans help them to be born, help them to wed, help them to die, and help their souls after death to obtain a state of bliss.[1]

> When I reached the High Department [School] I was attracted to the reform movement among the Sikhs, called the "Singh Sabha Movement." When I remember my early life I find that I was religiously inclined from a very young age. My two uncles and myself were the only three male members of the family when my grandfather died. My uncles were in service so I was chosen to perform his obsequies according the Hindu rites. I was very strict in following all the instructions of the village Pandit, though I was only nine years of age at that time [1891], in the belief that my grandfather who loved me very much when alive should derive full benefit from the rites that I was to perform for him for about two weeks...But the Sikh preachers told their audience that these rites and ceremonies were of no avail to the dead, so I began to study gurbani seriously and began to deliver lectures in Sikh gatherings.[2]

In 1897 when Kahn Singh Nabha, the erudite Sikh scholar, proclaimed through a vernacular tract that *Ham Hindu Nahin* (*We Are Not Hindus*), he brought almost four centuries of Sikh tradition to an end.[3] Until then the Sikhs had shown little collective interest in distinguishing themselves from the Hindus. Sikh notions of time, space, corporeality, holiness, kinship, societal distinctions, purity and pollution, and commensality were hardly different from those of the Hindus. Also the two shared the same territory, language, *rites de passage*, dietary taboos, festivals, ritual personnel and key theological doctrines. The

---

1. M.A. Macauliffe, *The Sikh Religion*, v. 1, Oxford: Clarendon Press, 1909, p. lvii.
2. Bhai Jodh Singh, "Jodh Singh Papers."
3. Khan Singh Nabha, *Ham Hindu Nahin* (Amritsar: Shri Guru Singh Sabha Shatabdi Committee, 1973; first Punjabi edition, 1898). Ironically this charter of Sikh separatism was initially published in Hindi. For a recent English translation see Jarnail Singh, *Sikhs, We Are Not Hindus* (Toronto: the author, 1984).

[Joseph T. O'Connell, Milton Israel, Willard G. Oxtoby, eds., with W.H. McLeod and J.S. Grewal, visiting eds., *Sikh History and Religion in the Twentieth Century* (S. Asian Studies Papers, 3) (Toronto: S. Asian Studies, Univ. of Toronto, 1988)]

construction of personhood within the two traditions and their solutions for existential problems were quite alike. In brief, the semiotic, cultural, affective and territorial universe of the Sikhs and Hindus was virtually identical.[4] These subjective and objective similarities were so striking that the colonial authorities for much of the nineteenth century found it very hard to distinguish between their Hindu and Sikh subjects. In the 1855 census in the Punjab the Sikhs and Hindus were lumped together in many districts of the province.[5]

The pluralistic framework of the Sikh faith in the nineteenth century allowed its adherents to belong to any one of the following traditions: Udasi, Nirmala, Suthreshahi, Khalsa, Sangatshahi, Jitmali, Bakhatmali, Mihanshahi, Sahajdhari, Kuka and Sarwaria.[6] Many of these Sikhs shaved their heads, freely smoked tobacco and hashish and were not particular about maintaining the five external symbols of the faith. In the absence of a centralized church and an attendant religious hierarchy, heterogeneity in religious beliefs, plurality of rituals, and diversity of life styles were freely acknowledged. A pilgrimage to the Golden Temple could be supplemented with similar undertakings to the Ganges at Hardwar or the shrine of a Muslim saint. Attending seasonal festivals at Benares or Hardwar was in no way considered a transgression of prevailing Sikh doctrines, whatever teleological studies may like to assert today. Contemporary vehicles of knowledge—myths, texts, narratives, folklore and plays produced by non-Sikh authors—were accorded a firm place within the Sikh cosmology. Far from there being a single "Sikh" identity, most Sikhs moved in and out of multiple identities, defining themselves at one moment as residents of this village, at another as members of that cult, at one moment as part of this lineage, at another as part of that caste and at yet another moment as belonging to a "sect." The boundaries between what could be seen as the centre of the Sikh tradition and its periphery were highly blurred. There simply was no single source of authority within the Sikh tradition and thus several competing definitions of what constituted a "Sikh" were possible. For this reason it is fundamentally futile to seek to define what was the essence of the Sikh faith in

---

4. This commonality is discussed at length in my "A World Reconstructed: Religion, Ritual and the Community Among the Sikhs, 1850-1901," Ph.D. dissertation, Faculty of Asian Studies, Australian National University, Canberra, 1987.

5. Ibbetson, a census commissioner for the Punjab, noted with great frustration: "But on the border land where these great faiths meet, and especially among the ignorant peasantry whose creed, by whatever name it may be known, is seldom more than a superstition and a ritual, the various observances and beliefs which distinguish the followers of the several faiths in their purity are so strangely blended and intermingled, that it is often impossible to say that one prevails rather than the other, or to decide in what category the people shall be classed." *Report of the Census of the Punjab, 1881*, v. 1, by D.C.J. Ibbetson (Calcutta: Superintendent of Government Printing, 1883), p. 101.

6. Unfortunately, except for the Khalsa, Udasis and Kukas, very little historical literature is available on the different traditions that constituted the Sikh faith. For instance, we hardly know what it implied to be a Sahajdhari or a Suthreshahi. The result is that much of the Sikh history is inscribed and read solely as the history of the Khalsa, which after all was only one of the several competing cultural codes within the polyphonic complex of Sikhism. Unless this erroneous situation be rectified, it will remain virtually impossible to explain the precise evolution of the Sikh tradition or answer how the Khalsa code ultimately came to establish its hegemony in the late nineteenth century.

the nineteenth century. Sikh personhood and practice for much of the nineteenth century implied a series of changing relationships and subjective moods.

However, in the late nineteenth century a growing body of Sikhs took active part in a systematic campaign to redefine their faith and purge it of what they saw as Hindu accretions and a Brahmanical stranglehold over their rituals. In 1905 Arur Singh, a manager of the Golden Temple, in a highly controversial move, ordered the removal of all the Hindu idols that had been lodged in the precincts of the holy shrine for several generations. What accounts for this dramatic inversion in attitudes, perceptions and relationships? Why did Sikhs suddenly develop this fetish for cultural boundaries that would permanently distance them from the Hindus? What was the source of these religious innovations? Existing literature lists four fundamental causes of this transformation: the competition between Sikh and Hindu middle classes to corner jobs and shrinking economic resources in trade and agriculture; the foundation of the Singh Sahba and the Arya Samaj, powerful Sikh and Hindu socio-religious movements respectively; efforts to gain greater representation in legislatures; and, finally the divide-and-rule policy of the British administration.[7]

Curiously some of the reasons proffered to account for the Sikh-Hindu divide in the 1900's were quite similar to the theories being put forward to explain the contemporary Sikh-Hindu conflict. Just as it is being suggested today that the Punjab crisis is rooted in the lack of adequate employment avenues for educated Sikh youth, historians have long argued that Sikh communalism at the turn of the century arose out of Hindu predominance in the civil service, urban professions and merchant capital. Similarly, the inability of the Akalis to capture enough seats in the Punjab legislative assembly may be matched with the Chief Khalsa Diwan's frustration at being under-represented in the then legislative councils. Finally, the accusations levelled against the Congress regime of consciously dividing the Sikhs and Hindus in order to stay entrenched in power are the same as those pinned on the door of the then British rule.

This striking correspondence in the reasons for the Hindu-Sikh estrangement at the turn of the century and the animosity between the two communities in the 1980's compels one to ask: does history perpetually repeat itself? Do people never change their categories of thought or the way they experience the world and act upon it? Is there no difference between one historical epoch and another? How important is human experience, desire and imagination in constructing and disseminating social meaning? Without in any

---

7. These reasons for instance are listed in the following works: Kenneth W. Jones, "Communalism in the Punjab, the Arya Samaj Contribution," *Journal of Asian Studies* 28 (1968), 39-54, and *"Ham Hindu Nahin:* Arya-Sikh Relations, 1877-1905," *Journal of Asian Studies* 32 (1973), 457-75; N. Gerald Barrier, "The Punjab Government and Communal Politics, 1870-1908," *Journal of Asian Studies* 27 (1968), 523-39; Richard G. Fox, *Lions of the Punjab* (Berkeley: University of California Press, 1985), pp. 122-30 and 161-74; Rajiv A. Kapur, *Sikh Separatism* (London: Allen and Unwin, 1986), pp. xiii-xiv. Different authors give greater or lesser priority to political, economic or administrative factors depending on the exact issues they are seeking to answer and their vision of history.

way denying the importance of what may be termed the pragmatic factors in the embitterment between Sikhs and Hindus, this paper endeavours to locate the cultural, or what will be referred to here as the semantic, sources of Sikh separatism.

With this aim in mind, the first section of the essay looks at what held the Hindus and Sikhs together for much of the nineteenth century. This issue is of critical importance for the subsequent analysis. Before considering conflict we obviously need to know more about cohesion. Historians generally take the harmony between Sikhs and Hindus in the nineteenth century for granted, as if it were a self-evident truth. What glued the two together calls for an explanation as much as the ensuing estrangement. It is my thesis that the absence of any malice between Sikhs and Hindus was the result of an elaborate cultural code in which members of the two traditions adhered to the same rules for social organization and *rites de passage*. The reasons for convergence between the two traditions having been explained, the second section examines what happened to these shared cultural norms. Once again the life-cycle rituals are used as a central illustration. By doing so, the paper arrives at certain conclusions that highlight the specific nature of Sikh separatism at the turn of the century.

I

Social and ritual practices in nineteenth-century Punjab were largely governed by the rules applying to households (*ghar*; literally, "house"; here, "household"), maximal lineages (*biradari*), clans (*got*) and caste (*zat*). What an individual did with his or her life, the values that guided him or her in this universe, the cultural equipment through which he or she interpreted daily experiences, the control over land, labour and patronage and the distribution of power were determined not by the framework of a single religious community but by what *biradari* or *zat* a person belonged to. Moreover, from the domestic domain to the politico-jural domain, access to material and ideological resources depended on a person's ability to establish genealogical rank or to influence those who had it. Such a mode of existence is reflected not only in the ethnographic and historical texts,[8] but also in the myths, legends and folklore of the Punjab. The popular folk songs of Hir-Ranjha, Mirza-Sahiban and Sassi-Punnun, recited by minstrels all over the province, illustrate both the existence of clan rules and how conflict, retribution and bloodshed followed when these rules were violated.[9] Often questions of honour and shame within the lineage

---

8. See Hamza A. Alavi, "Kinship in West Punjab villages," *Contributions to Indian Sociology*, n.s., 6 (1972), 1-27; Tom G. Kessinger, *Vilayatpur 1948-1968: Social and Economic Change in a North Indian Village* (Berkeley: University of California Press, 1974), pp. 37-38; Charles Joseph Hall Jr., "The Maharaja's Account Books: State and Society Under the Sikhs," Ph.D dissertation, University of Illinois at Urbana-Champaign, 1981, pp. 34-65.

9. Versions of these folk songs are reproduced in R.C. Temple, *The Legends of the Punjab* (Patiala: Language Department, Punjab, 1963; first published Bombay 1884-86), vols. 2-3, pp. 507-80 and 1-37 respectively.

were of far greater importance than religious loyalties. For the greater part of
the last century inter-personal transactions among people in the Punjab were not
therefore simply an extension of their religious traditions, but were embedded in
a complex idiom of kinship, patron-client relationships and asymmetrical
reciprocity. Religion, I would like to argue, is not, as has often been assumed, a
key to understanding the pre-British society. Why this is so is too complex a
question for a full discussion here,[10] but a few preliminary observations may
help to set the following discussion in context.

In the Indian religious tradition, unlike the Judeo-Christian, there was no
notion of a well-demarcated religious community possessing a centralized
ecclesiastical hierarchy. People did not conceive of themselves simply as
"Hindus" or "Sikhs." These categories overlapped and it is historically more
precise to speak in terms of a continuum or simultaneity of religious identities
rather than of distinct religious collectivities.[11] An "either-or" dichotomy is
often of very little value in conceptualizing Indian religious traditions.

It is not without reason that Indian languages do not possess a noun for
"religion" signifying a single uniform and centralized community of believers.[12]
Religion was primarily a highly localized affair, often even a matter of
individual conduct and individual salvation. For much of their history the
people in the subcontinent went on with their rituals, pilgrimages and acts of
religious piety without objectifying religion into an exclusive entity. Religious
traditions were based on local traditions and not on a pan-regional organization
of communities. Islam may have been the only exception to this, but then Indian
Islam, heavily coloured by Sufism, is of a radically different *genre* from its
counterpart elsewhere. The fact that religion was highly localized in not
particularly surprising for a peasant society. The innumerable anthropological
monographs on village communities in South Asia have made us conscious of
the autonomy of religious thinking and practices in the Indian countryside,
conceptualized in such diverse terms as folk beliefs, popular religion and "little
traditions."[13] Peasant settlements spatially removed from urban centres and
geared to a production system predominantly based on household production
and consumption had an inbuilt centripetal force. Among other things this
contributed to belief in an amorphous growth of local gods, deities and spirits.

10. I have done so elsewhere. See my "A World Reconstructed."
11. The "peculiarities" of the Indian religious tradition are increasingly coming to the surface as
social historians proceed with the task of an in-depth analysis of the religious situation in the
different regions of the subcontinent. On the lack of clear-cut religious identities in the United
Provinces see Sandra Freitag, "Religious Rites and Riots: From Community Identity to
Communalism in North India, 1870-1940," Ph.D. dissertation, University of California, Berkeley,
1980. For a similar report on Bengal see Rafiuddin Ahmed, *The Bengal Muslims* (Delhi: Oxford
University Press, 1981), pp. 4-5, 59-71 and 183-86.
12. There are also no specific Indian equivalents for "faith," "belief," "god," "monotheism" and
"polytheism." See R. Burghart and A. Cantile, eds., *Indian Religion* (London: Curzon Press, 1985),
p. viii.
13. For an overview see David Kinsley, *Hindu Goddesses* (Berkeley: University of California
Press, 1986), pp. 197-211.

It can also be argued that the peasantry as a class was unwilling to surrender its cultural autonomy to other social groups and often fiercely resisted any outside efforts at incorporation, particularly when such exercises were led by those who were also responsible for the extraction of revenues and services.[14] Each village in northern India would generally have a protective deity on the boundaries of the hamlet, which among other functions safeguarded its inhabitants from the pernicious influence of outsiders—be they people from other villages, malevolent spirits or the state. In order to cure sick cattle, face the vagaries of weather or obtain fecundity, the peasantry was willing to bargain with the most powerful sacred resource without bothering with religious labels. Such liberties with the sacred often vexed urban reformers and prompted their frequent jibes and moral campaigns against what they considered to be the superstition, ignorance and irrationality of the common folk. For the peasantry these cultural features often became an idiom of resistance.

Religion as a systematized sociological unit claiming unbridled loyalty from its adherents is a relatively recent development in the history of the Indian peoples. Once this phenomenon surfaced, probably sometime in the nineteenth century, it rapidly evolved, gained wide support and became reified in history. Out of this reification process it easily turned into something separate, distinct and concrete: what we today recognize as Hinduism, Buddhism and Sikhism.[15]

Therefore, when Tandon in a widely-quoted statement notes, "After all, we and the Sikhs stemmed from the same stock; most Hindus had Sikh relations, and intermarriage was common...We and the Sikhs had the same castes and customs, and they were always members of our brotherhoods—biradaris,"[16] it would have been far more accurate if he had made it clear that the question of religious identity was of no great importance, that the more enduring themes in the construction of personal identity in the Punjab had to do with the bonds of kinship and territoriality. For instance, when a Sikh Khatri married into the family of Hindu Khatris the question of religion was largely irrelevant; the most important normative consideration in this exercise of wife-taking and wife-giving was that both households belonged to the endogamous Khatri caste. Equally, the reception of a child into the world, the disposal of a corpse, the choice of a pilgrimage site, participation in seasonal festivals, in short the rhythms of day-to-day existence, were mediated by a network of kinship and caste. Leach, in his classic study of the Shans and Kachins in Burma, is quite correct when he notes, "Differences of culture...are structurally significant, but the mere fact that two groups of people are of different culture does not

---

14. See James C. Scott, "Protest and Profanation: Agrarian Revolt and the Little Tradition," *Theory and Society* 4 (1977), 1-38.

15. For a persuasive argument on these lines see W.C. Smith, *The Meaning and End of Religion* (New York: Macmillan, 1963).

16. Prakash Tandon, *Punjabi Century* (Berkeley: University of California Press, 1968), pp. 10-11.

necessarily imply—as has nearly always been assumed—that they belong to two quite different social systems."[17]

From the fact that Hindus and Sikhs shared positions within a single social structure, and from the "peculiar" nature of religion in Indian society, there flowed an important consequence: the religious categories "Hindu" and "Sikh" were ambiguous, fluid and fragile. This proposition can best be illustrated by following step by step the intricacies of *rites de passage* among the Sikhs. In all pre-industrial societies such rites tend to express the relationships among individuals and the society in which they live. By showing the absence of any distinctively Sikh life-cycle rituals, I would like to argue that Sikhs were encompassed by "Hindu" society.

Among Sikhs from the Khatri and the Arora castes, when a woman was pregnant, a ceremony called *ritan* was performed in the fifth or the seventh month.[18] The pregnant woman received a new set of clothing for the occasion as well as sweets from her mother, and the females from the *biradari* assembled to dress her up in the gift clothes and to share the sweets. On the birth of a son there was much rejoicing and exchange of gifts. The doors of the house were decorated with leaves from the *siris* (*Acacia sirissa*) tree and among the Jat Sikhs the image of an outspread hand was made with red dye on the outside walls of the house and an iron ring tied over the lintel. A lamp or a cow-dung cake was left to burn outside the mother's room, night and day, in order to protect the newborn infant from malevolent forces. Six days after the birth, the family priest or *purohit* was called to cast a horoscope for the newly born child.

In the post-natal phase the mother, because she was considered to be polluted, was kept in seclusion for a period varying from eleven to thirteen days, depending on the ritual purity of the caste to which she belonged. This period of impurity was most commonly called *sutak*, but was also known as *chhut*, especially in the north-west of the Punjab. On the eve of the thirteenth day, the females of the household started the purification rites by smearing the walls and floors of the house with a mixture of mud and cow dung. The earthen vessels which had been used during this period were then smashed and all metal vessels thoroughly cleansed. On the day itself the *purohit* lit a sacred fire in the house and sprinkled members of the household with holy water from the Ganges. In the case of certain castes, on the thirteenth day the mother gave away her old clothes to the midwife, who sometimes shared them with the Nain (the Nai's

---

17. Edmund Leach, *Political Systems of Highland Burma* (London: G. Bell and Sons, 1954), p. 17.

18. The following account of the life-cycle rituals, unless otherwise specified, is based on R.W. Falcon, *Handbook on Sikhs for Regimental Officers* (Allahabad: Pioneer Press, 1896; hereafter *Handbook*), pp. 48-54; A.H. Bingley, *Sikhs* (Patiala: Department of Languages, 1970 reprint; first published Simla, 1899), pp. 93-107; *Punjabi State Gazetteers, Phulkian States, Patiala, Jind and Nabha* (Lahore: The Civil and Military Gazette Press, 1901), pp. 231-37, and *A Glossary of the Tribes and Castes of the Punjab and North-West Frontier Province, Based on the Census Report for the Punjab, 1883, by the Late Sir Denzil Ibbetson, K.C.S.I., and the Census Report for the Punjab, 1892, by Sir Edward Maclagan, K.C.S.I., C.S.I.*, v. 1, compiled by H.A. Rose (Lahore: Superintendent, Government Printing, Punjab, 1919; hereafter *Glossary*).

wife). The latter brought with her some cow urine, green grass and nail-parer. After sprinkling the cow's urine over the mother with the grass, the Nain trimmed her patron's nails for the first time since her confinement. After all this had been done, the mother and the child were allowed to come out of the room in which they had been confined for a period of thirteen days. As on all auspicious occasions, oil was sprinkled on the ground outside the threshold by the Nain. The ritual cleansing over, the child was named either by a Sikh *granthi*, who after appropriate prayers opened the Adi Granth at random and used the first word of the first line of the page opened to coin a name, or, more frequently, by a Brahman who used his almanac to find a name. The mother was deemed to be fully purified only after forty days of confinement, after which she was allowed to enter the domestic kitchen and tend the hearth.

Compared to the rituals of birth, the proceedings for a marriage were far more complex. There was an immense variation in ceremonial not only among the different castes of Sikhs but also within caste groups and among Sikhs of different localities. Generally among the Jat Sikhs the village Nai or Brahman *purohit* would as a first step act as a go-between (*lagi*) opening negotiations between two households which could lead to an eventual marriage. If the discussions were successful, a betrothal ceremony would follow, when the go-between would be ceremoniously received by the boy's family and would put a mark on the brow of the future bridegroom and give him money and sugar from the girl's family. The actual time for the marriage was fixed by astrologers after consulting the horoscopes of the boy and girl.[19] Two or three months before the wedding, a letter called a *sahi chithi*, announcing the exact date of marriage, was dispatched by the girl's household in the care of a Nai. The days preceding a wedding were punctuated with several rites and observances: the beating of drums, singing and dancing, the propitiation of the nine planets, the tying of cotton threads on wrists and ankles, and worship by the bridegroom at an ancestral shrine and before a *jand* (*Prospis spicigera*) tree.

On the appointed day the bridegroom, accompanied by a *barat*, or wedding procession made up entirely of men, reached the bride's place. It was considered inauspicious for the procession to reach the scene of the wedding before sunset. On arrival the visitors were received by the girl's kin with loud singing and the beating of drums. Often, if the families could afford it, dancing girls were asked to participate in the rejoicing. The same night, after the feasting, the bridegroom was led to a special enclosure and the following ceremony called the *phera*, or circling of the fire, was performed.

A place was first marked off with four upright stakes joined by cross-pieces of wood at the top and the inside. This was covered with a red cloth called a *vedi*. Inside this enclosure were placed two red seats for the bridal couple. The

---

19. The most favourable season for marriage was spring, but marriages could also take place in the following months: Magh (January-February), Phagan (February-March), Baisakh (April-May), Jeth (May-June) and Har (June-July). The months considered inauspicious for marriage were Kattak (October-November), Poh (December-January), and Chet (March-April).

pair were seated and the Brahman who was going to perform the marriage rites marked the ground with a square divided into compartments, each representing a particular deity. These were worshipped in the name of the couple and the Brahman recited *shlokas* from the *shastras* asking the bride's parents to give up their daughter in marriage. A small fire was lit and the Brahman tied the hem of the girl's head-scarf to a piece of cloth which was placed over the shoulders of the bridegroom. Guided by a relative, he led the bride four times around the fire, which, as a deity, stood witness to the marriage. The bride then came to the front and circumambulated the fire three more times while the officiating priest recited verses from the sacred texts. The marriage was then complete and the couple left for the boy's house accompanied by the Nai's wife. But the marriage was not consummated; after spending a few days in the bridegroom's house, the bride returned to her parents' place, where she resided until she was finally made over to her husband at a ceremony called *muklava*, separated from the actual wedding by an interval of two, three, five, seven or nine years, depending on a decision by the girl's parents.

Much as in the case of marriage ceremonial, the Sikhs lacked any distinctive mortuary rite that could be described as a charter of corporate identity. "Sikhs," wrote Falcon, an officer with the British army, "follow the Hindu custom of dying upon the ground and of burning their dead, the dying person being lifted off the bed just before the death and placed upon the ground."[20] In cases where death had occurred too late for the body to be cremated before sunset, it was kept in the house for the night, during which time some five or ten of the deceased's kinsmen kept watch over the corpse.

The next morning, before being taken to the cremation ground, the body was washed and dressed with great care. It was taken to the funeral ground on a wooden bier by a relay of four men, followed by a procession made up of kinsmen and close associates. When the funeral procession reached half-way to the funeral grounds, water was sprinkled round the bier and the son or closest agnate smashed an earthen vessel on the ground. If the deceased happened to be an elderly person, a brass vessel was thrown on the ground and the mourning was replaced by rejoicing. On reaching the cremation ground a pile of logs was erected and the corpse laid on it.[21] Five balls of rice and flour called *pinda* were then placed on the corpse, and the heir, taking a sacred torch lit by a Maha Brahman, or impure funeral priest, lit the wooden pyre.[22] Following the cremation, all those who had joined the funeral procession took a bath to get rid of the pollution. The bones that remained unburnt, called *phul*, were collected

---

20. Falcon, *Handbook*, p. 53.
21. For a description of a funeral procession for an old Sikh, see R.E. Parry, *The Sikhs of the Punjab* (London: Drane's, 1921), pp. 34-35.
22. In the case of certain castes a different procedure was followed for the distribution of the *pinda*. One was placed on the deceased's breast before the bier was lifted. A second was offered as soon as the body was taken over the threshold of the house, a third when it had passed the village or town gates, a fourth when the funeral procession reached half-way and the fifth at the cremation ground. See *Glossary*, pp. 844-45.

on the third or the fourth day after the cremation, and the bereaved household made arrangements either to take them personally for immersion in the river Ganges at Hardwar or to send them in charge of the family Brahman. The period of mourning varied greatly among the different castes and depended on their ranking in the social hierarchy and ritual purity. In case of high-caste Sikhs it was eleven days for a son and three days for other agnates who had participated in the funeral rites. Those lower down in the social ladder could have periods of mourning lasting for up to forty days.

In cases where the deceased had died from unnatural causes such as hanging, drowning, poisoning or snake bite, or when death had occurred prior to his being shifted from a bed to the ground, close relatives went to Pihewa, a place in Ambala district, and there performed obsequies through the mediation of a Brahman. If this was not done, it was believed the relatives would be haunted by the spirit of the dead person, in the form of a *bhut* (if the deceased happened to be a male) or of a *churel* (if female). The chief mourner, normally the eldest son, went through a series of daily rituals during the period of mourning. He hung a clay pot with a small hole in its bottom on a *pipal* (*Ficus religiosa*) tree and had to fill it with water twice daily for ten days. Besides this he had to go through two other daily rites: to offer *pinda* in the morning and light an earthenware lamp in the evening. The eleventh day after the death saw the end of the period of pollution and was marked by the beginnings of the post-cremation rituals or *shraddh*. Balls of rice, ghee and sugar (termed *pinda dan*) were either fed to a crow or thrown into a river. Later kinsmen, friends of the bereaved and an odd number of Brahmans were given food. On the thirteenth day the Maha Brahman, the person who had supervised the cremation rites, was invited to the deceased's house and, if the departed person was a male, he was given an umbrella, a stick, a pair of shoes, a turban, the dead person's cot, wearing apparel and often a little opium. The *shraddh* ceremonies were often repeated on each anniversary of the death. The objective of such mortuary rituals was to earn merit for the deceased and reduce his sufferings.

What are the conceptual implications of this ethnographic description? First, ritual enactments are a condensed statement of the most deeply held values of a society. As metaphors of collective consciousness they inform of cultural boundaries, communicate notions of time, space and sacrality, endow people with a significant sense of personal identity and often reinforce social order. For instance, when mortuary rituals demanded of the chief mourner that he sleep on the ground for a period of eleven days, the injunction fulfilled simultaneously several of the rules alluded to above. Due to his polluted state the mourner was temporally and spatially separated from all his kinsmen. He was barred from eating "hot" foods, having sexual contact and changing garments—all mundane activities for a householder.[23] The chief mourner's liminal state conferred on

---

23. The pervasive category of "hot" as operative in popular Indian ritual or religious contexts embraces that which is calorically hot, or spicy, or passionate, and so on. —Editors' note.

him a unique identity at once sacred and dangerous. Only after fulfilling his ritual obligations that reiterated a certain vision of the cosmos and social reality could he be reintegrated with his family, kin and society. The symbols, gestures, formulae and emotions that make up a ritual performance help transform the chaos and vicissitudes of human existence into an ordered and meaningful sequence. More simply, to paraphrase Myerhoff and Moore, rituals help people overcome indeterminacy in life.[24] They banish "from consideration the basic questions raised by the made-upness of culture, its malleability and alterability,"[25] thus endowing social life with a certainty which on closer reflection it does not seem to possess. It is worth noting in passing that the meaning of the term *samskara*, widely used in lay parlance to denote the life-cycle rituals, is to "prepare," "refine" and to "complete."[26] In other words, these rituals (*samskaras*) have the power to distill and complete what is undistilled and incomplete in human life.

Secondly, there was hardly any difference between the way Hindus and Sikhs received a child into this world, contracted a marriage alliance or performed funerary rites. This tied them together into a common symbolic universe. A close look at the beliefs and practices encoded by the mortuary rites, commonly referred to as *shraddh*, illustrates this integration.[27] On death the soul of the deceased turned into a disembodied ghost or *preta*, becoming dangerous for itself and the living. By performing a sequence of rituals the grieving family aimed at creating an outer body for this ethereal spirit. For a period of ten days, as stated previously, a *pinda* was offered by the chief mourner in the name of the deceased; each of these rice or flour balls was to reconstruct a specific limb of the body. These offerings had to be made on the bank of a river or by some sacred tank. The chief mourner, facing south offered the *pinda* on top of a piece of *kusha* grass. At the end of the ritual the *pinda* commonly was put in the river, but it could also be fed to a crow, which was seen as a temporary embodiment of the *preta*, who signalled his acceptance of the offering by eating it. After ten days this exercise in reconstituting the body was complete and on the eleventh day it breathed and was fed. The next day the performance of an elaborate ritual enabled the deceased to join his ancestors. At last the marginal ghost (*preta*) became a venerable ancestor (*pitar*). It could now set out on its journey to the abode of ancestors. The entire corpus of Sikh mortuary rites was suffused with the myths, texts, practices and beliefs of the "twice-born" Hindu castes. Similarly Sikh rites at birth and marriage, despite

24. Barbara Myerhoff and Sally Falk Moore, eds., *Secular Ritual* (Amsterdam: Van Gorcum, 1977), pp. 3-24.
25. Ibid., pp. 16-17.
26. R. Nicholas and R. Inden, *Kinship in Bengali Culture* (Chicago: University of Chicago Press, 1977), p. 37.
27. For the following account I am indebted to Jonathan Parry, "Death and Digestion: The Symbolism of Food and Eating in North Indian Mortuary Rites," *Man*, n.s., v. 20 (1985), pp. 612-30.

the variations introduced by the innumerable *biradaris* and *gots*, were structurally not distinct from those of upper-caste Hindus.[28]

Third, Sikhs and Hindus both employed the services of the same ritual intermediaries—Brahmans, *purohits*, Nais and Maha Brahmans, to conduct their *rites de passage*. The result of all this was that the two were integrated into a common cultural universe and they shared the same grammar of social relations based on vertical ties of kinship and caste rather the horizontal solidarity of religion and community.

All this, no doubt, can be qualified to some extent. Within the pluralistic framework of Sikh tradition in the nineteenth century there was a significant Khalsa sub-tradition that did not blend very well with the amorphous state of the Sikh faith. The Khalsa Sikhs had their own notion of what constituted the Sikh past and more importantly they possessed a distinct life-cycle ritual in the form of *khande da pahul* or baptism rites.[29] Those who underwent this rite had to maintain the five well-known symbols of the Khalsa and in addition strictly to observe the injunctions laid down in the *rahit-namas* or manuals of conduct. These manuals most clearly manifest the aspirations and ethos of the Khalsa sub-tradition.[30] They visualized a considerably deritualized Sikhism, shorn of polytheism, idolatry and Brahmanical dominance. But a great deal of historical and linguistic research needs to be carried out before we can be sure how precisely the *rahit-nama* texts related to the aspirations of the Khalsa. However, one point is clear: in many ways the *rahit-nama* literature foreshadowed the homogeneous Sikh identity and religious boundaries of the late nineteenth century.

Identity formation is invariably a dual process. It is not sufficient for a group of people to think that they constitute a separate entity; those among whom they live and with whom they interact must also recognize this claim. Therefore the Khalsa's self-perception of being distinct from the rest of the civil population in the province did not automatically imply that they were accepted as such by others who belonged to the Sikh tradition or by Hindus. For instance, the commonly cited custom in many Hindu households of having one member become a Khalsa Sikh attests to the contrary. The Khalsa urge to strike a separate identity was further diluted by two factors: as yet it had not become mandatory for all Sikhs to undergo *khande da pahul*;[31] and the different sub-

---

28. For details on how similar the Sikh and Hindu life-cycle rituals were see Mrs. S. Stevenson, *The Rites of the Twice-Born* (London: Oxford University Press, 1920), and R.B. Pandey, *Hindu Samskaras: A Socio-Religious Study of the Hindu Sacraments* (Banaras: Vikrama Publications, 1949).

29. A detailed account of the rite and the procedures to be followed for the ceremonial is in Avtar Singh Vahiria, compiler, *Khalsa Dharm Shastar* (Amritsar: Sodhi Ram Narain Singh, 1914), pp. 137-43.

30. For seminal writings on the origins and evolution of the *rahit-nama* literature, see W.H. McLeod, "The Problem of the Panjabi Rahit-namas," in S.N. Mukherjee ed., *India, History and Thought: Essays in Honour of A.L. Basham* (Calcutta: Subarnarekha, 1982), pp. 103-26, and *The Chaupa Singh Rahit-Nama* (Dunedin: University of Otago Press, 1987).

31. British observers in the nineteenth century were always struck by how rarely the Sikhs underwent the passage-rite of initiation. R.W. Falcon stated: "The tendency is always in less

traditions constituting the Sikh movement had their own distinct rites of initiation.[32]   A large body of Sikhs in sub-traditions, who may be clustered under the generic term of *sahajdhari* Sikhs, underwent what was often referred to as *charan pahul*. In this rite the initiate was administered water sanctified through using it to wash either the feet or the toe of the right foot of a holy figure, generally a member of a Guru lineage such as the Bedis, Bhallas and Sodhis. Consequently, when it came to defining who was a Sikh, there was no ready-made or simple answer. According to a broad definition any person who accepted the teachings of Guru Nanak could qualify to be one, and by a narrow definition only those who had undergone *khande da pahul* qualified to be Sikhs. But which of these two standards was to be applied came to be determined only in the last few decades of the nineteenth century.

II

The story of how Punjabi society underwent massive structural and social change under colonial rule, how a large number of socio-religious organizations like the Brahmo Samaj, the Arya Samaj and the Singh Sabha came to be founded and how they started to battle over cultural, ideological and political issues, is by now fairly well established in historical literature and there is no need to repeat it in detail here.[33] For the purpose in hand, what is important to note is that colonialism fostered a new social *élite* among the Sikhs. This *élite* was new not so much in terms of its social origins but of its functions and, more importantly, the instruments of transmission (for instance, the printing press) that it appropriated. Many members of this new *élite* came from families and castes who enjoyed high ritual standing and controlled social resources not available to others. Equally, there were also men who did not have such privileged backgrounds. However, the proportion of these newer men compared to the former was still small. Together, they were emerging as a power-bloc the like of which never before had existed in the Sikh tradition. In pre-British society there had never been one societal group that sought to usurp the sole right to generate cultural meanings and define people's lives. For centuries a broad ensemble of professional groups—bards, genealogists, storytellers, healers, minstrels, shamans, local saints, diviners, among others—had mediated cultural conventions. Historically tied to particular clans, castes and localities, they had elaborated myriad "little traditions" that were largely kept alive through oral texts. During key events in the *rites de passage* a wide variety of social codes, myths and legends were communicated orally by the traditional culture-

---

essential matters to revert to the practice of ancient religion: take for example the great slackness there is at the present time in taking the pahul, very many who call themselves Singhs in the Singh tracts, omitting to take the pahul though adopting the surname and keeping some of the observances." *Handbook*, p. 21.
  32. Vahiria, *Khalsa Dharm Shastar*, p. 115.
  33. Background in N. Gerald Barrier, *The Sikhs and Their Literature* (Delhi: Manohar, 1970); Kenneth W. Jones, *Arya Dharm* (Delhi: Manohar, 1976), and Fox, *Lions of the Punjab*.

bearers. The result was a plurality of social visions and practices centred on numerous peasant communities.

But in colonial Punjab for the first time there emerged a restless new *élite* who cut across kin ties, neighbourhood networks and even caste affiliations. They soon came to monopolize the right to represent public morality and social values. Initially supported in this task by the British administrators, they were later backed by the lethal armies of advancing capitalism (e.g., commercialization and rapid communications) that eventually swept aside many of the older professional groups who had in the past underwritten and communicated local culture. The new cultural *élite* among the Sikhs aggressively subsumed a variety of Sikh sub-traditions, dissolving alternate ideas like asceticism under a monolithic, codified and reified religion. To do so, they established an extensive network of Singh Sabhas that spread from Peshawar in the west to Agra in the east, and from Srinagar in the north to Karachi in the south. By 1900 there were at least 116 Singh Sabhas spread over major urban centres, small market towns and large village settlements. The religious paradigm enunciated by these Sabhas, under the aegis of the new *élites*, began to gain currency because its dominant characteristics represented an unchanging idiom in a period of flux and change. Henceforth, Sikhs were required to speak and dream through one language, that of the cultural *élites*. Those who deviated or refused to mould themselves according to the standards of the "Great Tradition" were gradually displaced and consigned to the margins of the community. After considerable resistance, these marginalized groups finally turned their backs on Sikhism and went their own way. The older forms of Sikhism were displaced forever and replaced by a series of inventions: the demarcation of Sikh sacred space by clearing holy shrines of Hindu icons and idols, the cultivation of Punjabi as the sacred language of the Sikhs, the foundation of cultural bodies exclusively for Sikh youth, the insertion of the anniversaries of the Sikh Gurus into the ritual and sacred calendar and, most importantly of all, the introduction of new life-cycle rituals.

The result was a most fundamental change in the nature of the Sikh tradition. From an amorphous entity it was rapidly turning into a homogeneous community. And of all the competing entities, symbols and norms that went into constituting the Sikh movement, it was the Khalsa sub-tradition that came to imprint its image on the "new" community.[34] The Udasis, Nirmalas, and Nanakpanthis, the complex earlier referred to as Sahajdharis, came to be viewed as deviants. The Hindu-Sikh conflict was not, therefore, simply a question of two communities fighting it out with each other, but also had to do with the elimination of internal differences among the Sikhs. With the negation of many of the Sikh sub-traditions, a single Sikh identity began to crystallize in the first decade of this century. In contemporary literature this new identity was given the name "Tat Khalsa," and those within the Sikh tradition who were opposed to

---

34. On why and how this happened see my "A World Reconstructed."

its vision of the world came to be known as "Sanatan" Sikhs. The point is that while formerly there never was a standard Sikh identity for those outside the tradition to see, negotiate and compete with, under the Tat Khalsa's aegis such an identity came to be forged for the first time. The boundaries between what was Sikh and what was non-Sikh were no longer blurred; the Tat Khalsa had "framed" the community.

The influential Tat Khalsa began to do this as early as the 1880's by deriding the *rites de passage* practiced by the Sikhs. They were deeply conscious of the fact that a separate Sikh identity could not be attained as long as "Hindu" life-cycle rituals continued to be adhered to by the faithful. Since *rites de passage*, as argued previously, are the most fundamental statements of group identity, with a deep emotive content, Sikhs desirous of distancing themselves from Hindus could not be seen performing Hindu rituals. The Tat Khalsa, with the organizational support of the Singh Sabhas, started a massive campaign through newspapers, tracts and lectures to congregations (*diwans*) to replace the Hindu rites with new Sikh rites. Between 1884 and 1915 at least twenty-four manuals were produced to determine what sort of life-cycle rituals should be performed by the Sikhs. (This estimate does not include the polemical literature on the *rites de passage*. See the appendix to this chapter for a list of these life-cycle manuals).

The largest segment of these guides was made up of works on marriage rituals. Even when these books disagreed on the precise historical origins of these customs or the correct steps in a particular rite, a great majority of them derided existing ceremonials. The Tat Khalsa's condemnation of existing rites was based on three major factors: they were Hindu in origin, intent and purpose; Sikh Gurus were opposed to these practices and, therefore, had developed separate rites for their followers; and, finally, many elements within the prevalent rites smacked of superstition and backward thinking. Since the revised rituals radically departed from the pre-Singh-Sabha phase and also played a fundamental role in etching Sikh cultural boundaries, it is worth describing them in some detail.[35]

Soon after a child was born, a set of five verses from the Adi Granth was to be recited. Ten to twelve days later, five Sikhs were supposed to prepare *amrit* and administer it to the newborn baby in the presence of the Adi Granth. This done, the parents repaired to a *granthi* and asked him to name the child by consulting the Adi Granth, as described previously. There was no need to consult a Brahman or a *purohit* in the naming process. Also, it was undesirable to place amulets around the child or consider the mother to be in any way polluted. The pre- and post-natal practices from customary culture of the region, described as Hindu rites in the idiom of contemporaries, were simply discarded.

---

35. Unless otherwise stated, the following account is based on Bhai Suraj Singh Paracharak, *Gurmat Kaj Bivhar* (Lahore: Maluk Singh Subedar, 1913). Suraj Singh was a well-known Tat Khalsa publicist, and from 1900 onwards regularly wrote on Sikh history, rituals and the lives of contemporary Sikhs. He produced approximately eleven books.

All Sikhs—Jats, Khatris, Mazhbis—were required to perform the same rituals without any reference to their caste or *biradari* traditions.

The birth rituals having been transformed, a similar change was effected in marriage arrangements. Since Nais and the Brahmans came to be portrayed as cheats and parasites in the Sabha literature, it was recommended that the preliminary marriage negotiations be carried out without their intervention. When discussions were successful, they were to be followed by a simple betrothal ceremony. The date for the wedding was to be arrived at without consulting astrologers, and all months of the year were decreed to be auspicious for the occasion. Such old practices as asking Brahmans to officiate in the proceedings, using Nais to convey the letter announcing the wedding and arranging for dancing girls, Bhands and Mirasis to participate in the wedding processions were decreed to be anti-Sikh. When the wedding procession arrived at its destination it was not to be greeted with loud music or other forms of welcome, but with piously recited verses from the Adi Granth. The initial proceedings were to be concluded with the Sikh *ardas*. The final marriage ceremony, commonly referred to as Anand, was to be performed by the couple four times circumambulating the Adi Granth and not going around any fire. While this was being done, a set of four verses from the Adi Granth, composed by the fourth Guru, Ramdas, were to be recited. This did away with the ancient custom of reciting the *shastras* and other non-Sikh sacred texts.[36]

The Tat Khalsa were also unwilling to leave the funeral ceremony unchanged. Though the body is transitory it is also a means of projecting powerful social symbols. The environment of the corpse was seen to have as much potential for communicating communal identity as the body of a living person. If a death occurred, the following acts were deemed objectionable: transferring a dead body from the bed to the ground, placing a lighted lamp on its hand, having the bereaved family, cognates and friends wail and lament the departed. These widespread practices were judged to be Hindu and therefore of no import to the Sikhs. For Sikhs the manuals on passage rites recommended that the corpse be washed and dressed with particular care being taken to have all the "five k's" on the body of the deceased. At the cremation ground, before the wood pyre was lit, the Sikh *ardas* and a liturgical text, *Kirtan Sohila* (a collection of five hymns, three of them by Guru Nanak and one each by the fourth and the fifth Gurus), were to be recited for the peace of the departed soul.

While the body was being consumed by the fire, it had been conventional for the chief mourner to break the skull with a stick from the bier.[37] The Tat

---

36. Extensive background on ritual procedures in Taihal Singh, *Gurmat Riti Anusar Vivah Bidhi* (Lahore: Taihal Singh, 1903); Udham Singh, *Vivah Padhti Pati Parikarma* (Amritsar, published by the author, 1908); and Suraj Singh, *Khalsa Vivah Bhag Bidhi* (Amritsar: Bhai Chattar Singh, 1912).
37. According to a contemporary ethnographic text: "The smashing of the skull is said to be due to the idea that the life of a man is constituted of ten elements, nine of which cease their functions at death, while the action of the tenth continues for three days after death, causing the body to swell if it remains unhurt. The seat of this, the tenth, element is in the skull, which is accordingly smashed in order to set it free. Finally he [the chief mourner] pours over the skull a cup of ghi

Khalsa banned this practice from a Sikh funeral as it was considered to be in breach of the Khalsa mortuary rites. But their loudest opposition was reserved for two aspects of the former mortuary rites: carrying the ashes to the river, tank or canal, and holding a *shraddh* ceremony; such ceremonies were seen as bringing no merit to the deceased and only fattening the parasitical Brahmans.[38] The only rite Sikhs were supposed to perform was an uninterrupted forty-eight-hour recitation of the Adi Granth.

In order to encourage the widespread acceptance of these changed rituals, leading Sikh newspapers freely gave space to publicizing any *rites de passage* performed by a Sikh household in accordance with the new prescriptions, or what came to be called *gurmaryada*.[39] The large number of notices published on the life-cycle ceremonies in contemporary papers from as early as 1886 also tells us of the Tat Khalsa's growing success in bringing about a transformation in Sikh consciousness of ritual practices.   What initially were changes introduced by only a small minority gradually came to be accepted by the Sikh public at large.   The first overt signs of this decisive change can be seen in the controversy generated over the passage of the Anand Marriage Act.

With an increasing number of Sikhs at the turn of the century performing their marriage ceremonial according to the form prescribed by the Tat Khalsa, it suddenly dawned on the reformers that this mode of marriage had absolutely no legal or customary recognition. In the absence of such a sanction the civil courts could easily reject any marriage contracted through the *anand* rites, leading to endless problems over the status of children, distribution of wealth and inheritance. In addition, sections of the Arya Samaj began to ridicule Sikhs marrying by *anand* rites by suggesting that they were parenting bastards. Worried over the legal complexities and incensed by Arya Samaj propaganda, Tikka Ripudaman Singh, a Sikh prince with strong views on what Sikhism should be like and a former pupil of Kahn Singh of *Ham Hindu Nahin* fame, introduced an Anand Marriage Bill in the Imperial Legislative Council on October 30, 1908. It soon became apparent to the prince and his Tat Khalsa supporters that the enactment of the bill was not going to be easy. Rejecting customary conventions was one thing; turning them into a piece of legislation was an entirely different matter. The British administration, always afraid of any form of change, was not convinced of the merits of the proposed legislation; the Sanatan Sikhs had from the very beginning been opposed to any tampering

---

[butter], mixed with sandalwood and camphor. This rite of smashing the skull is called kapal kiria or the rite of the skull." *Glossary*, p. 847.

38. For an extensive broadside against the *shraddh* rites see *Khalsa Akhbar*, September 18, 1886, pp.3-5.

39. For examples see *Khalsa Akhbar*, June 25, 1887, pp. 7-8; October 8, 1887, pp. 6-7; December 29, 1898, pp. 7-8; September 27, 1895, pp. 5-6; May 15, 1896, p. 7; July 12, 1895, p. 6; July 31, 1898, p. 8.

with customary rituals and the Arya Samaj activists, keen on denying Sikhs a separate religious identity, forcefully rejected this new charter of separatism.[40]

In the face of this hostile reception the proposed legislation could have easily failed to pass, but the Tat Khalsa exhibited great perseverance and launched a massive campaign to drum up public support for the bill. Sikh publicists produced an unending stream of tracts stating the need for and merits of the Anand mode of marriage, and leading Sikh newspapers like the *Khalsa Samachar* and *Khalsa Advocate* were packed with articles disputing the claims of all those who objected to the codification of the marriage rituals.[41] Two claims were constantly reiterated in its defense; that the non-*anand* form of marriage was Hindu and Sikhs did not want to have anything to do with such alien customs; and that the third and fourth Sikh Gurus, Amar Das and Ramdas, had developed distinctively Sikh marriage rituals and therefore it was only logical that Sikhs adhere to these ancient rites.[42]

In a period of eleven months, from October 1908 to September 1909, over three hundred mass meetings were organized all over the province with the single objective of demanding the passage of the bill. Simultaneously almost 700,000 Sikhs petitioned the imperial administration in favour of the proposed enactment.[43] The British administration was duly impressed by these public manœuvres and on October 22, 1909 the bill became an Act of law. This success considerably boosted the Tat Khalsa position on *rites de passage*. The intensity and emotion with which the bill was defended illustrates the importance the Sikh public had come to attach to the newly invented rituals. Never before in colonial Punjab had the Sikhs come together on a common platform with such fervour as they did over the *anand* marriage controversy. This act for the first time legally codified a Sikh ritual, thereby providing Sikh separatism with state recognition; 1909, the year the Anand Marriage Act was legislated, can be viewed as a watershed in the history of modern Sikhism.

What do these changes in life-cycle rituals reveal? Earlier the stories, symbols and sentiments expressed in the *rites de passage* had had nothing to do with an autonomous Sikh tradition. Going to Hardwar to consign the ashes of a deceased relative to the Ganges and negotiating with a Hindu ritual specialist on the banks of the river, did not convey a separate Sikh identity. Similarly, listening to verses from the *shastras* at the time of a marriage had a very different connotation from recitation of verses from the Adi Granth. Instead of creating any boundaries between Sikhs and others, the earlier rituals in fact had emptied a person of any associations with the embryonic Sikh universe. The Tat

---

40. Background in K.S. Talwar, "The Anand Marriage Act," *The Panjab Past and Present* 2 (1968), 400-10.

41. For a forceful defense of the *anand* marriage ritual see Sardar Ajmer Singh, *Anand Vivah Par Vichar ka Khandan* (Amritsar: Sardar Ajmer Singh, 1908).

42. See Mohan Singh Vaid, *Gurmat Viraudh Binas* (Amritsar: the author, 1908).

43. *Government of India, Judicial Proceedings*, December 1908, 94-95 B, quoted in S.H. Khawaja, "Sikhs of the Punjab 1900-1915: A study of Confrontation and Political Mobilization," Ph.D. dissertation, University of Missouri, Columbia, 1980, p. 194.

Khalsa's transformation of these rituals, however, turned them into powerful bearers of the "new" Sikh consciousness. They came to dramatize the distinctions between "us" (Sikhs) and "them" (Hindus).

Ethnic differences are rarely based on any objective criteria. They are invariably constructed out of poetical discourses: a sense of place, a mode of dress and most importantly a specific interpretation of the past. For instance, the historical trajectory that was put forward to justify the *anand* marriage rites can usefully illustrate this enigmatic phenomenon.

> Guru Amar Das tried to batter down all the injurious caste barriers, and, incensed at this noble effort of the third Guru, the Hindus excommunicated those Sikhs of the Guru who in obedience to this teachings had ceased to observe caste. Among those Sikhs was one named Randhawa. When he wanted to marry his daughter, the Brahmins refused to come and officiate at the solemnization of the marriage, saying that having become a Sikh of Guru Amar Das he had ceased to be a Hindu, and thus had forfeited every right to have the marriage of his daughter performed according to Hindu rituals. Upon this the Sikh went to Guru Amar Das Ji, and said he was prepared to keep his daughter unmarried, but would on no account consent to the ceremony being performed according to the Hindus who were so wrath [*sic*] at his having given up the whimsical caste distinctions. Realizing the fix in which the Sikh was, the Guru ordered his son-in-law (afterwards Guru Ramdas Ji) to go and officiate at the marriage of the Sikh's daughter. It was on this occasion that four *lavan* were originally composed by the fourth Guru. The next noteworthy occasion on which the entire form prescribed conjointly by the third and fourth Gurus was observed was the marriage of the sixth Guru's daughter (Bibi Viro) at the village Jhabal in the Amritsar district.[44]

Two aspects in this putative genealogy of the *anand* marriage form written by a Sikh professor at the Khalsa College, Lyallpur, in the 1900's call for attention. First, it dates the Hindu-Sikh differences back to the sixteenth century. What was clearly a modern problem was endowed with an ancient history of animosity. Secondly, and more importantly, the differences are not expressed in a pragmatic matrix encompassing political economy or material interests but in a semantic idiom. On the one hand they have to do with issues of ritual purity and impurity and on the other with the poesis of passage rites. Differences in human society, be they ethnic, religious or political, are mostly internalized through subjective modes: myths, stories, rites and symbols. The corpus of the new ritual introduced by the Tat Khalsa put the faithful in touch with a specific past, one that simultaneously highlighted an exclusive Sikh ethos and also legitimized what Hobsbawm aptly describes as "invention of tradition."[45]

The "invented tradition" made it possible for the Sikh public to think, imagine and speak in terms of a universal community of believers united by uniform rites, symbols and scripture. The rules of the household, lineage, clan

---

44. Government of Punjab to Government of India, April 20, 1909, enclosure. Home Department Judicial Proceedings, July 1909, 55-56, quoted in K.S. Talwar, "The Anand Marriage Act," p. 401.

45. E. Hobsbawm and T. Ranger, eds., *The Invention of Tradition* (Cambridge: Cambridge University Press, 1983).

and caste that had governed many of the inter-personal transactions in the Punjab were gradually breached and there began to arise a vision of an undifferentiated community. However fleeting its presence may have been, its impact was to be experienced increasingly in the everyday life of the people of the province. The Tat Khalsa publicists also started instructing their co-religionists to marry only among the Sikhs. This may not have led to a spate of inter-caste marriages among Sikhs, but it at least introduced an element of religious identity into a key rite. The course had been set for the much-quoted pronouncements on the frequency of Hindu-Sikh marriages to become a cliché.

The withdrawal of the Sikhs from the former rites of passage meant that in due course they stopped relying on the ritual services of "Hindu" intermediaries like Brahmans and *purohits*. In the present state of research it is hard to specify at what precise moment Sikh intermediaries—the *bhais* and *ragis*—came to seize control of the transformed rites, but whatever the chronology of this transition, what needs to be underscored is that this played a crucial role in the formation of Sikh ethnicity. It is interesting to note that just as the Brahmans and *purohits* moved out and the *bhais* and *ragis* came in, there was a similar transposition in sacred formulae. While formerly Brahmanical verse was recited in one form or another at the times of birth, marriage and death, now the Adi Granth moved into a central position in the enactment of all rituals associated with the milestones of life. From being a guide to the mysteries of life, the Adi Granth became a rich resource for constructing an exclusive semiotic universe for the Sikhs.

The ritual changes introduced by the Tat Khalsa ultimately came to be inserted in the *rahit-namas*. In the present state of research it is not possible accurately to date the *rahit-nama* literature, but in 1910 and 1931 respectively the Chief Khalsa Diwan and the Shiromani Gurdwara Prabandhak Committee set up commissions to formulate a new *rahit-nama*, and the performance of the life-cycle rituals was made an integral part of the *rahit*. This had not been the case with most of the former *rahit-namas* and was a radical innovation.[46] The changes introduced by the latest *rahit-nama*, titled *Sikh Rahit Maryada* and published in 1950, were a tribute to the far-reaching implications of Tat Khalsa thinking on the construction of personhood within the Sikh community during the present century.

In sum, in this section I have argued that between 1880 and 1901 the life-crisis rituals were finally constituted into a communicative grid par excellence. They came to transmit simultaneously identity, a particular vision of history,

---

46. The following well-known *rahit-namas* contain no reference to the rules of passage rites (i.e., birth, marriage, death): the *Rahit-nama* of Prahlad Rai (or Prahlad Singh); the *Rahit-nama* of Nand Lal; the *Tankhah-nama* of Nand Lal; and the *Rahit-nama* of Desa Singh. The *Rahit-nama* of Chaupa Singh has no explicit mention of a marriage ceremonial for the Khalsa. There is a brief mention of passage rites in the following *rahit-namas* but no detailed exposition: the *Rahit-nama* of Daya Singh; *Prem Sumarg* and *Sau Sakhian* (unlike the Tat Khalsa, this apocryphal text backs the post-mortuary *shraddh* ceremonies). It is probable that *rahit-namas* that record *rites de passage* are of a later date than the ones that do not.

exclusivity and communal solidarity. An autonomous symbolic universe has always been a prerequisite for the cultural-religious identity of any universal religious community. The Tat Khalsa completed this task for the Sikhs. While the roots of the drive for this cultural autonomy may be traced by some scholars back to Guru Nanak, the reasons for its consolidation certainly lie entangled in the social history of late nineteenth-century Punjab. Rituals as much as any other force play a vital role in societal change and in the generation of communal solidarity. The oft-repeated rhetorical statement *Ham Hindu nahin* ("We are not Hindus") now had a subjective basis. Whatever it lacked was supplemented by further innovations in the spheres of language, history, theology, sacred space, religious calendar and territory.

III

Conflict in human societies cannot be understood without reflecting on how human actors interpret the world around them. Although we know a great deal about the changes Indian society underwent during the colonial period, e.g., the intense rivalry between anglicized *élites*, the peasant differentiation in the countryside and the role of merchant capital in Punjab's agrarian economy, we know far less about the changes in the Sikh view of the world, categories of thought and ritual action. My central contention is that if we want to understand fully the rift between the Sikhs and Hindus, we urgently need to know how their attitudes towards time, space, sacrality, body management, commensality, cultural transgression, rituals and inter-personal transactions shifted in the late nineteenth century.

This chapter, through a historical and ethnographic reconstruction, has argued that in pre-British Indian society people's consciousness and social cleavages were not so much influenced by categories of universal religious communities but, rather, had to do with principles of kinship, locality and caste. However, with the introduction of British rule and the massive transformation that followed, the very nature of religion changed. It increasingly became objectified and started mediating in social equations in a way it had never done before. Having obliquely noted this development, I went on to discuss how a new social group—the Tat Khalsa—usurped the right to speak on behalf of the entire Sikh tradition and in doing so injected new definitions of religion and community among the Sikhs. From this reconstitution of the Sikh tradition there followed a radical shift in the Sikh *rites de passage*. It was through these rituals that Sikhs became conscious of their distinct ethnic identity. How else, apart from these rituals, one must ask, could the Sikhs have perceived themselves as different from Hindus? The performance of each of these ritual acts continually communicated, reaffirmed and rehearsed a sense of the Sikh community. Each Sikh could now carry his religious identity into the most fundamental moments of this life and by doing so buttress the distinctive status of the Sikh community. When by the turn of the century these new rituals were firmly entrenched, there occurred a definite rupture in the Sikh and Hindu notions of how the universe is constituted and in their respective subjective experiences.

However, in the last analysis the answer to the Hindu-Sikh question, whether at the turn of the century, today or in the future, is an epistemological question. It depends on what we make of man and his universe. If we accept that human societies are always involved in spinning "webs of significance," to use Geertz's illuminating phrase,[47] then a definite rupture took place between Hindu and Sikh attitudes at the turn of the century. But if we take the view that the world is made up of utilitarian, pragmatic, resource-maximizing individuals and that narratives, experiences, rituals and cultural performances are mere epiphenomena (which some social scientists arrogantly dismiss as "false consciousness"), then nothing changed at the turn of the century. By this reading, Hindus and Sikhs at the turn of the century, as today, were quintessentially the same, and what is referred to as the "Punjab crisis" will disappear as did, in the eyes of some, the chasms that emerged in the late nineteenth century.

Appendix: Manuals of *rites de passage*

These twenty-four manuals on *rites de passage* written between 1884 and 1915 may be considered as an intermediate *genre* between the classic and modern *rahit-namas*.

Uttam Singh. *Khalsa Sanskar Pustak*. Lahore: Vidya Pustak Parkashak Press, 1884.
Attar Singh. *Khalsa Dharm Shastar Sanskar*. Amritsar: Amir Chand Press, 1893.
Avtar Singh Vahiria. *Khalsa Dharm Shastar*. Lahore: Arorabans Press, 1894.
Jhanda Singh. *Pahul ki Maryada ka Granth*. Lahore: Viddiya Press, 1895.
Giani Gian Singh. *Amrit Prakash*. Lahore: Arorabans Press, 1898.
Kahan Singh Nabha. *Gurmat Sudhakar*. Amritsar: Wazir Hind Press, 1901.   First published 1898 in Hindi.
Hakim Munna Singh. *Khalsa Dharm Sanskar*. Lahore: Mufid-i-Am Press, 1899.
Bhai Ram Singh. *Kitab Rasman wa Lag Chagh*. Amritsar: Chasma-i-Nur Press, 1899.
Sardar Jawala Singh. *Vivah Sanskar Bhag*. Amritsar: Wazir Hind Press, 1899.
Bhai Partap Singh. *Khalsa Dharm Sanskar Bidhi*. Lahore: Khalsa Press, 1900.
Manna Singh. *Khalsa Dharam Sanskar Bidhi*. Amritsar: Wazir Hind Press, 1901.
Sant Ganesh Singh. *Khalsa Vivah Padhti*. Lahore: Shri Gurmat Press, 1901.
Taihal Singh. *Gurmat Riti Anusar vivah Bidhi*. Lahore: Shri Gurmat Press, 1901.
Khalsa Kanya Vivah Sanskar. Lahore: Khalsa Press, 1905.
Shri Guru Granth Sahib Vichaun Lavan. Amritsar: Khalsa Tract Society, 1907.
Sant Hira Das. *Gurmat Samanya*. Ludhiana: Singh Sabha, 1907.
Sodhi Ram Narain Singh. *Khalsa Dharm Shastar*. Amritsar: Shri Gurmat Press, 1908.
Udham Singh. *Vivah Padhti Pati Parikarma*. Amritsar: Udam Singh, 1908.
Teja Singh Bhasaur. *Khalsa Rahit Prakash*. Bhasaur, 1908.

---

47. Clifford Geertz, *The Interpretation of Cultures* (London: Hutchinson, 1973), p. 5.

Avtar Singh Vahiria, compiler. *Khalsa Dharm Darpan*. Lyallpur: Bhai Pratap Singh and Sunder Singh, 1910.

Bhai Suraj Singh. *Khalsa Vivah Bhag Bidhi*. Amritsar: Bhai Chattar Singh, 1912.

Idem. *Gurmat Kaj Bivhar*. Lahore: Maluk Singh Subedar, 1913.

Avtar Singh Vahiria, compiler. *Khalsa Dharm Shastar*. Anandpur: Sodhi Ram Narain Singh, 1914.

Gurmat Prakash Bhag Sanskar. Amritsar: Chief Khalsa Diwan, 1915.

Sikh Politics in British Punjab prior to the Gurdwara Reform Movement

N. Gerald Barrier

The issues[1] and patterns predominant in the contemporary world of the Sikhs have their roots in the earlier experiences of the community. Many observers comment on the continuities between current ideological and personal struggles and the recent past, most notably Akali and Shiromani Gurdwara Prabandhak Committee (hereafter S.G.P.C.) politics after 1919. Others refer to more general social and cultural bases of Sikh perceptions and action, such as concern with honor, competition, alliances and rivalries based on personality, groups or region.[2] References to the pre-gurdwara-reform period tend to focus on one or two themes. The first involves the strengthening and institutionalization of Sikh identity, a process associated with the Singh Sabha period, ca. 1870-1919. During that time Sikhs supposedly revived ancient traditions and either revitalized existing institutions or created new ones. The Singh Sabhas are seen as protecting the Sikh faith and paving the way for a resurgence of Sikhism. The second theme involves relations with the British, revolving around efforts to present a loyal posture toward colonial rule while at the same time creating new political organizations. Dominant in the story is the Chief Khalsa Diwan (hereafter C.K.D.), begun in 1902, an association that for almost two decades remained at the center of Sikh and imperial politics. The C.K.D. generally is pictured as sometimes well-meaning, elitist, cut off from the masses and pursuing policies and strategies out of tune with the times or needs of Sikhs in the Punjab. Eventually the C.K.D. approach came to be seen as hollow, and Sikhs turned to an emergent and more dynamic network associated with the Akali Dal and the S.G.P.C.[3]

1. Research and writing of this essay have been supported by grants from the University of Missouri (Columbia) Research Council and the U.S. National Endowment for the Humanities.

2. Essays in Paul Wallace, *Political Dynamics of Punjab* (Amritsar: Guru Nanak Dev University, 1981); Robin Jeffrey, *What's Happening to India* (Holmes and Meier, 1986); and Joyce Pettigrew's research.

3. General overviews reflecting this perspective include Khushwant Singh, *A History of the Sikhs*, v. 2 (Princeton: Princeton University Press, 1966); Richard G. Fox, *Lions of the Punjab*

[Joseph T. O'Connell, Milton Israel, Willard G. Oxtoby, eds., with W.H. McLeod and J.S. Grewal, visiting eds., *Sikh History and Religion in the Twentieth Century* (S. Asian Studies Papers, 3) (Toronto: S. Asian Studies, Univ. of Toronto, 1988)]

Neither accepted interpretation of the pre-1919 period provides an understanding of the complex world in which Sikhs underwent a critical re-examination of their faith and priorities. The historical evidence produced by the Sikhs themselves—tracts, newspapers, organizational material[4]—suggests that the Singh Sabhas did not resolve all or even most of the myriad differences and divisions within the community. On the contrary, the competitions and conflicts of the time in many ways mirror the struggles over authority, legitimacy and control of resources that today can be found not only in the Punjab, but among Sikhs dispersed across the world. Similarly, the various types of political involvement prior to 1919 touch upon and perhaps illuminate the current twists and turns of Sikh politics. Viewing the politics of Singh Sabha leaders and the C.K.D. in terms of misguided loyalty or ineffective political strategy perpetuates a misunderstanding of the evolution of Sikh public life. Sikhs before the Akalis were struggling with hard decisions about alliances and the relationship between identity and action. Their battles were not as heroic as those of the Gurdwara Reform movement, but another look at what they were about and their successes and failures conceivably throws light on subsequent political patterns.

This paper examines some of the dynamics of early Sikh politics during British rule. The first section reviews the nature of the political system evolving after annexation of the Punjab. British policies and institutions contributed to shifts within Punjab political culture that affected the way Punjabis saw themselves and organized. Moreover, the British cultivated a particular set of relationships with Sikhs that influenced the growth of institutions and the way that individuals and groups assessed political alternatives. The next section examines how Punjabis, and especially Sikhs, responded to the new opportunities and potential dangers associated with the West and British rule. The third section describes the role of the C.K.D. in dealing with two related

---

(Berkeley: University of California Press, 1985); and Harbans Singh, *Heritage of the Sikhs* (Delhi: Manohar, rev. ed., 1984). Also on the C.K.D., essays by Surjit Singh Narang, "Chief Khalsa Diwan," in Wallace, *Political Dynamics of Punjab*, pp. 67-81; "Chief Khalsa Diwan," *Journal of Sikh Studies* 12, 97-108, along with treatment by Rajiv Kapur, *Sikh Separatism* (London: Allen and Unwin, 1986). A different evaluation based on the critical Punjabi documents of the period is provided by Harjot Singh Oberoi's essays and his dissertation at the Australian National University. Also, my earlier work on the Singh Sabha period (1970) and my forthcoming book on the emergence of modern Sikhism, ca. 1988.

4. Research on this period draws heavily on the tract literature and contemporary documents produced by the Sikhs themselves, as well as newspapers and journals. The Punjabi documents are surveyed in Barrier, *The Punjab in Nineteenth Century Tracts* (East Lansing: Michigan State University, 1969) and *The Sikhs and Their Literature* (Delhi: Manohar, 1970) and Gaur and Dimes, *Catalogue of Panjabi Printed Books* (London: Foreign Commonwealth Office, India Office Library, 1975). On the periodical literature, see Barrier and Wallace, *The Punjab Press, 1880-1905* (East Lansing: Michigan State University, 1970). This essay especially relies on the reports of individual Sikh organizations and four papers: *Khalsa Akhbar* (representing the views of the Lahore Singh Sabha), *Khalsa Samachar* and *Khalsa Advocate* (reflecting the views of the Singh Sabhas and Chief Khalsa Diwan) and *The Tribune* (a nationalist paper critical of Singh Sabha activities, especially those critical of Hindu practices and defining boundaries between Sikhs and Hindus). Also useful have been British documents in the Government of India Home Public and Political Files (GIPol) and Punjab government proceedings (London and Lahore). Some of the best recent scholarship is found in two journals, *The Journal of Sikh Studies* and *Panjab Past and Present*.

types of politics, resolving internal conflict within the community while at the same time fashioning a united Sikh response to changes within the political system. The discussion hopefully will stimulate a fresh look at a pivotal period in Sikh history as well as raise questions about sources and links between past and present.

The British, the Sikhs and the Punjab Political System

Ranjit Singh fashioned an empire first by building coalitions and then by slowly centralizing governmental and revenue institutions. Sikhs were active participants in politics under his regime. Regional groups and the remnants of the *misls* influenced alliances and the distribution of resources, while individual families gained increasing power within a locality or through close association with the military or civilian administration. Hindu and Muslim groups also were involved heavily in the public life of the Punjab and along with Sikhs aided in making the institutions of government function.[5]

The allocation of resources and influence tended to be in the hands of particular rural *élites*. In the west, Jat and Rajput Muslim families held land and power, with kinship groups influencing alliances as did attachment to shrines and religious leaders. The central districts had large estates and smaller domains controlled by Hindu, Muslim and Sikh tribes or castes (particularly Jats). *Biradaris* also were important there and to the east, where Hindu Jats were prevalent. Commercial and urban-oriented castes or tribes also played a role in politics, but wealth and influence arose from control of land and agrarian linkages.[6]

While British rule reinforced the communal tendencies spreading quickly after the 1870's, religious identity and patterns already were important elements in Punjab political culture prior to colonial conquest. Despite mixing of social and religious traditions locally, Muslims and Hindus (along with Sikhs) had maintained boundaries separating them from others and reinforcing sectarian identification. Each had religious *élites* and shrines, along with festivals, traditions of worship, educational institutions and patterns of pilgrimage. The demarcation between Hindus and Sikhs was not clear. Comments by observers in the mid-nineteenth century, as well as recent scholarship by specialists such as Harjot Singh Oberoi, indicate that in terms of social networks, ritual and religious understanding, Hindus and Sikhs were quite similar.

The British contributed to the evolution of a new political system by borrowing ideas and structures from the earlier regime and transferring new doctrines and institutions that gave Punjab politics a particular cast. A rough-and-ready administrative system rested upon a balance between personal rule by

---

5. The historiography on Ranjit Singh and the Sikhs of the Punjab during his regime has improved over the last two decades. Useful essays include those in J.S. Grewal and Indu Banga, eds., *Maharaja Ranjit Singh and His Times* (Amritsar: Guru Nanak Dev University, 1980) and in the recent proceedings of the Punjab History Conference.

6. Two forthcoming monographs by Ian Talbot and David Gilmartin, revisions of their dissertations, present a balanced view of the nature of the Punjab political system.

officers involved in local affairs and a separate judiciary that sometimes endangered the vaunted Punjab tradition of executive action. Added later were new legislative units, in the form of local committees and a provincial council, and an expanding intelligence operation designed to provide the rulers with accurate information about what Punjabis were thinking and doing.[7]

Despite talk of personal rule, however, Punjab administration rested ultimately upon use of indigenous institutions and developing support groups among Punjabis. From the beginning, the British ruled the province with appreciable help from those associated with former regimes. Over time, the Punjabi share in handling local matters increased. First as Extra Assistant Commissioners and then as Honourary Magistrates, members of Punjabi groups moved up within the executive and judicial branches. The Punjab tended to lag behind neighboring provinces in such matters, but by the 1919 constitutional reforms the legislative council and the patterns of recruitment in various branches of government paralleled those found elsewhere. Patronage for the perceived "natural leaders" of the Punjab, those identified and cultivated as supporters of the colonial government, played a vital role in early decisions about who would fill the new positions and places of power, but by 1900 elections and competition based on education and training became increasingly important in allocation of resources.

Although British administration in the Punjab never was monolithic and encompassed a variety of viewpoints and policies, several key assumptions influenced how the government functioned. These grew in part from the real or perceived dangers resulting from the "warlike" traits of the local population and the border situation, and also reflected how the early administrators saw themselves and the people they ruled. At the center of British oratory and action was a concern with image. Officers felt that they had brought India "from chaos to order" and saved the empire in 1857. That was due essentially to being known to the people and having their respect as legitimate rulers.[8] Punjabis supposedly held honor and *izzat* in high regard. A government that survived had to be seen as strong, decisive, tough, and yet fair and sensitive. The administrative fiats of John Lawrence, summary action during the mutiny and the more controversial responses to the Kukas and later communal riots all were part of a tradition that eventually became outdated but continued to shape the Punjab government's reactions to crisis. Being seen as a legitimate ruler also required active cultivation of support and accessibility. These elements were

---

7. Discussion of the administrative method of the Punjab is in my essays on Punjab politics cited in footnotes 9 and 11, and chapter 1 of my unpublished dissertation, "The Punjab Disturbances of 1907" (Duke University, 1966).

8. See documents on possible reorganization of civil administration, GI Home Public 1883, 227-94A; also the published memoirs of Punjab Indian Civil Service officers serving in the nineteenth century. Those by Beames, Elsmie, and O'Dwyer are useful, as are the writings of Darling and Thorburn.

highlighted in a document on "social and political intercourse with Punjabis" distributed widely to young officers.[9]

British views of communal patterns in their new province, as well as concern with being seen as judicious and fair, led the colonial power to balance the interests of the religious communities. There are frequent references in documents to Punjabis being bundles of sticks waiting to beat each other. Whether this was accurate or not, as in other situations, the British acted upon their assumptions. On some occasions divide-and-rule tactics were employed, but these tended to be short-term responses to an immediate situation and not a long-range policy. Only if the British controlled communal disturbance and acted so as to minimize overt conflict could the government survive.[10]

Also important was official regard to custom and existing institutions. The early attempts to respect customary law, social relationships and village institutions rested on the British assumption that the primarily rural Punjab population would be loyal if there was minimal dislocation of daily life. Initial responses to continuation of existing grants and land revenue arrangements reflected a variety of priorities (often conflicting), but the government tried to maintain a semblance of continuity where finances and local situations permitted. Such an approach became more difficult because of the direct and indirect results of British rule, so that the government was constantly trying to revamp the system and adjust laws and regulations to mitigate change. If particular economic changes threatened disruption and thereby seemed to present a political danger, steps had to be taken immediately. Dramatic instances included the Punjab Alienation of Land Act and the ill-fated Colonisation Bill of 1907.[11]

The decisions about allocation of resources and laws rested on the rulers' evaluation of whose help was judged vital for political control. At the heart of imperial strategy was the notion that a content "yeomanry," landed proprietors of the dominant agricultural tribes, always would support the government. This meant maintaining their economic viability as well as insulating them from disturbing elements from the cities such as moneylenders and politicians. Such attention was even more critical because some of the Muslim and Sikh tribes provided recruits for the police and military. Related to concern with rural conditions was maintaining support and influence through the "natural leaders" such as the landed aristocracy, *jagirdars* and *rais* and through close association with, and at times control over, religious leaders and institutions. In the experimental stages of "local government" in the Punjab, local magnates were

---

9. Reprinted in Barrier, "How to Rule India," *Panjab Past and Present* 5 (1971), 276-96.
10. Reviewed in Barrier, "The Punjab Government and Communal Politics, 1870-1908," *Journal of Asian Studies* 27 (1968), 523-40, and Punjab comments on press controls and communalism, Barrier, "To Rule India: Coercion and Conciliation in India, 1914-1919," in Dewitt Ellinwood, ed., *India and World War One* (Delhi: Manohar, 1978), pp. 75-108.
11. Background in Barrier, "Punjab Disturbances," *The Punjab Alienation of Land Bill of 1900* (Durham: Duke University, 1966), "The Punjab Disturbances of 1907," *Modern Asian Studies* 1 (1967), 353-83, and "The Arya Samaj and Congress Politics," *Journal of Asian Studies* 26 (1967), 363-79.

nominated to the new committees and councils so that their authority and influence would smooth administration.   Similarly, elections and broadened representation in handling the affairs of religious endowments were avoided because the "natural leaders" and pro-British priests would lose out to the politically unreliable (particularly lawyers and Western-style professionals).[12] The local government tended to have a "contamination" view of politics; that is, some elements in society were considered stable and loyal but constantly in danger of being engulfed or influenced from the outside.   The same approach was evidenced in official reactions to the Indian National Congress or disturbances such as in 1907 and 1919.   Outside agitators allegedly were stirring the calm waters of the province and manipulating Punjabis.[13]

British reaction to the Sikhs fluctuated, but in general, official policy toward the community mirrored the basic assumptions and strategies found in overall decision-making.   The government probably was more ambivalent toward Sikhs because of their recent political prominence, although the support from the former rulers and soldiers of Ranjit Singh's kingdom during the mutiny assuaged some official misgivings.   The continuing militancy of Sikhs, while considered very positive when channeled into imperial military activities, also kept alive suspicion and worry about them as a potential threat.   The rulers accordingly took the Sikhs very seriously and yet tried to avoid their being seen as either favored or distrusted.[14]

Discussion frequently revolved around three sections of the Sikh community.   Jat Sikhs were seen as among the most industrious farmers in India and the bedrock of loyalty in the countryside.   There was a tendency to picture them in an idyllic way, as simple folk characterized by strength, devotion to work and family, and as good allies when given resources and not provoked.[15]   The Sikh soldier, a second category watched and occasionally pampered, typically came from the rural stock and, therefore, the government had a dual reason for monitoring developments in central Punjab, where Jat Sikhs played a dominant role in agrarian matters.   Since British officers believed that the valor and even loyalty of their Sikh troops were closely linked with religious identity, as is well known, they went to great lengths to insure that each recruit was baptized, adhered to wearing the "five K's" associated with the Khalsa and had ample opportunity to worship and visit home for religious purposes.   By the 1880's, Sikh regiments came to symbolize a particular view of Sikhism, one quite separate from Hinduism, and furnished funds and other support for revivalists

---

12. Punjab government discussions of land alienation issues, and detailed evaluation of elections and strategy, GI Home Mun June 1882, 20-22A; Home Public March 1899, 92-120B. Ibbetson's note is representative of the general approach. Minute 27/21/1899, Public Feb. 1900, 231-34A.

13. The Punjab government response is evaluated in Barrier research on 1907 disturbances.

14. Discussion in minutes by John Lawrence and the ongoing debate over control of the Golden Temple, confidential memo, and analysis in Ian Kerr, "The British and the Administration of the Golden Temple in 1859," *Panjab Past and Present* 10 (1976), 306-21; "British Relationships with the Golden Temple, 1849-90," *Indian Economic and Social History Review* 21 (1984), 139-51.

15. A theme repeated frequently in settlement reports.   A similar outlook is also reflected in recruiting handbooks such as A.H. Bingley, *Sikhs: A Handbook for Indian Army* (1918).

who were trying to mobilize the general community.   The British role was recognized and appreciated by leaders of the Singh Sabhas.   In 1896, for example, the *Khalsa Akhbar* reviewed government policy and welcomed efforts to "maintain orthodoxy" and promulgate an authentic view of Sikhism.[16]

Finally, the government viewed Sikh aristocrats, the landed families and especially the rulers of nearby states as those who could assist in legitimizing the government and help in administering the province.   Grants, *jagirs*, places in *darbars*, honors and appointments to government posts were reserved for prominent Sikhs.   In reviewing policy toward grants for descendants of prominent Sikh families, for example, the British sometimes continued financial aid even when the original *jagir* had lapsed, as illustrated by decisions about a grant to the Sodhi family at Kot Guru Har Sahai, Ferozepur.   Noting their service during the mutiny and a place of prominence among Malwa Sikhs, the British awarded Rs. 3,508 annually to insure continued political influence.[17]   In other cases, the British felt that they had been too punitive toward key families after the Sikh wars and made more lenient, conciliatory arrangements.[18]

The British relationship with the Golden Temple at Amritsar illustrates official determination to be involved with and control a central Sikh institution as well as some of the ambiguities and conflicts that resulted.   Initially the British continued grants to the temple's dignitaries and then appointed one of their Punjabi officials, Sardar Jodh Singh, to manage the Darbar Sahib.[19] Evangelical officers, led by Robert Cust, soon questioned whether the British should support Sikh religious shrines and suggested that if Sikhs were left to themselves, the temple would fall to pieces, the sect would vanish and Sikhism would cease to be a political threat.   Key Punjab officials thought otherwise and continued to be part of the management of the shrine.   In the ensuing debate over specific controversies up through 1900, such as treatment of Mazhbi troops, audits of accounts, corruption of priests and avoiding implementing Act XX of 1863 (Religious Endowments Act, with provisions for setting up representative management committees), the government strengthened its resolve to supervise the temple.   If this were ended, the institution might decline along with Sikh co-operation and loyalty that had served the British well "in the past and may be of the utmost consequence" in the future.[20]

The official response to the Kuka movement and the events surrounding the attempt of Duleep Singh to return to the Punjab suggest other dimensions of British political maneuvering.   The spread of the revivalist Namdhari sect had

---

16. *Khalsa Akhbar*, Feb 14, 1896, 7; July 29, 1898, 3-4. Fox presents the argument in detail although he exaggerates the importance of the British role in strengthening Sikh identity.

17. GI For Internal, July 1885, 154-58A. The Foreign/Secret Proceedings, 1849-1859, are filled with voluminous documentation on how the British evaluated each *jagir*. The degree of loss and its implications are surveyed briefly in Harjot Singh Oberoi, "Bhais, Babas and Gyanis," *Studies in History* 2, 33-62.

18. For Financial March 1880, 88-90B.

19. There is an excellent treatment in Kerr's articles on the Golden Temple.

20. Comment by C.A. McMahon, Commissioner of Amritsar, 1882, Kerr, "British Relations," pp. 148-49.

been watched carefully by official agents and the rudimentary British intelligence system. The reports on the implications of the speeches and activities of the founder, Guru Ram Singh, were garbled and often conflicting. Some informants, including prominent Sikhs of the period (1860's), felt that the aims of the Kukas primarily were religious—reform of marriage, a simple lifestyle and a new emphasis upon spiritual matters, including acts of extreme devotion and reverence. Others highlighted the authoritarian nature of the sect and its attempts to establish a rudimentary administrative system paralleling that of the British.[21]   The matter never was officially resolved because a few members of the sect launched an attack on butchers and, as a result, many were summarily executed and their guru exiled. A review of the documents suggests strongly that the local government did not see the Kukas either as a great danger to the Raj or as a disloyal element that might turn other Sikhs toward revolt.

The mounting claims of Maharaja Duleep Singh and his efforts to return to the Punjab in the 1880's, however, did seem to pose more of a threat to Sikh loyalty. After a life of excess and conversion to Christianity, Duleep Singh rediscovered the Sikh faith and reconverted in Aden, where the British intercepted him and forbade his visit to India.   Duleep Singh had some sympathizers among Punjabi Sikhs, who attempted without success to whip up support for claims about land and even his throne.   Initially the central and Punjab governments were concerned about Sikh reaction and devoted a large portion of their police and intelligence network to gathering information on public opinion and the machinations of his associates.   Duleep Singh's subsequent support for Russian plans to invade India and his public pronouncements suggested that the elaborate precautions were overdone. A few Sikhs aligning with the Maharaja either were prosecuted or driven underground, and in general the issue receded, much to the nervous delight of the British and the urban leadership of the Singh Sabhas.[22]

Sikhs were but one of many political variables that the British had to consider as they attempted to maintain control over a province undergoing rapid social, economic and religious change.   Except for outbreaks of communal rioting and occasional localized disturbance, the local authorities felt very much in command.   That changed during the early years of the twentieth century.   The challenge of trying to reconcile a particular set of administrative values with a political system increasingly complex and difficult to manage forced the Punjab government to make a painful and often turbulent transition from bureaucrat to politician.   Alliances with support groups became more overt and public, as

21. Basic documents in Nahar Singh, *Gooroo Ram Singh and the Kuka Sikhs*, vols. 1-2 (New Delhi: Amrit Publishers, 1965, 1966), and critical essays by Ganda Singh, "Was the Kuka (Namdharai) Movement a Rebellion against the British Government?" *Panjab Past and Present* 8 (1974), 325-45, and W.H. McLeod, "The Kukas: A Millenarian Sect of the Punjab," *Panjab Past and Present* 8 (1974), 164-87.

22. History of events and most of the documents in Ganda Singh, *Maharaja Duleep Singh: Correspondence* (Patiala: Punjabi University, 1977).   A thorough biography of Duleep Singh is Alexander and Anand, *Queen Victoria's Maharajah, Duleep Singh* (New York: Taplinger, 1980).

limits on executive authority endangered personal rule. Hard decisions had to be made about allocation of resources in an era when Punjabis were mobilizing to insure their growth and survival. To support one set of groups or interests through legislative or executive fiat of necessity involved the potential alienation of their opponents. Former assumptions about who was important politically, the old networks, did not seem to be as valid, nor were the earlier methods of control as effective. Warnings, informal pressure, and influence had to be buttressed with new ways of dealing with political turmoil.

The new institutions transferred to the Punjab were bearing fruit in a way that the British had not anticipated. New professional classes were emerging, with economic, caste and religious interests. Politics moved beyond petitions and deputations, to the streets and countryside. Punjabis, including Sikhs, competed openly in every arena of public life, and pursued a range of political strategies to wrest from the British the goals of politics—legitimacy and resources.

Early Patterns of Punjab Politics

The emergence of a Western-style political system in the Punjab reflected both traditional and modern elements. Local and regional magnates controlling land and access to shrines continued to be seen as legitimate leaders by those linked by marriage, caste or tribal affiliation and dependency/authority relationships. Their prominence was reinforced by patronage and close association with the new government. Also present was a tendency for Punjabis to divide along religious lines based on their historical experiences prior to 1849. Although social and religious cleavages existed within the Hindu, Sikh and Muslim communities, inter-communal differences were commonly understood and affected public life. Moreover, years of struggle, local conflict and competition for converts had left a sense of distrust and insecurity. In the Sikh case this was reinforced by a tradition of martyrdom and lost empire. When Punjab communities re-examined their histories and reassessed who they were and what they wanted in the environment accompanying British rule, their respective legacies became accentuated and influenced their political roles.[23]

The modern components of the political culture derived in large part from Punjabi interaction with the ideas and institutions introduced by Western rule. The structure of politics changed. The British became the source of decisions about resources and access to power. They introduced new arenas of competition that encouraged a different kind of thinking about politics, such as the need to form associations, the development of improved communications and in general the search for effective means of focusing opinion and mobilizing

---

23. Background on communal tendencies in Barrier, "The Punjab Government and Communal Politics," "The Arya Samaj and Congress Politics," *Journal of Asian Studies* 28 (1969), 339-56 and Kenneth Jones, *Arya Dharm: Hindu Consciousness in Nineteenth Century Punjab* (Berkeley: University of California Press, 1975). As Harjot Singh Oberoi notes in his chapter in this volume, lines between Hindus and Sikhs were not fixed; however, the differentiation between Hindu/Sikh and Muslim definitely had historical and cultural roots.

support.   Although the colonial power relied extensively on traditional or "natural" leaders and distrusted agitation among emerging urban *élites*, its very presence encouraged competition and new forms of political organization. Moreover, English ideas about politics, culture and religion helped shape the new milieu. Exposure to Western ideology and history widened the worldview of Punjabis, while missionaries, Christianity and notions about society and progress stimulated cultural and intellectual responses.

Old and new, thus, were mixed in the evolving political patterns. The Anjuman-i-Punjab, for example, had a membership and program that incorporated traditional elements as well as a more Western orientation. One of the first political and cultural associations in the province, the Anjuman sponsored debates, discussed literature and education, and initiated proposals and agitation aimed at influencing official policy.[24]   Similar blends of groups and interests could be found in Hindu, Sikh, and Muslim organizations begun in the 1860's and 1870's.   As in other regions of India, however, an increasing number of activities tended to center around the work of a relatively small range of Western-educated or middle-class groups residing primarily in urban areas. Although initially Bengalis played a premier role, by the 1880's a distinctly Punjabi *élite* had emerged, drawing heavily on the castes, with traditions of administration and religious leadership and open to innovation.   Hindus and Sikhs of Vaishya origin were joined by Muslims of similar persuasion involved in law, education and government. The "new men" adopted Western forms of organization and tactics.   Their concerns tended to be limited and local, generally involving matters of economic or religious significance. They communicated among themselves and with the British through accepted mechanisms such as petitions, correspondence and the print media.[25]

Besides exhibiting characteristics found in other parts of India, the political culture of the Punjab had a parochial style and imagery that often cut Punjabis off from other Indians and at the same time endangered local co-operation. Punjabi aggressiveness and a pride in being brave and militant had roots in a variety of sources, including folk literature and the contemporary customs of Rajput and Jat tribes.   Also important was the frontier orientation with value placed on physical strength and a tradition of conflict.   Too, Punjabis seemed to share a sense of being behind the rest of India—an insecurity fostered by their relatively late start in securing Western education and the perceived lack of sophistication among the professional classes. Public statements and correspondence contained allusions to being "rough and ready," crude, strong, and brave. Some imagery was positive—the sword arm, the "lions of the Punjab," the defender of India—and others, negative—crudeness, lack of culture, a poor command of English and awkwardness.   Also present was emphasis on

24. Jeffrey Perrill, "The Anjuman-i-Punjab as a Common Interest Association and Symbol of Social Change in 19th Century Punjab," *Panjab Past and Present* 16 (1983), 343-70.
25. Surveyed in the various publications of Jones and Barrier; on the Muslims, see Peter Churchill, "Muslim Societies of the Punjab, 1860-1890," *Panjab Past and Present* 8 (1974), 69-91.

practicality and common sense, possibly associated with the commercial traditions among the Vaishya traditions.[26]

Factionalism and belligerence were common in Punjab public life. Between 1870 and 1900 hundreds of organizations came to the province. In many, whether secular or religious, struggles and political maneuvering over control of resources and legitimacy were prevalent. Punjabis tended to go public with their disputes in a very personal and provocative fashion. Editorials, correspondence sections and news accounts often referred to controversy and contained personal attacks, slander and innuendo. The history of public institutions in the Punjab abounds with incidents of confrontation and fission. Outside the province, Punjabis had a reputation for bullish, aggressive and erratic behavior.[27]

There also was a shared view of how personal or institutional struggles related to British authority. Accepting the official view of the government as the *ma-bap*, the parental source of justice and all important patronage, Punjab politicians emphasized their own loyalty and attachment to the Raj while simultaneously tarring opponents with the label of "seditious" or "trouble-making." British allies supposedly would be protected and given aid, whereas opponents would be injured by government fiat. Whether involved in cow riots, control of local councils or public demonstrations, Punjabis hurled charges of being "political" (by which was meant "anti-British") and of "sedition" in newspapers, tracts and correspondence.[28] Although collecting such information regularly, the British police agencies tended to downplay its importance and only rarely investigated the charges prior to 1900. The accusations, nevertheless, became a recognized pattern, providing the government with information as well as buttressing its central role among competing factions. In fact, the Punjab government resisted pressure in 1914 to set up a special review of the Punjab press on the grounds that ample warning already was being given:

> The factional feeling so strongly prevalent in the Punjab affords further safeguard against any prolonged dissemination of objectionable books. The vigilance of the Vernacular Press and its contributors may be trusted to draw attention to anything from which one side can hope to make capital at the expense of its opponents.[29]

26. Barrier, "The Arya Samaj," and "Punjab Politics and the Press, 1880-1910," in Margaret Case and N.G. Barrier, eds., *Aspects of India* (Delhi: Manohar, 1986); works of Lajpat Rai including the autobiography edited by V.C. Joshi and the reports of speeches by Punjabis at provincial political conferences and annual meetings of the Indian National Congress, ca. 1986-1906, reported in the Lahore *Tribune*.

27. Correspondence among Congress leaders (Naoroji and Mehta Papers, National Archives of India) reflects disdain for Punjab tactics and leaders. On factions, Jones (1975), essays in Gustafson and Jones (1975). Newspapers are the best sources for following the conflicts, supplemented by the British "Selections from the Vernacular Press" (Home Public and Home Political files).

28. Tactics discussed in Jones, *Arya Dharm* and "*Ham Hindu Nahin*: Arya-Sikh Relations," *Journal of Asian Studies* 32 (1973), 457-75; Barrier, "Muslim Politics in the Punjab," *Panjab Past and Present* 5 (1971), 84-127. The *Civil and Military Gazette* (Lahore) served as a forum for charges of disloyalty and at times actively cooperated with the government in trying to dissociate "loyal" elements from potentially seditious activity. The most extreme example of the "disloyalty" tactic surfaced during the aftermath of the 1907 disturbances.

29. PG to GI, 13C, Feb. 25, 1914; GIPol March 1914, 108-16A.

Politics and religious revitalization frequently were inseparable in the last decades of the century. Some alliances across caste and religious lines did occur, either through the auspices of a central association (the Lahore Indian Association made sporadic efforts to get professionals to co-operate on class or secular issues) or in response to a particularly threatening situation such as racism or a tax bill. Also, divisions within communal organizations often were as heated as those between religious sects because of the struggle to gain control over institutions and to be seen as the legitimate authority. Nevertheless, most of the politics in the urban areas revolved around the tendency of many Western-educated Punjabis to identify with parochial (especially loosely defined religious) groups rather than with a common class. Muslims, Hindus and Sikhs formed new associations to defend perceived interests and to attack opponents. The various programs reinforced identification complete with visions of a heroic past, a dangerous present and a future that required extensive mobilization of community resources. Organizations adopted modern agitational techniques and developed new communication networks including tract societies and a range of newspapers and journals. Battles were fought in street debates, by competition for prominence in councils and educational facilities and, occasionally, through the use of force (especially over kine slaughter, processions and respect for shrines). Despite the riots, Punjabis shared the assumption that the only way to influence the government and thereby to assure patronage was through accolades of loyalty and constitutional means. As in other parts of India, local politicians carefully avoided confrontation or pressuring the British. Instead, they used resolutions, deputations and demonstrations of public opinion as the primary vehicles for influencing imperial politics.[30]

The institutions and some ideology of the Singh Sabha movement resembled other Punjabi organizations such as the Arya Samaj and Muslim *anjumans*. The associations re-evaluated their traditions in light of contemporary demands and served to focus the attention of co-religionists upon issues and strategies. Unlike the others, however, at least one group of Sikhs addressed a special problem, that of trying to define and then promulgate a sense of identity and separate consciousness at a time when most Sikhs felt comfortable with little if any distinction between the beliefs and practices of Hindus and Sikhism. The efforts of particular Singh Sabha leaders to represent a view of a distinct Sikh tradition marked a decisive turning point in the evolution of the community.

From the outset, two groups of Sikh activists disagreed over correct doctrine and strategy. The earliest Singh Sabha in Amritsar, under the guidance of the Maharaja of Faridkot and Baba Khem Singh Bedi, supported the expansion of education among Sikhs and tried to defend the community against proselytization by Muslims and Christians. The Amritsar group tended to be elitist and represented traditional leaders such as Bhais, *gianis* and aristocrats.

---

30. For political assumptions and tactics, see Barrier, "The Punjab Government and Communal Politics," and "Mass Politics and the Punjab Congress in the Pre-Gandhian Era," *Panjab Past and Present* 9 (1975), 349-59.

On the central issue of whether Sikhs were Hindus, Baba Khem Singh Bedi aligned with Udasis and *sahajdharis* and was comfortable with portraying Sikhs as a reformist element within greater Hinduism. Led by lower-caste Sikhs, such as Ditt Singh, and professional or middle-class Sikhs involved in education or journalism, such as Gurmukh Singh and Jawahar Singh, the Lahore Singh Sabha championed an aggressive assertion of Sikh separateness and attacked popular customs, such as respect for caste and Hindu influence in ceremonies and shrines. Each grouping mobilized supporters and developed communication links with other urban and eventually rural Sikhs. The controversies raged with great heat and destructiveness for two decades. Eventually, however, the Lahore program of strengthening the boundaries and self-identity of Sikhs became prominent as other Singh Sabhas began to associate actively with the "neo-Sikh" or Tat Khalsa perspective. In addition to defending Sikhs against Arya Samaj attacks, the Singh Sabhas built schools and a college, opened orphanages, established archives and historical societies and produced a flood of polemical and scholarly literature on Sikh tradition.

Almost a hundred Singh Sabhas or related societies were scattered across the Punjab by 1900. A few even had been established in other parts of India, Africa, South and Southeast Asia. Each tended to mirror the concerns and personalities of local leaders. The Ferozepur Singh Sabha, for example, championed female education and improved home life as a means or revitalizing Sikh society. In Tarn Taran, Mohan Singh Vaid's interest in health, the sanctity of shrines and tract literature colored the tone and emphasis of the town's Singh Sabha and, for that matter, the network of other organizations in the vicinity. Bhasaur and Babu Teja Singh quickly became associated with a militant defense of Sikh doctrine and radical social experiments.[31]

What held these disparate groups and institutions together was an evolving sense of separate Sikh identity and commitment to defeating foes within the community as well as those outside. The pockets of Sikh activism also were linked by a set of channels and contacts. In addition to close social relations among leaders, the improved forms of communication made possible an effective network for the dissemination of information and, as necessary, rapid mobilization of Sikhs. The postal service facilitated the exchange of messages, while the railroads opened up opportunities for frequent, face-to-face communication. Regional and local meetings now could be attended with ease, and large *diwans* visited by hundreds and then thousands became common. The regular circulation of *jathas* (organized groups with a particular mission, generally preaching and reform tasks) extended Singh Sabha influence into Sind,

---

31. Overviews of the Singh Sabha movement in: Harbans Singh, *Heritage*; Khushwant Singh, *History of the Sikhs*; Barrier, *The Sikhs and Their Literature* (Delhi: Manohar, 1970); Gurdarshan Singh, "Character and Impact of the Singh Sabha Movement on the History of the Panjab" (dissertation, Punjabi University, 1972). On the diversity of interests, see Harjot Singh Oberoi's paper and his earlier publications. The links between the Punjab Singh Sabhas and immigrant groups are treated in Barrier, "Sikh Migrants and Their Homeland," in Barrier and Dusenbery, eds., *Sikh Migration and the Diaspora* (Delhi: Manohar, 1988).

the border regions and the most isolated village.   Festivals and regular celebrations of *gurpurabs* also brought Sikhs together.   Most importantly, the Sikhs were linked by an expanding publications industry consisting of several tract societies and a variety of newspapers.   The *Khalsa Akhbar* played an especially critical role in sending a message of reform and revival to Sikhs scattered around the world.   The paper also served as a conduit for news and commentary as Sikh correspondents sent in reports and raised questions about theological and social issues.[32]

The Singh Sabha activities encompassed three related types of politics. The first involved struggles among Sikhs over legitimacy and doctrine.   The rivalries and acrimony characterizing the early days of the Singh Sabhas are well known.   Lawsuits, social ostracism, attacks in the press and by street preachers and even "excommunication" and manipulation of edicts from traditional centers of authority were among the tactics employed.   As in the case of the Arya Samaj, sometimes the internal battles spilled over into other arenas.   Charges of disloyalty toward the British were leveled by Ditt Singh and his associates against members of the Amritsar Singh Sabha because of their real or suspected support for Duleep Singh, for example.   In the early 1890's, the location of Khalsa College became a political issue that involved not only the two constellations of Singh Sabhas but also the Arya Samaj and the government.[33]

A second and increasingly important dimension of politics focused on defending Sikh interests against other Punjabis.   Initially a few Singh Sabha leaders had participated in Arya Samaj meetings and contributed to the Dayanand Anglo-Vedic College Fund.   This relationship was damaged in the mid-1880's, however, because of published attacks on the Gurus and the persistent Arya claim that Sikhs were Hindus.[34]   Antagonism increased when Arya Samajists initiated a *shuddhi* (reclamation or purifying) movement that aimed first at bringing alleged Hindu converts to Islam back into the fold and then extended to converting lower-caste Sikhs and having them undergo public removal of hair.   Sikhs countered with their own *shuddhi sabhas*.   The Lahore Singh Sabha tried desperately and with little success to change Sikh social attitudes so that Mazhbis and others would not be vulnerable to Arya promises of equality.   The tract and journalistic warfare was bitter and ferocious.   Again, a favorite tactic was trying to charge opponents with disloyalty.[35]

The Singh Sabha emphasis upon Sikh bravery and martyrdom had the potential of stirring up old antagonisms toward the Muslims, but the literature of

---

32.   See the detailed review in Barrier, "Sikh Migrants," and comments in Ian Kerr's chapter in this volume.   On the Punjab and Sikh press see Barrier, "Punjab Politics and the Press," and Barrier and Wallace, *The Punjab Press, 1880-1905* (East Lansing: Michigan State University South Asia Series, 1970).   Only Harjot Singh Oberoi has made extensive use of the rich material in the *Khalsa Akhbar*.

33.   Events documented in Ganda Singh, *Bhagat Lakshman Singh Autobiography* (Calcutta: Sikh Cultural Center, 1965).

34.   Jones, "*Ham Hindu Nahin.*"   This essay, in various translations and often mutilated form, has been published by Sikh associations as an anti-Arya-Samaj tract.

35.   A survey of internal disputes is in *Bhagat Lakshman Singh Autobiography*.

the period suggests that Muslims were not seen as a persistent danger. The most sustained conflicts with Muslims involved *jhatka* meat. Sikhs and Muslims went to court or appealed to the British in cases where local butchering arrangements offended either community. The issue became more heated after the early 1900's, as did Sikh reaction to Ahmadiya claims about the Gurus and the superiority of Islam. The other major arena of competition was the municipal committee. In Lahore, Amritsar and Jullundur Sikhs attempted to insure a presence on the local committees so as to protect their interests. The Amritsar body was considered most important because of the committee's responsibility for public works and supervision of shops around the Golden Temple.[36]

Struggles between factions and with non-Sikhs generally involved a third party, the British, who controlled institutions and resources judged critical for political survival. Except for occasional lapses, such as the Duleep Singh incident, the Singh Sabhas uniformly maintained close contacts with the rulers and adopted a loyalist position. The link between Sikhs and the British was reflected in the constitutions of the Sabhas and in the public statements and journals associated with the movement. Individual Sikhs participated in the activities of local Indian National Congress organizations or in cow protection societies, but, except for representing community interests in an acceptable, constitutional fashion, the Singh Sabhas avoided pressing their demands. For example, during the discussions of language and primary education sparked by the Hunter Education Commission in 1882, Singh Sabhas prepared memorials opposing Urdu and Hindi as the language of the schools and urged emphasis upon Punjabi writing in the Gurmukhi script. Those resolutions, and the evidence given by prominent Sikhs such as Baba Khem Singh Bedi and Attar Singh Bhadaur, however, were couched in very pro-British and loyal language.[37] While editorials and letters in Sikh journals did criticize decisions by scattered British officers and persistently asked for more patronage, on the whole the Sikhs tended to consider themselves as one of the major pillars of British rule. The prevalent mood was aptly captured in a *Khalsa Akhbar* editorial, "How the Panth has Made Progress."[38] Under Ranjit Singh no special attention was given to the Sikhs and therefore the community had suffered problems. The British had recognized the importance of Sikhs and made possible a resurgence. In fact, the editorial concluded, British rule had been foretold by Guru Tegh Bahadur.

---

36. Based on reports in *Khalsa Akhbar*, 1889-1895, and British documents on Punjab municipal committees, PG Mun (India Office Library).

37. *Report by the Panjab Provincial Committee, Education Commission* (Lahore, 1882). Especially useful are memorials from the Sat Sabha headed by Attar Singh Bhadaur (pp. 561-62), the Sikh National Association (562-63), the Lahore Singh Sabha (pp. 563-64) and testimony of Attar Singh and Khem Singh Bedi (pp. 141-44, 304-12). The evidence reflects a divergence of opinion, especially over Urdu versus Punjabi. The Singh Sabha argued that Sikhs were falling behind in part because of Education Department policy. It offered a complete program for revamping education and assisting the Sikhs. The Sikh National Association, headed by Khem Singh and Gurmukh Singh, prepared a "Hunter's Singh Sabha Prize" to be given to the first female graduate of Punjab University who completed a degree in Punjabi.

38. *Khalsa Akhbar*, April 21, 1899.

The Sikh view of imperial rule was not unlike that of other Punjabis, except in two respects. First, those who claimed to represent the community (both the aristocrats and middle class leading the Singh Sabhas) appreciated that Sikhs were permanently a minority and therefore needed either alliances with non-Sikhs to bolster their influence or firm patronage from the British. The former strategy seemed impossible because of Arya militancy and ongoing attempts to delineate boundaries with Hindus. The Punjab government offered a more appealing avenue for strengthening Sikhs in education and employment. Moreover, close connection with the army buttressed loyalty. Sikh exploits of bravery such as occurred at Saragarhi in 1898 were celebrated with tracts and memorials. Anniversaries became occasions for public exchanges of best wishes between the Sikhs and the British.[39] The result? A persistent record of support for the British combined with pride in military service and distinction to produce an inflated view of Sikh importance and a concomitant over-reliance on imperial goodwill and rewards.

By the end of the nineteenth century Sikhs stood at an important juncture. Political conditions were changing swiftly. The structure and policies of the British impinged more directly upon community interests. In the legal arena, for example, Sikhs found themselves involved in court cases that touched on central issues such as control of gurdwaras, rituals, legitimacy of marriage arrangements and even the definition of "Who is a Sikh?" The latter question was dramatically raised in the judicial proceedings about Dyal Singh Majithia's will.[40] Almost simultaneously Sikhs began to question whether the traditional tactics of representing needs and relying upon British aid would suffice as the access to resources came to depend more on competition and elections. Numbers counted in such a world, and the British could not lean too far in making the Sikhs a priority. The tracts and journals suggest an awareness that Sikhs were falling behind and faced great danger from within and without.

The Chief Khalsa Diwan and Punjab Politics

In November of 1901 the Amritsar Khalsa Diwan convened a meeting of prominent Sikhs to discuss creating a central body that would co-ordinate and lead the Singh Sabhas. Officially inaugurated a year later, the Chief Khalsa Diwan began with twenty-nine affiliated Sabhas and by 1920 had over a hundred member institutions. During that time the C.K.D. was involved in a range of activities and became accepted as a major spokesman for Sikhs.[41]

---

39. Annual celebrations detailed in *Khalsa Advocate* and *Khalsa Samachar*. Special scholarships honored the Saragarhi "martyrs."

40. Background is in *Bhagat Lakshman Singh Autobiography*; see alo Teja Singh, *The Gurdwara Reform Movement and the Sikh Awakening* (Jullundur: Desh Sewak Book Company, 1922).

41. Surveys of the work of the C.K.D. are found in the following: Gurdarshan Singh Dhillon, "Character and Impact of the Singh Sabha Movement" (Ph.D. dissertation, Punjabi University, Patiala, 1972); Khushwant Singh, *History of the Sikhs*; Surjit Singh Narang, "Chief Khalsa Diwan," in Wallace, *Political Dynamics*, pp. 67-81; "Chief Khalsa Diwan," *Journal of Sikh Studies* 12

The Diwan had a formal constitution and a complex set of committees and procedures for going about its business.   The aims included promoting the welfare of the Khalsa Panth, propagating the teaching of *gurbani*, disseminating information on tradition and authentic sources and safeguarding the political rights of Sikhs.   The C.K.D. theoretically incorporated the perspectives and decisions of five major committees.   A general committee consisted of representatives from member institutions, members delegated by the *takhats* and the princely states and individuals who met fiscal and service criteria.   That committee elected an executive committee that met monthly and conducted most of the regular business, referring critical matters to the broader body.   The other three committees dealt with finances, advice (legal, administrative, religious) and life-members.

Although the rules set the boundaries and structures of C.K.D. operations, informal networks and procedures kept the association functioning.   Several leaders continued from the most active Singh Sabhas, such as Vir Singh, Mohan Singh Vaid, Takht Singh and Teja Singh Bhasaur, among others.   Sundar Singh Majithia had major input into the C.K.D., as he did with local journals and the Khalsa College.   The pressures of meeting local commitments and the distance of travel, however, meant that frequently there was a revolving group at the helm of the C.K.D., albeit with shared perspectives and personal connections.   The membership drew from the more aristocratic elements of Singh Sabhas as well as from the new professional classes.   In 1913, for example, almost half of the twenty members attending the General Committee session had B.A.'s, M.A.'s, or legal degrees.[42]

Trying to pinpoint C.K.D. decisions on certain issues is difficult because of the consultative system that evolved.   Matters frequently were referred to subcommittees, which had a mixed record of reporting back and making specific recommendations.   In general, the C.K.D. solicited public input on issues and spent considerable time discussing letters and differing opinions.   It frequently circulated documents to Singh Sabhas or published them in journals for public comment.   For example, the Diwan sent out a questionnaire about opening the Guru Granth Sahib in public meetings and decided on the basis of the replies (over 1,600) that the correct approach was to open the Granth in a room associated with the meeting but not in the public meeting hall.[43]   The finance committee, on the other hand, ran a tight operation.   Accountability was at the heart of all C.K.D. programs.

(1985), 97-108; Kapur, *Sikh Separatism*.   The British view is in Petrie's Criminal Investigation Department note.

42. Most of the reviews of the C.K.D. suggest that the organization was elitist, operated in a vacuum and represented the interests of an upper class personally tied to the British.   The C.K.D. documents and the range of activities in which C.K.D. proponents were involved suggest otherwise.   Several key Akali leaders such as Kharak Singh and Master Tara Singh participated actively in the early stages of the Diwan.   As Harjot Singh Oberoi notes, there was evolving in the Sikh community a new cultural *élite* not necessarily representing only one class or small segment of society.

43. C.K.D. minutes (available in mss. in Amritsar and in my collection), Aug. 5, 1915.

The C.K.D.'s role in politics should be considered within the context of its multi-faceted, expanding program. Of key importance was the mobilizing of fiscal and personal resources. Despite concern with matters spiritual, the practicality of the C.K.D. came out most clearly in its handling of finances. Too many donations were being wasted, according to the Diwan, and therefore regular audits of public enterprises should be conducted and the results publicized. In addition to publishing its own accounts, which after a few years amounted to thousands of rupees when the expanding network of C.K.D. institutions was included, the Diwan emphasized that all Singh Sabhas should circulate their reports. If such annual publication proved too expensive, the other options included summary statements in panthic newspapers as well as in the *Masik Pattar* (a C.K.D. newsletter with reports and summaries of Singh Sabha ventures).[44]

Human resources received equal, if not more, attention. The C.K.D. organized and paid for the circulation of *jathas* that travelled across India. Some were involved in preaching, in addition to the regular C.K.D. *updeshaks*, but others worked with *sahajdharis*, confronted the Arya Samaj or ministered to Sikhs. As in the case of many of its activities, these were not innovations, but the Diwan regularized the outreach program and provided both finances and publicity. Also related was sustained mobilization of Sikhs in local and regional meetings. The Diwan helped establish an annual schedule of *diwans* and urged that panthic disputes be taken up in these meetings and resolved constitutionally. The results soon became apparent. In 1906, for example, the Lahore district meetings attracted approximately 8,000 participants; one at Hazara, 5,000; the Bhasaur week-long discussions over 1,800; and a three-day session at Amritsar, at least 4,000 Sikhs.[45]

The C.K.D. also worked hard to strengthen its relationship with Sikh princes, who in the past had made extensive contributions to educational and humanitarian institutions.   Simultaneously, Diwan members attempted to monitor the publishing of authentic tracts and commentaries, judged to be essential elements in the expansion of panthic resources.[46]

Mobilizing resources involved strengthening communications among Sikhs. Building on the legacy of the earlier Singh Sabhas, the C.K.D. utilized two newspapers—the *Khalsa Samachar* in Gurmukhi and the English-language *Khalsa Advocate*—to disseminate reports and spark public awareness. The influence of the papers far exceeded the estimated circulation of around 4,000. Stories were read aloud in villages, and copies circulated among students and the

---

44. Circulation and implications are treated in Barrier, "Sikh Migration."
45. Reports in *Khalsa Samachar*, Feb.-April and July-Nov., 1906. Background on the *diwans* is in Barrier, "Sikh Migration."
46. *Khalsa Samachar*, Feb. 25, 1909, p. 7; also eight resolutions on the princes passed between 1907 and 1918. On the issue of published documents, see *Khalsa Samachar*, Feb. 28, 1906, pp. 10-11; May 2, 1906, pp. 3-4. One cause for concern was the reprinting of a controversial book by Sardha Ram Philauri, sometimes used as a text in Punjab University, Lahore, during the late nineteenth century.

army. Both also reached audiences in England, Africa, Southeast and East Asia, and North America. The two major newspapers, along with smaller ones sponsored by affiliated organizations, contained news about Singh Sabhas, editorials on political and religious issues, and correspondence columns. Designated correspondents from many of the Singh Sabhas sent in reports and resolutions on contemporary problems.[47] The journals served as scorecards as had the earlier *Khalsa Akhbar*, publicizing good deeds, donations and the mounting record of Sikhs who were following the Singh Sabha approach to ritual and rites of passage.[48] The Khalsa Tract Society was put on more firm financial footing and K.T.S. booklets, along with those from new tract societies in Peshawar and Tarn Taran, circulated broadly.

In addition, the personal and institutional ties among Sikhs were expanded. Even before the C.K.D., the location and variety of activities of Singh Sabhas suggest that the movement had spread well beyond the cities and towns into the countryside. The annual *diwans* both generated such contacts and mirrored the success of the efforts. The creation of Sikh schools in outlying areas further expanded the rural-urban network. Although more research is necessary to understand the breadth and significance of such developments, they were occurring and added a new dimension to the potential impact of the Singh Sabhas. Similarly, the institutionalization of the *updeshak* or missionary efforts by the C.K.D. augmented the sporadic efforts of the earlier period. The Diwan helped create schools for preachers, *ragis* and *granthis* and then systematically scheduled their activities. As was typical of C.K.D. priorities, these specialists were expected to submit detailed reports, which in turn were publicized to demonstrate the effectiveness of Sikh service and outreach. In reading the newspaper accounts of Singh Sabha and C.K.D. initiatives, one is struck by the rapid transmission of information and appeals, *benati*, among Sikhs scattered across the world. Hong Kong, East African and Canadian Singh Sabhas, for example, often responded to events and appeals within a few weeks of announcements in Punjab papers. The appeals also stimulated a substantial contribution network that tied specific Singh Sabhas to favorite charities, programs or the C.K.D. itself.[49]

Besides initiating contacts and helping to form more Singh Sabhas, the Diwan built orphanages and hospitals. Sikhs had to take care of their own, particularly in situations where Arya Samajists or Christian missionaries already had social-service agencies in place. As mentioned earlier, the Diwan also created or provided leadership for existing *updeshak* schools such as the one headed by Bhai Lal Singh at Gharjakh.

---

47. *Khalsa Advocate*, Feb. 22, 1905, p. 3.
48. Communication system in Barrier, "Punjab Politics and the Press," and "Sikh Migrants."
49. For example, extensive reports in *Khalsa Samachar* (Jan. 2, 1913) about villages and towns where Sikh ceremonies were conducted, involving birth, marriage and death; such reports appeared more frequently in the 1905-1914 period but seem to have begun declining in number during the war. Oberoi in this volume also discusses the rituals and reporting system prior to 1900.

Two new institutions require special mention. Sikhs had been discussing the formation of an educational conference since at least 1903,[50] and in 1908 the first annual Sikh Educational Conference was held. The conference served several functions. The meetings brought together thousands of Sikhs who discussed educational issues along with related problems such as the spread of Punjabi and government patronage. Resolutions and speeches often dealt with broader themes (history, tradition, the need for change, new approaches to the family). The publicity reached beyond the immediate audience, and the funds raised enriched not only the programs of the Singh Sabha sponsoring the particular session but other C.K.D. and local projects. The conference became virtually a ritual, a symbolic gathering of Sikhs who shared a common commitment and view of the world. It also further legitimized the leadership of the C.K.D.[51]

The other notable offshoot of the C.K.D. was the Khalsa Biradari and associated efforts to address the issue of untouchability within the Panth. Formed in 1908 after extensive discussions among Sikh leaders, the Biradari attempted to soften and ultimately eliminate Sikh negative attitudes toward the lowest castes such as Mazhbis, Rahtias and Ramdasis. Treatment of these groups had received publicity and a demand for action from the Lahore Singh Sabha and its affiliates since the 1880's. There had been a few dramatic episodes of conversions, marriages and public acceptance, but the C.K.D. highlighted awareness of the inconsistencies between the doctrine of Sikh equality and existing social practice. Much impetus came from continuing Arya Samaj efforts to claim those at the bottom of the Sikh social scale. The Diwan sent out teams, attempted conciliation in explosive situations and had some success in improving social contacts and admission to gurdwaras. As the *Khalsa Samachar* noted,[52] if the outcastes were accepted and given *amrit*, 50,000 new Sikhs would be added and the resources of the community expanded. The more conservative elements did not agree. The C.K.D. and the Educational Conference paid a price in terms of attacks and ostracism. When the Conference met in Amritsar (1910), for example, officials in the Darbar Sahib refused admission to a procession of delegates because of their stand on free access to Sikh shrines.[53]

Mobilizing resources, improving communications, and institution-building opened up new areas of competition and conflict among Sikhs. The fourth C.K.D. concern, therefore, was overcoming factionalism and finding ways to conciliate and unify the community. In a strong and perceptive editorial the

50. *Khalsa Samachar*, March 16, 1903, pp. 8-9.
51. C.K.D. educational efforts reviewed in Narotam Singh, "Chief Khalsa Diwan," *Journal of Sikh Studies* 8 (1981), 118-29; and Gurdarshan Singh, "Character and Impact."
52. *Khalsa Samachar*, Oct. 12, 1904, pp. 4-5.
53. *Khalsa Advocate*, Feb. 18, 1910, p. 7. Also *Khalsa Samachar* and C.K.D. reports in the spring of 1910. On Majha/Doaba conflict, *Khalsa Samachar*, Aug. 28, 1913, pp. 5-6, and C.K.D. proceedings, Aug. 19, 1917.

Khalsa Samachar commented on "our self-murdering policy."[54] Sikhs were their own worst enemies. Feuds threatened the life of Singh Sabhas and the C.K.D. and only if understandings could be reached and disputes cease would Sikhism survive. The Diwan devoted considerable energy to resolving conflicts.

The Diwan used its networks and influence to promulgate a distinct view of Sikhism. Sikhism was a separate religion with its own rituals, historical traditions and sense of identity. The leaders of the Diwan and Singh Sabhas generally pursued policies that would further delineate Sikh boundaries and remove any lingering Hindu influence. Their pressure and negotiations paved the way for the removal of idols from the Golden Temple in 1905 and, with their support, individual Singh Sabhas moved to criticize Hindu rituals and accretions in local shrines. Gurdwaras belonged to the Panth, the C.K.D. argued, and the drive to reclaim that ownership and the removal of Hindu elements accelerated. The successful fight to legalize *anand* marriage was another landmark. For the first time, literally hundreds of thousands of Sikhs were mobilized in meetings and petition drives. Also for the first time, a distinct Sikh marriage ceremony devoid of Hindu and Brahmanic influence was legitimized by the legislature and British authority. The C.K.D. went on to publicize other rituals seen as distinctly Sikh through the use of tracts, historical commentaries and proclamations.[55]

It would be misleading, however, to claim that the Singh Sabhas and C.K.D. uniformly believed that the only "true Sikhs" were *keshdhari* and *amritdhari* and that others such as *sahajdharis* were in fact Hindu.[56] Such a vision was too limited and intolerant in light of the diversity of those who looked upon themselves as Sikhs. *Sahajdharis* were considered part of the larger Sikh community as long as they worshiped in gurdwaras and saw Sikhism as separate from Hinduism. This was good political strategy at a time when numbers counted (although later, particularly after 1920, the issue took another turn), but it also made sense in terms of the accommodative approach the Diwan pursued in trying to maximize the personal and fiscal resources available for education and other projects.

The tendency of the C.K.D. to bridge such differences came out repeatedly in its proceedings. Levels of participation were designated so that while only baptized Sikhs served on committees, *sahajdharis* would give advice and assist in the organization.[57] Similarly, the Diwan issued a resolution that *sahajdharis* could play a full role in gurdwara services and participate in all respects

---

54. *Khalsa Samachar*, Aug. 16, 1905, pp. 3-5.
55. *Anand* marriage issues are reviewed in H.S. Oberoi's chapter in this volume; also see K.S. Talwar, "The Anand Marriage Act," *Panjab Past and Present* 2 (1968), 411-20.
56. Kapur, Fox and contemporary observers such as Ruchi Ram Sahni present this image, as do other recent studies by Gurdarshan Singh and Surjit Singh Narang. There is much confusion over "class" and "interests" in the existing secondary literature that needs to be clarified by careful study of the documents.
57. C.K.D. proceedings, 1903-1906. Committees were instructed to seek the advice and discuss issues with prominent *sahajdharis*.

including reading the Guru Granth Sahib in meetings.[58]   To avoid misunderstanding, the official paper of the C.K.D., the *Khalsa Advocate*, said that while many Sikhs identified with the Khalsa, *sahajdharis* were on the path of religious searching and must be kept within the Panth and incorporated completely.[59]

The refusal to make dogmatic statements and adopt a harshly restrictive view of membership and ritual did little to reconcile Sikhs who still continued to insist that Sikhism and Hinduism were synonymous. These Sikhs challenged the Diwan in the press, at meetings or by associating openly with Hindu organizations. The best-known example was the agreement of Gurbaksh Singh Bedi (son of Khem Singh Bedi) to serve as president of the Punjab Hindu Conference. On the basis of the letters sent to the C.K.D., the newspaper accounts and the correspondence from Singh Sabhas across the world, however, it appears that most Sikhs at least tacitly approved of the middle-of-the-road approach of the Diwan. The major exceptions were individuals and organizations who adopted a narrow, literal interpretation of Sikh tradition. The C.K.D. struggled to keep them within the organization.[60]

During its first decade the C.K.D. had remarkable success in fostering Sikh identity and strengthening institutions of the community. The C.K.D. stood at the center of an international network of Sikh organizations. Sikh rituals and publications were widespread and female education, care for orphans and training of students and religious specialists had increased dramatically. Divisions remained among Sikhs, but rival associations rose and fell. Some represented regional interests or rival groups. Others like the Majha Khalsa Diwan preferred to pursue their own activities, particularly gurdwara reform and *prachar*, but over time worked out co-operative arrangements and became part of the C.K.D. network.[61]

Much of the C.K.D.'s efforts were defensive. Attacks from the Arya Samaj persisted. The heightened sensitivity to external attack and the cry of "Sikhism is in danger" complicated the Diwan's strategy of winning patronage and benefits from the government while at the same time maintaining the loyal image of the community. The 1907 disturbances illustrated its problem. Several Singh Sabhas and *diwans* criticized British policies toward the canal colonies and revenue rates. The *Khalsa Advocate* joined in by congratulating the cultivators who by "constitutional agitation" had brought the government to see the folly of its projected water-rate increases.[62] The Amritsar Singh Sabha, on the other hand, held an earlier meeting that urged Sikhs to be cautious. Some

---

58. C.K.D. proceedings, Oct. 1, 1916.
59. *Khalsa Advocate*, July 15, 1904.
60. Background on Teja Singh and his fundamentalist program is in Harbans Singh, "The Bakapur Diwan and Babu Teja Singh Bhasaur," *Panjab Past and Present* 9 (1975), 322-32; Barrier, *The Sikhs*, surveys the issues and publications relating to Teja Singh's view of Sikhism.
61. Discussed in *Dukh Niwaran*, 1906-08, and Munsha Singh Dukhi's biography of Mohan Singh Vaid. The Diwan was replaced by a C.K.D. subcommittee on Majha *prachar*.
62. *Khalsa Advocate*, May 4, 1907, p. 3.

speakers at rural protests allegedly had claimed that Sikhs were now disloyal, particularly because of recent developments in Khalsa College. The Sabha resolved that such disagreements should not be misinterpreted. The enemies of Sikhism were trying to drive a wedge between Sikhs and the British.[63] Similarly, the *Khalsa Samachar* warned that Ajit Singh, a leading agitator, had claimed to represent all Sikhs and was even talking about Sikh mutiny. Actually, the paper claimed, Ajit Singh was an Arya Samajist who knew that every "real" Sikh was pro-British.[64] The unexpected repression in May shook the Sikh public, and they along with Hindus and Arya Samajists began a series of "loyalty" deputations to meet with the British. The C.K.D. was involved in several such activities and helped orchestrate Singh Sabha meetings that applauded British gestures of conciliation and warned Sikhs to avoid being seen as seditious.[65]

The 1907 events illustrate the frustrations among Sikhs in different localities and the problem of maintaining a united political stance. In addition to scattered episodes, the C.K.D. found itself locked in a spiral of conflict with the British over basic and volatile issues. One of the earliest involved Khalsa College. Between 1902 and 1907, the local authorities had become concerned about the internal administration of the Sikh institution. After a series of warnings and a student demonstration in favor of the Congress, the government struck. The issue was whether an unpaid Sikh engineer would be replaced by a paid British professional. Unwise and derogatory comments were made about the competency and sacrifice of the Sikh which, when published, sparked protest meetings across the Punjab. The British proceeded to take over the college by forcing on its administrators a new constitution that gave control to government officials and their allies.[66] The Diwan passed a resolution on the situation, but to no avail. Reluctant to lead an agitation against the government, especially in light of the unrest and charges floating around, the managing committee expressed its regrets and asked that Sikh public opinion be considered. At a general meeting two days later, Sikhs fought among themselves about strategy, and finally the matter was buried on the pretext of securing more information.[67]

The next sustained encounter with the Raj proved more favorable. Pressure had been growing to insure the legitimacy of a distinctly Sikh marriage (*anand*) devoid of all Hindu or Brahmanic influence. The C.K.D. had encouraged the simple marriage ceremony and given "panthic sanction" to advocates of *anand*.[68] During the months while the bill was being discussed in

---

63. *Khalsa Samachar*, April 3, 1907, pp. 1-2.
64. *Khalsa Samachar*, April 10, 1907, pp. 3-5.
65. Background on deputations and Sikh meetings in the *Civil and Military Gazette, Khalsa Advocate, Khalsa Samachar*, June-Aug., 1907.
66. Ganda Singh, *Khalsa College*. Resolutions on the College came from East Africa, Vancouver and Hong Kong, as well as from other Singh Sabhas in the Punjab.
67. C.K.D. proceedings, April 1907. Sundar Singh Majithia continued to work within the new structure but finally resigned four years later.
68. C.K.D. proceedings, Jan. 26, Oct. 18, 1908. Also see comments in *Khalsa Samachar*, Jan 6, 1909, p. 7.

the Governor General's Legislative Council, the Diwan mobilized the largest mass demonstrations ever seen in the Punjab. Regiments, Singh Sabhas outside India, large meetings in most districts—all produced petitions and memorials and thereby validated the C.K.D. claim that Sikhs as a community supported the measure. The Indian government had been lukewarm because of the Hindu objections, but the show of Sikh unity carried the day.[69] In a situation where the British had little or no vested interest the C.K.D. demonstrated its ability to influence decision-making. The passage of the bill evoked the usual Sikh response, cheers for the C.K.D. leadership and bursts of emotional rhetoric about the impartiality and benefits of British rule.

In several other areas, however, the Sikhs and the C.K.D. had a mixed record of gaining British support. The decennial census became a focus for agitation. The publication of the 1901 census stirred discussion about sects within Sikhism and calls for better co-ordination. Arya Samajists and Christians were growing in number, while Sikhs seemed to be in decline. Lower-caste and *sahajdhari* Sikhs were "dangling" between Sikhism and Hinduism and would topple in either direction unless Sikhs worked hard on social reform.[70] The government was pressured to change the forms and rules that in 1901 had meant that generally only *keshdharis* were returned as Sikhs. Instead, the Diwan asked that individuals might designate their religious affiliation without regard for symbols or specific doctrines. The British probably did not agree with the claim that "the very existence of the Sikhs is now in the balance." But the difficulties of trying to make administrative decisions in a heated census-taking situation and at least a nod toward the argument of "continued Sikh loyalty" led to the desired shifts. The size of the Sikh population and its literacy rate subsequently moved upward, reflecting altered census categories as well as the fruits of C.K.D. efforts in education and proselytization.[71] Other successes included having the *gurpurabs* placed upon the official calendar (first in the Punjab and later extended to all of India) and the gradual legitimization of Punjabi within educational circles, the railway system, and in the mails.[72] With regard to a perennial issue for Sikhs, the right to wear a turban in particular professional settings, the Diwan's resolutions on wearing the "national headdress" helped pave the way for turbans in the Indian Medical Service and in the London Inns of Law.[73]

Other initiatives were less successful. The C.K.D. methodically kept score of special honors, appointments and elections. Increasingly aware of their vulnerability as a permanent minority, Sikhs pressed for more patronage and

---

69. For background on the bill and agitation, see Talwar, "Anand"; also Gurdarshan Singh Dhillon, dissertation.
70. *Khalsa Samachar*, April 26, 1905, pp. 4-5. Also *Khalsa Advocate*, May 20, 1905, p. 2.
71. *Khalsa Advocate*, Nov. 25, 1910, p. 5. Discussions of census data are in Fox and Kapur.
72. *Khalsa Samachar*, Sept. 21, 1904, p. 7; resolutions, C.K.D. proceedings, 1904-08 (resolution on holidays, Oct. 18, 1903). Discussed extensively in GI Home Public 1903-05.
73. Resolutions and discussion of Educational Conference in *Khalsa Samachar* and *Khalsa Advocate*, April 1908.

weightage on the basis of a record of loyalty and contributions to the army and economy.   C.K.D. resolutions and editorials in its two papers continually commented on specific events and measured Sikh results against those of others. Out of 146 Extra Assistant Commissioners, for example, there were only 13 Sikhs; Sikhs were inadequately represented on the Amritsar Municipal Committee; no Sikhs were members of the Punjab University Syndicate.[74] One editorial might cheer the naming of three Sikh Rai Bahadurs as an indication of British happiness with the community[75] and a few months later note pessimistically that all three imperial honors were awarded to Muslims. What about the loyal Sikhs?[76] Much of the rhetoric, of course, was designed to pressure and keep Sikh interests in the limelight, but underneath the reporting and resolutions was a growing sense of being perpetually behind. The initial discussions of proposed legislative reforms in 1907 sparked calls for special protection and a number of seats equal to those available to Muslims. After all, it was argued, Sikhs had formerly ruled the Punjab and now were the loyal mainstays of British rule.[77] Comparisons with Muslims became more frequent, and the British were called upon to give Sikhs special help in conflict situations. In an incident over the burning of a gurdwara in Udarwal, for example, accused Muslims were found not guilty. Ignoring the judicial process, Sikhs charged the British with turning their back on allies.[78] Jhatka shops kept appearing as an issue, and the C.K.D. sent deputations to the British to preserve Sikh rights.[79]

The Singh Sabhas and the Diwan already were involved in trying to win British assistance in the struggle over control of gurdwaras. Discomfort over Hindu practices and mismanagement had led the Lahore Singh Sabha much earlier to challenge the rights of managers and local *granthis*. From 1895 onward, for example, *jathas* and annual *diwans* were present at Nankana in a sustained attempt to check misuse of funds and improve facilities. Confrontations and court cases were common at Babe-di-Ber in Sialkot. British officers gave limited assistance in Sialkot and also in Peshawar, where a *mahant* had sold considerable gurdwara property, but there were limits to executive intervention. For all practical purposes, the government had legalized the rights of the *mahants* and now felt obliged to honor their commitments.[80] The campaign to change practices in the Golden Temple had begun back in 1895 when objections were raised to idols and a picture showing Guru Gobind Singh worshiping Durga.[81]   The C.K.D. helped focus issues and through negotiations and

74. *Khalsa Samachar*, Feb. 22, 1905, p. 7.
75. *Khalsa Samachar*, July 2, 1908, p. 1.
76. *Khalsa Samachar*, Jan. 29, 1909, p. 3.
77. *Khalsa Samachar*, Sept. 18, Oct. 2, 1907, editorials.
78. *Khalsa Samachar*, Feb. 5, 1908, p. 3.
79. *Khalsa Samachar*, Feb. 5, 1908, p. 5. Also the *Khalsa Samachar* lobbied for special refreshment rooms in railroad stations where appropriate refreshments would be served and smoking forbidden. Conflict with Muslims increased, surveyed in Sarfraz Khwaja, *Sikhs of the Punjab* (Islamabad: Modern Book Depot, 1985).
80. Discussed in Teja Singh, *Gurdwara Reform*, pp. 84-136.
81. *Khalsa Akhbar*, Feb. 12, 1897, p. 5.

launching a province-wide agitation had partial success in Amritsar. Idols were removed in 1905 and almost simultaneously in Tarn Taran and occasionally a *pujari* would be forced to resign because of a haircut or to ask pardon for a misdemeanor.[82]   On the basic issue of selection of officials, day-to-day administration and accountability to the community, however, the Tat Khalsa Sikhs achieved little. Singh Sabhas might send in resolutions calling for the C.K.D. to name managers and play a key role in Golden Temple matters, but the British were determined to keep tight reins on the central Sikh institution.

The C.K.D. continued to deal with each new political problem by using the strategies that had met with success in the past—public meetings, resolutions, demonstrations, use of journals and tracts to mobilize support and personal or official negotiations with the British. Its leaders saw themselves in a broker role, trying to mediate differences and facilitate communication. The firing of Sikh policemen, for example, would stimulate an investigation and proposals to work out a compromise acceptable to officials and Sikhs alike.[83]   The increased political awareness of a range of Sikh organizations and groups, however, put mounting pressure on C.K.D. leadership to achieve more and at a faster pace. Their authority also tended to be questioned from another direction. Government policy toward Sikhs and the C.K.D. in particular was shifting. Responding to the growing tendency for Sikhs to press their demands aggressively, some officers were hostile toward the Tat Khalsa. In 1909, for example, the District Commissioner of Amritsar decided that Singh Sabha members could not be managers or *granthis* at the Golden Temple. The C.K.D. and the Sikh press perceived this as official insensitivity and a gross interference in Sikh domestic affairs.[84]   Had they known the depth of distrust within the Criminal Investigation Department (C.I.D.) and Punjab police, they would have been far more upset.

The 1907 disturbances had shaken the Punjab government. One result was a tendency to see conspiracy and danger behind any sustained public activity. The C.I.D. daily and weekly reports on the Punjab are filled with tales and warning. Much of the information is skewed, inaccurate and worthless, but the British relied on informants and an intelligence system and often acted upon misconceptions. Their interpretation of the Sikh revival and the C.K.D. is a case in point. In a much-quoted evaluation of Sikh politics, Petrie blends fact, fiction and conjecture into a web of conspiracy.[85]   Scattered speeches and tract material are laced together to suggest a Tat Khalsa threat to the government. Noting the similarity in organization and zeal between the Arya Samaj and the Chief Khalsa

---

82. Stories in *Khalsa Samachar* and *Khalsa Advocate*, Oct. 1917. Also *Khalsa Samachar*, Feb. 11, 1909, p. 2. Background on administration and reforms in Harjinder Singh Dilgeer, *The Akal Takht* (Amritsar: Punjabi Book Company, 1980); essays in Fauja Singh, *The City of Amritsar* (New Delhi: Oriental, 1978); Madanjit Kaur, *The Golden Temple, Past and Present* (Amritsar: Guru Nanak Dev University, 1983).
83. *Khalsa Advocate*, Dec. 16, 1910, pp. 3-4.
84. *Khalsa Samachar*, Aug. 26, 1909, p. 2.
85. Petrie (1911). The most recent studies rely heavily on the Petrie account for details and interpretation.

Diwan, he even suggests that they may combine in an anti-British campaign. With reference to Khalsa College, he claims that several on the managing committee are Aryas and that the Samaj has infiltrated the Sikh movement. Since Teja Singh was in London at a time when seditious pamphlets were sent to Punjab and had close relations with the C.K.D., that organization must have been involved with the tracts. A similar approach is found in the weekly C.I.D. reports on Sikhs. Every meeting received attention and even though most obviously were religious in nature lists of those attending and commentary are extensive. Any large meeting, such as the *diwan* held by the Lahore Singh Sabha in October, 1910, automatically became suspect.[86] The British did have information and some insight into the various factions among Sikhs, but the underlying theme was that of a once loyal community slipping into sedition. The result? The Sikhs were not to be trusted, and army units should be quarantined from Tat Khalsa influence. Since the British had helped legitimize the Singh Sabha view of Sikhism, that proved very difficult. One solution was to limit recruitment of Sikhs, particularly for foreign service. According to the Army Department, Jat Sikhs had become arrogant because of their desirability for police and military positions outside India and now had an "exaggerated idea of their own superiority."[87] The overall strategy was to avoid showing any sign of weakness toward the Sikhs and certainly not to meet their excessive demands.

Despite the reticence of both parties, several sets of events in 1913 and 1914 brought the British and C.K.D. into a close working relationship. In May 1913, the British tore down a small wall bordering the gurdwara at Rikabganj in Delhi. Earlier the government had made arrangements to acquire the border area by purchasing the land from the *mahant* and setting up a charitable trust. The purpose of the deed was to straighten the road leading to the new Viceregal palace and at the same time to improve the beauty of the area.[88] Within a few weeks news of the incident reached the Punjab and there was a massive outcry. A *rais* from Lyallpur, Harchand Singh, visited Delhi and, outraged by what he saw, helped organize protests against the British. The government attempted to misguide the Sikhs about the nature of the damage and, when that failed, fell back on the traditional tactic of securing support from within the Sikh community. Upset by the uncontrollable rage and challenged by Harchand Singh and his new Lyallpur-based paper, *Khalsa Akhbar*, the C.K.D. became involved in trying to settle the matter and co-operated with Hailey, Commissioner of Delhi, in negotiations. Sewa Ram Singh visited the site repeatedly and served as the C.K.D. emissary. Sikhs divided into two camps,

---

86. Home Pol Nov. 1910, 7-10B. Other reports are in Feb. 1909, 1-11B. The C.I.D. material must be verified with material in papers or other sources. The dates, content of speeches and lists of participating individuals are suspect. Similarly, the selections from the press often differ from the actual stories in Sikh papers.

87. GI Army Dept, April 1912, 1590A.

88. The most succinct and accurate account is Oberoi, "From Gurdwara Rikabganj to the Viceregal Palace," *Panjab Past and Present* 14, 182-98. Other background is in Sangat Singh, *Freedom Movement in Delhi* (New Delhi: Associated, 1972). Daily events are covered in the C.K.D. minutes, 1913, and the review in local Sikh journals.

but the beginning of the First World War prevented an escalation. Before a *shahid* group could liberate the gurdwara and rebuild the wall in 1920, the British permitted Delhi-based Sikhs to make the repairs.

One result of the C.K.D.'s role in the affair was the permanent alienation of an assortment of Sikhs who felt that the strategy of working with the British went against the interests of the community. This did not mean, as some observers claim, that the Diwan lost its legitimacy and fell from the center of the Sikh political stage. On the contrary, for the time being the willingness of the British to work with the Diwan reinforced its position. Also important in that regard was the naming of a new Lieutenant Governor, Michael O'Dwyer, who respected Sikhs and tried to conciliate them whenever possible. At a visit to Khalsa College, for example, O'Dwyer rehearsed the history of patronage given Sikhs and awarded the College another Rs. 10,000.[89] By coincidence, several court cases strengthened the Singh Sabha position. A gurdwara in Campbellpur was transferred to local Sikh control, and the High Court decided *anand* marriages were legal, even for converts, and, by inference, that Sikhs were quite separate from Hindus.[90]

The First World War further reinforced loyalty toward British rule. C.K.D. members along with the leadership of the Singh Sabhas rallied Sikh support for the war effort. The C.K.D. role was to focus energy and facilitate organization because enthusiasm for the imperial cause already was widespread both in the urban and rural areas. These efforts were rewarded by the granting of honors and official accolades about Sikh bravery and loyalty.[91] More tangibly, the Punjab government responded to yet another worldwide mobilization over the issue of wearing *kirpans* and recommended that their use for ceremonial purposes be permitted in the Punjab. No limits should be placed on length because Sikhs saw the *kirpans* primarily as religious symbols and not as weapons. The confidential notation on the issue indicates that the British feared another confrontation such as had occurred over Rikabganj. Perhaps the issue could be resolved quickly, and even if it had the appearance of a victory for the "neo-Sikhs," an exemption from the Arms Act was a wise tactic.[92] The C.K.D. was the political beneficiary of the popular decision, as it was to be again in 1917 when the Government of India replied to a C.K.D. resolution about extending the waiver and exempted the *kirpan* from the Arms Act throughout India.[93]

---

89. *Khalsa Samachar*, Oct. 20, 1913, pp. 4-5.
90. *Khalsa Samachar*, Feb. 12, 1914, p. 2; April 24, 1913, p. 4; *Khalsa Advocate*, Feb. 21, 1914, p. 3. O'Dwyer's attitude towards the Sikhs and Punjab politics is a theme in his autobiography (1925).
91. On the Sikh and overall Punjabi response to the war, M.S. Leigh, *The Punjab and the War* (Lahore: Punjab Government, 1922); Barrier, "To Rule India: Coercion and Conciliation in India, 1914-1919," in DeWitt Ellinwood, ed., *India and World War One*.
92. Noting and correspondence in GI Home Jud, June 1914, 245-47A.
93. Documents in GI Home Pol 1917, Feb. 17-18A; May 1917, 85-102A. On the Sikh view, *Khalsa Samachar*, Feb. 15, 1917, p. 2.

The return of the Sikh immigrants during the war, especially those connected with the Ghadar party, seemed to underline the importance of Sikh loyalty for British rule. Punjab Sikhs had raised funds to help immigrants in Canada and agitated against mistreatment of Indians in North America. The *Komagata Maru* events received great publicity in the press. Singh Sabhas and the Diwan held sympathy meetings, but following the shooting at Budge-Budge in September 9, 1914 and the various revolutionary activities of isolated Ghadar groups, sympathy turned to distrust and then rejection. The C.K.D. labelled the Ghadarites as "non-Sikh" and issued its now familiar call for Sikhs to demonstrate support for the government.[94] Even those Sikhs who had called for militant action over Rikabganj tended to disown the Ghadar conspirators. Although a few organizations were set up to co-operate with the British in preventing the spread of unrest in the countryside, the disinterest and even antagonism of Sikh farmers suggest that such efforts were not necessary. The Ghadarites had assumed that Punjabis were on the verge of revolt and found to their dismay a reasonably content population that handed them over to authorities as criminals.[95]

During the war the C.K.D. continued its dual role of strengthening Sikh institutions and protecting Sikh political interests by negotiations and lobbying with the British. Sikhs were prominent in recruitment, propaganda and raising funds. The organization was seen by the British and most Sikhs, or at least those associated with the hundred or so Singh Sabhas, as the political center for the community. The government consulted with the Diwan on several gurdwara cases and made it a conduit for contributions to the soldiers' relief fund. The Diwan also moderated internal struggles and set up conciliation committees. Increasingly, Sikhs came to see the C.K.D. as an authority in political and religious matters. A flood of correspondence asked for interpretations about correct ritual, accurate editions of the Granth and details concerning caste and social practice.[96]

The Diwan's prominence, nevertheless, made it vulnerable to pressure and accusation. Calls came from all directions for leadership in handling a problem or intervening to protect Sikh interest. At the same time, discontent with recruitment and British arrogance was spreading. Even the *Khalsa Samachar* and the *Khalsa Advocate* more frequently commented on acts of British injustice by 1917. Groups distrusting the C.K.D. strategy of moderate agitation and resolution kept pushing for action. They also formed a communications network involving tracts and newspapers (*Khalsa Akhbar* and *Panth Sewak* among

---

94. Discussed in Puri, *Ghadar Movement* (Amritsar: Guru Nanak Dev University, 1983), pp. 158-67; Kapur, pp. 67-68. On the wider issues, Dignan, *The Indian Revolutionary Problem in British Diplomacy* (New Delhi: Allied, 1983) and Hugh Johnston, *Voyage of the Komagata Maru* (Delhi: Oxford U. Press, 1979).
95. Ghadar perspectives are reflected in books by Sohan Singh Josh, including his history of the Ghadar and *Akali Morchon ka Itihas* (New Delhi: Peoples Pub. House, 1972). At the time, most Punjabis saw the Ghadarites as terrorists.
96. Approximately one-fifth of the resolutions in the 1916-17 period dealt with such requests, while double that number focused on administrative matters.

others) quite independent of that of the Singh Sabhas. The C.K.D. decided in February 1917 to defend its policies by circulating publicity in the Sikh press.[97] Those identified with the C.K.D., such as Bhai Takht Singh, also came under fire from the opposition, which charged mismanagement and wasting of panthic resources.[98]

The failure of Sikhs to receive what was considered a proper share of patronage and representation gradually eroded the Diwan's authority. Any sustained political discussions with the British brought forth the divisions just below the surface. In response to the Public Service Commission in 1913, for example, both the C.K.D. and Sikh groups aligning with Hindus sent resolutions and deputations to discuss the future of Sikhs in the bureaucracy. Sundar Singh Majithia was grilled extensively about the program of the C.K.D. and the degree to which it represented all Sikhs. Avoiding strict definitions, he said that "those who do not follow the doctrine of the Sikhs are non-Sikhs."[99] His view of Sikhs as separate from Hinduism was challenged by Gurbaksh Singh Bedi, who claimed to represent the vast majority of Sikhs except a "small party" tied to the C.K.D. To him, Hindus and Sikhs were inseparable and should be treated that way in setting up recruitment and other civil service arrangements.[100]

The political fortunes of the Sikhs were not helped by their record in open elections for the Punjab Legislative Council. Out of eleven seats, Sikhs won only one in 1912 and none in 1916. Even though the government subsequently appointed Sundar Singh and Gajjan Singh, the *Khalsa Samachar* still was bitter and drew a bleak picture of the future.[101] In a situation that would be repeated frequently in the 1920's, a controversy arose over the appointment of Gurbaksh Singh, who had presided over the Hindu Conference. The experience with elections, when combined with rising expectations because of the community's war record, set the stage for more aggressive assertion of Sikh rights.

In 1916 and 1917 the Diwan's resolutions and public demonstrations gradually moved from requests to demands. A series of documents was sent concerning Punjabi, jobs, and commissions in the army. These rights should be given not on the basis of numbers but on the centrality of Sikhs within the empire. At least one-third of all seats in representative bodies should be reserved for Sikhs. In addition, the Sikh contribution to the war effort should be recognized by moving a considerable number of eligible soldiers to officer status. Stung by the Lucknow Pact negotiated by the Congress and Muslim League, which left Sikhs out of the proposed Hindu/Muslim percentages in the impending legislative reforms, Sikhs were determined to get their fair share.

---

97. C.K.D. proceedings, Feb. 18, 1917.

98. *Khalsa Samachar*, Sept. 23, 1915, p. 3. The Akalis made similar charges two decades later but failed to forcibly seize the Sikh Kanya Mahavidyala, Ferozepur.

99. Sundar Singh evidence, *Royal Commission on the Public Services in India*: Appendix V.X (London, 1914, Cd. 7582), pp. 71-75. He claimed beliefs were primary and outward appearances less important.

100. *Royal Commission*, p. 126.

101. *Khalsa Samachar*, June 8, 1916, p. 3.

Rallies across the Punjab culminated in a meeting of representatives from the Sikh states, the *takhats*, Singh Sabhas and *diwans*. A small delegation also met with Secretary of State Montagu.[102]

Although the details of the confidential discussions on the Punjab franchise have not been examined thoroughly, neither the local government nor the home government was prepared to meet Sikh demands. Loyalty, a role in the army and prominence in education and agriculture did count for something so that Sikhs received approximately 18% of the seats in the reformed legislature. Before the final arrangements were in place, however, the C.K.D. already had lost its place of authority. Ironically, the British eventually relinquished control of Khalsa College to the Sikhs and made acceptable amends at Rikabganj, but those actions came long after the political eclipse of the Diwan.

The Punjab government's political assumptions and faulty intelligence system fanned the discontent culminating in the 1919 disturbances. From the British viewpoint, honor and *izzat* had to be maintained at any cost. The repression of an imagined rebellion led to the massacre at Jallianwala Bagh. Perhaps British power was temporarily buttressed by the savage repression, but the acts destroyed much of the credibility of O'Dwyer's government and alienated a large part of the population. The massacre also destroyed the remaining influence of the C.K.D. British concern with honor and maintaining order brought almost immediate dishonor to its sometime political supporter. Upset with the uncontrolled public demonstrations and still clinging to its views about politics and official patronage, the Diwan could not make a shift and provide leadership in opposing the British. The public response to its lukewarm criticism of atrocities and its call for tolerance was immediate and strong. An appeal to an earlier record, including alleged successes in having Sikhs identified in the reforms as a separate entity,[103] proved fruitless. Too, the Diwan faltered in handling the volatile situation relating to the gurdwaras. Again the conflict between a commitment to peaceful resolution of issues and the shifting expectations of Sikhs virtually paralyzed the organization. A few C.K.D. leaders attempted to work within a new Sikh political association, the Central Sikh League, but there too, they lost out to politicians who had been waiting in the wings.[104] Charges of elitism and false pride surfaced in a series of pamphlets and letters. The new radical paper *Akali* called for a broadened Diwan program and compromise meetings were set up to explore that possibility. Again a failure: the Diwan could not accept the tactic of direct action and confrontation as a means of protecting Sikh interests. When the key issue of gurdwara reform was resolved in the streets and legislative chambers, the C.K.D. was seen as a major political participant by neither the Akali Dal nor the British.

---

102. C.K.D. proceedings, June 3, Oct. 14, 1917. Background on constitutional issues is in Gurdarshan Singh, "Sikh Politics in the Punjab," *Panjab Past and Present* 3 (1969), 67-78, and Mohinder Singh, *The Akali Movement* (Delhi: Macmillan India, 1978); Kapur, also articles by Sukhmani Bal in the proceedings of the Punjab History Conference, 1981-83.
103. *Khalsa Samachar*, Jan. 1, 1920.
104. *Khalsa Samachar*, Sept. 16, 1920, p. 3; C.K.D. proceedings, Aug. 1, Oct. 31, 1920.

In retrospect, the Chief Khalsa Diwan may be seen to have made three key contributions to Sikh politics. The first was institutionalizing the Singh Sabha view of Sikhism as a separate religion with distinct rituals and a tradition devoid of Hindu influence. The resulting consciousness affected the way Sikhs looked at each other and the world around them. Without that consciousness, the mobilization of Sikhs spread across the world would have been impossible. There would have been no drive for protecting Sikh rights nor assertion of community control over the gurdwaras.

Secondly, the Diwan took existing but often disparate Sikh organizations and linked them together in an effective communication system. Efforts were focused and information and ideas disseminated over time and distance. This enhanced the sense of Sikh identity and mission and opened up new paths of collaborative action and also conflict. The *diwans*, conferences, district and provincial meetings, tracts and, most importantly, the journals and newspapers all were critical legacies from the Singh Sabha and C.K.D. era. Without them, there would have been no dissemination of Sikh rituals, no sustained communication and exchange of resources with Sikh immigrants, no network that could be activated for legislation over *anand* marriage and no Akali challenge to the community.

The final element was a strategy for dealing with internal division and survival as a minority community. Accommodation, negotiation and compromise were hallmarks of the Diwan. Sometimes its tendency to leave matters hanging, to avoid or postpone dealing with issues, to be not specific or rigid in doctrine was frustrating, but from the Diwan's perspective drawing lines finely or creating an "orthodoxy" that excluded individuals or groups from Sikhism was not in the Panth's best interests. The same approach pertained to external political arenas. Sikhs could not be totally self-reliant. Self-strengthening must be augmented with linkages and collaboration to give Sikhs leverage in gaining access to resources. More times than not, Hindus and Muslims were seen as opponents or at least as questionable long-term allies. Accommodation with the British therefore was a logical and strategic move. That required compromise and political maneuvering, with confrontation and conflict only as a last resort. In the formative stages of Punjab politics such an approach had worked reasonably well, but with the shifting of British priorities and the emergence of a new set of constitutional and public arrangements after 1919, the C.K.D. could not adapt quickly. Some of the C.K.D. leaders, such as Sundar Singh Majithia, pursued collaborative arrangements in the widened legislature and attempted to help Sikh interests through alliances with other political groups and the British. The C.K.D. as an institution, however, resumed its familiar task of trying to buttress Sikhism through education, toleration and institution-building. The new self-appointed representatives of the Sikhs, the S.G.P.C. and the Akali Dal, now had to face the problems of disunity, political alternatives as a minority, and defining what it meant to be a Sikh in a rapidly changing world. That process continues even today.

Akali Struggle: Past and Present

Mohinder Singh

While extremist slogans and violent actions of a few individuals have received global attention, little is known about the strong tradition of non-violence and passive suffering among the Sikhs dating back to the martyrdom of Guru Arjan. In recent times it was the Akalis who, during their peaceful struggle for gurdwara reform (1920-25),[1] were able to demonstrate the efficacy of the Gandhian weapon of peaceful *satyagraha* through their passive sufferings at Nankana Sahib, Guru ka Bagh and other centres of Akali activity. Gandhi was so much impressed by the Sikhs' strict adherence to the vow of non-violence that he often quoted their examples to other *satyagrahis,* such as those of Munshi Peta and Malegaon who failed to keep their vow. In the Akali victory in the Keys affair, Gandhi found vindication of his own policies and described the Akali triumph as the first decisive victory of forces of Indian nationalism.[2] Since the media in India and abroad have blown out of proportion violent actions of a few individuals, and an impression has come to be created that the Sikhs as a community have become violent and aggressive, it would be helpful to study their recent past to find out for ourselves that they have a long tradition of defending the meek and oppressed and that the recent phenomenon of killing innocent civilian population is alien to the Sikh tradition and has no moral or religious sanction.

Fighting against injustice and oppression is an essential component of early Sikh tradition. Its best example in Sikh history comes from Guru Tegh Bahadur, who challenged the authority of the Mughal Emperor on an issue that did not concern him directly and sacrificed himself for a cause (defending the right to wear *tilak* and *janeo*, two ritualistic symbols of the Hindus) in which he personally had no faith. And the latest example is that of the Akali *morcha* against the internal Emergency in India (July 1975–January 1977). In that instance the Akalis launched a powerful non-violent struggle against the denial

---

1. For a detailed account see Mohinder Singh, *The Akali Movement* (Delhi: Macmillan, 1978).
2. See for details Partha N. Mukherji, "Gandhi, Akalis and Non-violence: An Analysis in Retrospect," *Man and Development* 4, no. 3 (September, 1984); Amrik Singh, ed., *Punjab in Indian Politics* (Delhi: Ajanta Publications, 1985).

[Joseph T. O'Connell, Milton Israel, Willard G. Oxtoby, eds., with W.H. McLeod and J.S. Grewal, visiting eds., *Sikh History and Religion in the Twentieth Century* (S. Asian Studies Papers, 3) (Toronto: S. Asian Studies, Univ. of Toronto, 1988)]

of civil liberties, even when the Akali Dal itself as a political party was not banned as were other similar organisations. I should like to limit this chapter to the discussion of the Akali struggle in the twentieth century, with a brief account of three of its main phases, namely, i) the Akali movement for gurdwara reform (1920-25), ii) Akali agitation for a Punjabi Suba (1956-66) and iii) the recent Akali struggle beginning with the passage of the Anandpur Sahib Resolution in October, 1978, and going up to Operation Bluestar (June, 1984) and the tragic events that followed. Instead of giving a detailed narrative of the different facets, I prefer to mention briefly the main issues involved and attempt a comparative study of the manner in which the past and present Akali leadership handled the vital issues.

I

The Shiromani Akali Dal[3] has been launching powerful religio-political agitations since its inception in December 1920. A comparative study of its three most powerful agitations reveals some interesting facts, the most important of them being the role of the leadership. It shows how the Akali leaders in the past succeeded in channelling the popular religious upsurge during the Gurdwara Reform movement (1920-25) into a powerful instrument for India's struggle for freedom and brought the Sikh community into the mainstream of Indian nationalism. Three distinct features of the past struggle made it more effective than its later manifestations in the struggle for a Punjabi Suba and in the more recent Akali agitation (1978-84). The first was that the Akali leadership realised the value of press and public opinion. They not only started an English daily, *The Hindustan Times*, in addition to two vernacular papers, *Akali* (Urdu) and *Akali te Pardesi* (Punjabi), but also carried with them the non-Sikh population and the nationalist leadership. The second was that from the very beginning they eschewed violence and quickly disowned the violent activities of the splinter group, the Babbar Akalis. And third, the movement was never allowed to take a communal turn.[4]

It is interesting to note that while differences of opinion existed among the Akali leaders in the past they succeeded, in most of the cases, in rising above their personal interests and in evolving consensus on most of the crucial issues. And again, while individual leaders differed on approaches to various issues, they were clear about the main goals and could take a united stand on a commonly agreed programme. By contrast, the present leadership has failed to unite on more than one occasion, their vested interests and egos generally taking precedence over the interests of the community at large. The Janus-faced

---

3. For a detailed account see Harjinder Singh Dilgir, *Shiromani Akali Dal* (Punjabi; Jullundur: Punjabi Book Company, 1978).

4. See for details Mohinder Singh, *Akali Movement*, pp. 27-47; Gurbakhsh Singh Shamsher Jhabalia, *Shahidi Jiwan* (Punjabi; Nankana: Gurdwara Prabandhak Committee, 1938); Narain Singh, *Kujh Haad Biti, Kujh Jag Biti* (Punjabi; Delhi: International Sikh Brotherhood, 1966).

politics of the present leadership has created more problems than it has solved and is mainly responsible for the present impasse.

It was the vision of the Akali leaders like Baba Kharak Singh, Mangal Singh and Master Tara Singh that was largely responsible for widening the scope of the purely religious struggle and utilising the movement for creating political consciousness among the Sikh community. I find it difficult to agree with the authors of the popular literature on the subject such as Teja Singh[5] and Ruchi Ram Sahni[6], or with Barbara Ramusack[7], who describes the movement as "a purely religious affair." While I concede Ramusack's point that the Congress leadership used the Akali struggle to further its own programme of non-violent non-cooperation, I find it difficult to accept her argument that "in the Akali agitation over the Nabha affair the British government was able to discredit the S.G.P.C. in the eyes of the religiously inclined Sikhs." If it were so, why did the same government, which allegedly discredited the S.G.P.C. and declared it an unlawful association in 1923, withdraw the notification after the passage of the Sikh Gurdwaras and Shrines Bill in 1925 and recognise the Akalis as the sole spokesmen of the Sikh community with regard to the management of the historic Sikh shrines?

To my mind Nabha was a trial of the wisdom of the Akali leaders, who managed to take their movement from religion to politics (Guru-ka-Bagh to Nabha) and back to religion (in Jaito), where they were at their best. Without entering into any controversy with Barbara Ramusack and other scholars like Ajit Singh Sarhadi[8] and Baldev Raj Nayar,[9] I wish to reiterate that the Akalis' movement was not a mere movement of gurdwara reform. Most of the historic gurdwaras that mattered already had come under Akali control after the tragedy of Nankana in 1921 and the struggle was at its peak during the Guru ka Bagh (August 22, 1922–April 23, 1923) and Nabha-Jaito (September 29, 1923–August 6, 1925) *morchas*, where the main issues were other than gurdwara reform—i.e., cutting of wood from the land attached to the gurdwara in the first case and restoration of the Maharaja of Nabha to his throne in the second. Moreover, if the movement is to be labelled as "a mere movement of gurdwara reform," as most Akali well-wishers have unwittingly described it, then its achievement becomes meaningless because the gurdwaras were and unfortunately continue to be misused and mismanaged; only the persons and patterns have changed.

While corruption in the gurdwaras was there much earlier than the days of gurdwara reform, the very fact that an organised struggle could not be launched

5. Teja Singh and Ganda Singh, *Gurdwara Reform Movement and Sikh Awakening* (Jullundur: Desh Bhagat Yadgar Committee, 1922).

6. Ruchi Ram Sahni, *Struggle for Reform in Sikh Shrines*, ed. Ganda Singh (Amritsar: S.G.P.C., 1965), 1965.

7. "The Incident at Nabha," *Journal of Asian Studies* 28:3 (May 1969), reproduced in Harbans Singh and N.G. Barrier, eds., *Punjab Past and Present: Essays in Honour of Dr. Ganda Singh* (Patiala: Punjabi University, 1976).

8. Ajit Singh Sarhadi, *Punjabi Suba: The Story of the Stuggle* (Delhi: K.C. Kapur & Sons, 1970).

9. *Minority Politics in the Punjab* (Princeton: Princeton University Press, 1966).

before 1920 shows that there was lack of needed religio-political awakening among the Sikh masses. It was the cumulative effect of socio-religious reform movements such as the Nirankari, the Namdhari and the Singh Sabha, and purely political regional and national events, such as the agrarian unrest, the Rowlatt Bills agitation, the Jallianwala Bagh tragedy and the launching of a non-cooperative movement in the country, which encouraged the Sikhs to launch a powerful agitation against the corrupt *mahants* and the bureaucracy in the province, which was tacitly backing these vested interests. However, it was the tragedy of Nankana, in which Mahant Narain Das and the mercenaries hired by him killed over 130 peaceful Akali reformers, that proved a turning point in the history of the Akali movement and compelled the reformers to widen the arena of their struggle.

Mahatma Gandhi, who had then launched a larger movement of non-violent Non-Cooperation (1920-22), was greatly impressed by the example of non-violent resistance of the Sikhs. He was overwhelmed by the courage displayed by them in the Nankana tragedy and visited Nankana Sahib on March 3, 1921 to express his sympathy with the Akali reformers. In a specially arranged *shahidi diwan* he made a brief speech in Hindustani, in the course of which he said that the news of Nankana was so staggering that he would not believe it without confirmation.[10] The Mahatma strongly condemned the action of Mahant Narain Das and the mercenaries hired by him and described the martyrdom of Akali reformers as an "act of national bravery."[11]

Gandhi also advised the Akalis to broaden the scope of their initial struggle and reform the "bigger gurdwara," i.e., India, by joining the larger movement of Non-Cooperation. The Akali leadership accepted his advice and quickly joined the nationalist struggle by passing a formal resolution in favor of Non-Cooperation on May 5, 1921. Akalis' strict adherence to non-violence so much impressed the Mahatma that for quite some time the Nankana tragedy figured in his writings and speeches. While addressing the *satyagrahis* of Munshi Peta, he said, "I wish to see the bravery of Lachhman Singh and Duleep Singh in Munshi Peta. Without raising a little finger, these two warriors stood undaunted against the attack of Mahant Narain Das of Nankana Sahib, and let themselves be killed."[12] While comparing their resistance with the violent acts of the residents of Malegaon, Gandhi pointed out: "if these two brothers [Lachhman Singh and Duleep Singh] acted with great nobility at Nankana Sahib the residents of Malegaon had displayed an equal degree of heinousness."[13]

Gandhi was able to convince his lieutenants in the Congress to support the Akali movement and thus involve the Sikhs in the national movement, as had been done in the case of Muslims by taking up the issue of the restoration of the *khalifa* to his position in Turkey. With the Congress support the Akali struggle

10. *Collected Works of Mahatma Gandhi*, v. 19, pp. 396-97.
11. Ibid.
12. Ibid., v. 20, p. 67.
13. Ibid., p. 68.

against a foreign government became a synonym for reform in Sikh shrines. Akali agitation over the Keys affair and, later, their struggle at Guru ka Bagh are two important manifestations of the non-violent nature of the Akali movement.

Akali Agitation over the Keys Affair

The Golden Temple, the Akal Takht and the adjoining gurdwaras had come under the control of the Akali reformers in October 1920. Sardar Sunder Singh Ramgarhia, the Manager of the Golden Temple, was also holding the office of Secretary of the new Committee of Management appointed by the S.G.P.C. Realising the force of public opinion, he decided to fall into line with the party of reform and agreed to hand over the keys of the *toshakhana* to Baba Kharak Singh, newly elected President of the S.G.P.C. But before he could do so the Deputy Commissioner of Amritsar tried to forestall the Akali move by immediately sending an Extra Assistant Commissioner to collect the keys of the *toshakhana* from him. This led to the famous agitation called *Chabian da morcha*, in which thousands of Akali volunteers courted arrest and offered non-cooperation.[14]

After failing to contain the agitation, the government thought of isolating the Sikhs from the larger movement of Non-Cooperation by unconditionally releasing all the prisoners arrested in this connection and by returning the keys to Baba Kharak Singh. This surrender by the government was viewed by nationalist leaders in the country as a decisive victory for the forces of Indian nationalism. Mahatma Gandhi sent the following telegram to Baba Kharak Singh on the occasion: "FIRST BATTLE FOR INDIA'S FREEDOM WON. CONGRATULATIONS."[15]

Struggle at Guru ka Bagh

After suspension of Non-Cooperation in February, 1922, and the arrest of Gandhi and other Congress leaders, the government found the Akalis isolated and thought of "teaching them a lesson." An excuse was found in a complaint by the *mahant* of the Guru ka Bagh gurdwara that the Akalis were cutting dry *kikkar* (acacia) trees from the land attached to the gurdwara. Describing this as an act of "stealing of private property," the police started arresting the Akali volunteers. This led to another powerful Akali *morcha* at Guru ka Bagh, in which over 5,000 Akali volunteers courted arrest. But the government had to give in again by releasing them unconditionally and allowing them to cut wood from the land attached to the gurdwara.[16]

---

14. For a detailed account see Mohinder Singh, *Akali Movement*, pp. 43-49.
15. Xerox copy of the telegram is published in Ganda Singh, ed., *Some Confidential Papers of the Akali Movement* (Amritsar: S.G.P.C., 1965), p. 11.
16. For details see Mohinder Singh, *Akali Movement*, pp. 49-61.

The Nabha Affair and the Jaito *morcha*

In their hour of victory the Akali leaders took up the issue of the restoration of Maharaja Ripudaman Singh of Nabha to his throne.[17] For the first time there were serious differences of opinion among the leadership on the merit of the issue. The moderate members felt that the abdication was a "political issue" and, therefore, the S.G.P.C., which was a religious body, should not take up the question of the Maharaja's restoration. These members argued that if the Akali leadership felt that in deposing the Maharaja the government had injured the feelings of the Sikh community, the question should be taken up by the Central Sikh League, the newly formed political organisation of the nationalist Sikhs. While the issue was being hotly debated the extremists gained an upper hand as a result of their victory in the general elections of S.G.P.C. in 1923. The new executive not only endorsed the earlier decision on the Nabha issue but adopted a more aggressive tone. The Akali Dal also passed a formal resolution urging the S.G.P.C. "to raise a typhoon of agitation till the Maharaja was restored" and promised its wholehearted support in the struggle.[18]

What is worth mentioning here is the role that the press and public opinion played in the Nabha affair and in the subsequent Akali struggle at Jaito. Master Tara Singh, through his forceful articles in the two vernacular dailies, the *Akali* and the *Akali te Pardesi*, was able to arouse the sentiments of the Sikh masses by comparing the removal of Maharaja Ripudaman Singh to that of Maharaja Duleep Singh in 1849. In the *Akali te Pardesi* Master Tara Singh wrote:

> Lovers of the Panth, will you allow the guardians of Maharaja Duleep Singh to take charge of the Tikka Sahib of Nabha? Rise, hold *diwans* and deliver lectures. Every Sikh society should raise a storm of agitation against this treachery and deceit...Do not stop, be fearless and come forward.[19]

The Akali leaders also succeeded in enlisting the support of the Indian National Congress on the Nabha issue. In the Cocanada session of the Congress held in December 1923, the Nabha issue was hotly debated. In his presidential address Maulana Mohammad Ali remarked that "a better opportunity for civil disobedience, at least on a provincial scale, never presented itself ever since the arrest of the Mahatma." The Congress also passed formal resolutions supporting the Akali stand on the Nabha affair and described the official attack on the S.G.P.C. and the Shiromani Akali Dal as "a direct challenge to the right of free association of all movements for freedom."[20]

In the special session of the Congress held in Delhi in September 1923, a resolution was passed supporting the Akali agitation in Nabha. It was decided to

---

17. Ripudaman Singh, who ascended the Nabha throne on December 20, 1911, was forced to abdicate in favour of his minor son on July 9, 1923. While charges of maladministration were levelled against him the real cause of his deposition was his close association with the nationalist leaders and his sympathy for the Akali struggle. For a critical and scholarly article on consequences resulting from Ripudaman Singh's abdication see Barbara N. Ramusack, "The Incident at Nabha."
18. S.G.P.C. resolution quoted in file No. 628-3-P, Foreign-Pol, 1924, National Archives of India, New Delhi.
19. Issue dated July 9, 1923.
20. Report quoted in *The Tribune*, January 1, 1924.

send Congress observers there to get first-hand information about the developments. Jawaharlal Nehru, A.T. Gidwani and K. Santhanam, who went there for the purpose, were arrested as soon as they entered the state territory and were put behind bars. During their detention and subsequent trial in Nabha these observers not only gained first-hand knowledge about the Akali reformers and their movement but also got a chance to know about the high-handedness of the bureaucracy and the arbitrary nature of justice in the princely state of Nabha. During his encounter with the Akalis, Nehru became their great admirer and wished to prove "worthy of their high tradition and fine courage." The last paragraph of his original statement drafted in the Nabha jail on November 23, 1923 reads as follows:

> I was in Jail when the Guru-ka-Bagh struggle was gallantly fought and won by the Sikhs. I marvelled at the courage and sacrifice of the Akalis and wished that I could be given an opportunity of showing my deep admiration of them by some form of service. That opportunity has now been given to me and I earnestly hope that I shall prove worthy of their high tradition and fine courage. Sat Sri Akal.[21]

On noticing that the Akali leadership had managed to challenge the authority of the government on a political issue which was bound to create serious repercussions in other princely states also, the government came out heavily against the Akali leadership. Through a notification issued on October 12, 1923, the S.G.P.C., the Shiromani Akali Dal and various jathas organised by or affiliated to the Akali Dal were declared "unlawful associations."[22] After this notification mass arrests of the supporters of the Nabha agitation were ordered, and all the sixty members of the interim committee of the S.G.P.C. were arrested on charges of "treason against the King-Emperor." At the same time serious efforts were made by the official machinery to create divisions in the Akali ranks by propagating the notion that the Akalis were trying to "restore the Sikh Raj" under the cloak of the Nabha agitation—thus isolating them from their supporters in the Congress and other nationalist forces.

In the meantime Malcolm Hailey,[23] who as Home Member of the Viceroy's Council had been dealing with the Akali movement, took over as the Governor of Punjab. He followed a well-planned and carefully executed policy of splitting the Akali leadership, separating the religious issues from the political ones, opening new fronts to divide the resources of the Akalis, alienating the Hindus and Muslims and also the moderate Sikhs from the Akali cause and

---

21. The first hand-written draft by Jawaharlal Nehru was drastically changed by Motilal, who visited Nabha in connection with the defence of his son. It was the revised version that was actually read in the court. For the original draft see Mohinder Singh, Akali Movement, pp. 206-12. For the revised version see Ganda Singh, ed., Panjab Past and Present (October, 1970), pp. 425-31.

22. Order No. 23772 (Home Department), Judicial, October 12, 1923. For full text see Mohinder Singh, Akali Movement, p. 198.

23. Malcolm Hailey, who started his career as a Settlement Officer in the Sialkot district of the pre-Partition Punjab, understood the Sikh character much better than his predecessor and other British officials. A huge collection of his private papers in the India Office Library, London, which I consulted during 1974-75, throws new light on the British policy towards the Akali movement, some references to which are available in author's paper on the subject published in Pritam Singh, ed., Journal of Sikh Studies (Amritsar: Guru Nanak Dev University), 4:1 (February, 1977).

organising anti-Akali associations to put forward counter-claims. On consulting a large number of private and confidential letters exchanged between Malcolm Hailey and the higher authorities in Delhi and London preserved in the India Office Library, London, we find that Hailey was not interested in negotiating with the Akali leadership "till the whole Sikh attitude had been transformed and made more pliable." He felt that there had been too much inclination in the Punjab to let the Sikhs dictate terms and real peace was not possible till the government was able to dictate terms to them.[24] In one of his letters to the higher authorities in London, Hailey summarised his new policy in the following manner:

> I do not think that we can now gain any more by efforts at conciliation, for theirs is a peculiar mentality which will always take conciliation for weakness.[25]

For the purpose of strengthening the moderates against the extremists, Hailey encouraged the loyalist elements in the Sikh community to come out in open opposition to the Akali movement. He instructed the district-level officials to organise Sudhar committees in every district where there were Sikhs.

. Success of Hailey's policy is evident from the fact that he not only managed to create divisions among the Sikhs over the Nabha issue but also was able to influence a leader of the stature of Mahatma Gandhi, who suddenly advised the Akali leaders to suspend their agitation in Nabha. In his letter dated March 4, 1924, to the secretary of S.G.P.C., Gandhi advised the Akali leadership to think over the whole question afresh. Further, he informed them that he would be able to help only if they separated their agitation in Nabha, which in his opinion was a purely political question, from their movement of religious reform.[26] Here the Mahatma seems to have conveniently ignored the fact that it was he and his lieutenants in the Sikh League who had brought the Akalis from religion to politics and had persuaded them formally to join the movement of Non-Cooperation by launching a frontal attack against the bureaucracy.

As discussed in the preceding pages, it was Mahatma Gandhi who advised the Akalis to join the larger movement of Non-Cooperation during his visit to Nankana Sahib in March, 1921. At that stage, when the Akalis were engaged in a life-and-death struggle at Jaito, Gandhi's advice to suspend the movement and to drop the Nabha issue altogether was bound to weaken the Akalis further. It is interesting to note that when the Akali leaders expressed their inability to accept his advice and continued sending more *jathas* to Jaito, Gandhi started issuing open letters to the press expressing his doubts about the Akalis' adherence to the principle of non-violence. His references to the past incidents of the removal of Hindu idols from the precincts of the Golden Temple were bound to weaken the communal harmony which till then was being brought about by enlisting the

---

24. Letter dated July 2, 1924 from Malcolm Hailey to Sir Valentine Chirol, Hailey Papers, Mss Eur E. 220/6-A, India Office Library, London.
25. Ibid.
26. For the full text of Mahatma Gandhi's letters to the Akalis see Ganda Singh, ed., *Confidential Papers of the Akali Movement*, pp. 45-55.

sympathy and support of the Hindu and Sikh masses for the Akali cause. In his letters to the Akalis the Mahatma wanted them to give him an assurance that their movement was "neither anti-Hindu nor anti any other race or creed," and that they were not working for the "restoration of the Sikh Raj under the cloak of religious reform."[27] It is rather strange that in spite of the Akalis' clear demonstration of their strict adherence to the vow of non-violence—for which he himself had publicly praised their conduct—Gandhi failed to form a correct assessment of the Akalis and their movement and suddenly withdrew his support for their cause at a very critical juncture.

It is worth mentioning here that the Akali leaders of those days failed to fall into the trap and suspend their four-year-old agitation without achieving any of their goals. It seems that apart from the influence of the official propaganda machinery Gandhi was also biased against the Akalis by the reports on the Punjab being sent to him by K.M. Panikkar and Lala Lajpat Rai. The latter had reasons to feel upset over the recent developments in Punjab politics. The emergence of Baba Kharak Singh as a powerful Sikh leader, who also carried influence with the Congress and was well known for his staunch nationalist views, posed a danger to the exclusive leadership of men like Lajpat Rai in Punjab politics. Fortunately for the Akali leaders, when Gandhi suddenly withdrew his support from the Akalis during their life-and-death struggle in Nabha, other nationalist leaders like Madan Mohan Malaviya and Muhammad Ali Jinnah came to their rescue. On noticing that Hailey was not prepared to negotiate with the Akalis or the nationalists but was cleverly encouraging anti-Akali associations to draft a parallel bill, Malaviya tried to take the wind out of Hailey's sails by drafting a bill of his own in consultation with the Akali leaders in jail and by asking the Sikh members of the Punjab Legislative Council to move the same and the Hindu Members to support it.[28] In case the introduction of his bill was not allowed in the Punjab Legislative Council, Malaviya had the alternative of introducing it in the Central Legislative Assembly on the grounds that there was need for all-India legislation on the subject. Malaviya hoped to get his bill through with the support of the nationalist members of the Assembly. The moves of Malaviya and Jinnah compelled Hailey to come to terms with the Akali leaders, which resulted in the passage of the Sikh Gurdwaras and Shrines Bill by the Punjab Legislative Council in July 1925.[29]

While the passage of the bill put an end to the five-year-long Akali agitation, conditions imposed on the release of Akali leaders created divisions in their ranks. The moderate group accepted conditional release and captured the S.G.P.C., only to be dislodged by the extremists after their unconditional release a year later. While the British government tried its best to help the moderate

---

27. Ibid.

28. Hailey's letter of October 29, 1924 to Sir Alexander Muddiman, Hailey Papers, Mss. Eur E. 220/6-C.

29. For details of circumstances leading to the passage of the bill, see Mohinder Singh, *Akali Movement*, pp. 126-36. For the full text of the bill, see M.L. Ahluwalia, ed., *Select Documents of Gurdwara Reform Movement* (Delhi, 1985), pp. 286-364.

group, they could never again capture the S.G.P.C., which has since then generally remained under the control of the Akalis.

Whatever be their other failings, it goes to the credit of the past Akali leaders that they were clear about their goals and did not compromise on their basics. Akali achievement is significant not only in view of the large-scale participation of the Sikhs—though Sikhs constituted less than 2% of India's population, the number of Sikhs who courted arrest matched those arrested in connection with the country-wide movement of Non-Cooperation. Again, while Mahatma Gandhi withdrew his movement in 1922 without achieving any of the three goals (i.e., restoration of the *khalifa*, righting the Punjab wrongs, and *swaraj* within one year), Akalis did not suspend their agitation till they got a bill passed on lines acceptable to them. While the Akali leaders supported the Congress programme during subsequent agitations over civil disobedience and the Quit India movement, they did not hesitate to oppose the Congress when it came to defending the interests of the Sikh community. Thus the "much-maligned" Master Tara Singh quit his membership of the Working Committee of the Indian National Congress when the latter decided to boycott the British war efforts during World War II. If the Sikhs were still occupying important positions in the various services it was mainly due to the vision and foresight of Akali leaders like Master Tara Singh. It is becoming increasingly fashionable to blame the Akali leaders, especially Master Tara Singh, for not demanding or for refusing to accept a "Sikh homeland" as if the same were being offered to them on a platter, as was asserted by the late Sardar Kapur Singh.[30] Even some of the younger generation of Sikh scholars, particularly Gurmit Singh,[31] a Sirsa-based advocate, and Harjinder Singh Dilgir,[32] another advocate from Jullundur, have started supporting the above thesis and asserting that "there was a chance to get Khalistan and Master Tara Singh missed the opportunity."[33] There are others who feel that Master Tara Singh did not press for a homeland for the Sikhs because of pressure from Sardar Baldev Singh, who was the sole financier of the Akali Dal and had business interests in different parts of India. Since such an issue needs serious investigation and research, I do not wish to discuss this here except to point out that even if the British wanted to give the Sikhs a separate homeland they could not do so for a number of reasons, demography being the most important one. During a chance meeting with Lord Mountbatten in London in 1975, I pointedly raised this issue with him and was told that the British government never made such an offer to the Akali leaders.

It is relevant here to refer to the exchange between Sir Stafford Cripps and the Sikh leaders. Giani Kartar Singh, who was one of the members of the Sikh delegation that met Cripps to present the Sikh point of view prior to partition of

---

30. For a detailed account see Kapur Singh's booklet, *The Stupid Sikhs* (Vancouver: All Canada Sikh Federation, 1975).
31. See Gurmit Singh, *Failures of the Akali Leadership* (Sirsa: Usha Institute of Religious Studies, 1981).
32. Harjinder Singh Dilgir, *Shiromani Akali Dal* (Jullundur, 1978).
33. Gurmit Singh, *Failures*, p. 159.

India, pleaded that the Sikhs would not feel safe in either a united India or a Pakistan. They should have a province of their own where they would be in a dominant or almost dominant position. In reply to Sir Stafford Cripps, who asked what would be the area of the proposed Sikh State, Giani Kartar Singh suggested that it should be the whole of Jullundur and Lahore divisions together with Hissar, Karnal, Ambala and Simla districts of the Ambala division and Montgomery and Lyallpur districts. Now the Sikhs in the proposed area would have been a very small minority. It cannot be believed that the majorities would have migrated out to India and Pakistan to allow Sikhs to have a dominant position. Unless the Congress and Muslim League were to have agreed, the British government could not have turned out Hindus and Muslims from this area.

This is also confirmed by perusal of the correspondence between the British officials in Punjab and the higher echelons in Delhi and London. For instance, in one of his letters to the Viceroy of India, Sir Bernard Glancy, the Governor of Punjab, wrote:

> The Sikhs, although, as I have recently told you, are undoubtedly relieved by the rejection of the offer brought by Sir Stafford Cripps, are still feeling distinctly restive. Master Tara Singh and his lieutenants have found it an easy matter to stir up communal feeling at the alleged danger of the Sikhs being subjected to Muhammadan rule in the Punjab, and they are loath to cease from exploiting this opportunity. They will no doubt derive some degree of comfort from the sympathetic references made to Sikhs in the debates which have just taken place in Parliament, but it is to be hoped that these expressions of sympathy will not go to their heads and lead them to believe that "Khalistan" is regarded in responsible quarters as a practicable proposition. As you are well aware, the practical objections to "Khalistan" are even greater than those which lie in the path of Pakistan. Apart from the upheaval that would be caused by tearing out a large section of territory from the vitals of the provincial body politic, it is worth remembering that there is not one single district in which the Sikhs command a majority. Another illustration of the complexity of the problem can be placed on the results of the last census [of 1941] owing to the determination of all the communities to inflate their own figures, but it is true that a few years ago, though there are half a dozen Sikh States in the agency, there was only one state, the Muslim state of Malerkotla, where the majority of the population were Sikhs.
>
> The obvious course for the Sikhs to pursue is to seek a satisfactory basis for combining with the major community in the Province.[34]

As is well known, the demand for a Sikh homeland or Azad Punjab—where Sikhs were to hold the balance, with Hindus and Muslims being in almost equal number—was being made to counter the Muslim League's demand for Pakistan. Both the British government and the Akali leaders knew that the Sikhs did not constitute a majority in any particular area of the undivided Punjab. It was only after the partition of India and subsequent migration of the Sikhs from West to East Punjab that they got consolidated in one state and only after the merger of Patiala and East Punjab States Union (P.E.P.S.U.) with Punjab and its

---

34. V.P. Menon, ed., *Transfer of Power* (Princeton: Princeton University Press, 1957), v. 2, p. 7.

division on the linguistic principle in 1966, that they have come to constitute a nominal majority in the new state's population.[35]

II

While a detailed discussion on the Akali agitation for the creation of a Punjabi-speaking state is not possible in the present chapter it is worth mentioning that the very purpose for the creation of such a state seems to have been defeated. Contrary to the Akalis' expectation of perpetual domination in the newly created state, experience has shown that they have never been able to have a full term of a stable Akali ministry. While a common enemy (British rule) and a common cause (independence) kept the Congress and the Akalis closer to each other during India's struggle for freedom, cracks started appearing in their friendship soon after the country became independent in 1947. Akali anxiety to capture power at the provincial level and to "experience the glow of freedom" promised to them by Jawaharlal Nehru and other important Congress leaders, and the Congress policy of monopolising power at both the provincial and central levels, were bound to clash sooner or later. While in other states issues of statehood did not take communal shape, in the case of Punjab it became so. The agitation for the creation of Punjabi Suba[36] was spearheaded by the Akali Dal and Punjabi, which in fact was the language of the people of the Punjab at large, willy-nilly got associated with the Sikhs exclusively, with Akalis as its most vocal spokesmen. While Punjabi Hindus are to be blamed squarely for disowning their mother-tongue for political reasons, some of the Akali leaders should also share the blame for confusing the Punjabi Suba agitation with the call for a Sikh-majority state. Since the Congress leadership that ruled India was unwilling to consider seriously any proposal based explicitly on religious and communal grounds, the Akali Dal tried to present its demand before the States Reorganisation Commission in 1953, on linguistic patterns without emphasising the point of Sikh majority. As the Commission members had already been prejudiced as a result of Akali leaders' earlier arguments that "the Sikhs were promised the right of self-determination both by the British and the Congress leaders in 1946,"[37] the Akali demand for a Punjabi Suba was summarily rejected. Punjabi Hindus' opposition to the Suba was used by the Commission to argue that the "demand lacked general support of the people inhabiting the area."[38] The Commission had not only rejected the Akali demand but also questioned the validity of Punjabi in Gurmukhi script as the language of the people of Punjab, which made them feel humiliated.

---

35. At the time of the creation of the Punjabi Suba in November, 1966 the Sikh population was nearly 55%, while according to the latest census this had gone up to 63%.

36. For a critical account see Baldev Raj Nayar, *Minority Politics in the Punjab* (Princeton: Princeton University Press, 1966); Ajit Singh Sarhadi's pro-Akali account is available in *Punjabi Suba: The Story of the Struggle* (Delhi: U.C. Kapur, 1970). For a comparative study of agitations over language issues in Bihar, U.P. and Punjab see Paul R. Brass, *Language, Religion and Politics in North India* (Cambridge: Cambridge University Press, 1974).

37. Quoted in Sarhadi, *Punjabi Suba*, pp. 147-48.

38. Quoted in Paul Brass, *Language, Religion and Politics in North India*, p. 320.

After rejection of their demand for a Punjabi Suba the Akalis launched a powerful agitation to achieve their goal. The Congress-ruled Centre tried to contain the Akali agitation through the Regional Formula, which almost accepted the principle of division of Punjab.[39] The Akali Dal suspended the agitation and decided to merge with the Congress in contesting the 1957 Assembly elections. But the Akalis soon realised their mistake. Partap Singh Kairon, who became the Chief Minister of Punjab, did not have any sympathy with the Akali demand for a Punjabi Suba. Ironical as it may sound, this old Akali turned Congressman became the most powerful instrument in suppressing the Akali agitation for a Punjabi Suba in the years that followed. Without going into the details of the Akali agitation for a Punjabi Suba, what is relevant here is the point that the Akali leaders were clear about the issue. While there were differences of approach—with Master Tara Singh still airing his grievances against the Congress and accusing Nehru and others of going back from their promises to the Sikhs and new leaders like Sant Fateh Singh trying to give a regional tone to the Akali demand—all the leaders were united in their basic object of getting their demand conceded through peaceful agitation within the constitutional and democratic framework.

It was during the Akali agitation for a Punjabi Suba that a major development occurred. The leadership of the Akali Dal changed from the traditional non-Jat urban leadership to the newly emerging rural Jat leadership. Master Tara Singh,[40] a middle-class educated non-Jat leader, who had emerged on the scene during the Akali agitation for gurdwara reform in the 1920's and dominated Sikh politics for nearly four decades, was ousted by Sant Fateh Singh, his own hitherto little-known lieutenant. Fateh Singh till then was known more for his religious and social work in the Ganganagar area of Rajasthan and had little knowledge of, or interest in, Punjab politics.

Backed by a powerful Jat peasantry, Sant Fateh Singh introduced a secular note into Akali politics by presenting the Punjabi Suba demand as based on "purely linguistic consideration." "We do not seek a Sikh majority area," the Sant declared; "we are not concerned about percentages. We want the Punjabi Suba to comprise an area where Punjabi language is spoken regardless of the fact whether the Sikhs are in a majority or minority."[41] This shift in stand weakened Hindu opposition to the Suba demand. By another clever move the Sant and his followers succeeded in creating a wedge between the opponents of the Punjabi Suba by demanding Haryana and Punjabi Suba in one and the same breath. The new slogan had an electric effect in the Hindi-speaking districts, with the result that the Punjabi Hindus, who had been blocking the creation of a

39. Baldev Raj Nayar, *Minority Politics in the Punjab*, pp. 218-19.
40. While there is no standard biography on Master Tara Singh, details of his role in various movements are available in such works as Jawant Singh, ed., *Master Tara Singh: Jiwan, Sangarsh te Udesh* (Punjabi); Niranjan Singh, *Jiwan Yatra Master Tara Singh* (Punjabi) (Delhi: Navyog Press, 1968) and his autobiography in Punjabi, *Meri Yaad*.
41. *The Tribune*, October 30, 1960.

Punjabi Suba, were quickly isolated from the Haryanivis, who, for their own interests, became indirect supporters of the Punjabi Suba demand.

In the meantime some other developments took place which brought about a major change at the national level. Jawaharlal Nehru died on May 27, 1964, and Lal Bahadur Shastri became the new Prime Minister of India. In Punjab Partap Singh Kairon, the powerful Chief Minister of Punjab, was replaced by a rather weak non-Sikh named Ram Kishan. With this change in leadership at almost all levels, opposition to the Punjabi Suba demand started dwindling, and soon a Cabinet sub-committee was appointed to consider the question of formation of a Punjabi-speaking state which, ironically enough, became a reality in November 1966 with Indira Gandhi as the Prime Minister of India.

While the creation of a Punjabi Suba put an end to the long Akali agitation, the later history shows that it created more problems while solving one. The new Punjab was not the one the Akali Dal had demanded and hoped for. Since the division was made on the basis of the 1961 census, wherein a large number of Punjabi Hindus had been returned as Hindi-speaking for political reasons, a large area that was in reality Punjabi-speaking was left out of the new Punjab. Chandigarh, which was built on Punjab territory and out of the resources of Punjab as its new capital, was put under central control and declared a Union Territory and also joint capital of both Punjab and Haryana. Also, control of the Bhakra Dam and Madhopur and other water-control headworks was taken over by the Centre. All this gave the Akali leaders a new cause to revive their agitation for redressing their grievances and keeping their agitation alive. But in the meantime a new development had taken place.

For the first time the Sikhs had come to form a majority (55%) in one of the states of the Indian union, which created amongst the Akalis a hope of perpetual rule by emerging as the regional alternative to the Congress rule in Punjab. While up to the creation of the Punjabi Suba the Akali leaders had been united in their demand and clear about the major issues, creation of the Punjabi Suba and their lust for power created serious differences. In addition to capturing the S.G.P.C. and its resources, the Akalis now had another, much bigger, source of strength and weakness, that is, capturing political power in the new state. During the general elections of 1967, one year after the creation of the Punjabi Suba, the two Akali Dals—the Master and the Sant groups—worked at cross purposes. In trying to knock each other out, the two ended by capturing between themselves 26 out of 104 Assembly seats (Sant Akali 24 and the Master group 2). In the newly created Punjabi Suba the much-maligned Congress still emerged as the single largest party, with 48 seats. Since the Congress was unable to form the Ministry, all the non-Congress groups combined to form a coalition government in Punjab with Gurnam Singh as the chief minister. While it is not relevant to discuss ministry-making in Punjab, what is pertinent here is the fact that in their lust for political power the Akalis observed no scruples and betrayed not only the masses who had returned them to power but also the cause for which the Punjabi Suba had been formed. In quick succession Gurnam

Singh was dislodged by Lachhman Singh Gill and the latter was himself defeated when he failed to get the budget passed through the legislature. In the mid-term elections in February 1969 the Sant Akali Dal was returned as the largest party, with 44 seats, and Gurnam Singh again became the chief minister in an Akali-led coalition. During nearly two years' tenure as the Chief Minister of Punjab, Gurnam Singh faced various crises and awkward situations, the worst of them being Darshan Singh Pheruman's going on a fast for the inclusion of Chandigarh into Punjab and dying a martyr's death after having lived on water for seventy-four days.

While both the Akali leaders—Tara Singh and Fateh Singh—had broken their vows by going on fasts unto death and breaking them without achieving their goals, Pheruman, a veteran Congressman, put the Akalis to shame by living up to the Sikhs' tradition of never going back from the sacred oath. His martyrdom shook the conscience of the central government, which announced that Prime Minister Indira Gandhi would give her award on Chandigarh and other issues. The award, which was announced on January 29, 1970, gave Chandigarh to Punjab, in return for some Hindi-speaking villages of Chandigarh together with cotton-rich Fazilka and Abohar as a "compensation" to Haryana. This was a strange justice. Haryana was to be compensated (and this has become a live issue since then) for losing Chandigarh, which did not belong to it. For sheer political expediency and to discredit the Akalis in the eyes of the Sikhs, Haryana from this time onward was made a party to most of the issues that were to be raised by Punjab whether through the Congress or through the Akali chief ministers. And this would complicate matters in the years to come.

In Punjab Gurnam Singh was succeeded by Parkash Singh Badal, a rich landlord from the Giddar Baha area of the Malwa region, who formed with the Jan Sangh in March 1970 a coalition government that lasted barely one year. In the Punjab Assembly elections in 1972 Congress recovered most of the ground it had lost soon after the creation of the Punjabi Suba. After emerging as the largest party in the state assembly, with sixty-seven seats, the Congress formed a government in Punjab with Giani Zail Singh as the Chief Minister. Deeply rooted in Sikh tradition and having understood the Sikhs' psyche much better than his predecessors, Giani Zail Singh[42] took over from the Akalis many of their religious issues. By introducing a religious tone to Punjab politics Giani succeeded to a great extent in weakening the Akalis. But the result—growing communalisation of provincial politics—was disastrous. In an attempt to secure Sikh votes for the Congress, Giani organised one of the biggest religious processions, commemorating the march of Guru Gobind Singh from Anandpur near Bhakra Nangal to Damdama near Bhatinda. At the same time he tried to

---

42. Zail Singh started his career as a village preacher but later joined the freedom struggle as an activist of the Parja Mandal movement in the princely Sikh state of Faridkot. After Independence he became a minister in the Punjab cabinet and later rose to the position of Chief Minister of Punjab in March, 1972. In January 1980 he was inducted into the Central Cabinet as the Home Minister and later in July 1982 elevated to the office of President of India, the first Sikh to attain this exalted position in free India.

make inroads into the S.G.P.C. and the Akali Dal by promoting Dal Khalsa to oppose the Akalis in the S.G.P.C. elections. A good deal of literature dealing with recent Sikh problems points to Giani Zail Singh's involvement in the Bhindranwale phenomenon in Punjab politics.[43] For instance, Mark Tully has reported Zail Singh as having footed the bill for the inaugural meeting of the Dal Khalsa held in Aroma Hotel, Chandigarh, on April 13, 1978.[44]

III

In Akali politics unprecedented developments have taken place during the last decade. Gurcharan Singh Tohra, who got himself elected as the President of the S.G.P.C. in 1973 and has manœuvred to remain in position to date (except for a brief interregnum from March to November 1986) has proved to be the cleverest of the Akali politicians. In a well-written article, "Punjab and Mr. Tohra," Patwant Singh blames Mr. Tohra for most of the past and present troubles in Punjab. To quote him:

> The central fact which emerges out of a careful reading of Punjab's politics is that Mr. Tohra is the one who has woven the many webs in which the state and central governments have so frequently been trapped. By allowing Jarnail Singh Bhindranwale to use the shrine for his inflammatory politics, Tohra helped to place the Golden Temple, that sacred and exalted emblem of Sikhism, in the very eye of the political storm. It is entirely likely that its eventual destruction formed a part of his calculations, for he seems to have foreseen that an attack on the temple would do more to drive the Sikhs and the rest of India apart than any other event. What makes him doubly suspect is that he seems prepared to enact this scenario once again.[45]

Patwant Singh feared that Tohra's re-election as the President of the S.G.P.C. in November 1986 was fraught with dangers because "it could be the precursor of yet another calamitous collision over the Golden Temple," inasmuch as his very first action after being elected as the President of the S.G.P.C. on November 30, 1986, was to disband the special task force raised to keep the temple precincts free from undesirable elements. Other Akali politicians played their part equally "well" in falling into the trap of Indira Gandhi by creating conditions which led to the traumatic events of June 1984 and the disastrous consequences that followed.

Jagdev Singh Talwandi, who was ousted from the presidentship of the Akali Dal, tried to recover the lost ground by raising the slogan of more autonomy for Punjab, which became the basis of the controversial Anandpur Sahib Resolution of 1973. As if not to lag behind in the power struggle, the official Akali Dal adopted Talwandi's child. Though the Anandpur Sahib Resolution was passed in 1973, the Akalis did not press for its implementation when they came to power in Punjab in 1977 and also shared power with the Janata Party at the Centre. It was only after the Akali defeat in the Assembly

---

43. Amongst the best works on the subject is M.J. Akbar's *India: The Siege Within* (Harmondsworth: Penguin, 1985).
44. Quoted in *Amritsar: Mrs. Gandhi's Last Battle* (London: Jonathan Cape, 1985), p. 60.
45. *The Hindustan Times*, December 6, 1986.

elections in 1980 that they revived their old programme of agitation. In the meantime Jarnail Singh Bhindranwale,[46] who started as a religious preacher but rose to be a major force in Punjab politics as a result of backing from the Congress, put the Akali leaders on the defensive. Unless they could present something really radical there was little chance of their regaining their influence with the Sikh masses and competing with Bhindranwale, who made a sentimental and emotional appeal to the rustic Sikh youth of Punjab. It was in this spirit of competition with Bhindranwale in the field of religion and with the Congress in the field of regional politics that the Akalis formally launched their *Dharam Yudh morcha* on August 3, 1982, in the hope of getting some negotiated settlement on various long-pending demands of the Akali Dal.

Since recent Akali politics is not the area of my specialisation and as more competent scholars are likely to debate this problem, I would not like to go further into the details of this latest phase of the Akali struggle. What is relevant here, however, is to point out that although during the first two phases of their struggle, the Gurdwara Reform movement (1920-25) and the Punjabi Suba agitation, the Akali leadership was more or less united and was clear about the main issues, during the post-Punjabi-Suba agitation and especially during the Dharam Yudh *morcha* not only have the leaders remained ambiguous over various issues, but they have been working at cross-purposes. To discredit Longowal, Talwandi raised more extremist slogans. Similarly, Gurcharan Singh Tohra allowed Bhindranwale and his men to occupy the Guru Nanak Niwas and later move to the Akal Takht and helped his new ideology grow in the hope of reducing the popularity of Harchand Singh Longowal, whom he feared as a rival in Akali politics. And again, while Tohra managed to save himself during Operation Bluestar, he opposed the Punjab accord as something that would help Longowal and his men claim credit for solving the long-pending demands of the Akalis.

Strangely enough, the same Mr. Tohra, who opposed the Accord and its signatories, lent his support to Surjit Singh Barnala in ministry making and in the bargain got Major Singh Uboke, Prem Singh Chandumajra, Harbhajan Singh Sandhu and Basant Singh Khalsa included in the Barnala cabinet, leaving Parkash Singh Badal in the lurch. However, when he was forced to resign his presidentship of the S.G.P.C. he again joined hands with the Badal group and also helped extremists to regain their control over the Golden Temple. As pointed out before, after re-election to the presidentship of the S.G.P.C. in November 1986, Tohra's very first act was to disband the special task force raised to guard the Golden Temple against undesirable elements. What is happening in the Golden Temple these days is mainly the outcome of this wrong

---

46. During the post-Operation-Bluestar period, a number of journalists have tried to cash in on the myth of Bhindranwale, which has resulted in a large body of populist literature on the subject that cannot be described as serious or dependable biography of the late Sant. However, on various issues leading to Operation Bluestar and the consequences that followed, the best-edited work is Amrik Singh's *Punjab in Indian Politics: Issues and Trends* (Delhi: Ajanta Publications, 1985).

decision of Mr. Tohra. Mr. Amarinder Singh, scion of the royal Patiala family, who all these years has been a staunch opponent of Mr. Tohra and his politics, did not hesitate to join the Tohra-Badal combine after he resigned from the Barnala cabinet over the issue of police entry into the Golden Temple.

In the game of power politics Barnala has fared no better. The man who criticised the Congress government at the Centre for violating the sanctity of the Golden Temple by sending police and army into the sacred precincts, himself sent armed youth under the "command" of his son Gaganjit Singh to dislodge others whom he considered "undesirable" and later sent police into the holy precincts on April 30, 1986, thus lending legitimacy to the army action in June 1984. After the death of Sant Harchand Singh Longowal, who was the main source of strength of the Akali Dal, Mr. Barnala should have made efforts to carry with him important Akali leaders like Parkash Singh Badal and others to ensure unity in the party. It is a rather sad commentary that the Akali Dal, which had secured 73 seats in the Punjab Assembly elections in a house with a total strength of 117, was quickly reduced to a minority with the defection of Mr. Badal and 26 other Members of the Legislative Assembly (M.L.A.'s) belonging to his group. Instead of winning over Badal, who carried much influence with the Sikh farmers in Malwa and also enjoyed the confidence of a section of non-Sikhs, Barnala and his deputy, Balwant Singh, saw to it that Badal did not occupy any position of influence either in the Akali party or in the newly formed Akali government in Punjab.

Unfortunately, the Barnala-Balwant Singh combination started on the wrong note after the signing of the Punjab accord and the subsequent Akali victory in the provincial elections. They seem to have found in the Akali victory a personal triumph and not a mandate in favour of late Sant Longowal's slogan, "Unity within the party and reconciliation with rest of the nation." While forming the cabinet and reorganising the party, the Barnala-Balwant Singh faction made no secret of their monopolising power in the government and party on the pattern of what their patron Rajiv Gandhi was doing at the Centre. Instead of aligning himself with people without much political rooting, Barnala should have made a serious effort to accommodate Badal, especially when the latter was prepared to accept even the number two position in the cabinet. Maybe for personal reasons he did not want a deputy who was too strong, or perhaps he was under pressure from his advisors at the Centre not to have any truck with those who opposed the Punjab accord. Whatever may be the reason, Barnala and his group clearly had compromised the interests of the party and the community they claimed to represent.

Again, in order to stay in power Barnala and his supporters whisked away some forty M.L.A.'s to Chail and Simla in the neighbouring state of Himachal Pradesh to check them from joining the rebel group of twenty-seven that left the Barnala group of the Akali Dal over the issue of police entry into Golden Temple. To keep himself in power Barnala had to take the rather ignominious step of quickly adding twenty-one more legislators, including three dissidents, to the existing council of ministers. But Barnala alone cannot be accused of compromising his principles for political power. This is equally true of other Akali leaders.

As mentioned earlier, Gurcharan Singh Tohra first opposed the Punjab accord but later joined hands with Barnala in return for the latter's help for securing him another term as president of the S.G.P.C. and also for taking his protégés like Major Singh Uboke, Basant Singh Khalsa and Harbhajan Singh Sandu into the Barnala cabinet. Again, while Tohra criticised Barnala for the police entry into the Golden Temple and made a common cause with the breakaway group led by Mr. Badal, his protégés were not asked to give up their ministerial berths. Basant Singh Khalsa confessed that though he was unhappy over the issue of police entry into the Golden Temple "he did not want to leave the Barnala group and thus allow the Barnala government to be dismissed by the Centre the way it dismissed the minority government of G.M. Shah in Jammu and Kashmir." Unfortunately for Basant Singh Khalsa and others who very much wished to enjoy the benefits of remaining in power, the Barnala government was still dismissed by the Centre on the eve of the Haryana elections in spite of Mr. Barnala's toeing the central line and thus losing his credibility with the Sikh electorate over issues such as police entry into the Golden Temple, defying the *hukumnama* and extending full support to the state police chief, J.F. Rebeiro, in tackling the terrorist problem. After signing the accord with the Prime Minister of India, which promised, among other things, the transfer of Chandigarh to Punjab on January 26, 1986, the best thing for Barnala would have been to tender his resignation the moment he learned that the transfer had again been postponed by the Prime Minister. That would have at least partly helped him regain the lost credibility with the Sikh electorate in Punjab.

A careful comparison between the past and present Akali leaders shows that there has been a qualitative change since the days of the Akali movement. We no longer have men of stature like Baba Kharak Singh, Master Tara Singh and Sant Fateh Singh, who refused to bargain for personal or political benefits. In spite of his very close association with Jawaharlal Nehru and others in the Congress who occupied positions of power in free India, Kharak Singh refused to get any position or personal benefit, not even the pension as a freedom fighter to which he was legitimately entitled. Similarly Master Tara Singh refused to compromise the interests of his community over the issue of Sikhs' recruitment during World War II and resigned from the Working Committee of the Congress to help Sikhs get into the armed services. He had differences with the Congress, but he always kept the door for negotiation open. At no stage did he bargain for any political position by compromising with the Centre and sacrificing the interests of the Sikh community. In utter contrast, for the present leaders the S.G.P.C. and other gurdwara platforms have become ladders to climb to political power. The classic examples of this change of attitude are those of the president of the S.G.P.C. and the "head priest" of the holy Harmandir Sahib seeking nomination to the Rajya Sabha. While using religion for political agitations has been, and continues to be, the Akali forte, use of the S.G.P.C. and other religious platforms for furthering personal and political ambitions is a recent phenomenon fraught with dangers.

It is time Akali leaders learned from their past and rose above narrow prejudices and personal ambitions to provide much-needed leadership to the Sikh community. At the same time, the Government of India should give up its policy of dividing and weakening the Akali leadership, because a strong Akali leadership alone can act as a buffer between the government and the extremist element in Punjab and bring peace to the strife-torn state.

Fox and the Lions:
The Akali Movement Revisited

Ian J. Kerr

Has there emerged a satisfying explanation—satifying, that is, in general outline and direction such that specialists and informed outsiders find it reasonably accurate and interpretively plausible (correspondent and coherent)— to the following question: how does one explain the development of an intensified communal identity among the Sikhs in the first quarter of the twentieth century and the expression of that identity through vigorous political activity (what I hereafter refer to as the Akali movement)? The proposed explanation, moreover, should contribute to the development of validated models of socio-economic change, that is, models that have the capacity to explain the real past insofar as that past can be constructed. To approach the history of the Sikhs in any other way (e.g., as *sui generis*) is to doom Sikh studies to antiquarianism or to a kind of hagiology.[1] Of course, the exploration of such a question at the very least obliges me to identify some of the substantive and conceptual gaps that may exist in the current explantion.

But of what should a reasonably complete and satisfying explanation consist? Eric Hobsbawm has argued that to write the history of societies we must have "at least an approximate order of research priorities and a working assumption about what constitutes the central nexus or complex of connections of our subject, though of course these things imply a model."[2] He went on to argue that there was a tacit consensus among many historians as to what the working model, the set of priorities and assumptions, should look like, albeit

---

1. Although the angle of approach is somewhat different, the following two essays make a similar point: Mark Juergensmeyer, "The Forgotten Tradition: Sikhism in the Study of World Religions," in *Sikh Studies: Comparative Perspectives on a Changing Tradition*, ed. M. Juergensmeyer and N.G. Barrier (Berkeley: Graduate Theological Union, 1979), pp. 13-23; and, in the same volume, Ainslie T. Embree, "Locating Sikhism in Time and Place: A Problem for Historical Surveys," pp. 55-62.

2. E.J. Hobsbawm, "From Social History to the History of Society," in *Historical Studies Today*, ed. F. Gilbert and S.R. Graubard (New York: W.W. Norton and Company, 1972), p. 12.

[Joseph T. O'Connell, Milton Israel, Willard G. Oxtoby, eds., with W.H. McLeod and J.S. Grewal, visiting eds., *Sikh History and Religion in the Twentieth Century* (S. Asian Studies Papers, 3) (Toronto: S. Asian Studies, Univ. of Toronto, 1988)]

with his recognition of the presence of variant forms.[3] I suggest, therefore, that the following variant of Hobsbawm's working assumptions constitutes an appropriate standard against which to assess the adequacy of existing interpretations of the development of a Sikh communal identity conjoined to political militancy in the first quarter of this century.

The variant model which would seem suitable for the twentieth-century Punjab is as follows. One must begin with an historical environment whose dominant characteristic was the fact that the Punjab was in the advanced stages of induction into a new mode of production, the capitalist mode, through its integration into the evolving world economy under the aegis of a specifically Indo-centric variety of British colonialism. Thus, to diverge somewhat from Hobsbawm, this model cannot "work outwards and upwards from the process of social production in its specific setting."[4] Instead, one must give analytical priority to the external pressures generated on the Punjab by the world economy as mediated by the colonial situation—a mediation, however, that crucially included the British political and economic need to find and to retain collaborators within the population of the Punjab.[5] With this historical environment established, one should then pursue an explanatory strategy like that advocated by Hobsbawm, namely, the examination of the material environment as modified by human agency from which one moves to the evolving forces of production (the means of production, relevant demographic and labour processes) and on to the "structure of the consequent economy— divisions of labour, exchange, accumulation, distribution of the surplus, and so forth—and the social relations arising from these."[6] With this base established, one moves to the institutional and ideational elements of the society. This "structural" approach, however, must then be wedded to an exposition of historic change and transformation, within which the central dynamic, however poorly articulated, was the collective attempt of men and women to adapt to and to shape their life situations. Different collectivities, moreover, existed and were in competition with one another. The exposure of these societal tensions enables the historian to examine "collective consciousness, social movements, the social dimension of intellectual and cultural changes, and so on."[7]

The Punjab, as is well known, is virtually a test-tube example of change, transformation and resultant tensions in the period 1839-1987. Examples of new forms of collective consciousness, social movements and intellectual ferment abound. Students of the Sikhs and Sikhism have major opportunities to

---

3. Some historians argue that the consensus is beginning to break down. See Lawrence Stone, "The Revival of Narrative: Reflections on a New Old History," *Past and Present*, no. 85 (November, 1979), 3-24. Later in this paper I do argue for a role for the narrative at a certain point in the explanatory process.

4. Hobsbawm, "From Social History," p. 12.

5. A process explored in I.J. Kerr, "Imperial Rule in the Punjab, India, 1849-1872: A Partial Test of Ronald Robinson's Theory of Collaboration," *Journal of the Pakistan Historical Society* 29 (July, 1981), 149-75.

6. Hobsbawm, "From Social History," p. 12.

7. Ibid., p. 13.

contribute to worldwide debates. I do not suggest that the research program outlined above needs to be slavishly followed or that any particular study must pursue the entire program. I do, however, suggest that the program provides a test of completeness and satisfactoriness of an explanation and that it provides "a point of departure for reflections on those larger issues of scholarship that relate to the Sikh tradition" called for by the editors of the proceedings of the first Berkeley conference on Sikh studies.[8]

Do we have the makings of an explanation of the Akali movement that satisfies the research program outlined above? Had this question been asked five years ago or even two years ago, the answer would have been "no." Useful work had been done on the institutions and the ideas of the Akali movement, and some sound analysis of the political dimensions of the movement was available.[9] The economic "backbone," however, was largely unexamined, though its significance was often raised, as indeed it had to be for a generation of scholars raised on Thorburn, Darling, Calvert, Trevaskis and aware of the riches to be found in the decennial censuses, the district gazetteers, the settlement reports and the many publications of the Punjab Board of Economic Inquiry.[10] However, an attempt at a complete explanation of the type outlined above did not exist.

Richard G. Fox has changed the situation. His *Lions of the Punjab*, published in 1985, provides a "complete outline" explanation of the Akali movement and injects the history of twentieth-century Punjab into a number of debates which deal with the wider world and which are being conducted world-wide.[11] It is one of those books that, even in attempted refutation, will command the central ground for a number of years to come. It is a major achievement, in which Fox takes an existing body of information, much of which is fairly accessible in a variety of published sources, and fashions a new, persuasive analytical synthesis.

Let me touch upon a few of Fox's arguments in order to demonstrate that he does, for the main part, provide an explanation of the type I advocate above.

8. Juergensmeyer and Barrier, *Sikh Studies*, p. 1.
9. For example, Mohinder Singh, *The Akali Movement* (Delhi: Macmillan Company of India, 1978).
10. H. Calvert, *The Wealth and Welfare of the Punjab*, 2nd ed. (Lahore: Civil and Military Gazette, 1936); H.K. Trevaskis, *The Land of the Five Rivers* (London: Oxford University Press, 1928) and *The Punjab of Today: An Economic Survey of the Punjab in Recent Years (1890-1925)*, 2 vols. (Lahore: Civil and Military Gazette Press, 1931); M.L. Darling, *The Punjab Peasant in Prosperity and Debt*, 4th ed. (Bombay: Oxford University Press, 1947); S.S. Thorburn, *Musalmans and Money-lenders in the Punjab* (Edinburgh, 1886). An ill-digested summary of much of this type of material is to be found in B.S. Saini, *The Social and Economic History of the Punjab 1901-1939* (Delhi: ESS ESS Publications, 1975).
11. Richard G. Fox, *Lions of the Punjab: Culture in the Making* (Berkeley: University of California Press, 1985). I refer frequently to this book in the remainder of the paper, but I will only cite quotations. Among the debates to which Fox contributes is the on-going attempt to understand the nature, course and consequence of the capitalist world economy, within which there are a number of sub-debates, e.g., the mode-of-production debate. A good critical summary (albeit from within the Marxian tradition) of many of the contributions to that debate is provided by Anthony Brewer, *Marxist Theories of Imperialism: A Critical Survey* (London: Routledge and Kegan Paul, 1980). Also see T.S. Byres, "Modes of Production and Non-European Pre-Colonial Societies: The Nature and Significance of the Debate," *Journal of Peasant Studies* 12 (January-April, 1985), 1-18. Fox also pursues a debate within anthropology about the meaning of culture.

He begins with the penetration of the capitalist world economy into the Punjab under the aegis of British colonialism, whose objectives shaped and reshaped the nature of that penetration. The ascendancy over time of different and contradictory objectives generated different systems of agricultural production and labour in the Punjab, as characterized by the differences between the central Punjab and the Canal Colonies, which then came into competition with one another. The petty commodity producers of the central Punjab became increasingly disadvantaged and had to intensify their labour inputs to the point of self-exploitation in order to compete because of the labour-saving benefits major canal irrigation provided to the colonists. Unequal exchange was thereby established as value flowed from the less-favoured area to the more favoured area. Indeed, Fox's analysis of the different labour processes that arose from the differential means of production present in the area of well-water, as opposed to the area well watered, is masterful; it is a good example of the analytical application of the labour theory of value.[12]

To cut the first part of an intricate argument short, Fox produces a compelling description of the forces and relations of production in the agrarian sector of the Punjab as they had developed in their various and contradictory forms by 1920. He includes a discussion of the role of additional sources of employment, such as military service or migration overseas. The goal of his analysis is to show how and why the agriculturalists of the central Punjab were severely distressed by 1920 and thus, under the right circumstances, available to become supporters of the Akali reformers.

The Akali movement for Fox began as "religious reformism in Punjab cities and ended as anticolonial revolt in Punjab villages."[13] The urban beginnings were to be found in the growth of a reformed Sikh consciousness, expressed in the Singh Sabha movement, among lower-middle-class Sikhs who, partly in response to the Hindu militancy of certain Arya Samajists (a movement which lost political momentum and failed to become a vehicle for rural protest) affirmed their own Sikh identity, an identity which acquired an enhanced strength through the struggle to regain control of the Sikh shrines. Ironically, this struggle brought them into conflict with the British colonial authorities who supported the conservative *mahants* and *pujaris*. The urban reformers thus came to appropriate a "Singh identity," which had been created by the British as part of their recruitment and use of the Sikhs in British military service—an identity which had been enhanced and glorified during the First World War. Thus, in the immediate post-war context the "new" identity was used to induct an aggrieved rural population into a movement of mass protest which "equally expressed religious intent, anticolonialism and agrarian protest."[14] The first two elements in this heady mixture also proved attractive to the rural lower-middle class of the

12. Fox, *Lions*, pp. 52-78. Cf. Samir Amin, *Unequal Development: An Essay on the Social Formations of Peripheral Capitalism* (New York: Monthly Review Press, 1976), pp. 133-54.
13. Fox, *Lions*, p. 87.
14. Ibid., p. 178.

Canal Colonies, many of whom joined the protest despite their comparative affluence. The actual process of induction, Fox claims, was carried out by techniques similar to those used by British recruiting parties among rural Sikhs while the conduct of the protest campaigns often had military overtones.

Fox, I suggest, does give us an explanation of the Akali movement that in outline and direction is satisfying. Non-specialists, especially those who do not have South Asian research interest, will be attracted to Fox's arguments because he addresses wider issues within a framework which, if not universally accepted, is certainly widely known. (Those who do have such interests, even if the Punjab is not their specialty, will be better equipped to read *Lions of the Punjab* with the appropriate caution.) And he does contribute to the development and validation of models of socio-historic change; indeed, at times he becomes tendentious in his pursuit of a new concept of culture. I would further suggest to specialists in Sikh studies—among whom, I suspect, may be found those least favourably inclined towards the book—that an overly specialized criticism of Fox will leave his main arguments largely unscathed. The exposure of his omissions or his errors of substance will only have an impact if they can be shown to require fundamental modifications to his analysis or if a compelling counter-framework can be developed upon a substantive base shown to be more accurate. Another strategy is to accept the fundamental correctness of Fox's outline and approach and to ask how his account might be made more credible and coherent. I favour the latter strategy for approaching the question with which this paper began, namely, how one best explains the genesis and the course of the Akali movement.

Fox is no single-minded historical materialist (a species which, in any case, may exist only in the fervid imaginations of some neo-conservatives) who wants to argue "that a militant reformist Sikhism, the Singh identity that expressed it, and the Third Sikh War that enacted these beliefs existed or came into existence to express the deteriorating condition of the central Punjab cultivators as the colonial pattern of petty commodity production declined."[15] On the contrary, consciousness for Fox "is always historically contextualized and historically concrete; it is always in the making under particular conditions of time and place."[16] Fox, in fact, espouses a position close to that so effectively utilized in E.P. Thompson's *The Making of the English Working Class*.[17] However, central elements in Fox's account of the making of the Akali movement require scrutiny, and no element more so than the recruitment of Sikhs into the army and the role that played in helping to create a new Sikh identity. That identity, having been appropriated first by the urban Sikh reformers, was then used to mobilize rural Sikhs—or so Fox would have us believe. The new identity allegedly captured the frustration and militancy of the

---

15. Ibid., p. 105.
16. Ibid., p. 134.
17. A position whose theoretical dimensions are better followed in E.P. Thompson, *The Poverty of Theory and Other Essays* (London: Merlin Press, 1978).

cultivators and helped to direct those emotions to support the demand for shrine reform.

The first point one must make about the recruitment of Punjabis of all types into the British Indian army is how little we actually know, how little detailed research has been done.[18] The persistence of this situation continues to be surprising.[19] Scholars acknowledge the importance of the recruitment but continue to make that point by reference to the same tired old sources. But where is the detailed work based on the Military Proceedings of the Government of India and the Annual Army Caste Returns, to name but two bodies of sources readily available in London?[20] This research lacuna is a problem for Fox because he places much explanatory weight—in the leap from material conditions to human consciousness—on the formative and anticipatory consequences that the army policy had for Sikh identity formation. Fox reads a great deal into a few sources—sources like the army caste/class handbooks, McMunn and M.S. Leigh—that by their very nature provide a tautological expression of a particular kind of Sikh identity, a British view of the Sikhs, which the Sikhs, or some Sikhs, may or may not have accepted either in whole or in part.[21]

.A related point is that the Sikhs were not the only "martial race" recruited within the Punjab. If one reads the army handbooks dealing with non-Sikh groups one finds martial attributes, fine physiques, a tradition of military service and so on being ascribed also to various Muslim or Hindu castes and tribes.[22] And although the Sikhs produced a percentage of recruits during the First World War greatly in excess of their percentage in the population of Punjab, the fact remains that out of the 370,609 combatants recruited from the Punjab, 190,078 (51.4%) were Moslems and "only" 97,016 (26%) were Sikhs.[23] The Moslems, too, were demobilized into a context of material distress and political activity as were, for that matter, the Hindus.

I suspect that McLeod's position will prove closer to the truth. The army's insistence that Sikh recruits retain their traditional symbols, or obtain

---

18. We await the fruition of DeWitt C. Ellinwood's work, but see his "An Historical Study of the Punjabi Soldier in World War I," in *Punjab Past and Present: Essays in Honour of Dr. Ganda Singh*, ed. Harbans Singh and N.G. Barrier (Patiala: Punjabi University, 1976), pp. 337-62; DeWitt C. Ellinwood and C.H. Enloe, eds., *Ethnicity and the Military in Asia* (Buffalo: State University of New York, 1979); DeWitt C. Ellinwood and S.D. Pradhan, eds., *India and World War I* (New Delhi: Manohar, 1978).

19. It is an important and ready-made topic, though best left in many of its aspects to someone with a taste for quantification.

20. And probably only readily available in London these days, at least to historians working on Sikh topics given the situation in India. Some idea of what can be accomplished from these sources can be found in Ardythe Maude Roberta Basham, "Army Service and Social Mobility: The Mahars of the Bombay Presidency, with Comparisons with the Bene Israel and Black Americans" (Ph.D. dissertation, University of British Columbia, 1985).

21. Captain R.W. Falcon, *Handbook on Sikhs for the Use of Regimental Officers* (Allahabad: 1896); Captain A.H. Bingley, *Sikhs* (1899; reprint ed., Patiala: Languages Department, Punjab, 1970); Sir George MacMunn, *The Martial Races of India* (London: Sampson Low, Marston & Co., 1933); M.S. Leigh, *The Punjab and the War* (Lahore: Punjab Government, 1922).

22. For example, Lt. Colonel J.M. Wikeley, *Punjabi Musalmans* (Calcutta: Superintendent, Government Printing, India, 1922) and Major A.H. Bingley, *Jats, Gujars and Ahirs* (Calcutta: Superintendent, Government Printing, India, 1918).

23. M.S. Leigh, *The Punjab and the War*, p. 44.

them through the baptismal ceremony upon joining the army, was important but should not be overly emphasized. "The primary significance of the army policy was the economic opportunity which it afforded."[24] Pay, pay remittances to family, savings and pensions constituted the central nexus between the British Indian army and the Sikhs of rural Punjab. Indeed, Fox expresses a view similar to this in his second chapter. "It took remittances from both military service and laboring abroad to protect the agrarian system based on domestic ownership and family labor."[25] Moreover, a martial tradition and other cultural symbols suited to spur militant protest under the appropriate historical conditions existed among Sikh Jats (be they *amritdhari* or *sahajdhari*) before British rule in the Punjab. During the crucial yet still dimly understood later seventeenth- and eighteenth-century evolution of Sikhism it appears that the Panth was heavily influenced by the values and life-style of its increasing Jat membership. In fact, 1920-25 was almost a reprise of the period of Guru Hargobind, which one authority describes as follows: "The growth of militancy within the Panth must be traced primarily to the impact of Jat cultural patterns and to economic problems which prompted a militant response."[26] And, of course, the *jathas* of the Akali movement could draw inspiration from the *jathas* of the eighteenth century following Banda's execution in 1716.

British army policy, therefore, at best played an intensifying and sustaining role in Sikh identity formation, a role which was a part of the puzzle but not a major part. The Sikh Jats of the central Punjab did not need to adopt a reworked identity from urban, reforming Sikhs—and the contempt many Sikh Jats have for their urban Khatri and Arora brethren is often described[27]—since they already had a secure identity, which included a tradition of militancy, organized protest and, when necessary, violence. Sant Singh Sekhon's comments about the earlier 1960's could, I suspect, also apply to the earlier 1920's:

> It is a historical motive that attracts them to a political movement and not the Sikh religion. About any religious matter they are very latitudinarian. But when there is a mass demonstration (morcha) 90 percent of those arrested are Jats. The Congress has done a lot for us they think, but we cannot turn our backs on Panth (the Sikh community). It is a question of bravery, of communal courage. Group pride comes in! Have the Sikhs gone down before the government?[28]

It was precisely to a Jat identity that Lieutenant-Governor O'Dwyer appealed in one of his army recruiting tour exhortations in 1918: "if regard be had to

---

24. W.H. McLeod, *The Evolution of the Sikh Community* (Oxford: Clarendon Press, 1976), p. 55.

25. Fox, *Lions*, p. 48.

26. McLeod, *The Evolution*, pp. 12-13.

27. For example, Joyce Pettigrew, *Robber Noblemen: A Study of the Political System of the Sikh Jats* (London: Routledge and Kegan Paul, 1975), pp. 41-43.

28. Quoted in Joyce Pettigrew, "The Growth of Sikh Community Consciousness 1947-1966," *South Asia*, new series, 3 (December, 1980), 46.

available numbers the Mazhbi Sikhs have far surpassed the Jats...do the Jats view the Cavalry of Mazhbis with equanimity?"[29]

Fox's interpretation of the role played by the recruiting and organizational policy of the British Indian army (i.e., using caste and community as regimental building blocks) in helping to develop a particular Sikh identity is strained, overdone and finds the roots of a militant identity in a set of antecedent conditions which were, at best, tangential and contributory rather than central.

It is to Fox's credit, however, that he does seek to explain the mobilization historically rather than fall back upon the determinisms of cultural materialism and culturology (a kind of idealism in which cultural meanings determine social action). He, therefore, shares the problem that bedevils all reflective historians: how does one explain the collective or individual interventions of human beings in particular historical processes and situations? How does one describe the synapses between a particular set of material conditions, the human consciousness that arises thereupon, and the actions based on that consciousness that may follow? Regardless of my reservations about the particular explanation of the locus of Sikh identity provided by Fox, I admire his attempt to grapple both with a particular historical process and a major methodological and theoretical issue.

We may be most concerned about Fox and the Lions, but Fox himself also wishes to pursue some substantial epistemological chickens. The answer historians may have to give at this level of the explanatory paradigm is to resort to the detailed narrative in the attempt to engage in what W.H. Walsh called "colligation" or "the procedure of explaining an event by tracing its intrinsic relations to other events and locating it in its historical context."[30] There comes a point in any piece of historical explanation where human action can only be made intelligible by thorough and careful narration, the point where theory is made credible by dense reconstruction. And if there is a fatal flaw in Fox's work it is to be found in his inadequate and sometimes misdirected reconstruction. He gets caught between expectations generated by his theoretical approaches and his reliance on a limited and one-sided set of sources, into providing a reconstruction that in places corresponds poorly to the particular conditions in the Punjab in the early twentieth century within which the Akali movement developed. This paper, however, is not an exercise in methodological criticism or in theory construction, nor is it meant to be a review *per se* of *Lions of the Punjab*. I am interested in assessing the extent to which we now have a good explanation of the genesis, course and *dénouement* of the Akali movement. Richard Fox has made a major contribution to such an explanation, but he does leave some important considerations inadequately examined. I shall mention

---

29. Quoted in Stephen P. Cohen, *The Indian Army* (Berkeley: University of California Press, 1971), p. 71.
30. W.H. Walsh, *An Introduction to the Philosophy of History*, 3rd ed. (London: Hutchinson, 1967), p. 59. Also R.F. Atkinson, *Knowledge and Explanation in History* (London: Macmillan, 1978), esp. the note on p. 139. A recent treatment of some of these issues is Michael Stanford, *The Nature of Historical Knowledge* (Oxford: Basil Blackwell, 1986).

three that I think to be important parts of any overall explanation of how an Akali consciousness was made and was then made to act collectively in the aftermath of the First World War.

First, Fox provides only very brief mention of the Babbar Akalis. This is unfortunate because in their espousal and use of violence, among other characteristics, the Babbars represented a form of protest different from that presented within the same historical context by the main Akali movement. Indeed, the Babbar Akalis appealed to the poorer groups among the rural discontented, for whom the wider Akali movement, with its narrow focus on gurdwara reform and control, was in considerable measure a failure.[31] But why and how, one must ask, was the Akali movement as a whole able to feed upon rural distress without addressing some of the basic socio-economic demands of the distressed? A close comparison of the two Akali movements may help us understand both movements better. The Babbars, significantly, were rural protesters who had few, if any, links to the urban Singhs who figure prominently in Fox's explanation.[32]

Second, Fox does not provide an adequate consideration of the role enhanced communications played in the development of the Akali movement. A revolution in communications took place in the Punjab in the late nineteenth and the early twentieth centuries.[33] It is a revolution that continues today, but by 1919-20 it had already proceeded far enough to facilitate greatly the mobilization of the Sikhs and other Punjabis. The communication revolution helps us to explain how the movement developed and goes some considerable distance in helping to explain why the movement succeeded. It does not explain why the movement developed or why it took the form and direction that it did, although a certain intensity and speed of communication was probably a necessary prerequisite for the kind of mass mobilization that did occur. Appropriate communication networks must be present if the grievances of atomized individuals and small groups are to be shared in such a way as to make collective protest possible. Leaders and followers must be in regular communication if collective protest is to be organized, focussed and sustained. This requirement was well understood by the Babbar Akalis, who, despite their clandestine existence, went to considerable pains to keep villagers aware of the objectives of the movement. Their techniques included a mobile press, producing the *Babbar Akali Doaba* on a portable duplicating machine that had been bought with money extorted from a *lambardar*.[34]

---

31. Susan B.C. Devalle and Harjot S. Oberoi, "Sacred Shrines, Secular Protest and Peasant-Participation: The Babbar Akalis Reconsidered," *Punjab Journal of Politics* 7 (July-December, 1983), 33.

32. Cf. Fox, *Lions*, pp. 171-84 with Devalle and Oberoi, "Sacred Shrines," pp. 44-62.

33. Note in this connection N.G. Barrier's important contribution on the Chief Khalsa Diwan found elsewhere in this volume. Also note Barrier, "The Punjab Government and Communal Politics, 1870-1908," *Journal of Asian Studies* 27 (May, 1968), 529, where he states mass communications helped to spur the unrest and rioting in the late 1880's and early 1890's.

34. Devalle and Oberoi, "Sacred Shrines," pp. 51-52.

What I have in mind when I refer to a revolution in communications is a concept that encompasses the nature and the consequences of a major increase in the rapidity and intensity of the movement and/or dissemination of people, goods and ideas. In its broadest formulation it is a concept akin to the process of social mobilization described by Karl Deutsch, which can include education and the growth of literacy, urbanization, intensified economic interchange, and so on.[35] Paul Brass used elements of Deutsch's approach in his useful study of the role of language and linguistic symbols in the development of Sikh communal consciousness.[36] Much work, however, remains to be done and I believe that the later nineteenth- and twentieth-century history of the Punjab provides fertile ground for the application, testing and refinement of concepts like those advanced by Deutsch. Certainly communication of all varieties is a central component of the synapses that are present at the interface between the external and internal dimensions of human history, between material conditions and collective consciousness. Grievance must be articulated and shared in order to become a political reality. Or, as Lenin said: "politics begin where the masses are, not where there are thousands, but where there are millions, that is where serious politics begin."[37]

Of what did the revolution in communications that preceded and accompanied the Akali movement consist? How did it facilitate and intensify mobilization, such that we can understand better the substantial and effective organization displayed by the Akalis, and the impressive outpourings of protest activity as *jathas* large and small marched across the Punjab? How did it make possible the rapid feedback and response to confrontations such that large numbers of rural and urban Sikhs quickly became aware of what was happening and, in the emotional climate thereby generated, found themselves swept into the protest movement? Certainly there was such a revolution, on-going since the later nineteenth century, the centrality of which to the success if the Akali movement is captured in the following quotation from Mohinder Singh:

> Moreover, contrary to the Government's expectation that its repressive action [1922] at a remote village (Guru-ka-Bagh) would not attract sympathizers, spectators, press reporters and photographers, a large number of them continued to visit the place. They played a major role in exposing the brutality of the police by publishing accounts of such actions in the newspapers.[38]

The Punjab of the early 1920's was a place in transformation in terms of the improved means of communication, i.e., the technology of communications, including in the case of roads both roadbeds and the equipment that travelled thereon. Also in transformation was the intensity of communication: the flows of people, goods and content-bearing media such as newspapers, letters, books,

35. Karl W. Deutsch, "Social Mobilization and Political Development," *American Political Science Review* 55 (September, 1961), 493-514.
36. Paul R. Brass, *Language, Religion and Politics in North India* (London: Cambridge University Press, 1974), esp. chapter 6.
37. Quoted in E.H. Carr, *What Is History?* (New York: Vintage Books, 1967), p. 61.
38. Mohinder Singh, *The Akali Movement*, p. 57.

and telephone calls via the improving means of communication. An extensive railroad system existed by the turn of the century, from which in the early 1920's a burgeoning road system began to take over short-haul traffic in people and lighter goods. Metalled road mileage in 1920-21 was 2,937, while unmetalled roads covered 22,106 miles. These figures, however, only tell part of the story, since more bridges over rivers and *nullahs*, better interconnections, and the maintenance of many unmetalled roads as motorable in fair weather also contributed to better and faster communications.[39] By 1925 some 266 motor-cycles and 1,133 cars and trucks were travelling on Punjab roads—a far cry from the turn of the century, when bullock carts, *ekkas*, *tumtums*, and *tongas* were the main means of road transportation.[40] Road and rail transport in turn made for a more effective postal system. Post offices numbered 2,935 in 1921, and by 1931 every town and on average every thirteen villages were so served. The telegraph system was similarly well-developed (330 stations in 1921; 524 in 1931) such that the 1921 *Census* could report that "the most inaccessible spots have unexpectedly frequent deliveries" of postal materials and telegraphs.[41] In 1930-31 there were 126,229,278 letters delivered.[42]

By the early 1920's many Punjab towns had rudimentary telephone systems, and trunk lines connected the larger centres with one another and with the rest of India via Delhi. The decade 1920-21 to 1930-31 was a period of considerable expansion of the telephone system. The same decade saw the growth of radio communications.[43]

The peoples of the Punjab, in fact, were participants in a worldwide expansion of the means of communication. It was a transformation that occurred within the Punjab but also linked Punjabis more intensively and quickly to the wider world. This world extended to other parts of India, and beyond to the embattled, expatriate Punjabi communities in Canada and the United States. Their continuing struggles against discrimination helped to fuel the fires of discontent in the Punjab as news of those struggles flowed back to the Punjab via newspapers, pamphlets and letters. Insofar as the California-based Ghadar movement had influence, that influence depended on international flows of communication.[44]

---

39. *Census of India, 1931*, v. 18: *Punjab*, part 1 (Lahore, 1933), p. 40. A more descriptive account of road development is W.S. Dorman, "Highways in the Punjab, Past and Future," *Minutes of Proceedings of the Punjab Engineering Congress, 1919*, v. 7 (Lahore, 1919), pp. 3-24.

40. *Census, 1931*, p. 50. *Imperial Gazetteer of India. Provincial Series, Punjab*, v. 2 (Calcutta: Superintendent of Government Printing, 1908), p. 92.

41. *Census, 1931*, p. 52. *Census of India, 1921*, v. 15: *Punjab and Delhi*, part 1 (Lahore, 1923), p. 18.

42. *Census, 1931*, p. 52. The *Imperial Gazetteer of India, Provincial Series, Punjab*, v. 2, p. 93, contains a useful table for the years 1880-81, 1890-91, 1900-01, 1903-04, which details postal deliveries by categories (letters, newspapers, parcels, etc.) and in addition enumerates other important details like value of stamps sold, money orders issued and savings bank deposits. I have not seen anything comparable for the later decades.

43. *Census, 1921*, p. 18; *Census, 1931*, p. 52.

44. There is a developing literature on the Sikhs overseas. Among those with a Canadian focus are: T.G. Fraser, "The Sikh Problem in Canada and Its Political Consequences, 1905-1921," *Journal of Imperial and Commonwealth History* 7 (October, 1978), 35-55; Hugh Johnston, *The*

The changed communication environment had been recognized by the British during World War I in the conduct of their propaganda campaigns designed to ensure Indian support for the war effort. Punjabis, of course, were central objectives of the campaigns. Different media—newspapers, communiqués, public lectures, mass mailings, slide shows—were used as the British searched for the most effective way to convey their message. Most bizarre, but also revealing about the penetration of the postal system, was "a scheme to sell 'Loyalty' postcards."[45]   The British, however, seem to have been caught somewhat off guard when similar techniques were used against them by the Akalis.

The point seems to be irrefutable. The Akali movement was launched in a communication environment favorable to sustained mobilization. Moreover, the field of struggle was compact in size, relatively free from major physical barriers, culturally quite homogeneous (e.g., linguistically) insofar as the Sikhs were concerned, and tightly focussed on the issue of the control of the shrines. It was a very manageable protest; indeed, a casual student like myself cannot but be impressed with the organization and direction exhibited by the Akalis and be led from that observation to wonder just how "mass" a mass movement it in fact was.[46]   Might not ease of communication and rapidity of deployment of personnel (to objectives established by the Akalis to which the *mahants* and the British could only react after the fact) have enabled the reformers to maximize the impact of a relatively few, active protesters? Perhaps the "Third Sikh War" was more in the nature of a well-led, tactically oriented skirmish.

Voyage of the Komagata Maru: The Sikh Challenge to Canada's Colour Bar (Delhi: Oxford University Press, 1979); Norman Buchignani and Doreen M. Indra with Ram Srivast[a]va, *Continuous Journey: A Social History of South Asians in Canada* (Toronto: McClelland and Stewart, 1985). The Ghadar movement finds mention in all of these works but one should also read Emily Brown, *Har Dayal: Hindu Revolutionary and Rationalist* (Tucson: University of Arizona Press, 1975). Joseph T. O'Connell recently has published a very useful bibliographic survey of Sikhs in Canada: "Sikh Studies and Studies of Sikhs in Canada," *Studies in Sikhism and Comparative Religion* 5 (October, 1986), 154-73.

45. N. Gerald Barrier, *Banned: Controversial Literature and Political Control in British India 1907-1947* (Columbia: University of Missouri Press, 1974), p. 75. The whole book, of course, illustrates the British concern with controlling print media in India.

46. Fox has an interest in magnifying the size of the Akali movement, an interest captured in phrases like "massive rural protest" (p. 9), or in his repeated reference to the movement as the "Third Sikh War." Mohinder Singh, *The Akali Movement*, upon whom Fox relies for some of his information, also has an interest in stressing the presence of extensive participation. But even if we double the figure (25,000) of the number of Akali volunteers given by Mohinder Singh (pp. 100-1, table note) we only get 1.6% of the Sikhs in the Punjab (3,110,060) in 1921. This may or may not be "mass participation." Rajat K. Ray, "Masses in Politics: The Non-Cooperation Movement in Bengal 1920-1922," *Indian Economic and Social History Review* 11 (December, 1974), 343-410, touches on the same question during the same time period but in a different part of India. Regardless of the answer to the question, the Akali movement certainly exhibited a controlled type of participation in which mass activity was kept tightly focussed on the objectives established by the leadership and thus was unlikely to stray into other activities more representative of rural distress. Sumit Sarkar sees this kind of control as generally present in the struggles of Indian nationalists. See his *'Popular' Movements & 'Middle Class' Leadership in Late Colonial India: Perspectives & Problems of a 'History from Below'* (Calcutta: Centre for Studies in the Social Sciences, 1983). The significance of this for an investigation of the Babbar Akalis is obvious.

Nonetheless, it does appear that many Sikhs came to support, tacitly if not actively, the goals of the Akali movement. And why not? By the early 1920's Sikh literacy was on the increase, many newspapers and other forms of written materials were available and quickly distributed, and more Sikhs were students in educational institutions than at any previous time.[47] Moreover, the bare statistics on the growth of education and literacy only hint at the communication impact of the print media. For example, chains of interconnections magnified the impact of each newspaper.[48] The processes of social mobilization were at work—to cap which, a heavy-handed British administration and foolish *mahants* gave the Akalis one public-relations bonanza after another: Tarn Taran, Nakana, Guru ka Bagh, Jaito.

Mention of the process of social mobilization brings me to the third inadequacy of Fox's presentation. He does not explore sufficiently the uprooting that had taken place in rural Punjab, such that many Sikhs were ready for induction into the protest movement.[49] The increasing economic distress in the central Punjab, whose causes he exposes, was intensified and catalyzed by other, shorter-term crises. One such element (and Fox is aware of it) that requires much more research is the presence of many demobilized Sikh soldiers. These had been uprooted by their wartime experiences, including, for some, service on the Western Front, from which many of their brethren did not return—men whose Punjabi names remain carved in grim, massive monuments at Ypres and elsewhere in Flanders. The returnees faced an uncertain reintegration into a distressed agrarian economy. Some were inducted into the Akali cause.[50]

There were, indeed, many events and processes at work in the Punjab during the Great War and afterwards that can be identified as potentially uprooting. The Punjab, for example, was thrust to centre stage of the all-India nationalist struggle in 1919 as a result of the Amritsar massacre. This and other events need to be carefully looked at for their possible contributions to the processes of mobilization. However, the historian needs to avoid forgetting causal priorities in the attempt to provide a dense narrative.

One other "uprooting" that demands thorough examination is the great influenza epidemic of later 1918. This event represented an intense crisis for the Punjab and much of the rest of India. The number of deaths crammed into a few months was enormous: some 17 million Indians died, of whom at least a million

47. Brass, *Language*, pp. 300-9, provides most of the statistics.
48. *Census, 1921*, p. 317: "Actually for every paper printed or sold there are 20 persons who read its contents, or listen to it being read in the street of the smaller towns, or in the 'chaupals' of the larger villages, and the men who listen will in their turn pass on it [*sic*] at least part of the news to their women folk, or to friends and relations when visiting villages remote from lines of railway or off the main routes."
49. Deutsch, p. 494, argues that mobilization has two phases: "(1) the stage of uprooting or breaking away from old settings, habits and commitments; and (2) the induction of the mobilized persons into some relatively stable new patterns of group membership, organization and commitments."
50. Mohinder Singh, *The Akali Movement*, p. 57.

were Punjabis. Their death rates in rural areas exceeded 50 per 1000.[51] Parry, whom Fox uses in another context, observed some one hundred sick in the village Kulhur while "at the entrance to the village I counted no less than eighteen burning pyres, while remains of broken pitchers lay thickly about them, showing that many in the prime of life had died." At Ludhiana "deaths often exceeded one hundred a day."[52] The *Census* refers to choked hospitals while "dead and dying lay by the sides of the roads, burial grounds and burning ghats were strained beyond their capacity and corpses lay awaiting burial and cremation. Terror and confusion reigned supreme."[53] The short- and medium-term social, economic and demographic repercussions of this tragic event were substantial and influenced in many ways the course of Punjab history in the early 1920's. One also suspects, however, that the great wave of death had a psychological effect on rural Sikhs; in conjunction with other forces, it may have prepared them for induction into a religious cause. One does not have to accept the extreme positions of some psycho-historians in order to recognize the unsettling, uprooting, terrifying effect of this great epidemic.[54]

I began this chapter by advocating an appropriate research strategy for explaining the genesis and the development of the Akali movement. I then suggested that Richard Fox's recent book, *Lions of the Punjab*, was in accord with that strategy, that model if you will, and that the book does provide a satisfactory and reasonably complete explanation of the Akali movement. Indeed, I went further: I said the book was a major achievement as a work of analysis and synthesis.

Reasonably complete and satisfactory, however, does not mean correct in all of the book's aspects. It means that Fox meets in outline reasonable tests of coherence within a particular analytical framework and correspondence to the historical facts as we know them. Fox, in fact, meets the test of coherence more completely than he does the test of correspondence. Historians rightly will take exception to some of his assertions about the political and social conditions in early twentieth-century Punjab. His knowledge of the Sikhs, Sikh organizations and Sikh political life in that period needs development. I have suggested some of the ways in which I think Fox's presentations to be deficient or somewhat off-base. Most of the criticisms I have made focus on the "upper levels" of the explanatory paradigm: at the level of activated group consciousness, where one seeks to explain how and why a substantial number of people consciously

---

51. I.D. Mills, "The 1918-1919 Influenza Pandemic—The Indian Experience," *Indian Economic and Social History Review*, 23 (January-March, 1986), 1-40; *Census, 1921*, p. 61; Saini, *History*, p. 16. The effect of Mills' revisionist article is to increase the estimates of mortality attributable to the epidemic. The 1921 Punjab *Census* recognized that its figures under-recorded the death toll.

52. R.E. Parry, *The Sikhs of the Punjab* (1921; reprinted, Patiala: Languages Department, Punjabi University, Patiala, 1970), pp. 34, 36.

53. *Census, 1921*, p. 60.

54. W.L. Langer, the most *pakka* of diplomatic historians, came to argue for due attention to psychological factors in history during the later years of his career. See his "The Next Assignment," *American Historical Review* 63 (January, 1958), 283-304. Langer, in fact, specifically argued for attention to the psychological repercussions of the Black Death.

attempt to do something collectively about their life situation—or at least consciously choose to follow a certain set of leaders.   The making of consciousness, Akali or any other, is a difficult thing for an historian to reconstruct.   Richard Fox's greatest contribution is to expose with considerable clarity the outlines of the longer-term socio-economic transformation in which the Akali movement was imbedded.   However, we still need a clearer explanation of how a particular superstructure came to interact with that socio-economic base such that the demand for gurdwara reform became a "mass" movement.   Fox, though, shows us the way.   I hope the book gets the attention it deserves.

The Shiromani Gurdwara Prabandhak Committee and the Politicisation of the Sikhs

Attar Singh

In one form or another the Shiromani Gurdwara Prabandhak Committee (S.G.P.C.) has remained, ever since its inception in 1925, central to what may well be defined in the terms coined by Jawaharlal Nehru as Sikh religious nationalism. Such a description is even more apposite for the situation obtaining during the last four decades after Independence. For the Punjabi Suba agitation launched by the Shiromani Akali Dal with the thinly veiled object of carving out a Sikh-majority state soon after Independence, the Committee provided both the rallying point and the launching pad. The agitation was based in the Golden Temple complex directly under the control of the S.G P.C. and it was justified by the Sikh political doctrine of inseparability of religion and politics. These campaigns were conducted in the typical format of Akali *morchas* evolved during the Sikh Gurdwara Reform movement in the early twenties. The models of the *morcha* were provided by some of the famous *morchas* such as Chabian Da *morcha*, Guru ka Bagh *morcha* and Jaito *morcha*, all occurring immediately before the passage of the Sikh Gurdwara Act in 1925. Organised essentially as a regular display of collective non-violent defiance of state authority, these *morchas* came to be associated with sending out bands of volunteers known as *jathas* every day over a considerable period of time to attract public notice and make dramatic impact. This required both a safe assembling point for the volunteers pouring in from all over and the starting point for the *jathas* to proceed from, and also involved a safe sanctuary for the organisers of the *morchas* and camping arrangements for the volunteers. These *morchas* proved to be an effective means for political mobilisation.

At least two of the major Akali *morchas* in 1955 and 1961 were allowed by the S.G.P.C. to be conducted from the precincts of the Akal Takht within the Golden Temple complex where the volunteers took their oaths before marching out in passive resistance.

[Joseph T. O'Connell, Milton Israel, Willard G. Oxtoby, eds., with W.H. McLeod and J.S. Grewal, visiting eds., *Sikh History and Religion in the Twentieth Century* (S. Asian Studies Papers, 3) (Toronto: S. Asian Studies, Univ. of Toronto, 1988)]

Apart from these two *morchas* in pursuit of the Sikh political goals, another Akali *morcha* was launched in 1975 in protest against the promulgation of "Emergency" in India extinguishing all civil liberties and fundamental rights. It did not have an exclusive Sikh political content, and was therefore greatly appreciated by a wide spectrum of political opinion in India that would otherwise have looked askance at the mixing of politics and religion by the Akali Dal. In 1982, however, the *Dharam Yudh morcha*, started originally by Sant Jarnail Singh Bhindranwale and later on adopted by the Shiromani Akali Dal, proved to be the most cataclysmic of all. The ramifications of this *morcha* are as yet far from being spent, and the role of the S.G.P.C. in the initiation and the tragic *dénouement* of the whole complex of events leading therefrom has been of primary significance. The chain of events triggered by the annual election of the office-bearers of the S.G.P.C. on November 30, 1986, has engulfed the Sikh world in an unprecedented turmoil, the resolution of which is not yet in sight.

The S.G.P.C. is as yet a live organism as much for the Sikh masses as for the rest of India, involving all sorts of theological, social and economic contradictions and drawing in a vast multitude of people at different levels of perception and participation. To start with, I would like to draw attention to the constitutional ambivalence built into the very formation of the S.G.P.C. The Shiromani Gurdwara Prabandhak Committee derives its institution from an act of the Punjab Legislature (Gurdwaras Act 8 of 1925), which was enacted primarily "to provide for the better administration of certain Sikh Gurdwaras." This act has been amended and adapted no less than 35 times through legislative action of the state. On the analogy of this act, the Indian Parliament adopted the Delhi Gurdwaras Act 82 of 1971, which in certain regards is more radical in theo-political content than the Punjab act. Legislative sanction of the state for setting up an autonomous religious organisation implies that the state had to intervene to provide a system for regulating a part of the religious concern of a section of the people. This act of the state may be further seen to indicate that the Sikh people had failed to devise a self-management of their "historical and other major shrines" and had to invite the support of the state in conducting a part of their religious affairs. What is odd about this situation is that a purely religious arrangement should depend for legitimacy on an act of the state.

This superimposition of the state on "church" affairs, especially as it was brought about by a long drawn-out struggle of gurdwara reform carried on by the followers of the faith, implies the failure of the "church" to evolve a self-determined, self-perpetuating and self-reliant system of administration. But the continuing demand for enactment of an All India Sikh Gurdwara Act, which incidentally formed a part of the Memorandum of Settlement signed between Rajiv Gandhi, Prime Minister of India, and the late Sant Harchand Singh Longowal, the then President of the Shiromani Akali Dal, on July 24, 1985, may be interpreted as a firm indicator that the Sikh "church" welcomes the support of the state, at least in the matter of its continued institutionalisation.

The procedure adopted for the institution of the S.G.P.C. further contributes to the inherent political significance and role of the Committee. The Gurdwara Reform movement had two major components: first, the transference of control of the Sikh gurdwaras from the hereditary custodians known as *mahants* to the Sikh community as a whole; and second, creation of a representative instrument to discharge the function called forth by such transference. Several factors combined to make this movement converge upon the widely shared concern of the Sikhs in the early twenties for being recognised as a distinct identity, an entity that had been shattered and fragmented after the fall of the Sikh kingdom in 1849. Here it will be worthwhile to remember that in the formation of the S.G.P.C., the disinherited Sikh mind found a symbol of its corporate existence to enshrine the memories of its past glory, a substitute for the theo-political personality negated by the end of the Sikh supremacy in 1849. The shift from state to "church" as the rallying point for saving the community from falling apart and for demarcating and strengthening the group boundaries led to perceiving the "church" as a substitute for the state and marshalling all its might as a force for conservatism against the forces of modernisation, of which the secular state is a prime motivator and instrument.

The stout resistance by the *mahants* and the ruthless opposition of the British government to the movement generated a unity of struggle and purpose in the community with a wide and deep spread, the like of which had never been witnessed since the fall of the Sikh kingdom in 1849. In its turn this unity of struggle and purpose led to politicisation and mobilisation of the Sikhs, especially from amongst the emergent middle castes and classes: the professionals, the urban middle classes and the peasantry (i.e., land-owning agriculturalists).   Reinforcing the rising passions and expectations, the movement was rewarded with a system involving the entire community in the institution of the S.G.P.C. The Committee was to be selected on the basis of adult franchise, which at that time was not operative even for the state legislature, based as it was on restricted franchise. It was quite natural that the procedure of periodic renewal of the mandate through elections should lend to the elected body an overall popular mandate mixing religious content with political intent. Moreover, the organisation of elections on such a wide scale demanded a political organisation, which was met by the formation of a religio-political party known as the Shiromani Akali Dal. All the political campaigns proceeding from the movement of Sikh religious nationalism were led by the Shiromani Akali Dal both before and after Independence.

The relationships between the Shiromani Gurdwara Prabandhak Committee and the Shiromani Akali Dal, whether in power or in opposition, have ranged from co-ordinational to oppositional contradictions and have fostered factionalism both in the community and in the Dal. There have been several instances, including the one recently witnessed wherein the S.G.P.C. invoked the religious authority of the Akal Takht and its *jathedar*, an appointee of the S.G.P.C., against even the President of the Shiromani Akali Dal and the

Akali Chief Minister. It did so even though the S.G.P.C. itself is a product of the Shiromani Akali Dal's political organisation. The Akal Takht so far is directly under the control of the S.G.P.C.

This was a repetition, with a wider sweep, of what occurred in 1979 when the President of the S.G.P.C., Gurcharan Singh Tohra, and the President of the Shiromani Akali Dal, Jagdev Singh Talwandi, who had fallen out with the then Akali Chief Minister, Parkash Singh Badal, petitioned to the Akal Takht chief to seek punishment of the latter on all sorts of personal failings and political misdeeds. At that time the then Chief Minister out-manœuvred the *jathedars* and managed to be awarded a favourable verdict from Sadhu Singh Bhaura, the then *jathedar* of the Akal Takht. In 1980, the differences and ego-conflicts between the top leaders of the Akali Dal were so grave that as an escape from the ugly situation they sought the intervention of the Akal Takht *jathedar* to release the list of the party candidates. This action was later on interpreted by the Supreme Court as religious interference in the general elections, leading to the disqualification of an Akali Member of the Legislative Assembly, H.S. Fattenwala, from seeking election to the Parliament or the State Assembly for six years.

This theo-political instrument was again activated after the defeat of the Akali Chief Minister's faction in the annual election of the office-bearers of the S.G.P.C. on November 30, 1986. Through the new *jathedar* of the Akal Takht appointed by the new Executive Committee, attempts were made not only to discipline the Akali Chief Minister, Surjit Singh Barnala, but even to call into being a new Akali Dal with the immediate aim of forcing the ruling Akali Dal out of office. The basic contradiction lies in the fact that the S.G.P.C. is constituted by the members elected to the committee as the nominees of the Shiromani Akali Dal. These nominees, after election on the party ticket, appoint the *jathedar* of the Akal Takht, who may then confront the party in the exercise of his "supreme authority" and even come out in total conflict with the very party of which the S.G.P.C. and the Akal Takht chief are the creatures.

In another way, this phenomenon can be interpreted as the inherent contradiction between the "church" absolutism and the politico-democratic base of the Sikh "church." In the world history of "churches" of different faiths the Sikh "church" is unique, in that while it is a creation of the democratic processes, with periodic elections by the electorate comprising not the clergy but the laity, it should demand absolute authority. The absolutist "church" and the democratic relativism of its constitution constitute a paradox that generates intra-community pulls and pressures and factional and ideological conflicts, on the one hand, and the conflict between the Sikh "church" (shaped by the S.G.P.C.) and the state on the other. The conflict involving the S.G.P.C. is not with the Union government alone. It is much more vigorously pursued with the Punjab state government, especially when Punjab is ruled by the Akali Dal itself, and stems essentially from the fervently fostered myth that the S.G.P.C. represents an authority superior to the state and that the latter is answerable to it rather than *vice versa.* Typical of the conflict has been the S.G.P.C. antagonism towards successive Akali governments led by the late Justice Gurnam Singh, Lachman Singh Gill, Parkash Singh Badal and S.S. Barnala. There is a deeper significance to it than that predicated by ego-conflicts: the structuring of the S.G.P.C. as an institution quite similar to the state legislature has come to be associated in the collective consciousness of the community with the inherent authority to legislate upon all its concerns, theological, political, social and cultural.

A reference to the original Sikh Gurdwara Act of 1925 shows that the Shiromani Gurdwara Prabandhak Committee was initially conceived as some sort of a federating institution, with only a supervisory role over the local committees managing the Sikh shrines in exercise of local autonomy. Originally, only two shrines were to be directly administered by the S.G.P.C., namely Shri Akal Takht Sahib, Amritsar, and Shri Takht Keshgarh Sahib, Anandpur Sahib. All other shrines, either clubbed together on the city basis or individually, were to be administered by the local committees. Similarly, the funds available for the functioning of the S.G.P.C. were to be provided from one-tenth of the savings of these committees. This situation, with the authority and the resources of a popularly elected body being severely restricted, generated a desire for expansion, originally jurisdictional and later on functional as well. The Committee, described by some as the "parliament of the Sikhs," with its executive committee, perceiving itself as the "religious government," pursued relentlessly the demand for extension of its direct authority to cover as many gurdwaras as possible. With the amendment of 1945 the local committee of the Golden Temple was abolished and the management of the whole complex was transferred to direct control of the S.G.P.C. From then on this process has continued so unrelentingly that under an ordinance issued by the Governor of Punjab in November 1986, even the gurdwaras with an annual income of Rs. 25,000 (less than $2,000 U.S.) were transferred to the direct control of the S.G.P.C.

Exercising direct control over hundreds of gurdwaras now within the present Indian states of Punjab, Haryana and Himachal Pradesh, the S.G.P.C. has virtually transformed them into its field operational centres. In addition to providing direct access to the funds of all the gurdwaras, this arrangement also placed vast patronage in the hands of the S.G.P.C. by way of cadre recruitment, thereby giving it the visible character of a state within a state.

Jurisdictional expansionism has been matched with functional expansionism as well. As pointed out earlier, the functions initially entrusted to the S.G.P.C. were restricted to better administration of certain Sikh gurdwaras. From this managerial role the Committee started assuming the authority of the Sikh "church" and branching out in theological as well as non-religious directions. In the absence of any challenge or resistance from within the community, the Committee has grown into an authoritarian agency that brooks no dissent or even conscientious objection.

As a matter of fact, the S.G.P.C. has assumed to itself prescriptive power over all the religious, quasi-religious, semi-religious and religio-political concerns of the followers of the faith in all their broad contexts. In purely "church" matters the S.G.P.C. has contributed a great deal to define Sikh identity in a much more restricted manner than that admitted even in the Sikh Gurdwara Act itself. The cumulative effect of various Sikh religious and social reform movements had emphasised Sikh distinctiveness from Hindus, but the admissibility of the Sikh sects other than the Khalsa order, such as the Udasis, the Nirmalas, the Sewa Panthis, the Sahajdharis, the Namdharis, Nirankaris, etc., had never been questioned or restrained. This is reflected in the definition of the "Sikh" given in the Gurdwara Act of 1925. But in actual practice the working of the S.G.P.C. marginalised all these sects and cults, some of which were even pushed out, such as the Sant Nirankaris. All but those adhering to the order of the Khalsa had to content themselves with the passive role of worshippers, finding it more and more difficult to seek or acquire participation in the affairs of the S.G.P.C. Such a divergence of the reality from the concept was, interestingly enough, formalised in 1971 by the Indian Parliament, which transformed the all-inclusive definition of the Sikhs and shrines of the Sikh Gurdwara Act of 1925 into an all-exclusive definition by including the requirement of wearing unshorn hair. The process towards this new definition, initiated and encouraged by the British Indian Army regulations, was further consolidated by the S.G.P.C. It contributed a great deal to the self-awareness of the Sikhs not only as an expression of their distinctive faith but also as an outer cover for a self-contained political identity of the Sikhs. In a resolution adopted by the S.G.P.C. in 1980 the Sikhs were declared a distinct "nation" (*qaum*) with all political ramifications implicit in the term.

Apart from promoting the concept of Sikh nationalism in the field of politics, the Committee also invested the Sikh institutions, especially the Akal Takht, with unprecedented authority not confined to the questions of Sikh theology and Sikh orthodoxy and Sikh orthopraxy. The S.G.P.C. went in a big way to establish educational institutions, both professional and non-professional. It also instituted, as if it were a university, "national professorships in Sikhism." All the three Sikh scholars and activists who were invested with this distinction projected a radical approach towards promotion of Sikh religious nationalism.

It will be seen from the above that the tendency towards expansionism, both jurisdictional and functional, has been inspired by a desire to draw all the secular concerns of Sikhs towards the supremacy of the "church," a move that in a way is diametrically opposed to the process of secularisation in the contemporary world, which tends to draw more and more sectors of secular activity away from the jurisdiction of the "church." This lends to Sikh politics a theocratic character deriving its sanction from the dominion of the divine rather than the human world.

It is a measure of the acceptance of the political role of the S.G.P.C. that even secular political parties such as the Indian National Congress and the

Communist Party of India involved themselves on various occasions within the elections to the S.G.P.C. Notwithstanding the discouraging results of such endeavours, the basic political concern of these parties has been to secure, through contesting these elections, a foothold among the Sikh peasantry (agricultural land-holders), which has over the years come into total and unshared dominance with the S.G.P.C., pushing out its original collaborators, the urban middle classes. A major political significance of the S.G.P.C., through which the influence and the resources of the gurdwaras are marshalled towards promotion of the political interests of the Shiromani Akali Dal, lies in the fact that it has been the breeding ground for the Sikh politicians, a fair number of whom can be found even in the Congress and the Communist parties. This is so because the electoral base of the Punjab Legislative Assembly or Indian Parliament for the Sikh voters is the same as that for the S.G.P.C. Election to the S.G.P.C. is one way of projecting a Sikh hopeful as a representative of his particular constituency. It is therefore often said that for the Sikh politicians the road to Chandigarh or New Delhi lies via Amritsar, the headquarters of the S.G.P.C.

In the revival and transformation of the institution of the *jathedar* of the Akal Takht, as invested with the "supreme authority" in matters both sacred and secular, can be located the search of the S.G.P.C. for a visible symbol of the body corporate of the faith. The present Gurdwaras Acts make no reference to the authority of the office of *jathedar* or the mechanism for its exercise. But in actual practice, the "exalted office" has increasingly been functioning as the sovereign or the "president of the religious republic," with the S.G.P.C. chief as his prime advisor. The proposed bill for an All India Gurdwara Act, recently under consideration by the S.G.P.C., seeks specifically to institutionalise the office as one of "supreme authority," as beyond the pale of the laws of the land. Correlating this total concentration of powers in a visible symbol with the demand for bringing all the gurdwaras in India under the direct control of the S.G.P.C., one is confronted with a phenomenon the Indian state never before had to deal with. On a workable resolution of this potential crisis of the state-"church" relationship will depend the direction the politicisation of the Sikh community may take. The fate of the S.G.P.C., the main mechanism of Sikh politicisation for the last more than six decades, is bound inexorably with the choice of that direction.

The Crisis of Sikh Politics (1940-1947)

Indu Banga

A crisis in Sikh politics was created by the growing spectre of Pakistan in the 1940's. The Punjab formed the cornerstone of the strategy of the Muslim League. All Punjabis reacted to the League's demand in some form or other. While the Muslims were gradually won over to the idea of Pakistan, the Hindus and Sikhs opposed it from different platforms. The opposition of the Sikhs, however, was the strongest; they saw Pakistan as presenting a grave threat to their cultural heritage, economic position and political future. This paper is essentially an analysis of the politics of the last decade of colonial rule from the perspective of the Sikhs in the Punjab.

In the 1940's the organised political opinion among the Sikhs was represented mainly by the pro-government Chief Khalsa Diwan and its legislative wing, the Khalsa National Party, the pro-Congress Central Akali Dal, the Sikh Congressites, the Sikh Communists and the Shiromani Akali Dal. The Shiromani Akali Dal under the leadership of Master Tara Singh gradually emerged as the leader of the Sikh political opinion against the Pakistan idea.[1] In the process, the Akali Dal acquired a political identity distinct from the Indian National Congress, and also dealt independently with the British Indian government, the Unionists, the Hindu Maha Sabha and the Muslim League.[2]

The crisis of Sikh politics unfolded in four distinct stages, marked by : i) the Lahore resolution of the Muslim League demanding separate states for Muslim majority areas (March 1940); ii) the Cripps proposals conceding Pakistan in principle (March 1942); iii) the C.R. formula, suggesting on behalf of the Congress separation of the Muslim majority areas (July 1944); and iv) the beginning of "direct action" by the Muslim League (August 1946).

---

1. Master Tara Singh (1885-1967) was the president of the Shiromani Gurdwara Prabandhak Committee (S.G.P.C.) from 1936 to 1944, and he also remained the president of the Shiromani Akali Dal for most of this period. Barring temporary retirement from politics for a few months in 1944, he remained preeminent in Sikh affairs throughout the 1940's.
2. In order to keep the main thrust of the discussion clear, factions of the Shiromani Akali Dal have been deliberately left out of this discussion.

[Joseph T. O'Connell, Milton Israel, Willard G. Oxtoby, eds., with W.H. McLeod and J.S. Grewal, visiting eds., *Sikh History and Religion in the Twentieth Century* (S. Asian Studies Papers, 3) (Toronto: S. Asian Studies, Univ. of Toronto, 1988)]

I

The Punjab was the only region in British India with three communities of considerable importance.[3] With over 55% population in the 1940's, Muslims formed the majority in the province; they also dominated in the ruling Unionist Party. Though less than 30%, Hindus outnumbered others in business and professions. The number of the Sikhs was only about half that of Hindus, but they played a role in the political, economic and cultural life of the province that was far in excess of their numerical proportions.

In fact, of all the communities in the Punjab, the Sikhs perhaps had the strongest identification with the region.[4] Over four-fifths of the Sikh population was living in the Punjab; their Gurus were born there; their religion had flourished there; they had been its rulers immediately before the advent of the British. Nearly one-half of the "aristocracy" in the Punjab still belonged to the Sikh community.[5] The Sikhs cultivated the richest lands in the Punjab and paid more than 40% of the land revenue and water rates. They maintained over 400 self-supporting educational institutions; they had also achieved the highest literacy rate in the province.[6] Their electoral strength was double in proportion to their numerical strength; it was proportionately much more than that of the other two communities in the Punjab.[7] Until recently they had formed 20% of the total Indian army.[8] But the Sikhs formed only a little over 12% of the population in the Punjab in 1941, and even in combination with the Hindus, they could not balance the Muslim majority in the province.

Since the 1930's the Sikhs, particularly the Akalis, had been expressing resentment against the "anti-Sikh" and "communal" policies of Sikander Hayat Khan's Unionist government in the Punjab.[9] They had been agitating against

---

3. According to the census of 1941, the community-wise population of the Punjab was :

Muslims	16,217,242
Hindus, including Scheduled Castes	7,550,372
Sikhs	3,757,401
Others	893,804
Total Population	28,418,819

Satya M. Rai, *Legislative Politics and Freedom Struggle in the Punjab, 1897-1947* (New Delhi: Indian Council of Historical Research, 1984), Appendix VIII, p. 343.

4. The Punjab was "their all in all." The Sikhs claimed the Punjab to be their "homeland," their "holy land" and "their body, their soul, and their very life": "The Sikh Memorandum to the Sapru Committee," *The Tribune*, April 17, 1945.

5. *Chiefs and Families of Note in the Punjab*, ed. G.L. Chopra (Lahore, 1940), Appendix: Revised Pedigree Tables.

6. Nicholas Mansergh, ed., *The Transfer of Power, 1942-47* (London: Her Majesty's Stationery Office, 1970-83; cited hereafter as *T.P.*), v. 1, The Sikh All Parties Committee to Sir S. Cripps, March 31, 1942, Document 467, pp. 582-88. This memorandum, incidentally, is the best reflection of the self-image of the Sikhs and their aspirations in the 1940's.

7. In 1930, with a population ratio of 11.1%, the Sikhs had a voting ratio of 24%. In the case of the Muslims, the corresponding figures were 55.2% and 43.7%, while the figures for Punjabi Hindus were 32.0% and 32.1%, respectively: K.C. Yadav, *Elections in Punjab* (New Delhi: Manohar, reprint 1987), Table 6.

8. Khushwant Singh, *A History of the Sikhs*, Vol. 2: 1839-1947 (Delhi: Oxford University Press, 1978), p. 213, n. 37.

9. K.L. Tuteja, *Sikh Politics (1920-40)* (Kurukshetra: Vishal Publications, 1984), pp. 173-207.

the low proportion of the Sikhs in the services and the government, restrictions on the sale of *jhatka* meat in government institutions, control on the sale of *kirpan*, and discouragement of Gurmukhi in primary schools. They also protested against the introduction of the bills amending the Gurdwara Act of 1925 and the Alienation of Land Act of 1901 as anti-Panth and anti-peasant, respectively. They had been particularly exercised over the bill on behalf of the Muslims claiming ownership of the Shahidganj gurdwara in Lahore. The Sikhs attributed these measures to the statutory Muslim majority reinforced by the Communal Award of 1932, which they condemned vehemently.[10]

The Lahore Resolution of the Muslim League, passed under the presidentship of Muhammad Ali Jinnah in March 1940, now presented the prospect of permanent Muslim domination in the Punjab.[11] The idea of a Muslim majority state called "Pakistan" had been in the air since 1930, and the idea of a physical division of the country had been underlined by the Muslim League throughout 1939.[12] Therefore, despite its "vagueness," the Lahore Resolution soon acquired the name "Pakistan Resolution."[13] In the context of the "communal" politics of the Unionist government, "Pakistan" signified "Muslim rule" to the Sikhs and an end to their political aspirations, economic advantages and cultural traditions. Already, there was evidence of growing tension between the Sikhs and Muslims in the Punjab.[14]

Therefore, even before the Lahore Resolution of March 1940 the Akalis had been expressing concern over the Pakistan idea and opposing the granting of any further concessions to Muslims.[15] About sixty prominent Akali leaders, including Master Tara Singh, Sampuran Singh and Pratap Singh, decided to go to the Ramgarh session of the Congress, just a few days before the League session at Lahore, to impress upon the Congress leaders that they should not give further concessions to Muslims under coercion. The Akali leaders maintained that if the Congress yielded to the Muslim League's demand, the Sikhs would also stand on "their rights as an important minority."[16]

---

10. Ibid., p. 156. In fact, under the so-called "Communal Award," 88 seats in the 165-member Punjab Legislature had been reserved for Muslims. The Hindus and Sikhs had 44 and 33 seats respectively.

11. In its Lahore session of March 22-24, 1940, the Muslim League demanded grouping of the Muslim-majority provinces in the northwest and northeast "to constitute Independent States." It made no mention, however, of "partition" or "Pakistan." Ayesha Jalal, *The Sole Spokesman: Jinnah, the Muslim League and the Demand for Pakistan* (Cambridge: Cambridge University Press, 1985), p. 58, n. 51.

12. S.R. Mehrotra, "The Congress and the Partition of India," *The Partition of India: Policies and Perspectives*, ed. C.H. Philips and Mary Doreen Wainwright (London: George Allen and Unwin, 1970), p. 207.

13. B.R. Nanda, "Nehru, the Indian National Congress and the Partition of India," in Philips and Wainwright, p. 166. The League's resolution was dubbed "Pakistan Resolution" first by the Hindu press; see Sikander Hayat Khan's speech in the Punjab Legislative Assembly, reproduced in V.P. Menon, *The Transfer of Power in India* (New Delhi: Orient Longmans, reprint 1979), p. 444.

14. Azim Husain, *Fazl-i-Husain: A Political Biography* (Bombay: Longmans Green & Co., 1946), pp. 287-96; also Tuteja, *Sikh Politics*, pp. 180-81.

15. In the first All India Akali Conference, held at Atari on February 12, 1940, concern was expressed over the "Pakistan idea voiced by some"; see Nripendra Nath Mitra, *The Indian Annual Register* (cited hereafter as *IAR*), 1940, v. 1, pp. 56-57.

16. *The Tribune*, March 11, 1940.

With this background, the Akalis understandably reacted strongly to the "Pakistan Resolution" of the Muslim League. At the Akali conference held at Anandpur just a day after the conclusion of the League session, the Akali leaders Giani Dhanwant Singh and Master Ajit Singh severely criticised the "Pakistan Scheme."[17] Giani Kartar Singh declared that the mere thought of subjection to "Muslim Raj" embodied in the idea of Pakistan was "nauseating."[18]   The Shiromani Gurdwara Prabandhak Committee (S.G.P.C.) announced that it would not co-operate with Sikander Hayat Khan in the war effort so long as he did not leave the Muslim League.[19]   In an anti-Pakistan conference at Lyallpur the Akalis condemned Jinnah's two-nation theory.[20]   Master Tara Singh, president of the Shiromani Akali Dal, said in his address to the Uttar Pradesh Sikh Conference that the League's demand might mean "a declaration of civil war"; to realise it the Muslims would have to "cross an ocean of Sikh blood."[21]   The S.G.P.C. and the Akali Dal celebrated the Ghallughara day and about 20,000 Sikhs gathered at the Akal Takht and vowed to oppose the Pakistan scheme.[22]

The reactions of other political groups among the Sikhs were equally strong. The Khalsa National Party declared that the Sikhs "would not tolerate for a single day the undiluted communal Raj in the Punjab."[23]   Baba Kharak Singh of the Central Akali Dal declared that the Sikhs "shall not allow India to be vivisected."[24]   The Central Khalsa Youngmen Union announced that the Sikhs would "never let the so-called Pakistan Scheme materialise."[25]   Some angry reactions even asked for "Khalsa Raj" from Jammu to Jamrud and for a "Khalistan" under the Maharaja of Patiala.[26]

As the year progressed, the anti-Pakistan utterances of the Sikhs began to reflect their increasing anxiety because of the ambivalent stand taken on this issue by the Indian National Congress. The immediate reaction of the Congress leaders to the Lahore Resolution of the League was very strong. For Gandhi it was "an untruth"; for Nehru, "an insane suggestion"; for C. Rajagopalachari, "a medieval conception"; and for Maulana Azad it was "meaningless and absurd."[27]   The Congress leaders did not believe that the Muslims of India would support the League's demand, but they felt that they could not oppose it if the Muslims wanted it. By May 1940 the Congress leaders had made it clear that the Congress would not use coercion to resist the demand for Pakistan.

17. Ibid., March 27, 1940.
18. Ibid., April 2, 1940.
19. Ibid., April 5, 1940.
20. Ibid., April 8, 1940.
21. Ibid., April 18, 1940.
22. Ibid., May 28, 1940.
23. Ibid., March 29, 1940; also *IAR*, 1940, v. 1, p. 257.
24. *The Tribune*, April 11, 1940.
25. Ibid., April 18, 1940.
26. Ibid., May 21, 1940 and April 7, 1940; also Kailash Chandra Gulati, *The Akalis: Past and Present* (New Delhi: Ashajanak Publications, 1974), p. 88. Master Tara Singh, however, was quick to clarify the position of the Shiromani Akali Dal that it stood for the "Congress Principle of Swaraj" and the "rule of all communities." *The Tribune*, May 29, 1940; also *IAR*, 1940, v. 1, pp. 356-58.
27. B.R. Nanda, "Nehru, the Indian National Congress and the Partition of India," pp. 166-67.

However, there was no formal announcement of the Congress stand on Pakistan until April 1942.[28]

Meanwhile, the "August offer" of Viceroy Linlithgow (1940) reassured the League that power could not be transferred to Indians unless they arrived at some mutually agreed position.[29]   To expedite the transfer of power, C. Rajagopalachari, a senior member of the Congress Working Committee, offered the prime ministership to a nominee of the Muslim League, with a cabinet after his choice.[30] This "sporting offer" made on August 23 only strengthened the apprehensions of the Akalis about the appeasement of the League by the Congress. The Akali Dal criticised the "sporting offer" as "unjust, undemocratic and anti-national" and demanded that the Congress should reiterate its position with regard to the "Pakistan scheme." The Akali Dal clarified its own stand: "For winning freedom, the Sikhs will remain with the Congress, but not for establishing Pakistan. We want freedom but not a change of masters."[31] Master Tara Singh accused the Congress of bowing before Muslim obstinacy (zid) and forgetting its promise to the Sikhs made in 1929 in its Lahore Resolution that it would protect the interests of the minorities and take no action affecting them without their approval.[32] He declared that in matters related to the "Pakistan Scheme" and communal disputes the Sikhs henceforth were on their own.[33] The Congressite Sikhs, too, opposed the "sporting offer" and the League's demand, but they also defended the Congress and criticised the stand taken by Master Tara Singh and the Akali Dal.[34]

In early September the question of Sikh recruitment in the war was combined with the growing resentment over the Congress stand on Pakistan. Recruitment to the army was important to the Sikhs not only as a major avenue of employment but also because of its relevance for their role as "a substantive force" in Indian and provincial affairs.[35] After the Gurdwara Reform movement (1920-1925) the proportion of the Sikhs in the army had been reduced from 20% to 13%;[36] the war appeared to present a good opportunity to regain the lost

---

28. S.R. Mehrotra, "The Congress and the Partition of India," pp. 209-14.
29. Jalal, The Sole Spokesman, pp. 62-63.
30. The Tribune, August 26, 1940; also, Menon, Transfer of Power, p. 95.
31. The Tribune, September 11, 1940.
32. In its Lahore Resolution of 1929 the Congress assured "the Sikhs, Muslims and other Minorities" that "no solution" of communal questions "in any future Constitution would be acceptable to the Congress that did not give full satisfaction to the two parties concerned." Pattabhi Sitaramayya, History of the Indian National Congress, I (New Delhi: S. Chand and Co., 1935), p. 64.
33. The Tribune, September 18, 1940.
34. Ibid., October 8, 1940; October 23, 1940.
35. Stephen Oren, "The Sikhs, Congress and the Unionists in British Punjab, 1937-1945," Modern Asian Studies, 8:3 (1974), p. 407. There were over 120,000 Sikh combatants during World War I. In its report the Simon Commission had noted the exceptional contribution made by this small community" to the fighting force during the World War. T.P., v. 1, D. 467, p. 583.
36. Correspondingly, the proportion of Punjabi Muslims and Pathans rose from 26% in 1914 to 4% in 1930: B.R. Ambedkar, Pakistan and the Partition of India, quoted in Khushwant Singh, History of the Sikhs, v. 2, p. 213, n. 37.

position. The entire Sikh Panth from the "prince to the peasant" was united in the win-the-war effort.[37]

The Akali Dal was initially divided over this issue because of the Congress stand of non-cooperation in the war effort until the declaration of war aims and the assurance of the grant of independence.[38] The Akalis had hoped that they would be able to reconcile the Congress position with Sikh participation in the effort. Master Tara Singh believed in the potency of the army for the freedom and safety of the country and felt convinced that Indians should take advantage of the opportunity offered by the war to raise the strength of the Indian army and to open armament factories. If the British lost India would also lose. He regarded the recruitment of the Sikhs also as a check on what he saw as aggressive Muslim communalism. He therefore wrote to Maulana Azad and sent a copy of that letter to Mahatma Gandhi that even if the Congress was "compelled to have recourse to civil disobedience to exert moral pressure on the government, it should do nothing to prevent recruitment to the army."[39] Mahatma Gandhi disapproved of Master Tara Singh's suggestion and said that there was no common ground between the Congress ideology of non-violence and Master Tara Singh's belief in the rule of the sword. The Mahatma therefore advised him to be "either fully nationalist or frankly communal."[40] Master Tara Singh in his reply underlined that the Congress too believed in non-violence only as a matter of policy; it had offered its services in the war effort if its demand for independence was conceded; the objective of the Congress was independence and not civil disobedience or non-violence for its own sake.[41] In September, Master Tara Singh resigned from the All India Congress Committee because of Congress president Maulana Azad's "rigid and insulting stand" on the war effort.[42]

Pandit Nehru attributed the differences between the Congress and the Akali Dal to the latter's "dual and non-committal attitude," which was "at complete variance with the fundamental policy of the Congress."[43]   The Sikh Congressmen dubbed the Akali leadership "communal" and "anti-national" and found their strong opposition to Pakistan and the Communal Award "ridiculous" in view of their advocacy of cooperation with the British, who were in alliance with Jinnah. The pro-Congress Sikhs revived the Congress Sikh League, and Mangal Singh, a staunch Congressite, condemned the Akali leaders as "traitors."[44] The Akalis reacted strongly to political invective. At a political

---

37. This was said by Sant Singh, minister of Kapurthala state. *The Tribune*, October 10, 1940; also *IAR*, 1940, v. 2, p. 323.
38. *The Tribune*, September 10, 1939; October 12, 1939; also Menon, *Transfer of Power*, p. 61.
39. Quoted in S.L. Malhotra, *From Civil Disobedience to Quit India* (Chandigarh: Panjab University, 1979), p. 128; also Jaswant Singh, *Master Tara Singh: Jiwan Sandesh te Uddesh* (Amritsar, 1972, in Punjabi), pp. 163-67.
40. Malhotra, *Civil Disobedience to Quit India*, p. 128.
41. Ibid., pp. 130-131; Jaswant Singh, *Master Tara Singh*, pp. 167-72.
42. *The Tribune*, September 20, 1940.
43. Ibid., October 16, 1940.
44. Rai, *Legislative Politics*, 269; also *The Tribune*, September 20, 1940 and October 16, 1940.

conference in Amritsar, Master Tara Singh felt justified in asking the Sikhs not to rely on any one's word but to improve their own strength so that no one could betray them, whether the Congress or the government.[45]

Thus, the Akali and the Congress leadership were speaking on different wave-lengths. Even when the Congress found the division of the country "distasteful," most of the Congressmen, following Mahatma Gandhi, thought that Pakistan, whatever it might mean, "could not be worse that the foreign domination."[46] While the Congress regarded accommodation with the Muslim League as the likely price to pay for freedom, the Akalis saw it as putting an end to the freedom of the non-Muslims in the Punjab. The Akalis were therefore prepared to postpone the attainment of independence if Pakistan could be stalled. Convinced of the legitimacy of their respective positions, the Shiromani Akali Dal and the Congress parted company before the end of 1940. The following year saw the Akalis supporting the war effort and the Congressmen participating in the individual *satyagraha* against India's entry into the war.

II

Early in 1942, when the war came perilously close to India, the British War Cabinet sent Stafford Cripps to win over Indian support for the war. Recognising India's right to frame its own constitution after the war, Cripps' proposals envisaged a loose federation giving the provinces the right to opt out of the Indian Union.[47] This clause was the "first public admission of the possibility of Pakistan."[48] Jinnah felt pleased, as it assured Pakistan after the war "if the Muslims wanted it."[49] The Congress Working Committee in its resolution of April 2, 1942 turned down the Cripps proposals because of "the novel principle of non-accession for a province." But the committee could not think of "compelling the people of any territorial unit to remain in an Indian Union against their declared and established will."[50] As far as the Sikhs were concerned, both the government and the Congress had conceded the League's demand in principle. Now Jinnah had only to produce majority support to establish his case.

The Sikh deputation consisting of Master Tara Singh, Baldev Singh, Jogendra Singh and Ujjal Singh met Stafford Cripps on March 27 to apprise him of the viewpoint of the Sikh All Parties Committee.[51] Master Tara Singh

---

45. *The Tribune*, October 31, 1940.

46. Quoted in S.R. Mehrotra, "The Congress and the Partition of India," p. 211.

47. Draft Declaration for Discussion with Indian Leaders (as published), March 30, 1942, *T.P.*, v. 1, D. 456, p. 565.

48. Amery to A. Hardings, March 2, 1942, ibid., D. 208, p. 283.

49. *The Tribune*, March 28, 1942. The "provincial option" was seen as "definitely a victory for Jinnah." When it was offered in 1942 the "Pakistan Resolution" was only two years old and the League's position in the Muslim majority province was none too strong. Menon, *Transfer of Power*, p. 438. Also Jalal, *The Sole Spokesman*, pp. 75-76.

50. Quoted in S.R. Mehrotra, "The Congress and the Partition of India," p. 214.

51. The All Parties Committee, which had met earlier in New Delhi, felt bitter and outraged over the utter disregard of the position of the Sikhs in the past and present. It considered the Cripps proposals as "a betrayal of the Sikh cause." *IAR*, 1942, v. 1, p. 149.

expressed his firm conviction that since the provincial option was to be exercised by a bare majority, the Punjab would "never come into a general union" and the Sikhs would never tolerate "Muhammedan rule, open or disguised."[52] Since the draft proposals could not be modified the Sikh leaders felt convinced that the British had merely enacted a "charade" to concede the League's demand.[53] The memorandum of the Sikh All Parties Committee to Cripps conveyed their determination to resist "by all possible means, the separation of the Punjab from the All India Union."[54] They demanded adequate protection of their position through the division of the present Punjab into two provinces so that the Sikhs could have "the decisive voice as a large balancing party" between Hindus and Muslims.[55]

During April and May, various Akali Jathas and Singh Sabhas all over the Punjab categorically opposed the Cripps proposals and expressed their solidarity with the stand taken by the All Parties Committee. They assured the Akali leaders of all support in this hour of crisis for the Panth.[56] Master Tara Singh described the situation as "very critical" and asked the Sikhs to prepare, if need be, for single-handed struggle.[57] Baba Kharak Singh of the Central Akali Dal also declared that "so long as there was a single Sikh there could be no Pakistan in the Punjab."[58] The supporters of pro-government Kirpal Singh Majithia too expressed opposition to Pakistan.[59]

The general expression of solidarity against the government on the issue of Pakistan unnerved the provincial authorities. They were particularly worried about the "unprecedented intensification of bitterness" between the Sikhs and Muslims and its adverse effect on the war effort.[60] Since any understanding between Jinnah and the Akalis seemed impossible, the British appear to have prompted Sikander Hayat Khan to have an agreement with the Akalis to diffuse the "dangerously strained" situation.[61] The Unionist leader too was in need of support in the Legislature as within two years of the Lahore Resolution more than seventy Muslim Unionists were said to be inclined towards the Muslim League.[62] With his commitment to the unity and autonomy of the Punjab, his

---

52. Reported by Ogilvie to Pinnell, March 30, 1942, *T.P.*, v. 1, D. 455, p. 564. The Sikhs regarded themselves "as being in danger of everlasting subjection to an unsympathetic and tyrannical Muhammedan Raj." Glancy to Linlithgow, April 14, 1942, ibid., D. 625, p. 772.

53. *The Daily Akali* (Punjabi), April 1, 1942 and April 3, 1942; also *IAR*, 1942, v. 1, p. 149; *T.P.*, v. 1, D. 440, p. 536.

54. The Sikh All Parties Committee to Cripps, March 31, 1942, *T.P.*, v. 1, D. 467, p. 583.

55. Note by S. Cripps, March 27, 1942, ibid, D. 396, p. 496.

56. For example, *The Tribune*, March 27 and 31, 1942; April 8-9 and 14-17, 1942. In fact, the Baisakhi celebrations of April 1942 turned into anti-Pakistan rallies attended by thousands opposing the Cripps proposals. Also, *The Daily Akali*, April 6, 8-9 and 25, 1942 and May 4 and 16, 1942.

57. *The Tribune*, April 5, 1942.

58. Ibid., April 8, 1942; also *IAR*, 1942, v. 1, p. 399.

59. *The Tribune*, April 6, 1942.

60. Glancy to Linlithgow, March 4, 1942, *T.P.*, v. 1, D. 236, p. 321; also Linlithgow to Amery, March 9, 1942, ibid., D. 287-88, pp. 383-85; Note by Major General Lockhart, February 25, 1942, ibid., D. 180, p. 239.

61. Churchill to Roosevelt, March 7, 1942, ibid., D. 271, p. 364; also Note by S. Cripps, March 24, 1942, ibid., D. 371, pp. 464-65.

62. Linlithgow to Amery, March 7, 1942, ibid., D. 269, p. 362.

communal harmony meetings and his resignation from the League's Working Committee in May, Sikandar now appeared to be much less communal to the Akalis.[63] Both sides felt that the void created by the death of Sunder Singh Majithia, the leader of the Khalsa National Party, in December 1941 could be filled more effectively by Baldev Singh, an Akali legislator and a wealthy Jat. Baldev Singh formed a new United Sikh Party in the Legislature in March 1942, and replaced Dasaundha Singh of the Khalsa National Party in the Punjab Cabinet within a fortnight of the pact with Sikander Hayat Khan in June 1942.[64]

The Sikander-Baldev Singh pact was an attempt at a limited co-operation between the Akalis and the Unionists and at mitigating what were seen as the adverse effects of "Muslim domination." It covered nearly all those issues that had been agitating the minds of the Sikhs before the League's resolution in 1940, such as legislation on religious matters, the share of the Sikhs in services, teaching of Punjabi in Gurmukhi and facilities for *jhatka* meat.[65] It was meant to remove the existing irritants without involving sensitive issues like a statutory Muslim majority. It was the last joint political effort of the Punjabis of all the three major communities for unity and communal harmony within the existing framework.[66] The pact left the Akali Dal free to pursue its political programme against the government and the Pakistan scheme.[67]

The Sikander-Baldev Singh pact was condemned by the Congressite and Communist Sikhs and by the Central Akali Dal. Baba Kharak Singh demanded Baldev Singh's resignation.[68] Sant Singh referred to the "absurdity" of the pact, because while Baldev Singh sat with the government, the Akali Party sat in the opposition.[69] The Communists alleged that the Akalis were ready to grab "any crumbs that might come their way."[70] The Akalis themselves became impatient

---

63. In fact, Sikander Hayat Khan's famous "Hands off the Punjab" speech in the Punjab Legislative Assembly on 11 March 1941 was seen as "a unilateral declaration of independence" from Jinnah. Jalal, *The Sole Spokesman*, pp. 67, 83. For extracts, Menon, *Transfer of Power*, Appendix I, pp. 442-58. The formation of the Khalsa Defence of India League in January 1941 to aid the war effort also brought the Akalis closer to the Unionists. For further detail, Oren, "The Sikhs, Congress and the Unionists," pp. 409-11.
64. The terms of the pact were embodied in a letter of Sikander Hayat Khan to Baldev Singh. For the text see Rai, *Legislative Politics*, Appendix x, pp. 345-47; also, *The Tribune*, 16 June 1942.
65. For example, *The Tribune*, December 21, 1939; February 29, 1940; July 22 and 24, 1940; December 6, 1940; and January 15, 1941.
66. Baldev Singh explained later that he entered into this pact "for removing the besetting curse of inter-communal bitterness in the Punjab." *IAR*, 1944, v. 1, p. 227. The Unionist Party appeared to be "a non-communal organisation" also in view of the determined opposition to Jinnah by Sir Chhotu Ram, the influential Jat leader from Haryana and a minister in the Punjab Cabinet. Oren, "The Sikhs, Congress and the Unionists," pp. 416-17.
67. Baldev Singh made the pact in his "personal capacity" with the "moral support" of the Akali Dal, but without committing it "in any way." Master Tara Singh in the Akali Conference in September 1942, *IAR*, 1942, v. 2, p. 299; also Jaswant Singh, ed., *Master Tara Singh*, pp. 134-37.
Penderal Moon, a British officer serving the Punjab in the 1940's, also saw the pact as an effort "to stall Pakistan." Moon, *Divide and Quit* (London: Chatto and Windus, 3rd impression 1964), p. 31.
68. *IAR*, 1943, v. 1, pp. 297-98. Baba Kharak Singh was addressing the Akhand Hindustan Conference at Roomi in district Ludhiana on June 19-20, 1943.
69. Ibid., 1944, v. 1, p. 196.
70. G. Adhikari, "On the Question of Sikh Homeland," originally published in *People's Age*, 4:25, December 1945, and reprinted in *Marxism Today*, 4 (May-July 1986), p. 9.

with the pact, as its only tangible results had been Jogendra Singh's joining the Viceroy's Executive Council in July 1942, and the Khalsa National Party's joining the Baldev Singh group in the Legislative Assembly in March 1943. The death of Sikander in December 1942 and the relatively weak position of the new Premier, Khizr Hayat Khan, vis-à-vis Jinnah had dimmed the prospects of any gain. Master Tara Singh was constrained to admit in 1943 that Baldev Singh's ministry alone could not protect Sikh interests. He pleaded for its replacement by the Azad Punjab scheme as the "only proposal" that could protect the Sikhs from the domination of a single community.[71]

"Azad Punjab" was the name given to a province envisaged in the memorandum of the Sikh All Parties Committee to Stafford Cripps.[72] This "ideal province" was to be created after separating eastern Punjab and two canal-colony districts from the Muslim-majority western Punjab.[73] Its population was to be so balanced—about 40% Muslims, 40% Hindu and 20% Sikh—that the Punjabis would be free of the domination of any single community. Hence, the name "Azad Punjab."[74] The Punjab thus reconstituted was to have "joint electorates, with no reservation of seats." The Hindu and Sikh minorities in the Muslim majority province in the north-west were to get 25% and 15% weightage respectively.[75] The river Chenab was later proposed to be the dividing line between the two provinces "after taking into consideration the population, property, land revenue and historical traditions of each of the three communities."[76]

During 1942-43, the Azad Punjab scheme evoked strong reaction from various quarters, particularly from the Congressite and Communist Sikhs, the protagonists of the Akhand Hindustan and the Hindu leaders of the Punjab, all of whom dubbed it communal, anti-Hindu, anti-national, reactionary and opportunistic.[77] The Sikhs of the Rawalpindi division, which was situated on the other side of the Chenab, were particularly vocal. They dubbed the scheme as "suicidal" and Master Tara Singh as "Pakistanist" and "an agent of British Imperialism."[78]

---

71. Master Tara Singh was presiding over a Sikh conference at Dhundial held on October 3-4. *IAR*, 1943, v. 2, p. 301.
72. *T.P.*, v. 1, D. 467, pp. 586-87; also D. 455, p. 564. The name "Azad Punjab" was mentioned first in a resolution of the All India Akali Conference at Dahela Kalan on July 24, 1942. Sadhu Singh Hamdard, *Azad Punjab* (Amritsar: Ajit Book Agency, 1943, in Urdu, 2nd ed.), p. 48.
73. This was essentially a reiteration of the demand for "territorial rearrangement" of the province made by the Sikhs in 1931 at the Second Round Table Conference. See Rai, *Legislative Politics*, pp. 36-37.
74. Jaswant Singh, ed., *Master Tara Singh*, p. 146; also *IAR*, 1942, v. 2, p. 301.
75. *The Tribune*, March 15, 1943; September 6, 1943; also *IAR*, 1943, v. 1, pp. 294, 300.
76. *The Tribune*, June 6, 1943; also *IAR*, 1943, v. 1, p. 298. In the Sikh All Parties Memorandum to Cripps, however, the river Ravi was proposed to be the boundary between eastern and western Punjab. *T.P.*, v. 1, D. 467, p. 586.
77. For example, *The Tribune*, February 8 and 9, 1943; August 9, 1943; and December 8, 1943. Also *IAR*, 1943, v. 1, pp. 297-98; v. 2, pp. 295, 303.
78. *IAR*, 1943, v. 2, pp. 300, 302-03, 305. Also, *The Tribune*, February 2, 1943; June 22, 1943. The anti-Azad Punjab conferences were organised at different places in the Rawalpindi division, with the Congressite leaders Baba Kharak Singh and Sant Singh mostly being in the forefront.

Master Tara Singh clarified that, far from being anti-national or another Pakistan, Azad Punjab was intended to be an alternative to the division of the country. It was in fact a move to "cripple" the Pakistan scheme. By changing the boundaries of the Punjab, "we can take out the overwhelming majority of the Hindus and Sikhs from Muslim domination" and "get rid of the present Pakistan."[79] Azad Punjab was certainly not "a Khalistan on the Pakistan principle," and Ujjal Singh wished that "a happier name" had been selected for this demand, which was intended to be a province within the Union of India.[80] In the anti-Pakistan conference held at Damdama Sahib, Giani Kartar Singh categorically stated that "we wanted neither 'Hindu Raj,' nor even the 'Sikh Raj.' What we advocate is joint rule of all parties and communities, guaranteeing safeguards and religious freedom to all the inhabitants of the country."[81]

It is clear in retrospect that the demand for a separate province was rooted in a genuine fear that the Sikh community would be "lost forever" if Pakistan were established.[82] The British also admitted that the Sikh interest was "definitely centred on the Punjab" and that bitterness between Sikhs and Muslims was increasing.[83] The Azad Punjab scheme was essentially a defensive strategy adopted in response to the recognition of the idea of Pakistan by the government through the Cripps proposals and by the Congress through its resolution of April 2, 1942.[84]

Having broken with the Congress, the Akalis were looking for allies. The "common menace" of Pakistan induced the Akali leaders to make common cause with the Hindu Mahasabha. During 1942-44 they opposed the League's demand and the Cripps proposals from common platforms.[85] But their joint endeavours could not go far. Even when they underlined the common cultural heritage of Sikhs and Hindus, the emphases of the leaders speaking from common forums varied with their respective communal identity. While the Sikh leaders underlined the common socio-cultural and political ties, the Hindu

---

79. *The Tribune*, March 15, 1943; also *IAR*, 1943, v. 1, pp. 294, 303.

80. *IAR*, 1943, v. 1, pp. 298-99. Ujjal Singh clarified that the Akalis "only wanted the separation of the original Punjab from the western districts annexed to it by Maharaja Ranjit Singh just as Sind was separated from Bombay and Orissa from Bihar."

81. *The Tribune*, March 15, 1943.

82. Ibid., October 5, 1943; also *IAR*, 1943, v. 2, p. 301. "If the Punjab is gone everything is gone" was the general feeling expressed at the Dhundial Sikh conference held on October 3-4, 1943.

83. Note from Geoffrey de Montgomery, Governor of the Punjab (1928-33), circulated by the Secretary of State on March 8, 1942. *T.P.*, v. 1, D. 276, p. 371; also Documents, 236 and 271, pp. 321 and 363-64, respectively.

84. The contemporaries were unable to see the Azad Punjab scheme as an attempt at rationalising the provincial boundaries because of the fear, mutual distrust and political rivalry with which the political atmosphere was charged. Following them, some late works have misunderstood the sequence of things or treated Azad Punjab as the demand for a separate Sikh state. See Khushwant Singh, *History of the Sikhs*, v. 2, pp. 253-54 and n. 18; Gulati, *Akalis*, p. 95; Kirpal Singh, *The Partition of the Punjab* (Patiala: Punjabi University, 1972), p. 9; Rai, *Legislative Politics*, p. 290; also, Satya M. Rai, *Punjab since Partition* (Delhi: Durga Publications, 1986), pp. 56-57.

85. *The Tribune*, March 29 and 31, 1942; April 2, 5, 9, 13 and 20, 1942. Also Rai, *Legislative Politics*, p. 272.

leaders like Raja Narendra Nath and Gokal Chand Narang talked of the "inherent oneness" of the principles of Sikh and Hindu religion and called Sikhs the "protectors" and the "sword arm" of the Hindus.[86] The Akalis did not relish the Hindus' not recognising the distinct socio-religious identity of the Sikhs. In the Akali conference at Lahore in June 1943, reference was made to "a very minor quarrel" existing between the Sikhs and Hindus, and it was noted that even this could be resolved if the Hindus "ceased to ask the Sikhs to declare they were Hindus."[87] Culturally, the Sikhs and Hindus had much in common, but it was "clearly for the Sikhs to say" whether they were Hindu or not, and not for the Hindus to insist that the Sikhs were Hindu.[88] Master Tara Singh expressed unhappiness also over the anti-Sikh bias and propaganda of the Hindu press of the Punjab.[89] Nevertheless, there was a genuine desire to have some kind of common front against the Pakistan scheme and the Akali Dal and the Hindu Mahasabha tried to work together for some time. In the middle of 1943 it was agreed that the Akalis would not support the Muslim League in the Punjab and that the Hindu Mahasabha would not object to the Azad Punjab scheme or the League-Akali coalition in the North West Frontier Province (N.W.F.P.).[90]

At the Akhand Hindustan Conference at Delhi in October 1944, the Akali leaders promised wholehearted support to the Hindus in their fight for the integrity of India.[91] The speeches of the Hindu leaders, however, ranged from rational to emotional and even to blatantly communal.[92] "All Indians owed it to their country to maintain its integrity"; there were ways and means by which "the largest measure of provincial autonomy could be made compatible with some kind of federal control," said Dr. Radha Kumud Mukerjee in his presidential speech. "Hindustan is the land of the Hindus, and the Sikhs, Muslims and Christians are all Hindus," said Dr. B.S. Moonje, the vice president of the Hindu Mahasabha. "Everyone who lives in India is a Hindu"; "India is not the land of the Qur'an, but the land of the Gita," declared V.D. Savarkar, the president of the Mahasabha. Such rhetoric and all-embracingness could not possibly sustain the enthusiasm of the Akalis, who were particularly sensitive about Savarkar's "Hindudom" absorbing the "Sikh brotherhood."

In their anxiety to counter Pakistan the Akalis did not hesitate to explore the possibility of some understanding with the Muslim League. Stafford Cripps had advised the Akali leaders to negotiate with the Congress and League for securing the maximum possible protection, which could even mean "a semi-autonomous district on the Soviet model" within Pakistan.[93] L.S. Amery also

86. *IAR*, 1943, v. 1, p. 295 and 1944, v. 1, pp. 196-98.
87. Ibid., 1943, v. 1, p. 297.
88. *The Tribune*, July 18, 1943.
89. *IAR*, 1943, v. 1, p. 297, and 1943, v. 2, p. 301.
90. *The Tribune*, July 17 and 18, 1943. Also Rai, *Legislative Politics*, p. 295.
91. *IAR*, 1944, v. 2, p. 230.
92. Ibid., pp. 229-30.
93. Note by S. Cripps, March 27, 1942, *T.P.*, v. 1, D. 396, p. 496; also, March 31, 1942, D. 466, p. 581.

visualised that the Sikhs would throw "all their weight against non-adhesion," which might oblige Jinnah to offer them "a special position" in the Punjab.[94] Pakistan was still not a certainty and, as Amery wrote to Linlithgow, it was "up to Indians themselves to prevent Pakistan by mutual concession."[95] Initiative in this direction seemed necessary in view also of the reports of the increasing incidents of violence and provocation against non-Muslims and of the public meetings and demonstrations in favour of Pakistan.[96] Moreover, as a result of government support, the League had been able to gain ground in Bengal (April 1942), Assam (August 1942) and Sind (October 1942).

It was in this context that the Akalis explored the possibilities of arriving at some kind of understanding with the League. Sikander Hayat Khan's defensive stance towards Jinnah prompted Baldev Singh to approach the League leader in late 1942, but the talks broke down on the question of "Pakistan."[97] After the death of Sikander in December 1942, his successor, Khizr Hayat Khan, tried to run the Unionist government with the help of non-Muslim groups led by Chhotu Ram, the influential Hindu Jat leader from the Haryana area, and Baldev Singh, the leader of the United Sikh Party in the Legislature. The continuation of this tricommunal government was the very negation of the principle of Pakistan. Jinnah hoped that the Akalis would support the League against the Unionists if some of their demands were met. Giani Kartar Singh reportedly met him in Bombay, but could not arrive at any agreement on the issues on which the League and the Akali Dal held irreconcilable positions.[98] Probably neither expected much out of these exploratory talks. There appears to have been no serious discussion of any terms of co-operation between the League and the Akalis in the Punjab.[99]

However, the Akali leadership had concurred in Ajit Singh Sarhadi's joining the coalition ministry in the N.W.F.P. in May 1943. This coalition was based on an agreement containing eleven clauses providing safeguards for the Hindu and Sikh minorities in the province. It was also agreed that "the question of Pakistan would be suspended and shelved during the coalition ministry."[100] Like the Sikander-Baldev Singh pact, this coalition and the terms of its agreement were consistent with the main concern of the Akali Dal to neutralise

---

94. Ibid., D. 542, p. 674. Amery was addressing a press conference on April 7, 1942.
95. Ibid., April 3, 1942, D. 517, p. 633.
96. For example, *The Tribune*, April 8, 16, and 27, 1942; July 10 and 16, 1942; and August 6, 1942.
97. Oren, "The Sikhs, Congress and the Unionists," p. 412.
98. *The Tribune*, November 23, 1943; also, Jalal, *The Sole Spokesman*, p. 97, n. 59. [See Patwant Singh's chapter in this volume for a later (1946) meeting between Jinnah, Kartar Singh, *et al*. —Editors' note.]
99. The "negotiations" between the Muslim League and the so-called "pro-Muslim League faction" of the Akali Dal, led by Giani Kartar Singh, could not amount to much, as the two organisations held almost irreconcilable positions on Pakistan. See Oren, "The Sikhs, Congress and the Unionists," p. 418. Cf. Rai, *Legislative Politics*, p. 295; Baldev Raj Nayar, *Minority Politics in the Punjab* (Princeton, New Jersey: Princeton University Press, 1966), pp. 91-92.
100. Ajit Singh Sarhadi, *Punjabi Suba: The Story of the Struggle* (Delhi: U.C. Kapur & Sons, 1970), p. 73. Jinnah in fact was "irrelevant" in the politics of N.W.F.P.; see Jalal, *The Sole Spokesman*, p. 116.

the League's bid for total power in the region. It was also an attempt to protect the interests on the non-Muslims in the N.W.F.P. In this the Akali Dal had been influenced by the strategy of the Hindu Mahasabha to form a "workable" coalition with the League wherever its ministry seemed "inevitable."[101] However, the critics of the Akali Dal like Baba Kharak Singh and Durlab Singh and Sikh Congressmen referred to the coalition as "a blunder," "a somersault," a "stab in the back" and an "opportunist and reactionary policy" that caused "irreparable loss to the Sikh interests."[102]

In early 1944, Jinnah tried to consolidate his position among the Muslim legislators of the Punjab.[103] But he failed to prevail upon Khizr Hayat Khan to merge the Unionist Party with the Muslim League on the basis of the Sikander-Jinnah pact of 1937.[104] In the Muslim League Conference in June, Jinnah felt obliged to take the offensive and declare that the "Unionist Party did not exist"; it had only been "an instrument" for lowering the prestige and influence of the Muslim League in the province. Jinnah even denied that he had a pact with Sikander Hayat Khan in 1937: "There could not be a pact between a leader and a follower." He also asserted that it was open to the League to terminate the League-Unionist or any other coalition.[105] Jinnah nevertheless failed to make a serious dent in the Unionist Party or erode its mass base. In fact, by this time, "his shares in the political market had begun to deteriorate."[106] He therefore simultaneously expressed readiness to come to any "fair and equitable" settlement with the Sikhs and "publicly" requested the Sikh leaders to "acquaint" him with their proposals.[107] Baldev Singh reacted strongly to Jinnah's condescending tones: it was evident from the "unilateral repudiation" of its pacts by the Muslim League that it treated its pledged word lightly and that the Sikhs would greatly hesitate to rely on any future promises made by the League.[108]

---

101. Sarhadi, *Punjabi Suba*, p. 73; also pp. 74-79 for Sarhadi's defence against the criticism of the "coalition" by the Congress.

102. *The Tribune*, May 19, 1943; September 15, 1943; December 18, 1943; also *IAR*, 1943, v. 2, pp. 227-28, 302, 306. Cf. Gulati, *Akalis*, pp. 103-4.

103. Khizr Hayat Khan's allegiance was Jinnah's "passport to the centre" issued by a Punjab ministry. Jalal, *The Sole Spokesman*, p. 85. Jinnah asked Khizr Hayat Khan that his ministry call itself the Muslim League coalition, and that the League Assembly members should belong to one and not to two parties. Khizr, however, could not accede to this, as it not only amounted to interference in provincial affairs but also challenged the very basis and secular claims of the Unionist Party. Ibid., p. 93.

104. In October 1937, following the Muslim League's loss in the elections, and to buttress Jinnah's claims as the accepted Muslim leader, Sikander Hayat Khan had allowed Jinnah to speak for the Punjab at the Centre. But the All India Muslim League was to have no say in the Punjab's affairs, even though Sikander had agreed to bring his followers nominally into the Punjab League, ensuring the obliteration of an independent League in the province. Ibid., p. 39.

105. *IAR*, 1944, v. 1, pp. 222, 224.

106. Glancy to Wavell, August 23, 1944, *T.P.*, v. 4, D. 671, p. 1224; also Jalal, *The Sole Spokesman*, pp. 94-98.

107. *IAR*, 1944, v. 1, p. 229.

108. Ibid., pp. 227-28.

III

In July 1944, C. Rajagopalachari came out with a refined version of his offer of April 1942 so that the League's claim for separation might be accepted to secure the "installation of a national government."[109]   This "C.R. formula" proposed the basis of a settlement with the League in return for its co-operation with the Congress in the "formation of a provisional interim government." Essentially, it allowed the inhabitants of the "contiguous districts" with absolute Muslim majority to decide the issue of separation from Hindustan on the basis of plebiscite, retaining by mutual agreement common interests like defence, commerce and communication. The terms were to come into effect only after the transfer of power by the British. The C.R. formula had the approval of Mahatma Gandhi and it became the basis of the Gandhi-Jinnah talks in July-October 1944.[110]   The talks, however, broke down because of Jinnah's insistence on having a completely independent state covering all the six "Muslim majority" provinces in their entirety, that is, the Punjab, the N.W.F.P., Sind, Baluchistan, Bengal and Assam.[111]

The discredited C.R. formula and the abortive Gandhi-Jinnah negotiations, however, appeared to prove the worst fears of the Akalis that the pledge of 1929, given by the Congress, which had been regarded as some kind of insurance for the protection of the minorities, would be forgotten when it came to appeasing the League.[112]   The Sikhs by and large saw the C.R. formula as a betrayal; their survival was at stake, but they were "nowhere in the picture."[113]   With the exception of the Communists,[114] the Sikhs expressed their resentment against the C.R. formula from various platforms, the most important and the most vocal being the "All Parties Sikh Conference" convened in Amritsar on August 20-21, 1944 by Master Tara Singh.[115]   The Akalis understandably were the most incensed and outraged. Master Tara Singh asked: "If you can not force a

---

109. Menon, *Transfer of Power*, p. 139; also *IAR*, 1942, v. 2, pp. 206-7 for Rajagopalachari's letter to Mahatma Gandhi, dated July 18, 1942.

110. *IAR*, 1944, v. 1, p. 111, and v. 2, pp. 51-52, 129-30, 130-32.

111. Jinnah dismissed the C.R. formula as offering "a shadow and a husk, a maimed, mutilated and moth-eaten Pakistan." But he was pleased that at least in his personal capacity Gandhi had accepted the principle of partition. The Gandhi-Jinnah talks also strengthened Jinnah's hand at the time when his prestige had fallen considerably. Menon, *Transfer of Power*, p. 163.

112. See note 32 above.

113. *The Tribune*, August 4, 1944. Master Tara Singh held that, being the "most vitally affected community in India," the Sikhs should in fact have been the "major community in the negotiations." *IAR*, 1944, v. 2, p. 220.

114. In the Sikh Communists Conference held at Amritsar on September 11, 1944, speeches in support of Mahatma Gandhi and the Congress as well as the League's demand were made by, among others, Baba Sohan Singh Bhakna, Teja Singh Swatanter, Sohan Singh Josh and Durlab Singh. *IAR*, 1944, v. 2, pp. 215-17. The Communist Party supported the League's demand for self-determination for Muslims, because it "defined a nationality by the single criteria [sic] of common religion": Bhagwan Josh, *Communist Movement in Punjab 1926-47* (Delhi: Anupama Publications, 1979), p. 171; also Rai, *Legislative Politics*, pp. 300-4. Cf. Jalal, *The Sole Spokesman*, p. 96.

115. With the convening of the "Panthic gathering" against the "Raja-Gandhi formula," Master Tara Singh came out of his temporary retirement from politics subsequent to his resignation from the presidentship of the S.G.P.C. and the Shiromani Akali Dal a few months earlier. Jaswant Singh, ed., *Master Tara Singh*, pp. 149-50.

minority to stay in India, how can you force another minority to go out of India?"[116] He nevertheless hoped that it might still be possible to present the Sikh case before Mahatma Gandhi, and he requested him to meet a Sikh deputation. Mahatma Gandhi assured Master Tara Singh that he would not come to a final settlement without consulting Sikh opinion, but he appeared to have "bypassed" his request to meet a Sikh deputation.[117]

The general mood at the "All Parties Sikh Conference" was therefore one of exasperation and anguish. Santokh Singh, the Leader of the Opposition in the Punjab Assembly, said that "no one, not even ten Gandhis, had a right to barter away the Sikhs."[118] The first resolution emphatically condemned and rejected the "Raja-Gandhi formula" and declared that no settlement reached without previous consultation with the Sikhs and without their consent would be binding on them. A resolution moved by Mangal Singh turned out to be the most significant. It underlined the opposition of the Sikhs to the division of India and wanted the creation of a position wherein the Sikhs would not remain under the domination of a Muslim or Hindu majority, and in which they would get the same rights in all provinces as had been given to other minorities. It was clearly a reiteration of the demand for Azad Punjab as a province in the Indian Union. By an amendment, however, it was turned into a demand for an independent Sikh state.[119]

Despite the explosive tenor of many speeches, the Sikh state was seen as the last and not a very welcome choice. The preference of the Panthic gathering was clearly for "equal rights like brothers" and a "common rule of all communities"; for "a composite cabinet of all communities" under a "national government." Even when Master Tara Singh declared for the first time that "the Sikhs were a nation" he had underlined that "they wanted to live in this country as honourable people";[120] they "could not be forced to go out of a united India—into Pakistan."[121] Giani Kartar Singh asked, "if Pakistan was to come out of compulsion because Mr. Jinnah's demand could not be resisted, why not give an independent state to the Sikhs also?"[122] The All India Akali Conference (Lahore, October) repeated the demand for a separate state in similar qualifying terms.[123] The opposition of the pro-Congress groups among the Sikhs to the C.R. formula was a bit subdued; they were also opposed to the Akalis. By the

---

116. *The Tribune*, August 11, 1944.
117. Ibid., August 21, 1944. To Durlab Singh Mahatma Gandhi later on wrote that his "association with Rajaji in his formula could not affect the Sikh position in the slightest degree even if Quaid-i-Azam Jinnah accepted it." His meeting a Sikh deputation therefore was "unnecessary" in view of his "absolute assurance." Ibid., November 15, 1944; also *IAR*, 1944, v. 2, p. 222.
118. *IAR*, 1944, v. 2, p. 213.
119. Ibid., pp. 210-11, 211-15.
120. Ibid., p. 213; also *The Tribune*, August 21, 1944.
121. *IAR*, 1944, v. 2, p. 215.
122. Ibid., p. 213.
123. *IAR*, 1944, v. 2, pp. 218-21. The demand for a Sikh state was repeated in similar terms in the "Sikh memorandum" to the non-partisan Sapru Committee: *The Tribune*, February 3 and 23, 1945; also Jaswant Singh, ed., *Master Tara Singh*, pp. 194-96.

beginning of 1945, however, the Shiromani Akali Dal clearly emerged as the "premier organisation of the Sikhs" and their "largest party."[124]

The post-war developments towards full self-government were initiated by Viceroy Wavell's broadcast on June 14, 1945, proposing a new Executive Council to be entirely Indian except for the Viceroy and the Commander-in-Chief. Discussion of the Wavell plan and a new constitution began at Simla (June 25–July 14, 1945), wherein representatives of all the major political parties participated. "Tara Singh's Sikh Party" was recognised as the representative organisation of the Sikhs and Master Tara Singh himself as their spokesman.[125] He was happy that the Executive Council was to have one Sikh representative. He successfully withstood Maulana Azad's pressure that the Akali Dal should send "an agreed Sikh name" through the Congress.[126] In the course of the deliberations at Simla Master Tara Singh did not slacken his opposition to Pakistan. By this time the government had begun to consider the "pursuit of the Pakistan doctrine" as an "alarming menace to peace" in the Punjab.[127] On the whole, the position of the League appeared to be "rather weak" in early 1945.[128] The Simla conference, however, ended as a fiasco due largely to Jinnah's insistence that the League alone could represent the Muslims.

Prime Minister Attlee's Labour government took office on July 26, 1945 and began to expedite matters towards full self- government. Elections to the central and provincial Assemblies were announced on August 21. On September 19, the Viceroy announced his plan for convening a Constituent Assembly and forming an Executive Council representing the main Indian political parties. The newly elected provincial legislatures were to elect their representatives to the Constituent Assembly and to consider the Cripps proposals of 1942.

The All India Akali Conference (Gujranwala, September) rejected the Wavell plan, based as it was on the already discredited Cripps proposal, but decided to fight the elections to the provincial Assembly because the formation of the Constituent Assembly and the freedom and integrity of India depended upon the result of these elections. The Akalis were determined to oppose Pakistan through "concerted Panthic action."[129] "The Sikh Panth would resist

124. *The Tribune*, January 10, 1945; April 1, 1945.
125. Note by Sir F. Mudie, October 13, 1944, *T.P.*, v. 5, D. 55, p. 108. In fact, as early as September 1944, Master Tara Singh's name was being proposed as the representative of the Sikhs in the forthcoming conference; see note by Sir E. Jenkins, September 6, 1944, ibid., D. 6, p. 14.
126. Wavell to Amery, July 9, 1945, ibid., D. 577, p. 1210.
127. Note by Sir B. Glancy, October 26, 1944, ibid., D. 70, p. 143. Glancy in fact insisted that "we should do our utmost" to expose the "inherent flaws" in the Pakistan doctrine.
128. Sumit Sarkar, *Modern India, 1855-1947* (Madras: Macmillan India, reprint 1985), p. 416. The League ministries in Bengal and N.W.F.P. had fallen, and in Sind and Assam they existed on "Congress sufferance"; Khizr Hayat Khan's Unionist ministry in the Punjab had openly broken with Jinnah in mid-1944. For detail see Jalal, *The Sole Spokesman*, pp. 84-125.
129. *IAR*, 1945, v. 2, p. 168.

Pakistan to the last man," declared Ishar Singh Majhail while unfurling the *nishan sahib* in the presence of over 100,000 people.[130]

The Akalis felt compelled to go to the elections on the Panthic ticket because the League was going to the polls on the issue of Pakistan. Separate electorates also made it imperative for the Akalis to consolidate Sikh opinion in opposition to Pakistan. However, in view of the weak position of the League in the Muslim majority provinces in early 1945, the Akali Dal relegated the demand for a separate state to the background.[131] It nevertheless decided to fight the election independently of the Congress and other political organisations. Master Tara Singh declared that the Panth could not rely on any organisation: "The Communists and the Congress supported Pakistan, and the Hindu Mahasabha which opposed it did not count."[132] Ujjal Singh also advised the Sikhs to "fight for their rights alone," because the Congress had failed to realise how Pakistan was going to affect the Sikhs in the Punjab.[133] The Congress, on the other hand, could not appreciate the Akali assertion that there was no contradiction between the Panthic ticket and nationalistic aspirations. It denounced the Akali Dal as a communal party like the Hindu Mahasabha and the Muslim League. Attitudes were hardening on both sides. The Congress suspended Babu Labh Singh, president of the Akali Dal, from its membership and Mangal Singh resigned from the Congress on this issue. After much effort on both sides, an Akali-Congress compromise was effected only for four seats, the strongholds of the Communists.

The election results showed significant shifts in the party position since 1937.[134] Winning 22 seats now, in contrast with the 10 seats in 1937, the Akalis were able to consolidate their position by eliminating the Communists and the other Sikh rivals. The Congress, too, emerged much stronger, winning 51 seats as compared to 15 in 1937. It won 10 Sikh seats but only one Muslim seat. The Muslim League won a massive victory, capturing 75 out of 86 seats as against only two in 1937. The Unionists could win only 20 seats as against 90 in 1937. Within one year the Muslim League had replaced the Unionists as the representative of Muslims and as a political force in the Punjab.[135] The League, however, needed the support of another party in the 175-member Assembly to form the government, but a compromise could not be effected with the Congress and the Akali Dal, so an Akali-Congress-Unionist coalition under Khizr Hayat

---

130. Ibid, p. 164. Babu Labh Singh, the president-elect, was taken in a two-mile-long procession accompanied by sixty Akali Jathas carrying swords and Sikh flags and shouting anti-Pakistan slogans.
131. Ibid., p. 167. In the resolution passed at the Akali conference in September 1945, stress was laid on the promotion of the "freedom, unity, integrity and welfare of our beloved motherland."
132. Ibid., p. 166.
133. Ibid., p. 167.
134. *The Tribune*, February 17, 1937; February 24, 1946; also Menon, *Transfer of Power*, p. 230. Cf. Rai, *Legislative Politics*, pp. 222, 316.
135. During 1945, the Muslim League had effectively appropriated the base of the Unionists among the Muslim landed gentry, religious leadership and the peasantry. It already had a fairly strong urban support, particularly among students and professional classes. For detail, see Jalal, *The Sole Spokesman*, pp. 138-51.

Khan took over the government in March 1946. Despite its majority, the League had to sit in the opposition, a position which the Punjabi Leaguers could not accept for long.

The clear victory of the Muslim League in the elections had convinced the Akalis that the British were going to concede "Pakistan in some shape or form."[136] The demand for a separate state for the Sikhs in the Punjab "as their homeland and holy land" was revived by the Akali Dal in the meeting of its Working Committee on March 22, 1946.[137] Their memorandum to the Cabinet Mission in April 1946 is the clearest exposition of their determination to oppose Pakistan in "unequivocal" terms. They also asked for the abolition of the statutory Muslim majority to ensure the Sikhs "an effective voice" in the administration of the country. Alternatively, they asked for a new province to be carved out "as an additional provincial unit in the united India." The Sikhs would demand a separate state, it was added, if the Muslim demand for Pakistan was going to be conceded.[138]

As if to realise the worst fears of the Sikhs, the Cabinet Mission scheme, announced on May 16, gave the "substance of Pakistan" to the League and "liquidated the position of the Sikhs in their homeland."[139] It proposed a loose confederal structure in which Muslims had the chance of dominating north-western and north-eastern provinces of the country. It provided for compulsory provincial grouping, the Punjab going to the Muslim-majority group B. But there was no provision for safeguards for the Sikhs as had been provided for the Muslim and Hindu minorities, even though the Sikhs had been recognised as one of the "three main communities" in India.[140]

The Panthic Conference held at Amritsar on June 10, 1946 reflected an acute sense of crisis and desperation among the Sikhs.[141] Their "cry for justice and protection of the legitimate rights had gone unheard"; it was "a grave hour for the Sikh Panth"; there was an "attempt to enslave us for ever," an attempt "to atom bomb the Sikhs." It was a question of survival for the Sikhs and they prepared to give a tough fight to the British government. A representative body called the Pratinidhi Panthic Board was appointed, with Indian National Army Colonel Narinjan Singh Gill as its chairman. This Council of Action decided first to explore all avenues through negotiations with the Congress and the Muslim League before starting a triangular struggle or *morcha* against the

---

136. *The Tribune*, March 11, 1946; March 6, 1946.
137. Khushwant Singh, *History of the Sikhs*, v. 2, p. 259, n. 5.
138. *IAR*, 1946, v. 1, pp. 200-201; also Rai, *Legislative Politics*, Appendix XII, 348-49; *T.P.*, v. 6, D. 56, pp. 138-41.
139. This was stated in the resolution passed at the Panthic Conference convened on June 10, 1946. *IAR*, 1946, v. 1, pp. 203-4. In his letter to the Secretary of State, dated May 25, 1946, Master Tara Singh underlined the anxiety of the Sikhs who had been placed under "perpetual Muslim domination." Ibid., pp. 201-2.
140. The Statement of the Cabinet Mission and the Viceroy, May 16, 1946, 18 (c): Menon, *Transfer of Power*, Appendix IV, p. 471. The "three main communities" were "General, Muslim and Sikh."
141. *IAR*, 1946, v. 1, pp. 202-5.

government and the two major political parties. It meanwhile decided to boycott the interim government and the Constituent Assembly.[142]

The Congress Working Committee, presided over by Jawaharlal Nehru on August 9, appealed to the Sikhs "to reconsider their decision to boycott the Constituent Assembly."[143] It admitted that "injustice had been done to Sikhs" by the Cabinet Mission and assured the Sikhs that the Congress would give "all possible support in removing their legitimate grievances and in securing adequate safeguards for the protection of their just interest in the Punjab." The Committee appealed to the Sikhs to "reconsider their resolution of boycotting the Constituent Assembly." Meanwhile, on July 29, the Muslim League had rejected the Cabinet Mission scheme and given a call for "direct action."[144] The Pratinidhi Panthic Board decided to "give the Constituent Assembly a fair trial" and to cast their lot with the Congress on August 14, precisely a year before the foundation of Pakistan.[145] Two days later, on August 16, the "direct action" in Calcutta unleashed an orgy of violence which soon spread to other parts of India, including the Punjab.

IV

Events moved fast during the last year of colonial rule. Jawaharlal Nehru's Interim Cabinet was sworn in on September 2, with Baldev Singh as the Sikh member. The League joined it on October 26, but refused to join the Constituent Assembly. Its cooperation with the Congress hinged on parity at the centre and the "compulsory grouping" at the provincial level. On January 5, 1947 the Congress finally, albeit with reservations, accepted the grouping clause of the Cabinet Mission scheme. This placed the Sikhs, much to their dismay, under a permanent Muslim majority rule. Master Tara Singh and Giani Kartar Singh termed it a "betrayal" of the Sikhs, and Mangal Singh asked for the "partition of the Punjab into two parts."[146] A persistent agitation by the Muslim League in the Punjab brought down Khizr Hayat Khan's coalition ministry on March 2. This was followed by Governor's rule in the Punjab and widespread riots in which the Sikhs bore "the main brunt of the communal fury."[147] The Congress Working Committee was constrained to admit in its meeting on March 8 that "the tragic events" of the last six weeks in the Punjab had necessitated "a division of Punjab into two Provinces," separating the "predominantly Muslim part" from "the predominantly non-Muslim part."[148]

---

142. The decisions to boycott the interim government and the Constituent Assembly were taken respectively on June 22 and July 5.
143. *T.P.*, v. 8, D. 114, p. 180; also *IAR*, 1946, v. 2, p. 105.
144. Despite Jinnah's statement that "this day we bid good bye to constitutional methods" and that "we have also forged a pistol and are in a position to use it," "direct action" was intended primarily to be civil disobedience against the government and secondarily non-cooperation with the Congress. Menon, *Transfer of Power*, pp. 283-84. "No one, however, had a clear idea of the shape 'direct action' would take." Jalal, *The Sole Spokesman*, p. 212, n. 14.
145. Text of the resolution, August 14, 1946, *T.P.*, v. 7, D. 158, p. 243.
146. *The Tribune*, January 7 and 9, 1947, quoted in Gulati, *Akalis*, p. 128.
147. Menon, *Transfer of Power*, p. 419.
148. Ibid., p. 347; also Rai, *Legislative Politics*, p. 326.

Meanwhile, on February 20, Prime Minister Attlee had announced his government's decision to hand over power to Indians at the latest by June 1948.[149] The new Viceroy, Mountbatten, took over on March 24 to effect the transfer of power. Within a month of his arrival it became clear to all concerned that the division of the country between India and Pakistan could not be averted. Various strategies were now adopted by the Akali Dal to keep the Sikh population together. The Sikhs were spread all over the Punjab without being in a majority in any single district of the province. The Akalis revived the idea of "Sikhistan" between the rivers Jamuna and Chenab "on the basis of Sikh landed property, Sikh sacred shrines and Sikh interests."[150] Mountbatten made it clear that "Sikhistan" was not possible and that whatever the dividing line, nearly half of the Sikh population would fall in Pakistan.[151] Giani Kartar Singh then toyed with the idea of the "Sikh State joining Pakistan," securing special privileges and concessions for its government.[152] However, the Akalis had "committed themselves so deeply to the partition of the Punjab" that it was "difficult and perhaps impossible for them to take a different line."[153] They were making "business-like and serious" preparations for "civil war" and were determined to "fight to the last man if put under Muslim domination."[154] Jinnah also did not give them any "coherent and acceptable guarantee of their security" within Pakistan.[155] Their parleys with the League remained at best a strategy to secure as much of the area inhabited by the Sikhs for the Indian Punjab as possible.[156] In fact, in their talks with the Viceroy, the Akali leaders had "repeatedly" asked for partition of the province.[157] They also tried their utmost to secure the Chenab to be the boundary between the East Punjab and Pakistan as "a lasting solution to the communal problem."[158] They insisted also on the "provision for

---

149. Menon, *Transfer of Power*, Appendix IX, pp. 507-8. Power was to be handed over either "as a whole to some form of central government for British India, or in some areas to the existing provincial governments." Thus, more than one successor authority was envisioned for independent India.
150. Larry Collins and Dominique Lapierre, *Mountbatten and the Partition of India*, Vol. I (New Delhi: Vikas Publishing House, 1982); Viceroy's personal reports, May 8, 1947, p. 126.
151. Ibid., May 1 and 8, 1947, p. 125.
152. Record of an interview between Mountbatten and Jinnah, April 26, 1947, *T.P.*, v. 10, D. 229, p. 452. Besides the deep personal involvement of Giani Kartar Singh, who hailed from the canal colony district of Lyallpur, the Viceroy too was interested in avoiding the partition of the province. Collins and Lapierre, *Mountbatten*, Viceroy's personal reports, May 1 and 9, 1947 and June 5, 1947, pp. 125 and 128, respectively. In fact, on this issue there was reportedly "a split amongst the Sikhs," with Master Tara Singh and Baldev Singh opposing Giani Kartar Singh; see Thompson to Corfield, June 2, 1947, *T.P.*, v. 11, D. 22, p. 38.
153. Cf. Nayar, *Minority Politics*, pp. 91-94.
154. Collins and Lapierre, *Mountbatten*, Viceroy's personal reports, April 9 and 24, 1947, pp. 122 and 124, respectively; Jenkins to Mountbatten, April 30, 1947, *T.P.*., v. 10, D. 263, p. 506.
155. Baldev Singh to Mountbatten, June 2, 1947, *T.P.*, v. 11, D. 36, pp. 67-70; also Menon, *Transfer of Power*, p. 344.
156. Cf. Nayar, *Minority Politics*, pp. 91-94.
157. Minutes of the meeting of the Viceroy with Indian leaders, June 2, 1947, *T.P*, v. 11, D. 23, p. 41; also Broadcast by Mountbatten, ibid., D. 44, p. 87.
158. *IAR*, 1947, v. 1, p. 244. This was emphasised by Master Tara Singh, Giani Kartar Singh and Baldev Singh in their meeting with Mountbatten in New Delhi on April 18, 1947. It was reiterated in a convention of the Hindu and Sikh legislators from the Punjab held in New Delhi on

transfer of population and property," without which "the very purpose of partition would be defeated."[159]

Mountbatten finally prevailed upon Jinnah to agree to the partition of the Punjab and also of Bengal by conceding the right of self-determination to the non-Muslim minorities in these provinces. The Mountbatten plan of June 3 provided for the division of India into two sovereign states. The East Punjab section of the provincial Assembly met on June 23 and voted for partition by a majority vote.[160] The Boundary Commission was appointed in early July and on August 17 it awarded thirteen out of the twenty-nine districts of the Punjab to the Indian Union. The crisis for the Sikhs was thus resolved with the partition of the Punjab.

V

In sum, the crisis of Sikh politics began with the demand of the Muslim League for the division of the country, with the Punjab going to the Muslim-majority state of Pakistan. The Akalis viewed this demand as a threat to everything they valued: their heritage, their lands, their political interests and, above all, their identity as a distinct community. The outbreak of war and the preparedness of the Congress to appease the League for the "larger cause" of freedom only deepened the crisis.

At the outset, most people in the country took the League's demand as a "bogey" or one of the many "airy" schemes floated in those days. The Punjabi Hindus and the Congressite Sikhs took it seriously but hoped by and large that the danger would somehow be averted by stressing the unity and integrity of India. While the Communist Sikhs supported the idea of Pakistan, the Akalis articulated its implications for the non-Muslims in the Punjab and embarked on a course of opposition. The Akali leaders insisted on the unity of India, but if the Punjab could not be saved from going to Pakistan, they demanded change in provincial boundaries. The Azad Punjab scheme, the demand for a separate state, and partition were parts of a single strategy. In fact, the empirical content of their various demands remained nearly the same. The Akali leaders were trying to save the region between the Jamuna and the Chenab, broadly comprising the divisions of Ambala, Jullundur and Lahore in addition to the canal colony districts of Lyallpur and Montgomery, from passing under

May 2, 1947. Ibid., p. 245. In fact, the Sikhs and Hindus from the Punjab, including those belonging to the Congress, stuck to this position till the announcement of the boundary award.

159. This was stated in a resolution jointly passed by the Working Committee of the Shiromani Akali Dal and the Pratinidhi Panthic Board of June 14, 1947. Quoted in Kirpal Singh, *Partition*, p. 35. They had been hoping that 85% of the Sikhs would remain in India and the remaining 15% would be transferred from Pakistan to India.

160. The Punjab Assembly met amidst demonstrations and communal disorders. The West Bengal section of the Assembly had already met on June 20 and had voted for partition. However, unlike the Punjab, Bengal had "no local political deadlock," but it had to be partitioned "for broadly similar reasons." Collins and Lapierre, *Mountbatten*, Viceroy's personal papers, April 2, 1947, p. 121; also Menon, *Transfer of Power*, pp. 347, 435.

"perpetual Muslim domination."[161] What they tried to secure was not an area in which Sikhs were dominant, but an area in which no single community was in a position to dominate the others, and in which the political, economic and cultural interests of the Sikhs could be safeguarded.[162]

Finally, the implacable opposition of the Akalis to the League's demand convinced the British authorities that the Sikhs meant to oppose Pakistan by all the means at their command. The Congress leadership also realised that even if the League's demand were to be conceded, it would be unfair to oblige the non-Muslim minorities to remain in Pakistan. The Viceroy finally prevailed upon Jinnah to agree to the "mutilated and moth-eaten" version of Pakistan which he had rejected earlier. East Punjab was thus in a certain sense a gift of the Akalis to independent India.

---

161. The Akalis had been hoping that the "other factors," such as landed property, religious and cultural institutions and the "historic role" of the Sikhs would weigh in their favour and make up for their small numbers. Baldev Singh to Mountbatten, June 2, 1947, *T.P.*, v. 11, D. 36, p. 70.

162. It must be emphasised that the demand for a "Sikh State" before 1947 was not a programme given to the masses. It remained confined to the political parleys of the leaders and should not be confused with the recent demand for "Khalistan" by a section of the Sikh community.

Sikh Minority Attitudes
in India's Federal System

Paul Wallace

Indian federalism, in both its governmental and political aspects, serves as a dual-edged sword, either exacerbating or ameliorating relations within the Sikh community and Sikh relations with non-Sikhs. Central government policies and, more importantly, policy implementation affect every state within the Indian Union. States as geographical entities are constantly involved in a tug-of-war over the distribution of national resources. That is a normal bargaining relation between the Center and the states in every federal system. India's situation is rendered more complicated than that of the United States, or of Australia or West Germany, by the overlapping of political with cultural boundaries. Switzerland, perhaps, is the closest analogue to India, but it lacks comparative saliency in terms of size and level of economic and political development. Canada's Quebec province is closer to a state in the Indian situation.

Prophets of doom had been predicting the dismemberment or balkanization of India even before the emergence of a terrorist movement in Punjab in 1981. Ethnic differences revolving around one or more ascriptive characteristics, such as religion, language, caste and tribe, are most commonly invoked as divisive factors that India's federal system will be unable to contain.[1]

An anthropologist, Harold Gould, in reviewing some of the major pessimistic newspaper and scholarly accounts from as early as the 1950's, suggests that such pessimism itself may be ascriptive, inherited form the colonial period. He concludes that "some of the abhorrence which many Indian intellectuals feel toward their political system" stems from a "deep-seated

---

1. One of the earliest, most influential books emphasizing India's fissiparous tendencies is Selig S. Harrison, *India: The Most Dangerous Decades* (Princeton: Princeton University Press, 1960). Its cover jacket starkly asks the pessimistic question, "Can the Nation Hold Together?" Harrison, in the 1950's, sees striking similarities between India and the pre-World War I Austro-Hungarian Empire. Regionalism and caste lobbies, along with the passing of India's nationalist "tall leaders," in his view, open the prospect for the "balkanization" of India. In particular, see chs. 3, 4, and pp. 319-23.

[Joseph T. O'Connell, Milton Israel, Willard G. Oxtoby, eds., with W.H. McLeod and J.S. Grewal, visiting eds., *Sikh History and Religion in the Twentieth Century* (S. Asian Studies Papers, 3) (Toronto: S. Asian Studies, Univ. of Toronto, 1988)]

belief" in their political inadequacy bequeathed by an idealized British model and transmitted through British education.[2]

Despite the periodic waves of pessimism, India has been remarkably resilient in coping with a succession of federalist problems. The integration of the princely states tested newly independent India. This was followed by the political crucible of states' reorganization in the 1950's and 1960's. Continuing federalist developments include the designation of Mizoram as India's twenty-third state in 1987 as part of a political compromise with a two-decades-long insurrectionary movement.[3] No part of India has been immune from state pressures on the Center, nor from periodic central efforts to increase the power of the Center at the expense of the periphery. In the 1980's, Kashmir and Punjab in the northwest, Assam and West Bengal in the east, and the southern states of Andhra Pradesh and Karnataka have all been contentious domains of federalist struggle.

Punjab, nonetheless, by 1987 began to appear unique and perhaps intractable. Non-violent agitations continued, as in the successful movement of the 1960's for a Punjabi or Sikh majority state, but by 1981 there was as well a terrorist movement, part of which at least proclaimed the goal of Khalistan, an independent Sikh state. Repression in the form of Operation Bluestar utilized the military in June 1984 to storm the Golden Temple in Amritsar. Many of the premier separatist leaders were killed, including Sant Jarnail Singh Bhindranwale, and martial law was imposed throughout the state. Force did not succeed. Neither did the political accord between Prime Minister Rajiv Gandhi and Akali Dal leader Sant Harcharan Singh Longowal in June 1985. A window of political opportunity appeared to open with the Accord and the elections that brought the moderate Akali Dal to power in Punjab in September 1985.[4] For the first time since the onset of systematic violence, central and state political authorities seemed to be working in harmony. Moreover, the high election turnout of 67.58% exceeded the preceding 1980 and 1977 election totals despite well-publicized dissident Sikh demands for a boycott.

A favorable political climate dissipated as the Rajiv-Longowal accord failed to be implemented. By early 1986, the Punjab problem appeared to have reverted back to 1984. Sant Bhindranwale's seminary, the Damdami Taksal, provided new fundamentalist leaders, his father headed a dissident Akali Dal, and new extremist recruits continued to be provided by the All India Sikh Student Federation (A.I.S.S.F.). The sense of *déja vu* became more enhanced as

---

2. "On the Apperception of Doom in Indian Political Analysis," in Paul Wallace, ed., *Region and Nation in India* (New Delhi: Oxford and Indian Book House, 1985), p. 297.
3. Mizo National Front leader Laldenga made the transition from a civil-war insurrectionist to a freely elected Chief Minister of the new state. India's central government, earlier the enemy of the Mizo movement, engineered the compromise. Prime Minister Rajiv Gandhi had the highest Mizo title of *Thangchhuah* conferred upon him by Laldenga. *India Today* 12:5 (March 15, 1987), 12.
4. The Akalis won 73 of the 117 seats, followed by the Congress (I) with 32, six for the Bharatiya Janata Party (including two seats won in December), and six won by other parties and independents. For complete results and a comparison with the 1980 elections see Paul Wallace, "The Sikhs as a 'Minority' in a Sikh Majority State," *Asian Survey* 26:3 (March, 1986), 374.

the military again moved into the Golden Temple complex in Amritsar on April 30, 1986, following the declaration of the formation of Khalistan by the Kahlon faction of the A.I.S.S.F. The code name selected this time, Operation Search, sounds like a variant of Operation Bluestar. Unlike the 1984 military assault, however, there was no significant resistance to the commando operation nor were any major extremist leaders captured.[5]

Politically, the action split the ruling Akali Dal. Former Akali Dal Chief Minister Parkash Singh Badal and Gurcharan Singh Tohra, long-time head of the Sikh temple management committee, the Shiromani Gurdwara Prabandhak Committee, resigned from the Akali Dal on May 2 along with two cabinet members, Amarinder Singh and Sukhjinder Singh.[6] The ruling Akali Dal, which had come to power in September 1985 with almost a two-thirds majority, became a minority government on May 8, when 27 of its 73 M.L.A.'s became a separate Akali group within the Assembly.[7]

Punjab in 1987 presented a federal dilemma. Terrorist killings the preceding year totaled approximately 700, went to about 80 a month during the first part of the year, and increased after the advent of President's Rule in May to more than 100 a month. An appreciable number of Hindus, particularly from the districts bordering Pakistan, had fled to Haryana and Delhi.[8] Political formulas were conspicuous by their absence, while military force, in the form of ever-increasing numbers of central reserve police in addition to the Punjab police, at best could contain the high level of terrorism.

Comparisons with Northern Ireland provided the prospect of an ominous future. The power of the state pitted against the intractable nature of the extremist movement could result in a lengthy deadlock. Such is the prospect presented by Punjab's police chief, Julio Francis Ribeiro, India's foremost professional police officer. In a candid press conference on January 3, 1987, he admitted that the war against terrorism would be a long drawn-out one, as "it had come to stay." People in Punjab, he suggested, must learn to live with terrorism as the people in Europe were doing.[9] Eliminating terrorism was not possible, he stated a week later, as "it is in the heart and mind of those perpetrating it in the cause of misplaced sentiments of philosophy." Police and paramilitary forces rather than the army, he concluded, could control terrorism "to a manageable extent as had been done in Ireland."[10]

5. *The Times of India*, April 30 and May 1, 1986, p. 1; *The New York Times*, May 1, 1986, p. 3; *India Today*, May 31, 1986, pp. 8-13.

6. *The Times of India*, May 3, 1986, p. 1.

7. Ibid., May 3, 1986, p. 1.

8. More than half of the killings in Punjab in 1986 took place in the border districts of Amritsar and Gurdaspur. *India Today* 12:2 (January 31, 1987), 15; *Christian Science Monitor*, May 13, 1987, 12; *India Today* 12:24 (December 31, 1987), 12.

9. *The Times of India*, January 4, 1987, p. 1.

10. Ibid., January 10, 1987, p. 9. With the imposition of President's rule, sixty additional companies of paramilitary forces were distributed throughout the state in addition to the existing 55,000 police and paramilitary forces. *India West*, May 15, 1987, p. 1.

A Northern Ireland scenario for Punjab focuses on the law and order problem while neglecting a careful examination of the issues and process that led to it. Rajiv Gandhi's accord with Sant Longowal in June 1985 did identify major issues and begin a productive process. It simply floundered in the face of non-implementation and the inevitable political complexities, including the Center's relations with Haryana, internal Congress Party problems, rising Hindu militancy and the fragmentation of the Akali Dal in Punjab.

Re-examination and renewed efforts instead of resignation offered the only prospects for breaking the Punjab deadlock. Instead, New Delhi attempted to postpone further any meaningful initiatives by declaring President's rule on May 11, 1987.[11] Direct central government rule over Punjab failed to benefit the Congress Party in the adjoining state of Haryana in June 1987 as the alliance led by Devi Lal won four-fifths of the Assembly seats. At best, President's rule has allowed a breathing space while Prime Minister Rajiv Gandhi has sought to revitalize a leadership position shaken by alleged scandals, poor Congress Party electoral results, and international problems with India's neighbors.

Political expressions by Sikhs toward India's central government revolve around two related axes. One focuses on center-state relations with Sikhs geographically concentrated in one state within India's federal system. A second dimension revolves around Sikh minority attitudes in Punjab, which exist despite their apparent numerical, economic and political dominance. Federal concerns in terms of a Punjab-centered identity are quite different from religious distinctiveness or religious separatism. Failure to distinguish between them in terms of public policy lies at the core of the Punjab problem. A workable political process must encompass both of them.

Center-State Relations

Sikh federal concerns are not markedly different from those of the other major religious community within Punjab. Hindus as well as Sikhs share a Punjab orientation toward the need for enhanced state autonomy on development issues such as water, power and industrial development. Both of the state's major communities support the long promised transfer of Chandigarh to Punjab even though approximately seventy per cent of Chandigarh's population is Hindu.[12]

Clearly the most controversial and provocative document which attempts to set forth Sikh positions toward Indian federalism is the Anandpur Sahib resolution, which first appeared in October, 1973. Political separatism is the charge from both opponents and proponents. Granting the demands for greater autonomy, from the central government perspective, undermines the integrity of

---

11. *Christian Science Monitor*, May 13, 1987, p. 12.
12. The 1971 figures were 71.68% Hindu and 25.45% Sikh. Census of India 1971, Paper 2 of 1972, *Religion*, p. 108.

the Indian Union.   At the same time, refusal to grant them, the Akali Dal charged, "was itself paving the way for Khalistan."[13]

Political rhetoric flowing from all concerned parties muddled the normal process of political bargaining. Political documents have to be assessed in terms of their political context. That is the first point: the Anandpur Sahib resolution is a *political* statement. Moreover, it is not one statement, but a series of statements changed according to the existing situation and the group which authors the revised version.

It originated at the birthplace of the Khalsa, where Guru Gobind Singh in 1699 had established the physical and symbolic elements of what subsequently became mainstream or orthodox Sikhism. A militant Sikh Khalsa (brotherhood) defending itself from Mughal repression underwent an initiation, adopted the name Singh ("lion"), and accepted baptism, uncut hair and other identifying characteristics that distinguished them from other religious communities.

Anandpur Sahib in 1973 represented a roughly analogous political situation, although clearly less threatening than in 1699. An election defeat of the Akali Dal in 1972 had removed it from power in the State Assembly. It went from being the largest single party in the previous 1969 elections, with 43 seats in the 104-seat Assembly, to 24 in 1972 (compared to 66 for the Congress Party). Out of power, the Akali Dal utilized the symbolically potent venue of Anandpur Sahib to pass a series of resolutions which in effect challenged the ruling Congress Party at the state and national levels while simultaneously attempting to rally political support. The Resolution then receded into the background as one more example of the many statements emanating from various states in India which periodically seek increased state autonomy. Subsequent events, including the Emergency promulgated by Prime Minister Indira Gandhi in 1975 and the Akali Dal return to power in 1977, further buried the 1973 Anandpur Sahib resolution.

Ironically, in view of later events, the reactivation of the Anandpur Sahib resolution begins at least partly as a counter to the public declarations for a Khalistan expressed at the 54th All India Sikh Educational Conference held in Chandigarh on March 17-18, 1981. Until this time, support for the extremist concept of a completely autonomous or independent state remained largely outside India, being promoted by Jagjit Singh Chauhan, a former Punjab minister residing in England. As the self-appointed president, he issued non-accreditable Khalistan passports, sought membership in the United Nations, raised funds and attempted to develop a following, primarily from overseas Sikhs.

Surprisingly, the conservative Chief Khalsa Diwan-sponsored educational conference served as the forum for the Khalistan appeal in 1981. Ganga Singh Dhillon, a Sikh businessman from the United States, unexpectedly associated himself with the Khalistan movement as he publicly called for a separate Sikh

---

13. *The Tribune* (Chandigarh), April 14, 1981, p. 3.

state with associate membership in the United Nations.[14] Khalistan banners then were paraded before a large gathering of Sikhs who came to celebrate the Holi festival at Anandpur Sahib a week after the educational conference. Extremist Dal Khalsa and Nihang Sikhs raised Khalistan slogans.[15]

Moderate Sikh political leadership, led by Sant Harcharan Singh Longowal, tactically must have felt threatened by yet another challenge to the Akali Dal's position as the leading party among the Sikhs. Several dissident Akali Dals already contested the dominant Longowal Akali Dal. Jagdev Singh Talwandi led the most notable opposition, exercising a more militant and communal posture. Talwandi had been president of the dominant Akali Dal until his expulsion following the Akali defeat in the 1980 elections.[16] In addition to what can be considered as conventional political parties in Punjab, Sant Jarnail Singh Bhindranwale by this time was leading a major Sikh revivalist movement increasingly attractive to Sikh youth.

Longowal's Akali Dal reacted strongly to the Khalistan demands raised in Chandigarh and Anandpur Sahib, charging that they "were being raised at the instigation of Congress (I) leaders."[17] Akali Dal legislative leader Parkash Singh Badal, a former Akali Chief Minister and later in 1986 a dissident himself, asserted that the Chief Khalsa Diwan provided "a pro-Government and pro-Congress (I) stage."[18]

In this highly volatile political context, the moderate Longowal Akali Dal decided to focus on the Anandpur Sahib resolution with its thrust on increased autonomy for Punjab as the major Sikh issue rather than Khalistan and separatism. In the narrow political sense of linking the three major Sikh groups under the moderates' umbrella the tactic succeeded. Separate *morchas* or agitations were launched and unified. Talwandi's Akali Dal started its agitation in April 1982. Bhindranwale followed with a movement focused on the release of All India Sikh Student Federation leader Amrik Singh in July. Longowal led a separate *nahar roko* agitation to block work on the Yamuna-Sutlej link canal. The three movements coalesced on August 4, 1982 with the Anandpur Sahib resolution as a joint demand headed by Longowal as the overall "dictator."

One interpretation from an Indian business journal described the Akali tactic as a "masterful stroke" which enabled the Longowal Akali Dal "to forge an alliance between the religious consciousness of the Sikhs and the political and economic demands of the Jat Sikh capitalist farmers."[19] Eminent novelist and journalist Khushwant Singh concluded that the Akali Dal (L) purpose was to

14. *The Tribune* and *Indian Express*, March 18 and 19, 1981.
15. *National Herald*, March 22, 1981, p. 6.
16. Robin Jeffrey, *What's Happening to India?* (London: Macmillan, 1986), pp. 142-43. A more detailed analysis of the background to the split in the Akali Dal, beginning with the breakup of the Janata Party at the center, is provided in Paul Wallace, "Plebiscitary Politics: India's 1980 Parliamentary Elections in Punjab and Haryana," *Asian Survey* 20:6 (June, 1980), 612-33.
17. *The Tribune*, April 14, 1981, p. 3.
18. Ibid.
19. Bharat Bhushan, "The Punjab Business: Rich Farmers Bid for Power," *Business India*, June 6-19, 1983, p. 59.

"destabilize the Congress government through agitation."[20]   A third interpretation stressed the cost to the moderate Sikhs, as the alliance with the extremists "has successfully alienated opposition parties with whom they could share a political future."[21] Each of these varying analyses points to the political complexity, the potential benefits and risks faced by each of the competing yet allied groups.

It is clear, especially in retrospect, that militant tactics, however non-violent, could promote a more favorable context for the continuing extremist and violent movement led by Bhindranwale.   Longowal needed meaningful concessions from New Delhi so as to enable a return to a more conventional political process.   His Akali Dal could compete effectively with the other two more militant groups under normal conditions. They were disadvantaged in an extremist competition. In this important sense, Longowal's Akali Dal presented a moderate Sikh position by focusing on the Anandpur Sahib resolution.

Negotiations between the Akali Dal and New Delhi began on October 10, 1981 and continued periodically until 1984. Not one, but several versions of the Anandpur Sahib resolution became involved. It is doubtful that the original 1973 version ever received serious consideration in regard to the center-state provisions. Its version of state autonomy would have restricted central authority to defense, foreign relations, currency and general communications for all states. Clearly, New Delhi could not treat this seriously.

But a reformulated version had been passed by the All India Akali Conference held at Ludhiana on October 28-29, 1978. Most important, the earlier demand limiting the Center to only four spheres had been radically altered to an endorsement of "the principle of State autonomy in keeping with the concept of Federalism." The most specific part of the Resolution on this subject is the statement that "it has become imperative that the Indian constitutional infrastructure should be given a real federal shape by redefining the central and state relations and rights."[22]

In this form, the Akali Dal formulation is in the mainstream of extended efforts over time by various states and groups to redress the balance in what has been described as India's "quasi-federal" system tilting toward the unitary side. Constitutional scholar K.C. Wheare categorized India's system as quasi-federal as early as 1953. He emphasized such centralizing features as the Emergency powers, President's rule, the Center's power to alter state boundaries, the incorporation of state constitutions within the Union constitution, and the dominant role of the Center in financial matters.[23] A selective list of major efforts in re-examining and recommending changes to Indian federalism includes the Administrative Reforms Commission in the 1960's, the Rajamannar

---

20. Khushwant Singh, "The Genesis of the Hindu-Sikh Divide," in Amarjit Kaur et al., *The Punjab Story* (New Delhi: Roli Books International, 1984), pp. 8-9.
21. Ayesha Kagal, *The Times of India*, December 19, 1982, p. 6.
22. Government of India, *White Paper on the Punjab Agitation* (New Delhi, July 10, 1984), pp. 72-73. Texts of the Akali Dal resolutions and demands are included in the White Paper.
23. K.C. Wheare, *Federal Government*, 3rd ed. (London: Oxford University Press, 1953).

Committee appointed by the Tamilnadu Government in 1977, and resolutions submitted by all five southern Chief Ministers in July 1978, including two opposition Congress (I) Chief Ministers.[24]

There were, however, subsequent versions of what collectively has been labeled the Anandpur Sahib resolution. Talwandi's militant Akali Dal during its agitation in April 1981 returned essentially to the original 1973 Resolution emphasizing the emasculated Center provisions. Adding to the confusion, Longowal's Akali Dal specified forty-five demands in September 1981 and a revised list of fifteen demands in October 1981. Item 9 in the list of fifteen demands reverted to limiting the Center to "Foreign Affairs, Defence, Currency and Communications."[25]

Consequently, it is clear that not one resolution, but a basket of Anandpur Sahib resolutions, sat before the negotiators and in a kaleidoscopic, changing manner. Certainly, this could be confusing as well as capable of exploitation. Each of the contending Sikh groups in addition to the Center could pick and choose in making a particular case. But this is the stuff of politics. Bargaining and compromise are possible in a situation of varying and even conflicting positions. But political will proved lacking in the period 1981-1984 giving way to Operation Bluestar, a military response. Thirteen months later, however, a new Prime Minister chose not to treat the issue of increased state autonomy as tantamount to secession. Nor did the leading Sikh spokesman. The Rajiv-Longowal accord of July 1985 referred the portions of the Anandpur Sahib resolution relating to center-state relations to the Commission headed by retired Supreme Court Justice R.S. Sakaria, which had been appointed in March 1983.[26]

Demands posited in the various Anandpur Sahib resolutions and in supplementary statements, range from the most general to those that are very specific. Resolution 1 of the August 1, 1977 Longowal "authentic English version"[27] begins with a general statement of the need to recast center-state relations: "it has become imperative that the Indian constitutional infra-structure should be given a real federal shape by redefining the central and state relations."[28] Centralization of power is condemned and decentralization is advocated. Other resolutions with important center-state ramifications include the redrafting of the tax structure, the control of water works to be located in Punjab, parity relations between the prices of agricultural produce and industrial raw materials, changes in the land reform laws, a redistribution of the Ravi-Beas waters, and the establishment of six sugar and four textile mills in the state so as "to implement its agro-industrial policy."[29]

---

24. For further details of these unsuccessful efforts see Paul Wallace, "Center-State Relations in India: The Federal Dilemma," in James R. Roach, ed., *India 2000: The Next Fifteen Years* (Riverdale, Maryland: The Riverdale Company, 1986), pp. 146-65.
25. Government of India, *White Paper on the Punjab*, pp. 61-65.
26. The Accord was read out to members of both Houses of Parliament on July 24, 1985. *The Times of India*, July 25, 1985, p. 1.
27. Government of India, *White Paper on Punjab*, p. 69.
28. Ibid., p. 72.
29. Ibid., pp. 73-78.

Underlying these and other demands or complaints is the widespread attitude in Punjab that it suffers discrimination from the Center. Partly, this is attributed to the Center's concern with Punjab as a border or front-line state with Pakistan. Accordingly, the Center has resisted efforts in Punjab, stemming from both communities, to allow more significant industrialization. An oft-cited figure in Punjab is that eighty per cent of the bank deposits by Punjabis are invested outside the state. Economic neglect or discrimination by the Center also is part of the charge that of "over Rs. 22,000 crores spent on the public sector industries, less than 2% have been invested in Punjab."[30]

More objective sources provide corroborating data. According to a governmental report, out of total central investment in all the states in non-departmental undertakings, essentially industrial and commercial, as of March 1979, Punjab's share was only 2.2% of the total.[31] Even lower figures are reported by the Centre for Monitoring the Indian Economy (Bombay) in its November 1980 publication, Volume 2. Punjab accounts for only 0.9% of central government investments in "projects in hand."[32] It should be emphasized that the time period for these data is just prior to the onset of the disturbances which seriously began to affect Punjab in 1981.

Punjab consistently lacks heavy and even medium-scale industry. Nonetheless, the stereotype persists in India itself that the state is bursting with prosperous small-scale industry. The bustling industrial centers of Ludhiana, Jalandhar (Jullundur) and Amritsar provide a visual picture of small-scale entrepreneurs proliferating along the Grand Trunk Road and expanding in all directions. These small-scale industrial *bustis* are the sites for Satish Saberwal's "mobile men."[33]

In fact, small scale industry is largely limited to eight industries: woolen textiles and hosiery, steel re-rolling, cotton textiles, cycles and cycle parts, cotton ginning and pressing, agricultural implements and machine tools, sewing machines and parts, and sports goods.[34] Small-scale industry has proved to Punjabis, Sikhs and Hindus alike that their work ethic and entrepreneurial ability can succeed in the industrial as well as the agricultural sector. Yet the necessity for industrial permits, government licenses, central-government-determined location sites, and investment funds controlled or channeled by the central

---

30. The Council of Sikh Affairs, *The Anguish of Punjab: The Sikhs Demand Justice* (Chandigarh, ca. 1983), p. 29. I.K. Gujral, in *Mainstream*, states that it "was commonly believed that about two-thirds of Punjab's bank deposits get invested outside Punjab." August 14, 1982, p. 13. Quoted in Jeffrey, *What's Happening to India?* p. 80.

31. Bureau of Public Enterprises, Ministry of Finance, *Annual Report on the Working of Industrial and Commercial Undertakings of the Central Government* (New Delhi, 1980), cited in R.S. Johar, "Decentralization of Industrial Development with Special Reference to Punjab," in Johar and J.S. Khanna, eds., *Studies in Punjab Economy* (Amritsar: Guru Nanak Dev University, 1983), p. 206.

32. Ibid., p. 206.

33. Satish Saberwal, *Mobile Men: Limits to Social Change in Urban Punjab* (New Delhi: Vikas, 1976).

34. Johar and Khanna, *Studies in Punjab Economy*, p. iii.

government is seen as constraining further industrialization.   Moreover, industrialization is seen as essential for the state.

"Prosperous Punjab" is a relative notion. It does have India's highest per capita income, with the 1980-81 figure of Rs. 2,771, and the provisional 1981-82 total of Rs. 3,164. That compares to the all-India averages for the two years of Rs. 1,559 and Rs. 1,758.[35] Punjab's per capita income nonetheless remains markedly lower than U.S. $300 per year. In this context of relatively less poverty and high expectations, Punjab's agriculturally based economy is not expected to provide the lead as it already is highly developed. Industry is seen as the major growth sector as without new technological breakthroughs it is "unrealistic to assume that agriculture will continue to spearhead Punjab's economic advance [as in the] last 15 years."[36]

Industrialization also is needed to redress Punjab's imbalance between rural and urban poverty. Estimates by the Government of India in 1978 placed 34.9% of the state's urban population under the augmented poverty line as compared with 17.4% of the rural population.[37] These figures may be low, but they provide a fair indicator of the relative discrepancies between the two sectors.

As part of the basic economic structure, it also is recognized that water and power are critical. Controlling the headworks of rivers which flow through Punjab and/or receiving an adequate and assured distribution of the water is seen as essential. Early completion of the Thein Dam and constructing a nuclear power plant in Punjab are consistently advocated as means of meeting rural and urban power needs.

Thus, many of the demands in the Anandpur Sahib resolution, however poorly or militantly formulated, reflect a frustration in the state with what are viewed as central constraints on more effective planning and implementation. Increased state autonomy is at least partly a code term for more control by Punjab of its human and material resources.

Sikh Minority Attitudes

Punjab's center-state differences are significant, but perhaps no more remarkable in the recent past than those of numerous other states.[38] Center-state problems are more likely to become major crises when an ethnic dimension fuels the fire, such as provided by language in the cases of Assam and Tamilnadu, or religion as in Kashmir and Punjab. It is notable that despite the extreme poverty

35. Government of Punjab, *Statistical Abstract of Punjab 1983* (Chandigarh: The Economic Adviser to Government, 1984), pp. 98-99.

36. K.S. Gill, "Agricultural Development in Punjab," in Johar and Khanna, *Studies in Punjab Economy*, p. 6.

37. Seventh Finance Commission of the Government of India (Appendix IV, 1978, p. 239), as cited in Johar and Khanna, *Studies in Punjab Economy*, pp. 159-60.

38. A number of examples are explored in Wallace, "Center-State Relations in India," in Roach, ed., *India 2000*.

and low levels of development in Uttar Pradesh, Bihar and Madhya Pradesh[39] cultural nationalism[40] has not flared in a comparable manner in this Hindi-speaking, Hindu heartland. Sikh minority attitudes are central to the Punjab problem despite their apparent numerical, economic and political dominance.

Sikhs constituted 60.75% of Punjab's population in 1981 as compared to 39.93% for Hindus. This clear majority is tempered by the fact that the total of 10.19 million Sikhs in Punjab and 13.07 million in India as a whole is dwarfed by the Hindu total of 549 million, as well as by Muslims who totaled 75.5 million in 1981. Sikhs are only 1.96% of India's population as contrasted to the Hindu majority of 82.64%, the Muslim population of 11.35%, and even the Christian total of 2.43%.[41]

Even the numerical majority within Punjab is of recent origin and based on an insecure memory pool and view of the world. Prior to the partition of the Punjab between India and Pakistan in 1947, Sikhs were but the third largest religious community in the Punjab. They composed only 12% of the population as compared to 35% for the Hindus and 51% for the Muslim majority. Following partition and the exodus of Muslims, Sikhs remained a decidedly minority community with 33.3% of the population as compared to the Hindu majority of 63.7%. They became a majority only in 1966 with the advent of the Punjabi Suba. The dominant Hindu areas became the new state of Haryana, while Hindu-majority hill districts joined Himachal Pradesh.

Cognitively the historical minority position continues. Moreover, minority attitudes are maintained by Sikhs by the apprehension that the recently achieved 60% majority may be declining. It was widely believed in Punjab that the Sikh majority had shrunk to 52% in the 1980's.[42] Explanations of the decline tended to focus on Sikh out-migration to other parts of India and to Sikh-established areas in many parts of the world, as well as to the large inflow of migrant farm workers from Hindu areas in Uttar Pradesh, Bihar, Rajasthan and even from as far away as Orissa. The fact that data on the religious composition of the population from the 1981 census, while tabulated, was not released until July 1985 remains unexplained. The *Statistical Abstract of Punjab 1983*, for example, provides detailed information from the 1981 census for an enormous number of categories. Yet, it uses the 1971 census data on religion. The 60.75% Sikh majority in 1981, according to the census, is a slight increase from the 1971 figure of 60.2%. One goal of the terrorist movement certainly is to drive Hindus from Punjab and, through counter-reactions to Sikhs elsewhere in India, stimulate the latter to return to Punjab.

---

39. Their per capita incomes for 1980-81 were: Bihar, Rs. 927; Uttar Pradesh, Rs. 1,272; Madhya Pradesh, Rs. 1,134; as compared to the all-India average of Rs. 1,559. Government of Punjab, *Statistical Abstract of Punjab 1983*, pp. 98-99.

40. See Marguerite Ross Barnett, *The Politics of Cultural Nationalism in South India* (Princeton: Princeton University Press, 1976), ch. 1.

41. Government of India, *Census of India 1981, Household Population by Religion of Head of Household*, as reported in the *Indian Express*, July 21, 1985, pp. 1, 10.

42. *Business India*, June 6-19, 1983, p. 67.

Minority attitudes also are involved in the economic sector even though Sikhs, as the driving force of Punjab's Green Revolution, provide the most successful example of agricultural development in India. They constitute the rural majority in all of Punjab's districts with the sole exception of Hoshiarpur. By contrast, Hindus are the majority in the urban areas. Thus, for example, Sikhs compose 91.4% of the rural population in Amritsar District while Hindus are a 54.9% majority in the urban areas. In Patiala, Sikhs have a rural majority of 64.7% while the Hindu urban majority is 63.6%.[43]

Rural Sikhs, particularly Jat Sikhs who dominate in rural areas, had turned Punjab into India's most successful agricultural area even before the advent in the 1960's of the new high-yielding varieties of grain associated with the Green Revolution. Land consolidation, canal and tube-well irrigation, power from the Bhakra-Nangal Dam and a new agricultural university already provided an excellent infrastructure. State support for such continuing developments had been present at least since the advent of British rule,[44] and became enshrined in the Punjab Alienation of Land Act (1900) and in the policy of the ruling Unionist Party during the inter-war period.[45] State policy continued to provide supports for agriculture in the post-independence period regardless of shifting political party patterns and higher or lower degrees of political stability.[46] These crucially important supporting elements have been generated and utilized to advantage by the hard-working, industrious rural population.[47]

Consequently, Punjab could take advantage of the Green Revolution to a remarkable degree. It occupies only 1.6% of the area of the country, but it provided 73% of the India-wide procurement of wheat and 48% of rice in 1980-81.[48] Only Mexico produces more per acre of wheat, and Punjab is second only to Japan in per-acre production of rice. Cotton, potatoes and sugar cane also have flourished.[49] Even with the unsettled political conditions resulting from the terrorist movement, record agricultural production continues. Per capita rural income in Punjab is almost three times that of the national average.[50]

---

43. Tabulated from Government of India, *Census of India*, Paper 4 of 1984, pp. 494-517.
44. Himadri Banerjee, *Agrarian Society of the Punjab, 1849-1901* (New Delhi: Manohar Publications, 1982), pp. 201-2.
45. See Norman G[erald] Barrier, *The Punjab Alienation of Land Bill of 1900* (Durham, North Carolina: Duke University Commonwealth Studies Center, Monograph 2, 1966), and Paul Wallace, "Peasant Mobilization in India and the Contemporary Political Significance of Sir Chottu Ram," *Indian Journal of Political Science* 41:4 (December 1980).
46. For an excellent comparison between Indian and Pakistani Punjab that focuses on public policy and the role of the state see Elizabeth Hollister Sims, "Rural Development and Public Policy: Agricultural Institutions and Technological Change in the Indian and Pakistani Punjab," Ph.D. dissertation, University of California, Berkeley, 1985.
47. Kusum Nair, *Blossoms in the Dust: The Human Element in Indian Development* (London: Gerald Duckworth, 1961), pp. 102-15. M.S. Randhawa, *Out of the Ashes* (Punjab: Public Relations Department, 1955).
48. S.P. Mehra, *Punjab Today: An Economic Overview* (Jalandhar: New Academic Publishing Co., 1983), p. 128.
49. Manohar Singh Gill, "The Development of Punjab Agriculture, 1977-1980," *Asian Survey* 23:7 (July, 1983), 832-34.
50. Punjab from 1976-77 to 1978-79 had an average per capita rural income from agriculture of Rs. 1,627 compared to the all-India average of Rs. 638.

Why then, given this record of long-time and continuing agricultural success, do Sikhs have minority attitudes in the economic sector? One part of the explanation stems from the affluence that is so visible in Punjab. Large parts of the population have been left behind, creating stark contrasts in a small state. The productivity of three districts, Ludhiana, Jalandhar and Patiala is approximately 75-100% higher than that of the lowest districts of Bhatinda, Hoshiarpur and Faridkot.[51] Even more striking is that estimates of the percentage of the rural population living below the poverty line range between 17.5% and 33%.[52]

Compounding these elements of rural poverty in Punjab is the marked change in land holdings comparing 1970-71 with 1980-81. Marginal and submarginal holdings, defined as below 1 hectare (2.47 acres) have fallen from 33.73% of all holdings to 19.21%. Small holdings between 1 and 2 hectares were about 19% for both decades. These two categories were the only ones to record a decrease in number. There were 320,245 fewer marginal holdings in 1980-81, and 60,715 fewer small holdings. Medium holdings, between 4 and 10 hectares, recorded the largest single increase with 21,317.[53] These are land holdings typically supporting families. The absolute number of individuals affected, therefore, must be several times higher.

It is possible that many of these families continue to work in rural areas. Wage rates for agricultural labor in Punjab are high by Indian standards. Day rates for ploughing increased by over 100% from Rs. 7.94 to Rs. 16.04. These are state-wide averages; Green Revolution areas are even higher.[54] On the other hand, higher poverty levels in the urban areas suggest that many and possibly the bulk of the former marginal and small agriculturalists, primarily Sikhs, migrate to the many small towns and few cities.

It appears that not only poor Sikhs are migrating to urban areas, but wealthier ones as well. H.K. Manmohan Singh reports that out-migration is greater than in-migration to Green Revolution areas and that the wealthier tend to leave while the poorer come into the area.[55] Some of these poor may be the landless former marginal and small landholders. It is more likely that the need for agricultural labor is met more by the migrant labor from other states on which Punjab has now become dependent.

51. S.S. Grewal and P.S. Rangi, "Imbalances in Growth of Punjab Agriculture," in Johar and Khanna, *Studies in Punjab Economy*, pp. 51-54.

52. G.S. Bhalla and Y.K. Alagh, "Green Revolution and Small Peasants: A Study of Income Distribution in Punjab Agriculture," *Economic and Political Weekly*, May 7, 1982, p. 876. H.K. Manmohan Singh, "Population Pressure and Labour Absorbability in Agriculture: Analysis and Suggestions Based on Field Studies Conducted in Punjab," in Johar and Khanna, *Studies in Punjab Economy*, pp. 400-2.

53. Compiled from data furnished in Government of Punjab, *Statistical Abstract of Punjab 1983*, pp. 150-51. The original data are from the Agricultural Census of Punjab, 1980-81, which was based on a 10% sample survey.

54. Ibid., pp. 406-7.

55. H.K. Manmohan Singh, "Population Pressure," in Johar and Khanna, eds., *Studies*, pp. 400-2.

Thus, one comes full circle to the case made in an earlier section of this article for industrialization in Punjab. Hindus and Sikhs, all Punjabis, join in this felt need. But the Sikh intensity would appear to be more recent and rapidly increasing. Successful Jat Sikh farmers increasingly are attempting to branch out into trading and investment in industry, where they confront non-Jat Sikh trading castes and the dominant Hindu urban groups.[56] Their children attend Guru Nanak Dev University, Punjabi University and a host of colleges. There they learn a new life style, but find it difficult to compete against the more sophisticated urbanites.[57]

Poor and wealthy alike confront the low level of industrialization. Punjab ranked only tenth among Indian states for national income generated in the factory sector in 1977-78, two places lower than in 1965-66.[58] One estimate is that every year there is an increase of 100,000 in educated unemployed youths. An Amritsar police official states that it is probable that "five percent of them will get involved in terrorist activities or extremism."[59]

Various items in the Anandpur Sahib resolution, therefore, relate to both the agricultural and industrial sector. Some represent a prosperous Jat Sikh view, as in the demand that the "prices of agricultural produce should be fixed on the basis of the returns of the middle class farmers," or in the demand for complete "nationalisation of the trade in foodgrains." At the same time, it is recognized that there is a "growing gap between the rich and poor" in rural areas, and there is a need to establish agro-industries in the rural areas so as "to relieve the growing population pressure in the urban areas."[60]

Politically, Sikhs are dominant in Punjab, especially after the spectacular election victory of the Akali Dal in the September 1985 elections. But, as the opening section of this chapter indicates, political dominance is ephemeral. Sikhs are no more homogeneous than other religious communities in India, and perhaps less so. Dominant landed Jat Sikhs in rural areas normally cannot depend on political support from non-Jat Sikhs who are agricultural laborers and those who provide various services. Mazhbi, Rai, Cheemba, Ramgarhia and Lohar Sikhs are more likely to support the Congress or Communist parties. Sikh merchant castes such as the Khatris and Aroras have their own orientations.

Cross-cutting the varied social composition of Sikhs is the ever present factionalism. In 1987, before President's rule on May 11, there were the ruling Akali Dal headed by Surjit Singh Barnala, dissident groups headed by Parkash Singh Badal and Jagdev Singh Talwandi respectively, and several smaller groups each claiming to represent the true Akali Dal. There even is a small

56. Bharat Bhushan, "The Punjab Business," pp. 50-70.
57. Donna Suri, "Portrait in Black: Notes From a University Hostel in Punjab," in Paul Wallace and Surendra Chopra, eds., *Political Dynamics of Punjab* (Amritsar: Guru Nanak Dev University, 1981), pp. 257-63.
58. R.S. Johar, J.S. Khanna and P.S. Raiky, "Industrial Development in Punjab: A Study in Characterization, Case for, and Constraints," in Johar and Khanna, *Studies*, p. 155.
59. Suresh Arora, Superintendent of Police Headquarters, Amritsar, as quoted in *The Washington Post Weekly Edition*, January 19, 1987, p. 18.
60. Government of India, *White Paper on the Punjab Agitation*, pp. 86-87.

Master Tara Singh Akali Dal although his dominance ceased in 1960 and he died in 1967. The extremist movement provides its own spectrum ranging from Bhindranwale's father, Baba Joginder Singh, who heads the United Akali Dal, to the Damdami Taksal, the All India Sikh Student Federation and shadowy terrorist groups with various names.

Central to the Sikh minority attitudes in the political area are Congress Party efforts to develop and exploit differences within the dominant Akali Dal. Tactics have included contesting through a front group in the elections to the Sikh controlled temple system, the S.G.P.C., and using the power of the government at the state and national levels.[61] It is widely believed in India that the Congress (I) assisted Sant Bhindranwale from about 1978 in order to widen the differences within the Akali Dal.[62] Highly respected columnist Kuldip Nayar concluded that little did they realize at that time that they were creating a Frankenstein.[63]

Even with a victory in the September 1985 elections, the Akali Dal could not translate a clear majority in the State Assembly into a resolution of the Punjab problem. Neither the centrally appointed Mathew Commission in January 1986 nor the Venkataramiah Commission in July was able to effect the transfer of Chandigarh to Punjab. Militant Sikh opposition to the Sutlej-Jamuna link canal receives less public attention, but is an equally explosive issue. In turn, the impressive political support to the Surjit Singh Barnala Akali Dal government dissipated both internally and externally. As *The Times of India* editorialized, "the inevitable failure of the Union government to implement the basically flawed Punjab accord has been overtaken by a renewed struggle for leadership of the Sikh community."[64]

Reduced to minority status by splits, and dependent on opposition party support, the Barnala government almost instinctively blamed its deteriorating position on the central government. At the same time, it remained dependent on Congress (I) support in the State Assembly and looked to Delhi for actions which would help to restore its political influence. President's rule, consequently, is not a surprise. Minority attitudes in this dependent context are clear. Instead of there emerging from the September 1985 election the possibility of a Khalsa Raj not thwarted as in the past by the Center, as one commentator suggested,[65] the Center once again has become the enemy as perceived by major elements of the Sikh population.

61. Paul Wallace, "Religious and Secular Politics in Punjab: The Sikh Dilemma in Competing Political Systems," in Wallace and Chopra, *Political Dynamics of Punjab*, pp. 13-17. J.C. Anand, "The Punjab: Akalis in the Coalition," in K.P. Karunakaran, ed., *Coalition Governments in India* (Simla: Indian Institute of Advanced Study, 1975), pp. 237-50.
62. Ayesha Kagal, *The Times of India*, September 12, 1982. Joseph Lelyveld, *The New York Times Magazine*, December 2, 1984, p. 43.
63. Kuldip Nayar and Khushwant Singh, *Tragedy of Punjab: Operation Bluestar and After* (New Delhi: Vision Books Pvt. Ltd., 1984), p. 31.
64. *The Times of India*, January 28, 1986, p. 8.
65. Janardan Thakur, *The Times of India*, October 13, 1985, p. 1.

Conclusion

Sikh minority attitudes in Punjab have been conditioned by the political, constitutional and governmental patterns arising from India's centralizing federal system. The Anandpur Sahib resolutions of the 1970's and 1980's symbolize the felt need for increasing autonomy; for a lessening of the centralizing tendencies of the ruling party and government. In this respect, Sikhs and Punjab as a whole are not markedly different from other Indian states. All desire additional resources from the Center and less central control.

Punjab's situation is exacerbated by the ethnic factor arising from its Sikh population. Minority attitudes underlie Sikh political behavior despite the community's apparent numerical, economical and political dominance in the state, and not without cause. Majority characteristics in fact are fragile and seldom attainable. Sikh reality is of a heterogeneous community in a period of rapid social and economic change. Sikh identity, nonetheless, is a powerful force capable of mobilization under conditions where the religious community is perceived to be in danger. The Anandpur Sahib resolutions also relate to these concerns.

The combination of federal constraints and minority attitudes has contributed to periodic Sikh agitations. Achievement of a Sikh majority state in 1966 did not resolve fundamental Sikh concerns. In addition to the basically non-violent militancy of the past, terrorism since 1981 has been added to Sikh political expression.[66] Punjab in the 1980's became India's problem state to a degree that surpasses earlier crises involving such states as Kerala, Tamilnadu, West Bengal, Andra Pradesh and Assam.

Three models are suggested as possibilities for coping with the demands and movements symbolized by the Anandpur Sahib resolutions and the movements propelled by the terrorist, extremist and militant movements since 1981 in Punjab. Accommodation in the tradition of the nationalist movement and the Nehru-led Congress Party is one option. Consociational arrangements between the respective *élites* provides another version of accommodation. Third, the possibility of the enhancement of a regional identity which provides an overlay to the religious community identities and minority attitudes is conceivable within the federal polity of India.

---

66. It must be emphasized that terrorism in the past related to one stream of the nationalist movement, the Ghadar Party. See Harish K. Puri, *Ghadar Movement: Ideology, Organization and Strategy* (Amritsar: Guru Nanak Dev University Press, 1983). Neither of the two major Sikh movements prior to 1981 employed violence as a tactic. Both the Gurdwara Reform movement of the 1920's and the Punjabi Suba movement of the 1960's modeled themselves on Gandhian non-violence strategy. Rajiv Kapur in his recent book, *Sikh Separatism: The Politics of Faith* (London: Allen and Unwin, 1986), provides a meticulous and carefully researched examination of the 1920's movement. He carefully documents the non-violent thrust of the movement, in contrast to the violence of the opponents. His title, however, is misleading as he fails to distinguish clearly between religious and political separatism. Consequently, he infers a relationship which did not develop in the pre-independence period. Nor is political separatism, Khalistan, the goal of more than a small minority among the Sikhs in contemporary Punjab.

These three options are not mutually exclusive. On the contrary, a combination of all three would appear to be essential to deal with the basic problems. A workable process would be abetted by a reversal of the long-term trend in India toward centralization. Decentralization in the form of increased autonomy and responsibilities for the states is necessary in political reformulation.

Accommodation necessitates the forging of political linkages across the core support bases of individual political parties. Mahatma Gandhi's and Nehru's Congress Party served as an umbrella for a wide spectrum of social groups as well as a fly-over or bridge for groups formally outside the party. Accommodation could enable the effective political expression of India's diversity: "not just a system providing means of competition and conflict but also a coalitional arena in which both ruling and oppositional groups can enter their diverse claims."[67]

Punjab has a notable record of accommodation politics which tends to be almost forgotten during periods when agitations dominate. Akali Dal alliances at different points in time with the Congress Party, the Hindu-dominant Jan Sangh, and its leadership of the broad coalition following the Emergency are reflective of accommodation politics. Neither can the Akali Dal election victory in September 1985 be interpreted along strictly religious lines. Voting along "strictly communal lines should have resulted in the Akalis getting 61 percent of votes or thereabout" instead of the 38.4 percent it received.[68] It also is notable that the Akali Dal, a Sikh political party, had three Hindus and one Muslim elected under its banner.

Consociational arrangements emphasize the role of *élites*[69] within the state, and between them and New Delhi. Identifying and being sensitive to the first order concerns of the major communities on such matters as language, religious institutions and the broad outlines of state resource allocations are essential. In brief, the consociational arrangements place emphasis on sensitive, responsive and responsible leadership.

Sant Fatch Singh adhered in important respects to the principles of consociational politics in leading the Akali Dal movement toward the achievement of Punjabi Suba in 1966, and in executing subsequent alliance politics with the Hindu dominant Jan Sangh. Most importantly, he redefined Punjabi Suba from communal to language criteria. Redrafting state boundaries on a linguistic basis became acceptable in the 1950's, while changes based on religion were politically unacceptable. In fact, Punjab became a Sikh majority state. But the political formulation enabled the Sikh Akali Dal and Hindu Jan Sangh leaders to cooperate successfully until the consociational arrangement collapsed in 1979.

---

67. Rajni Kothari, *Politics in India* (Boston: Little, Brown & Co., 1970), p. 421.
68. Lolita Ghose and Ashok Lahiri, "Was Punjab Poll Communal?" *Indian Express*, October 12, 1985.
69. For a sophisticated discussion of consociational politics see Arend Lijphart, *The Politics of Accommodation: Pluralism and Democracy in the Netherlands* (Berkeley: University of California Press, 1968).

Elite-driven formulations, as the above example illustrates, can dissipate even after long periods of working satisfactorily. The scholarly literature on consociational polities recognizes its somewhat fragile nature. A notable review of six major books on the subject concludes: "Ironically, the consociational model is coming under considerable stress at the very moment at which it is belatedly being recognized on the map of comparative politics."[70] Nonetheless, despite their several weaknesses, consociational approaches continue to be explored in regard to countries which often are characterized as manifesting a fragmented political culture. Austria, Belgium, the Netherlands and Switzerland are the states most often used as models, both positive and negative, of consociational politics. Northern Ireland and the developing countries of Africa and Asia increasingly are beginning to be so considered.[71]

Neither accommodation nor consociational politics appears to provide long-term solutions in isolation. Broader-scale relationships, as in the accommodation mode, along with the leadership and nurturing elements of consociationalism, would appear to be essential. Regionalism is a third element that can provide an overarching link to what otherwise seems to be deteriorating into a fragmented political culture in Punjab.

An emphasis on Punjab's regional identity can be a two-edged sword. India's newly independent central government hesitated to approach the redrafting of state political boundaries on the basis of linguistic lines due to a fear of regionalism turning into separatism. States' reorganization, however, provides evidence that regionalism can enhance national as well as local integration. Hindus and Sikhs in Punjab share a common culture. They even speak the same language, although they use different scripts and different names for it. In 1964, two years before the advent of Punjabi Suba, I asked a stenographer in the Punjab State Assembly how he knew which language—Punjabi or Hindi—to record for an M.L.A. "They all speak Punjabi. I know which script they wish to have recorded," he replied.

Politics is not necessarily a zero-sum game. Multiple identities can be reinforcing rather than mutually destructive. In the words of a Guru Nanak Dev University political scientist, "There is no inherent contradiction between the Hindu-Sikh identities, Punjabi identity and the national identity."[72] Conversely, high levels of internal differences weaken the state in relation to the Center. Enhanced Punjab regionalism could simultaneously strengthen the state and Indian federalism.

---

70. Hans Daalder, "The Consociational Democracy Theme," *World Politics*, July, 1974, p. 618.
71. Jurg Steiner, *European Democracies* (New York and London: Longman, 1986), ch. 13, "Consociational Decision Making," pp. 201-16.
72. M.S. Dhami, "Punjab and Communalism," *Seminar*, no. 314 (October, 1985), p. 38.

Part Three
History and Society:
Diaspora

Conceptions of Sikh Culture in the Development of a Comparative Analysis of the Sikh Diaspora

Norman Buchignani

Introduction

This paper is concerned with certain definitional and theoretical issues in comparative Sikh diaspora studies. Section I outlines the major concentrations of contemporary research done on Sikhs overseas. It also contends that the present diversity of interests evident in this research, while worthwhile in itself, poses a challenge to the theoretical integration of diaspora studies. In particular, divergent research foci generate equally divergent notions of Sikh culture, which must be reconciled in order that theoretical integration may proceed more smoothly. Sections II and III consider the range of conceptions of culture presently in use in diaspora research and assess the implications that each of these has for the development of a comparative understanding of Sikhs overseas. The paper ends with a set of summary conclusions about the future of comparative diaspora studies and the role of conceptions of culture within it.

I

Studies of the Sikh Diaspora and Issues of Comparison

The Sikh diaspora today is over a hundred years old, large, and rapidly growing. Historically, it had a significant impact on Indian affairs, those in the Punjab in particular. It was episodically involved in key issues in receiving countries as well. Since the diaspora today is so much bigger, more prosperous, better organized and less impeded by ethnic and racial discrimination, its social importance is many times greater than before. With respect to India, it is currently deeply tied to the debate over Khalistan and Sikh ethnocultural rights in Punjab. Its religious impact, not to mention the effects of remittances, people and ideas flowing back to India, is considerable. A significant proportion (5-8%) of all Sikhs now live overseas, and with respect to educated, well-off Sikhs this

[Joseph T. O'Connell, Milton Israel, Willard G. Oxtoby, eds., with W.H. McLeod and J.S. Grewal, visiting eds., *Sikh History and Religion in the Twentieth Century* (S. Asian Studies Papers, 3) (Toronto: S. Asian Studies, Univ. of Toronto, 1988)]

proportion is far higher. Within an ever-increasing range of receiving countries, Sikhs are coming to the fore in a wide range of visible and ethnocultural minority group issues from minority group cultural rights to issues concerning the elimination of racial prejudice and discrimination. Throughout history, the saga of Sikhs overseas has also been potentially important from a social science point of view. In both the present and the past, the wide-ranging situations of Sikhs worldwide have presented important examples of ethnic and race relations and of minority group family and community organization.

Considering both their societal impact and social science potential, it is not surprising that the Sikhs' diaspora has received increasing (though still somewhat sparse and uneven) research attention since the first serious studies of such overseas communities were done in the 1920's.[1] Research activity has in fact increased precipitously (admittedly, from a minute trickle to a small stream) since 1970. Since the beginning, studies of diaspora Sikhs done in the general metaphor of ethnicity and race have been prominent: studies of ethnic and race relations, and of community and family development and change in the context of minority group conditions. Recently, the growth of Sikh studies has begun to shift this balance somewhat. Some researchers primarily interested in homeland Sikh cultural, religious and political development have extended their interests to the diaspora, and a few others long involved in diaspora studies have made an increasing commitment to understanding the specifically Sikh aspects of the diaspora equation.

This rapid growth aside, it would be wrong to suggest that the present corpus of research on Sikhs overseas constitutes a mature, well-integrated, theoretically well-supported intellectual discourse. Even now the yearly output is such that it is relatively easy to keep up with the total corpus of material. Indeed, this is a virtual necessity irrespective of one's particular research concerns, there being far too little research overall to restrict one's literature scope any more than this. We can, however, have every confidence that the present upward swing in research interest will continue for some time into the future.

It is, consequently, critical to begin asking questions about how this growing body of information might be better integrated and more explanatorily powerful.[2] It would be fair to say that diaspora research is now well into its initial phase of development: that characterized by the production of increasingly sophisticated case studies done from many points of view and for many purposes.[3] Such an initial evolutionary development is to be expected. Even so, the rise of high-quality diaspora Sikh case studies argues for far greater attention being placed on how this material might be integrated into a mature, theoretically powerful, highly interactive discourse.

---

1. Ch'eng 1931; Das 1923; U.S. Senate, Immigration Committee 1911.
2. This builds on an initial statement by Barrier and Juergensmeyer, 1979.
3. As paradigm examples, see Helweg 1985; Bhachu 1981, 1985; LaBrack 1980; Johnston 1987 and Barrier 1987.

It should be stressed that this evolutionary path is far from inevitable. Topically, diaspora Sikh studies are not like, say, the study of the French Revolution. In this latter case, the very topic has determined certain constraints on discourse, and most researchers are drawn from a single academic field; there are a great many scholars who have spent their whole lives studying the French Revolution, and the great majority of them are historians. Theoretically, Sikh diaspora studies cannot depend on the kind of unity of discourse generated in more homogeneous domains like the study of social interaction. Hence, without an awareness that theoretical and topical integration poses clear benefits, and without serious attention to how such integration might be achieved, it may never come about.

Indeed, the lack of such integration has already had some rather serious, albeit rather obvious, negative consequences for diaspora studies. These include a considerable duplication of topical research effort without the consequent benefit of inductive theoretical integration, the relatively rare use of comparative controls on generalizations about Sikh belief and behaviour made on the basis of single case studies, the sparsity of discourse on apparent contradictions or differences between case studies, and the utter lack of any scientifically driven attempt to fill obvious research voids.

Central to the development of more integrated Sikh diaspora studies is the issue of *comparison*:   comparison of Sikhs in particular places with other minority groups there, and comparison of research findings on the diaspora with the immeasurably greater research corpus on Sikhs in the Punjab.[4] Only through comparison will we be able to disentangle the determinants of Sikh heritage from determinants of context; through orderly comparison lies the only route to theoretical integration.   At present, there is obviously a certain degree of comparative integration evident in the diaspora literature, but this integration typically fails to cross the divisions separating certain basic domains of research from others.

In the broadest sense, one sees today two, arguably three, basic lines of inquiry within Sikh studies. By far the predominant line of inquiry could be broadly characterized as studies of Sikhs overseas as ethnocultural communities. This research is typified by basically descriptive or case-specific analytical research on such things as patterns of family and community development, migration, employment and value change. It would be fair to say that the orienting metaphor for such studies is that research is being done on *new communities* that happen to be Sikh.[5] They are done characteristically by individuals whose primary research backgrounds are anthropological and whose

---

4. Major qualifications on the latter claim are in order. There are a great many studies of Sikhs in the Punjab, but I would venture to say that far more *urban* community studies have been done in the diaspora than in the Punjab. Even anthropological research in the Punjab has a strong rural bias.

5. See Anwar 1976; Aurora 1967; Ballard 1973, 1978, Ballard and Ballard 1977; Bhachu 1981, 1984, 1985; Buchignani and Indra 1985; Chadney 1976, 1984; Chan 1979; Desai 1963; Ghuman 1980; Helweg 1977, 1980; Joy 1984; Kalra 1980; LaBrack 1983; LaBrack and Leonard 1984; Lal 1976; Leonard 1982; Thompson 1970.

primary concerns are as likely topical (e.g., family studies or network analysis) as they are Sikh. There is, however, a growing minority of researchers doing this kind of work whose central commitment is to the study of diaspora Sikhs *per se*.[6]

One might wish to distinguish further within this research those studies done under the metaphor of Sikhs as *minority groups*.[7] Although in many instances this separation of minority-relations research from community studies is a bit arbitrary, one can nevertheless see a distinct core of studies which have been done in the orienting frame of ethnic and race relations, where the primary concern is with intergroup role relations, patterns of ethnic identity and identification, prejudice and discrimination, the role of Sikhs in the context of human rights, and issues of integration, acculturation and assimilation. This research also tends to see "Sikhness" as somewhat secondary, in this case to minority group status. Once more, though, a small group of researchers have demonstrated a primary commitment to studying Sikhs.[8]

Granted this division, the third basic variety of diaspora research is that motivated by a primary interest in Sikhs, their religion and culture; it is often done by individuals grounded in an understanding of Sikhs in their homeland.[9] Naturally, the focal research questions vary accordingly. Two are fundamental: How does the diaspora context affect Sikh culture and social organization? And how do activities of Sikhs in the diaspora affect Sikhs in the homeland, and *vice versa*? Typically, research interests here are on things deemed central to the Sikh experience—religion, family and politics in particular. Here the orienting metaphor is that of Sikhs who happen to be migrants or minority groups.

Beyond this threefold topical division there exists another critical dimension of contemporary Sikh diaspora studies: diversity of theoretical and/or subtopical interest. Reflecting its new and somewhat marginal status, there are very few full-time researchers worldwide who have made their central research commitment to the study of Sikhs overseas: Chadney and Dusenbery on Sikhs in Canada; LaBrack and, hopefully, Leonard on Sikhs in the United States; Helweg, Bhachu, Ballard and Cole on Sikhs in Britain. To these might also be added those few individuals who have become involved in diaspora studies as a temporary outgrowth of a primary research involvement in Punjab Sikh history: Barrier, Juergensmeyer, McLeod. More typically, though, researchers have been led to do some Sikh research at some point in their lives for primarily theoretical or social reasons: interest in the dynamics of race relations, concern over racial discrimination, interest in studying aspects of multicultural education, and so on.

6. This would include Bhachu, Chadney, Dusenbery, Helweg and LaBrack.
7. See Aurora 1960; Beetham 1970; Brooks 1975; Buchignani 1977, 1978, 1980a, 1980b; Buchignani and Indra 1981a, 1985, 198-; De Witt 1969; Dusenbery 1981, 198-b, 198-c; Indra 1979; Johnston 1979; Kuepper *et al.* 1975; Leonard 1984, 1985, 1987; Mathur 1970; Remmer 1972; Robinson 1984; Scanlon 1975; Uberoi 1964; Wood 1983.
8. For example, Ballard, Dusenbery and Leonard.
9. See here Barrier 1979; Brooks and Singh 1978; Buchignani and Indra 1981b; Chaudri 1973; Dusenbery 198-a; Helweg 1983; LaBrack 1979; McLeod 1979, 1985.

The bulk of British, Canadian and American research has arisen this way. Predictably, this latter research is very heterogeneous and rarely reflects a deep understanding of Sikh diaspora issues. It is almost never well integrated with other studies of the diaspora.

This diversity of interest is, of course, entirely justifiable. The complex lives of diaspora Sikhs do, after all, intersect all three of the basic orientations above, and Sikhs do become involved in a host of social issues worthy of research. Moreover, there is no necessary contradiction between there being an even broader variety of case-study-level research interests than presently exists and substantial theoretical integration. At the same time, such a sharp set of research divides as those which presently separate one kind of Sikh study from another do pose rather formidable barriers to higher-level integration, primarily because the divergent orienting metaphors organizing research cast basic research issues into different moulds, in effect in each case creating a different construction of reality.

Without some awareness of it, this divergence of research reality constructions can seriously limit the future integration of diaspora Sikh studies. Otherwise, researchers with a significant commitment to Sikh studies will tend to talk past each other, will attempt to compare the incomparable, and will engage themselves in a host of disputes that appear to be empirical but arise from divergent theoretical and definitional orientations. Without such integration among core researchers the contributions of the far more numerous dilettantes will continue to be significantly less fruitful than otherwise would be the case.

Perhaps the most central such potential source of grief concerns something quite primal, implicated in such questions as:

- For research purposes, how is Sikh culture to be defined?
- What are the consequent implications of alternative definitions on how Sikh culture is portrayed and on research foci at the case-study level today?
- What implications does the use of these alternative conceptions of Sikh culture have for the comparative process?

The remainder of this paper is devoted to investigating these core questions. However, this exercise must be prefaced by a brief aside on definitions and definitional analysis. First, it should be stressed that social science definitions are essentially arbitrary. Their appropriateness should not be gauged by their "match with the world" but rather by their usefulness to the research process. In the case of Sikh diaspora studies, because there exists a rather wide range of research agendas, it would be unrealistic to propose that one might ever be able to fashion a universal definition of Sikh culture adequate for all situations. Rather, analytical effort is far better used to disentangle the implications which alternate definitions have, such that the comparative process might integrate these at a somewhat higher level.

Second, it must be appreciated that "culture" *per se* is almost never the actual object of research. Indeed, virtually all social science research can proceed quite well without reference to the word or concept; British social anthropology managed this quite nicely for more than thirty years. In this regard, definitions of culture here serve primarily as markers of particular theoretical orientations towards the relative weighting and articulation of belief and behaviour in Sikh diaspora studies; the latter are of course critical factors in any attempt at theoretical integration.

In addition, any discussion or evocation of the integration of a given field must not beg the question of integration for what purpose. In this case, certain basic objectives are taken as non-controversial:

1. That integration must not detach the Sikh diaspora from the homeland.
2. That integration must not detach groups and individuals in the diaspora from the dynamics of their own self-creation.
3. That integration must not neglect the constraints of the societal and cultural contexts surrounding Sikhs in the diaspora.
4. That integration must strengthen the connections between empirical findings on Sikhs overseas and social science theory.

In addressing these issues, empirical examples are a useful aid to ground otherwise abstract discussion. Such examples are drawn chiefly from the rich, eighty-year-long experience of Sikhs in Canada.

II

Subjectively Based (Mentalist) Conceptions of Sikh Diaspora Culture

Diaspora Sikhs are at once culture-bearing groups (however "culture-bearing" is defined), community-based ethnic groups, and minority groups living in the context of much larger and more powerful majority groups. Moreover, these three things are highly intertwined empirically. Minority group status can accentuate ethnic identity, with consequent effects on the retention of both cultural ideas and behaviours; endless other permutations are possible also. Consequently, any serious analytical conception of Sikh diaspora culture should at least acknowledge the literature on ethnicity. Hopefully, it should do far more, and should draw on this literature for guidance in addressing relevant issues. This is, of course, already being done, for, as was noted above, a considerable proportion of Sikh diaspora research has focused on ethnic and race relations.

This form of diaspora research naturally reflects contemporary analytical biases in ethnic and race relations.[10] It would be fair to say that subjective, actor-centered views of what constitutes ethnicity and the source of ethnic social organization predominate today, especially in anthropology. The central concerns are with such things as:
- individual and collective identity maintenance;
- patterns of identification by others;
- the allocation of ethnic significance to certain beliefs and behaviours;
- the effects such allocations of significance have on cultural retention;
- presentations of ethnic self;
- patterns of intra- and inter-group relations and social organization.

Being, as they are, heavily based on social-psychological theories of role, exchange, rational choice and symbolic interaction, contemporary orientations in ethnic research place the primary locus of culture at the level of ideas. In essence, from this perspective Sikh diaspora culture would be equated with the shared beliefs and values held by people identified as Sikh. This is a rather conventional anthropological definition of culture. However, in research practice "culture" is usually seen more narrowly, inasmuch as a central theme of the approach is actor salience. Thus, studies focus on those particular cultural values and beliefs which appear to be tied to (and, especially, are symbolic of) personally held ethnic identity—to those identified by Sikh individuals as characteristically Sikh. Both in studies done of Sikhs in this vein and in ethnic research more generally there is usually definitional silence as to what constitutes ethnic cultural *behaviours*. As implicitly defined by research concentrations, ethnic behaviour is that which has conscious salience as such, either to "ethnics" themselves or to others.

Variants of this conception of Sikh diaspora culture—as being primarily located in the mind and as having essentially symbolic behavioral expression—are common in Sikh diaspora community and family studies, and they naturally predominate in contemporary (as contrasted with historical) studies of Sikh relations with others. They do not always predominate in research done from a Sikh studies point of view.

What are the implied costs and benefits of using this notion of Sikh diaspora culture and the research agenda that goes with it?

Consider the potential benefits first. Perhaps the greatest attraction of this approach is that it provides a relatively complete "generative" model, linking Sikh diaspora belief to individual behaviour, community social organization and inter-group relations. In this model enculturated, ethnically sensitive sets of individuals find "Sikhness" of some importance to their conceptions of their personal selves. For various self-interested purposes (e.g., presenting statements of solidarity and difference, self-interest, peer pressure, etc.) they

---

10. At least with respect to research on contemporary Sikhs. This has *not* primarily been the case with respect to diaspora Sikhs in the past, who have been dealt with primarily in the context of legal-political issues and chronological history. For an exception see Leonard 1984, 1985, 1987.

consciously seek to generate role-contextualized, situationally constrained behaviour which symbolizes to them or others their identity and group allegiance. The actual degree to which such behaviour is manifest is a function of individual and collective Sikh resources and alternative choices, as well as the numerous constraints of the societal context in which they operate. Patterned Sikh diaspora behaviour thus may develop in disparate ways in different contexts, even though it is grounded on identical core values. The degree to which these presentations of self are acknowledged by others as valid depends on the degree to which there can develop a pattern of reciprocity of role presentations between given individuals.[11]

From the point of view of the development of comparative Sikh studies this model must be in certain respects compelling, for it allows one to develop theoretical unity across a range of empirical examples of Sikh behaviour that may on the surface appear quite divergent. For example, intermarriage rates between Sikh pioneers in Canada and others (say, between 1904 and 1950) were virtually nil,[12] whereas pioneers from absolutely the same background living in California during the same period intermarried extensively with Mexican-Americans.[13] Context, especially the differing racial views and class backgrounds of Mexican Americans and European Canadians, clearly explains part of the difference. So do the differing economic conditions under which Sikhs operated in these two places. One cannot explain these intermarriage rates by invoking a substantial divergence of cultural values or beliefs, or individual resources. Similarly, such a model might easily explain the active entrepreneurial tradition of India-born Sikhs in Britain (leaving aside the obvious business tradition of East African Sikhs there) and the relative paucity of such activities in Canada. Racial discrimination clearly disproportionately drives British Sikhs into entrepreneurial activity. It could also easily address the high residential concentration of Sikhs in Britain as compared with those in Canada and especially those in the United States (exclusive of the Yuba City area of California).

Indeed, perhaps better than any other, this approach allows one to reconcile a fundamental discrepancy of Sikh diaspora culture that will be considered more fully in subsequent sections: everywhere, Sikh diaspora cultural *behaviour* diverges dramatically from that of the Punjab, even among the most recent immigrants. For example, consider a typical Sikh family in Calgary, Alberta, one year after their arrival in Canada. Paid jobs, working for non-Sikhs; neighbours, not Sikh; house furniture, men's and children's clothing, all "Canadian"; the source of most material goods and services, non-Sikh. And yet this is manifestly not a simple case of nearly total, instantaneous "culture loss." If this is to be deemed "acculturation," one must massively qualify the distinction between

---

11. See Buchignani 1981 for a more detailed exploration of reciprocity in South Asian inter-group relations.
12. Buchignani and Indra 1985.
13. LaBrack and Leonard 1984; Leonard 1982.

behavioral acculturation and change in *values and beliefs.* In many instances the latter can be powerfully conserved among immigrants despite such values and beliefs having rather limited behavioral expression.

This approach also allows one to operationalize a proposal at least tacitly made by almost all Sikh researchers and yet rarely empirically demonstrated: that there actually *is* a relatively clear hierarchy of core Sikh values and beliefs, and behavioral responses based on them, which are of such subjective importance to the majority of Sikhs that they will put considerable energy into their preservation. Often one sees in diaspora studies an unsubstantiated and too facile shift from arguments about *Punjabi* Sikh cultural priorities (or even worse, from prescriptive idealizations of what Sikhs ought to do) to the identification of these same priorities with those in the diaspora. Naturally, everyone is well aware of the long-term effects of acculturation in the diaspora, and hence is cognizant of the fact that, say, East African Sikhs in Britain do not have the same cultural priorities as do those who have emigrated directly from India.[14] Still, neither has the contention that there are core values that transcend a given case been given much research attention, nor has there been anywhere near a full appreciation of the nearly instantaneous ways in which identity, self-interest considerations, and context can modify behavioral priorities. A key case in point is the massive shift among North American adult male Sikhs towards exhibiting the visible markers of a *keshdhari* Sikh since the time of Operation Bluestar.

In this sense, case studies done in this subjectivist mode drawn from a range of contexts can aid comparative integration by providing a proving bed for assertions about the depth and priority of Sikh cultural commitment and about the relative stability of putative Sikh core values and beliefs. For example, it is an almost stereotypic contention that Sikhs tend under certain conditions to band together in common cause against outside threat. On the one hand, instances supporting this assertion are easy to find in the Canadian experience; when faced by racial oppression Sikh pioneers united this way in 1907, just as did contemporary Sikhs after Operation Bluestar. On the other, greater comparative analysis based on this subjectivist model would allow one to move to the next stage: towards developing a theory of Sikh response to threat that specifies the conditions and constraints under which such responses operate. Similar arguments could be made with respect to a wide range of Sikh values concerning such things as marital and family relations, institution formation, and the like. In each instance, grounding culture in the realm of ideas might allow a considerable degree of general unity to arise out of disparate behavioral practice.

Of course, the present research fascination in anthropological ethnic studies with symbolic markers of ethnicity is tailor-made for addressing the obviously important empirical instances of ethnic marker use among diaspora Sikhs:

---

14. See Bhachu 1985.

issues such as the wearing of the five *kakars*, as well as patterns of identification of ethnic markers by others.

And finally, this kind of approach is critical to establishing a cross-societal theory of Sikh relations with others. As Doreen Indra and I have discussed at great length elsewhere, the comparative race- and ethnic-relations literature itself is characterized by a high degree of theoretical integration, and the integration of Sikh studies with this literature will provide yet another avenue of comparative generality to crosscut the diaspora literature.[15]   It will also reduce otherwise predictable efforts to "re-invent the wheel" as Sikh case studies, decontextualized from this ethnic and race relations literature, uncover yet another aspect of ethnic and race relations already commonplace in the discourse.

At the same time, there are good reasons for not committing exclusively to a fully subjective, choice- and decision-making model of Sikh cultural ideas and their expression. In particular this is so because of two basic considerations: its inability to incorporate fully what we would wish to know and the methodological problems inherent in the implementation of such a research orientation.

Perhaps the key difficulty of the former sort is that the allocation of greater ethnic Sikh significance to certain values and beliefs does *not* correspond in any simple fashion to the degree to which those cultural values and beliefs with higher significance are actually manifest in behaviour. Neither does it alone allow a straightforward explanation of the degree to which actual diaspora Sikh behaviour is similar to, or different from, that of Punjabi Sikhs, the majority group, or other ethnocultural minority groups in the same context.

Of course, at one level this is an automatic consequence of behaviour being a function of contextual variables, as was considered above. Here, I refer to a quite different set of mechanisms. In many respects, the generative model of Sikh behaviour used in subjectivist approaches begins with a hierarchy of Sikh diaspora values and beliefs, which are then constrained by contextual and rational choice factors from being fully expressed. The model suggests an "economy" of expression, wherein individuals and groups must make strategic choices about which behaviour to activate when faced with limited resources applicable to their expression. Virtually every case study of diaspora Sikhs illustrates that such a model of cultural expression is far from being a complete explanation of Sikh behaviour, for many such manifest behaviours are maintained with little reference to core values of any kind.

A case in point would be the nearly exclusive use of spoken Punjabi by Canadian Sikh pioneers throughout their lives. Few learned English before they came to Canada, and even fewer gained any proficiency with it thereafter. Virtually every second-generation Sikh Canadian of the subsequent era (1920-1950) spoke fluent Punjabi. One might infer from this (given the subjectivist model of cultural expression) that this almost total linguistic

---

15. Buchignani and Indra 198-.

retention implied that a very high value was being placed on Punjabi, either for symbolic purposes or because of a "decision" that the benefits of Punjabi use outweighed those of its replacement with English. There is in fact little support for either conclusion. This high degree of language retention seems better accounted for by far more "mechanical" forces. Punjabi was the first language of the pioneers. They were all adults when they came to Canada, and they did not come from a culture where an ideology of adult learning was particularly strong. They were socially segregated, thus limiting their access to spoken English; they were able and indeed preferred to work together. Of course, one could counter that in the "economy" of cultural maintenance this could be interpreted as being a "rational" decision, in that Punjabi could be maintained with little effort or cost whereas learning English would have provided few new benefits. There is undoubtedly some truth to this counter-argument, but note the changed argumentative ground: now language persistence is reduced to an "automatic" consequence of ease of maintenance in the context of social isolation rather than to its having high symbolic value.

The same kind of argument may well hold for the *majority* of behavioral cultural patterns among diaspora Sikhs. Whether such patterns are or are not the same as those of the majority group, for example, is in many instances symbolically quite irrelevant to all concerned; hence symbolic considerations are minimal determinants of their expression. Instead, they are the automatic consequences either of being the only such behavioral patterns available in the Sikh *repertoire* (in the case of many patterns divergent from mainstream practice) or else are majority-group practices of little symbolic load that are either convenient or functionally necessary to acquire.

This is not to suggest that one could or should dispose of consciousness or of beliefs and values in the explanation of such behavioral manifestations. The point is simply that in many instances of patterned Sikh diaspora behaviour the non-symbolic, "automatic" persistence of culture as well as the non-symbolic determinants of context frequently are important determinants in their own right. In addition, the strong association of the appellation "ethnic culture" in a behavioral sense to only those things which *are* ethnically salient is far too restrictive a base upon which to build general Sikh studies. In both these respects, the integration of diaspora studies must clearly consider the shape and consequences of a wide range of objective cultural practice. On this, more later.

There are also some rather deep methodological difficulties involved in subjectivist research strategies that have important implications for the development of a comparative synthesis.[16] These difficulties arise from the simple fact that we cannot get "inside people's heads" to observe directly what Sikh diaspora cultural values, beliefs, priorities and choices actually are. All of these things must be inferred from statements about them made by individuals,

16. See Buchignani 1982 for a more extensive theoretical discussion of this issue; Buchignani 1987 addresses this methodological problem in the context of research on South Asians in Canada.

or else must be inferred from behaviour.   The chief problem with such inferences is that they are in some ways profoundly circular.   One must infer actor-level subjective significance from patterned action, yet the very model that is thereafter used to explain such patterned behaviour depends on the same values that such behavioral observations have just supposedly identified. Moreover, this process is highly prone to the error of attributing symbolic significance to behavioral patterns through the unwarranted conclusion that if a given set of Sikh cultural behaviours is significantly different from those of the majority group, this must stem from symbolic determinants.

III

Objective (Behavioral) Conceptions of Sikh Diaspora Culture

Prior to 1970 virtually all so-called ethnic studies used a predominantly behaviorally oriented conception of ethnic or minority group culture.   This was true of those with roots in the early Chicago school of ethnic- and race-relations sociology and anthropology (1920-1940), and it was also true of subsequent work done through the acculturation and culture-contact orientations of the period 1940-1970.   Such objectivist approaches to ethnic culture thereafter quickly lost their pre-eminence, to the extent that they are now viewed by most ethnic- and race-relations theoreticians with considerable disdain as being atheoretical and unreflective of reality.

In social science one must always view such a polar paradigm shift with some suspicion.   For reasons I have considered elsewhere the book on objective approaches is by no means theoretically closed.[17]   Moreover, theoretical disdain notwithstanding, most community-based and Sikh-studies-oriented research done on the diaspora in fact concentrates heavily on Sikh culture as behaviour, even if such behaviour is now rather routinely explained with respect to belief and values.   Does this imply that such research is misguided and that it is consequently unlikely to provide a strong base for comparative synthesis?   The answer depends rather strongly on which of the several possible variants of the objectivist approach is chosen.   In any case, concern with Sikh cultural behaviour *per se* hardly needs any justification in itself.

A.   Diaspora Sikh Culture as That Which Punjabi Sikhs Do

Perhaps the most common option one sees in the diaspora literature is clearly based on an *a priori* interest in either Sikh culture *per se* or in observed differences between Sikh minority group and majority group cultural behaviour. This approach would equate Sikh culture with (1) those objective behavioral patterns which are learned, shared and transmitted within groups identified as Sikh, and (2) those which are clearly the same as, or derivative from, objective Punjabi Sikh practice.   This is the predominant (albeit usually implicit)

---

17. Buchignani 1982, 1988.

definition used by most researchers in the Sikh-studies tradition, and it is most certainly the most prominent folk conception, Sikh and non-Sikh, also.

This formulation is naturally well founded, at least in some respects. For those involved in contemporary Sikh studies, it is perfectly legitimate to wish to chart out the continuity and changes in key Sikh practices close to the hearts of those in this tradition: patterns of religious expression, of marriage, and so forth. For those of us with an interest in the history of the diaspora, observations of behaviour are the overwhelmingly preponderant data, and much of this data addresses continuities and changes in Sikh source culture. It would, therefore, be foolhardy to deem such historical information second class simply because beliefs and values may be in some ways theoretically primary. Some sort of modelling based primarily on behaviour is therefore necessary to consider adequately the historical situation. For those addressing issues such as Sikh socio-economic access and patterns of inter-group relations, behavioral data is critical also, particularly to analyses of the interplay between Sikh cultural retention (culture being defined as above) and the degree to which individuals have full access to the societal reward system.

Naturally, observations of Sikh behaviour also avoid the nasty problems of inference mentioned above in reference to subjectivist approaches, at least superficially. Some concentration on behavioral cultural difference is of course a necessary adjunct to analyses of the maintenance of Sikh identity, beliefs and values in the diaspora, inasmuch as little significant cultural difference at the level of ideas can be maintained without some kinds of behavioral support.

Theoretically, studies of objective cultural difference also allow the possible integration of diaspora studies into the literature on cultural pluralism, and through this route allow yet another means to integrate Sikh studies as a function of the host context.

At the same time, there are some deep potential difficulties in the use of this conception of Sikh culture for the purposes of theoretical comparison. First of all, this view produces what may be termed the "dismal view" of Sikh cultural persistence in the diaspora. It is dismal in the sense that it suggests a subtractive model of "real" diaspora Sikh culture wherein Sikh immigrants initially have a full measure of Sikh culture before they leave the Punjab, but even at the time of initial settlement in receiving countries they are able to enjoy at best half a cultural loaf. Thereafter, processes of acculturation inevitably and inexorably reduce this cultural residue of "true Sikh culture."

Realistically, diaspora Sikhs in *all* industrialized countries behaviorally exhibit rather little of this kind of "roots culture," even as new immigrants. This has been true historically as well as at present. Consider once more those early pioneers in Canada. Facing very high levels of social discrimination and having few class resources, they were hardly strong candidates for substantial acculturation. And yet from a strictly behavioral point of view a great many (I would argue most) of their cultural traits were soon indistinguishable from those of the majority group. An even greater proportion were strictly parallel with those of other culturally unrelated Asian minorities, especially the Chinese. Socially isolated, most without families, and yet able to work in the company of one another, early immigrants at least were able (or required) to maintain strong informal community, language and certain aspects of religious practice. By objective standards, contemporary Sikh Canadian immigrant behaviour is even more similar to that of the majority group, and shares many broad patterns with contemporary immigrant groups from Asia and Southern Europe.

Undoubtedly, understanding such massive shifts in behavioral patterns is of critical importance to the development of comparative Sikh studies, and ought not therefore to be neglected. These changes are every bit as important as the continuities with Punjabi Sikh culture so deeply valued by those who subscribe to this approach. The "culture loss" metaphor, though, has this very effect: it makes "original" Sikh cultural maintenance something problematic, something worthy of research—while at the same time making behavioral acculturation non-problematic, with its consequent neglect in research. Moreover, if carried out primarily at an objective level, such "before and after" immigration comparisons, in addition to being tacitly invidious, tend to give short shrift to the fact that *Punjabi* Sikh behavioral patterns are hardly monolithic. Rather, they typically allow a wide range of acceptable alternatives, some predominating in one person, group or context, others elsewhere. Therefore, the standard of comparison by which "true" Sikh diaspora culture is to be judged is in itself problematic, though in this approach it is rarely considered so.

Finally, it is difficult to conceive how any other primary theoretical base could be provided to explain the persistence and change of pre-immigration Sikh culture patterns, save for the subjectivist model presented above. In essence, many issues of behavioral culture are theoretically reducible to issues of consciousness, belief and values. At a secondary level there are, of course, purely behavioral and contextual ways of explaining non-symbolic, "automatic" cultural persistence. But the difficulty faced by any attempt to go in this direction is that this explanatory route has been grossly neglected in ethnic studies generally. Sikh-studies researchers venturing in this direction would be travelling in rather uncharted theoretical territory.

B. Diaspora Sikh Culture as That Which Diaspora Sikhs Do

A few others have chosen to opt for the other major objectivist alternative: the use of only consideration (1) in the above definition. Sikh culture is equated with those patterned behaviours that are learned, shared and transmitted by people identified as Sikh. It has been this approach in particular that has been much derided by theoreticians of ethnicity as being naïve, even useless. It is also given rather short shrift by those enamoured of "true" Punjabi Sikh culture. For the purposes of addressing ethnicity *per se*, such a definition may well be counter-productive, but comparative Sikh studies cannot be simply reduced to questions of ethnic and race relations.

The primary value of this approach is that it does not seek to make the always somewhat artificial distinction between what aspects of culture are "truly Sikh" in origin and which are derived from "mere acculturation." The approach considers *all* the patterned behaviours of individuals in Sikh communities to be relevant without any *a priori* judgments about which behaviours are "really" Sikh. Such global definitions are virtually the exclusive preserve of those who study community organization and development, where attempts to apply the previous criterion of "true Sikh culture" are always transparently inappropriate. At this level, the concentration is on "patterns *of* living," usually with there being some attempt to reconcile these behavioral observations with Sikh-held "patterns *for* living" through something approaching the subjectivist model referred to above.[18]

One might expect that such an approach might provide rather little potential for comparative studies, inasmuch as such an all-encompassing definition would seem to detach case studies from their Sikh roots and because the variability of context-specific acculturative forces might seem to admit of such great variation as to preclude meaningful comparison. These are indeed potential dangers, but they are not necessary ones. For example, if one compares the total corpus of contemporary Sikh Canadian practice with that of other recent Asian immigrant groups, one sees powerful parallels despite obvious differences in "original cultures"—however the latter might be defined. The same thing would hold for cross-group comparisons made in the British or American contexts. Clearly, in each instance the dual dimensions of common immigrant status and common host society are critical; from this we must conclude that in many ways Sikhs are immigrants and members of particular societies first, and Sikhs second. This underlines a serious weakness in present Sikh diaspora studies: a nearly total lack of nation-specific comparison between Sikhs and other similarly situated ethnocultural groups in such countries. Were one to have access to these (and access is in part dependent on a rather global definition of Sikh culture), the next stage of theoretical integration would be to merge these sets of nation-specific observations into a more general contextual typology of industrialized and Third World contexts as they impact on Sikhs and others.

And, of course, similar arguments support the development of integration along other lines. In many situations Sikhs are also primarily men or women, working or middle class, first or second generation; and yet, although noted in some case studies, these points have not been well developed in a comparative sense at all.

---

18. Cf. Bhachu 1985.

IV

Towards a Theoretical Synthesis

As has been argued throughout, there are no strong theoretical or empirical reasons for claiming that one of the various definitions of culture and related orientations presently in use in Sikh diaspora studies should be used to the exclusion of others. At the same time, one should not therefore conclude that all such definitions are of equal priority or utility. In a broad sense, it seems incontestable that mentalistic conceptions have a considerable degree of theoretical and causal priority over objectivist ones.

This is true in several senses. First, objective cultural behaviour is better explained through reference to mental processes, beliefs and values than *vice versa*. Secondly, while the choice- or decision-making models that inevitably arise out of mentalistic conceptions of culture "over-rationalize" the explanation of behaviour, they nevertheless are the primary theoretical route we have available to an understanding of the Sikh diaspora experience. When they are tied to symbolic interactionism, the generative quality of these models also allows the comparative integration of widely divergent behavioral practice. Equally powerful purely behaviorally based theories are not presently available. This theoretical priority does not therefore suggest that case study research on diaspora Sikhs should concentrate on beliefs and values at the expense of behaviour. It does suggest that those concerned primarily with the latter are under considerable obligation to ground their observations at least partially in the realm of ideas.

Moving to a more general level, I might leave off with a few final points about the future development of more integrated Sikh diaspora studies. First, whatever their immediate research concerns, researchers in the field should be aware of the constraints of their theoretical perspectives. Alternative definitions of Sikh culture were demonstrated here to have profound implications for how research proceeds and for how it might be integrated, but this is only one of many such factors that have similar implications. Second, this does not suggest that synthesis need only come through the rise of a monolithic, homogeneous theoretical perspective: this would be profoundly dysfunctional and is an unrealistic goal in any case. Still, contemporary researchers should become more aware of the need to integrate the research discourse. This could be done minimally through the development of a greater appreciation of the findings of others and the integration of such findings into one's own work. Inasmuch as other studies of necessity come from differing perspectives, this form of integration would be more than just empirical; it would also begin to build stronger bridges between alternative theoretical and definitional points of view. Finally, researchers should begin to consider the option of research that is explicitly comparative rather than being grounded in a particular case study. In this regard, I do not mean programmatic pieces like this one; such theoretical exercises have their place, but they are no substitute for empirical research.

References

Anwar, M. *Between Two Cultures: A Study of Relationships between Generations in the Asian Community.* London: Community Relations Commission, 1976.

Aurora, Gurdip Singh. "Indian Workers in England: A Socio-historical Survey of Indian Workers in England." M.Sc. thesis, Economics, University of London, 1960.

———. *The New Frontiersmen: A Sociological Study of Indian Immigrants in the U.K.* Bombay: Popular Prakashan, 1967.

Ballard, C. "Family Organization Among the Sikhs in Britain." *New Community* 2 (1973), 12-24.

———. "Arranged Marriages in the British Context." *New Community* 6 (1978), 181-96.

———. "Family Organization in a Wider Context: Jullunder and Mirpur Compared." *New Community* 11 (1983), 1-2.

Ballard, R.; and C. Ballard. "The Sikhs: The Development of South Asian Settlements in Britain." In J.L. Watson, ed., *Between Two Cultures: Migrants and Minorities in Britain.* Oxford: Basil Blackwell, 1977.

Barrier, N. Gerald. "The Role of Ideology and Institution-Building in Modern Sikhism." In Mark Juergensmeyer and N. Gerald Barrier, eds., *Sikh Studies: Comparative Perspectives on a Changing Tradition.* Berkeley: Graduate Theological Union, 1979, pp. 41-51.

———. "Sikh Immigrants and Their Homeland: The Transmission of Information, Resources and Values in the Early Twentieth Century." Paper presented at the Conference on the Sikh Diaspora, University of Michigan, 1987.

Barrier, N. Gerald; and Mark Juergensmeyer. "The Sikhs and the Scholars." In Barrier and Juergensmeyer, eds., *Sikh Studies: Comparative Perspectives on a Changing Tradition.* Berkeley: Berkeley Religious Studies Series, Graduate Theological Union, 1979.

Beetham, D. *Transport and Turbans: A Comparative Study in Local Politics.* Oxford: Oxford University Press, for the Institute of Race Relations, 1970.

Bhachu, P.K. "Marriage and Dowry Among Selected East African Sikh Families in the United Kingdom." Ph.D. dissertation, University of London, 1981.

———. "East African Sikhs in Britain: Experienced Settlers with Traditionalistic Values." *Immigrants and Minorities* 3:3 (1984), 276-95.

———. *Twice Migrants: East African Sikh Settlers in Britain.* London: Tavistock, 1985.

Brooks, D. *Race and Labour in London Transport.* London: Oxford University Press, for the Institute of Race Relations, 1975.

Brooks, D.; and K. Singh. "Ethnic Commitment Versus Structural Reality: South Asian Immigrant Workers in Britain." *New Community* 7:1 (1978).

Buchignani, Norman. "A Review of the Historical and Sociological Literature on East Indians in Canada." *Canadian Ethnic Studies* 9:1 (1977), 86-108.

———. "Accommodation, Adaptation and Policy: Aspects of the South Asian Experience in Canada." In K.V. Ujimoto and G. Hirabayashi, eds., *Proceedings of the Second Colloquium on Asians in Canada.* Guelph: University of Guelph, 1978, pp. 30-71.

———. "Accommodation, Adaptation and Policy: Dimensions of the South Asian Experience in Canada." In K. Victor Ujimoto and Gordon Hirabayashi, eds., *Visible Minorities and Multiculturalism: Asians in Canada.* Toronto: Butterworths, 1980[a], pp. 121-50.

———. "South Asians and the Ethnic Mosaic: An Overview." *Canadian Ethnic Studies* 11:1 (1980[b]), 48-68.

———. "The Social and Self Identities of Fijian Indians in Vancouver." *Urban Anthropology* 9:1 (1981), 75-98.

————. "Anthropological Approaches to the Study of Ethnicity." *Occasional Papers on Ethnic and Immigration Studies*, 82-13. Toronto: Multicultural History Society of Ontario, 1982.

————. "Social Science Research on South Asians and Canada: Retrospect and Prospect." In Milton Israel, ed., *The South Asian Diaspora in Canada: Six Essays*. Toronto: Multicultural History Society of Ontario and Centre for South Asian Studies, University of Toronto, 1987, pp. 113-41.

————. "Ethnic Phenomena and Contemporary Social Theory: Their Implications for Archaeology." *Conference Proceedings, 18th Annual Chacmool Conference.* Calgary: University of Calgary, 1988.

Buchignani, Norman; and Doreen Indra. "Inter-Group Conflict and Community Solidarity: Sikhs and South Asian Fijians in Vancouver." *Canadian Journal of Anthropology* 1:2 (1981)[a], 149-57.

————. "The Political Organization of South Asians in Canada," in J. Dahlie and T. Fernando, eds., *Ethnicity, Power and Politics in Canada.* Toronto: Methuen, 1981[b], pp. 202-32.

————. "Canadian-Sikh Ethnic and Race Relations, and Their Implications for the Study of the Sikh Diaspora," in N.G. Barrier and V.A. Dusenbery, eds., *The Sikh Diaspora.* Delhi, Manohar, forthcoming 1988.

Buchignani, Norman; and Doreen Indra, with Ram Srivast[a]va. *Continuous Journey: A Social History of South Asians in Canada.* Toronto: McClelland & Stewart, 1985.

Chadney, James G. "The Vancouver Sikhs: An Ethnic Community in Canada." Ph.D. dissertation, Michigan State University, 1976.

————. *The Sikhs of Vancouver.* New York: AMS Press, 1984.

Chan, Sucheng. "Overseas Sikhs in the Context of International Migrations," in Mark Juergensmeyer and N. Gerald Barrier, eds., *Sikh Studies: Comparative Perspectives on a Changing Tradition.* Berkeley: Graduate Theological Union, 1979, pp. 191-206.

Chaudri, J.J.M. "The Emigration of Sikh Jats from Punjab to England," in A. Mayer, ed., *Social Science Research Council Report*, Project HR 331-1. London: Social Science Research Council, 1973.

Ch'eng, Tien-Fang. *Oriental Immigration in Canada.* Shanghai: Commercial Press, 1931.

Das, Rajani Kant. *Hindustanee Workers on the Pacific Coast.* Berlin: Walter de Gruyter, 1923.

Desai, Rashmi. *Indian Immigrants in Britain.* London: Oxford University Press, 1963.

DeWitt, John, Jr. *Indian Workers Associations in Britain.* London: Oxford University Press, 1969.

Dusenbery, Verne A. "Canadian Ideology and Public Policy: The Impact on Vancouver Sikh Ethnic and Religious Adaptation." *Canadian Ethnic Studies* 8:3 (1981), 101-20.

————. "The Sikh Person, the Khalsa Panth and Western Sikh Converts," in J.K. Lele *et al.*, eds., *Boeings and Bullock Carts: Rethinking India's Restructuring.* Leiden: E.J. Brill. Cited as "198-a."

————. "Punjab Sikhs and *Gora* Sikhs: Conflicting Assertions of Sikh Identity in North America." Mimeo. Cited as "198-b." Cf. his chapter in this volume.

————. "On the Moral Sensitivities of Sikhs in North America." In O. Lynch and P. Kolenda, eds., *Consuming Passions: Emotion and Feeling in Indian Culture.* Forthcoming. Cited as "198-c."

Ghuman, P. "Bhattra Sikhs in Cardiff: Family and Kinship Organization." *New Community* 8:3 (1980).

Gonzales, Juan L. "Asian Indian Immigration Patterns: The Origins of the Sikh Community in California." *International Migration Review* 20:1 (1986), 40-54.

294   Norman Buchignani

Gupta, Santosh P. "The Acculturation of Asians in Central Pennsylvania." Ph.D. disseration, Pennsylvania State University, 1969.

Helweg, Arthur W. "A Punjab Community in an English Town: A Study in Migrant Adaptation." Ph.D. dissertation, Michigan State University, 1977.

———. *Sikhs in England: The Development of a Migrant Community.* Delhi: Oxford University Press, 1980.

———. "Emigrant Remittances: Their Nature and Impact on a Punjabi Village." *New Community* 10:3 (1983).

———. *Sikhs in England: The Development of a Migrant Community.* Delhi: Oxford University Press, 2nd ed., 1985.

Indra, Doreen. "The Portrayal of South Asians in the Vancouver Press, 1905-76." *Ethnic and Racial Studies* 2:2 (1979), 164-87.

James, A. *Sikh Children in Britain.* London: Oxford University Press for the Institute of Race Relations, 1976.

Johnston, Hugh. *The Voyage of the Komagata Maru: The Sikh Challenge to Canada's Colour Bar.* Delhi: Oxford University Press, 1979.

———. "Patterns of Sikh Migration to Canada, 1900-1960." In the present volume.

Joy, Annamma. "Work and Ethnicity: The Case of the Sikhs in the Okanagan Valley of British Columbia." In Rabindra Kanungo, ed., *South Asians in the Canadian Mosaic.* Montreal: Kala Bharati, 1984.

Juergensmeyer, Mark. "The Ghadar Syndrome: Immigrant Sikhs and Nationalist Pride," in M. Juergensmeyer and N.G. Barrier, eds. *Sikh Studies: Comparative Perspectives on a Changing Tradition.* Berkeley: Graduate Theological Union, 1979, pp. 173-90.

Kalra, S.S. *Daughters of Traditions: Adolescent Sikh Girls and Their Accommodation to Life in British Society.* Birmingham: Diane Balbir Publications, 1980.

Keupper, W.B.; G.L. Lackey; and E.N. Swinerton. *Ugandan Asians in Britain: Forced Migration and Social Absorption.* London: Croom Helm, 1975.

LaBrack, Bruce. "Sikhs Real and Ideal: A Discussion of Text and Context in the Description of Overseas Sikh Communities," in Mark Juergensmeyer and N. Gerald Barrier, eds., *Sikh Studies: Comparative Perspectives on a Changing Tradition.* Berkeley: Graduate Theological Union, 1979, pp. 127-42.

———. "The Sikhs of Northern California: A Socio-historical Study." Ph.D. dissertation, Social Sciences, Syracuse University, 1980.

———. "The Reconstitution of Sikh Society in Rural California." In G. Kurian and R. Srivastava, eds., *Overseas Indians: A Study in Adaptation,* pp. 215-40. New Delhi: Vikas, 1983.

LaBrack, Bruce; and Karen Leonard. "Conflict and Compatibility in Punjabi-Mexican Immigrant Families in Rural California: 1915-1965." *Journal of Marriage and the Family* 46:3 (1984), 539-56.

Lal, B. "East Indians in British Columbia (1904-1914): A Historical Study in Growth and Integration." M.A. thesis, History, University of British Columbia, 1976.

Leonard, Karen. "Marriage and Family Life Among Early Asian Indian Immigrants." *Population Review* 25:1-2 (1982), 67-75.

———. "The Pahkar Singh Murders: A Punjabi Response to California's Alien Land Law." *Amerasia Journal* 11:1 (1984), 75-87.

———. "Punjabi Farmers and California's Alien Land Law." *Agricultural History* 59:4 (1985), 549-62.

———. "Pioneer Voices: Reflections on Race, Religion and Ethnicity." Paper presented at the Conference on the Sikh Diaspora. Ann Arbor: University of Michigan, 1987.

Mathur, Laxman P. *Indian Revolutionary Movement in the United States of America.* Delhi: S. Chand, 1970.

McLeod, W.H. "The Sikhs of the South Pacific," in Mark Juergensmeyer and N. Gerald Barrier, eds., *Sikh Studies: Comparative Perspectives on a Changing Tradition.* Berkeley: Graduate Theological Union, 1979, pp. 143-58.

————. *Punjabis in New Zealand.* Amritsar: Guru Nanak Dev University, 1985.

Remmer, Malcolm. *Race and Industrial Conflict: A Study on a Group of Midland Foundries.* London, 1972.

Robinson, V. "Asians in Britain: A Study in Encapsulation and Marginality," in C. Clarke, D. Ley and C. Peach, eds., *Geography and Ethnic Pluralism.* London: Allen and Unwin, 1984.

Scanlon, T. Joseph. *The Sikhs of Vancouver: A Case Study of the Role of the Media in Ethnic Relations.* Carleton University: Mimeo, 1975.

Thompson, M. "A Study of Generational Difference in Immigrant Groups, with Particular Reference to the Sikhs." M.Phil. thesis, University of London, 1970.

Uberoi, Narindar. "Sikh Women In Southall." *Race* 6:1 (1964), 34-40.

United States Senate, Immigration Commission. "Report of the Immigration Commission: Immigrants in Industries, Part 25: Japanese and Other Immigrant Races in the Pacific Coast and Rocky Mountain States." Washington, D.C.: Government Printing Office, 1911.

Wood, John R. "East Indians and Canada's New Immigration Policy," in G. Kurian and R. Srivastava, eds., *Overseas Indians: A Study in Adaptation.* New Delhi: Vikas, 1983, pp. 3-29.

Patterns of Sikh Migration to Canada, 1900-1960

Hugh Johnston

The Sikh community in Canada is over eighty years old, but it has all the appearances of a new immigrant community; and, like all new immigrant communities, it is very much oriented towards its homeland. An obvious explanation is the large immigration that has taken place in the last twenty years. But the older elements of the community, the families that can trace their histories in Canada to the first decade of this century, have also remained remarkably attached to the Punjab. Their fathers, or grandfathers, or uncles first entered the country at a time of comparatively unregulated immigration, between 1903 and 1908. In 1908 the door was shut to further immigration from India, and little immigration was permitted for the next half-century. What happens to a population of immigrants admitted over the course of a few brief years and then denied renewal by immigration for the next forty or fifty years? The Sikh community did not disappear, and it did not assimilate. It remained at once a tiny, isolated fragment within the Canadian context and an integral, although distant, part of the Punjabi world centered in India.

A few Sikhs came to British Columbia in 1903 and launched an immigration of more than 5,000 over the next four years. Spokesmen for the principal carrier, the trans-Pacific steamer service of the Canadian Pacific Railway, called it a spontaneous movement. The steamer spokesmen did so defensively. Sikh immigrants replaced some of the C.P.R.'s lost steerage traffic from Hong Kong following the introduction of a higher head tax on Chinese immigration. A special agent of the Dominion Government, in a secret report in 1907, held the C.P.R. responsible for this new immigrant "invasion."[1]   So did the Deputy Minister of Labour, W.L. Mackenzie King, in his Royal Commission Report of 1908. The C.P.R.'s counter-explanation was given by the General Superintendent of the Trans-Pacific Service when he testified before King's

---

1. Public Archives of Canada (hereafter P.A.C.), Borden Papers, T.R.E. McInnes to Frank Oliver, Minister of the Interior, Oct. 2, 1907, copy.

[Joseph T. O'Connell, Milton Israel, Willard G. Oxtoby, eds., with W.H. McLeod and J.S. Grewal, visiting eds., *Sikh History and Religion in the Twentieth Century* (S. Asian Studies Papers, 3) (Toronto: S. Asian Studies, Univ. of Toronto, 1988)]

commission.[2] It was as follows: Sikh interest in Canada had been generated by Indian troops who had seen the country on their way back from Britain to the Orient a couple of years before. This explanation has been much repeated and it has a basis in fact.[3] Yet there were other ways that information could reach the Punjab. Dr. A. Nugent, a Presbyterian missionary, worked with Sikhs in Vancouver for several months in 1907. He was told by some that the first to come to Canada had been to Australia previously and had travelled a great deal.[4] For explaining the genesis of Sikh migration to Canada, these stories are inconclusive and uninstructive. One way or another, adventurous individuals were bound to find their way to North America. They might have come and gone without notice. Their arrival became remarkable when others followed in appreciable numbers; and that happened when the right circumstances prevailed.

By all accounts the migration began among Sikhs in Hong Kong. The fever then reached back to India, and most of the immigrants who followed came directly from home.[5] Once the interest was evident, the C.P.R.'s agents in Calcutta assiduously circulated advertisements throughout the Punjab.[6] Some immigration was generated by a labour contractor, D.R. Davichand, a Punjabi who had earlier spent five years in Australia. He sent tickets to men in the Punjab, particularly in the Ferozepur district, and he posted bonds for many who arrived with insufficient funds to clear immigration.[7] Most men, however, arrived at their own expense and without the assurance of work. The C.P.R. recruited them as a carrier, not as a potential employer.[8] Davichand was probably responsible for no more than five per cent of them. And, without the enthusiastic letters and reports from an advance guard, they would not have chosen to come. In this way, twenty or thirty immigrants in the first twelve months, became forty-five in the second, 387 in the third, 2,124 in the fourth and 2,623 in the fifth.[9] Over 40% of these men were concentrated in three large

---

2. W.L. Mackenzie King, *Report of the Royal Commission into the Methods by Which Oriental Labourers Have Been Induced to Come to Canada* (Ottawa: King's Printer, 1908), p. 75.

3. Norman Buchignani and Doreen Indra with Ram Srivast[a]va, *Continuous Journey: A Social History of South Asians in Canada* (Toronto: McClelland and Stewart, 1985), pp. 5-6.

4. United Church of Canada Archives, Presbyterian Church in Canada, British Columbia Mission to East Indians, Mr. Nugent's Report *re* Hindoos at Vancouver, 1907.

5. According to American immigration statistics, in 1905, 70 East Indians immigrated directly from India, 17 from British North America (Canada), and 58 from elsewhere (including Hong Kong). In 1907, the figures were 883 from India, 89 from British North America, and 100 from elsewhere. Out of 483 East Indians in the Dillingham Commission sample, 402 had been agriculturalists and only 16 had been soldiers before emigrating. U.S. Senate, *Report of the Immigration Commission: Immigrants in Industries, Japanese and Other Immigrant Races in the Pacific Coast and Rocky Mountain States*, part 25, v. 1, 61st Congress, 2nd Session, Doc. no. 633 (Washington: Government Printing Office, 1911), pp. 327-28.

6. King, *Report*, pp. 77-79.

7. Ibid., pp. 78-80; *The World*, Vancouver, July 20 and 30, 1906. According to the July 20 story in *The World*, Davichand had by then placed 300 Sikh and Hindu labourers in Vancouver mills.

8. McInnes to Oliver, Oct. 2, 1907.

9. These are June-to-May figures from 1903 until 1908. During the 1903 calendar year, 10 East Indians arrived; and by October 1, 1904, the total was 57. In the fiscal year 1904-05, when East Indians were first separated from the other category in the annual report of the Department of the Interior, 45 arrived. The figures are given in Buchignani and Indra, *Continuous Journey*, p. 7, with an estimate of 30 for 1902-04. See P.A.C., RG 76, file 536999, W.G. Parmelee, Deputy Minister,

contingents: the 696 who arrived on the *Tartar* in November 1906, the 901 on the *Monteagle* in September 1907, and the 547 on the *Tartar* in October, 1907.[10] Most arrived late in the season without immediate work or shelter and suffered great privation in their first few weeks or months in the country. Their reports would have reduced immigration in succeeding years even if the Canadian Government had not brought it to a stop by regulation in 1908.

The precise timing of this immigration was determined by economic and political realities. It began as soon as independent immigrants from the Punjab were able to pay the cost of travel halfway around the world and find employment at North American wages on arrival. The responsiveness of Punjabi villagers to reports of jobs in Canada was a product of their integration into the international economy. That integration had proceeded briskly during the preceding thirty years as the Punjab rail system expanded from 400 miles in 1873 to over 3,000 in 1903 and as its system of irrigation canals grew from 2,744 miles to 16,893.[11] In rural Punjab this development encouraged a shift away from domestic crops (millet, sorghum and other coarse grains) to export crops (wheat, cotton, and sugar cane). In 1904, Indian wheat exports to Great Britain exceeded those of Russia and the United States, and the Punjab controlled a major part of the Indian trade.[12] The exports that left the Punjab provided the cash and credit that made distant travel possible for peasant farmers. Land, worth twenty rupees an acre in 1875-76, and thirty rupees in 1886-87, rose to nearly eighty in 1900-01. Land prices fell by 18% in 1901-02 as a consequence of the restrictions imposed by the Punjab Alienation of Land Act of 1901, but they recovered within two years (before the immigration to Canada started) and reached ninety-eight rupees an acre in 1907-08.[13] In 1907, the cost of a passage from Calcutta to Hong Kong and from Hong Kong to Vancouver was 201 rupees, a substantial investment for a typical landholding family with four or five acres. Fifteen or twenty years before, when Punjab land prices had been lower, but trans-Pacific travel just as expensive, it would have been prohibitive. A trans-Pacific steamer service had operated between Vancouver and Hong Kong since 1887. Sikhs and other North Indians, who had been recruited for work in Singapore, Hong Kong and elsewhere in the Far East since the late 1860's, had outposts on the Pacific.[14] Having found work in

Trade and Commerce to J.A. Smart, Deputy Minister, Interior, Oct. 19, 1904, and Oliver to Governor-General-in-Council, Oct. 29, 1907.

10. *Daily News Advertiser*, Vancouver, shipping columns, Nov. 15, 1906, Sept. 12, 1907, Oct., 10, 1907; P.A.C., RG 76, file 536999, Frank Oliver to Governor General, Nov. 18, 1907.

11. H.H. Calvert, *The Wealth and Welfare of the Punjab* (Lahore: Civil and Military Gazette Press, 1922), p. 107.

12. *Pannell's Reference Book* (London: The Granville Press, 1906), p. 704; Eric Stokes, *The Peasant and the Raj: Studies in Agrarian Society and Peasant Rebellion in Colonial India* (Cambridge: Cambridge University Press, 1978), p. 263.

13. G.S. Chhabra, *The Social and Economic History of Punjab, 1849-1901* (New Delhi: Sterling Publishers, 1968), p. 312; Himadri Banerjee, *Agrarian Society of the Punjab* (New Delhi: Manohar, 1982), p. 103.

14. Kemial Singh Sandhu, *Indians in Malaya: Some Aspects of their Immigration and Settlement, 1786-1951* (Cambridge: Cambridge University Press, 1968), pp. 73, 123-27.

Australia in the 1890's and then having been barred by Australian legislation in 1901, they were ripe for Canada. Nonetheless, a spontaneous emigration over such a distance could not have been financed by a less prosperous rural community than the Sikhs, and they could not have managed it much earlier than they did.

Most of the emigrants were young men in their twenties who had raised their passage money in India without assistance from anyone in America— friend, relative, or contractor. American immigration figures show that 93.5% of all Indians arriving in the U.S. between 1908 and 1910 paid their own fares.[15] The Dillingham Commission, which completed a forty-one-volume report on immigration for the U.S. Congress in 1911, obtained personal data on 474 Indian labourers on the Pacific coast. Most of these men had entered the U.S. through Canada, and they represent a sample of the migration to both countries. Among them, 23 (5%) were under eighteen years of age and 288 (61%) were eighteen to thirty years of age.[16] This sample probably over-represents the over-thirty and under-eighteen groups. Among 1,372 men who landed in Victoria in October and November of 1907, 1,223 (89%) were (or said they were) in the age range eighteen to thirty.[17] None was under eighteen and only 47 (3.8%) were thirty-five or over. The oldest was forty-five. A significant proportion had wives in India. In the Dillingham Commission sample, 215 (48.8%) were married, and in the 1907 sample of men landing at Victoria, 863 (62.9%). The bachelors were mostly younger men, twenty-one and under and, while not yet married, as closely tied to their families at home as their married companions. Of 79 Indians surveyed in the states of Washington and Oregon in 1908, 31 had sent an average of $139.35 home that year despite scarcity of work: 18 to wives, 9 to parents and 3 to brothers (and one who did not specify).[18]

The Dillingham Commission estimated that 85% of Indian immigrants in those years were Sikhs.[19] On the *Komagata Maru*, which was turned back from the port of Vancouver in 1914, 76% of the 291 passengers identified by caste were Jat Sikhs.[20] The rest were Sikhs of other castes and Hindus and Muslims from the same districts. This was a migration primarily from the central and most densely populated districts of the Punjab. But it was the product of mobility, enterprise, and opportunity rather than population pressure. It was a

15. U.S. Senate, *Reports of the Immigration Commission: Statistical Review of Immigration, 1820-1910*, 61st Congress, 3rd Session, Doc. no. 756 (Washington: Government Printing Office, 1911), p. 360.
16. U.S. Senate, *Reports of the Immigration Commission: Immigrants in Industries, Japanese and Other Immigrant Races in the Pacific Coast and Rocky Mountain States*, part 25, v. 1, 61st Congress, 2nd Session, Doc. no. 633 (Washington: Government Printing Office, 1911), p. 339.
17. Information tabulated from manifests of steamships *Monteagle* and *Tartar*, which arrived at Victoria from Yokohama Sept. 11 and Oct. 9, 1907. Manifests are on microfilm reel T 512, P.A.C. A total of 1418 East Indians arrived on these two ships, but 46 entries in the manifest are illegible or incomplete.
18. U.S., Senate, *Immigrants in Industries, Japanese*, p. 347.
19. Ibid., p. 337.
20. *Report of the Komagata Maru Committee of Inquiry* (Calcutta: Superintendent Government Printing, India, 1914), Appendix iv, list of passengers.

migration in which the most successful land-owning caste in the Punjab participated and few others. It took place during a decade in which the population of the central districts dropped sharply. Between 1901 and 1911, epidemics of the plague were responsible for one death in four, and the death rate exceeded the birth rate by 2%.[21] The loss was accentuated by continuing migration to the Canal Colonies of West Punjab, where Jat peasants could obtain allotments of as much as fifty-five acres in contrast to their holdings of three to ten acres in the central districts.[22] In comparison to the demographic impact of epidemics and internal migration, overseas migration was insignificant. If population pressure was a stimulus to leave, it should have been a greater stimulus ten or fifteen years earlier. Moreover, the plague was more devastating in the female population and left an imbalance between sexes that freed some men for overseas travel. By 1911, males outnumbered females by five to four.[23] The number of emigrants directly affected by this disproportion, however, was small because a majority were married, and a majority of the unmarried were young.

If the *Komagata Maru's* passenger list is a guide, potential emigrants were spread in small numbers and in unequal proportions throughout the Jat Sikh districts. More than half of the *Komagata Maru* passengers were from the Malwa districts between the Sutlej and Jamma rivers. A quarter were from the Mahja districts between the Bias and Ravi. A twelfth or thirteenth were from western Punjab. And only about an eighth were from the Doaba area between the Bias and Sutlej, although that is the area that developed the strongest ties with Canada. The *Komagata Maru* reflected the geographical distribution of Jat Sikh population in the Punjab. The largest contingents on the ship came from Amritsar and Ferozepur, the districts with the largest Jat Sikh populations. The Doaba districts of Jullundur and Hoshiarpur had smaller Sikh populations, and their contingents were correspondingly smaller. In British Columbia, Doaba men predominated. A list of leading activists and informants in the Vancouver Sikh community in 1914 identifies 24 out of 28 as men from either Jullundur or Hoshiarpur. The files of the immigration department yield the villages and districts of origin for almost 500 Indians residing in British Columbia in the 1920's and 1930's. Over 60% of these men were from Jullundur and Hoshiarpur; 14% were from Ferozepur; 7% were from Ludhiana; and less than 20% were from other districts. Perhaps the Doaba men were the most numerous element of the original migration, or perhaps they were the ones that stayed when others went back. The matter asks for explanation, not simply on the evidence of the *Komagata Maru*, but because in Malaya, which was a stepping

---

21. James Douie, *The Punjab, North-West Frontier Province and Kashmir* (Cambridge: Cambridge University Press, 1916), p. 98.

22. To take the example of one colonization area, the number of immigrants from Amritsar, Jullundur, Gurdaspur, Hoshiarpur and Ludhiana in the Chanab Colony in the Lyallpur District rose from 221,445 in 1901 to 280,232 in 1911. See Himadri Banerjee, *Agrarian Society of the Punjab* (New Delhi: Manohar, 1982), pp. 41-42.

23. Douie, *The Punjab*, p. 99.

stone on the way to Canada, only about 20% of the Sikh population was from Doaba.[24] Even if the emigration was more concentrated in two districts than the others, it drew only a few men from any one village.[25] Distant travel was limited to those with cash or credit whose families could spare the manpower. For these reasons, men travelled from their homes singly or in pairs, and by the time they accumulated in large numbers they represented many districts and hundreds of villages.

Sikh immigration to British Columbia began in the early years of an unprecedented economic boom in Canada that lasted, with one twelve-month interruption, until 1913. More immigrants entered the country in those years than in any other comparable period before or since.[26] The boom gathered force in 1903, when the Federal Government launched the construction of two transcontinental railway lines, the National Transcontinental and the Grand Trunk Pacific, paralleling the existing Canadian Pacific line. It was fed by the rapid expansion of settlement over the vast regions of the prairie west, and by the development of the mining regions of British Columbia, Alberta, and northern Ontario. Carried along in this boom was the forest industry of British Columbia, which found a primary market for lumber in the new prairie settlements as well as in the Kootenay and Crows Nest Pass mining districts and in exports to the United States.[27] On the strength of forestry and mining, the population of British Columbia increased by 120% between 1901 and 1911; and in the brief five years that Sikhs and other Indians enjoyed unrestricted entry to Canada, the population of Vancouver doubled.

Sikhs who arrived in small numbers in 1903 and 1904 readily found work. Those who followed in 1905 and 1906 had similar success, although they suffered initially when they disembarked 500 or 600 at a time without any indoor accommodation or immediate job to go to.[28] They were hired to do rough outdoor work for which there was an insufficient supply of white labour. The largest number were taken on by sawmills and shingle mills, particularly in the lower Fraser Valley-Vancouver region and on Vancouver Island, but also in the interior of British Columbia. Many others, however, were employed on railway construction or on railway maintenance gangs, on construction sites, on cattle farms, in orchards, and in salmon canneries. As a rule they were paid less than

---

24. Sandhu, *Indians in Malaya*, p. 124.
25. On the *Komagata Maru* there were, for example, 53 individuals from 37 villages around Ferozepur and 9 individuals from 9 villages in the Hoshiarpur area. A sample from a later period shows the same pattern. In 1939, when immigration officials were registering illegal East Indian immigrants, the 31 men from Ferozepur who came forward were from 21 villages and the 84 from Hoshiarpur were from 55 villages. So it was with men from other districts as well.
26. Dept. of Manpower and Immigration, Canada, *Immigration and Population Statistics* (Ottawa: Information Canada, 1974), p. 31, table 3.1.
27. *Report of the Forest Branch, Department of Lands, B.C. Sessional Papers*, 1914.
28. P.A.C., RG 76, file 535999, Falk Warren, retired Colonel in Royal Artillery, India, to Undersecretary of State for India, Nov. 22, 1906, copy; A.S. Munro, Immigration Agent, Vancouver, to W.D. Scott, Nov. 26, 1906, telegram; and E. Blake Robertson, Assistant Superintendent of Immigration to Scott, Dec. 27, 1906. *Vancouver Daily Province*, Nov. 17, 19, 24, 1907.

white men for the same work and they were preferred because they were less likely to leave.[29]

They were mobile, nonetheless, and went wherever opportunity beckoned. Half of them quickly crossed the American border because they could get higher wages in the sawmills and on the railway gangs of Washington and Oregon.[30] In these states they did not obtain a secure foothold. Indians earned a reputation as strikebreakers after they were used to replace striking Italian railway workers in Tacoma, Washington; and a white riot in Bellingham, Washington, discouraged employers from taking them on subsequently. Railway work led Sikhs from Washington and Oregon into California; and by the summer of 1908 they were employed as fruit pickers in the orchards of the Sacramento valley.[31] Their mobility, however, did not take them across the Rockies, nor did it get them into the metalliferous mines and coal mines of the Kootenay and Crows Nest Pass regions of eastern British Columbia and Alberta. Miners' unions opposed the employment of alien workers (those who were not Canadian, British or American), but mine owners brought in Finns, Slavs, and Italians nonetheless.[32] Hostility towards Asiatics was more intense than towards other alien workers, but that alone would not have excluded them. What kept Sikhs out of the Kootenay and Crows Nest Pass mining camps and what stopped them from crossing the Rockies was the competition of other immigrant groups brought in from the east by rail at subsidized immigrant rates. These rates were available only as far as Calgary; and while they helped to feed labour into southeastern British Columbia, they did little for the coastal region.[33] The $500 head tax on Chinese immigrants introduced in 1904 created further shortages in an undersupplied coastal labour market. This was the market that offered employment to Sikhs.

From the moment Sikhs first landed in British Columbia, they faced the hostility of civic authorities as well as of the labouring public. The mayor and council of Vancouver tried to prevent them from coming into the city on disembarkation by putting up a police cordon to keep them in the dock area until they could be loaded onto trains bound for jobs in the interior. They came back as fast as they were sent away. When 150 Sikhs abandoned work on the hydraulic mines of the Okanagan, the Vancouver press blamed the weather: a

---

29. P.A.C., RG 76, file 536999, A.S. Munro to W.D. Scott, Director of Immigration Aug. 16, 1906; Falk Warren to Undersecretary of State for India, Jan. 2, 1907, copy; McInnes to Oliver, Oct. 2, 1907; J.H. MacGill to Scott, Jan. 21, 1909; *Daily New Advertiser*, Vancouver, Oct. 19, 1906, p. 3; *Vancouver Daily Province*, Nov. 30, 1906; U.S. Senate, *Immigrants in Industries, Japanese*, pp. 330 and 352-53; Buchignani and Indra, *Continuous Journey*, pp. 17-20.

30. P.A.C., RG 76, file 536999, W.D. Scott Memorandum, Oct. 23, 1907.

31. U.S. Senate, *Immigrants in Industries, Japanese*, pp. 331-37.

32. Donald Avery, *"Dangerous Foreigners": European Immigrant Workers and Labour Radicalism in Canada, 1896-1932* (Toronto: McClelland and Stewart, 1979), pp. 25-33.

33. The British Columbia Lumber and Shingle Manufacturers Association, in September 1906, asked the C.P.R. to extend the immigrant rates from Calgary to Vancouver because shortage of labour on the coast was crippling the logging industry and affecting the sawmills. *Vancouver Daily Province*, Sept. 21, 1906.

mild Okanagan autumn was too cold for them.[34] In all likelihood, these men were simply searching out the best work and wages available and came back to Vancouver where employers were waiting for them. A survey in November, 1909, showed some Sikhs working as far east as Fernie, near the Alberta border.[35] Others would have followed if the best openings had been there.

Five years of rapid expansion in British Columbia were arrested in 1907-08 by the economic impact of a major depression in the United States. Canadian lumber prices, which had risen by 70% in the preceding six years, fell more than 20% in 1907 and lumber mills cut back production.[36] The information system that drew Asiatic labour into the province was too slow to shut off the supply with the first economic downturn. In the fall of 1907, as lumber mills laid off thousands of men, immigrants from China, Japan, and India arrived in increased numbers.[37] The Vancouver anti-Oriental riot of September, 1907, was a consequence. At this point, the Canadian Government took steps to check Oriental immigration and to stop immigration from India completely. The depression lasted twelve months. In the latter half of 1908, the economy picked up and the mills reopened. An estimated 2,500 Indians remained in the province;[38] but without more immigration from India, this community was destined to keep only a marginal and shrinking share of the labouring jobs in British Columbia.

Between 1909 and 1913, the number of lumber mills in British Columbia increased from 215 to 334 and the province's productive capacity in lumber rose by 89%.[39] For Indians this growth created no new opportunities. Lumber mill operators adjusted to the post-1907 realities and sought to make work and wages attractive to white labour. The change can be illustrated with figures from Fraser Mills in New Westminster. In 1907, the company employed 120 Indians and twenty to thirty white men. Subsequently, the company recruited French Canadians and other white labour; and while they expanded their operations, they kept fewer and fewer Indians. They employed sixty-three in 1908 and twenty-nine in 1931 although their work force by then had grown to 653.[40]

An American recession, beginning in 1913, affected British Columbia on the eve of the First World War. Lumber production fell by 30% in 1914 and it declined further the following year. Revival came in 1916, but only in 1917 did British Columbia lumber production pass 1913 levels. In the autumn of 1914,

---

34. *Vancouver Daily Province*, Oct. 6, 15, 19 and Nov. 28, 1906.
35. P.A.C., RG 7, G 21, file 332, Copy of W.C. Hopkinson's diary, Nov. 1909–Jan. 1910.
36. Report of the Forestry Commission, *British Columbia Sessional Papers*, 1911.
37. Total Asian immigration was 399 in 1904-05, 2,327 in 1905-06, 4,258 in 1906-07, and 12,623 in 1907-08: P.A.C., RG 76, file 806018, W.D. Scott to Francis W. Giddens, Dept. of Labour, Dec. 11, 1908.
38. P.A.C., RG 7, G 21, file 332, E.J.E. Swayne, Governor of British Honduras, to W. Collet, Administrator, British Honduras, Dec. 20, 1908, enclosed in Governor-General Dispatch to the Colonial Secretary, Jan. 7, 1909.
39. Forestry Commission, *B.C. Sessional Papers*, 1911; Stephen Gray, "Forest Policy and Administration in British Columbia, 1912-1928" (Ph.D. dissertation, Simon Fraser University, 1982), table 2, p. 11.
40. M. Jeanne Meyers Williams, "Ethnicity and Class Conflict at Maillardville/Fraser Mills: The Strike of 1931" (M.A. thesis, Simon Fraser University, 1982), pp. 7-9, 25.

about half of the Sikhs in British Columbia left the province for India. From the Pacific coast states of Washington, Oregon, and California there was a comparable exodus. The San Francisco-based Ghadar party was encouraging men to raise the banner of mutiny in India while Britain was at war in Europe. The governments of India and the Punjab took the Ghadar threat seriously and saw dangerous intent in the return of so many.[41] Most of these men were Ghadar sympathizers, but lack of work helped decide them to go home. By March of 1915, 3,200 emigrants had returned to India from overseas; 8,000 came back during the first two years of the war.[42] About half of these men were from North America.[43] A survey conducted by an immigration officer, late in the summer of 1915, reported that only 1,099 Indians remained in British Columbia. Of these, 750 were located in Vancouver and vicinity, 200 in Victoria and 149 in the interior. Most were working in lumber mills, a few on farms, some on railways, and some were unemployed. Hundreds had left, according to this report, because jobs were scarce.[44]

In 1918, the Deputy Minister of Labour for British Columbia reported only 567 Indians employed in industrial work in the province (including those in the forest industries but not those in agriculture).[45] The total population at that time could not have been much over 700. With the growth of the British Columbia coastal forest industry in the post-war period, the number of Indian wage earners increased until it peaked in 1923 at 1,151. The annual figures reported by the Deputy Minister of Labour suggest a considerable return of men who had been in Canada before, particularly between 1921 and 1922. By the census of 1921, there were only 951 Indians in the province, of whom 784 were employed in industrial jobs. A year later, the number employed exceeded the 1921 census population by 183. Others were self-employed. In 1922, Indians owned and operated six lumber companies, seven logging camps, two shingle mills, two grocery stores, fifty firewood outlets and twenty-five farms.[46]

The community's share of the labour market contracted somewhat after 1923, ranging between a high of 980 employed and a low of 750 over the next six years. This happened despite continued growth in coastal forest production and rising employment in the province generally. In these years, Indians were restricted more and more to the lumber industry, which meant, for most, sawmills, but also included planing mills, shingle mills, logging camps, logging

41. G.S. Deol, *The Role of the Ghadar Party in the National Movement* (Delhi: Sterling, 1969), pp. 108-48.

42. Sir Michael O'Dwyer, *India as I Knew It, 1885-1925* (London: Constable, 1926), pp. 196, 204.

43. In January, 1914, the East Indian population in Washington, Oregon, and California was an estimated 4,450; by the 1920 census it had dropped to 1,898 despite some immigration. National Archives of the United States, Dept. of Labor, Immigration Service, file 52903/110, Commissioner, Angel Island to Commissioner General of Immigration, Jan. 23, 1914, and detailed breakdown of the 1920 census in the same file.

44. P.A.C., Borden Papers, M.R.J. Reid to R. Clogstoun, Sept. 11, 1915.

45. Annual reports of the Deputy Minister of Labour, British Columbia Sessional Papers.

46. R.K. Das, *Hindustani Workers on the Pacific Coast* (Berlin and Leipzig: Walter de Gruyter, 1923), p. 27.

railways, and lumber dealerships. The numbers employed elsewhere, in the pulp and paper industry, the building trades, food processing, etc., declined from 130 in 1918 to 9 in 1928. The British Columbia public and the governments it elected did not accept Indians, Chinese or Japanese as rooted elements of the population of the province; and the comparative prosperity of the 1920's did nothing to allay anti-Oriental feeling. Government policy was aimed at reducing the economic spheres of these groups.[47] Most attention was directed at the Chinese and Japanese because their numbers were greater, but Indians suffered the same hostile climate.

In the early years of the Great Depression, between 1930 and 1932, Indians lost over 500 jobs in British Columbia.[48] As the economy slowly improved from 1934 to 1937, they were less successful than whites in getting jobs back. Some sustained themselves in the fuel business, delivering firewood, coal, and sawdust, or in other small businesses. Others chose to go back to the Punjab. The first two years of the Second World War created no new opportunities; and, at the low ebb, in 1941, there were scarcely 700 men in the province either employed or in business for themselves.

The fluctuation in numbers of Indians employed in British Columbia over the course of three decades suggests a continuing movement between Canada and India that immigration figures do not reveal. Among other immigrants who came to North America as general labourers without wives or families, the percentage that went home, sooner or later, has been high. For Italian immigrants to the U.S. between 1908 and 1924, the out-migration rate has been calculated at 45.6% of the in-migration; among Greeks it was 53.7%, and among Bulgarians, Montenegrans and Serbians it was 87%.[49] Some of these people came and went more than once. Between 1899 and 1910, 14% of the Italian immigration to the United States was made up of returnees, i.e., those coming to the United States a second or third time. More remarkable were Chinese immigrants to the United States in the same years, among whom 64% were returning after visits home.[50]

For Indians, American figures are incomplete. They indicate a net gain through immigration between 1910 and 1920 of close to 2,000.[51] Yet the 1920 census shows a sharply reduced Indian population, particularly in the Pacific coast states, where 1,898 were enumerated in place of 4,191 ten years earlier. Several thousand men had slipped out of the country unrecorded—through Mexico, perhaps, or through Canada. Canadian statistics are no better. The Immigration Department reported neither emigration nor returning immigration.

---

47. Ken Adachi, *The Enemy That Never Was: A History of the Japanese Canadians* (Toronto: McClelland and Stewart, 1976), pp. 139-53; Harry Con, Ronald J. Con, Graham Johnson et al., *From China to Canada: A History of the Chinese Communities in Canada* (Toronto: McClelland and Stewart, 1982), pp. 135-45.
48. Annual reports of the Deputy Minister of Labour.
49. Thomas J. Archdeacon, *Becoming American: An Ethnic History* (New York: The Free Press, 1983), p. 139.
50. U.S. Senate, *Statistical Review of Immigration, 1820-1910*, p. 359.
51. Das, *Hindustani Workers*, table iv, pp. 10-11.

It provided figures for people entering Canada for the first time only. One can get some idea of the amount of travel between Canada and the Orient from the fourth-class Oriental steerage figures for C.P.R. steamships. In the years 1911 through 1919, C.P.R. steamers, on the route linking Hong Kong and Yokohama to Victoria and Vancouver, carried 83,578 Oriental steerage passengers inbound to Canada and 49,927 outbound to Asia.[52]   By comparison, total Asiatic immigration in these years was only 37,493. Moreover, while the C.P.R. was the major carrier, it was not the only carrier; it competed with Japanese and American lines.

Nothing illustrates the circulation of men between British Columbia and the Punjab better than the tally of illegal Indian immigrants made by the Canadian Government in 1939.[53]   There were 622 Indians in industrial jobs in British Columbia at that time; and the male population fifteen years of age and over, could not have been much over 800. (By the census of 1941 it was 741). For political reasons—to avoid a provocative issue in Canadian-Indian relations while the empire was at war—the Canadian Government promised amnesty to Indians who had entered the country illegally.[54]   The Director of Immigration expected fifty or sixty men to come forward, but, by the end of the year, he had a list of 218. In other words, 25% or 30% of the Indian men in the province were illegal immigrants. Some had entered Canada from the United States; a few had come as students or visitors or had jumped ship; and a majority had passed themselves off as returning immigrants or the sons of landed immigrants.[55] These men, judging from the biographical details of one-third of them, ranged in age from mid-twenties to fifties; and at least half had come to Canada in the early 1930's in the worst years of the Depression. Their biographies suggest the restless travel and circuitous routes that connected the Punjab and British Columbia.[56]   One example will serve. This man arrived at the port of San Pedro, California en route to Mexico in July, 1924. In 1926 he surreptitiously entered the United States, and early in 1931 he slipped into Canada. From 1931 to 1937 he was in India; and in 1937 he had returned to Canada. A number of these illegal immigrants had worked their way north from Mexico. Many had spent from one to six years in India since coming to Canada. Of these illegal immigrants 43 subsequently applied for permission to bring in relatives.[57]   Eight of the 43 had children born in India one year or more after the fathers first arrived in Canada. Another seven had wives who would have been under the

---

52. Annual reports of Department of Trade and Commerce, *Canada Sessional Papers*.
53. P.A.C., RG 76, file 536999, List of East Indian illegal registrants during 1939 at Victoria and Vancouver, from District Superintendent, Vancouver, May 23, 1947.
54. Ibid., O.D. Skelton, Undersecretary of State for External Affairs, to F.C. Blair, Director of Immigration, 9 Sept., 1939; Buchignani and Indra, *Continuous Journey*, pp. 92-93.
55. P.A.C., RG 76, file 536999, F.W. Taylor, District Superintendent, to Commissioner of Immigration, Nov. 20, 1939.
56. F.C. Blair, Memorandum for file, September 19, 1939; D.P. Pandia to F.C. Blair, May 12, 1941, enclosing list of newly registered men who wish to bring in their families.
57. Pandia to Blair, May 12, 1914, enclosing list. Comparison of lists shows that these men were among the 218 registered in 1939.

customary marriage age when their husbands emigrated. Three others left for India within a month of being registered—two of them to get married.

These men represent a common pattern, not just among the illegal immigrants, but in the whole community. Illegal immigration was made easier because so many men went home for extended periods and were willing to sponsor an "adopted" son or to sell Canadian papers to someone else. In the early years, the Canadian immigration department did not provide Indians with documentation when they left the country, although they systematically registered out-going Chinese. The policy was deliberate and designed to make return more difficult.[58] However, Indians were allowed back in, even if they had been away for more than a year, if they could prove previous residence by presenting a steamship ticket, a tax receipt, or a property deed with their name on it, or by passing the scrutiny of immigration officers. The question of lost domicile was poorly defined in law; and officials accepted a plausible document or story rather than risk losing a challenge in court. In 1913, the immigration department began to register Indians out for absences of twelve months.[59] From 1921 on, they registered Indians out for three years; and they granted extensions. There is evidence of considerable traffic back and forth as early as 1911-1914. About 300 Indians left Canada for India in 1911 alone.[60] Between 1930 and 1932, over 100 men applied to bring in sons they claimed were conceived during visits home seventeen or eighteen years before.[61] (They wanted to get their sons into the country while they were still eligible, before they passed their eighteenth birthdays.) Some of these applications may have been fraudulent, but they tell us what was considered plausible, not just by the applicants, but by the immigration officers who dealt with them.

Many men raised families in India while working much of their lives in North America. Some went home repeatedly, and the births of their children were spread over many years. A man who applied for permission to bring his family to Canada in 1924 had children born in India in 1908, 1918, and 1922, although he had originally immigrated before 1908. An applicant in 1930 had children born in 1909, 1922, 1923, 1926, and 1927.[62] This was the experience of not just one generation, but of two. M—— belongs to the second generation of Indian-born Sikhs in British Columbia. His father came to Canada in 1906, left in 1909, and came back in 1912. He (the son) came to Canada with his father in 1927, left in 1930, came back in 1936 and left in 1939. Father and son spent the war years in India. The son returned first, and the father did not come

58. P.A.C., RG 76, file 536999, L.M. Fortier, for Superintendent of Immigration, to W.W. Cory, Deputy Minister, Interior, June 17, 1912, and J.H. MacGill, Immigration Agent Vancouver to W.D. Scott, Oct. 25, 1911.

59. Ibid., M.R.J. Reid, Immigration Agent, Vancouver, to E.W. Brodie, General Passenger Agent, C.P.R, Vancouver, Sept. 20, 1913 and M.R.J. Reid to S.N. Reid, Canadian Immigration Inspector at Seattle, Nov. 18, 1913.

60. Ibid., J.H. MacGill, to W.D. Scott, Jan. 22, 1912.

61. Ibid., List of letters issued for East Indian boys to enable them to join fathers in Canada, Oct. 1930–Oct. 1932.

62. Ibid., List of outstanding East Indian applications at Victoria, B.C., as at July 31, 1933.

back until 1954. At that point, immigration officials questioned his status as a Canadian resident, but after some hesitation they let him in.[63] A—— is a Canada-born Sikh. His grandfather came to Canada in 1908. His father was born in India in 1910 and came to Canada at the age of 16 in 1926. He returned to India in 1937 and stayed there until 1950, unable to travel during the war and delayed by the events of 1947.[64] The men of these two families were polyseasonal migrants who kept their families and maintained their homes in India for more than forty years after they first came to Canada.

There were virtually no women among the pioneer immigrants. The 1911 census shows only three women in British Columbia out of a population of 2,292. As a matter of policy, the C.P.R. did not carry women in its fourth-class Asiatic steerage and that meant that it cost more for them to emigrate.[65] In any case, the attraction was work, not life in Canada, and men had no incentive to bring dependents. The orders-in-council that barred Indian immigration after May-June 1908, made no exceptions for wives and children; after that, men already in the country were unable to bring in their families if they sought to do so. This remained the case for eleven years. It is unlikely that many women would have come at that time, whatever the law was. Over 5,000 Indians immigrated to the United States between 1908 and 1920.[66] Yet there were only 98 Indian females in the whole country by the 1920 census, and only 27 in the Pacific coast states, where the Sikh population was concentrated. Nonetheless, in 1911, Indians in British Columbia mounted a campaign for the admission of wives. Officials suspected that issue had been taken up by activists in the Indian community for strategic reasons because it was more likely to evoke sympathy than the question of male immigration.[67] If the only appeal had been to public sentiment in British Columbia, the agitation would have achieved no results for several decades. The Secretary of State for India, however, pushed the Canadian Government to make some concession, pointing to the damage the issue was doing to the morale of Sikh troops.[68] In 1918, after three years of negotiation, the Canadian Government agreed to admit the wives and minor children (under eighteen) of Indians legally resident in the country. The new regulations became effective in 1919.[69]

In the twelve years that followed, up to March 31, 1931, only 172 women immigrated. In the Depression years, fewer came—only sixty-nine in the ten

63. Interviewed in Vancouver, Sept. 1983.
64. Interviewed in Vancouver, Nov. 1984.
65. From the C.P.R. Pacific Steamship Service and Royal Mail Line brochure for 1906-07 on p. 7: "Asiatic Steerage. Chinese, Japanese and other Asiatics only will be booked in this class. Females will not be carried in Asiatic Steerage."
66. Das, *Workers*, pp. 10-11.
67. Vancouver City Archives, Stevens Papers, copy of "Private Memorandum re Hindu Immigration: Particularly with reference to the present agitation for the admission of wives and families of the Hindus now resident in Canada," Jan. 26, 1939.
68. Austen Chamberlain, to Robert Borden, Sept. 10, 1915, cited in Ministère des Affaires Extérieures, *Documents relatifs aux relations extérieures du Canada* (Ottawa: Queen's Printer, 1967), pp. 658-59.
69. Buchignani and Indra, *Continuous Journey*, pp. 65-66.

years up to March 31, 1941.[70] It cost more to maintain a family in Canada than in India. While wages were good, employment for Indians was limited, and the situation was insecure for the Sikh community as a whole and for individuals within it. The social environment was alien and hostile and the pull of home and village strong. For these reasons, for every man who brought out his wife, several did not.

Official figures show an immigration of 431 Indian children and 135 men between 1919 and 1941. Most of the children were boys, and many of them were sixteen- or seventeen-year-olds who were brought in as minors while they were still eligible. Similarly, many of those classified as adults were young men who had applied to immigrate before they were eighteen, but who had arrived in Canada subsequently. By 1931, Fraser Mills in New Westminster had been employing Indians for a quarter of a century. Although the number had shrunk, there were still twenty-nine there that year. This group of twenty-nine included twenty-three married men. Only seven of those men had brought their wives to Canada.[71] This situation characterized the community as a whole. Men had accepted separation as the price of employment in Canada, and this attitude was slow to change.

The 1941 census found 1,465 Indians in Canada with 91.7% of them in British Columbia. Through legal immigration, illegal immigration, and natural increase, at least 600 Indians had been added to the Canadian population between 1931 and 1941, yet the census count showed an increase of only sixty-five. This means that almost 40% of the people present for one census were not there for the next. An analysis of the age and sex composition of the Indian community reveals how tentative its roots were after the passage of almost forty years.[72] The community included 424 Canada-born children, of whom 356 were born in British Columbia. Most of these children were under ten years of age, and very few were over fifteen. In British Columbia the adult population (fifteen years and over) was 82.8% male. About 25% of the women who had immigrated over the preceding twenty years had since left, either temporarily or permanently. At the time of the census, 442 of the men were old enough to be pioneers, although some were not, having immigrated illegally later on. Most of the pioneers had been between eighteen and thirty in 1908, and they were now in their fifties and early sixties. The oldest were in their eighties. Another 290 or 300 men belonged to the post-1908 generation of immigrants. There were two men for every woman between the ages of fifteen and fifty; but there were twenty men for every woman over fifty. Although some men married women considerably younger than themselves, it is still evident that few

---

70. Figures calculated from annual reports of the Superintendent of Immigration, Department of the Interior, and, subsequently, Department of Immigration and Colonization, *Canada Sessional Papers*.
71. Williams, "The Strike of 1931," table iv, p. 27.
72. P.A.C., RG 76, file 536999, Memorandum for the Under-Secretary of State for External Affairs concerning the position of the East Indian group under Dominion and Provincial Legislation, 10 August, 1945, Appendix B (census data).

pioneers ever lived a married life in Canada and that most of the families were those of younger men.

Over half of the women who immigrated before 1950, did so in the seven years from 1924 to the spring of 1931, four-fifths in the fourteen years from 1921 to the spring of 1935.[73] Their productive child-bearing years were concentrated between 1930 and 1942; and most of their children reached school age after 1939.[74] Some went on to high school, but the majority did not. The number of Indian children attending schools in British Columbia rose steadily until 1948, when 644 were enrolled. In the next few years, there was a marked decline in numbers as this cohort passed through the system. Only in the 1950's did the first generation of Canada-born children reach marriage age. As a rule, families sought partners for their children in India. They did so to reinforce cultural ties, and because it was difficult to find a boy or girl in the small Canadian Sikh population who was from the right caste, sub-caste, and village, and who was acceptable in all other respects. In 1949, the Indian community lobbied for the right to bring in fiancées; and from 1951 on they were able to do so.[75] Only sixteen brides and fourteen grooms had arrived by the end of 1955.[76] Some young men went back to India to be married and returned with their brides as wives. Nonetheless, the formation of second-generation Sikh families was only partially under way by the mid-1950's.

The status of the Indian community improved in 1947 when Indian citizens in British Columbia obtained the right to vote, and in 1951 when the Canadian Government amended its immigration regulations after negotiations with the Republic of India. The old regulations had limited immigration to the wives and unmarried children under eighteen of Indians who were resident citizens of Canada. (Most Indians in the country were deemed to be citizens by virtue of long residence, even if they had not formally applied for papers.)[77] The new regulations introduced a quota of 150 citizens of India a year, not including the husbands, wives and unmarried children under twenty-one of Canadian citizens, who were admissible without quota restrictions.[78] The quota made possible the entry of independent immigrants, unrelated to Canadian citizens and from communities in India which, as yet, had no foothold in Canada. It also made

---

73. Calculation based on figures in annual reports of the Department of Immigration and Colonization. In addition to the steerage passengers one adult female arrived in 1918-19, one in 1919-20, as saloon passengers.
74. In 1925-26, 20 East Indian children attended schools in B.C., in 1929-30, 67; in 1933-34, 116; in 1939-40, 264; in 1942-43, 309; in 1948-49, 644; and in 1952-53, 372. See Reports of the Public Schools of the Province of British Columbia, *British Columbia Sessional Papers.*
75. P.A.C., RG 76, file 3-33-15, pt. 2, Resumé of East Indian immigration to Canada showing concessions granted since 1945, signed C.E.S. Smith, 21 Jan., 1958.
76. Ibid., RG 76, v. 714, India quota list.
77. Memorandum for the Under-Secretary of State for External Affairs, 10 August, 1945, p. 2, section 8.
78. Ibid., RG 76, file 3-33-15, pt. 2, Memo: Information on Canada-India Immigration Agreement, 1957, signed by Laval Fortier, Deputy Minister, Citizenship and Immigration, Aug. 1, 1957.

possible the admission of fiancées and relatives previously excluded. In April, 1957, under a new agreement with India, the quota was raised to 300.

In the first five years (1951-1955), 419 quota immigrants and 187 non-quota immigrants (husbands, wives and children) arrived in Canada from India.[79] The number of close relatives that Sikhs in Canada wished to sponsor was small, but the number of more distant male relatives considerable.[80] In the administration of the quota, a tug-of-war developed between officials of the Department of Immigration and the Sikh community, which put pressure on the minister through local members of Parliament (a practical benefit of the right to vote).[81] The officials wished to reserve as many places as possible for independent immigrants with professional or other special qualifications, arguing that these people were more easily integrated and more acceptable to the Canadian public than general labourers admitted as the relatives of Canadian citizens.[82] In assigning places to relatives, they tried to give priority to close relatives: to the wives and unmarried children of recently arrived immigrants (who had to come within the quota), to parents or to fiancées. On the other hand, the Sikh community in Canada applied far more frequently for brothers than for wives, for sons than for daughters, and for nephews, male cousins, and brothers-in-law than for parents.

In 1952, for the sake of expediency, the whole quota was allocated to applicants from Canada and, consequently, was made up largely of adult male relatives. From 1952 through 1956, the Immigration Department attempted to reserve 100 quota numbers for applications made in India.[83] The immigration attaché in New Delhi was overwhelmed with applications; and for the first two years he simply acted as a screen, rejecting most of the applications and sending the best ones to Ottawa for decisions. After 1954 he was authorized to assign quota places on his own, but the system still worked against the independent applicant without relatives in Canada. From 1951 to the end of 1956, two-thirds of the quota went to sponsored relatives rather than to independent immigrants and their dependents.[84] In 1957, when the quota was raised to 300, the minister set aside 225 spots for applications from Canada. In the next year officials were able to reduce this to 150. Up to that point, Sikhs in Canada had monopolized

-----

79. Ibid., Laval Fortier, Deputy Minister, Citizenship and Immigration, to Jules Léger, Under Secretary of State, External Affairs, Aug. 17, 1956, copy. All of the quota spots had been assigned; but almost half of the people cleared for immigration under the quota had not immigrated by the end of 1955.

80. Ibid., Fortier to the Minister, Citizenship and Immigration, Oct. 28, 1954.

81. A note from J.W. Pickersgill, Minister of Citizenship and Immigration on a departmental memo that mentions special pleading in East Indian quota cases: "I would prefer to give Fulton his two grandnephews and Pearkes his two nephews—but put one over to 1955 in each case. Others O.K." Pearkes and Fulton were opposition M.P.'s. See Fortier to the Minister, Oct. 28, 1954.

82. RG 26, file 3-33-15, pt. 2, Fortier to the Minister, April 16, 1957.

83. Resumé of East Indian Immigration to Canada, Jan. 21, 1958, and Fortier to the Minister, Oct. 28, 1954.

84. My analysis of the quota list (RG 76, v. 714).

the quota; and they had done so despite activity in the immigration office in Delhi, which had been receiving close to 100 applications a month.[85]

For this reason, the quota admitted many men destined for the general labour force, and comparatively few professionals. Only 10% of the quota spots went to professionals and their dependents from 1951 through 1956, and even as late as 1959, less than 30%. No more than one in six or seven of these professionals was a Sikh.[86] The annual figures reported by the immigration department disguise these features of the immigration from India because the tables listing immigrants by occupation use the category "East Indian" without regard to country of origin. Of so-called East Indian immigrants arriving from 1953 through 1959, less than three-quarters came from India. Fourteen per cent were immigrants from the United Kingdom with United Kingdom citizenship. The rest were from Pakistan, Ceylon, the West Indies and elsewhere.[87] In the 1950's, more "East Indian" professionals came from these countries than from India; and few professionals from India were Sikhs.

Similarly, most of the increase in the immigration of women and children that became apparent after 1955 was among non-Sikh immigrants. Sikhs continued to go to British Columbia, while Ontario and Quebec absorbed most of the other South Asian immigrants.[88] The 1961 census reflected the higher level of female immigration among non-Sikhs. In the Ontario South Asian community, although it was new, females were 44% of the population. In British Columbia they were only 38%. The persistent imbalance between sexes among the Sikhs of British Columbia was the result of an immigration heavily weighted towards males that had exceeded the natural increase of a small group of settled families. The dominant element in the adult population, numerically and politically, was the India-born. This was the case and had always been the case, although the community was nearly sixty years old.

The original immigration from the Punjab to British Columbia, in the five years up to 1908, had been a spontaneous movement, financed in India, of young men who came not as independent immigrants, but as contributing members of families in villages and on land in the Punjab. In a period of rapid economic expansion in Canada, these men obtained a limited niche in the British Columbia coastal lumber industry. The possibility of enlarging that niche, or of exploiting beyond it, was cut off for half a century by the immigration barrier erected by the Canadian Government in 1908. Through boom times and bust (with the exception of the years 1918-22), the Punjabi Sikh share of jobs in British Columbia tended to shrink, principally because employers realized that this

85. P.A.C., RG 76, file 3-33-15, pt 2, C.E.S. Smith, Director, Dept. of Citizenship and Immigration, to Deputy Minister, Aug. 1, 1956.

86. My analysis of the quota list.

87. Annual reports of the Department of Citizenship and Immigration, *Canada Sessional Papers*.

88. To the present, Sikhs remain concentrated in B.C. Although the 1981 census showed more people of Indian origin in Ontario than in B.C., Sikhs were distributed: 40,940 in B.C., 16,650 in Ontario, and 10,120 in the rest of the country.

reservoir of labour could not be tapped any further, and looked elsewhere. Having come to Canada without thought of settlement, few Sikh immigrants reconsidered, although many stayed for years or for the rest of their lives. Under these circumstances, some men made repeated visits home and there was a constant exchange of population between British Columbia and the Punjab. British Columbia to the Punjab was rather like Newfoundland seen from Devon and Cornwall in the seventeenth and eighteenth centuries: a distant place of employment for men. Inevitably, families established themselves in British Columbia, but the community remained an immigrant community without the benefit of free immigration for half a century. A more open immigration policy might not have changed matters radically. Among Sikhs in Malaya, family immigration did not begin until after 1945.[89]   Canadian Sikhs, in the 1950's, were tied to family and village in their land of origin with an intensity shared by few other immigrant communities of the same age in Canada; and the Sikh population in the Punjab with familial connections in Canada was far more extensive than the small number of Sikhs in Canada might have suggested.

89. Sandhu, *Indians in Malaya*, p. 125.

Ethnicity Confounded:
Punjabi Pioneers in California

Karen Leonard

Attempts to understand ethnicity and its relationship to social class and religious affiliation have generated scholarly inquiry and debate in the social sciences for decades. After Barth's important work,[1] most scholars have moved away from viewing ethnicity as "primordial," i.e., as ascribed to a group that is largely biologically self-perpetuating (endogamous), with group members sharing values, institutions, and a field of communication and interaction.[2] Recent work has pointed to individual exercise of "situational ethnicity"[3] and the role of the state in determining ethnic identity.[4] In an unpublished essay, John Comaroff states that ethnicity is constituted by specific historical forces and cannot be used to explain other phenomena, being itself a product in need of explanation. Further, he argues that it is the marking of ethnic identities in relation to others, not the substance of ethnic identities, that is primordial, and this marking is rooted in "the asymmetric incorporation of structurally dissimilar groupings into a unitary political economy."[5] Finally, he talks of ethnicity taking on the appearance of an autonomous force, and, paradoxically, becoming stronger in the cultural sense as class differentiation proceeds within the designated group. (Here he observes that both Weber and Marx had the historical process going the other way, with primordial affinities based on status giving way to affinities based on class.)

Comaroff draws on historical and contemporary material from Africa to illustrate his points, but his analysis applies equally well to rural California, where I have studied a systematically bi-ethnic community known as the "Mexican-Hindus." Unlike most immigrants from India, the Punjabi pioneers in early twentieth-century California married women not of their background,

---

1. Barth 1969.
2. Narroll 1964.
3. Cohen 1978, pp. 387-89.
4. Brass 1985.
5. Comaroff 1984, p. 9.

[Joseph T. O'Connell, Milton Israel, Willard G. Oxtoby, eds., with W.H. McLeod and J.S. Grewal, visiting eds., *Sikh History and Religion in the Twentieth Century* (S. Asian Studies Papers, 3) (Toronto: S. Asian Studies, Univ. of Toronto, 1988)]

women of a different religion and national origin: they married Hispanic women, both Mexican and Mexican-American.   (As we shall see, state laws helped determine their choice of spouses.)   These couples and their children were termed "Mexican-Hindu" by the rural California communities in which they lived.   There are "Japanese-Mexicans" and "Chinese-Mexicans,"[6] but we know little of their family life.   The Chinese in Mississippi, some of whom married black women, have been studied too, but again the mixed marriages have been little emphasized in the work.[7]   In fact, there seem to be few systematically bi-ethnic communities like the Mexican-Hindus, and there is no detailed socio-economic study of such a bi-ethnic community.[8]   I have used historical sources and interviews to follow the immigrants and their descendants, examining the choices they made with implications for ethnicity; I have also reconstructed the historical circumstances that played a large part in shaping those choices.   Here is a community so small and idiosyncratic that the state took no official notice of it, a community that lasted only one, possibly two, generations in any structural sense; yet its history tells us a great deal about ethnicity, the relationship of ethnicity to social class and religion, and the flexibility and persistence of ethnicity over time.

The origins of the Mexican-Hindu community lie in the Imperial Valley and its development as a center of agricultural production after 1907.   The Valley is located in California's southeast corner along the border with Mexico. The building of the American hemisphere's largest irrigation system there drew ambitious men from all over the world.   Although Anglos dominated, the 1920 census shows many other groups represented.   Especially numerous were Mexicans, Japanese, and blacks, followed by Canadians, Swiss, Germans, English, Greeks, Italians, Irish and Portuguese.[9]

Among the early arrivals in the Imperial Valley were Punjabi immigrants from India's Northwestern Frontier Province.   These Punjabis, predominantly Sikhs, were continuing a long-standing practice whereby farming families in the Punjab sent one or more sons out of the Punjab to earn money.   Punjabis constituted a disproportionate part of the British Indian military and police services.   They worked throughout the British Empire, in the Middle East,

---

6. There were a few Japanese-Mexicans in the Imperial Valley, but nothing has been written about them.   The large community in Mexico has been the subject of a master's thesis by Chizuko Watanabe, "The Japanese Immigrant Community in Mexico: Its History and Present" (California State University, Los Angeles, 1983).   Chinese-Mexicans are somewhat more numerous in the Valley and especially across the border in Mexico; no systematic work appears to have been done on them.

7. James W. Loewen, *The Mississippi Chinese: Between Black and White* (Cambridge, Mass.: Harvard University Press, 1971) is excellent on race relations but offers few details of family life for the early Chinese-black families; Robert S. Quan, *Lotus among the Magnolias* (Jackson: University Press of Mississippi, 1982), scarcely mentions such families.

8. Susan Benson's fine *Ambiguous Ethnicity: Interracial Families in London* (Cambridge: Cambridge University Press, 1981) is a model of research on ethnicity within families, but her couples are not part of any one community.

9. U.S. Bureau of the Census, *Fourteenth Census of the United States*, v. III, *Population, 1920* (Washington, D.C.: Government Printing Office, 1923), pp. 109, 113, 123-24.

Africa, Southeast Asia and the China treaty ports;[10] the largest number of those in California came from service in Shanghai and Hong Kong or through relatives in service there. Once in California, they worked in the lumber industry, in railroad building, and in agriculture. Most were Jat Sikhs, from landowning families in the central Punjab. They began as migrant laborers, moving in groups around the state with a "boss man" who knew English and contracted for the group with employers.

Americans called these Punjabi immigrants "Hindus," a term which simply denoted those who came from Hindustan or India. It had a strong pejorative content at first. Stereotyped as the least desirable of the immigrants from Asia, uneducated peasants with particularly obnoxious beliefs and habits, the Hindus were not wanted even as laborers. Their appearance in the Imperial Valley was heralded by alarmed headlines when they were brought in to pick the cotton crop in 1910.[11] Only a few years later their movement out of the labor category to become landowners aroused more apprehension;[12] they and the Japanese were contrasted unfavorably with the Mexicans, who were allegedly content to remain in their place.[13] The thinking of the time, that various national and ethnic groups filled different niches in the economic system, is quite clear in the contemporary sources, which constantly compared the Hindus to others involved in agricultural labor.[14]

For the Punjabi men, the term "Hindu" was a religious misnomer. In fact, 85% to 90% of the men were Sikhs and another 8-10% were Muslims; a very small percentage were actually Hindus. I have argued elsewhere[15] that religion was not a major component of their identity in the early decades in the United States and I want to reiterate that point here: the Punjabi language and its regional culture united the Punjabi men across religious lines. Partnerships formed to lease and farm agricultural land included Sikhs, Muslims, and Hindus in the Imperial Valley; local associations did the same. The Sikh temple founded in Stockton in northern California in 1912 included Muslim and Hindu men in its political, social and religious activities. Finally, the men were extremely political. Sensitive to their status as colonial subjects, they thought Americans saw them as slaves to the British.[16] They formed the Ghadar party in 1913 in California, a militant nationalist party which sent money and men back

10. Barrier 1987, pp. 11-16; Wood 1966, pp. 14-16.
11. *Holtville Tribune*, September 16, October 21, 1910.
12. *Holtville Tribune*, January 24, February 4, 1918.
13. "We need the labor of the Mexicans. They are not like the Japs and Hindus. They don't come to stay. They are satisfied to labor," said the secretary of the El Centro Chamber of Commerce (Robert Hays) in 1928. Paul Taylor, field notes for his book, *Mexican Labor in the United States, 1927-1930*, ed. by Abraham Hoffman, 72-77. Bancroft Library, University of California, Berkeley.
14. Evaluations differed from region to region, but the Hindus generally earned negative remarks in the early years. An exception is the interview with Mr. William Richardson, retired foreman of the Lucius Powers Ranch in Sanger, who found the Indians the best of all classes of labor, better than Japanese, Mexicans, Greeks, Armenians, and white laborers. Interview No. 90, February 18, 1925, Survey of Race Relations, Hoover Institute, Stanford. (Thanks to Sucheng Chan for reference to this source.)
15. Leonard forthcoming (a).
16. Puri 1980, p. 129.

to the Punjab for terrorist activities against the British. They also formed regional (Malwa, Doaba) political groups in the 1920's, after factionalism splintered the Ghadar effort to some extent.[17] The men worked together, formed social, religious and political institutions in California, and were self-identified and identified by others as "Hindus." One could argue for a male ethnic group, if such a thing made any sense, particularly in the central and northern areas of the state, where more of the Punjabi men stayed bachelors.

But in the south, in the Imperial Valley, many of the Punjabi men married and formed families. Most of them had been married in India and had left families there, but those who decided to stay in California faced a difficult choice. The restrictive immigration laws prevented them from bringing their wives; the same laws prevented the men from visiting India and returning to the U.S., since they could not be readmitted legally. They could live as bachelors in the U.S. or they could marry local women. If they wanted women to live with them, to cook and clean for them, to bear their children, they had to look to local women, and the women they turned to were overwhelmingly Mexican and Mexican-American (see the appendix for origins of spouses and regional distribution of couples).

There were many reasons for choosing Hispanic women. Mexican women were beautiful; they resembled Punjabis physically. Mexicans and Punjabis had a similar material culture, a rural way of life with similar types of food, furniture, etc. Mexicans and Punjabis shared an initially low class status in California.[18] But it was more than a matter of individual choice, for there were early marriages or affairs with Anglo women and with black women too. The fact was that miscegenation laws prohibited marriages across racial lines in California until 1948, and most California county clerks saw the Punjabi men as colored, or "brown," the word they used most often to describe the men in the blank on the marriage license for race. Thus the women the Punjabis married also had to be perceived as "brown," and that generally meant Hispanic women. So, it was Hispanic women whom they could marry legally. Finally, why did they choose to marry their women, rather than just live with them? One answer is that they did not always marry them.[19] Another answer is that marriage generally gives men power over women, and the Punjabis did not expect marriage in the U.S. to be substantially different from what they knew back in India.

---

17. On the militant Ghadar party, see Vatuk and Vatuk 1969 and Puri 1980, 1983. For the Malwa Sudharak Society, see Civil Suit 25280, San Joaquin County, 1932, and its appeal to the California Supreme Court in 1936, 54 P2d 1099 5 C2d 405. For disputes, see Jane Singh's interview with Mrs. Puna Singh, transcribed tape, *Gadar* collection, University of California, Berkeley, pp. 14-15, and notes from Jane Singh's interview with Kesar S. Dillon, 1976, tape 3, side 2.

18. LaBrack and Leonard 1984.

19. Marriage licenses could not be found for all couples; I searched sixteen county record offices and assume that many more marriage licenses do exist. I included on my master list all those relationships that produced children or that lasted long enough for people to mention them as a couple.

Hispanic women were available primarily in southern California. Mexican migration to the U.S. was just beginning in the decade of the 1910's, fueled by the Mexican Revolution and its attendant political and economic turmoil, and it was beginning along the southern border with Mexico. In Texas and California, where cotton was being cultivated by the Punjabi men with the help of Mexican immigrant labor, these bi-ethnic marriages initiated the Mexican-Hindu community. There was a status difference in the very earliest marriages between wealthy "Hindu" farmers from Holtville and Mexican women working in their fields.[20] Other Punjabi-Mexican marriages followed, usually reflecting the same status difference. There was also an age difference, the men characteristically being in their 30's and 40's and their brides in their teens and 20's. The women were almost all Catholic, but the marriage ceremonies were civil ones, and the signatures of bride and groom alike testified to illiteracy or a low level of literacy.[21] Rudimentary English or Spanish served as a common language.

At the time these marriages began to occur, ethnic similarities between the men and women were most striking. Like Mexicans,[22] the Punjabis were discriminated against by white society; if anything, initial opinion of them was even more strongly prejudiced. At least half of the women were, like the men, pioneers in a new country and from a group entering the same economic niche. The men were learning Spanish, to deal with Mexican agricultural laborers and to speak to their wives. Some Punjabi men adopted Spanish names or nicknames: Miguel for Magyar, Andreas for Inder, Mondo for Mohamed. The Mexican-American influence may have been preceded by Spanish influence in the Philippines: one man, for example, had taken the name Vicente during his stay there on the way to California and had enjoyed a flirtation with a local girl. In San Francisco, the early Muslim immigrants went into business selling tamales to sailors. Finally, the very first conjugal relationship documented, in 1913, was a common-law marriage with an Hispanic woman.[23]

Once initiated, the Punjabi-Mexican marriage pattern became well established. The first brides recruited other women, their relatives and friends, for marriages with Punjabi men. Sisters with small children who had been deserted or widowed were called from Mexico to marry Punjabis. The men travelled too, some from northern California to Texas for marriages (and journeys took much

20. Sher Singh and Gopal Singh, wealthy cotton farmers in Holtville, married Antonia and Anna Alvarez on Nov. 7, 1916, and July 16, 1917, respectively: Imperial County Recorder's Office, marriage license numbers 5:164 of 1916 and 5:388 of 1917; interview with descendant Harry Chand, Live Oak, 1982.

21. These conclusions come from my analysis of 111 California marriage licenses, which record age, occupation, marriage performer, and signatures.

22. For the situation faced by Mexicans, see Paul S. Taylor, "Mexican Labor in the United States: Imperial Valley," *University of California Publications in Economics*, vol. 6, no. 1 (Berkeley, California, 1928).

23. Mola Singh, life story interviews, for his experiences in the Philippines (Selma, 1982); Salim Khan, "A Brief History of the Pakistanis in the Western United States" (unpublished M.A. dissertation, History, Sacramento State University, 1981), for the San Francisco food vendors; specifically for tamales, Joe Mallobox (El Centro, 1982). The first common-law wife was murdered by her husband: *Contra Costa Gazette*, October 25, 1913 (brought to my attention by Harold Jacoby, who refers to it in his unpublished manuscript of 1978).

longer in those days).[24] One Sikh from the Imperial Valley took the train to El Paso, looking for the nieces of a Mexican woman working for him. He knocked on the wrong door, and the mother and three daughters on the other side of it mistook him at first for a Turk because of his turban, but in a few days he and his bride and her mother and sisters were on the train back to El Centro. His partners married the sisters and eventually the mother also married a Punjabi Sikh.[25] This was a typical pattern; many sets of sisters or female relatives married partners and formed joint households out along the irrigation canals or country roads. The women's network was strengthened further with the birth of children, when the *compadrazgo* system of fictive kinship drew upon the women's relatives and friends as religious sponsors. Punjabi men stood as godfathers to each other's children in this basically Catholic system, but they were not central to it.

How can these bi-ethnic marriages be understood? The reaction of the dominant Anglo society in rural California provides some insights. Hostile headlines greeted the first filing for a marriage license by a Punjabi in the Imperial Valley. The reporter seemingly disapproved of this indication that the Punjabis meant to stay, and also questioned the legality of a Punjabi-Mexican marriage.[26] A marriage two years later aroused even more antagonism, for the woman involved was white, the sixteen-year-old daughter of her Punjabi groom's white tenant farmer! Other Punjabis were involved with white women in the Imperial Valley in the early years. Not surprisingly, white society came to sanction the marriages to "Mexican girls" and even helped the Punjabi men control them.[27]

By turning to the lower-status Hispanic group for women, the Punjabis ceased to threaten white society. They may even have strengthened their relationship with white men, because Punjabis and whites were prejudiced against Hispanics. By marrying women whom they were not expected to bring into their business and social dealings with white men, the Punjabis built male comradeship that rested on a tacit exclusion of their wives and families.[28]

---

24. Twenty-eight marriage licenses from Las Cruces, New Mexico (where people went from El Paso because of the Texas three-day waiting period between license and ceremony) show grooms from Yuba City, Marysville, and Fresno, as well as El Centro, Calipatria, and towns in Arizona. Fifteen of the brides were from Mexico, thirteen from Texas and New Mexico (Doña Ana County Recorder's Office, New Mexico).

25. This was Kehar Singh Gill, who married Matilde Sandoval: Interview with Mary Garewal Gill (Holtville, 1981), daughter of Lala Sandoval, who came and married Sucha Singh Garewal, Kehar Singh Gill's partner, and Lala Sandoval Garewal, Mary Garewal Gill, Silveria Chell and Bob Chell (Holtville, 1982).

26. *Holtville Tribune*, March 16, 1916; this first marriage license was not utilized, and Sher Singh took out another one (for another woman, too) later: *Holtville Tribune*, November 10, 1916.

27. *El Centro Progress*, April 5, 1918, trumpeted "Hindu Weds White Girl by Stealing Away to Arizona" about B.K. Singh's marriage. Another wed a white woman in 1918 (Mit Singh and Jessie Powell, San Diego, June 14). Mola Singh told me of his affair with a white woman and the lawsuit it brought against him (Selma, 1982); in the same interview Mola Singh recounted an episode from his second marriage to an Hispanic woman, when he got advice from a local judge on how to control his Mexican wife.

28. Anglo bankers and farmers close to Punjabi farmers almost never met their wives and clearly preferred it that way.

Similarly, Anglos, Punjabis, and Mexicans were all prejudiced against blacks, brought in to pick cotton in the same decade; the Punjabi association in the Imperial Valley cautioned its members not to marry black women.   An association member justified the policy as a desire to avoid connection with the lowest status group in American society.[29]

One interpretation of these bi-ethnic marriages was Dadabhay's theory of "circuitous assimilation" (1954), which proposed that the Punjabi men were assimilating into American society by way of a subculture.   He thought that discrimination and a high rate of intermarriage drove Asian Indians into the Mexican-American subculture, which readily accepted them.   But that was not the case.   The relationship was asymmetrical; the Punjabi men had no women to give.   They took wives only from the Hispanic community and they were prejudiced against that community, on the whole.   Despite some friendships and several cases of parents-in-law living with their daughter and her Punjabi husband, few Punjabi men were close to their Mexican relatives or other Mexicans.   The one instance I found of a Punjabi-Mexican partnership ended in lawsuits.[30]   Punjabi men may have classified the women as close to them in culture, but they clearly viewed Mexicans as a group as "other."

Mexican men strongly objected to these marriages; there were instances of violent retaliation against the women and the Punjabi men involved.[31]   Several women testified to derogatory comments and name-calling by Mexicans because of their marriages, and it is striking that the majority of the *compadrazgo* relationships formed to sponsor baptisms, confirmations, and first communions of the children drew upon Punjabi men and their Hispanic spouses rather than upon Hispanic couples.[32]   The *compadrazgo* system did not integrate the Punjabi men into the Catholic Church or the Mexican-American community; it strengthened relationships among members of the Mexican-Hindu community. In effect the women were cut off from their community when they married Punjabis; they did not draw their husbands into the Mexican-American community.

The first decade of Punjabi-Hispanic marriages may have promised to establish a community.   Certainly the Mexican-Hindu couples did visit each other and hold dinners and dances.   They produced many children, and the *compadrazgo* system linked them through their children.   But as time went on,

---

29. *Constitution and By-laws of the Imperial Valley Hindustanees' Welfare and Reform Association* (Imperial: n.d., p. 7) discouraged marriages with "negroes" and "other women who are undesirables"; interview with Bagga S. Sunga (El Centro, 1981).

30. Imperial County Civil Case no. 35078 of 1961; interview with Judge Lehnert (Brawley, 1981).

31. *El Centro Progress*, [month torn off] 9, 1918, for the story of a race riot resulting from an oath of vengeance made by several Mexicans who went to a Punjabi-Mexican couple's home to attack them; *Holtville Tribune*, March 9 and 10, 1922, for the story of the abduction of two brides of Punjabis to Mexico and their beating there. The latter was confirmed by the daughter of one of the abducted women, Janie Diwan Poonian (Yuba City, 1982).

32. Interviews with Nellie Soto Shine and Caroline Shine Sunghera Resendez (Huntington Beach, 1982); and Lala Garewal Gill, Silveria Chell, Bob Chell, and Mary Garewal Gill (Holtville, 1981).

both external and internal circumstances changed, and the changes threatened the fragile bonds between Hispanic women and Punjabi men. Although many couples proved to be exceptions, on the whole a process of distancing occurred, not so much because of the substantive content of the two ethnic identities but because of state laws, differential stratification within the two groups, and the changing social evaluation of the groups by the dominant culture. The women too, like their Mexican relatives and countrymen, gradually came to be viewed as "other" by the Punjabi men, and many fathers treated their Mexican-Hindu children with considerable ambivalence.

Federal and state law changed, and treated Punjabis and Mexicans differently with respect to immigration and citizenship. In 1917, Asia immigration was prohibited under the Barred Zone Act.[33] In 1923, the Thind decision by the U.S. Supreme Court made Asian Indians ineligible for U.S. citizenship and therefore subject to California's Alien Land Laws.[34] These laws provided that "aliens ineligible for citizenship" could not own or lease agricultural land, potentially cutting the Punjabis off from their livelihood. Punjabis and Mexicans now had very different rights under the law and very different access to the political process. To complicate this further, the Hispanic wives, both Mexican-born and American citizens, lost their citizenship or their eligibility for it by marrying an alien ineligible for citizenship. This was the provision of the federal Cable Act, in effect from 1922 through 1931. So the wives, who might have been used to holding land on behalf of their husbands, were unable to do so legally during the crucial 1920's.[35] Some men did put land in the names of their wives (the extent to which the Cable Act was actually enforced in the Imperial Valley is unclear) and regretted it when divorce or marital conflict threatened their control of that land. Land could be put in the name of one's mother-in-law or brother-in-law, but this proved even riskier. So the Punjabi men turned to Anglo landowners, lawyers, and judges to hold land for them and to honor verbal leases.[36]

The Punjabis had begun leasing and buying land soon after their arrival in the Valley. Many had secured large loans from local banks to grow cotton. A bank official recalled that the Punjabis got such loans at a time when Mexicans could not even walk in the door of his bank.[37] By the time the Alien Land Law

33. The 1917 Immigration Law also contained a provision (meant for Europeans) which stopped Mexican immigration until its suspension for Mexicans, a provision requiring a literacy test and an $8.00 head tax. Mario Garcia, "On Mexican Immigration, the United States, and Chicano History," *The Journal of Ethnic Studies* 7:1 (spring 1979), p. 83.
34. Jacoby 1958; Melendy 1981; Lesser 1985.
35. Although later allegations abound, there is no contemporary comment about "Hindus" gaining access to land by way of these marriages. The 1923 Thind decision subjecting them to the Alien Land Law came after the marriage pattern was well established. Had these marriages been instrumental in giving the Punjabis control of land, the white establishment presumably would have opposed rather than accepted them. On the other hand, a shared prejudice against Mexicans can be seen in the way Anglo friends, lawyers, and judges in the Valley helped Punjabis retain their land when some put it in the names of their wives' relatives and then had to fight off attempts to claim it.
36. Leonard 1985.
37. Former president of the Holtville Bank, Keith Savage, for the statement about Mexicans (Holtville, 1981); for the loans, see Laguna Niguel Federal Archives, Federal Bankruptcy Records,

was applied to them, the "good farmers" among them were already allied with members of the white power structure. Punjabis set up corporations involving absentee landowners in order to continue farming (following the example set by the Japanese, against whom the Alien Land Laws had been directed). After that strategy was challenged in 1933-34 by an Imperial County Grand Jury investigation and subsequent indictment, they turned to their children, American citizens, putting land in their names and managing it as guardians through the Probate Court. Significantly, the Cable Act had been repealed by this time, and land could be put in the name of wives.[38] Yet most men preferred to put the land in the names of their minor children, either through caution learned from the bad experiences of a few or through a desire to assert the strongest possible control over the nominal landholders.

Although the legal discrimination put the Punjabi men at a disadvantage *vis-à-vis* Mexicans, it was the Punjabis who were moving up in the local stratification system. The strategies used to evade the Alien Land Law make it clear that many Punjabi farmers had carved out places for themselves in the agricultural economy and won the backing of important figures in local politics. As Joyce Pettigrew has argued,[39] the patron-client system back in the Punjab had been based on reciprocal rather than asymmetrical relationships; Punjabis compete in a spirit of equality, and the men in California strove for that competitive, nonsubordinate position.

At the same time, Mexicans and Mexican-Americans in the Valley remained in the laboring class. The same year that the Punjabis were brought to trial for conspiring to evade the Alien Land Law (essentially for becoming members of the "grower" class), union organizing by Mexicans and Filipinos brought violence and federal intervention to the Imperial Valley and worsened relations between Anglos and Mexicans there.[40] No Punjabis were involved with the labor movement; as self-identified landowners, their interests lay with the Anglo establishment,[41] whatever the origin of their wives in California.

Far from being a haven from economic and political struggles in Imperial Valley agriculture, the home often was the site of domestic power struggles. Divorce was common.[42] It was not possible back in the Punjab, but the Punjabis

---

L.A. District Court, Indexes 1 and 2 (1917-29) where some 70 Hindu cases, almost all from the Imperial Valley, are recorded.

38. Some wives did hold land, and for many men besides their husbands; these tended to be the white and black wives, and among the Mexican-Hindus, the wives of the more prosperous men. Observation based on interview notes for couples and court records of probate cases.

39. Pettigrew 1975, pp. 19-20, 46-47.

40. Devra Anne Weber, "The Organizing of Mexicano Agricultural Workers: Imperial Valley, and Los Angeles 1928-34, An Oral History Approach," in *Aztlan*, 3:2 (1972), 302-47; James Gray, "The American Civil Liberties Union of Southern California and Imperial Valley Agricultural Labor Disturbances: 1930, 1934," Ph.D. dissertation, History, University of California, Los Angeles, 1966.

41. Mola Singh said about himself in 1919 at the age of 22: "I hired people to chop cotton...some were black, almost all were Mexican. I spoke Spanish to them, English to the judges" (Selma, 1982).

42. Leonard and LaBrack 1984.

in California learned that women could initiate divorce proceedings and ask for division of community property, custody of the children and alimony. The court records detail the complaints. The women resented being told to cook and clean for their husbands' partners; they resented being restricted when they wanted to visit their mothers or go out dancing with friends; they resented the stinginess of men intent on saving money to buy land. The men thought the women did not work hard enough on household and child care, socialized too freely with other men, and spent money carelessly. Women in the joint households quarreled with each other or with the other men; they made love to their husbands' partners or would not make love to their husbands' partners;[43] in sum, they were hard to control.

Remarriage was also common, and while it is not surprising that the Punjabi men continued to "choose" Hispanic women (the miscegenation laws were voided only in 1948), they frequently chose ones who had been married to other Punjabis before. The women were not so constrained by the miscegenation laws, and they did choose a wider range of partners. But they, too, often remarried within the Mexican-Hindu community, with Punjabis who had been married to Hispanic women before.[44] Prejudice by Mexican men may have continued against women who had married Punjabis; but the original motivation for many of the women, greater economic security, still held good as well.

Children were born and raised, and their coming increased the complexities of home life in this community. The children had to be named, and the overwhelmingly Hispanic names indicated the women's power in the domestic sphere. Only a few sons received Indian first names, usually by way of an affidavit of correction filed by the father years later. Fathers sometimes tried to get their sons called by Punjabi names; one sought the help of an Anglo neighbor in writing those names down so they could be used.[45] Names sometimes revealed conflict; in one divorce case, the parents fought over children whom they called by different names, the mother using Hispanic ones, the father Punjabi.[46]

As the naming pattern reflects, the language used in most Mexican-Hindu homes was Spanish. The dominant influences on the children were their mothers, their mothers' relatives, and frequently, older stepsisters and brothers fathered by Mexican men.[47] The religion in which most children were raised

---

43. One husband killed his wife when she would not make love to other Punjabis; another husband killed his partner for making love to his wife. *Brawley News*, April 16, 1921, and Imperial County, County Clerk's Office, criminal case no. 1031 of 1921 for the first instance; *Imperial Valley Press*, Dec. 1, 1938, for the second.

44. Divorce and remarriage statistics will appear in my forthcoming book (manuscript in preparation).

45. Elizabeth Harris (Holtville, 1981).

46. Imperial County Clerk's office, civil case no. 19314 of 1940. In another case, 19588 of 1940, a son was referred to as "Mario or Sunder."

47. Many women brought children into their marriages with Punjabis. In a set of 66 women for whom maternal fertility could not be computed, 24 women of the 66 brought 3.2 children each with

was Catholicism. This was not a contested matter but simply a "natural" result of leaving the child-raising to the women. Punjabi fathers, often illiterate and untrained in the finer points of their own religious beliefs, continued to practice Sikhism, Islam, or Hinduism to varying extents and taught their wives and children respect for all religions.[48]

The Punjabi men transmitted little of Punjabi culture to their wives and children. The immigration laws and other discriminatory policies against Asians made it useless to teach the children Punjabi or even tell them about Punjabi society, some fathers felt; others were working too hard to communicate much to their families.[49] Many descendants remarked that their fathers had not talked much to them about India, terming the men "grouchy" or "hard"; language problems may be responsible for some of this impression. Children's imperfect understanding of their fathers' homeland can be seen in their versions of the caste system.[50] Even the village names, very significant to the men and known orally to the women and children, are spelled with hesitation today and can seldom be located on a map.

There were two important exceptions to the pattern of Punjabi cultural loss. The domain of food was one. Cooking in the homes drew from both Mexican and Punjabi cuisine, and the men taught their wives to cook chicken curry, roti, and various vegetable curries. Some men made lemon pickle and other specialties. Food prohibitions according to religious custom were enforced in some families, particularly among the Muslims. Another important exception concerned disposition of the body upon death. The Sikhs insisted upon cremation, then not common in America, and they took photographs of the body with a turban on in a coffin so that relatives in India could see the man had remained a Sikh (never mind that the partners, friends and family around the coffin wore no turbans).[51] The Muslims purchased "Hindu plots" in rural cemeteries and carried out orthodox burial ceremonies for one another. On their tombstones, their names, the names of their fathers, and the names of Punjabi villages and districts were written in Urdu script; only the other men from India

---

them (completed family size averaged 6.4 children per woman).   Leonard, manuscript in preparation.

48. One educated wife (Julia Villa Deen, with a fourth-grade education from the Yuma, Arizona, schools) did convert to Islam, but she was an exception. The two or three Sikhs said to convert to Catholicism continued to be Sikh and were cremated when they died. Mola Singh said, when I asked him if he hadn't wanted his children brought up in his religion: "No, I didn't, I don't care. The church here may be Catholic, that's OK; the story of Jesus Christ is OK; you go your Church, I go my church; one God...Not different religions. Make different names...believe God, only one God" (Selma, 1982).

49. Janie Diwan Poonian told of her father's teaching them Punjabi and telling them about the Punjab, until one day when he said he would do it no longer, for there was no reason for them to know these things in America (Yuba City, 1982); Teresa Garewal (Holtville, 1981) said that when she married a Hindu, another Hindu offered her money but her husband did not accept, saying, "We are not in our country."

50. Leonard forthcoming a.

51. Such a photograph appears in the appendices to the paper written in an anthropology seminar by Allan P. Miller, "An Ethnographic Report on the Sikh (East) Indians of the Sacramento Valley," unpublished manuscript, South and Southeast Asia Library, University of California, Berkeley, 1950.

could read them. But the wives were buried in the Mexican Catholic sections of local cemeteries, and so were the children.[52] Here the marking of "self" and "other" definitely put the men in one category and the women and children in another.

In the families, the children grew up acquiring the substance of a Mexican-American ethnic identity, and they were generally perceived as Hispanic by the larger society. People called them "Mexidus" behind their backs. Singh became a Mexican name to many in the Imperial Valley. The school system, an important enforcer of boundaries in rural California, automatically enrolled most Mexican-Hindu children in schools on the Mexican side of town, regardless of their actual residence.[53] They were the objects of prejudice there—often the Mexican children were harder on them than others—but certainly their familiarity with Spanish and Mexican-American culture, and their identification with it by others, was reinforced.

Reactions to this marking as Hispanic were predictable, although they differed by class and region. Many of the Mexican-Hindu children, especially those from the better-off families, grew up insisting that they were "Hindu," not Mexican. Some of the better-off children brought pressure to bear on the lower-class ones to keep away from Mexican friends. In other instances (near Phoenix, Arizona, for example), wealthy Mexican-Hindu families avoided contact with lower-class Mexican-Hindus entirely. Children brought up in relative isolation from other Mexican-Hindus enjoyed meeting others like themselves, whether at the Stockton temple or in the orchards and fields on the labor circuit.[54]

Adolescence brought new tensions within these families as the Mexican-Hindu boys and girls began dating. Punjabi fathers had strong ideas about whom their children should marry. At this time, the men talked about caste and regional differences stemming from the Punjab: Sikhs and Muslims, Malwa and Doaba, or Jat and Chuhra, should not intermarry. But the mothers had little knowledge of these social markers and little sympathy with their application in California. The children had even less sympathy with their fathers' views on dating and marriage.[55] In the Imperial Valley, the children of Punjabis organized a Hindustani Club primarily for social purposes. Significantly, an age

---

52. Interviews with Olga Dad Khan (Sacramento, 1982) and Verdie Abdullia Montgomery (Sacramento, 1982); observation at the Hindu plots in Sacramento City Cemetery and the Evergreen Cemetery, El Centro. Julia Deen and Juanita Chavez Abdulla are the only wives buried in Hindu plots, the former in Sacramento and the latter in El Centro.
53. See Paul S. Taylor and Edward J. Rowell, "Patterns of Agricultural Labor Migration within California," *Monthly Labor Review*, Nov. 1938, 980-90, for details of the school system (they used school attendance figures by race to estimate migration timing and impact).
54. Mrs. Wheat (El Centro, 1981); Caroline Shine Sunghera Resendez (Huntington Beach, 1982); Karmelita Kakar (San Jose, 1982). "Singh" is not recognized as an Asian Indian name by younger people in the Imperial Valley: Irene Brinkman (Imperial, 1981); anonymous student in Duane Metzger's University of California, Irvine, class (Irvine, 1984).
55. Elizabeth Deen Hernandez quoted her mother as saying to her father when she wanted to date a "Rae" (Arain) and her Rajput father objected, "What is this caste thing? We're all Americans here" (Los Angeles, 1981). Some fathers wanted their daughters to marry older bachelor Punjabis, and although seven young Mexican-Hindu daughters did so, most of them divorced their husbands within a few years.

clause stipulated that there could be no members over forty, a clause intended to keep the fathers from interfering![56]

Given the pride most Mexican-Hindu children felt in their "Hindu" blood and the close associations they formed with others like themselves (friendships, the Hindustani Club), one might predict some tendency towards endogamy, or marriage within that group. But as the Mexican-Hindus married, their least preferred partner, for both men and women, was another Mexican-Hindu.[57] This can be explained partly by the tendency to marry outside the community entirely, in order to avoid the father's attempts to arrange marriages within it. But to understand this fully, we need to look again at the Punjabi immigrants and socio-economic stratification within that group by the 1940's. The smallness of the community, the competition and rivalry within it, meant that people knew each other well, often too well.

Very early, differentiation within the "Hindu" group produced landowners and leasers, "store men" and labor contractors, as well as migrant laborers. Those who were upwardly mobile were marked by their better knowledge of English and good relationships with Anglo growers, lawyers, and bankers. To a certain extent, they were also marked by their marriages. The Punjabi immigrants were predominantly rural residents in California, but some Punjabis and other South Asian immigrants (6% or less of the total California population of Asian Indians) lived in Los Angeles and San Francisco.[58] The urban men tended to be well-educated professional people, and many of them had married white women.

Political leaders in the Punjabi immigrant community, particularly those in cities and in central and northern California, were prejudiced against the family society centered in the south, and formed few links with the Mexican-Hindu children. The urban, educated men led the fight for political rights for South Asians in the U.S. Although they turned to the Punjabi farmers for financial support, they were critical of the marriages with Hispanic women and tended to understate their numbers and importance. Thus at the same time that Dadabhay found a proportionately large number of marriages to Hispanic women and proposed "circuitous assimilation" to Mexican-American society, another researcher on the Punjabi immigrants, Jacoby, saw significant acculturation to Anglo society. But Jacoby worked with the English-speakers active in the drive for legal equality and seriously underestimated the number of marriages with Hispanic women.[59]

---

56. *Holtville Tribune*, March 11, 1946, reported that the International Good Neighbors Club was helping to organize Indian youth and senior clubs in the Imperial Valley; it reported March 11, 1946, that the young people were forming an independent club instead. For the forty-year clause, Mary Garewal Gill (Holtville, 1981) and Domingo (Kishen) Singh Deol (Riverside, 1981).

57. Leonard, manuscript in preparation, analysis of California marriage licenses 1949-69.

58. See Brett H. Melendy, *Asians in America* (New York: Hippocrene Books, 1981), tables vii, viii, and ix, pp. 255-57, for the state and urban-rural breakdowns.

59. Harold Jacoby, "East Indians in the United States: The First Half-Century," unpublished manuscript, 1978 (field work done in the early 1950's).

Another political network linking the urban and rural immigrants was that centered on India, primarily the Ghadar party in the early decades, but to some extent the regional Malwa and Doaba associations active in the Central Valley towns as well. These efforts called upon the Punjabi farmers throughout California for financial support and personal commitment to the freedom and welfare of India. The leaders of these activities, many of them bachelors, came from the San Joaquin and Sacramento valleys. Since wives typically resented both the financial drain and the occasional violence characteristic of these Punjabi activities, the Imperial Valley family society produced fewer leaders and participants in all of these political activities.

The Mexican-Hindu children participated even less than their fathers in the Punjabi men's political activities. Citizens by birth, they were not concerned with the drive for U.S. citizenship. One Punjabi political leader, a bachelor in the U.S., expressed contempt for the children because they took full legal rights for granted; they had not been disenfranchised and forced to fight for their rights.[60] Without knowledge of the Punjabi language or Indian society and politics, the Mexican-Hindu sons were not recruited for the Ghadar party and other political activities either. The Stockton Sikh temple was an important meeting place for the Mexican-Hindu families, certainly, and the non-Indian wives and children participated in the social activities over the years. However, their ignorance of the Punjabi language was a major barrier to their participation in the political activities important to the Punjabi men.

Yet largely because of political developments, the decade of the 1940's was a crucial one for the Mexican-Hindu community. The children were coming of age, making decisions about marriage and occupations, and coming into conflict with their fathers over these decisions. The fathers were aging, and their wives, about twenty years younger in most cases, often sided with the children. These were difficult years for Mexican-Hindu family life in any case, but added to the internal tensions were others caused by the lifting of the legal constraints that had played so large a part in shaping the men's decisions in California. Not only did U.S. law change in 1946, making South Asians eligible at last for citizenship and therefore for landowning in California, but India and Pakistan achieved independence as nations in 1947. These momentous events had a tremendous impact on the Punjabi immigrants in California.

Finally given the opportunity, many of the early immigrants became U.S. citizens and sponsored the immigration of close relatives from India and Pakistan. The possibility of contact with one's first wife and/or children, after years of sending money or of total silence, had ominous implications for the second, Mexican-Hindu, wife and children. A few men took their American wives to visit their home villages. But some Punjabis divorced their wives in America and brought over Indian wives and sons. Others brought over nephews or grandsons and attempted to integrate them into their lives in California. A

---

60. Bagga S. Sunga (El Centro, 1981).

few sold their properties and retired to the Indian subcontinent, taking their money with them.[61]

The disposition of their property was a major concern of the aging immigrants, perhaps as important a concern as that about the proper disposition of the body at death. Now, at the end of their lives, the Punjabi men suddenly had the opportunity not only to put their land in their own names at last, but they had a choice of whom to leave it to. They could bring over only close relatives, but even the few relatives who came from 1946 to 1965 produced significant changes in the structure of the immigrant communities in California. The Mexican-Hindus found the newcomers were rivals to family property and disputed the claim of Mexican-Hindus to be "Hindu."

New names were invented to reflect the changing social realities. The new immigrants came from not one nation but two, India and Pakistan, and this partition back in India produced one in California. Fiercely proud to be no longer slaves of a colonial power but men from free new nations, the Punjabi pioneers identified with the new nations and divided sharply along religious lines for the first time in California. The designation "Spanish-Pakistani" was coined to describe the Muslims and their descendants and differentiate them from the Mexican-Hindus.[62]

Soon another new name was necessary. The pioneer "old Hindus" had to be distinguished from the flood of South Asian newcomers who came to the U.S. after the 1965 changes in the federal immigration law. These newcomers were, by and large, well-educated professional people, from all over India and not just the Punjab, but there was an influx of Punjabi peasants. The Yuba City-Marysville Punjabis in northern California had made relatively few marriages with local women. They sponsored rural Punjabi immigrants, at first relatives and then the relatives of relatives. This new Punjabi community up north[63] soon dominated in numbers and influence in arenas like the Stockton Sikh temple. The "old Hindus" were put on the defensive with respect to their "liberalization" of temple practices. Some of the old-timer Sikhs grew beards and put on turbans again. Aging Muslims helped newcomers establish a mosque in Sacramento. It was possible to view the Mexican-Hindus as an historical mistake, no longer (if ever) part of the immigrant community.

The developments stemming from the new immigration laws added stresses to those produced by socio-economic stratification and family rivalries

61. Isabel Singh Garcia (Yuba City, 1983); Mary Singh Rai (Yuba City, 1983); Mary Garewal Gill (El Centro, 1982).
62. Olga and Salim Khan (Sacramento, 1982); Sally and Niaz Mohamed Jr. (Brawley, 1981); Verdie Abdullia Montgomery (Sacramento, 1982).
63. Researchers of this new community took the "social change" perspective analyzed by Avruch (1987: 328) and looked for the assimilation of "traditional" immigrants through "modernization": Wenzel 1968 and Bradfield 1971. Dadabhay and Jacoby were also working with this paradigm in their earlier studies, as was Chakravorty (1968), who worked in the Imperial Valley but concentrated on the better-off farmers supporting the Sikh temple established there in 1948. Bruce LaBrack has done excellent work on the Yuba City community from the mid-1970's and his book is forthcoming.

within the Mexican-Hindu community. Members of the second generation responded differently to the pressures on them and the choices open to them. The poorer families tended to be closer to Mexican-American culture. In some such families, conflict with the father or his countrymen produced lasting anger or fear, alienating descendants from their Punjabi and Indian heritage.[64] In others, even where the Punjabi men were said to have "become Mexican," incoming daughters-in-law found a pride in Hindu ancestry which denigrated Hispanic ancestry.[65] Only one Punjabi-descended farmer in the Imperial Valley has renounced his "Hindu" name (Singh) and taken up leadership of the Mexican-Americans there.[66]

Personal names, always significant for this community, assumed even greater importance. Name changes by the children show interesting patterns over the life cycle, changing orientations towards ethnicity over time. Names on birth certificates were overwhelmingly Hispanic, but names on marriage licenses tended to reflect the ethnicity of the intended spouse. That is, Rudolfo at birth would be Rudolph at marriage if he was marrying an Anglo but Rudolfo if his bride was Hispanic. A few years later, that same man might put Kishen as his name on his children's birth certificates, and an informant would explain that in those years he was helping his aging father make decisions about his property. Some changed their names officially for professional reasons. For example, Spanish-language radio announcers changed their names from Singh to their mother's name, and a Mexican-Hindu farm supplier who hoped to do business with new immigrant farmers from India began using his Punjabi first name. Others changed their names officially to avoid identification with Punjabi immigrants in northern California, where the rapid increase in the immigrant population was leading to rising prejudice.[67]

Having grown up struggling against prejudices, few Mexican-Hindus have "invented a tradition" that glorifies their fathers and their heritage.[68] They are realists; at best there is a nostalgia for the days of the "old Hindus," when bachelor uncles came to the family homes to eat, drink, talk, and play with the children. But Mexican-Hindus did have a shared identity in the Imperial Valley in which they took pride. One man told me he had been called Mexican-Hindu all his young life, by everyone including state authorities like those who issued driving licenses in the Imperial Valley. His was a migrant laborer family. Working near Sacramento when the United States entered World War II, he

---

64. Karmelita Kakar (San Jose, 1982); Yolanda Singh (Santa Ana, 1983). And three sons refused to be interviewed, saying they were really Mexican or had nothing to say about their Hindu side.

65. Mr. and Mrs. Francisco Singh (Selma, 1983). Franciso said about his father: "My Dad turned Mexican. He brought us up, six or seven boys and one girl, after mother died. He didn't teach us much about India. When he said things we all just laughed at him, six or seven boys, not much chance."

66. Fernando Sanga (Brawley, 1981).

67. Isabel Singh Garcia (Yuba City, 1982); Alfred Sidhu (Sacramento, 1982); Leonard, "A Note on Given Names and Chicano Intermarriage," *La Red*, 1984, 4-5.

68. Terence O. Ranger and Eric Hobsbawm, *The Invention of Tradition* (New York: Cambridge University Press, 1984.) One person who romanticizes the old days is ridiculed by others.

enlisted in military service there, giving his race as "Hindu and Mexican." The clerk put him down as Caucasian, and he protested. "Well," she said, "if you're not Mongoloid or Chinese, you're a Caucasian as far as the Feds are concerned." This was a shock to him, an introduction to a wider world and, in some sense, a loss.[69]

Many Mexican-Hindu descendants do still claim to be "Hindu," whether their names are Maria Singh, Jose Akbar Khan, or Angelita Chand. Some of them contributed to the new Sikh temple in Yuba City, although they gradually stopped going to the temple to help cook the food there. They hold a Christmas dance in Yuba City (complete with *mariachi* band), where the strongest challenge to their legitimacy is posed by the new Punjabi community of some 8,000 people. They may have rebelled against their fathers as teenagers, used Anglicized or Hispanic names rather than Indian, or married outside the Punjabi and Mexican-Hindu network; but today many talk proudly of their fathers and the other "old Hindus" and contrast them favorably with the newcomers from the Punjab.[70]

The Mexican-Hindu experience is a striking illustration of the historical construction and reconstruction of ethnicity. State policies set a context in which the Punjabi men and Hispanic women "chose" to marry and create a bi-ethnic community in the Imperial Valley. The asymmetric incorporation of racial and ethnic groups into the rural California economy and the views of the dominant Anglo society towards those groups helped determine Punjabi and Hispanic attitudes towards each other over time, even *within* the families. The provisions of California laws concerning divorce and access to agricultural land had an impact on power within the families, affecting gender and generational relations. Finally, changes in the federal laws regulating citizenship and immigration broadened the opportunities for the Punjabi men after decades of constraint and enabled them to exercise power over families and property at the end of their life cycles, power exercised perhaps more vigorously because it was so long withheld.

For the Mexican-Hindu children, growing up and experiencing the consequences of both internal and external pressures, ethnic identity could be defined in several ways. They were identified by others as Mexican-Hindus; most often, they chose to define themselves as "Hindu." But the meaning of "Hindu," and of "Mexican-Hindu," the content of those ethnic identities, was unique to the American southwest. "Hindu" in California meant something totally different from "Hindu" in the father's homeland (and half the mothers

---

69. Alfred Sidhu (Sacramento, 1982).
70. Caroline Shine Sunghera Resendez (Huntington Beach, 1982); Isabel Singh Garcia (Yuba City, 1982). See Leonard forthcoming (b) for Mola Singh's lament about the changing temple practices forced through by the new Sikh immigrants. And Isabel Singh Garcia's long letter to the editor of the *Yuba City Valley Herald*, printed under the title "They Are Too Hindus" (April, 1983), says that: "The East Indians of today would like to forget we exist...Our mothers allowed their husbands to bring their brothers, sisters and nephews in the 1950s and helped them to adjust to our way of life, and the cycle has repeated itself over and over and over. But the new breed did not keep the quality up."

were not from Mexico). Being "Hindu" caused strong emotional reactions, either rejection of or commitment to, that ethnic identity. For those who chose to assert it, it became strong enough to withstand the prejudice expressed by political leaders among the early immigrant Punjabis and by new immigrants from India, strong enough to withstand even the second generation's own consciousness of its lack of knowledge of the Punjab and India. Class differentiation within the Mexican-Hindu community did not prevent the intensification of the "Hindu" identity, and indeed cannot predict who will assert it. "Hindu" is still a useful marker in parts of rural California, an ethnic identity with a history and force all its own.

References

Avruch, Kevin. "The Emergence of Ethnicity in Israel." *American Ethnologist* 14:2 (1987), 327-39.

Barrier, N. Gerald. "Sikh Immigrants and Their Homeland: The Transmission of Information, Resources, and Values in the Early Twentieth Century," in N. Gerald Barrier and Verne A. Dusenbery, eds., *The Sikh Diaspora: Migration and the Experience beyond Punjab.* Delhi: Manohar; and Columbia, Missouri: South Asia Books, forthcoming 1988.

Barth, F., ed. *Ethnic Groups and Boundaries: The Social Organization of Cultural Difference.* Boston: Little, Brown & Co., 1969.

Benson, Susanfine. *Ambiguous Ethnicity: Interracial Families in London.* Cambridge: Cambridge University Press, 1981.

Bradfield, Helen. "The East Indians of Yuba City: A Study in Acculturation." M.A. thesis, Anthropology, Sacramento State College, 1971.

Brass, Paul. *Ethnic Groups and the State.* London: Croom Helm, 1985.

Chakravorty, Robindra. "The Sikhs of El Centro: A Study in Social Integration." Ph.D. dissertation, Anthropology, University of Minnesota, 1968.

Comaroff, John L. "Of Totemism and Ethnicity: Consciousness, Practice and the Signs of Inequality." Unpublished paper, 1984.

Cohen, R. "Ethnicity: Problem and Focus in Anthropology." *Annual Review of Anthropology* 7 (1978), 349-403.

Dadabhay, Yusuf. "Circuitous Assimilation among Rural Hindustanis in California." *Social Forces* 33 (1954), 138-41.

Garcia, Mario. "On Mexican Immigration, the United States, and Chicano History." *The Journal of Ethnic Studies* 7:1 (spring 1979), p. 83.

Jacoby, Harold S. "More Thind Against than Sinning." *The Pacific Historian* 11:4 (1958), 1-2, 8.

———. "East Indians in the United States: The First Half-Century." Unpublished manuscript, 1978.

Leonard, Karen. "A Note on Given Names and Chicano Intermarriage." *La Red* 52 (1982), 4-5.

———. "Punjabi Farmers and California's Alien Land Law." *Agricultural History* 59:4 (1985), 549-62.

———. "Pioneer Voices from California: Reflections on Race, Religion, and Ethnicity," in N. Gerald Barrier and Verne A. Dusenbery, eds., *The Sikh Diaspora: Migration and the Experience beyond Punjab.* Delhi, Manohar; and Columbia, Missouri: South Asia Books, forthcoming 1988. Cited as "forthcoming (a)."

————. "Immigrant Punjabis in Early 20th-Century California: A Life History," in Sucheng Chan, ed., *Intersections: Studies in Ethnicity, Gender, and Inequality.* Cited as "forthcoming (b)."

Leonard, Karen; and Bruce LaBrack. "Conflict and Compatibility in Punjabi-Mexican Immigrant Families in Rural California, 1915-1965." *Journal of Marriage and the Family*46:3 (1984), 527-37.

Lesser, Jeff H. "Always 'Outsiders': Asians, Naturalization, and the Supreme Court." *Amerasia* 12:1 (1985-86), 83-100.

Loewen, James W. *The Mississippi Chinese: Between Black and White.* Cambridge, Mass.: Harvard University Press, 1971.

Melendy, Brett H. *Asians in America.* New York: Hippocrene Books, 1981.

Narroll, R. "On Ethnic Unit Classification." *Current Anthropology* 5 (1964), 283-312.

Pettigrew, Joyce. *Robber Noblemen: A Study of the Political System of the Sikh Jats.* Boston: Routledge & Kegan Paul, 1975.

Puri, Harish K. "Ghadar Movement: An Experiment in New Patterns of Socialisation." *Journal of Regional History* (1980), 120-41.

————. *Ghadar Movement: Ideology, Organisation and Strategy.* Amritsar: Guru Nanak Dev University, 1983.

Taylor, Paul S. "Mexican Labor in the United States: Imperial Valley," *University of California Publications in Economics*, vol. 6, no. 1 (Berkeley, California, 1928).

Taylor, Paul S.; and Edward J. Rowell. "Patterns of Agricultural Labor Migration within California." *Monthly Labor Review*, Nov. 1938, 980-90.

Vatuk, Sylvia; and Ved P. Vatuk. "Protest Songs of East Indians on the West Coast, U.S.A.," 63-80, in Ved Vatuk, ed., *Thieves in My House: Four Studies in Indian Folklore of Protest and Change.* Varanasi: Vishwavidyalaya Prakashan, 1969.

Watanabe, Chizuko. "The Japanese Immigrant Community in Mexico: Its History and Present." M.A. thesis, California State University, Los Angeles, 1983.

Weber, Devra Anne. "The Organizing of Mexicano Agricultural Workers: Imperial Valley, and Los Angeles 1928-34, An Oral History Approach." *Aztlan* 3:2 (1972), 302-47

Wenzel, Lawerence. "The Rural Punjabis of California: A Religio-Ethnic Group." *Phylon* 60:29 (1968), 245-56.

Wood, Ann. "East Indians in California: A Study of Their Organizations, 1900-1947." M.A. thesis, Anthropology, University of Wisconsin, 1966.

Table 1

Spouses of Asian Indians in California, 1913-1949

Types of Spouses

Counties	Hispanic		Anglo		Black		Indian		American Indian		Total	
	No.	%	No.	%	No.	%	No.	%	No.	%	No.	%
Yuba Sutter Sacramento San Joaquin	45	50.6	25	28.1	9	10.1	8	9	2	2.3	89	23.6
Fresno Tulare Kings	38	76	11	22	0	0	1	2	0	0	50	13.2
Imperial Los Angeles San Diego	221	92.5	12	5	6	2.5	0	0	0	0	239	63.2
Totals	304	80.4	48	12.7	15	4.0	9	2.4	2	.5	378	100

Source: Karen Leonard, family reconstitution from county records
(vital statistics, civil and criminal records)

Punjabi Sikhs and Gora Sikhs: Conflicting Assertions of Sikh Identity in North America

Verne A. Dusenbery

Introduction

Sikhs claim that theirs is the youngest major "world religion" and that the teachings of the Sikh Gurus (preceptors) are universal in their truth and applicability. Yet, until recently, Sikhism remained essentially a regional faith, one found among thirteen to sixteen million Punjabis living in India and in scattered Punjabi communities abroad. Over the past five centuries, as the Sikh community in Punjab grew in size and strength, it drew members from the indigenous Punjabi Hindu and, to a lesser extent, Punjabi Muslim communities. But despite more than a century of Sikh migration to other parts of the world, the community has remained an insular one. And norms of endogamy and non-proselytization have ensured that heretofore there has been no significant move on the part of non-Punjabis to embrace the Sikh religion. During the past fifteen years, however, several thousand young North Americans have made unprecedented claims to Sikh identity and have sought to have their "conversion" to the Sikh *dharma* ("religion," "moral duty," "way of life") recognized by both Punjabi Sikhs and the world at large.[1]

In the Punjab, the reaction to these *gora* ("white") Sikhs, as the Western converts are commonly called by Punjabi Sikhs, was, at least initially, quite

1. This paper draws on fieldwork conducted in 1978-79 in Vancouver, British Columbia, with Punjabi Sikhs and Gora Sikhs and on fieldwork conducted in 1972 and 1974 in the western United States and Canada with the Healthy, Happy, Holy Organization (3HO). It benefits from continuing archival research and from ongoing conversations with Sikhs throughout North America. This is an extensively revised and expanded version of a paper first presented in a symposium entitled "The Assertion of Group Identity: Symbolic Approaches" at the 56th Annual Meeting of the Central States Anthropological Society, Ann Arbor, Michigan, April 9-12, 1980. I would like to thank the other members of that symposium and members of the seminar on South Asian ethnosociology at the University of Chicago (winter 1983) for their helpful comments. I would particularly like to thank McKim Marriott and W.H. McLeod for their constructive criticisms of earlier drafts. The paper's flaws remain mine.

[Joseph T. O'Connell, Milton Israel, Willard G. Oxtoby, eds., with W.H. McLeod and J.S. Grewal, visiting eds., *Sikh History and Religion in the Twentieth Century* (S. Asian Studies Papers, 3) (Toronto: S. Asian Studies, Univ. of Toronto, 1988)]

positive.[2] Sikh leaders commented favorably on the apparent devotion and ritual piety of the converts and held them up as evidence to Punjabi Sikh youth and to non-Sikhs of Sikhism's appeal and relevance to the modern world. In North America, however, the response of Punjabi Sikhs was, from the start, considerably more restrained. Punjabi Sikhs in North America—including the growing number of second- and third-generation Canadians and Americans of Punjabi Sikh descent—had previously had a virtual free hand in defining for themselves and for the wider public what it meant to be a Sikh. Now this exclusivity was being challenged, and many Punjabi Sikhs thought it prudent to wait and see how the Gora Sikhs would assert their new-found Sikh identity before endorsing their claims and embracing the converts as fellow Sikhs.

This paper explores one aspect of the relationship between the small, but well-organized and highly vocal, group of North American Sikh converts— almost all of whom are members or former members of the Healthy, Happy, Holy Organization (or 3HO) and its religious arm, Sikh Dharma[3]—and the larger, but more diffuse and diverse, population of North Americans of Punjabi Sikh ancestry. The paper suggests that certain of the differences that have arisen between the Gora Sikhs and the Punjabi Sikhs over the assertion of a Sikh identity can be understood as deriving from differing cultural presuppositions about the nature of persons and groups. It argues that contrasting, culturally informed interpretations of Sikh teaching and practices have led the two groups to apply different standards in evaluating each other's assertions of Sikh identity. And it concludes that half a world of difference lies between the "radical egalitarianism" of North American converts and the "unity in diversity" perspective of Punjabi Sikhs, approaches that have led the converts to regard most Punjabi Sikhs in North America as no longer Sikhs and most Punjabi Sikhs in North America to regard Gora Sikhs as, at best, Sikhs of a very different kind.

Sikh Egalitarianism and Social Diversity

Sikh informants and Sikh apologists have commonly emphasized for Western audiences the degree to which Sikh doctrine constitutes a radical

---

2. We italicize *gora* as a non-English word when it appears as a term, but capitalize it without italics when it functions as a proper name referring to a particular group, like Khatri or Mazhbi Sikhs. —Editors' note.

3. Admittedly, there have been isolated instances of other Westerners of non-Punjabi ancestry becoming Sikh through intermarriage or individual conversion. Perhaps the most notable of these converts is the Englishwoman, Manjeet Kaur (a.k.a. Mrs. Pamela M. Wylam), the co-editor of the *Sikh Courier* of Gravesend, England. The members of Sikh Dharma are, however, the most numerous, visible, and organized of the *gora* ("white") Sikhs. There are currently some three thousand or more members of Sikh Dharma, including approximately five hundred minor children. They can be distinguished by their distinctive white *bana* (uniform of the Khalsa) and by their turbans for women. All are *keshdhari* ("hair-bearing") Sikhs, and a vast majority of the adults have undergone the *amrit pahul* (initiation into the Khalsa). Most Sikh Dharma members live in or near one of the approximately one hundred 3HO ashrams located throughout North America and in several overseas cities. Membership has held steady over the past decade, which suggests that new converts and children born to members balance those lost to the group by death or departure. Of those who have left the group, an unknown percentage have remained Sikhs; while others, including some of the past leadership, not only have left the organization, Sikh Dharma, but also have totally dissociated themselves from the Panth.

departure from Hindu ideology. Thus, they have pointed to the anti-caste pronouncements of the Sikh Gurus and to Guru Gobind Singh's formation in 1699 of the Khalsa Panth ("Brotherhood of the Pure")[4] as evidence of the Sikh obliteration of caste hierarchy. True, some have noted that the institution of inter-caste commensality and consociation in Sikh worship did not lead to inter-caste marriages, even among the Gurus, and that dropping Hindu caste and clan names in favor of the Sikh name-titles, "Singh" (lion) for males and "Kaur" (princess) for females, did not push awareness of one's caste affiliation from public consciousness.   However, at least in the South Asian context, Sikh teachings and ritual practices have stuck out as radically egalitarian;[5] and the differences in Sikh and Hindu ideology, rather than similarities in social organization, have been emphasized in giving substance to the claim that Sikhism is not only a unique and separate religion but one significantly free of caste distinctions.

Whether in deference to Sikh sensibilities or for lack of familiarity with Sikh social practices, South Asianists have by and large given only passing attention to the question of caste in the Sikh Panth.[6] We are indebted, therefore, to the historian W.H. McLeod for two articles that address directly the persistence of caste observances among Sikhs. It is McLeod's contention that what the Sikh Gurus meant by their teachings and demonstrated through their actions was that "whereas they were vigorously opposed to the *vertical* distinctions of caste they were content to accept it in terms of its *horizontal* linkages." Thus, he argues, what they were concerned to deny were (1) the "soteriological significance of caste" and (2) the "justice of privilege or deprivation based upon notions of status and hierarchy," while continuing to

---

4. Guru Gobind Singh's use of "Khalsa" seems to have connoted initially that the band of dedicated followers was his "own" or "special" community. Secondarily, the connotation of "pure" has come to be associated with the name Khalsa. Panth, literally "path," refers to the band or community of Sikhs. —Editors' note.

5. See, e.g., Cole and Sambhi 1978, p. 144; J. Singh 1981.

6. Louis Dumont, for one, is conspicuous in his silence on the issue of caste among the Sikhs. Indeed it is unclear whether he considers the Sikhs to be a renunciatory Hindu sect or a non-Hindu group, although we may infer from what he says of both renunciatory sects and non-Hindu religions in South Asia that he assumes the Sikhs to "have at the very least *something of caste despite modifications in their ideas and values*" (1980, p. 277, emphasis in the original) since "a sect cannot survive on Indian soil if it denies caste" (1980, p. 269). Presenting a contrasting model, Veena Das, building on the work of J.P. Singh Uberoi (1967), argues that the essence of the heterodoxy of rebel sects—including the Sikhs—is their "negation of the conceptual order of Hinduism" (1980, p. 55); but, she argues, the thrust of the negation is not an attack on the caste system itself but on "the special position of Brahmins as holders of *inherent* ritual merit within the conceptual scheme of Hinduism" (1980, p. 87, emphasis in the original).   As if to give substance to this latter interpretation, Satish Saberwal attributes the slackened caste observances in the Punjab to an undermining of the religious supremacy and socio-political influence of the Brahmins (1976, pp. 1-13) but suggests that the egalitarian ideology of Punjabi Sikhs, Muslims, Christians and Arya Samajists has been used selectively "to knock the Brahmin down *but to try, if possible, not to concede much opportunity to the lower castes readily*" (1976, p. 30, emphasis in the original). Cf. Marriott and Inden 1974, 1977, for an analysis of caste without recourse to religious/sociopolitical, orthodox/heterodox, or ideology/practice dualisms. According to Marriott and Inden: "The Sikhs believe that through initiation they incorporate their teachers, who are believed to be perfect and divine, even though human...[and] that they attain liberation while still belonging to their many original castes" (1974, p. 988).

accept the "socially beneficial pattern of horizontal connections."[7] McLeod does not deny hierarchical overtones in the ranking of local Sikh caste groups but argues that the Sikh Panth is and always has been of "heterogeneous constituency," being composed of various largely endogamous groups (Punjabi, *zat*; Hindi, *jati*) whose social interaction and status have taken different forms at different times and in different places, yet who continue to assert their own and confirm one another's common membership in the Sikh Panth.

McLeod's formulation, however foreign its solid geometric imagery may be to describing the fluid realities supposed by South Asians, strongly suggests that Punjabi Sikhs do not find it problematic to assert their similarities as Sikhs while simultaneously maintaining other diversities and dissimilarities among themselves as Punjabi persons. Such diversity among those calling themselves Sikhs is not only a matter of the different *zat* groupings to which Punjabi persons continue to belong; it is also a matter of different ritual practices which Punjabi Sikhs follow. For instance, two groups which might in the West be considered "orthodox" and "heterodox" Sikhs, i.e., long-haired *keshdhari* Sikhs and clean-shaven *sahajdhari* Sikhs, are generally regarded by Punjabis as simply different kinds or degrees of Sikhs. In light of prevailing Western conceptions, the persistence of caste observances in the face of Sikh "egalitarian" teachings and a tolerance of diverse—including what appear to be "unorthodox"—practices by those calling themselves Sikhs may be considered problematic issues by Western observers.[8] But given the radically different cultural conceptions of persons and social identities they hold, there is no reason to expect these to be problematic issues for Punjabis. Indeed, this paper suggests that the conflicting assertions of Sikh identity and mutual misunderstandings arising in North America between Punjabi Sikhs and Gora Sikhs follow from the radically different cultural assumptions each brings to the interaction.

Punjabi Persons and Sikh Practices[9]

The Punjabi term *zat* (like its Hindi cognate and synonym, *jati*), is commonly rendered as "caste," since it refers, among other things, to certain named, loosely ranked, hereditary, primarily endogamous, occupational groupings in Punjabi society that Western-oriented social scientists wish to assimilate to their notion of "caste." But as McKim Marriott and Ronald Inden have convincingly argued,[10] the terms *zat* and *jati* can refer to "all sorts of categories of things" (e.g., male beings as differentiated from female beings; human beings as distinct from animals or divinities) and to a "whole range of earthly populations" (e.g., regional groupings, religious communities,

---

7. McLeod 1974; 1976, pp. 88-91, emphasis in the original.
8. See, e.g., Juergensmeyer and Barrier 1979, pp. 2-3.
9. This section owes much to the "South Asian ethnosociology" of McKim Marriott, Ronald Inden, Ralph Nicholas and their students (e.g., Inden 1976; Inden and Nicholas 1977; Kurin 1974; Marriott 1980; Marriott and Inden 1974, 1977). For a more elaborated presentation of the analysis herein, see Dusenbery (forthcoming).
10. Marriott and Inden 1977, p. 230.

occupational categories, ethnic groups) for which the term "genus" and its plural, "genera," seem the most appropriate gloss. Since South Asian genera are ordered paradigmatically, not just taxonomically, each person belongs simultaneously to several kinds of genera. They are intersecting classes.

For Punjabi Sikhs, the most important distinctions of persons within Punjabi society are those based on religion (between Sikhs, Hindus, Muslims, etc.), those based on occupation (between agriculturalist Jats, mercantile Khatris and Aroras, artisan Ramgarhias and Ahluwalias, service Mazhbis and Ramdasis, etc.) and those based on regional origins (between peoples of the regions of the Punjab called Majha, Doaba, and Malwa). These different kinds of persons—by ancestry members of different human genera—are understood to possess different natural substances and moral codes deriving from, respectively and simultaneously, their objects of worship, their means of subsistence and their territory. Persons' generic substances and codes for conduct of persons are therefore not immutable. New substances and new moral codes—altered modes of worship, subsistence, and territory—may transform persons over time.

Being a Sikh, for a Punjabi, implies having one of these kinds of generic features through having incorporated into one's person the natural substance and moral code for conduct of the Sikh Guru (preceptor). Receipt of the Guru's coded substances makes those who bear them partly alike in their personal natures and, without making them alike in other ways, makes of them a recognizably distinct worship genus, the Sikh Panth. But different categories of persons may be recognized within the Sikh Panth based on the kind and degree of Sikh worship substances they have incorporated into their total persons. Minimally, those who incorporate the natural sacred sound (*gurbani kirtan*), the visual emanations (*gurdarshan*), and the edible "benefits" (*karah parshad*) of the Guru and who mix with other Sikhs in the communality of the *sangat* (congregation) and the commensality of the *pangat* (communal dining hall) may be considered *sahajdhari* (lit. "one who bears a light-weight [burden]") Sikhs. At the other extreme, those who incorporate the *amrit* (a "nectar of immortality" including sugar, water, steel and the Guru's word), shared in the course of the *amrit pahul* (initiation) ceremony, become *amritdhari* (lit. "nectar-bearing"; the common Christian-style translation is "baptized") Sikhs and members of the Khalsa Panth.

These *amritdhari* Sikhs, having achieved a higher state of Sikh regeneration through being further united with the Guru's substance and following a stricter moral code appropriate to the Khalsa, are thought capable of uniting others into the Panth by administering the *amrit* to initiates. Standing between the light-burdened *sahajdhari* Sikhs and the more heavily burdened *amritdhari* Sikhs are the *keshdhari* (lit. "one who bears hair [or a lion's mane]") Sikhs, who maintain the outward Khalsa form (including the uncut hair and other visible markings) without benefit of having incorporated the *amrit* and without the corresponding obligation and prestige of observing the full Khalsa *rahit maryada* (lit. "prestigious code of discipline"). Finally, *patit* (lit. "fallen";

the common Christian-style translation is "apostate") Sikhs are those who once having accepted the *amrit* no longer follow the Khalsa *rahit* (discipline). As their name implies, they are considered to have fallen in purity and rank and thus to be no longer able to induct others into the Panth.

If Punjabi persons are constituted as members of the Sikh Panth (worship genus) through their incorporation and manipulation of Sikh worship substances, they nevertheless continue to belong to their occupational, territorial, and other human genera. Nowhere is this composite nature of the Punjabi Sikh person more clearly illustrated than in the matchings of persons which characterize marriage practices. In keeping with the Guru's injunctions, Sikhs by and large marry other Sikhs; but they marry Sikhs who are relatively more or less like themselves, that is, those with whom they share not only the same worship substances and code of conduct but also the same occupational and territorial coded substances. The fact that endogamy within the Sikh Panth co-exists with an overwhelming preference for "caste" endogamous marriages and, to a slightly lesser extent, regionally endogamous marriages suggests not that there is some problematic contradiction between Sikh teachings and practices, but rather that Sikh ritual transactions, while making Punjabi persons partially alike *as Sikhs*, do not constitute them as completely identical persons.

Thus, it should not be surprising to find, as McLeod's work makes clear, that persons of different genera may assert their Sikh identity in different ways. For instance, the numerically dominant and influential Jats, though derived from what is sometimes considered a middling Hindu caste, have risen to an elevated rank, especially within rural Punjabi society; and, as McLeod notes, "the Jat Sikh commonly assumes a considerable freedom with regard to observance of the Khalsa discipline....In his own eyes and those of other Jats he remains a Sikh even if he cuts his beard or smokes tobacco."[11] This does not necessarily hold true for other *zat* groups. Though traditionally over-represented in the *sahaj-dhari* category, once having accepted the visible Sikh markings of a *keshdhari*, the urban Khatris and Aroras have generally maintained the outward form strictly, for "if a Khatri [or Arora] shaves he is regarded as a Hindu by others and soon comes to regard himself as one."[12]

The case of what traditionally have been regarded in Punjabi society as lower-caste and outcaste groups is particularly illuminating. As a vehicle of upward mobility, membership in the unpartitioned Khalsa has held considerable appeal. The full, public assertion of Sikh identity entailed in Khalsa member- ship—or, at the very least, the maintenance of *keshdhari* markings—visibly distinguishes the lower-caste Sikh from his Hindu caste-mates and is essential to the acceptance by others of his claim to being a Sikh. Writing of two such groups, McLeod notes that they have never "observed to any significant degree the practice of calling themselves Sikhs without observing the outward forms of

---

11. McLeod 1976, p. 98.
12. Ibid.

the Khalsa. For them this would destroy any social advantage implicit in the title of Sikh. Indeed, the title would not have been accepted as valid."[13] Such a group's transformed nature generally leads its members to take up new occupations and to avoid undertaking marriages with Hindu or Muslim caste-mates. And these actions eventually have led most such groups to be given corporate names distinct from those of their former caste-mates. But despite impressive gains in wealth and reputation made by some of these groups,[14] their partial transformations are rarely acted upon as outweighing other differences included in the group's original nature; and Sikhs of other, more highly reputed, castes generally maintain a policy of non-marriage with them.

It is in light of this understanding of Punjabi persons and Sikh practices that the Punjabi Sikh experience in North America and the conflicting assertions of Sikh identity made in North America by Punjabi Sikhs and Gora Sikhs begin to make sense.

From the Dominance of Jats to a Diversity of Zats

The first substantial Punjabi migration to North America occurred during the first decade of the twentieth century. From that point until the mid-to-late 1960's, the overwhelming majority of Sikhs in North America were Jats from Doaba (the plains area of Punjab between the Beas and Sutlej rivers). The original Sikh immigrants were predominantly laborers and farmers who had served in the Indian army. Most came to North America as sojourners, intent on making their fortune and returning home to the Punjab to retire in comfort on the family farm. The vast majority of these early immigrants eventually settled in British Columbia, where they became concentrated in lumber and lumber-related industries, or in California, where they pursued the traditional Jat occupation as agriculturalists. When, after long and arduous struggle, they were finally permitted to sponsor as immigrants their families left behind in the Punjab, it was their Jat Sikh wives, children and relatives who came to join them. And it was these original immigrants, plus an intermittent flow of legal and illegal immigrants, and their offspring, who kept alive a Punjabi Sikh presence in North America in the face of significant isolation from the homeland and alternately hostile and indifferent treatment from the host societies.

Individual non-Jats apparently mixed freely with their fellow Punjabi Sikhs and suffered little obvious social impairment on account of caste. In California, the first "East Indian" elected to the U.S. Congress, Dalip Singh Saund, was a Ramgarhia Sikh. In British Columbia, Mayo Singh, a Mahton Sikh, became a millionaire mill-owner and pillar of the Sikh community. Nevertheless, it was Doabi Jat Sikh practices that largely defined the Sikh identity as it developed in North America. One aspect of this Jat dominance was spreading indifference to the maintenance of the Khalsa *rahit*. In time, a majority of male Sikhs in North

13. McLeod 1974, p. 83.
14. See, e.g., Marenco 1974; McLeod 1974; Saberwal 1976; K. Singh 1977, p. 120.

America were clean-shaven and turbanless. And eventually most Sikh institutions, including the *gurdwaras* (temples), came to be dominated by clean-shaven Sikhs. New immigrants were urged to shave before or upon arrival in North America so as to facilitate their social and economic adaptation. Administration of the *amrit pahul*, and thus initiation into the Khalsa Panth, virtually ceased. Most Jats in North America designated themselves and their families as Sikh by virtue of their birth and upbringing; and, unless they did something actively to refute the assumption (e.g., convert to Christianity or marry a *gora*), that designation was generally not challenged by their fellow Jats.

Whereas British policies in India—especially the requirement that Sikh troops maintain Khalsa *rahit*—had helped to reinforce Khalsa discipline among Jat Sikhs,[15] Canadian and American policies and attitudes worked against the maintenance of the outward Sikh forms. Punjabi Sikhs in North America perceived their beards and turbans to be an impediment in their dealings with non-Sikhs, and most felt obliged to give them up. While this may have made them more acceptable to the non-Sikh public, it did little to change their identities in North America. In their own eyes they remained, for the most part, Doabi Jat Sikhs. And to the wider North American public, clean-shaven or turbaned, Jat or non-Jat, they were (with individual exceptions) regarded as "Hindoos" or "East Indians," Canadians and Americans being by and large insensitive to confessional or caste differences within the broader ethnic category.

Naming practices were also affected by North American customs and attitudes. The importance attached to surnames in North American culture and the convention of patronymical inheritance produced a number of onomastic anomalies for Punjabi Sikhs living in North America. Whereas in rural Punjabi society, "X Singh" could be further identified as "X Singh of Y village" or "X Singh, son of Z Singh," and "A Kaur" could be further identified as "A Kaur, wife of Y Singh" or "A Kaur, daughter of Z Singh," North American conventions led not only to a proliferation of "Mr. Singh" but to the creation of "Mrs. Singh" and "Miss Singh" as well. Pressure from the wider public for a differentiation of "Singhs" and the Sikhs' own discomfort with the effects of Western naming customs led to modifications in Sikh naming practices. Some Sikhs began to use their family's village name in Punjab as a last name, but by the 1950's it became conventional to use the name of one's *got* ("clan"; exogamous grouping within the *zat*) as a last name, reserving "Singh" and "Kaur" for use as middle names. Since *got* names are usually indicative of *zat* as well, Jat identities came to be strongly signaled.

If such accommodation was furthered by the homogeneity which prevailed in North America's Sikh population, that homogeneity did not altogether suppress the development of factional splits for which Punjabis—and Jat Sikhs

15. See Barrier 1970, p. xl.

in particular[16]—are well known. The homogeneity of the community and the chain migration did, however, allow most new immigrants to be incorporated into established social networks (*biradari* or *baradari*, "brotherhood") of fellow Jat Sikhs who were often kinsmen or village-mates. As a result, the established residents were able to guide the newcomer's adaptation to the new social environment, providing initial housing and job contacts and alerting the newcomer to appropriate local social convention. Of equal importance to the Sikhs, and helping to explain the practice of seeking spouses from India, the newcomer was one who renewed substantive ties to the homeland and provided a conservative counterbalance to any too radical deviation from Punjabi Sikh practices.

The Sikh population in North America began to change rapidly in the late 1960's, and once again the changes were in part the consequence of social policies over which the Sikhs themselves had little control. In the mid-1960's, in response to accusations that their immigration policies were implicitly racist, the Canadian and American governments liberalized their immigration regulations, making it considerably easier for unsponsored individuals of non-European backgrounds to gain residence. As a result, immigration of Punjabi Sikhs increased dramatically, not only from India but from the United Kingdom, East Africa, East and Southeast Asia and Fiji as well. During the past two decades, a number of new Punjabi Sikh communities have emerged in North America, especially in the larger metropolitan areas where Sikh professionals have found employment. In the long-established communities of British Columbia and California, old-timers and their descendants have been confronted by newcomers unbeholden to the old-timers for sponsorship, not necessarily having common *zat* membership and often pushing a visible Khalsa Sikh identity which most old-timers and their offspring had come to regard as an unnecessary encumbrance. Thus, changes in the character of the Sikh population in North America have been profound. Distinctions came to be felt not only between long-time residents and recent immigrants, between "traditionalists" and "modernists," and between India-born and North America-born, but also among those of different national origins or country of last residence, family regional origins in the Punjab, caste, class and—with the emergence of Gora Sikhs—ethnic or "racial" origins.

To the extent that their fellow Punjabi Sikhs in various countries have constituted their "significant others," Punjabi Sikhs in North America have remained sensitive to Punjabi differentiations of persons and human genera. The Jat Sikh population had been aware of *zat* relations, and by and large followed Punjabi endo-marital convention, although Jats had traditionally been somewhat "looser" (i.e., more hypergamous) in this regard than other Punjabis.[17] But as

---

16. See Pettigrew 1975.
17. McLeod 1976, p. 84. See the work of Karen Leonard (1982) on what she calls "Mexican-Hindu" marriages, i.e., some 380 liaisons contracted in California between Punjabi immigrants and Mexican and Mexican-American women in the period from the late 1920's to 1950. As Leonard

most spouses were sought in India and most of one's fellow Sikhs in North America were also Doabi Jats, caste and regional identity had been a relatively infrequent consideration in Sikh social life in North America. The North America-born were raised with far greater concern for the negative consequences for family honor (*izzat*) that would follow from marrying a *gora* (white male) or *gori* (white female) than from marrying the "wrong" kind of Punjabi Sikh. Indeed, the reputed differences in personal natures of Punjabis of different occupational, territorial or worship genera paled in comparison to the contrasts that parents drew between Punjabi and Western culture and character.

However, with the increase in non-Jat and non-Doabi immigration during the past two decades has come a greater emphasis on the supposed differences in character and temperament of different kinds of Punjabi Sikhs and increased concern that care also be taken to avoid "improper" (i.e., caste or regionally exogamous) marriages with Sikhs of different kinds. The use of *got* names as last names has conveniently made one's *zat* affiliation public knowledge and those who for whatever reason refuse to use a *got* name are often suspected of trying to obscure low-caste or out-caste origins. To foreclose any suggestion that their personal natures have degenerated as a consequence of transactions undertaken in North America, Punjabi Sikhs of all kinds continue to value actions which serve to "nourish and sustain"[18] ancestral occupational, territorial and worship genera. This has led them to minimize certain transactions with alien others (particularly with *gora* society, but also with other "kinds" of Sikhs) and to maximize transactions with persons of one's own kind. Such concern is manifest not only in formation of factions, in socialization of children and in arrangement of marriages, but increasingly also in the differentiation of Sikh gurdwaras and secondary institutions by caste, by regional origins and by ritual practices of members.[19]

It is into an increasingly diverse Punjabi Sikh population in North America that the Gora Sikhs have recently interjected themselves full-force. The reception they have received from Punjabi Sikhs in North America has been shaped in important ways by the Punjabi Sikhs' response to their own internal diversity and by Punjabi Sikh understandings of persons and human genera.

acknowledges, "the Mexican-Hindu community in California was a transitory one" (LaBrack and Leonard 1984, p. 535), and the offspring of these liaisons were neither socialized into Punjabi culture nor particularly welcomed in California's renascent Sikh communities.
18. Marriott and Inden 1977, p. 231.
19. In 1980, for instance, Vancouver, British Columbia, had three main gurdwaras. One was predominantly Malwai, while the other two were predominantly Doabi. The local Ramgarhia Society, founded in 1972, has talked seriously of Ramgarhias building and maintaining their own Sikh gurdwara, as the numerically and proportionally larger Ramgarhia communities have done in the U.K. and East Africa. Followers of Sant Meehan Singh, a product of the Nanaksar movement, have recently opened their own gurdwara. And even the local Naxalites have their own "Desh Bhagat Temple." Diversity of persons is increasingly reflected in diversity of institutions.

American and Canadian Sikhs of 3HO/Sikh Dharma[20]

In 1968 Harbhajan Singh Puri, a Khatri Sikh whose family had resettled in New Delhi during the post-partition exodus from Pakistani Punjab, quit his job as a customs official at Delhi International Airport at Palam and left for Canada to take a job as a yoga instructor. Upon reaching Toronto, he found that the promised job had fallen through, but with the aid of a Punjabi Sikh benefactor-sponsor, he was able to settle in Los Angeles, where he began teaching yoga courses at the East-West Cultural Center. Now calling himself "Yogi Bhajan," Puri proved to be a compelling teacher. Having found a receptive core of students, he soon established an *ashram* (spiritual commune) for them. There he taught his "Kundalini Yoga: The Yoga of Awareness," offered occasional "Tantric Yoga Intensives," and imposed upon his followers the structure and discipline of what he called "the healthy, happy, holy way of life." In 1969, the Healthy, Happy, Holy Organization (or 3HO) was formally incorporated as a tax-exempt educational organization. Puri was now sending his newly-trained "student teachers" to other cities in North America to teach Kundalini Yoga classes and to establish additional 3HO *ashrams*. During the early 1970's, the primary orientation of the organization was towards recruiting new members through the yoga classes and establishing new *ashrams* where, Puri now claims, members were being purified and prepared to accept their calling as Sikhs. At this point, however, Puri "continued to teach about Sikh Dharma in an indirect way."[21] 3HO members, most of whom were young white, middle-class American and Canadian refugees from the counter-culture, tended to regard themselves not as Sikhs but as "yogis" and "yoginis" or, in Puri's terminology, "shaktimen" and "shaktis."

Puri had, however, slowly begun to disclose his own Sikh background and introduce Sikh teachings to his closest followers. In 1971, he took eighty-four of them to India, where they visited the Golden Temple and surrounding shrines. At the Akal Takht ("throne of the Timeless One," the highest seat of Sikh religious-cum-temporal authority) the group was cordially received and Puri was honored for his missionary work. Returning home with what he represented to be the mandate to spread the message of Sikhism in the West, Puri began to supplement and supplant his primarily yogic explanation of the "the healthy, happy, holy, way of life" with a more explicitly Sikh account. Puri now also began to use the title "Siri Singh Sahib," a title which he claimed had been given him by the Shiromani Gurdwara Prabandhak Committee (the organization legally empowered to control historic and other Sikh gurdwaras in the Punjab) and which he rendered, liberally, as "Chief Administrative and Religious Authority for the Sikh Dharma in the Western Hemisphere." In 1973 he was successful in having the Sikh Dharma Brotherhood (later recast in non-gender-specific language as, simply, "Sikh Dharma") officially registered as a tax-

20. For greater detail on the development of 3HO, see Dusenbery 1973, 1975.
21. Khalsa and Khalsa 1979, p. 119.

exempt religious organization legally empowered to ordain Sikh ministers, who would have the authority to perform marriages, provide the last rites and administer the *amrit pahul* ceremony.

Puri's own transformation from "Yogi Bhajan" to the "Siri Singh Sahib" corresponded roughly with a change from a primarily yogic to a primarily Sikh identity on the part of 3HO members. The change did not happen overnight; but once convinced by Puri that what he was calling the "healthy, happy, holy way of life" was that of an orthodox Sikh, most 3HO members did not hesitate to make a formal commitment to their new religion. And Puri provided unprecedented opportunities for 3HO members to express their commitment, introducing Sikh initiations and minister ordinations in addition to holding the more traditional *amrit pahul* ceremony. The resultant change from a yogic to Sikh identity on the part of 3HO members also corresponded to a change of emphasis within the organization from the aims of recruiting new members and establishing additional *ashrams* to those of maintaining the established group, raising a second generation and establishing credibility as upholders of Sikh orthodoxy in North America. With respect to the latter task, the new American and Canadian Sikhs, as they called themselves, exhibited all the fervor and self-assurance one might expect from new converts to any faith.

Whereas most Punjabi Sikhs in North America had been content to keep a low profile, often regarding their visibility as a handicap and sometimes sacrificing their beards and turbans as a necessary adaptation to the demands of life in North America, the new American and Canadian Sikhs of 3HO have asserted their right to a full public expression of their version of Sikh orthopraxy and have sought aggressively to have their "religious rights" recognized by the North American public. In these efforts, they have made effective use of the media and of administrative and legal channels. 3HO has actively courted publicity and their "exoticness" (e.g., white clothing, beards, turbans, *ashrams*, mass marriages and strange "Indian" names) and their "good works" (e.g., drug rehabilitation programs, free kitchens) have made them "good copy." More significantly, with rare exception,[22] what media exposure they have received has been uncritical in accepting the converts' claim to represent orthodox Sikhism in North America. And such claims have been further reinforced by rulings of human-rights officials and the courts. In a number of cases successfully brought by 3HO members (e.g., for seeking exemption from hard-hat and dress-code requirements), North American officials have found the petitioner, as a Khalsa Sikh and a member of Sikh Dharma, to be a Sikh in good standing exercising a legitimate right to the practice of the Sikh religion. All of this activity has made the converts known beyond what their numbers might otherwise warrant. Punjabi Sikhs in North America, in particular, have been made well aware of the existence of the Gora Sikhs, even if they have personally had little or no interaction with them.

---

22. See "Yogi Bhajan's Synthetic Sikhism," *Time*, Sept. 5, 1977.

Gora Sikhs: Persons of a Deviant Sect or a Different Genus?

It would be inaccurate to suggest that so diverse a population as that of North American Sikhs of Punjabi ancestry has responded uniformly to the assertion of Sikh identity by Gora Sikhs. While few would deny the theoretical right of non-Punjabis to become Sikhs, fewer still accept the idea that Puri and the Gora Sikhs have the authority to speak for all the Sikhs of North America. Beyond that, however, the category "Gora Sikh" is such a new and in many ways anomalous one that it has taken time to sort out reactions. Early accounts of Gora Sikh-Punjabi Sikh interaction in the Los Angeles area[23] and in northern California[24] reported that initial receptivity to the converts' involvement with the established Sikh gurdwaras gave way to increasing discomfort on the part of Punjabi Sikhs. Agehananda Bharati discusses some of the reasons for the mixed feelings: "Punjabis candidly admire the strict Sikh ritual discipline of the 3HO, and grudgingly their teetotalitarian ways. [But] they do not approve of the uniformization of the 3HO, especially the 3HO women; and they resent the superior ways the 3HO displays towards them."[25] In many of their practices, Gora Sikhs seem insensitive to the meanings their actions may have for Punjabi Sikhs. They insist, for instance, that all-white clothing (a mourning color in Punjab associated with widows), turbans for women (almost unheard of among Punjabis, for whom a turban is a male symbol par excellence), vegetarianism (not a general Sikh—and particularly not Jat Sikh—practice) and yoga (varieties of which were said by the Sikh Gurus to be incompatible with the life of a householder enjoined upon Sikhs) are all orthodox Sikh practices. Yet, at the same time, most 3HO members lack fluency in Punjabi language beyond the memorization of a few *shabads* (hymns), even though for Punjabi Sikhs the Punjabi language and Gurmukhi script are intimately bound up with Sikh worship. Furthermore, the assertiveness of 3HO women and familiarity between the sexes, although restrained by North American standards, seem excessive to many Punjabis. And finally, the veneration of Puri by 3HO members verges on what Punjabi Sikhs regard as Hindu-like idolatry. Some of the insensitivity on the part of 3HO members may grow out of naïveté and reflect unfamiliarity with Punjabi culture, but some is based on a principled decision that Sikh "religious" norms—as understood by Gora Sikhs through Puri's presentation of them—must supersede parochial "ethnic" (i.e., Punjabi) custom.

The Goras' assertion of their Sikh identity has tended to provoke one of two responses from Punjabi Sikhs in North America. Some would deny altogether the claims of 3HO members to be Sikh. They maintain that despite the superficial appearance of adhering to Khalsa *rahit*, the Goras have not incorporated Sikh worship substances comparable to those maintained by other persons of the Sikh Panth. Among 3HO practices that are commonly cited as

---
23. Fleuret 1974.
24. LaBrack 1974, 1979; Bharati 1980.
25. Bharati 1980, p. 249.

inconsistent and incompatible with the Sikh *dharma* are: inclusion of Kundalini and Tantric yoga practices as a form of Sikh mysticism; distortions of *gurbani* and misquotations and mistranslations from the Adi Granth (the Sikh holy book, which is itself considered to be the reigning Guru); questionable legitimacy and efficacy of *amrit pahul* ceremonies conducted for and by 3HO members; veneration and reverence accorded Puri over and above that appropriately reserved for the Sikh Gurus, the Adi Granth, and the seats of Sikh spiritual authority; and, finally, formation of organizational structures and an ecclesiastical hierarchy independent of, inconsistent with, and at cross purposes to, the traditional Panthic organization.[26]   Together, such considerations lead many Punjabi Sikhs in North America to regard 3HO as a deviant sect or cult with Puri as its "false *guru.*"[27]

A number of parallels have been drawn between 3HO/Sikh Dharma and (a) other North American religious cults and (b) schismatic or breakaway sects in India claiming to be Sikh.   Punjabi Sikhs note that young North Americans seem unusually susceptible to religious cults and to brainwashing at the hands of authoritarian cult leaders.   Some cynically admire Puri for living the easy life off his gullible North American followers; but most express concern that 3HO members' willingness to take Puri's idiosyncratic teachings as Sikh orthodoxy means that they will accept anything Puri tells them and that their loyalty to Puri will come before their loyalty to the Panth.   In the wake of the mass suicide-murder at the People's Temple in Jonestown, Guyana, Punjabi Sikhs asked whether 3HO members might not be capable of the same or a similar act of blind fanaticism.   And in the context of the current Punjab crisis they ask: if Puri were to take issue with a ruling (*hukumnama, gurmata*) normally considered binding on the entire Panth, would his followers respect Puri's dictates or the collective decision of the Panth?

---

26. Sikhism has generally been free of an elaborate hierarchy of religious functionaries.   Any good Sikh can serve as a *granthi* (reader of the Adi Granth); and the title *giani* (learned one), a term of respect used in reference and address for Sikh "priests," does not require formal certification. Since the death of Guru Gobind Singh in 1708, the eternal Sikh Guru has been said to reside jointly in the Panth and the Granth.   Decisions in the name of the Guru Panth may in theory be made by any five good Sikhs in consultation with the Guru Granth Sahib.   In practice, the *jathedars* (lit., "commanders"; commonly, "high priests") of the five historic *takhats* ("thrones") constitute an exalted *panj pyare* ("five beloved").   *Hukumnamas* (decrees) issued on their behalf from the Akal Takht are considered authoritative.   The functionary appointed by the Shiromani Gurdwara Prabandhak Committee who serves in the role of *jathedar* of one of the *takhats* is respectfully addressed as "Singh Sahib" ("Lord Singh").   The title attaches to the role, not to the person.   Puri's appropriation of the title "Siri Singh Sahib" (lit. "Exalted Lord Singh") is seen by many Punjabi Sikhs in North America as suggesting that he considers himself superior even to the *jathedars* of the *takhats.*   Most refuse to acknowledge either his use of the title or his right to it.   Equally infuriating to many Punjabi Sikhs has been Puri's liberal bestowal of the titles "Mukhia Singh (Sardarni) Sahib" and "Singh (Sardarni) Sahib" on, respectively, his newly-created "regional ministers" and "ministers" of Sikh Dharma.

27. The Punjabi Sikh writer, Trilochan Singh, following a visit to North America to investigate the phenomenon of Western Sikh converts, came to share the views of many Punjabi Sikhs in North America who have been critical of Puri, 3HO and Sikh Dharma.   His work (1977) criticizes the group for deviations from mainstream Sikh practices and characterizes the group as a "Tantric Yoga cult."

Recent events in the Punjab also awaken Punjabi Sikh concerns for what can happen if deviant sects which claim to be Sikh are not repudiated at an early stage in their development. Standing out in the minds of many Punjabi Sikhs in North America are the clashes that have taken place in recent years in the Punjab between Sikhs and members of the Sant Nirankari Mandal. This is a group which claims descent from a nineteenth-century Sikh reformist movement and whose leaders maintain an outward Sikh form and use the Adi Granth in public ceremonies. But it is a group that the main body of Sikhs accuses of slandering the Sikh Gurus, misinterpreting and mistreating the Granth, elevating its own leader to the status of Guru and mocking Sikhism in its practices.[28] Several years of clashes between Sikhs and members of the Sant Nirankari Mandal culminated in a fatal encounter in Amritsar on April 13, 1978, and the subsequent assassination of the Sant Nirankari leader in 1980. The provocative actions of the Mandal, and frustrations with the Congress (I) government for allegedly aiding and abetting the provocations, eventually led to a *hukumnama* (decree) issued from the Akal Takht repudiating "pseudo-Nirankari" claims to being Sikh and ordering Sikhs to cease interaction with members of the Mandal. Some Punjabi Sikhs in North America argue that a similar repudiation should be made of Puri and his *gora* followers. In fact, resolutions that would declare Gora Sikhs of 3HO to be non-Sikhs and would bar them from participating in Punjabi Sikh institutions have been introduced for consideration by local Sikh societies in North America.

The fact that such resolutions have not been passed should be one indication that this negative view of the Gora Sikhs as a deviant sect is, for the present, a minority one. Indeed, it is more common to hear the Gora Sikhs referred to as "good Sikhs" than as "non-Sikhs." The majority of North American Sikhs of Punjabi ancestry seem willing to look past the Gora Sikhs' idiosyncrasies to note their visible Khalsa form and apparent adherence to Khalsa discipline. This is not to imply that most Punjabi Sikhs in North America are in full accord with the Gora Sikhs' representation of Sikh orthodoxy. Although there are areas of substantive agreement (e.g., the significant support given the Gora Sikh efforts to establish a Sikh "religious right" to maintain the beard, turban and other Sikh symbols), there is much about the Gora Sikhs' assertion of their identity that Punjabi Sikhs find alien. What I suggest has happened is that, given the Punjabi notion of the person that underlies the "unity in diversity" of the Sikh Panth, the majority of Punjabi Sikhs acknowledge the converts' claims to being Sikh but nevertheless regard them as persons of a very different—and lower—"kind."

It is not altogether surprising that Punjabi Sikhs should model their relations with Gora Sikhs along the lines of relations between Punjabi Sikhs of different kinds. When asked to explain to non-Punjabis and to their own North America-born youngsters the persistence of *zat* consciousness and *zat* endogamy

---

28. See, e.g., Guru Nanak Dev Mission, n.d.

in North America, Punjabi Sikhs commonly explain that people of different Punjabi ancestral occupational, territorial and worship communities are known to have different tastes, temperaments and ways of doing things which bind them to others of their own "kind" (*zat*) but which make them difficult to mix with— and unthinkable as recipients of one's daughter in marriage. In short, there are among Punjabi Sikhs many different "kinds" (*zat*) of people. Such a generic explanation, while doubtless understating Punjabi notions of purity and honor, could easily be applied to make sense of the otherwise anomalous category "Gora Sikh."

It is important to realize that most Punjabi Sikhs regard North America not only as alien territory but as a land which all too easily can lead those who inhabit it to undertake indiscriminate and dharmically inappropriate actions that might lower their personal natures. The Western culture of North America is, thus, suspect; and *gora* is a term with pejorative overtones. To be too *gora*-like (esp., to marry a *gora/gori* or to convert to Christianity) is to risk bringing into question the reputation or honor (*izzat*) of the collectives (e.g., family, *got, zat*) of which one is a part and to face possible social, if not physical, death. Indeed, before its application to Western converts to Sikhism, the term "Gora Sikh" was applied censoriously to any Punjabi Sikh whose personal nature was thought to have degenerated as a consequence of improper, "Western" behavior. Thus, the new Gora Sikhs of 3H0/Sikh Dharma, even when recognized by Punjabi Sikhs as "good Khalsa Sikhs," are persons who bear the alienating stigma of being *gora*. And this, in turn, affects the way that Punjabi Sikhs interact with them.

Understanding the Gora Sikhs to be Sikhs of a very different "kind" allows Punjabi Sikhs to excuse the many idiosyncrasies and insensitivities they detect in Gora Sikh actions. In fact, every idiosyncrasy or apparent insensitivity to Punjabi Sikh cultural conventions is further confirmation of the *goras'* alien nature. Thus, even when accepting as appropriate Gora Sikh participation in gurdwara functions and other activities of the Sikh Panth, most Punjabi Sikhs in North America remain circumspect in their interactions with Gora Sikhs. While they might be willing to honor publicly a Gora Sikh for *seva* (service) rendered to the Panth, few would go as far as to give their daughters in marriage to persons of what is, in effect, a very different "ethnic" genus.

In accepting Gora Sikhs as partially transformed *goras* who share a common membership in the Sikh Panth but who in other ways remain alien persons, Punjabi Sikhs are responding much as they have to conversions of low-caste and outcaste Punjabis. From a Punjabi perspective, "conversion" to Sikhism consists of partial inclusion, intersection, or union into the Sikh Panth and depends on recognized transformations in one's personal nature. Those whose ancestral substance has not been marked previously or marked consistently with Sikh worship substances have generally found initiation into the Khalsa Panth (or, at the very least, attainment of *keshdhari* markings and conduct) crucial to public acceptance of their transformed nature. Thus, like Punjabi converts from low-caste and outcaste groups, Gora Sikhs have found it crucial to their assertion of Sikh identity that they maintain Khalsa *rahit*. And like such Punjabi converts, Gora Sikhs have found that, while entrance into the Panth has resulted in improved markings in the eyes of other Sikhs, it has not removed all differences associated with the converts' original natures. Despite the fact that they, like such Punjabi converts, have avoided undertaking marriage with former "caste-mates" (i.e., non-Sikh *goras*), Gora Sikhs have not yet been accorded by other Sikhs a corporate name which would de-emphasize their *gora* origins. In light of the policy of non-marriage (or, at best, hypergamous marriage) which Sikhs of highly reputed castes maintain with low-caste and outcaste Punjabi converts, it is not surprising to find that Punjabi Sikhs of all kinds maintain a policy of non-marriage with Gora Sikhs. Gora Sikhs are after all the most recent and most alien of all converts, and their transformed nature is still untested.

Punjabi Sikhs in North America: Apostate or Retrograde Persons?

If it has served the purpose of a majority of Punjabi Sikhs in North America to treat the Gora Sikhs as Sikhs of a different—and somewhat dangerous and originally inferior—human genus, it has hardly satisfied the Gora Sikhs to be so treated. The source of the converts' discontent goes straight to their interpretation of Sikh teachings, and to the radical egalitarianism they find in Sikhism. It is their understanding of Sikh egalitarianism that leads them to assert a version of Sikh orthodoxy which Punjabi Sikhs in North America find either deviant or different. And it is the same principle that, in turn, leads the Gora Sikh to repudiate many practices of North Americans of Punjabi Sikh ancestry.

The Gora Sikhs make some crucial—and, I would argue, typically North American—assumptions about religion and about persons. They believe that persons are whole and impartible social units, i.e., that the "individual" is a non-divisible entity, and that common personal identity implies full equality. They hold that religious identity is essentially spiritual and personal, achieved through a full and conscious doctrinal choice (e.g., through spiritual rebirth, confirmation, conversion) rather than ascribed as a fact of natural birth. And they regard religious norms as universal, absolute and inviolable, entailing faithful adherence to some moral code of conduct equally enjoined on all believers and protected as a "religious right." This contrasts with the assumptions they hold about forms of social identity, which they associate with the facts of one's origins and biological descent, e.g., race, gender, national origin, ethnicity, and caste. These are regarded as essentially communal and non-volitional forms of social identity, and the associated norms of social action are understood to be arbitrary, ephemeral and legitimately adaptable in different social settings. In short, the Gora Sikhs are religious absolutists and cultural relativists, arguing that universal religious "codes for conduct" can be distinguished from and take precedence over particularistic cultural conventions. They thus distinguish that which they identify as a uniquely Sikh duty from that which they regard as mere Punjabi or North American custom. And they hold it incumbent on all would-be Sikhs in all places and at all times consistently to manifest their Sikh identity by maintaining identical Sikh religious practices.[29]

The Gora Sikhs take the creation of the Khalsa in 1699 by Guru Gobind Singh, the last living, human Guru, as a crucial event in the evolution of a distinctive Sikh identity. And they regard undergoing the *amrit* ceremony as crucial in the personal assertion of Sikh identity. They argue that Guru Gobind Singh's intention in setting forth the Khalsa *rahit* was (a) to provide the uniform standards by which to distinguish his Sikhs from other members of society (i.e., to give them a unique and distinct identity) and (b) to establish in concrete terms the total (not partial) equality of all those who would assert that identity. Such an interpretation is hardly extraordinary in the context of contemporary Western ideology, where "the fusion of equality and identity has become established at the level of common sense."[30] However, set against the understanding given these events by most Punjabi Sikhs, the implications of the Gora Sikh interpretations are radical indeed.

For one thing, because of the central place they give to the Khalsa *rahit* and to the distinctive visible form that Guru Gobind Singh gave his followers, the Gora Sikhs argue that one is not truly a Sikh without wearing the so-called "five Sikh symbols" or "five k's": the *kesh*, unshorn hair (covered by a turban); the *kanga*, a wooden comb; the *kirpan*, a sword; the *kara*, a steel bracelet; and the *kach*, a loin-and-thigh undergarment. In fact, the Gora Sikhs take these observable aspects of the Khalsa *rahit* as a necessary index of Sikh identity. This leads them to reject the notion that there might be different kinds of Sikhs following different codes of conduct and having incorporated varying degrees and kinds of Sikh worship substances. Such a reaction is, of course, culturally informed. As Louis Dumont has cogently noted, "[South Asians] will apply a rank where we in the West would approve or exclude."[31] Arguing that terms like "hereditary Sikh" and "clean-shaven Sikh" are contradictions in terms and that *sahajdhari* Sikhs are "not yet fully Sikh" and *patits* (as "apostates") are "no longer Sikhs," the Gora Sikhs have tried to exclude such people from participation as equals in Sikh affairs and have challenged their right to call themselves Sikhs. To explain why there should be so many of precisely these persons within the Punjabi Sikh communities of North America, the Gora Sikhs suggest that such people have "sold out" their religious principles to achieve the easy life in North America.[32]

If such a position has effectively alienated the Gora Sikhs from those who for many decades constituted perhaps the majority of all Sikhs in North America, it has not led them in the long run to take any less critical a view of those who have maintained the visible Sikh symbols. While the former are

29. Dusenbery (1981) discusses the radical differentiation of religion and ethnicity in North America (a differentiation of domains not found in Punjabi culture) and explores the implications of this differentiation for Sikh identity and institutional development in Vancouver.
30. Dumont 1980, p. 16.
31. Dumont 1980, p. 191.
32. See, e.g., Premka Kaur 1973, 1975.

considered "too North American to be good Sikhs," the latter are often found to be "too Punjabi to be good Sikhs." In particular, the Gora Sikhs are sensitive to signs of "caste consciousness" (a term used broadly to refer to any form of distinction or discrimination of persons among Sikhs), "subordination of women" (a term used broadly to refer to any form of sex-role differentiation in Sikh practices) and any other evidence of hierarchical or parochial behavior that the Gora Sikhs regard as inconsistent with Sikh "egalitarian" teachings.

This conviction leads the Gora Sikhs to take strong stands against a number of established conventions within the Punjabi Sikh communities of North America. As might be expected, they object on principle to caste or regional or ethnic endogamy among Sikhs, arguing that for Sikhs the only legitimate requirement for marriage should be that both partners be good Sikhs. While somewhat skeptical about the present feasibility of marriages between themselves and Punjabi Sikhs (since, they argue, it is so hard to find a North American of Punjabi heritage who is a good Sikh), they have no objection in principle to such marriages. In fact, some were obviously disappointed that Puri gave his own daughter in marriage to another Khatri Sikh rather than to one of his *gora* followers.

In yet another stand against what they regard as retrograde "caste consciousness," Gora Sikhs raise objections to the use of *got* names by Punjabi Sikhs in North America, arguing that Guru Gobind Singh intended the equality of all Sikhs to be indicated by their common name-titles as well as by their identical external form. As part of their own assertion of their new Sikh identities, Gora Sikhs have been given Sikh names, originally using "Singh" and "Kaur" as last names but more recently adopting "Khalsa" as a non-gender-specifying last name. Ironically, while their intent has been to assert the equality of all Khalsa Sikhs, the fact that they have been virtually alone among Sikhs in adopting this convention means that the last name "Khalsa" now indexes their membership in the Gora Sikh *biradari* (i.e., in Sikh Dharma) in almost precisely the same manner as the use of *got* names indexes the *zat* membership of Punjabi Sikhs.

One final example should suffice to make clear the way in which the Gora Sikhs' version of Sikh orthodoxy has served to separate them from the Punjabi Sikhs of North America. The Gora Sikhs interpret the Gurus' teachings on the equality of men and women not simply as testifying to their equality in the eyes of God and in their ability to accept the coded substances of the Guru but as mandating their equal place in every other aspect of Sikh religious life. Thus, the Gora Sikhs object to what they regard as the "subordination of women" in Sikh affairs and have pushed for an expanded role for women in the Sikh gurdwaras (e.g., as officiants and participants in Sikh services and as members of the management committees of the temple societies). And it is this same insistence on the equality of Sikh males and females that has led the Gora Sikhs to interpret the Khalsa *rahit* as requiring turbans for women as well as men.[33] As with so many of the Gora Sikh efforts to push their brand of radical egalitarianism, the attempts to get Punjabi Sikh women in North America to don turbans and take a more public—and to Punjabi Sikhs a more "male"—role in gurdwara affairs have been remarkably unsuccessful.[34] The net effect has been merely to reinforce the Punjabi Sikh impression of the *goras'* alien natures and to increase the Gora Sikh frustration at the failure of the Punjabis to live up to what the North American converts take to be essentials of the Sikh religion.

Conclusion

This paper has argued that the conflicting assertions of Sikh identity on the part of Gora Sikhs and Punjabi Sikhs in North America follow from significantly different assumptions about the nature of persons and social identities. It has suggested that the "radical egalitarianism" of the Gora Sikhs (i.e., the insistence that a common identity as Sikhs mandates a uniform and unitary set of beliefs and practices for all Sikhs) is significantly informed by the understandings of individual persons and totalizing social identities common in Western cultures. And it has suggested that the "unity in diversity" of the Punjabi Sikhs (i.e., the acceptance of multiple *zat* ties among Punjabi persons and varying degrees or levels of incorporation within the Sikh Panth) is significantly informed by understandings of composite persons and partially shared identities common in South Asian cultures.

As North Americans who could be expected to assert their Sikh identity in a way intelligible to the wider North American public, it is not surprising that the Gora Sikhs have had notable success in convincing the North American media and courts of their orthodoxy. In such situations, they address themselves to an audience which shares with them the same cultural assumptions. On the other hand, to the extent that Punjabi Sikhs in North America look to other Punjabi Sikhs as their significant others, they too can find continuing support for their assertion of Sikh identity. Punjabi Sikhs elsewhere with whom they share the same cultural assumptions do not consider most Punjabi Sikhs in North America to be degenerate and non-Sikh, but continue to match their children in marriage to them as persons of the same kind. Thus, to the extent that they look,

---

33. As Paul Hershman notes, in Punjabi Sikh culture "a woman...wearing a top-knot becomes as a man" (1974, p. 290). Hershman here mentions specifically the male role adopted by some Sikh widows in village Punjab. The only turban-wearing Punjabi Sikh women in North America whom I encountered in the late 1970's were those from families influenced by Bhai Sahib Randhir Singh's *jatha* (quasi-military "detachment"). Bhai Randhir Singh was a product of the Bhasaur Singh Sabha and the reformist ideology of Babu Teja Singh Overseer, whose "almost fanatical alterations" in Sikh practice included "that women be given equality in all ceremonies and wear the five k's" (Barrier 1970, pp. xxvi-xxvii, xxiii-xxiv).

34. These positions grow out of radical egalitarian assumptions rather than out of radical feminist ideology. 3HO's own "Grace of God Movement for the Women of the World" is explicitly opposed to the North American "women's liberation" movement. 3HO pushes the complementarity of male and female sex roles. Nevertheless, women have from the first taken an active and public role in 3HO and Sikh Dharma; and they seem unwilling to relinquish their public role in dealings with Punjabi Sikhs.

respectively, to non-Sikh North Americans and to non-North American Sikhs, each group continues to be reinforced in its assertion of Sikh identity. The conflicts arise most clearly in confronting one another.

But mutual misunderstanding need not be the inevitable and final result of this cross-cultural interaction. As I have suggested elsewhere,[35] there are indications that second- and third-generation North Americans of Punjabi Sikh ancestry may increasingly share current Western cultural assumptions about persons. With the Gora Sikhs having begun to send some of their children to India for schooling, second-generation Gora Sikhs may come to appreciate Punjabi cultural assumptions better than their convert parents have. If, in the face of current misunderstandings and conflicts, a true cross-cultural dialogue can be initiated, then it is possible that ongoing interaction, discussion, negotiation and debate will generate better mutual translations of the distinctive definitions of Sikh identity maintained by Gora Sikhs and Punjabi Sikhs in North America.

References

Barrier, N. Gerald. *The Sikhs and Their Literature*. Delhi: Manohar Book Service, 1970.

Bharati, Agehananda. "Indian Expatriates in North America and Neo-Hindu Movements," in J.S. Yadava and V. Gautam, eds., *The Communication of Ideas*. New Delhi: Concept Publishing, 1980, pp. 245-55.

Cole, W. Owen; and Piara Singh Sambhi. *The Sikhs: Their Religious Beliefs and Practices*. London: Routledge & Kegan Paul, 1978.

Das, Veena. *Structure and Cognition: Aspects of Hindu Caste and Ritual*, rev. ed. Delhi: Oxford University Press, 1980.

Dumont, Louis. *Homo Hierarchicus: The Caste System and Its Implications*, rev. ed. Chicago: University of Chicago Press, 1980.

Dusenbery, Verne A. "'Why Would Anybody Join...?' A Study of Recruitment and the Healthy, Happy, Holy Organization." B.A. honors essay, Anthropology, Stanford University, 1973.

———. "Straight→freak→yogi→Sikh: A 'Search for Meaning' in Contemporary American Culture." M.A. thesis, Anthropology, University of Chicago, 1975.

———. "Canadian Ideology and Public Policy: The Impact on Vancouver Sikh Ethnic and Religious Adaptation." *Canadian Ethnic Studies* 13:3 (1981), 101-19.

———. "The Sikh Person, the Khalsa Panth, and Western Sikh Converts," in Bardwell L. Smith, ed., *Religious Movements and Social Identity: Continuity and Change in India*. Leiden: E.J. Brill, forthcoming.

Fleuret, Anne K. "Incorporation into Networks among Sikhs in Los Angeles." *Urban Anthropology* 3 (1974), 27-33.

Guru Nanak Dev Mission. *Sikhism and the Nirankari Movement*. Patiala, Punjab: the author, n.d.

Hershman, P. "Hair, Sex and Dirt." *Man*, n.s., 9 (1974), 274-98.

Inden, Ronald B. *Marriage and Rank in Bengali Culture*. Berkeley: University of California Press, 1976.

---

35. Dusenbery 1981, pp. 110-11.

Inden, Ronald B.; and Ralph W. Nicholas. *Kinship in Bengali Culture*. Chicago: University of Chicago Press, 1977.

Jagjit Singh. "Egalitarian Society," in *The Sikh Revolution*. New Delhi: Vikas, 1981, pp. 115-35.

Juergensmeyer, Mark; and N. Gerald Barrier. "Introduction: The Sikhs and the Scholars," in Juergensmeyer and Barrier, eds., *Sikh Studies: Comparative Perspectives on a Changing Tradition*. Berkeley: Graduate Theological Union, 1979, pp. 1-9.

Khalsa, Shakti Parwha Kaur; and Gurubanda Singh Khalsa. "The Siri Singh Sahib," in S.P.K. Khalsa and S.K.K. Khalsa, eds., *The Man Called the Siri Singh Sahib*. Los Angeles: Sikh Dharma, 1979, pp. 117-31.

Khushwant Singh. *A History of the Sikhs, v. 2: 1839-1974*. Delhi: Oxford University Press, 1977.

Kurin, Richard. "Sect Formation and Definition in the Indian Context: The Sikh Case." M.A. thesis, Anthropology, University of Chicago, 1974.

LaBrack, Bruce. "Neo-Sikhism and East Indian Religious Identification." Paper presented at the Midwest Conference on Asian Affairs, Kansas City, Kansas, November 1974.

———. "Sikhs Real and Ideal: A Discussion of Text and Context in the Description of Overseas Sikh Communities," in M. Juergensmeyer and N.G. Barrier, eds., *Sikh Studies: Comparative Perspectives on a Changing Tradition*. Berkeley: Graduate Theological Union, 1979, pp. 127-42.

LaBrack, Bruce; and Karen Leonard. "Conflict and Compatibility in Punjabi-Mexican Immigrant Families in Rural California, 1915-1965." *Journal of Marriage and the Family* 43 (1984), 527-37.

Leonard, Karen. "Marriage and Family Life among Early Asian Indian Immigrants." *Population Review* 25 (1982), 67-75.

Marenco, Ethne K. *The Transformation of Sikh Society*. Portland, Oregon: The HaPi Press, 1974.

Marriott, McKim. "The Open Hindu Person and Interpersonal Fluidity." Paper presented at the meeting of the Association for Asian Studies, Washington, D.C., March 1980.

Marriott, McKim; and Ronald B. Inden. "Caste Systems," *Encyclopædia Britannica*, new 3rd ed. Chicago: Helen Hemingway Benton, 1974, "Macropædia," v. 3, 982-91.

———. "Toward an Ethnosociology of South Asian Caste Systems," in K. David, ed., *The New Wind: Changing Identities in South Asia*. The Hague: Mouton, 1977, pp. 227-38.

McLeod, W.H. "Ahluwalias and Ramgarhias: Two Sikh Castes." *South Asia: Journal of South Asian Studies* 4 (1974), 78-90.

———. "Caste in the Sikh Panth," in *The Evolution of the Sikh Community: Five Essays*. Oxford: Clarendon Press, 1976, pp. 83-104.

Pettigrew, Joyce. *Robber Noblemen: A Study of the Political System of the Sikh Jats*. London: Routledge & Kegan Paul, 1975.

Premka Kaur, Sardarni. "Rejoinder." *The Sikh Review* 21 (232), (1973), 52-56.

———. "Listen, O 'Patit' and Learn." *Gurdwara Gazette* 46:4 (1975), 4-13.

Saberwal, Satish. *Mobile Men: Limits to Social Change in Urban Punjab*. New Delhi: Vikas, 1976.

Trilochan Singh. *Sikhism and Tantric Yoga*. Ludhiana, Punjab: the author, 1977.

Uberoi, J.P. Singh, "On Being Unshorn," in *Sikhism and Indian Society* (Transactions of the IIAS, 4). Simla: Indian Institute of Advanced Study, 1967, pp. 87-100.

"Yogi Bhajan's Synthetic Sikhism: The Leader of 3HO Inspires Devotion and Hostility." *Time*, September 5, 1977, pp. 70-71.

Sikh Identity in England:
Its Changing Nature

Arthur W. Helweg

For people who want to understand migrant identity formation, the Sikh community in England is an excellent group to study. Mobility is a prominent theme in Sikh history, and there is a wealth of information on Sikh society. In the eighteenth century many Sikhs formed adaptable bands to survive persecution.[1] Under the British Raj, they scattered to various parts of the Empire, so that by the end of the Second World War, Sikh communities were prominent in Australia, Burma, Canada, Cambodia, China, East Africa, Fiji, Kenya, Malaya, New Zealand, the Philippines, Singapore, Thailand, the United States and Uganda.[2] In the last three decades, Sikhs have entered Britain, Canada and the United States in considerable numbers.[3] Now, 10% of the approximately fifteen million world Sikh population live outside of India,[4] and many of those living in India reside outside Punjab. Sikhs in England have been the focus of many studies which vary from literature and language to culture and social organization.[5] The data for this paper are based both on the author's field work and on literature concerning Sikhs in England.

To understand migrant Sikh identity of the present day, one is required to focus on a community that has been unusually mobile over the last three decades. Rapid transportation, telegraph, telephone and postal services have facilitated communication. People travel from one side of the globe to the other within two days and make an instant phone call or send a telegram which can reach many remote areas within hours. Money is transmitted across national boundaries with electronic rapidity. These facilities enable an expatriate to remain closely involved with his or her home community while residing

---

1. Harbans Singh 1985; Khushwant Singh 1963.
2. Helweg 1979.
3. Barber 1986; Buchignani and Indra 1985; Chadney 1984; de Lepervanche 1974, 1984; Helweg 1986a.
4. Iqbal Singh 1986.
5. Tatla and Nesbitt 1987.

[Joseph T. O'Connell, Milton Israel, Willard G. Oxtoby, eds., with W.H. McLeod and J.S. Grewal, visiting eds., *Sikh History and Religion in the Twentieth Century* (S. Asian Studies Papers, 3) (Toronto: S. Asian Studies, Univ. of Toronto, 1988)]

thousands of miles away. One can continue to be an active participant in local affairs in spite of the vast distance separating one from one's place of origin.

Development of Migration Studies

Traditionally, migration studies have concentrated on four broad topics: 1) causes of population shifts, 2) social-psychological concerns of immigrant adaptation, 3) social problems caused by immigration, and 4) the nature and dynamics of migrant groups and individual social networks. The vast majority of these studies use a static model that only considers the dyadic interaction between host and immigrant societies.[6] This is especially true when examining questions concerning identity.[7] With the worldwide communications revolution, researchers need a comprehensive model because international affairs as well as the ongoing interaction with the culture of origin impinge on migrant behavior. Also, there is a dearth of knowledge concerning the impact of population out-flow on the place of origin which includes the effects and processes of return migration.[8] It is only in the last fifteen years that the field of migration studies has begun to consider both ends of the population movements.[9] More recently, the works of Hendricks and Helweg have shown that the home society can have an ongoing influence on its emigrants and directly influence the host community—an influence that can last for generations.[10]

Nancy and Theodore Graves laid the theoretical base for understanding a three-way interactional relationship. They argue that these three social arenas must be considered to comprehend the behavior of expatriates: 1) the sending community, 2) the migrant groups, and 3) the receiving society, for a three-way diachronic process is taking place. The

> adaptive responses displayed by each of these three groups affects the problems confronting the others and the options open for their solutions. Thus the more holistic our view of the adaptive process, the more realistically we can understand and assess what is happening within each.[11]

When we examine migration in a holistic framework, many of the issues that were formerly treated as separate processes are placed in a proper context. In other words, the broader approach conforms more to the actual situation of recent immigrants because it considers the ongoing interaction these communities have on one another in spite of their geographical dispersion. In essence the home, host and migrant communities may mutually influence each other as if they were in the same geographical location. They should be treated as three parts of a unit rather than as distinct communities.[12]

---

6. Bryce-Laporte 1980; Jackson 1969; Jansen 1970; Kasdan 1970; Shaw 1975.
7. Glazer and Moynihan 1975; Barth 1969.
8. Connell, Dasgupta, Laishley and Lipton 1976; Oberoi and Singh 1980, 1983.
9. Gmelch 1980.
10. Hendricks 1974; Jeffrey 1976; Helweg 1978, 1979, 1986a, 1986b.
11. Graves and Graves 1974.
12. In the situation of the Sikhs, there may be more than three communities involved. For example, Sikhs who lived in East Africa, moved to Britain, shifted to Canada and finally settled in the United States have many more influences than just the sending, receiving and migrant groups.

As this paper will show, the identity[13] of a migrant group like the Sikhs in England changes in response to what happens in their place of origin, their new abode, and the stage of development the community has reached.[14]   An understanding of these ethnic dynamics is aided by using Merton's formulation of reference group behavior. Merton argues that a group's relationship to other groups influences behavior.[15]   Owen Lynch has added to Merton's ideas by identifying three of many possible reference groups, which are: 1) reference group of imitation, (group emulated), 2) reference group of identification (community in which people claim membership) and 3) negative reference group (people hostile to them).[16]   The present study adds a fourth category, reference group of evaluation (the community whose consensual agreement socially ranks the individual or group).[17]

People Studied

The Sikhs are a religious community that is highly respected for its assertive, innovative and militant behavior. A scholar, E.J.B. Rose, recognizes Sikh attributes when he writes, "the Sikhs are perhaps the most mobile and versatile people in the whole of India."[18]   Their founder, Guru Nanak (1469-1539), preached commonality between Hindu and Muslim; but there was no peace as rulers executed two of their Gurus and invaders massacred many disciples. Guru Gobind Singh (1666-1708), their tenth and last human Guru, proclaimed the Granth, Sikh scripture, to be their Guru after his death. He also transformed his followers into the Khalsa, a soldier-saint brotherhood.   He gave them the mission to "uphold right in every place and destroy sin and evil; that right may triumph, that good may live and tyranny be uprooted from the land."[19]   He gave his followers the moral justification for warfare in preaching that, "when all other means fail, it is righteous to draw the sword."[20]   With those ideals, tradition has it, he instructed Sikhs to wear the "five k's," which symbolize righteous militancy.

Guru Gobind Singh was assassinated; and subsequent eighteenth-century Sikh history was a cycle of rulers and invaders slaughtering and Sikhs avenging so that at times it seemed that rivers of Sikh blood flowed through the Punjab. For a brief period of glory, Maharajah Ranjit Singh (1780-1839) established a Sikh kingdom under his rulership. But disunity and intrigue among the ruling families followed his death, and the region was annexed by the British in 1849.

---

13. The concept of identity as used in the present literature varies and almost all definitions have problems (Barth 1969). In this study, however, the focus is on the group's culture (values, meanings and beliefs) and how the group defines and maintains its boundaries in relation to other communities.
14. Helweg 1986b.
15. Merton 1957.
16. Lynch 1968.
17. More research needs to be done, but the reference group of evaluation may only be significant for migrant communities.
18. Rose 1969.
19. Khushwant Singh 1983, pp. 41-46.
20. Ibid.

Recognizing the militaristic qualities of the Sikhs, the English classified them as a martial race and incorporated them into the Indian Army. Their loyalty to the crown was crucial for the British to maintain control in South Asia, and the Sikhs were handsomely rewarded with land grants and preferences in the armed forces. Their experience in the military acquainted them with opportunities throughout the Empire and they took advantage of them by emigrating.[21]

In 1947 when the Punjab was partitioned between India and Pakistan, many Sikhs were left destitute and resources were taxed. When news of opportunities abroad reached them through friends, relatives and travel agents, many decided to take advantage of them and England was a primary destination for Sikh emigration.[22] It was in this post-Second World War era that Sikhs from rural Punjab and other South Asians emigrated to England in significant numbers. Like other Asian and West Indian immigrants, they aided the United Kingdom's industry in the post-war recovery period by supplying cheap and needed unskilled labor.

By 1960, Sikhs realized that immigration prohibitions in the U.K. would be implemented. Relatives, friends, wives and children of those South Asians already in England were sponsored to the United Kingdom. They wanted their friends and consanguines to enter before the immigration option was closed. Thus, there was an extraordinary increase in the size of the Indian community of Gravesend, the focus of this study, and the Asian population in Britain generally. The expulsion of Asians from Uganda in 1972 caused many more Indians and Sikhs to settle in the U.K., swelling their ranks to the present count. There are about 1.25 million people of South Asian origin in Britain. This category includes those from India, Pakistan, Bangladesh and Sri Lanka and East Africans of Asian heritage. They form about 2.2% of Great Britain's population.[23] About 400,000 of these are Sikhs from India's Punjab.

Gravesend, Kent, is located on the outskirts of London's industrial sector. Like other port cities in England, it had a few Indians living there intermittently. Its paper, cable, rubber, printing, cement, engineering, shipbuilding and ancillary enterprises provided jobs that attracted immigrants. The 1980 census showed that Indians comprised 5,184 of Gravesend's total population of 94,756. Of these, 70% were Sikh Jats.[24]

By 1980, the Sikh community in Gravesend was losing its categorization as an immigrant community, for 45% of its members were born in England. Also, their cultural emphasis on education and obtaining skilled technical capabilities changed their class position. Initially, Sikh immigrants were agriculturalists from rural Punjab. By 1985, 20% of the wage earners were professionals.

---

21. It must also be kept in mind that during India's independence movement, the Sikhs suffered proportionately more than any other community (Harbans Singh 1985, pp. 319-35).
22. Helweg 1986a.
23. Hiro 1979.
24. These numbers are an under-representation of the South Asian contingent because the census only identified ethnic groups by place of birth. The actual figure may be forty per cent higher (Helweg 1986a).

Commercially, the Indians were making their impact: owning sixteen chemist shops, four pubs, one automobile repair garage, a number of green grocers, two laundromats, a bicycle shop, an electric goods shop, four grocery stores, five driver training schools, three market stalls, one children's boutique, one clothing factory, two construction companies and a tobacco and sweet shop. The Sikh economy of Gravesend had shifted from one that was dependent on the wider society to a generative economy where they were creating jobs and capital.

Punjab, their homeland, is the most prosperous region in India, boasting the highest per capita income (Rs. 3,1640 or U.S. $420), percentage of irrigated areas (79%), agricultural production (82% of its total area is under cultivation), number of tractors (60,000), milk yield and per capita milk consumption (production averages 2.45 kg and 4.31 kg per day from cows and buffaloes respectively and average per capita consumption is 443 grams per day), life expectancy (66.8 years for males and 61.9 years for females) and wages paid for agricultural laborers (Rs. 1,450 annually). Also Punjab was the first to launch an integrated rural development program.[25]

The village of Jandiali, Punjab, from which many of Gravesend's Sikhs emigrated to Britain, is a Sikh community located halfway between the cities of Jullundur and Ludhiana. This village has sent over two-thirds of its 1,608 members to England. Other emigrants are scattered in the north Indian states of Rajasthan and Uttar Pradesh. Yet others are in New Zealand, Australia, Canada, the Philippines and the United States. Since 1972, labor opportunities have developed in Dubai, Iran and other Middle Eastern countries. While most Jats went to England, the bulk of Chamar males and specialist castes gained economic enhancement in the oil-rich countries.[26]

Interaction of Sikhs in Gravesend and Jandiali[27]

The adaptation of England's Sikhs falls into four phases: premigration, freedom, conflict, and settlement.[28] Although the exact point where one phase ends and the other begins is not precise, the important consideration is the changing nature and influence of the three-way interactional process as the community develops.

Premigration is the period before any substantial migration process develops. The information transmitted between the sending and receiving groups is frequently inaccurate, stereotypical and exaggerated. In the case of both the Punjabis and the English, there was direct and indirect influence before the Jandiali-Gravesend migration stream developed.

---

25. Iqbal Singh 1986; Wallace 1986; *Statistical Handbook of Punjab.*
26. Helweg 1986a.
27. Most of the data for this section were acquired by the author's fieldwork. Research in Jandiali and Gravesend in 1970-71 was supported by an NDFL Fellowship and in 1977-78 by the Faculty Research Abroad Program of the Fulbright-Hays Program, U.S. Department of Education. Fieldwork in 1981-82 was financed by the Smithsonian Institution, and study in Gravesend was further supported by a Faculty Research Grant and Fellowship by Western Michigan University in 1985 and travel grants in 1986 and 1987.
28. Helweg 1986b.

Sikh villagers had mixed perceptions of the Raj. Their being preferred for military service contributed to their pride and sense of superiority. They also respected Britain's success in establishing political and economic stability. But the inevitable experience of discrimination and dissatisfaction produced revolutionary movements like the Ghadar Party.[29] A few Jandialians participated in the movement. The villagers also felt a sense of autonomy and maintained that though the English may have controlled the central government, Jandiali was insulated from direct rule. They proudly claimed, "we have never been ruled by a foreign power." Also the British were considered dirty and sexually immoral.[30] At the turn of the century, Punjabis who ventured abroad were often placed in the polluted category. People assumed they would carouse with white women and become drunk with liquor. At the same time, associating with the colonial rulers, going to England, or being able to manipulate the British, afforded an individual economic and political advantage.

From the perspective of reference group behavior, the group of identification for Punjabi Sikhs was their Sikh community. Their village was their reference group of evaluation. As the above shows, the British were both a negative reference group and a group of imitation. There was a love/hate relationship with the English, but the esteem aspect led to England's being a focus for immigration. Post-partition suffering in the Punjab, combined with exaggerated reports of opportunities in Britain, caused Jandiali's Sikhs to respond to the migration opportunity.

Newspaper articles in English, Hindi, Gurmukhi and Urdu described the prosperity abroad without considering deficiencies. One letter illustrates the nature of the information being sent back to Jandiali.

> My job in Gravesend is very easy. I go to work at 8 a.m. and push the green button to make the machine go. I sit in my chair until mid-morning, when I push the red button to stop the machine and take a half-hour tea break. After tea, I return and push the green button to make the machine go and sit in my chair until lunch. At lunchtime I push the red button to stop the machine, take an hour off until 1 p.m. when I return. I push the green button again to make the machine go. At tea-time in the afternoon, the red button is pushed to stop the machine and we take a half-hour off for tea, and then again I push the green button to start the machine until it is time to go home at 5 p.m. Then, I push the red button and stop the machine. For this I make Rs. 1,800 a month.

To a villager averaging Rs. 200 a month—if he had a successful harvest— England was paradise. When emigrants visited home, they wore new clothes, bought prior to leaving the U.K. for India, and spent money on relatives and friends in Jandiali as if the assets were inexhaustible. Those emigrants returning, especially in the 1950's, boasted of their success abroad and they were

---

29. Khushwant Singh 1966, ch. 12. The Ghadar Party was a revolutionary movement that functioned from around 1902 to 1915, although the Communists appealed to its leadership as late as 1925. It was primarily a movement by Sikhs.

30. British habits such as bathing in a tub (sitting in one's own dirt) and using a handkerchief are considered filthy. Also, it is the stereotype held by the Indians that Westerners are sexually much looser than the people of India.

generally covered in the press. A clerk in the post office was referred to as a "postal official," a sweeper at Bowater Scott Paper Company was an "employee at Bowaters," a typist for the local borough council was a "member of the borough civil service." Later on, the myth of England as a paradise was further supported by the tales of travel agents and smugglers who wanted client fees. The emigrant's position in England may have been lowly, but in Jandiali, he was a *bara sahib*, an important person whose emigration increased not only his esteem but also that of his kin group. The tales of wealth and success in Britain were compatible with the esteem villagers had for the British. They had seen the power of the Raj and recalled lavish parades as well as the grand lifestyle of the British in India. Exaggerated stories of success by emigrants were nothing new, but the esteem Punjabi Sikhs held for the British in reference group orientation helped to make such stories credible and contributed to the massive outflow of Sikhs to Britain.

The *freedom* phase is that wherein the men emigrate and wives and children remain behind. Thus, the immigrant community is composed primarily of males, and social controls are lacking. During this stage, the immigrants perceive themselves as sojourners and plan to return to their homeland with a fortune within a year or so. In the case of the Jandiali-Gravesend migration process, the freedom phase lasted from 1950 into the 1960's, when India-England migration was relatively free of restrictions. Males left their wives and children in Jandiali with the goal of entering Britain, acquiring a fortune and quickly returning to India with enough wealth to live a life of comfort and opulence. During this time, Indians relied heavily on the advice of friends and relatives. The start of the Sikh community in Gravesend came about when Bhuta Singh founded an employment service and provided laborers to build an oil refinery near Gravesend on the Isle of Grain. Many Sikhs responded and, for a fee, he provided jobs and housing and took care of bureaucratic requirements. One of these early laborers was Bhajan Singh of Jandiali. Bhajan Singh encouraged and helped his village mates to migrate to Gravesend and take advantage of the opportunities. Being a sponsor gave him prestige at home and in England.

Since they considered England a temporary abode, men worked insatiably hard, logging 90 hours a week. They wanted to earn money fast, and when they learned that the white English did not like to work on weekends, they filled the void. Their concern was not with how much money they earned per hour, but how much was acquired totally. If there was a job that paid £1/50 per hour without overtime and another that paid £1/00 with overtime options on weekends, the latter was accepted. As a result, some chose difficult piecework over steady employment. Although construction did not have the security of a factory job, it would pay more money, which would enable them to return to the Punjab sooner.

The men lived in crowded conditions—thirty or more men to a three-bedroom house. Men slept in shifts; when one left for work another took his cot.

Their social center was the pub, where they quenched their thirst with a glass of beer or ale. The arrangements were meager, but it was temporary and there was promise of greater prosperity and power upon returning to the Punjab.

Men were so busy making their fortune that caste rules were overlooked. Proud high-caste men performed demeaning jobs which involved cleaning latrines and sweeping cigarette butts—work they would never do in the Punjab. They tolerated work beside a low-caste individual, as they only wanted money and enhancement of social position in their home society. For expediency, many Sikhs discarded their turbans and shaved their beards because employers hesitated to hire a man with long hair that might get caught in machinery. For these Punjabi males in England, their primary goal was making money and enhancing their *mann* or *izzat*,[31] prestige, in India.

Indian men arriving in England in those early years were aided by South Asians already present. Indians relied heavily on each other, and there was little distinction between Sikh or Hindu, Indian or Pakistani. Other established villagers often took in wandering South Asians from the streets. They protected one another's reputations and did not write back to India concerning the detrimental behavior of an acquaintance unless they were hostile to him.

The reference group behavior during this time underwent changes. The group of identification for the Sikhs of Gravesend was still Sikh, but what that meant differed from what it meant in India. Some argued, "Guru Nanak shaved and so we are just as good Sikhs as those with beards." Also, there was less of an ethnic boundary among the communities of South Asian origin. Being from the subcontinent was enough to establish an affinity for helping and socializing. Even caste rules upheld by Sikhs in India became less important. Different castes worked and socialized together.

The Sikh immigrants in England did, however, remain apart from their English hosts and were in turn ignored by them. The English were not a negative reference group, but there was a feeling of superiority in that the Sikhs felt they were physically stronger than the whites. The group of evaluation remained the home village. They sent money back and behaved so that *mann* in the home village would be maintained or enhanced. It was to the village that they expected to return and it was in their village that they invested monetarily, socially and politically. In the early years communications with Jandiali were not efficient and reliable. Thus, Sikhs in England were not subject to pressures to obey rural social strictures. Even if a critic wrote back telling of one's deviant behavior, it was discounted as a rival trying to destroy one's character.

The ramifications of the reference-group orientation resulted in economic, social and political changes in Jandiali. Bhajan Singh and his family acquired social esteem and political power in Jandiali. Prior to emigration, they were a low family. Once a substantial emigration process was in place, village youth

---

31. *Mann* is the Punjabi word for *izzat*, which refers to the communal evaluation of a family. It is a cultural goal to work so that the kin group is held in high esteem by the community (Helweg 1986a, pp. 12-21).

aspired and dreamed of going to England, becoming rich, and returning *bara sahibs*, like Bhajan Singh.

Jandialians judged a man's success abroad according to wealth he sent back or displayed in the village. If a male earned in England and sent money back to his family and relatives, his kin group was proud. Dahya reports that over 50 per cent of a Pakistani emigrant's earnings were transmitted to his village via official channels and additional amounts via the black market.[32] That figure held for Jandiali's emigrants also. If a male, on the other hand, went to England and forgot about those in India, the family was shamed for not raising a proper son. There was more at stake for the relatives in the village than just getting money. They wanted to maintain family honor and this could only be done if the male member in England continued to show loyalty and concern for his family in his home village.

Not only did Bhajan Singh and his family gain political power, but others who associated with the emigrant faction gained esteem. Sajan Singh was one. His family was poor, but his father and brother emigrated to England and left Sajan behind to maintain the family farm. Along with that joint property, Sajan Singh managed the land of other village mates who had gone to England and entrusted their small holdings to him. In all, he farmed forty acres (although only seven belonged to him), owned a tractor and tube-wells. Sajan Singh also helped many families migrate to England, and became the spokesman for his less affluent village mates and the lower castes. By helping these people he acquired the status and influence of their *sarpanch* (head of the ruling village council), although the actual title belonged to the wealthiest man in the district.

Whenever any villager or *emigré* needed help to look after a relative, handle money in Punjab, care for land or promote a village project, he approached Sajan Singh, being confident that it would be satisfactorily and expeditiously accomplished. Sajan Singh's situation illustrates that one does not have to leave to reap the benefits of emigration. By helping those abroad with their assets in the village, he gained the necessary resources to become a man of power in Jandiali. Sajan Singh and Bhajan Singh later joined forces to present a challenge to the existing leadership of Jandiali, thereby creating social and political tensions in the village.

The *conflict* phase results when the immigrants' families are present and they have to deal with the cultural clashes of the immigrant and host communities. Their goal may still be to return to their land of origin, but social control mechanisms are establishing themselves in the host country.

By 1960, racial tensions had started developing in British society, causing the imposition of immigration restrictions. Fearing the closing of access to this land of prosperity, Gravesend Sikhs, like other South Asians in Britain, sponsored kinsmen, village mates, wives, children and friends to England. People who had not planned to leave India, decided to emigrate, reasoning, as

---

32. Dahya 1973.

did one man, "Why not go to Britain? I may never have this opportunity again. If I am unhappy, I can always return to India." Even the rich of Jandiali, as well as professionals in Jullundur and Ludhiana, emigrated for fear that they might miss out on opportunities in England. Thus, the composition of the England-Punjab migration stream swelled to include the economically well off and those with professional qualifications.

Families were united as men brought their wives and children to England. They also realized, as one Sikh put it, "all Parliament has to do is pass a law and we will have to leave." It was not just the opportunities in the U.K. that motivated migration but the fear of being deprived of the option to emigrate. The economic conditions of the village had vastly improved by 1960, and Punjab in general was classed as moderately prosperous.[33] Thus, it was the fear of losing the option to migrate that caused the massive influx into Britain, not the push of scarcity in the home region. The legislation produced an effect opposite to Parliament's intention—immigration increased rather than decreased.

The arrival of family members resulted in village norms being imposed on a population that had lived in cultural freedom. It was described by one Gravesend Sikh who stated, "We have one foot in England and one foot in India and it hurts in the middle." In the presence of wives, children and village mates, the males could no longer behave as they pleased. They came under the close scrutiny of their home village. Punjabi women abroad wrote home and portrayed a true representation of life in Britain. Since it was their responsibility to guard the honor of both their husbands' and their own families, they pressured their spouses to adhere to village norms. Parents wanted to set a good example for their children. The increased communications with India had made all doubly careful and conscious of their behavior, for their goal was to be highly respected in Jandiali, where they planned to resettle.

The explosive influx of Indians after 1960 created fears among the host community. White Gravesenders were unhappy with the obvious impact the presence of large numbers of Indians had made on their town. The racial clashes and friction in East London were exaggerated by politicians and reported daily in the British press. Discrimination became a major issue, and although a Sikh in Gravesend may not have experienced unfavorable treatment, he read about it in the papers or heard reports on television, realizing that his presence gave offense to many.

The British fear of being overrun was accentuated by the 1972 influx of Asians expelled from Uganda. Although many of these African Asians were well-qualified professionals and educated individuals who made a valuable contribution to British society, they were not accepted. Asians in Gravesend were blamed for taking jobs which rightfully belonged to the English. In certain cases the Punjabis had seniority over English whites. However, it was the immigrants' willingness to work overtime, on weekends and night shifts that

---

33. Ballard and Ballard 1977.

kept unemployment low among their ranks.   The National Front[34] marched through Gravesend and caused a great deal of fear among the Indians.   There was further resentment against the immigrant group because Indian children were very competitive in school and often scored over English children for academic honors.

In the terms of reference for group behavior, the group of identification was still Sikh, but the meaning of that shifted to a more rural orientation in cultural values and goals for the elders.   The shaven Sikhs did not suddenly become shorn, but more men started growing their beards and fulfilling family obligations in India.   Thus, the village became their group of imitation.   Sikh parents in England imposed restrictive norms on their children.   These were more conservative than what was actually the case in the Punjab.   The British became the negative reference group because of immigration restrictions and racism developing in English society.   In addition, the Sikhs did not want their children to emulate white culture.   Since they planned to return to India, where many had parents and family back in the village, Jandiali was still their reference group of evaluation.

A ramification of this changed identity was that Sikhs in Gravesend were caught between conflicting cultural demands.   For example, Sikhs had learned that trimming their hair and beards increased their marketability for jobs while in England.   Such action often broke the hearts of their parents in Punjab, for religious dictates maintained that unshorn hair was crucial to spirituality and masculinity.   The Gravesend Sikh male was torn between his desire to get a good job in England by compromising Sikh practices and not to cause parental anguish or set a bad example for his children.

A few returned to India, but life there was difficult.   They neither had knowledge nor business experience in Punjab and quickly lost their fortunes.   Others were unhappy without English amenities.   It may not have been any one thing in particular, but life in the village, especially for women, was difficult.   Having savored privacy in Gravesend, females preferred England, where they were the mistresses of their houses without having to yield to a mother-in-law.   Teenagers returning to the village had their share of hard times.   Young boys found their Punjabi language inadequate and part-time jobs for youth in Punjab were limited and frowned upon by elders.   Thus boys became bored.   Girls, because of their chaperoned and restricted life in England, did not face the same problems to the same degree as boys.   Youngsters were unhappy and wanted to return to their British way of life.

As a result, the Sikhs in Gravesend emphasized the cultural differences between themselves and the English.[35]   They worked to instill their heritage and

---

34. The National Front is a political party based on the premise of white racial superiority. It is reminiscent of the doctrines of Adolf Hitler and has the swastika as its symbol. It became visible in the 1970's and is still noticeable.

35. This is not to imply that the English did not do their part to maintain social separation. The point here is that it was a conscious endeavor among Gravesend's Sikhs to raise a distinction between themselves and the English host society.

pride into the second generation and to keep their children from absorbing the host culture and becoming "Brown British." Therefore, the migrants continued their interest in their place of origin, reacting to elections and politics in India as if these directly affected them. Immigrant vernacular newspapers described Indian riots, elections and political figures in detail. There was a dichotomy. On the one hand, Gravesend Sikhs did not want their children to become British. Yet, they were unwilling to give up the good life and wealth of England. The longer they stayed the more they wondered whether they had made a wise decision. They could see their second generation already resisting their source culture and emulating some British norms.

The second generation changed their focus. Boys with academic abilities preferred not to work in factories and opted for professions that were marketable on a world-wide basis. Thus, accounting, engineering and medicine were given priority over subjects like history, sociology, art and others that were not lucrative. Even if the child was artistically inclined, he succumbed to parental pressure and went into a more profitable field. Sikh youngsters were highly motivated and studied hard. They had seen their elders slave on assembly lines and did not want that life for themselves.

Elders were strict with their children, and this caused psychological conflicts. Indian boys attended school with English girls, but were forbidden even to talk with a female on the street. An Indian youngster conversing with a white girl was reported to his parents by another Sikh. Yet, youngsters saw their English friends at school behaving freely. Gravesend Sikh girls were required to come directly home after school without the interaction with friends that was the case among English girls.

These youngsters, raised on the "English Telly" and taught by English school teachers, were confused as to which values to follow. At home they respected their elders, lived for the family and had their marriage arranged. In school, they were ridiculed by their teachers and friends, who told them that such practices were inhumane and archaic. Contemporary British culture dictated a high emphasis on individualism, not submitting to the group, and choosing one's life partner. All these were in opposition to what Indian children were taught at home.

Children were taught a glorified version of Indian village life by their elders, causing them to long for India. However, a visit to rural Punjab was enough to convince them that the village was not an alternative. Also they were ignorant about the opportunities and luxuries of urban India; they considered all South Asia to be like their parents' village. Thus, to them, all India was undesirable in comparison with life in Gravesend.

The Gravesend Sikhs countered Western influence with strictness, holding language classes in the gurdwara and conducting instruction in Punjabi and Sikh culture. The elders also downgraded English norms and tried to stop their offspring from interacting with the whites. The influence from India continued to be strong. Gravesend Sikhs preferred spouses from India for their children.

They desired arranging marriages with spouses of rural background because of the high regard villagers were supposed to have for the elderly. For those with a daughter, they could keep her home if married to a boy from India, for the village lad was loyal and beholden to his wife's family for sponsoring him. Since these boys seldom had kin support in England, the balance of power shifted in favor of the female and her family.

Although parental logic was valid, the marriage of a village-raised child to an English-bred Punjabi was seldom compatible. Village boys expected their wives to cook at any time convenient to them. A girl working full time had to wait on her husband in the middle of the night after his pint of ale in the pub with his buddies. He expected her to walk behind him, keep her head covered and behave modestly like the village women. Sikh girls raised in England resisted these practices.

In response to the increased racial animosity in Britain, many second-generation Indians felt that they deserved the benefits they received in Britain. Unlike their parents, who felt they were guests in England and should be grateful, the youngsters argued that the British had exploited their country for several hundred years and had no reason to resent the U.K. Indians. In response to parties like the National Front and other forms of racism, they adopted a "fight fire with fire" doctrine.

It was also a time when more complex social boundaries developed in the Gravesend Sikh community. Initially the Sikhs were a unit, but as their numbers increased, divisions developed between those from East Africa and those from India. Also urban Sikhs had little in common with Sikhs of rural origins and those with beards felt the shaven contingent were not true Sikhs. Even caste differences arose as Ramgarhias and Jats emphasized their distinctiveness. The divisions in the Gravesend community were not, however, as prominent as elsewhere in England where the Sikhs of East Africa had their own gurdwaras, associations and networks.

In the meantime, divisions arose in the village also. Emigrants and their associates emphasized their distinctiveness from the other villagers. They showed off their appliances and clothes that came from England. Some returnee Sikhs made a point of using English words periodically even though they did not know English. They wanted to emphasize that they were from England.

Even the casual visitor to Jandiali in 1970 saw new multi-storied farm houses outside the village. A few England returnees on holiday were visible around the village. Being an England returnee, however, began to lose its former charm and prestige. It was no longer enough to be an English migrant or have a son or relative in Britain. Now, the emigrant had to have a decent job. If a man was a janitor, villagers in Jandiali lost respect for that individual; but when he returned to Jandiali for a visit, they were cordial towards him and his family. The emigrant was unaware of comments like, "He is a mere slave or a lowly sweeper in England; he is nothing." The emigrants did not realize the true feelings the villagers had towards them. In spite of the demeaned status of the

English emigrant, anyone who was not wealthy openly sought opportunities to emigrate. The Sikhs in Gravesend had no difficulty marrying their boys to educated girls in India and demanding high dowries. The uneducated girls from Gravesend were sought in Punjab for this provided access to England.

The political and economic situation of the village also underwent change. Sajan Singh, with the support of Bhajan Singh, had capital, and with the support of poor Jat families, Ramgarhias and other castes, he challenged the ruling family. Inflation hit Jandiali and made it necessary for a middle-class family to have relatives in England in order to maintain a decent living standard. Jandiali began to develop an externally dependent economy, meaning that the influx of outside capital enabled it to maintain its prosperity. In the case of Jandiali, there were over Rs. 1 million of visible assets acquired by money earned in England. Emigrant money built houses, bought tractors, dug tube-wells, acquired land and financed public amenities. Six of the eight tractors were paid for with emigrant money; most of the tube-wells were financed by Sikhs overseas, as were practically all the houses built after 1960. In addition, Jandiali's co-operative bank boasted a sizable surplus which exceeded Rs. 3 million in assets. This wealth in Jandiali did not include capital invested by emigrants in businesses in England and areas of India and of Punjab outside Jandiali.

The inflation rate is shown in the rising land prices. An acre of land in Jandiali cost Rs. 4,000 in 1954, but by 1968 it had risen to Rs. 12,000. In 1971 land was Rs. 25,000 per acre and by 1978 the cost was Rs. 30,000. Not only had the price risen drastically, but in 1970 it was difficult to buy land at any price. Landholders, whether in Jandiali or England, were not willing to sell the land which was their security.

Emigrants not only sent capital to Jandiali; they also communicated innovative ideas and modern agricultural technology. Relatives and friends abroad continually sent different varieties of seeds and information concerning new farm techniques. Sikh Jats tried these new methods and, if successful, they implemented them. Those individuals who had money and security from abroad could afford the risk of trying new techniques, thus becoming the opinion leaders of their village and surrounding area. Although Jandiali farmers keenly listened to farm programs on the radio and closely watched experiments conducted at Punjab Agricultural University, Ludhiana, they were often ahead of those sources because of information and shipments of new varieties of seeds from relatives in England, California or British Columbia. During this period, the Indian government allowed Punjabis abroad to send gifts to their relatives in the homeland. The Massey-Ferguson Tractor Company, between October 24, 1968 and August 31, 1970, delivered 1,038 tractors to Punjab, paid for in sterling by Indians in England.

Emigrants in Gravesend and Leamington Spa also provided capital for paving roads, building two schoolhouses, constructing two wedding houses, and collecting enough money for a new gurdwara. Without emigration, Jandiali and the Punjab might have been the scene of scarcity and poverty instead of being a prosperous region of India.

In the village, either rich Jat landowners or those with external support from their emigrant kin could afford to pay high wages to the itinerant workers and buy farm machinery. For those who had neither strong outside contacts from emigrants nor a rich background, village life became miserable. The inflation rate in the village increased more rapidly than their means to maintain a good living standard. In fact, with the mass emigration from Jandiali, emigrating or having close contacts with emigrants was the only way to survive for the middle income and poor. Although emigrant remittances were to decrease rapidly, 1978 revealed a visible increase in the external economy of Jandiali over the preceding two decades. Jandialians had a new gurdwara at the cost of Rs. 1.3 *lakh* (Rs. 130,000) and had invested R. 8 *lakh* (Rs. 800,000)—primarily pounds sterling donated by migrant villagers in England—in a bus business and a loan company. The latter two enterprises were headed by Sajan Singh. Jandialians in the seventies claimed that money continued to come back, but not to the same extent as in the sixties.

Most Jandiali emigrants held onto their land, which was managed by a friend or relative. It was very important for the Sikh in Gravesend to keep his land in the Punjab in spite of the shortage of labor caused by emigration. Interestingly, most of the work was done either by mechanization or by migrant workers from Uttar Pradesh who came to Punjab because of the higher wages. Jandiali emigrants continued to play an active role in village affairs, even though they resided in England. A group of emigrants donated money to build the new village place of worship to fulfill Bhuta Singh's dream of having a gurdwara in Jandiali with a tower so high that one could see Phagwara, which was three miles away, from its top. The *zaildar's*, or headman's, group resisted the new construction, but the emigrant faction won. The poorer Jat element had initially emigrated to England from Jandiali to make money, but an additional consequence was that they subsequently had power to influence village affairs.

In the case of emigrant villages like Jandiali, at first Jats had gone abroad mostly to England and some to Canada; but in the late seventies, large contingents of Chamars and other specialized castes, such as Tarkhans and Lohars in particular, ventured to the Middle East, sending money back to increase their family's wealth in the village. They, too, were encouraged by agents, like the early Jats had who had gone to England.

The *settlement* phase arrives when the immigrant community becomes a permanent part of their new abode—when returning is no longer a viable option.[36] In other words, they have changed from an immigrant community to a minority group.

---

36. The article (Helweg 1986b) which provides the framework for this study was written long before it was published. In relation to that study, the Sikhs of Gravesend have now reached the settlement stage.

The Gravesend/Jandiali Sikh migration had virtually stopped by the 1980's. England had initiated restrictive legislation so that only certain categories of family members could be admitted.[37] Thus their numbers did increase, but only slightly. There were many other factors that would affect Sikh immigrant identity. In 1981, Britain's cities exploded in racial violence, and Gravesend was not immune to those influences. Events in India also made their mark. The invasion of the Golden Temple by army troops, the assassination of Mrs. Gandhi and the massacre of Sikhs in Delhi all were to impinge on Sikh perceptions and identity formation in England.

In terms of reference group behavior the group of identification was still Sikh, but what that meant differed according to place of origin, caste and sect membership and generation. There was such animosity between those who were for Khalistan and those opposed that some of those advocating a moderate political stance feared for their safety. Sikh identity in England was not with India either. They were a group of their own. The group of emulation for the Sikhs in England was no longer the village. Those in England saw themselves as above their village counterparts, as those in India perceived themselves as more pure and superior to the emigrants. Those in England developed their own lifestyle. They emulated their own community, which also became their reference group of evaluation. However, the negative reference group became the British. Discriminatory practices and violence increased, and the Sikhs in England, like other minorities, resented such treatment. Thus the negative attitude toward the English host community increased. Even in the village, reference group behavior was evident as those who had emigrant affiliations accentuated their distinctiveness from the others. They formed their own political group and used their assets to control village politics.

The ramifications of this changed identity were many. When the Festival of India was held in Britain in 1981, some South Asians held a "Counter Festival" which emphasized Indian immigrant culture. As one boy stated, "We are not white British nor are we lackeys of the Indian government. We have our own culture to communicate." Yet, when India won the World Cup in soccer, the Sikh immigrants cheered and sweets were passed out to passing motorists as they traversed Southall, the Indian quarter in London.

Ties with India and the influence of the land of origin are still prominent. Bringing a girl from India for a spouse is still preferred over marrying an individual born and raised in England. In addition, the influence from India has been dramatic since the conflict in the Punjab has taken on an increasingly communal note. Sikhs and Hindus in England are more separate and some Sikhs and Hindus who have been friends for many years now find their relationship strained. In Gravesend, social pressure is such that a person who does not support the movement for Khalistan as a Sikh homeland is considered immoral

---

37. In the case of the United States, consanguine relationships were a loophole for immigration. The regulations in England varied periodically (Klug and Gordon 1983).

or not a true Sikh. One Sikh reflected the views of many when he said, "We all know that violence for Khalistan is not the way to do things, but the sentiment is such that if you voice your opinion, you will be condemned." When the Indian army entered the Golden Temple, there were mass demonstrations against the action and Gravesend Sikhs as well as other emigrant Sikhs have sent a great deal of money back to India to support the revolutionary movement.[38]

The situation has become more ambivalent for Sikhs in England, as the following two quotations illustrate. The first is by a fifty-year-old man who had worked in England but planned to return who said, "We have lost everything. India is no longer our home and yet we do not belong in England either. Where do we go?" A young shaven Sikh who had gone home almost every other year said, "I can't return to India any more. The militant Sikhs automatically shoot anyone without a beard, and I am shaven." Whether the above statements reflect reality is not important for our purposes. The crucial thing is how Sikhs perceive the situation because it is on perceptions that behavior is based.

Conclusions

As this study shows, the interactional relationship between the host, home and migrant communities is ongoing and changes as the immigrant community develops in its overseas abode. The foregoing account of the Gravesend-Jandiali migrants shows that there has been a three-way interactional relationship between the emigrant, receiving and sending communities. And the nature and strength of the transactional relationships among these three communities have changed as the migration process has developed over time. During the *premigration* phase, the communication link between the prospective receiving and sending communities transmits inaccurate and stereotypical information. In the *freedom* phase, males are free of many social strictures. The important factor is perception in the home community. Thus, money is remitted to help dependents in the sending community. The *conflict* phase is a time of social tension and rapid change. Wives, children and other family members come and assert adherence to norms of the home society. In the meantime, they have also to live within the dictates of the receiving culture, which imposes its own rules. The trauma becomes more acute as the second generation comes into prominence. During this time, return to the home village continues to be popular as a goal for many to achieve. The receiving society, however, can no longer ignore the new people settling in their midst and has to deal with the new population which has become a matter of concern. The *settlement* phase is when the immigrant community becomes permanent. This does not mean that emigrants lose interest in their homeland, but direct involvement with their natal community may be absent or decrease considerably. However, such traumas as the invasion of the Golden Temple raise overseas Sikh concern and involvement in India.

---

38. Chandran 1985; Chhabra 1984; Ray 1986.

This study illustrates that there is a strong ongoing interaction among the sending, receiving and migrant communities; each of the three groups must be considered in every stage of development. Further work needs to be done to enable us to understand better the effects of emigration upon host, home and migrant societies and to clarify the international relationships among these. To do so well, one needs a holistic approach.

References

Ballard, Roger; and Catherine Ballard. "The Development of South Asian Settlements in Britain," in James L. Watson, ed., *Between Two Cultures; Migrants and Minorities in Britain*. Oxford: Basil Blackwell, 1977, pp. 21-56.

Barber, John. "A Troubled Community." *Macleans* 99 (June 25, 1986), 19-23.

Barth, Frederik. "Introduction," in F. Barth, ed., *Ethnic Groups and Boundaries: The Social Organization of Cultural Difference*. Boston: Little, Brown, 1969, pp. 9-38.

Bryce-Laporte, Roy Simon, ed. *Sourcebook on the New Immigration: Implications for the United States and the International Community*. New Brunswick, N.J.: Transaction Books, 1980.

Buchignani, Norman; and Doreen M. Indra, with Ram Srivast[a]va. *Continuous Journey: A Social History of South Asians in Canada*. Toronto: McClelland and Stewart Ltd., in association with the Multiculturalism Directorate, Department of the Secretary of State and the Canadian Government Publishing Centre, Supply and Services, 1985.

Chadney, James G. *The Sikhs of Vancouver*. New York: AMS Press, 1984.

Chandran, Ramesh. "United Kingdom: Tackling Terrorism." *India Today* 10:22 (1985), pp. 28-29.

Chhabra, Aseem. "Thousands of Sikhs Protest." *India Today* 14:37 (1984), pp. 1, 14.

Connell, John; Biplab Dasgupta; Roy Laishley; and Michael Lipton. *Migration from Rural Areas: The Evidence from Village Studies*. Delhi, Bombay, Calcutta, Madras: Oxford University Press, 1976.

Dahya, B. "Pakistanis in Britain, Transients or Settlers?" *Race* 14:3 (1973).

Fanon, Frantz. *The Wretched of the Earth*. New York: Grove Press, 1963.

Glazer, Nathan; and Daniel P. Moynihan. *Ethnicity: Theory and Experience*. Cambridge, Mass.: Harvard University Press, 1975.

Gmelch, George. "Return Migration," in *Annual Review of Anthropology*, v. 9. Palo Alto, California: Annual Reviews Inc., 1980.

Graves, Nancy B.; and Theodore Graves. "Return Migration," in *Annual Review of Anthropology*, v. 3. Palo Alto, California: Annual Reviews Inc., 1974.

Harbans Singh. *The Heritage of the Sikhs*. New Delhi: Manohar, 1985.

Helweg, Arthur. "Punjabi Farmers: Twenty Years in England." *India International Centre Quarterly* 5:1 (1978).

————. *Sikhs in England: The Development of a Migrant Community*. New Delhi: Oxford University Press, 1979.

————. *Sikhs in England*, 2nd ed. New Delhi, Bombay, Calcutta, Madras: Oxford University Press, 1986[a].

————. "Indians in England: A Study of the Interactional Relationships of Sending, Receiving and Migrant Societies," in M.S.A. Rao, ed., *Studies in Migration: Internal and International Migration in India*. Delhi: Manohar, 1986[b].

Hendricks, Glen. *The Dominican Diaspora*. New York: Teachers College Press, 1974.

Hiro, Dilip. "Indians in Britain." *India International Centre Quarterly* 6:3 (1979).

Iqbal Singh. *Punjab under Siege: A Critical Analysis*. New York, London, Toronto, Sydney: Allen, McMillan and Enderson, 1986.

Jackson, J.A., ed. *Migration*. Cambridge: Cambridge University Press, 1969.

Jansen, Clifford. ed. *Readings in the Sociology of Migration*. London: Pergamon Press, 1970.

Jeffrey, Patricia. *Migrants and Refugees: Muslim and Christian Families in Bristol*. Cambridge: Cambridge University Press, 1976.

Kasdan, Leonard. "Introduction," in Robert F. Spencer, general ed., *Migration and Anthropology*. Seattle: American Ethnological Society and the University of Washington Press, 1970.

Khushwant Singh. *A History of the Sikhs*, v. 1: *1469-1839*; and v. 2: *1839-1864*. Princeton: Princeton University Press, 1963-66.

———. "Sikh Power." *Across the Board*, June 1983, pp. 41-46.

Klug, Francesca; and Paul Gordon. *Different Worlds: Racism and Discrimination in Britain*. London: The Runnymede Trust, 1983.

Kritz, Mary M.; Charles B. Keely; and Silvano M. Tombs, eds. *Global Trends in Migration*. New York: Center for Migration Studies, 1981.

de Lepervanche, Marie M. "A Boat Load of Grandfathers." Ph.D. thesis, University of Sydney, 1974.

———. *Indians in a White Australia: An Account of Race, Class and Indian Immigration to Eastern Australia*. Sydney, London, Boston: George Allen & Unwin, 1984.

Lynch, Owen. "The Politics of Untouchability: A Case from Agra, India," in Milton Singer and Bernard S. Cohn, eds., *Structure and Change in Indian Society*. Chicago: Aldine Publishing Company, 1968.

McNeill, William H.; and Ruth S. Adams. *Human Migration: Patterns and Policies*. Bloomington: Indiana University Press, 1978.

Mehta, Ved. *Daddyji*. New York: Farrar, Straus and Giroux, 1972.

Merton, Robert. *Social Theory and Social Structure*. Glencoe, Ill.: The Free Press, 1957.

Naisbitt, John. *Megatrends*. New York: Warner Books, 1982.

Oberoi, A.S.; and H.K. Manmohan Singh. "Migration, Remittances and Rural Development: Findings of a Case Study in the Indian Punjab." *International Labour Review* 109:2 (1980).

———. *Causes and Consequences of Internal Migration: A Study in the Indian Punjab*. Delhi: Oxford University Press, 1983.

Page, Barbara. "Postindustrialism," in *Encyclopedia of Sociology*. Guilford, Connecticut: The Dushkin Publishing Group, 1974, pp. 219-20.

Papademetriou, Demetrios G. "Effects of Emigration on the Sending Countries: Some Thoughts and Parallels between the American and Recent European Experiences with 'Labor Emigration,'" in Roy Simon Bryce-Laporte, ed., *Sourcebook on the New Immigration: Implications for the United States and the International Community*. New Brunswick, N.J.: Transaction Books, 1980.

Porter, John. "Ethnic Pluralism in Canadian Perspective," in Nathan Glazer and Daniel P. Moynihan, eds., *Ethnicity: Theory and Experience*. Cambridge, Mass.: Harvard University Press, 1975.

Ray, Shantanu. "Militant Chief Admits Canada Ties." *Indian Abroad* 16:49 (1986), 1, 5.

Rose, E.J.B. *Colour and Citizenship: A Report on British Race Relations*. London: Oxford University Press, 1969.

Shaw, R. Paul. *Migration: Theory and Fact*. Philadelphia: Regional Science Research Institute, 1975.

Swanson, Jon. "The Consequences of Emigration for Economic Development: A Review of the Literature." *Papers in Anthropology* 20:1 (1979), 39-56.

Tatla, Darshan Singh; and Eleanor M. Nesbitt. *Sikhs in Britain: An Annotated Bibliography.* Coventry: Centre for Research in Ethnic Relations, University of Warwick, 1987.

Tinker, Hugh. *A New System of Slavery: The Export of Indian Labour Overseas 1830-1920.* Bombay: Oxford University Press, 1974.

————. *The Banyan Tree: Overseas Emigrants from India, Pakistan and Bangladesh.* New York, Delhi, Karachi: Oxford University Press, 1977.

Wallace, Paul. "The Sikhs as a 'Minority' in a Sikh Majority State." *Asian Survey* 26: 3 (1986), 363-77.

The Presentation of Sikhs in Recent Children's Literature in Britain

Eleanor M. Nesbitt

Introduction

Children are profoundly influenced by early images. The characterisation of people of a particular sex, race, religion or occupation helps mould their presuppositions and behaviour in later life. For this reason anti-racist and feminist groups have monitored children's literature for potentially damaging stereotypes of racial groups or sexist gender roles and have campaigned for the removal of offending publications from libraries. In this paper I examine the emergence of children's literature concerned with Sikhs and Sikhism. I note the growing but different importance attached to this by Sikhs and by (non-Sikh) educationists and publishers, and I comment on the depictions of Sikhs in relevant fiction and non-fiction.

During a recent search for junior literature presenting Sikhs I examined thirty commercially published British books intended for younger readers ranging from infants to school leavers. Of these the ratio of books published from 1980 to 1987 to books published in the 1970's was more than 2:1, and none had appeared earlier than 1970.

Reasons for Children's Literature on Sikhs

The reasons for the appearance in the 1970's and 1980's of children's books that portray Sikhs are interrelated and are inseparable from recent history. Sikh migration to Britain came to general public notice during the 1960's. The earlier princely visitors and the trickle of ex-servicemen, students and pedlars swelled after 1945 into a more plentiful flow of male Sikhs and others from the Indian subcontinent to supplement indigenous labour in post-war industry and transport. Wives and children arrived later and gurdwaras were established. There were many Sikhs among the Asians entering Britain from newly-independent East African countries in the 1960's and 1970's. The visible

[Joseph T. O'Connell, Milton Israel, Willard G. Oxtoby, eds., with W.H. McLeod and J.S. Grewal, visiting eds., *Sikh History and Religion in the Twentieth Century* (S. Asian Studies Papers, 3) (Toronto: S. Asian Studies, Univ. of Toronto, 1988)]

presence of Asian communities in many British cities excited particular concern in educational circles.

The decision to provide extra English tuition for immigrants' children gave way to awareness of the need for multicultural education for all pupils. It was realised that the curriculum and library should be less ethnocentric. This was necessary in order to increase children's understanding of the varied society in which they were growing up. It was felt that children of different racial and religious backgrounds should find themselves represented in the teaching materials. The local presence of culturally diverse groups was seen as a rich human resource with potential for extending the content of subjects across the curriculum and throughout the age range. The racial attitudes and underlying values of teachers and educational writers were also challenged, with the hidden curriculum receiving scrutiny. Meanwhile, continuing instances of racial discrimination and culture-conflict in the news laid on writers of young people's literature an urgent responsibility to awaken a sympathetic understanding of characters from diverse ethnic and religious backgrounds.

In keeping with this multicultural perspective the underlying principles of the only statutory school subject, Religious Education, were also being rethought. According to most Local Agreed Syllabuses for Religious Education published since 1975, a major aim of the subject has been to increase pupils' understanding of world faiths.[1] This involves the teachers not only in communicating such information as key concepts, distinctive rituals and faith history but also in enabling pupils to empathise with the religious experience of others. Recent writing in Religious Education recommends that teachers encourage pupils to share with one another their knowledge and personal experience of religion.[2] Teachers are urged to select some of their material from the life experience of children and young people belonging to different religious traditions in Britain.[3]

To make multicultural education across the curriculum, and multi-faith Religious Education in particular, a reality, teachers and pupils required appropriate books. Books on Sikhism are now essential, for the reason that Sikhism is examined in the General Certificate of Secondary Education and is also an "A" level examination subject for one examination board.[4]

Sikh Concern

While educationists were promoting multicultural materials in which Sikhs and other communities featured, concerned Sikh adults had become determined to provide literature in English on Sikhism for Sikh children. Their perspective and motivation naturally differ from the interests of non-Sikh educationists, authors and publishers, but arise from the same situation of a growing Sikh

---

1. E.g., Birmingham 1975, Hampshire 1978, Berkshire 1982.
2. E.g., Grimmitt 1982.
3. E.g., Gates 1982.
4. For details of Sikh studies in public examinations see Cole 1987 and Buddle 1987.

diaspora in Britain. The literature they have produced has been a valuable source of information for teachers.

By 1969, the year of Guru Nanak's five-hundredth anniversary, many Sikh parents had realised that their children were growing up in Britain in virtual ignorance of Punjabi language and in a school environment in which Sikhism played no part.[5] Indeed, some values enshrined in the education system or informing peer group behaviour ran counter to Sikh teaching or to Punjabi cultural ethos. In October 1969 five thousand copies of *Guru Nanak for Children* were printed for free distribution, and in January 1970 the Sikh Missionary Society (UK) Gravesend was inaugurated. Since then numerous booklets, mainly in English, have been distributed free of charge, although the idiom and presentation were not always appropriate for young children growing up in Britain. Finance did not permit lavish productions with colour illustrations. Now the Sikh Missionary Society has risen to meet contemporary educational needs with *The Sikhs and Their Way of Life*.[6] This is comparable to the Canadian publication, *Sikhism: A Resource Book for Teachers*.[7]

Under the auspices of the Sikh Missionary Society the year 1986 saw the inception of the Sikh Religious Education Advisory Council (UK). Among its objects are:

> to develop and evaluate teaching materials in Sikh Religious Studies in cooperation with bodies specialising in curriculum development and to make such materials available to LEA's [Local Education Authorities], schools, colleges and other appropriate bodies.[8]

Concerned Sikhs have not only realised the increasing need for their youngsters to be taught soundly in English about their faith. They have also been disquieted by the content of publications from other sources. In these they have found factual errors and a difference in emphasis from what they would wish.   In some cases they suspect deliberate attempts to undermine Sikh "orthodoxy."

When Coventry Education Authority's Minority Group Support Service published *How a Sikh Prays*,[9] a conscious decision was taken to include photographic reference to a Sikh boy with short hair, since a high percentage of local male Sikhs are not *keshdhari*. The resulting indignation of some local Sikhs, who made representations to the Local Education Authority, is an indicator of the high importance which they attach to portrayal of Sikhs in children's literature.

Sikh concern about the presentation of their tradition has been intensified by escalating political unrest in their homeland, Indian Punjab. In 1984 tension between Sikh interests in Punjab and the central government came to a head in the storming of the Sikhs' holiest shrine by the Indian army. Sikhs came to

---

5. Grewal 1987.
6. Sacha 1988.
7. Singh 1985.
8. Memorandum of Association of the Sikh Religious Education Advisory Council (UK).
9. Minority Group Support Service 1979.

worldwide media notice as never before, and publishers' readiness to consider books focussing on Sikhs grew. Since June 1984 young British Sikhs have increasingly turned to the literature to learn about their religious and historical tradition and to help them forge a viable individual identity.

Despite the work of dedicated Sikh Missionary Society writers— Gurbachan Singh Sidhu and others—and the publications of Surjit Singh Kalra, the authorship of books on Sikhs for children produced by mainstream British publishers has been largely non-Sikh, though in consultation with Sikh advisors. Exceptions are Davinder Kaur Babraa, Sukhbir Singh Kapoor, Ranjit Arora, Piara Singh Sambhi and Daljit Singh. To date published junior fictional writing on Sikhs is totally non-Sikh.

A significant current initiative is the Birmingham Sikh History Project. For a year a team of Sikhs and others, working under the auspices of the Sikh Youth Service, are researching the history of the Birmingham Sikh community. They intend to produce educational packs for schools. These will focus not only on local Sikh history but also on earlier Sikh history and on the festival of Baisakhi.

Issues Involved in the Presentation of Sikhs and Sikhism

The issues are complex. Among individuals who share a common faith identity there are inevitably differences of emphasis. No one publication can do justice to all these. Not all books about Sikhs are primarily intended to give a normative account of Sikhism. Some are intended to present the Sikh community in all its diversity.[10] In Religious Education material the ideal form of Sikhism can be presented but not inculcated. Writers need an understanding of the sociological complexities (such as the subsidiary marriage practices characteristic of families of Bhatra caste) and of Sikhs' religious sensitivities in order to make informed decisions on emphasis and content. In one case one suspects that the writer was not fully aware of the distinctive features of the particular community whose practices are so vividly portrayed.[11]

The Sikh dissatisfied with a book produced by non-Sikhs may identify the shortcomings as stemming simply from ignorance. There is naturally fear that Sikhs' separate identity is being undermined by any public affirmation as Sikh of individuals who lack the outward signs of orthodoxy and commitment or by the inclusion of practice contrary to the Sikh code of discipline.

Since Sikh children are learning the fundamentals of their religion through school teaching and school books, Sikhs are justified in their concern, especially at the present juncture. At a time when the Punjab crisis and calls for separatism have heightened sensitivities and made the question of Sikhs' identity of burning importance, the allegiance of a growing diaspora generation, unfamiliar with the language of the scriptures, poses questions for the future of the community. In this crucially formative period of Sikh history the writings of

---

10. E.g., de Souza 1986.
11. Bennet 1985.

some scholars and lay people, both for adult and junior readers, can be argued to have a weakening or divisive effect upon a community whose weakness could serve inimical political interests.

For the purposes of this paper I shall divide published children's literature on Sikhs and Sikhism into three categories—non-fiction for primary school children (5-11 years), non-fiction for secondary school pupils (11-18 years) and junior fiction (5-18 years). Since fiction and children's books published in Britain may not be readily available to all readers, the bibliography includes a note on each title.[12]

Non-Fiction for Primary School Readers

Books for primary school children are lavishly illustrated with colour photographs of Sikhs in Britain. They present particular children and their families. Joan Solomon's Bobbi has short hair.[13] Olivia Bennett's Sikh family are all *keshdhari*, but the Sikh wedding could be misleading, since rather than concentrating on the religious ceremony it shows far from universal subsidiary marriage customs.[14]

Lyle and Aggarwal also introduce their readers to Sikhism through individual Sikh children. The approach is a good one; books such as these should be in school libraries regardless of the ethnic composition of particular schools and their immediate neighbourhoods. From contact with a number of books of this type children see a fuller picture of life as a Sikh child in Britain than is possible from any single book in this category.

Non-Fiction for Older Pupils

For secondary-school-age children Butler, Cole and Sambhi present an uncontroversially "orthodox" Sikhism. So do Kapoor and Arora. Harrison plumps for as visually unrepresentative a Sikh family as possible: father, mother, Amardip and Rema all have short hair. By following this family from India to Britain, and back on a holiday in the Punjab, readers are able to enter into their Sikh contemporaries' experience, a valuable exercise in imaginative understanding of children from an Indian Punjabi background.

De Souza's book portrays the lives of three dissimilar Sikh families and will be a useful addition to the literature on school library shelves. He ventures into the Southall community in some detail and attempts to elucidate the Khalistan question. Earlier books for junior readers had avoided tackling the political unrest and identity crisis of contemporary Sikhs. Not so Beryl Dhanjal. Her *Sikhism* in the series "Dictionaries of World Religions" presents the faith refreshingly in alphabetically arranged topics including Sikh identity, nationalism, sects and Bhindranwale. Dhanjal does not dodge the issues but marks a new departure in writing for secondary pupils with her trenchant expositions.

---

12. Most of the annotations appear also in Tatla and Nesbitt 1987.
13. Solomon 1980a and 1980b.
14. Bennet 1984 and 1985.

Daljit Singh and Angela Smith enable us to see Sikhs not only in Punjab and Britain but also in North America, not only Punjabi heirs to the tradition but also Western converts. The potential universality of the Sikh faith is apparent. From other books it appears as an ethnic religion.

Not all books for school use now aim to cover Sikhism in a general way. Three books focus on festivals, two of them on the particular festivals of Baisakhi and Guru Nanak's birthday, although Davidson's focus is sharpest in the title, which belies the unnecessarily general contents.[15]   These books all include visual and textual reference to Sikhs in Britain.

Sikhism receives mention in many books presenting several world religions, often thematically. Space does not permit the inclusion or discussion of these in this paper, nor the references—some quite erroneous—to Sikhs in books on such topics as immigrant communities.[16]

Junior fiction

This covers the age range from lower juniors (*Kamla and Kate*) to young adults (*The Turban-Wallah*). Junior fiction is not confined to the printed page. A Sikh character has appeared in BBC television's series *Grange Hill*, set in a multiracial London comprehensive school. *Running Scared*, teenage fiction by a best-selling London headmaster, was televised by the BBC in 1986.

Among junior fiction involving Sikh characters *Running Scared* is unusual for focussing on a girl (Narinder Kaur Sidhu). She and her friend, Paula Prescott, are the central characters. Rupinder Singh (*Hari's Pigeon*), Terry Singh (*Double Dare*) and Amrik Singh (*Kamla and Kate*) are all boys. Ganda Singh (*The Man in the Red Turban*) is a travelling salesman.

In *The Devil's Children* we see Sikhs through the eyes of an English girl, as we see Amrik in *Kamla and Kate*. But in this and the other stories (apart from *The Devil's Children*) we are invited to see the world through the Sikh characters' eyes as well—particularly in *Hari's Pigeon*. This is written as the diary of a Sikh boy whose father has married an English woman. The last page of *Hari's Pigeon* gives readers a helpful summary of Sikhism,[17] and in each case the writers provide informative detail along the way:

> It was an order of the Guru 300 years ago that all Sikhs are called Singh. It means "lion." (Dickinson 1970, p. 131.)
>
> (Sikhs) carry five signs... (Ibid., p. 31.)
>
> They aren't allowed to eat beef in their religion. (Ibid., p. 78.)
>
> Sikh boys must never cut their hair. (Gavin 1983, p. 85.)
>
> All Sikhs are Singhs but all Singhs aren't Sikhs. (Ibid., p. 87.)

---

15. Cole and Sambhi 1986; Davidson 1982; Kapoor 1985.
16. For discussion of books in these two categories see Nesbitt 1987.
17. Dickinson 1970, p. 93.

The scripture (the Guru Granth Sahib) receives mention.[18]   Ashley's description of the *akhand path* (continuous reading) at Baisakhi (major Sikh festival) helps readers unfamiliar with Sikh practice to visualise the scene:

> the granth on its cushion was carried head-high from the granth-room up those stairs and within minutes the akhand path had begun...the granth uncovered from its ornate cloth and the people, the whole Khalsa, singing to the accompaniment of tabla and harmonium.   "There exists but one God...self-existent, great and compassionate."

Scriptural passages from the morning and late evening prayers are quoted in Martin, which describes an *amrit* ceremony in the Punjab[19] and a Sikh's cremation in Australia.[20]

In this novel and in *The Turban-Wallah* the gurdwara plays an integral role in the plot.   The turban and uncut hair figure in the stories, and the *kara* (steel wristlet) and *kangha* (wooden comb) are mentioned by Dickinson, Griffiths, Ashley, Martin and Webster, e.g.,

> With a flick of his wrist to shake down his steel kara he took a look at his watch. (Ashley 1986, p. 94.)

The *kirpan* and *kachh* are also mentioned by Martin.   Similarly other glimpses into Punjabi life leave the impression that the writers have been doing their homework.   Martin spent some months in India among Sikhs.

Whereas the other stories are more or less convincingly set in contemporary Britain, *The Man in the Red Turban* is a hawker in Australia during the Depression of the 1930's and Dickinson's Sikhs, *The Devil's Children*, are projected into an imaginary future when everyone in Britain has destroyed machines in a contagious madness.   In this, the earliest by over a decade of the fiction under discussion, Sikhs were used because a community of people "already resident in Britain, cohesive among themselves, good mechanics, different from the British in dress and behaviour" were necessary for the story to be told.[21]   In this fantasy the Sikhs are presented as idealised and alien, they were "like a procession in fancy dress"[22] (for some reason the women wear saris, not *salwar kamiz*), spoke a "strange language,"[23] "like the call of a bird."[24]   To the villagers they are "the devil's children," surely a most unfortunate title.   They exemplify the now somewhat discredited "martial race theory":

> We are a soldier people. (p. 31)

> You fight well, like a Sikh. (p. 28)

and they reminisce about military life.[25]

---

18. E.g., Dickinson 1970, p. 83; Griffiths 1982, p. 35, where the naming of Hari's eldest cousin's baby boy is described; Webster 1984, p. 19, "the glitter of the cloth that covered the Holy Granth"; and Ashley 1986, p. 173.
19. Martin 1970, p. 97.
20. Ibid., pp. 108 ff.
21. Dickinson, personal communication, 1987.
22. Dickinson 1970, p. 13.
23. Ibid., p. 19.
24. Ibid., p. 17.
25. Ibid., p. 63.

By contrast, Webster and Ashley set their Sikhs firmly in authentic-sounding inner-city areas and write from firsthand knowledge of British Sikhs. Narinder and Rupinder are not stereotypical Sikhs. Particular real-life situations are explored by Griffiths and Gavin. In *Hari's Pigeon* the Sikh boy is coping with adjustment to an English stepmother; in *Double Dare* Terry lives in a children's home; in *Kamla and Kate* Amrik is a new arrival from a village apparently untouched by mechanisation. In both these books by Jamila Gavin the cultural distance between the Sikhs' Indian background and life in Britain is emphasised, or rather, exaggerated. Amrik appears strange to his new class-mates, and Britain appears strange to him—no soil underfoot, no wells, no *chapati* for school lunch—but the writer shows how a common bond supersedes the cultural differences when Amrik wins everyone's respect by walking on his hands. The other books—all for older readers—make a similar point: the gur-dwara and school sharing a minibus (Webster), the Sikh girl and her white friend falling victims to the same protection racket (Ashley), even the initially hostile villagers and the Sikhs finding common cause against violent marauders (Dickinson). Ganda Singh, like the Williams and other Australian families, is a victim of economic depression. Hari's predicament—adjusting to a parent's remarriage and drawing consolation from his pet bird—could be that of any child, just as Terry could be any orphan. The writers share a certain moral stance in this sympathetic portrayal of Sikhs as rich in distinctive culture yet not so different from everyone else after all.

It is through their exploration of what it feels like to be a young Sikh growing up in the west that writers of fiction have a significant opportunity to engage readers' imagination and help them to identify in some measure with teenage Sikhs' discovery of a viable self-identity. In *The Devil's Children* learning judo in self-defence against racial intolerance[26] and the children's facility in English[27] appear to be the only indications of the effect of settlement in the West. No *sahajdhari* (or short-haired) Sikhs are mentioned. In the characters of Hari, Rupinder and Narinder we see Griffiths, Webster and Ashley delve a little deeper into the pulls of religious tradition on the one hand and of conformity to non-Sikh norms on the other as young people forge a new identity distinct from their parents':

> "but the difference is I'm English Sikh, see? I'm a new sort. You're Punjabi Sikh and I'm London Sikh." (Ashley 1986, p. 89.)

> "One day," Rupinder said, "I shall cut my hair and leave off this turban, break with tradition." (Webster 1984, p. 103.)

> "Now Artar had grown a beard and he wears a turban...I think I would like to look like that when I'm grown up like my dad in the wedding photo." (Griffiths 1982, p. 41)

Children's literature has escaped the trend, encouraged by certain publishers of adult literature on Sikhs and other Asians, to concentrate on a left-

---

26. Dickinson 1970, p. 80.
27. Ibid., p. 40.

wing, feminist interpretation with the emphasis on racism, oppression and the cruelty supposed to be inherent in arranged marriages.[28] The Sikhs in the books surveyed above are exercises in speculative empathy, not the product of first-hand experience of living as a Sikh in Britain. One now looks forward to reading junior fiction by writers who are themselves Sikh.

Bibliography

Aggarwal, Manju. *I am a Sikh*. London: Franklin Watts, 1984.
    A book aimed at 5- to 9-year-olds. Illustrated with excellent colour photographs, it portrays a nine year old Southall Sikh boy's family. The gurdwara, worship, the five Sikh symbols, how to put on a turban, dress, eating, music and a wedding are topics covered.

Arora, Ranjit. *Sikhism*. Hove: Wayland, 1986.
    A book in the Religions of the World series. Topics mentioned include places of worship, Sikh women, Sikhs today. The colour illustrations are fine but the text too brief to provide more than an introduction.

Ashley, Bernard. *Running Scared*. London: Franklin Watts, 1986.
    Central to this work of teenage fiction, serialised on BBC television, is the friendship between Paula Prescott and Narinder Kaur Sidhu. Both girls' families are victims of an East End protection racketeer.

Babraa, Davinder Kaur. *Visiting a Sikh Temple*. London: Lutterworth, 1981.
    The focus is on the Woolwich Gurdwara in South East London, but there is much useful information on gurdwaras in general and some aspects of Sikh religion. Contains photos of Sikhs worshipping.

Bennett, Olivia. *Kikar's Drum*. London: Hamish Hamilton, 1984.
    See below.

———. *A Sikh Wedding*. London: Hamish Hamilton, 1985.
    These two books for primary-school children portray a Sikh family in simple text with excellent photographs. In the first Kikar buys a traditional drum and proceeds to the gurdwara in Bow. The second shows Kikar's sister's marriage including Punjab village customs.

Buddle, V. "Sikhism at 'A' Level," in W.O. Cole and E.M. Nesbitt, eds., *Sikh Bulletin* 4 (1987), 32-33.

Butler, D.G. *Life among the Sikhs*. London: Edward Arnold, 1980.
    Book derives from plays originally produced by Radio Manchester. The plays revolve around two English children who ask questions about other faiths.

Cole, W. Owen. *A Sikh Family in Britain*. Oxford: Pergamon, 2nd ed. 1985.
    Focusses on Sikh beliefs and practices in the context of everyday life in Britain. Aimed at middle and secondary school students, the book is a good introduction to the Sikh faith.

———. "Sikhism at GCSE" in W.O. Cole and E.M. Nesbitt (eds), *Sikh Bulletin* 4 (1987), 29-31.

———. *Thinking about Sikhism*. London: Lutterworth, 1980.
    A good general introduction to the faith for secondary students.

---

28. Wilson 1978; Shan 1985.

Cole, W. Owen; and Piara Singh Sambhi. *Baisakhi.* Exeter: Religious and Moral Education Press, 1986.
> This illustrated book in the Living Festivals Series- portrays the Baisakhi festival as celebrated by Sikhs in Punjab and in Britain.

———. *Meeting Sikhism.* London: Longman, 1980.
> Part of a series on world religions for secondary and primary school students. The book focusses first on Sikhs in the Punjab. Unit 5 deals with Sikhs in Britain, reasons for migration, a Sikh family and the Sikh way of life in Britain.

———. *Sikhism.* London: Ward Lock, 1973.
> For secondary pupils, this book covers the origin and growth of Sikhism, basic beliefs and practices, life and worship.

Daljit Singh and Angela Smith. *The Sikh World.* London: MacDonald, 1985.
> An excellent book aimed at schools. It has some photographs of gurdwaras in Britain.

Davidson, Margaret. *Guru Nanak's Birthday.* Exeter: Religious and Moral Education Press, 1982.
> This book in the Living Festivals Series devotes only Chapter 4 to the Sikh festival. Pp. 24-27 mention the celebrations in Britain, with photographs of the Exeter gurdwara.

Dhanjal, Beryl. *Sikhism.* London: Batsford, 1987.
> In the Dictionaries of World Religions series. The series is specifically intended to cater to General Certificate of Secondary Education courses. Bhindranwale, Sikh identity and the "martial races theory" are given entries.

Dickinson, Peter. *The Devil's Children.* London: Gollancz, 1970.
> In this story for children of middle school age Dickinson describes how, when England turned furiously against modern technology, a band of Sikhs ("the devil's children") remained unaffected. Nicky Gore, a lonely, frightened girl, joins the Sikhs in their trek out of London. They move into a deserted farm but meet with hostility from the villagers until both communities face a common threat.

Farnecombe, Anne. *Our Sikh Friends.* Redholm: Denholm House Press, 1978.
> One of a series intended to help junior and middle school age children gain a better understanding of people of different faiths. Factual information is conveyed by reference to an imaginary family; illustrated with line drawings.

Gates, Brian. "Children Prospecting for Commitment," in R. Jackson, ed., *Approaching World Religions.* London: John Murray, 1982.

Gavin, Jamila. *Ali and the Robots.* London: Methuen, 1986.
> A Sikh character figures in the story "H.C. Goes to school."

———. *Double Dare and Other Stories.* London: Methuen, 1982.
> Stories about children from diverse ethnic backgrounds. Terry Singh, the hero of "Double Dare," is an orphan. He discovers that his father had come from India to study, married an English girl and died in an accident. After various adventures tinged with the supernatural Terry meets his grandfather, Jaswal Singh, from India. For children of middle-school age.

———. *Kamla and Kate.* London: Methuen, 1983.
> Stories for children about two friends. Chapter 8 recounts the arrival of a new pupil, Amrik Singh, in their class.

Grewal, Balwant Singh. "Growth of the Sikh Missionary Society UK and Development of Its Work," in W.O. Cole and E.M. Nesbitt, eds., *Sikh Bulletin* 4 (1987), 1-12.

Griffiths, Helen. *Hari's Pigeon*. London: Hutchinson, 1982.
This story of a child's reaction to his father's remarriage is told in diary form. Hari's father, a Sikh, has married an English wife, against much opposition from both families. Hari is horrified at having to share his father and submerges himself in looking after a pigeon which he rescues from a cat. Details of Hari's Sikh background are brief but ever present. Intended for readers of middle-school age.

Grimmitt, M.H. "World Religions and Personal Development," in R. Jackson, ed., *Approaching World Religions*. London: John Murray, 1982.

Harrison, Steve. *Amardip and Rema: Two Sikh Children Visit India*. London: Macmillan, 1986.
Illustrated story of a Sikh family. It shows the parents' migration, their employment, the children at school and their experiences on a visit to Punjab.

Kapoor, Sukhbir Singh. *Sikh Festivals*. Hove: Wayland, 1985.
This book, intended for children of middle-school age, includes photographs of Sikhs and gurdwaras in Britain.

————. *Sikhs and Sikhism*. Hove: Wayland, 1982.
This presents the history and practices of Sikhs in India.

Lyle, Sean. *Pavan is a Sikh*. London: A. and C. Black, 1977.
The everyday life of a Sikh boy and his family in Britain. Excellent colour photos.

Martin, David. *The Man in the Red Turban*. London: Hutchinson, 1970.
The central character is Ganda Singh, a hawker in Australia during the Depression of the 1930's.

McLeod, W.H. *The Way of the Sikh*. Amersham: Hulton, 1986 (new edition).
A sound and simply written survey within the range of most pupils from 9 to 13 years of age. It mentions Sikhs arriving in Britain and the possibility of visiting gurdwaras in Britain.

Minority Group Support Service. *How a Sikh Prays*. Coventry Education Authority, 1979.
Black and white photographs and text aimed at primary children showing a Coventry Sikh boy in the gurdwara.

Mohinder Singh. *Sikhism: A Resource Book for Teachers*. Vancouver: Sikh Education Society, 1985.
A compilation for British Columbia's optional secondary-school course on world religions.

Nesbitt, Eleanor. "Sikhism in Books for Primary and Secondary School Readers," *Resource* (University of Warwick) 9:3 (summer 1987), 3-5.

Sacha, Gurinder Singh. *The Sikhs and Their Way of Life*. Southall Sikh Missionary Society, 2nd ed. 1988.
An extremely useful compilation of material on the gurus, Sikh history, religious beliefs and practices and culture, illustrated with black and white photographs and line drawings.

Sambhi, Piara Singh. *Understanding Your Sikh Neighbour*. London: Lutterworth, 1980.
A good and brief introduction to Sikhism seen through the life of a family in Britain. It features the Sikhs' coming to Britain, the birth and naming of a child, a visit to the gurdwara, a visit to Punjab and a marriage.

Shan, Sharan-Jeet. *In My Own Name*. London: The Woman's Press, 1985.
A Sikh woman's autobiography.

Sidhu, Gurbachan Singh; G.S. Sivia; and Kirpal Singh. *Guru Nanak for Children*. Gravesend: Sikh Missionary Society, 1969.

Stories of Guru Nanak's life illustrated with black and white pictures below which are printed key verses of the Guru's teaching.

Solomon, Joan. *Bobbi's New Year*. London: Hamish Hamilton, 1980.

Continues the story of the same Sikh family as above. Baisakhi celebrations are featured. The pictures are excellent.

————. *News for Dad*. London: Hamish Hamilton, 1980.

About the everyday life of a Sikh family in Britain. Excellent colour photos for primary school children.

de Souza, Allan. *The Sikhs in Britain*. London: Batsford, 1986.

In the Communities in Britain series. This is designed for teenage readers. It focusses on three families and provides background on Sikh history and migration to Britain, ending with "Khalistan, land of the Khalsa."

Tatla, Darshan Singh; and Eleanor M. Nesbitt. *Sikhs in Britain: An Annotated Bibliography*. Coventry: Centre for Research in Ethnic Relations, University of Warwick, 1987.

Webster, Len. *The Turban-Wallah: A Tale of Little India*. London: Oxford University Press, 1984.

A sensitively recounted story, dedicated to "the Sikhs of Britain" and intended for secondary-school-age pupils. It tells how Rupinder Singh, nicknamed Ruby, "the turban-wallah," falls in love with Tara, a Hindu girl, whose parents disapprove of the relationship. The author portrays both teenagers' family backgrounds in a sympathetic way.

Wilson, Amrit. *Finding a Voice*. London: Virago, 1978.

The experiences of some of Britain's South Asian women recounted in their own words.

The Sikh Diaspora:
Its Possible Effects on Sikhism

Owen Cole

The story of the establishment of Sikh communities outside India and other parts of Asia is a fascinating one, but it lies beyond the scope of this paper, which is really concerned with the consequences of this dispersion for Sikhism, perhaps for religious studies and also for interfaith dialogue.

It may be debated whether there is such a thing as "Sikhism," it being argued that there are only Sikhs and Sikh communities,[1] individuals and groups of men and women who follow the revelation given to Guru Nanak and his nine successors as laid down in the Guru Granth Sahib.[2] However, the conclusion of this writer, from taking part in discussions with Sikhs in Britain as well as India, is that there is a perceived, objective reality which they regard as Sikhism. This consists of certain beliefs and practices and, above all, the Sikh form of the "five k's," especially uncut hair, as well as the turban in the case of men. There is also a yardstick, the idea of the casteless egalitarian society inaugurated by Guru Nanak, finalised by Guru Gobind Singh and conveniently outlined in the *Rahit Maryada*.

In the Punjab, at least until the present religio-political crisis developed in the 1980's, there seems to have been no need for Sikhs to consider their own identity more carefully. This was also true in East Africa, where they, with other Asians, Hindu or Muslim, formed a coherent and self-sufficient group placed

---

1. See, for example, Wilfred Cantwell Smith, *Towards a World Theology* (New York: Macmillan, 1981), pp. 157-59. This view is also common among anthropologists and sociologists in Britain who have an interest in Sikh communities. Religious-studies specialists often give greater attention to the self-image which a religion seeks to convey.

2. W.H. McLeod, *Textual Sources for the Study of Sikhism* (Manchester: Manchester University Press, 1984), p. 79, quotes the *Rahit Maryada* definition as, "any person who believes in God, in the ten Gurus, in the Sri Guru Granth Sahib, other writings of the ten Gurus, and their teachings; in the Khalsa initiation ceremony instituted by the tenth Guru, and who does not believe in any other system of religious doctrine." The Delhi Sikh Gurdwaras Act, 1971, is more explicit in requiring that a Sikh must keep "unshorn hair." No one who trims or shaves his beard or *kesh* may vote in elections for the Shiromani Gurdwara Prabandhak Committee, and only *amritdharis* may stand as candidates. Some British gurdwaras are also insisting on these requirements. Issues of self-definition are likely to concern diaspora Sikhs for many years.

[Joseph T. O'Connell, Milton Israel, Willard G. Oxtoby, eds., with W.H. McLeod and J.S. Grewal, visiting eds., *Sikh History and Religion in the Twentieth Century* (S. Asian Studies Papers, 3) (Toronto: S. Asian Studies, Univ. of Toronto, 1988)]

between the British colonisers and the Africans. In other parts of India no problem existed because the Punjab homeland was only a train or, even more cheaply, a tiring bus journey away. In those areas of the British Commonwealth where Sikhs have settled in small numbers, and in other parts of Europe, they have had to survive as best they might, and here issues of identity do arise. It would be extremely interesting to know how they have achieved this. However, at an experiential level it is only possible for me to consider the British scene.

What characterises British Sikhs is, first, the intention of most of them to be only temporary migrants. But for the immigration legislation of the 1959-62 period, some men would never have come, others would not have stayed, and a large proportion of their dependents would never have seen Britain. The myth of return persists among many Sikhs, diluted by those who came from East Africa who, consciously preferring Britain to India, have no intention of returning to the Punjab, and by the growth to parenthood of the children of the Punjabi immigrants.[3] British-born, these young people may have an idealised view of the Punjab, an expressed sentimental desire to go there, rather like the *hiraeth* of the Welsh, and a strong Sikh identity. However, the reality is that they will stay in Britain. They and their children will constitute emotional ties keeping the older Sikhs, the pioneer migrants, here.

A characteristic already stated is that of a strong sense of identity among the young. Partly this is explained by the racism which they have encountered. Their parents did not notice it, or ignored it. They did not always, or often, compete for jobs in a way that would have caused hostility and resentment. Prudently they settled where employment of a menial nature was plentiful. Like most migrants they were adaptable and undemanding. In common with many Indians they had a respect for the white man. Their children, not content with following the parental example, academically well qualified and expecting to be treated on their merits, aware of an unconscious, insidious, but in their minds real, policy of assimilation, are adopting the Sikh outward form in increasing numbers. The oppression, as they see it, of Sikhs by the Indian government, is encouraging them to stress their distinctiveness all the more. The Sikh Youth Federation has won control of a number of gurdwaras, especially those where the membership is predominantly Jat, from their elders.

Among other Sikh groups which have invited Sikhs to re-adopt the Sikh outward form must be mentioned the Akhand Kirtani Jatha and the Nishkam Sevak Jatha. Of course these two expressions of Sikhism have very different aims and are completely distinct in their origins. The Akhand Kirtani Jatha owes its inspiration to the example of Bhai Randhir Singh (1878-1961). He was one of many Sikhs who dedicated his life to India's freedom struggle. He was also a Sikh of devotion and knowledge. This mystic was imprisoned by the British for his participation in the Ghadar movement, which declared war on

---

3. This issue is dealt with in considerable detail by Parminder Bhachu, in *Twice Migrants: East African Sikh Settlers in Britain* (London: Tavistock Press, 1985).

them on August 5, 1914.[4] The Jatha combines his devotionalism and concern for liberty. Overnight performances of hymn-singing, lasting twelve hours at a time, are undertaken by devotees who must be *amritdhari* and vegetarian. Women wear a *keski* under their *chunnis.*

The Nishkam Sevak Jatha owes its existence to Sant Puran Singh, also known as Kerichowale Baba. He was a Ramgarhia Sikh who came from Kerichowale in Kenya. Probably many more Sikhs than the ten thousand that the police estimated attended his funeral in Birmingham in 1983.   With gurdwaras in Birmingham and now in Leeds, the Jatha is growing in numbers and is strong in influence. Sant Puran Singh supported the Sikh protest against the judgment of Lord Denning in the famous Mandla case, when a headmaster refused to let a Sikh boy wear his turban at school, a judgment eventually reversed by the House of Lords.[5] It, too, emphasises the taking of *amrit*, respect for the Guru Granth Sahib, and vegetarianism as well as opposing the drinking of alcohol. Sikhism, nothwithstanding allegiance to the Guru Granth Sahib, has always owed much to the devotion and charisma of individuals. These two examples indicate that this influence continues. These and other groups, sometimes influenced by only locally known *sants*, are helping Sikhs recover or discover respect for the Sikh physical form as well as spiritual and ethical values. The young often find their authority, discipline and purposefulness compellingly attractive. During the next decade, certainly if the Punjab crisis continues and British society remains racist in the eyes of young people of Asian, African and Caribbean backgrounds, these movements within Sikhism, and the Sikh Youth Federation, are likely to increase in popularity and influence. The situation is also ripe for *sants* to emerge from the British Sikh population.

A method of promoting this resurgence is camps organised by one of these groups or the Sikh Missionary Society (U.K.).[6] These are often based in gurdwaras or school premises, rather than being held under canvas, unreliability being the only reliable feature of a British summer. At these camps young people learn Punjabi, musical instruments, how to conduct Sikh ceremonies, Sikh history and philosophy. They also discuss issues that arise as a result of growing up in Britain and enjoy playing games. Camps could have an important role to play in developing the spirituality and other qualities of the next generation's leaders.

---

4. The Ghadar movement is placed in the context of the Sikh contribution to the freedom struggle in India by Harbans Singh in his sweeping survey entitled *The Heritage of the Sikhs* (Delhi: Manohar, 1985), pp. 263-65 and 286.

5. March 24, 1983. This decision and the Motor-Cycle Crash Helmet (Religious Exemption) Act, 1976, which exempted "turban-wearing followers of the Sikh religion from the requirement to wear a crash helmet when riding a motor-cycle," should have settled the turban issue in Britain, but it has been raised again by health and safety-at-work regulations requiring the wearing of hard hats on building sites and similar locations. The matter has not yet been resolved.

6. The work and considerable achievements of the Sikh Missionary Society (U.K.) are described by Balwant Singh Grewal in *Sikh Bulletin*, no. 4 (1987), 1-12; the bulletin, published in Chichester, is edited by W. Owen Cole and Eleanor M. Nesbitt.

Another characteristic of the British Sikh community is its size. Statistics relating to ethnic minorities in Britain are notoriously misleading. No attempt at computation is made in national censuses. However, the number is likely to be over 300,000 and may be approaching 400,000.[7] This makes it the largest community outside India. Surprisingly it has never organised itself well, though many self-styled national leaders, committees and councils have emerged over the years. When there is a crisis, usually associated with the right to wear the turban, a certain cohesion quickly becomes manifest. The intense sense of democracy and equality which Sikhs have perhaps disguises this underlying unity and conceals it from view. It is often remarked of Sikhs that, like Jews, they are likely to be assimilated in times of peace and harmony. Paradoxically, holocausts and persecution trigger off survival instincts. Sikhs frequently point to the reign of Maharaja Ranjit Singh as the period when they came nearest to extinction. Stories of atrocities in the Punjab and support for Khalistan are resulting in the resurgence of a strong self-awareness among Sikhs who might otherwise have been assimilated.

The future of such young people will be taken up later. For the moment, as an aside, it might be allowed to pursue the Sikh-Jewish similarity. Each community is very distinctive in terms of language, form and culture. The two are also small in numbers worldwide. Neither of them is a missionary faith. This factor may well explain the way in which they are constantly aware of being threatened. They declare that they seek only to survive. Their members may often be successful in many enterprises, but they are not culturally competitive. They only respond to what they perceive as threats. They do not seek to convert the people among whom they live.

A final characteristic, relevant to this discussion, has to do with the previous paragraph and the circumstances in which Sikhs now find themselves. Comparatively small in numbers, they are threatened, like all religions in Britain, with secularisation. While Muslims might react against this aggressively, denouncing it, Sikhs do not. However, their numbers are large enough for them to believe that remedies can be found. It is these possible responses which will concern us in the rest of this paper.

All the major Sikh social sub-groups seem to be present in Britain: Khatris, Aroras, Ahluwallias, but especially Bhatras, Jats and Ramgarhias. Beyond these come Balmikis and Ravidasis. Early communities developed between the two world wars in port areas such as Cardiff, Southampton, East London and Manchester. The first settlers were often Bhatra traders who went from door to door selling household goods from large suitcases. In the 1950's they were followed by Jats, members of the landowning class of the Punjab, and Ramgarhias, skilled craftsmen and artisans from the towns. They settled together in the same districts where housing was cheap, in cities where work was

---

7. Kim Knott examines this problem in "Calculating Sikh Population Statistics," *Sikh Bulletin*, no. 4 (1987), 13-22.

plentiful, places like Slough, Coventry, Leicester, Bradford, Leeds and Birmingham, as well as Southall. They worked side by side in factories or on building sites. At the level of marriage the groups maintained their distinctiveness, but usually there was one gurdwara. With the passage of time, an increase in wealth, inner rivalries, and the pressure of Sikhs from East Africa, many of them Ramgarhia, a significant development has been the establishment of separate gurdwaras. Sometimes the reason has been geographical. Sikhs living in one area of a city for reasons of employment may not be able to reach the gurdwara because of inadequacies in the public transport system. Often, however, group rivalry has played a part. Ramgarhias may be irked by Jat domination or, sometimes, the latter's lack of emphasis upon the uncut hair, the turban and the avoidance of alcohol. For whatever reasons the name Ramgarhia appears outside some recently built gurdwaras.

Indian scheduled or *dalit*[8] classes are strongly represented in Britain. Members of these groups, often being of Punjabi origin, worshipped in gurdwaras, but it is now possible to come across Balmiki or Ravidasi Sabhas, especially in the Midlands. Both are to be found in Coventry, as well as four gurdwaras, one belonging to the Nanaksar movement. This one example demonstrates an underlying lack of cohesion in the Sikh Panth, or a wish on the part of sub-groups to retain their distinctive identities. It sometimes alarms Sikhs who wish to present a picture of unity to non-Sikhs, in contrast to the diversity which is Christianity. Many young Sikhs accept the divisions, going along with their parents' views and explanations. Some regard them critically, as contrary to the teachings of the Gurus. The present tendency is towards proliferation, which probably indicates wealth and security. The Sikhs have been hit by the recession and high unemployment of the early 1980's like other groups, but they have coped with it successfully on the whole and demonstrate the signs of economic prosperity.[9]

Many white members of British society remain completely ignorant of Sikhs and other so-called immigrant communities, even in the cities where they have settled. Sikh divisions mean nothing to them. Where they do matter is in the area of education, especially religious education. Most textbooks on Sikhism faithfully present the traditional Sikhism in the approved, idealised post-Singh-Sabha form. There is nothing to be objected to in this, at one level. People may complain about stereotyping, but if students do not begin with the norm, that is, Sikhism's portrait of itself, where else can they start? To use such a phrase as "some Sikhs," at the beginning of every sentence or paragraph is only to create uncertainty and confusion. However, the teacher soon comes to replace the

---

8. Although *harijan* is a word which has become popular following Mahatma Gandhi's use of it, the classes to whom it refers now seem to find it patronising. "Child of God" can also refer to a person whose natural father is unknown. *Dalit*, "oppressed," is being increasingly used as a self-description.

9. Information about many of the groups mentioned in this paper can be gleaned from articles listed in *Sikhs in Britain: An Annotated Bibliography*, by Darshan Singh Tatla and Eleanor Nesbitt, 1987, published by the Centre for Research in Ethnic Relations, University of Warwick.

monochrome view of Sikhs as a caste-denying egalitarian group when one becomes aware of the proliferation of gurdwaras. Some will have begun to do so through discovering the different way in which boys and girls are treated in terms of education. Some families have equal aspirations for the achievements of their sons and daughters, and exercise the same discipline upon both, but many girls face more restrictions than their brothers and are not encouraged to think of a career other than that of being a wife and mother. Teachers who probe more deeply become aware of a dowry system which persists despite being condemned by the Gurus.

Sikh children are far more likely to learn about their religion in school than in the gurdwara. Lamentably, inadequate as the provision for religious education in school may be, nevertheless, it is a compulsory subject in the curriculum. It may be taken in public examinations, and Sikhism features in most Agreed Syllabi.[10] A few gurdwaras still make little or no provision for their children to learn about their religion. Often the emphasis is upon learning Punjabi, and although the content may be stories from the *janam-sakhis*, there is no structured teaching of the faith. The young are expected to acquire it at home from their parents, or pick it up in the gurdwara despite their inadequate Punjabi. The consequence of this situation is that many teenagers and adults educated in Britain are aware of the difference which exists between the Sikh ideal and the reality. A few have converted, denouncing their parents and community as hypocrites, apparently finding a church which they considered faithful to the teachings of Jesus. Others have remained "Indian," "Asian," "Punjabi" or "Sikh" in some nebulous non-religious way. The numbers may not have been great and the Punjab crisis may have put the brakes on these kinds of rejection and alienation, but the matter has only been shelved. Sikhism in Britain is under scrutiny from within and without regarding the extent to which it is faithful to its ideals. (It is not unique in this respect. All religions, including Christianity, face the same predicament, but because Christianity is the dominant religion culturally and has engaged openly in self-criticism, it is not in the position of Sikhism in Britain.)

A recurrent question in the rest of this chapter is whether Sikhism is an expression of Punjabi culture or something more. So far the form of defense to which Sikhs are resorting as they face the threat of British society is linguistic. Gurdwaras concentrate on teaching language; appeals are made to local education authorities to provide mother-tongue teaching in schools. I have never challenged the worth of mother-tongue teaching. Coming from a Welsh

---

10. The 1944 Education Act made religious education a compulsory part of the curriculum for schools in England and Wales. What may actually be taught is determined by "Agreed Syllabuses" which each local education authority must produce. These are agreed, hence the name, between church bodies, teachers' associations and elected members of the local council. It is now customary for Sikhs as well as other religious groups to be represented on agreed syllabus conferences, wherever they are present in appreciable numbers in a locality. Sikhism can also be studied in public examinations; see W. Owen Cole, "Sikhism at GCSE and A level," *Sikh Bulletin*, no. 4 (1987), 29-31.

background, though sadly speaking only English, I welcome bilingualism and value the retention of parental culture. The comments I am about to make should be considered within that context. Thus although one may visit a gurdwara school and be impressed by two hundred children learning Punjabi there, one is aware that there are many times that number not attending the school or gurdwara, unable to communicate in any depth with their parents in Punjabi. It is also impossible for local authorities to provide language facilities in every school where there are children whose parental tongue is not English— though they could do much more than they do at present to help! However, the linguistic solution is going to become increasingly ineffective with the passing of time.

The Punjab crisis poses the question of whether Sikhism is an expression of Punjabi culture in a different form. Is Sikhism a Punjabi socio-political movement or a religion? It is possible to visit gurdwaras where pictures of the Guru have been replaced by those of Sant Jarnail Singh Bhindranwale and paintings of the destruction of the Akal Takht done by a Muslim artist. *Ragis* may sing *shabads* from the Guru Granth Sahib, but spiritual discourses have been replaced by political harangues. Older members of some gurdwaras are shifting their allegiance to others, e.g., Jat to Ramgarhia, to free themselves from the politics, threats and outbreaks of violence. In at least two gurdwaras, legal proceedings have been instituted by one group of members to wrest control from another.

The focus of Sikh worship is the Guru Granth Sahib. It could well emerge as the significant focus of the debate which is beginning about the nature of Sikhism: is it a Punjabi movement, religious or political, confined to Punjab and Punjabis or is it a world religion, whatever is meant by that term?

The attention which Sikhism has received because of its appearance in the West, and especially in Britain, coinciding as it did with the quincentenary of the birth of Guru Nanak in 1969, has resulted in its being regarded as a world religion in schools, institutes and colleges of higher education, though not so much in universities. Noss and Parrinder seem to have been the first writers of books on the world religions to have included a section on Sikhs.[11] Although American publishers and scholars may give them little attention,[12] the British story is very different. Sikhism features in most modern studies of religion.

---

11. John B. Noss, *Man's Religions* (New York: Macmillan, 1949). He and other writers were influenced by J.N. Farquhar's *Modern Religious Movements in India* (New York: Macmillan, 1915), which saw Sikhism as derived from the teachings of Kabir. Geoffrey Parrinder's *Book of World Religions* (London: Hulton, 1965), was probably the first school text book to include Sikhism. Most general works now include the religion which also featured in the Open University Course, "Man's Religious Quest" (AD.208). However, it is not widely taught in British universities and there is not yet a lectureship in Sikh studies.

12. The fact that John Clark Archer's *Faiths Men Live By* (New York: Nelson, 1934) escaped this chapter's attention confirms one's suspicion that the influence of Archer's textbook was limited to North America. Archer devotes one of his seventeen chapters to "The Sikhs and Their Religion," consciously avoiding (p. 309) the title "Sikhism". —Editors' note.

Sikhism has become aware of itself as a world religion for the first time since, perhaps, the days of Guru Arjan. Until the current crisis, it was becoming increasingly confident and open. Now it faces anxieties both from without and within. Externally, there is the challenge of scholarship, which any movement must accept if it emerges from relative obscurity onto the world stage. It may not welcome the attention it receives. Sikhs have not always been happy with the results of Western non-Sikh scholars or of their own adopting similar analytical approaches.[13]

The suspicions of critical analytical scholarship (conducted by outsiders but also by some of their own academics) which Sikh scholars sometimes express may be explained in a number of ways. Sikhs have been struggling for survival and for their religious liberty intermittently since the days of Emporor Aurangzeb. Before the British annexed the Punjab in 1849, the Ludhiana mission had already been established by Americans (1844). During the rest of the century the Arya Samaj sought to win Sikhs for Hinduism, and missionaries attempted to convert them to Christianity. The prospect was such that Macauliffe decided to record the story of Sikhism before the religion disappeared. He was premature. Both Arya Samaj and Christian missions failed to achieve these aims. However, some Sikhs believe that since Independence the Indian government has replaced the Arya Samaj as the instrument of Hinduisation and that Western missionaries have adopted a new strategy, one of seeking to undermine Sikhism by the use of the modern critical methods which skeptics used, with some success, against Christianity. In the present anxious climate there is a feeling that Sikhism is engaged in a guerrilla war. Friend cannot be distinguished from foe. The dispassionate scholar does not exist. The Sikh who questions the received tradition and the non-Sikh who claims to be adopting an objective approach, be it phenomenological or historico-critical, must not be surprised or dismayed at finding the warmth and openness of Sikh hospitality sometimes tinged with hostility. It is a sign of the times and, one hopes, something very temporary.

It is with these considerations that I turn to my remaining points, especially those which relate to the use of the Guru Granth Sahib in British gurdwaras. Mention has already been made of the language issue, of strenuous attempts by some gurdwaras and the belated response of some local education authorities to the need for Sikh children to be taught the language which their predecessors once acquired naturally. The consequences for families in which a language gap is growing between parents and children is bad enough, but there is also the

---

13. See *Journal of Sikh Studies* 4:1 (February, 1977). A review of Joyce Pettigrew, *Robber Noblemen* (London: Routledge & Kegan Paul, 1975), Ethne K. Marenco, *The Transformation of Sikh Society* (Delhi: Heritage Publishers, 1976), and W.H. McLeod, *The Evolution of the Sikh Community* (Oxford University Press, 1976), suggested that these three studies constituted a conspiracy against Sikhism rather than being unrelated, coincidental accounts. In *The Sikh Review*, January, 1976, hostility to Fauja Singh's research into Guru Tegh Bahadur's martyrdom was openly expressed. *The Sikh Messenger*, spring 1987, carries an article by Daljit Singh critical of Western studies of Sikhism, as does the editorial.

problem of religious illiteracy. Sikhism is now a religion of a book. The question is being asked by Sikhs: can that book be installed as the focus of worship in its translated form? One gurdwara secretary has already been discouraged from using Trumpp's version[14] for a Baisakhi *akhand path* in which he intended to invite interfaith participation. It was only the inadequacy of the translation that prevented this significant event's taking place. At a recent Sikh-Christian consultation,[15] the possibility of an English one-volume version of the Guru Granth Sahib's being installed in British gurdwaras was discussed. One Sikh claimed to have seen an Arabic copy used in a building in Dubai, but indicated that a Qur'an had also been present and was not sure that the place was a gurdwara. During and after a plenary discussion, some Sikhs remained silent, but a number of others rejected the possibility outright, saying that even to raise the issue was mischievous and unnecessarily controversial, and suggesting that this was a Christian assault upon the holy book, their Guru. The most that could be conceived was the use of English for lectures and sermons and the reading of passages from such a version. However, to install a translation would be inconceivable. The reason given for this was not the impossibility of translating the rich poetry of the scripture, but the nature of the book. It is the embodiment of the Guru. Consequently, its Gurmukhi form is not something with which anyone should tamper. It, not just the message, is sacred. To the question of which languages Guru Nanak used in Tibet, Baghdad or diverse parts of India, the reply is that, linguist though he was, the words of revelation were always in Gurmukhi, a term used both of the script and the language of revelation.

From this kind of discussion and comments received from Sikhs in India when the subject of translating the Guru Granth Sahib has been raised, it is possible to conclude, with some confidence, that British gurdwaras will use English translations, perhaps treating them with some dignity. They might be put on the kind of folding reading supports already used for the Qur'an and copies of the *Bhagavad Gita* or *Ramayana* in mosques and Hindu temples. However, the Gurmukhi original will still be the focus of worship. Perhaps the day will come when it will continue to be installed but few will be able to read it, and it will be rare to discover anyone who can translate it directly. There are already many British Sikhs who find its sixteenth-and seventeenth-century language, coupled with its terse poetry, difficult. Perhaps, as a counter-measure, Sikhs can be found who speak of receiving *darshan* through the sound of the words.[16] This, they argue, is sufficient, though to understand would be even better, they concede.

---

14. Ernest Trumpp, *The Adi Granth* (New Delhi: Munshiram Manoharlal, 1970, reprint of the 1877 edition). It is incomplete, unsympathetic, and a distortion of the teachings of Sikhism.
15. This, the third of its kind, was held at Campion House, Hounslow, under the auspices of the United Reformed Church (November 7-9, 1986).
16. To receive *darshan* in the Indian religious context is to be allowed to make contact with the holy person or object, and benefit thereby, through *seeing*. Here the analogue proposed draws upon the sense of hearing. ...Editors' note.

So far in this discussion I have mentioned the kinds of things which are happening or are the subject of speculation among Sikhs. I wish to move towards the conclusion by suggesting from my knowledge of Sikhs in Britain that the diaspora faces a number of options which become basically reduced to two, with variants on each.

The first is to become more Punjabi. By doing so Sikhs would make real and actual a stereotype of a Punjabi society that has never existed. They would be endorsing and giving validity to what happened to some extent under the process of institutionalisation which began with the Kartarpur community and went on for another two centuries, a process which was finalised as an ideal by the Singh Sabha movement.[17] By this I mean that the Singh Sabha movement's scholars provided a portrait of a Sikhism created by the Gurus in its entirety which had continued unchanged since 1708. It seems clear from a fairly cursory reading of Sikh history that although Khalsa Sikhism existed, many other modes of Sikh life were also to be found between the time of the Gurus and the late nineteenth century, when pressure exerted by Christian missionaries and members of the Hindu Arya Samaj forced Sikhs to re-assert their distinctiveness or be converted to Christianity or assimilated into Hinduism. The response to that crisis was to give such a stress upon the Khalsa ideal that it became rehabilitated and accepted as the norm after a long period when it had been one among several others. Normative Sikhism might be said to be encapsulated in the *Rahit Maryada*, an important document of a kind rare, if not unique, in the history of religions. However, it could be argued that it frees Sikhism from Punjabi culture, at least potentially. There is nothing in it about arranged marriages or restricting the freedom of girls to follow careers or wearing particular forms of clothing (other than the injunction to keep the "five k's"). These, however, are being stressed by some Sikhs in their reaction to secularisation, and claimed to be essential aspects of the religion.

The consequence of this stress on the Punjab is likely to be a closed Sikhism ultimately not welcoming the Western presence in any form, be it social contact or the interest of outsiders at the level of study and scholarship. Such an inward-looking Sikhism is difficult to imagine; it appears so contrary to the outgoing Sikh psyche, spirit and approach to life. However, anxiety and suspicion can affect personality in unexpected ways.

The other choice is for Sikhs to rediscover the essence of Sikhism as enunciated by the Gurus. Once again the basis can be the Khalsa form and the *Rehat Maryada* but the outlook would be that which seeks to emulate a Guru Nanak who travelled widely in response to a divine command to be a world teacher, recalling humanity to a spirituality and godliness of living which it had forgotten. This, it can easily be argued, is just as much an idealised impression

---

17. On the Singh Sabha movement see such studies as Khushwant Singh, *A History of the Sikhs* (Oxford University Press, revised 1977), volume two; Harbans Singh, op.cit.; W.H. McLeod, *The Evolution of the Sikh Community* (Oxford University Press, 1976); and chapters by H.S. Oberoi and N.G. Barrier in this volume.

of Sikhism as any other. That cannot be denied. Granting that it may be as difficult to discover what the so-called essence of Sikhism is or has been, as it is to discover the Christian ideal as found in the historical Jesus, nevertheless it is a task to which Sikh scholars might return. It interested them to a considerable degree at the time of the quincentenary of Guru Nanak, but since then countering the work of W.H. McLeod and responding to the Punjab crisis have preoccupied them to a major extent.[18]

Is the essence of Sikhism, as preached by Guru Nanak, true? And do the following quotations faithfully express it? If so, what are the consequences for Sikhs?

> Guru Nanak was a truly cosmic personality. He found the world in straits and chaos and protested against the growing misrule of the princes and priests. He mentioned, without fear or favour, the difficulties of the common man....Guru Nanak stood for the rights of the common man and objected to his exploitation in any form....Guru Nanak, the spiritual Healer of the modern age, offered an individual an efficacious remedy for the misguided and the spiritually sick. Not that there was any lack of so-called religious people in India, but their religious practices had lost all meaning and brought about no transformation. Guru Nanak went deep into the history of sick souls and provided them with the relief and nourishment they needed. Among his admirers were men of different faiths whom he had treated spiritually....The dynamism of Guru Nanak's message will save the modern world from global annihilation and the erosion of human values.[19]

The distinguished philosopher and onetime President of India, Sarvepalli Radhakrishnan, wrote:

> In the tradition of India, Nanak Dev believes in religion as realisation, *anubhava*. Those who adopt this view subordinate ritualistic practices and credal definitions. Nanak Dev does not believe in the ultimacy of the distinctions between the Hindu and the Mussulman. He goes beyond these distinctions and fosters a religion of spirit which is universal in character....Nanak Dev affirms the possibility of holy life in all religions. This philosophy of ecumenism, which is now becoming popular, was anticipated by the Sikh Gurus. No wonder that the Adi Granth, which is the sacred scripture of the Sikhs, contains the utterances of holy men of both Hinduism and Islam.[20]

Such quotations could be multiplied indefinitely. They speak of a Sikhism which was finding its place among the world's religions. But the Guru Nanak anniversary issues of the *Sikh Review* or *Spokesman Weekly*, nowadays, not surprisingly, often concentrate their attention on other aspects of the faith—opposition to intolerance or injustice, for example.

---

18. Conversely, the work of McLeod has had a positive reception among many other Sikh scholars, themselves appreciative of the role of authentic, though critical, historical scholarship. ...Editors' note.

19. "Guru Nanak: World Teacher," a lecture delivered by Dr. Gobind Singh Mansukhani in 1969, at James Graham College, Leeds, and published by the Central Committee of Sikh Temples in Great Britain, pages 18-20.

20. The introductory essay, pages 1 and 2, in *Guru Nanak, His Life, Times and Teachings*, edited by Gurmukh Nihal Singh (New Delhi: Guru Nanak Foundation, 1969).

Sikhism stands at a crossroads, not for the first time in its history, and again not for the first time it is there less by choice than by circumstance. It faces a number of possibilities.

It can become an essentially political movement, stressing the "five k's" and turban and even being firmly religious as it campaigns to prevent the sale of alcohol and tobacco in the Punjab and wherever it can exert influence, but bereft of the spirit of openness and tolerance, even respect for the rights of others, that existed in the days of Guru Nanak or Guru Tegh Bahadur. This, I suppose, might be described as Sikh fundamentalism similar to that of other religions in parts of the world where they are feeling threatened.

It might settle for being a *qaum*. This word conveys the notion of a coherent religious group bound together by ties of language and ethnicity. In Sikh terms it would be a group of people adhering to the Khalsa form, regarding the Punjab as their homeland, speaking Punjabi and preserving a culture based on that of the Punjab. Its spirituality might be strong, but it would be inward-looking and in terms of the diaspora steadily diminishing in numbers, especially if it could not maintain marriage links with India because of the immigration policies of the country of settlement.

A third way is for Sikhism to regard itself as a world religion capable of existing and prospering anywhere, contributing its distinctive spiritual and human insights with those of other religions to the benefit of humanity as a whole. In a country like Britain, where stress is being placed upon equality of race and gender, the Sikh ideals are thoroughly in place and congenial to the developing values of society. Perhaps, in a country searching for spirituality and discipline, the Sikh way of life has further contributions to make.

This third response seems to be the one most in keeping with the teachings of the Gurus. It may require compromises on matters of language and dress, perhaps the use of the vernacular, be it French, German or English, to an increasing extent in gurdwaras alongside the reading of the installed Guru Granth Sahib written in Gurmukhi (the kind of compromise found in Judaism comes to mind). Such developments are already being discussed in the diaspora and will have to be faced as a matter of necessity as young Sikhs leave the Punjab further and further behind.

Where authority will lie in this worldwide Sikh religion is another issue which will have to be addressed one day. The Shiromani Gurdwara Prabandhak Committee and the Takhts are unlikely to command the respect of Western Sikhs in the twenty-first century. Perhaps North American or British Sikhs will set up their own national councils and give them some kind of authority.

As an outsider I can only watch with concerned and friendly interest. Even to raise some of the questions and issues contained in this paper is to run the risk of being regarded as a mischief-maker seeking to subvert the Sikh religion. Such is not my intention. On the contrary, it is the result of the welcome that I have been given by Sikhs who see theirs as a world religion and who have encouraged me to learn about their beliefs and practices and be interested in their developments and crises.

The diaspora is not an insignificant part of Sikhism. It may account for some fifteen per cent of total numbers. It has done much to enhance the prosperity of the Punjab materially as British Sikhs, for example, send money to their homeland to enrich farms, businesses, and provide more comfortable dwelling houses for their relatives. However, it has also been responsible for a brain drain. This has been increased by the current turmoil in the Punjab, which has also diminished the desire of many Sikhs to return to the Punjab. This movement is bound to impoverish Sikh culture in the Punjab intellectually, but it will also have social consequences for the diaspora. Sikhs in the West, as individuals and as communities, are now highly influential, not perhaps at a national level politically, but that will come. There will be Sikh members of Parliament.

As yet the British diaspora, at least, has not thrown up its own students of religion. (The concerns of migrants are much more with the problems of settlement and establishing a sound economic foothold than with the "leisure" pursuits of academics.) However, the time will come when this happens and British-born scholars and *sants* appear. Then the diaspora will move into its second phase, one no longer conditioned by its Punjab origins and a need simply to survive.

In these days of turmoil and anguish, when those who have friends, Hindu and Sikh, also Muslim and Christian, in the Punjab and India, it is more than usually difficult to consider the future of Sikhism. It may be that the form and expression of the religion in its homeland will be unaffected by developments among the diaspora. After all, Anglican and Roman Catholic Christianity have, as yet, been very little moved by developments in those denominations in the United States, South America or Africa. The lack of interest which I have often found among Indians for their compatriots who have made their homes abroad could continue.

So far no mention has been made of the importance of Sikhism for interfaith dialogue. This is now an important activity of Christian theologians. Concern for mission has not ceased, but there is a new spirit present in the churches. Christians are distinguishing between the essential faith and culture, and they are realising that what they gave to India, Africa or South America was the gospel dressed up in European clothes that were unsuitable for the new countries into which it was introduced. Now they are more respectful of the indigenous cultures. With this humility goes an affirmation that God was already present in Africa, for example, in the tribal religions, or in India in Hinduism, Sikhism and Islam, before the missionaries came. The need to be informed about these religions is now acknowledged. This goes further for some Christians who become aware of the richness of Sikh spirituality and the authenticity of Sikh beliefs and wish to enrich their own. A sharing takes place as Sikhs also explore Christian insights. This dialogue between people of different religions will increase as Britain becomes more aware of itself as a multi-faith society and as certain preconditions are met. Among these are a sense of security, a willingness to trust each other, and the recognition of the spiritual worth of traditions other than one's own. The outgoing nature of Sikhs and the commitment of their Gurus to a classless, egalitarian, pluralistic society are already making them a community respected by Christians. This raises self-esteem as Sikhs take their proper place among the great world religions.

Conclusion

The ultimate question raised by the existence of the Sikh diaspora is this: is it necessary to be or become a Punjabi to be a Sikh? Did Guru Nanak, through his journeys, demonstrate that the message of Sikhism was to be universal? This is the inference that anyone who studies his life is invited to draw. He is to be seen as God's messenger in the *kal yug*, to those adherents of the great religions who had put religiosity and ritual first and forgotten the eternal message revealed through the *rishis* and prophets. If he did enunciate that universal message, then Sikhism, as it turns inwards in an understandable response to circumstances, may be in danger of losing sight of its *raison d'être*. It would not be the first movement to do this, by any means. However, it would seem strange if, within a generation of their beginning to regard themselves as a world religion, not in the sense of numbers and distribution but as a faith able to exist in any land and capture or inspire the heart and mind of any human being, Sikhs were to forsake that destiny and become the minor sect on the periphery of Hinduism where many Indians and indologists always located them.

Long ago Sikhs decided that they were not Hindus. Whether they are to be seen as an independent world religion with their own spiritual dynamism responding to more than the serious political events of the Punjab, perhaps with some form of world council, is something those interested in the Sikh religion will watch with interest in the closing years of this century. The answers will be provided, I suggest, by the Sikhs of the dispersion—especially those born in the West but aware of the spiritual riches of their heritage. They stand at a frontier with little from their history or the *Rahit Maryada* to guide them. In religious terms they have to depend on the spiritual teachings of the Gurus and the living presence of the Satguru.

Sikhs in the Diaspora cannot help responding to being a minority. The form and pace of change will depend upon factors which are external to them, like racism, which is at present provoking a return to Sikh identity in its Punjabi form, or the ease with which spouses may be brought into Britain from the Punjab. As this becomes more difficult, and if even the *ragis* who make regular tours find it hard to obtain visas, then British Sikhs will become quickly distanced from India, especially if the dispute in the Punjab is resolved. It will have to develop its own resources. However, a tradition which includes among its principles equality of sex, race, class and religion and is small enough in numbers to have a distinctive ethos,[21] should have no difficulty in responding to the challenge of the late twentieth century effectively.

21. Readers wishing to place this and other papers in the book in context might consult the following studies: W.O. Cole and P.S. Sambhi, *The Sikhs: Their Religious Beliefs and Practices* (London: Routledge & Kegan Paul, 1978, reprinted 1986); Harbans Singh, *The Heritage of the Sikhs* (New Delhi: Manohar, reprinted 1985); and W.H. McLeod, *Textual Sources for the Study of Sikhism* (Manchester: Manchester University Press, 1984).

Part Four
Comments on Recent Events

The Sikhs and the Challenge
of the Eighties

Patwant Singh

There is nothing unusual in the violence which the votaries of the Sikh faith have experienced in the five hundred years since it was founded. Most new movements face such hostility. What is unfortunate in this case is that it was directed at a wholly peaceful reform movement whose only aim was to synthesise the best of two great religions, Hinduism and Islam. But the towering rage of the Sikhs at the torture and beheading of Arjan, their fifth Guru—a scholar and saint and compiler of their sacred scriptures, the Guru Granth—was to change their future course as also of India's history. His brutal murder was to carry the Sikhs into unremitting wars for two hundred years and more, with the Mughal rulers of India as well as with the hordes that poured down periodically from the mountain passes in the north. The faith's prolonged baptism by fire was to cast its people in a special mould of militancy and self-confident *élan*.

Because the five hundred years from its inception till the present time have been bloodier than those experienced by most other religions, the lore and legends of the Sikh faith are woven around the valorous deeds of those who died defending it. Through conquests and defeats their sense of pride and destiny never left them. Each experience on the battlefield contributed in its own way to either a greater glorification of the ideals of their faith or a renewed resolve to restore its standing to a level higher than ever before.

This is the mosaic in which are reflected the colours and patterns of events that for centuries have influenced the Sikh psyche. Their history, of far shorter span than other faiths', has for that reason an immediacy which till today continues to sustain their emotions and self-esteem. A sense of this backdrop is necessary for understanding Sikh attitudes and actions and the making of more recent events, especially of the last forty years.

The tragedy of the crisis which is casting a lengthening shadow on India as the eighties draw to a close is that these proud people—who for generations have fought for the defence of India—are today wondering whether they themselves have a future in India. That all Sikhs are hostile to the country of their birth—or

[Joseph T. O'Connell, Milton Israel, Willard G. Oxtoby, eds., with W.H. McLeod and J.S. Grewal, visiting eds., *Sikh History and Religion in the Twentieth Century* (S. Asian Studies Papers, 3) (Toronto: S. Asian Studies, Univ. of Toronto, 1988)]

ranged against it—is not the existing political reality of India. It is a falsehood that reflects the disgraceful role of large segments of India's national press, which first distorted the perfectly legitimate demands of the Akali Dal, the Sikh political party—but by no means representative of all Sikhs. These then extended that fraudulent interpretation to question the patriotism of not only Akalis, but of the entire community: "Every feature of Sikh politics has pushed the Sikh community towards internalising a sense of deprivation, towards separateness, towards separation."[1]

Not only have bigotry and communal bias of the press, and the subtle game played by the government-controlled media like radio and television, helped set the Hindus and Sikhs on a dangerous course of confrontation. Some of the newspapers are even intent on rewriting the historic role of the Sikhs during India's independence movement. Fortunately, historical facts, once established, are not so easily changed. Some of these facts relate to the period immediately preceding the end of British rule.

During the climactic countdown to India's independence in 1947, it was clear to the two groups that would inherit power, the Congress and the Muslim League, that they were playing for extraordinarily high stakes in which the ultimate prize was the Indian subcontinent. The Sikhs knew it too, but with a crucial difference. They were not looking for a separate homeland. India was their home; they had always seen themselves as an integral part of it. They were not seeking to dismember still further the land of their birth. What exactly was the Sikh position as the time of India's independence drew near? Since there is no dearth of authoritative archival material on it, just two or three instances are given to show the brazen nature of the present charge against them.[2]

Sardar Hardit Singh Malik, a distinguished member of India's civil service during British rule and in post-Independence India, played a crucial role in setting the Sikh position in perspective quite early on. This followed a momentous meeting between the Sikh leadership and Mohammad Ali Jinnah in 1946. It was a period of vigorous lobbying by the major groups who were to inherit power after Independence. The initiative for winning over the Sikhs to the Muslim League's point of view came from Jinnah. In a message to the Maharaja of Patiala he proposed a meeting but seemed reluctant to go to Patiala for it. Sardar Malik, the prime minister of Patiala State, favoured the idea of a meeting on neutral ground, which he eventually arranged at the New Delhi home of his brother, Sardar T.S. Malik. The five persons who met there were the Maharaja of Patiala, Sardar Malik, Master Tara Singh, Giani Kartar Singh and Mr. Jinnah.

The Muslim leader, according to Sardar Malik,

was the most friendly and explained to us that he was most anxious that the Sikhs should accept Pakistan and agree to live there after it was created, and

---

1. Arun Shourie, "The Politics of Pandering," *The Indian Express*, May 12, 1982.
2. See the chapter by Indu Banga in this volume for details of this period. —Editors' note.

he went on to explain that if we did that he would agree to everything that we would wish for to safeguard our interest as a minority.[3]

Sardar Malik thanked him for his generosity but said: "You will have a Cabinet, a Parliament, the Judiciary, the Armed Forces. What exactly will be our share in all these?" Mr. Jinnah replied by telling a story of Zaghlul Pasha, Egypt's virtual ruler after the country became independent. When a delegation of the Copts, Egypt's influential Christian minority, went to see the Pasha to seek guarantees that would secure their position in the new Egypt, he asked them to ponder carefully what they wanted and bring back their demands in a written document. At their second meeting, when the Copt leader handed the written demands to him, Zaghlul Pasha, without even reading it, wrote "I agree" on the document. Jinnah then added, "This is how I will deal with you—as Zaghlul Pasha did with the Copts."[4]

The Sikh leaders, according to Sardar Malik, were not even agreeable to the establishment of Pakistan, let alone having any dealings with it. After their conversation with Jinnah and a brief discussion amongst themselves, they decided to take steps to counter any false propaganda that might be started following the meeting. Sardar Malik records that on that very day

> I went and saw U.N. Sen [Sir Usha Nath Sen, a veteran journalist], who wielded considerable influence in press circles in those days and was an old friend, and I said to him, "My friend, I have never asked you to do anything for me, but today I have a request to make, a very important request." I then told him about the meeting with Jinnah and added, "I want you to see to it the *The Statesman* carries on its front page the next morning the headline in the largest letters, 'The Sikhs will under no circumstances accept Pakistan.'" Sen promised to do his best and sure enough the next day the *The Statesman* carried the headline that I had asked for. And that was our answer to Jinnah. We could have had Sikhistan if we wanted, as that was what Jinnah was really hinting at, because he knew fully well that we could never agree to live in Pakistan. That was the price he was offering us, to agree to Pakistan.[5]

A little earlier, the Punjab's Governor Glancy had informed the Viceroy, Lord Wavell, that "if Pakistan becomes an imminent reality we shall be heading straight for bloodshed on a wide scale; non-Muslims, especially Sikhs, are not bluffing. They will not submit peacefully to a government that is labelled 'Muhammadan Raj.'"[6]

The price the Sikhs paid, once their stand became clear to the Muslim League, is graphically described by Alan Campbell-Johnson in his book, *Mission with Mountbatten*. He recorded his impressions during a visit with the Mountbattens to Kahuta near Rawalpindi. The time was early 1947, and Lord Louis Mountbatten had taken over as Viceroy from Wavell. It was a time when few doubts were left about the impending partition of the subcontinent, nor about the lines along which it would be partitioned.

---

3. Hardit Singh Malik, "Khalistan: Let us Keep our Cool–1," *The Indian Express*, November 12, 1981. The ensuing quotations by Malik are from this article.
4. Ibid.
5. Ibid.
6. N. Mansergh and Penderel Moon, *The Transfer of Power, 1942-1947*, v. 6 (London: Her Majesty's Stationery Office, 1976), p. 72.

We arrived to find that the havoc in the small town was very great. Picking our way through the rubble, we could see that the devastation was as thorough as any produced by fire-bomb raids in the war. This particular communal orgy involved the destruction of Sikhs and their livelihood by Moslems.[7]

Leonard Mosley, in *The Last Days of the British Raj*, recounted the ruthless massacre of the Sikhs in Rawalpindi in March 1947, when the Muslims turned upon them and, in a welter of ferocity, murdered two thousand of them.[8] In no part of West Pakistan was there any respite: neither in Lahore, Sheikhupura, Sailkot nor Gujranwala districts, nor in the towns. V.P. Menon, who had a ringside seat throughout that critical and eventful period, observes in his book, *The Transfer of Power in India*, that:

one must appreciate that the Sikhs had been driven out of their homes contrary to all their hopes and expectations; that they had been deprived of their lands and property, their shrines and holy places; that their losses in men and property had been comparatively greater than those of any other community affected by the communal upheaval; that nearly forty percent of the entire Sikh community had been reduced to penury and had become refugees with the necessity of having to start life afresh.[9]

The point is not that it was only the Sikhs who paid a heavy price, or that a staggering forty per cent of them were reduced to penury. The Hindus also shared a terrible ordeal, but with a difference: the Sikhs had been offered a way out, but had rejected it. It is necessary to reiterate this because those who have set themselves the task of rewriting history will distort even these indisputable facts.

Some writers have tried, somewhat laboriously, to prove that separatism is endemic to Sikh politics. In search of evidence to support this foregone conclusion—currently very popular in India's communally charged atmosphere—they have reached back to the Punjab Census Report of 1891, to a pamphlet by Lieutenant Governor M. Macauliffe (1903), then through the Montague-Chelmsford reforms (1932), the Cripps proposals (1942) and the All Parties Sikh Conference of 1944 to the Cabinet Mission's visit of 1946 and much more.

Quite understandably, no mention is made in such writings of other, more telling, facts. For instance, when in 1906 Lord Minto, then Viceroy of India, readily conceded the Muslim demand for separate electorates and reservation of Muslim seats in the legislatures, the Sikhs asked for no such accommodation. The Congress Party, in fact, setting aside principle in favour of political expediency, in 1916 concluded a pact with the Muslim League accepting and endorsing the concept of separate electorates.

Sikh demands for the reorganisation of Punjab during British rule have also been distorted to convey an entirely different meaning. So have Sikh concerns

---

7. Alan Campbell-Johnson, *Mission with Mountbatten* (London: Robert Hale, 1952), p. 79.
8. Leonard Mosely, *The Last Days of the British Raj* (New York: Harcourt, Brace and World, 1961), p. 213.
9. V.P. Menon, *The Transfer of Power in India* (Bombay: Orient Longmans, 1957), pp. 432-33.

in respect of their language, script, shrines and social customs. If the purpose of such deliberate misinterpretation of historical facts was to provide a scholastic underpinning to the prevailing communal prejudices in India, it has succeeded. The standing of the country's Sikh community has been compromised through these misinterpretations by communally biased writers and their papers. Yet the truth is that, instead of being separatists, the Sikhs, by rejecting Jinnah's overtures and those of the British, who sounded them out as well prior to the transfer of power, made no distinction between "Sikh interests" and the interests of a soon-to-be-independent India.

They looked upon India, whether before or after Partition, as the land of their birth, in which their saints and savants had founded their faith. To them the Hindus were not an alien people, but a people from whom they had sprung, to who they had married their sons and daughters, with whom they had shared their agonies and ecstasies, and whose friendship had been a part of their experience of growing up, as it had been of the generations before them. The Sikh stand at the time of partition was an outcome of their inviolable emotional involvement with their motherland, India, the unbecoming propaganda by today's commentators notwithstanding. Their misgivings were to arise in the post-Partition years, as they saw with dismay their Hindu friends, neighbours and relations disown their common mother tongue, Punjabi. But we shall come to that later.

Some of the sacrifices made by the Sikhs during the years when the drive toward independence was gaining momentum can also bear retelling because their courage and commitment during those crucial decades is not being spared attack in the current obsessive urge to denigrate them. Also these very sacrifices were to provide the cutting edge to the movements against colonial rule. They need be told again.

Let us take a look at the price Sikhs paid for securing India her independence. Of the 2,646 persons sentenced to life imprisonment in the Andamans, 2,147 or 80% were Sikhs. In the protest meeting at Jallianwala Bagh, which is acknowledged as the turning point in India's freedom struggle, the majority of the persons gunned down by the British troops were Sikhs. In the Indian National Army formed by Subhas Chandra Bose to fight the British in World War II, 12,000 out of the total of 20,000 were Sikhs, and so on. These figures, of course, have to be seen in relation to the fact that the Sikhs are only 1.9% of India's population!

It is against these stark facts of the freedom struggle and the period preceding Partition that the falsity of the current coverage of Punjab events must be judged. Consider, for instance, India's foremost newspaper, *The Times of India*. Under the editorship of Girilal Jain, it has over the last few years consistently vilified the Sikhs at every turn and more recently taken to rewriting history as well. Consider what the editor had to say about the role of the Sikhs (Akalis!) in the struggle for India's independence in an article under his own by-line in August 1986:

A myth has been built, and it is currently sought to be reinforced, about the heroic role of the Akalis in the independence struggle. This witting or unwitting distortion of the truth cannot but add to the prevailing confusion and aggravate the tragedy that is threatening to overwhelm the Sikh community...the Akalis, let us face it, were not an independent Sikh component of the larger freedom movement...they were the products of a British inspired movement amongst the Sikhs which emphasised their separateness from the Hindus. This emphasis was not accidental. It was part of the well-established 'divide and rule policy.' The Akalis, of course, had their problems with the British but these related to their view of Sikh interests; these had nothing to do with India's independence.[10]

What this makes clear is that the first and foremost challenge before the Sikhs is to re-establish the primacy of truth in the face of a communally biased media's ongoing campaign of disinformation. At present, they have neither a national daily, weekly nor fortnightly of their own which can objectively and convincingly counter the distortions of the articles and editorials in some of the national dailies, not to mention the bias of the government-controlled radio and television. (As we shall see further on, India's government-controlled television went beyond bias; it was positively instigative in whipping up mob hysteria against the Sikhs in the period immediately after Mrs. Gandhi's assassination). The dice—as regards projecting a balanced picture of events—are heavily loaded against the Sikhs. That the Sikhs have made no effort to fill this lacuna is a sad reflection on their failure to comprehend the importance of communication in the current crisis. What is being hammered home into the Indian public's consciousness through such writings is the recurring refrain of the Sikhs as separatists, as if all that Sikh politicians have to do is tell these fifteen million proud, energetic and independent-minded people that separation is the goal of the community and they will accept it. This would be a laughable premise but for the invidiousness of the accusation. Despite the extent to which the Sikhs have been savaged by recent events, the majority of them even now are not for separation, leave aside being separatist at the time of Independence.

In view of the sustained media onslaught against them—based on the premise that since public memory is short-lived, recent mistruths, if persuasively purveyed, are more easily accepted than distant and half-remembered realities— it is worth identifying those events whose impact on Sikh sensibilities helped to create serious tension in the otherwise convivial relations between Punjabi Hindus and Sikhs.

It is not as if their relationship was free of strains earlier. The Arya Samaj movement, started at the end of the nineteenth century, had first introduced them. Its denigration of Sikh philosophy and scriptures, and a corresponding emphasis on the use of the Hindi language and script, had gained it an impressive following in urban Punjab at the expense of the cohesiveness between the two communities. But these strains—not too dissimilar to those experienced by different social groupings in other societies—had been kept in

---

10. Girilal Jain, "What Ails the Sikh Community," *The Times of India*, August 11, 1986.

check by the maturity and magnanimity of the communities concerned. The language controversy, however, and the reorganisation of the states after Independence, were to prove more corrosive. Their effect on the psyche of the Sikhs, and their far-reaching consequences for the stability and social fabric of India, are yet to be fully analysed.

The idea of reorganising the provinces (which is how the states were referred to under British rule) along linguistic lines first took shape in 1920, when the Congress Party in its new constitution reorganised its country-wide Pradesh Congress committees on the basis of language. Later, in 1929, the Nehru Report committed the Congress to the restructuring of India on linguistic lines. Again, just two years prior to Independence, in 1945, Dr. Pattabhi Sitaramayya, president-elect of the All India Congress Committee, in his inaugural address reiterated his party's resolve to redraw the state boundaries of India on the basis of language.

After the transfer of power the party had second thoughts. The dangers of unleashing linguistic chauvinism on a fledgling republic were perceived more realistically. The euphoria of a period in which pledges could be made without having to face the challenge of implementation was replaced by more practical considerations. It was realised that the narrow outlook of language lobbies could undermine the larger promise of a free India. But the pressures grew. Ironically, Jawaharlal Nehru's own belated resistance to a reorganisation his father had recommended twenty years earlier was unable to stand up to the language zealots.

Even prior to the reorganisation itself, the ground was being laid not only for alienating the Sikhs but for the future political and social instability of India as well. Soon after Independence a resolution was moved in Jullundur's Municipal Committee to the effect that the committee's business should be conducted in Hindi. Why? Because Jullundur—in the heartland of post-Partition Punjab—was, so it was contended, a Hindi-speaking city! Then, literally on the eve of the 1951 census operations in Punjab, the late Lala Jagat Narain, general secretary of the Punjab Pradesh Congress, sponsored a campaign to get Punjab's Hindus and Harijans to declare Hindi as their mother tongue. Over forty-two years earlier, during the monsoon season in 1909, the Arya Samaj had invited the Rahtias, Ramdasis and Mazhbis (classified as the lower castes) to a meeting in Jullundur, always an epicentre of the Arya Samaj movement. The purpose of the meeting was to discuss "measures to uplift them," which meant to align them more firmly with the movement through inducement and influence.[11] Lala Jagat Narain, a staunch Arya Samajist, was patronised by the Punjab Congress Committee, who recognised his potential as a political foil to the Akali and Sikh appeal in the Majha and Doab areas of Punjab. This political move, essentially a marriage of convenience between Congress ambitions in Punjab and Arya Samaj fundamentalism, eventually was to erode the traditional Hindu-Sikh ethos in

11. Fortnightly Reports on the Punjab, August 14, 1909. National Archives.

Punjab. It was a Pyrrhic victory for the protagonists of Hindi, because even as it provided cause for satisfaction to Punjab's urban Hindu bourgeois and the Jullundur-based language press owned by it, it tore Punjab's social, cultural, and linguistic fabric down the middle. As Prof. Jaswant Singh Phul, of India's Janata Party, put it: "A patent lie was given a communal complexion." It would prove to be an act of great folly.

What made Punjab's Hindus deny Punjabi as their mother tongue? It was a delayed outcome of the seeds of communal chauvinism sown by the Arya Samaj. The Samaj's antipathy to the founder of the Sikh faith Guru Nanak Dev, and its refusal to acknowledge Gurmukhi as a script for Punjabi language eventually led to the rejection of the language itself. And this is where the irony of the events of 1906 and 1951 has been lost sight of. In 1906 the Muslims, a minority, wanted to separate from the Hindu majority by demanding separate electorates. In 1951 the Hindus, the majority community, sought to separate themselves from a minority, the Sikhs, on the grounds of religion, i.e., Hindi for the Hindus. In effect, it is such segments of Punjab's Hindu society, and not the Sikhs, who were and continue to be separatists!

Even more astonishing attitudes were to surface at the time of the actual reorganisation of states. They reflected an increasing bias against a Punjab that was beginning to be politically subverted from within by politicians of the majority community and the prevalent Congress culture. The two committees set up by the government of independent India to report on the feasibility of reorganization on linguistic lines, while endorsing the idea for other states, excluded the northern states from it, especially Punjab. The reason? As the Dar Commission (one of the two appointed) rightly pointed out, "nationalism and sub-nationalism are two emotional experiences which grow at each other's expense," and the reorganisation of India on "mainly linguistic considerations is not in the larger interests of the Indian nation." After this assertive expression of its concern, it equivocated, "it (reorganisation) was a grave risk, but one that had to be taken." In its report of December 10, 1948, it recommended—despite its reservations—the formation of Andhra, Karnataka, Kerala, and Maharashtra on linguistic lines!

To the Sikhs it seemed odd that whilst the demands of the Telugu-, Kannada-, Malayalam- and Marathi-speaking peoples were to be conceded, the government was not even prepared to include the demand for a Punjabi-speaking state in the Dar Commission's terms of reference. But the tables against them were to be turned still further. Since at the instigation of fundamentalist organisations like the Arya Samaj and of politicians of similar ilk a substantial number of Hindus in Punjab were disowning Punjabi as their mother tongue, the demand for a Punjabi-speaking state was, in the public's mind, slowly beginning to be seen as a demand for a Sikh state. In the course of time a purely linguistic demand which India's other linguistic groups had also made, and which the Congress Party had declared its goals in 1929, was in Punjab's case labelled as a separatist demand! The media willingly spread this falsehood.

Since the Akalis are usually made to appear the odd ones out in what is fancifully seen as the serene give-and-take of Indian political life, what *was* their demand? It was for a unilingual Punjabi-speaking state. In their proposal to the States Reorganisation Commission for a unilingual Punjab, the Hindu population would have been 57% as against 43% Sikhs. In effect the Akali demand was for a Hindu majority state and not a Sikh Suba. The States Reorganisation Commission rejected their proposal. The reason given for the rejection was that it was not supported by the Hindus of the Punjab, who were then 70% of the population of composite Punjab.

This refusal of Punjab's Hindus to have anything to do with a language they said was that of the Sikhs—even though for generations they had used and acknowledged it as their own language—was what converted the linguistic principle into a communal confrontation in Punjab. Even after the States Reorganisation Act was passed in 1956 on the basis of one language for one state, Punjab and Bombay were left bilingual. As was to be expected, Bombay too—because of the influence its people could exercise in the framing of national policy, which the Sikhs could not—was reorganised into the states of Maharashtra and Gujarat on May 1, 1960.

The Sikhs once again registered the humiliating fact that it was more political clout and less political principle that would count in post-Independence India. The time-table of the country's linguistic reorganisation provides proof of this:

States formed:	On:
Andhra Pradesh	October 1, 1953
Kerala	November 1, 1956
Karnataka	November 1, 1956[12]
Maharashtra	May 1, 1960
Gujarat	May 1, 1960
Punjab	November 1, 1966

Six years later, long after the formation of other linguistic states, and after a bitter struggle that killed many, sent several thousands to jail, and left permanent scars on communal relations in Punjab, a heavily truncated Punjabi Suba was eventually formed on November 1, 1966. Even at the end its creation was lacking in grace. The Shah Commission, established to determine the lines along which the further partition of Punjab on the basis of language would take place, was asked to make its recommendations with "due regard to the census figures of 1961." Thus, many Hindu-majority areas, where Punjabi was spoken but had been disowned in the census, were left out of the new Punjab. Akali protests against this term of reference given to the Commission were ignored. Chandigarh, built as the new capital of Punjab after Partition, was no longer a part of it. Justice Gurnam Singh, the Akali Chief Minister of the state, in a letter written in 1969 to the then Prime Minister, Mrs. Indira Gandhi, observed: "The

_____
12. The state of Mysore was formed on November 1, 1956. The name was changed to Karnataka in 1973 with a few *talukas* added.

terms of reference of the Shah Commission were framed on communal lines by your Home Minister." Mr. Gulzari Lal Nanda, the Home Minister, was described by Mr. Singh as a man with a communal outlook.

In the end, instead of a genuine unilingual Punjabi state with 57% Hindu population as demanded by the Akalis, a Punjab based on false and communally motivated figures of the 1961 census was formed with 61% Sikh population. A communal Punjab, for which they had never asked, was finally forced on the Sikhs.

The communalising of Punjab's politics was the work of small-town language zealots buttressed by the country's short-sighted political leadership of the time. It was not the work of the Akalis. But sadly, in part due to the state's composition and the manner in which it had come into being, Akali politics would also take a sharp communal turn that would eventually endanger both the community and the country.

Before we look at this tragic phase in Punjab's politics, it will be appropriate to spell out the second challenge which faces the Sikhs: the imperative of overcoming the resentments and mistrust generated by the events of the fifties and sixties. Without this they will not be able to muster the drive and determination required to deal with the current problems. Once the Punjabi Suba had been created, the Sikhs accepted it despite their reservations. They made it prosper and they can do infinitely more for it in the years ahead. Having dealt with the first challenge, which is to counter a communally biased media's misreporting on Punjab, the second challenge before the Sikhs is to start looking at the future, not the past.

Irrespective of how persuasive a case to the contrary is made, the inability of the Akalis to wrest political power from the Congress on their own merits, even after Punjab became a Sikh majority state, was in large measure responsible for their increasingly communal stand through the seventies. The Panth was not in danger then, though their recurring refrain on these lines did eventually endanger it. It also influenced some Sikhs into believing it.

What cannot be overlooked either is that their communal refrain was not an isolated phenomenon. In the new political ethos which was beginning to pervade the country, giving a perverse twist to its democratic ideals and the electoral process, an appeal to communal and religious sentiments seemed in order. The appeal to caste as an acceptable electioneering strategy was gradually and insidiously extending itself to the more dangerous realm of religion. The communal factor was coming home to roost and the Akalis seemed willing to cash in on it.

It was, unfortunately, a negation of their principled stand on the language issue. If, in their perception, Sikh interests could at the same time be best served by a genuinely linguistic and much larger Punjab—even though they would be a minority in it—it was unprincipled of them to opt for a communal line now. Clearly their aim was to wrest the Sikh vote away from the Congress. But ignored in their electoral calculus was the fact that they could have more effectively convinced the voters by providing them irrefutable evidence of the Congress Party's own predilection for cashing in on the communal element, and the shortcomings of its programs and policies in respect of Punjab's industrialisation, communication links, power shortages, and such. They could have applied themselves to the meticulous preparation of a blueprint for the economic and administrative revitalisation of the state. The electorate would have responded, because Punjabis are pragmatic people. They can tell the difference between a genuine and a spurious product. Religion need not have come into the electoral debate.

In the absence of a constructive strategy on the one hand, and given only the raw appeal of religious passions on the other, there could be no way of predicting the eventual outcome of emotions aroused by the zealots' appeal, or of predicting whether feelings once aroused to dangerous levels could be controlled. In the event, the Akalis were to find themselves outwitted by functionaries of the ruling party, who were planning to give events an even more dangerous turn in an already tense Punjab.

Quite simply, the Congress strategy aimed at destroying the Akali party itself: more immediately, the state's Akali-Janata coalition government formed after the Congress defeat in the 1977 elections following the Emergency. The Akalis had been anathema to the ruling party because of their sustained opposition to the Emergency throughout its duration. In the estimation of Congress strategists, the time had come to settle scores with the Akalis: to break the Akali Dal. That the democratic process does not entail the destruction of opposition parties, but only the countering of their electoral appeal with more convincing alternatives, was too fine a point for the hatchet-men of the Congress Party.

The Congress plan, as is well known by now, quite literally called for the "creation" of a religious leader who with messianic zeal would help wean Sikh votes away from the Akali-Janata coalition and in favour of the Congress, and who would later help dismantle the Akali Party itself. Jarnail Singh Bhindranwale was the man Sanjay Gandhi and Giani Zail Singh (Punjab's former Chief Minister) chose for this role. He was the new religious leader who with Congress support would be used to neutralise the Akali Dal's appeal to the Sikhs. If this goal required him to provoke communal passions, so be it. And if, aside from mocking the Akalis, he also pushed them towards more militant postures, so much the better: it would help discredit them still further in the eyes of the nation. If it caused irretrievable damage to the already strained communal relations in the state—well, that was politics. The time was 1977-78.

As was to be expected, communal relations did progressively deteriorate as excessive communal oratory found its echo in increasing violence and the criminalisation of politics. Throughout, it was the Congress Party—and not the Akalis—who provided protection to the forces that were stoking communal fires.

The irony underlying India's political life is that with radio and television in the iron grip of the government of India, and the press communalised to a great extent—though with a few worthy exceptions—these significant milestones in the deterioration of communal relations in Punjab are deliberately pushed into the background. Consciously ignored is the fact that many of the state's most senior Congress politicians who towards the end of the seventies stoked communal fires are today in positions of respectability bestowed by a grateful ruling party. In contrast, first the Akalis and then the entire Sikh community have been branded guilty of the crimes they did not commit.

No objective assessment of Jarnail Singh Bhindranwale can overlook the fact that, though a man of impressive scholarship in Sikh scriptures, he allowed himself to be used for the dubious political purposes of the ruling party. In the process, he staked the lives of thousands of his co-religionists without a specific plan or purpose in sight. Equally, when he finally broke with his mentors, he failed to perceive that the Congress mandarins would in a complete turnabout not only destroy him but also the standing and self-esteem of all Sikhs. A pliant media would help project him as a prototype of the beliefs and aspirations of all Sikhs. The resulting aim of the lurid propaganda would be to provide justification for the final, physical assault on that exalted symbol of Sikh faith, the Golden Temple. Jarnail Singh Bhindranwale did what no Sikh Guru had done in the past: he placed the supreme emblem of Sikhism in the direct line of fire.

The serenity of this noble place of worship, sacred to all Sikhs the world over, was traded for political goals. A truly heroic alternative would have been to face the adversary in the open, not to invoke the sanctity of a sacred shrine for self-protection. In this the Akalis also stand condemned. As I wrote at the time:

> It was clearly the responsibility of the Akalis and the SGPC to prevent the sanctity of the Golden Temple from being destroyed. The Akalis had the power to prevent this, but failed to use it. For this they stand indicted in the eyes of most Sikhs. But this failure has to be seen in the context of the low level to which the political process in Punjab had been reduced by the opportunism and deceit of politicians in their pursuit of power. As Akali efforts to negotiate with New Delhi failed and they returned empty-handed after each attempt, so, their cynicism with regard to Bhindranwale's intemperate and base pronouncements increased. If he was embarrassing the government, which in turn was embarrassing them, so be it.[13]

But what they overlooked was that by then not only the Akalis but all Sikhs were being discredited as less and less distinction was made between the two. The blurring of this distinction was no oversight. It was part of a larger design to which the country's far from unfettered press was lending itself. The media were making *all Sikhs* appear as accessories to the excesses of a few, and holding them accountable:

> It is 11 p.m. in the history of the Sikh community. It must reverse the clock. It is still possible to do so. But time is running out. The community must demand that the agitation be called off. The Sikhs must heed the warning before it strikes midnight.[14]

---

13. Patwant Singh, "Around the Punjab Impasse," *The Indian Express*, October 20, 1984.
14. Girilal Jain, "The Sikhs Are in Danger," *The Times of India*, March 7, 1984.

The indoctrination of the Indian public by large sections of the national and language press, has helped create nearly irreversible cleavages between the Hindus and the Sikhs. Fortunately this is true only of the Hindi-speaking population of the Union. Except for stray cases there is no estrangement in the case of the Sikhs and the people of the non-Hindi-speaking areas of the country. When, in time, a serious study is carried out to assess the damage done to the nation's social and political fabric by communally biased editors, columnists and reporters, it will be seen how small men with large pretensions abused their privileged positions to push the country to the very brink of disintegration.[15]

Apart from being described as separatists and secessionists, on whom every gesture of conciliation and tolerance was seemingly wasted, they were now put on notice. Based on the militancy of the few in the Golden Temple, a widespread resentment was gradually but surely being whipped up against the Sikhs. When the final assault on the Temple was mounted, it would have the sanction of large segments of the country. The assault itself would glorify the government—and thus the ruling party—which would be shown as conciliatory but unflinching when it came to a threat to the country's unity and integrity. Whether or not a threat did actually exist was immaterial. National leaderships have, through the ages, conjured up threats from the minorities in order to consolidate their hold on the majority.

Since all Sikhs had by then been made to appear hostile to a Hindu India, the Congress, as its savior, could naturally expect the Hindu vote in the next elections, which were but six months away. If in the process tanks and artillery had to be used to destroy a sacred heritage, well, it could not be helped.

There is no question that the S.G.P.C., under the stewardship of Gurcharan Singh Tohra, was equally culpable not only in allowing the dignity, grace, and tranquillity of the Golden Temple to be compromised but also for endangering its very existence. Mr. Tohra's reasons for doing it are unclear. As an obvious element in the Congress strategy of discrediting the Sikhs was the misuse of the

---

15. This aspect of the continuing tragedy of India in the eighties has not been highlighted, either through objective and intelligent analysis, or to the extent it deserves. But the few articles and essays which have appeared on the subject do forcefully make the point. Amongst these are two: "Shame: The Media and the Delhi Riots" and "Conspiracy of Silence" by Jugnu Ramaswamy, which appeared in the January and February 1985 issues of *Imprint* magazine. This writer's own essay, "The Distorting Mirror," which appeared in the book, *Punjab: The Fatal Miscalculation*, also describes the appalling role of the media, especially some of the national dailies.

For an overview of the Indian press—its coverage, structure and control, and the factors which determine the parameters within which it functions—"The Indian Press," in the *Far Eastern Economic Review*, July 18, 1985, provides interesting reading.

Amongst recent books, *Punjab: The Fatal Miscalculation* (edited by Patwant Singh and Harji Malik and published from Delhi by Patwant Singh) covers, with its four essays and fifteen articles, the entire genesis of this problem, a problem which results not only from the communalising of Indian politics but their criminalisation as well. This combination has placed Indian democracy on the razor's edge of survival. The book also carries an extensive bibliography of recent articles and books on Punjab. See also: Kuldip Nayar and Khushwant Singh, *Tragedy of Punjab: Operation Bluestar and After* (New Delhi: Vision Books, 1984); V.D. Chopra *et al.*, eds., *The Agony of the Punjab* (New Delhi: Patriot, 1984); Pramod Handa *et al.*, eds., *Punjab Crisis: Context and Trends* (Chandigarh: Centre for Research in Rural and Industrial Development, 1984); Mark Tully and Satish Jacob, *Amritsar: Mrs. Gandhi's Last Battle* (London: Jonathan Cape, 1985).

Golden Temple, it is difficult to accept that a man of his intelligence was unable to see through it. Were other senior Akalis like Sant Harchand Singh Longowal and Parkash Singh Badal also unable to comprehend this game plan? This question too has to be asked. But since the Golden Temple's affairs are managed by the S.G.P.C., its president, Mr. Tohra, must bear the ultimate responsibility for inviting the retribution which was visited on the altar of Sikh faith.

The third challenge before the Sikhs, then, is to establish necessary checks to ensure that their exalted shrines are never again made pawns in the games of politicians. In view of the reprehensible indifference to the sentiments of the Sikhs shown by the government of India in June 1984, the community must give serious thought to the administration of their places of worship so that there will be no excuse again for ordering artillery and armour against their shrines. It is not a part of the valorous traditions of the Sikh faith to use the hallowed precincts of gurdwaras for unholy purposes. A handful of Sikhs, no matter how piously well-intentioned, must not be permitted to take over with brute force places of prayer, meditation and solemn ritual. The sanctity of the temples cannot be left to their whims.

A logical outcome of this is the crisis of political leadership, which is making a mockery of the very qualities for which the Sikhs have always been noted. The present Akali leadership has largely failed to measure up to the tasks before it. So the fourth challenge before the Sikhs is to restore the primacy of merit in selecting their political representatives.

It is unedifying to see persons belonging to one of the most inspired and democratic faiths in history look to smugglers, religious bigots and power brokers for support during elections. This is by no means the normal practice of Sikh politicians in Punjab, but if even a few are guilty of it they disgrace Sikh traditions of personal integrity and self-denial. Equally disgraceful is the conduct of the cabals and factions within the Akali party which are making the governance of the state impossible. The self-centred concerns of the hierarchy of the Akali Dal are deeply disturbing. Obsessed with political ambitions, to the exclusion of ideology, loyalty or even common decency, they are dismantling the constructive perspective of the party.

Now for the demand of Khalistan, an independent Sikh state. There is a percentage of the Sikh population in India—a very small one as yet—that is of the view that the formation of Khalistan is inevitable no matter how long it takes, or the extent of bloodshed its creation will involve. Fortunately, the number of Sikhs who subscribe to this view, whether in Punjab or outside the state, is still small. But this can change overnight. Any untoward act or incident could trigger large-scale violence leading to a migration of populations: to multitudes on the move, seeking the security of their own people and carrying with them their bitter hurt, anger and vengefulness. After this, it would only be a matter of time before the final, fateful countdown to yet another partition of the country.

Instead of facing up to this danger with a sober sense of responsibility and maturity, those in elective office, public life and editorial positions in India would have us believe that no one in India will accept another partition. Nobody wants to see India partitioned, certainly not the majority of the Sikhs. But it is good to remember that when there are two parties to a dispute, the tendency of one of them to ignore views of the other can in time lead to an ugly showdown, especially if each is equally committed to having its way. A similar refusal to face up to facts was shown in 1947. Just as the implications of the deteriorating situation at that time were never comprehended in their entirety, a realistic sense of the consequences of allowing the present political stalemate in Punjab to continue is not being shown today.

It is brashly assumed that the country can be kept together by force. This is a dangerous assumption. The tendency is to cite the role of the military in northeastern India as a model. But what is ignored is the difference between the people, the regions and their borders. These differences should be obvious to any but the most myopic. If the army is asked to control Punjab, it would, as was pointed out in a recent survey, "only serve to destabilise Punjab as a solid base of military operations in case of a war with Pakistan."[16]

No army can fight an enemy with its own population in an angry mood, certainly not a population with martial traditions and a large number of highly trained ex-servicemen in its midst. It would be one of history's most tragic miscalculations to assume that military rule is the panacea for the present troubled state of Punjab.

Force has never been a substitute for statesmanship. It is the ultimate folly to be mesmerised by it, to use it to solve political problems. The disinclination to deal with explosive political issues expeditiously and on a political level could in time create an uncontrollable situation that would lead inevitably to a split in the country. Khalistan would literally be forced on the country through inaction or delayed political action. The danger of this, it appears, is yet to be fully realised.

After the violent events of 1984—the assault on the Golden Temple and the tragic assassination of Mrs. Indira Gandhi and the subsequent massacre of the Sikhs—it was statesmanship that pulled the country back from the brink. But the respite was short-lived. The hopes raised by the accord reached between Prime Minister Rajiv Gandhi and Sant Harchand Singh Longowal on July 24, 1985, were shattered within months of its signing. The communal lobbies around the Prime Minister were able to blunt the brilliant initiative of the two who signed the Accord. When a workable proposition, the Punjab accord, was finally available, it was just as quickly trampled underfoot: by the Centre, which waffled unforgivably in its implementation (the Centre did not display the political will needed to enforce its commitment to issues such as the immediate transfer of Chandigarh to Punjab), and by the Akali Dal, which, given to a

---

16. "Punjab: What Can be Done?" *India Today*, December 31, 1986, p. 24.

tradition of internecine warfare, split and caused political havoc in the state. The Centre, in fact, first betrayed the Accord through its mishandling of the Abohar-Fazilka issue, and the Akalis were later outraged when a commission that had been appointed said that 70,000 acres would have to be given up by Punjab in lieu of Chandigarh.[17]

Even this account errs in detail if it does not report that the Akali Dal did not split till three months after the Centre had failed to transfer Chandigarh to Punjab on January 26, 1986. With the government of India turning its back on the very first commitment it had pledged itself to honour under the Accord, Mr. Surjit Singh Barnala[18] "was already a politically doomed man." It is New Delhi's intransigence that pushed the state back into a phase of renewed violence, not the dissensions within the Akali Dal. The government cannot evade responsibility for the pass the state has come to. Whilst it would be wrong to gloss over the shortcomings of the Akalis, it would be equally incorrect to attribute to them failures which were caused by the Centre's lack of statesmanship and foresight and its refusal to stand by its commitments.

Is this refusal the main reason for the renewed violence in Punjab since early 1986? No, it is not. It is one of the reasons, though not the only one. Two other powerful motivations have driven segments of the Sikh population in the state to take to arms. The first of these is the astounding unconcern of the government of India in the matter of punishing those who claimed the lives of 2,717 persons in the first four days of November 1984. Of these, 2,146 persons were killed in Delhi. In the same period in Delhi,

> Sikh educational institutions, several large and many small houses were burnt. Trucks, taxi cabs, three-wheeler scooters, cars, motor cycles and scooters were burnt in their hundreds. Movable property, cash and jewellry were stolen or destroyed. Factories and business premises, together with their machinery and stock in trade, were looted, damaged or destroyed. A disturbing feature of this occasion is that for the first time in the history of mob violence in India, a systematic attack was made on places of worship. Of about 405 gurdwaras in Delhi some three-quarters are reported to have been damaged or destroyed.[19]

Can any administration of a civilised country refuse to punish those who commit such crimes? Does New Delhi believe it can? Or that the Sikhs will reconcile themselves to the government's reluctance to bring the criminals to book? If there is understandable outrage against the killing of innocents in Punjab, and investigating agencies are apprehending suspects all over the country every day, is there any justification for not showing equal zeal in apprehending those who killed or caused to be killed thousands of innocent Sikhs in November 1984? By what perverse logic are the killers of Sikhs in Delhi and elsewhere immune to prosecution?

---

17. Ibid., pp. 24, 25.
18. The Chief Minister who headed the Akali ministry in Punjab after his party came into power in the September 1985 elections in the state. He was removed from office by the union government in May, 1987.
19. Report of the Citizens' Commission, headed by Justice S.M. Sikri, former Chief Justice of India, 1985. pp. 35 ff.

Easily the most flagrant instance of independent India's declining standards where constitutional proprieties are concerned was the government's stand in the aftermath of these massacres. It refused to enquire into them! They were viewed as a natural response of the people to Indira Gandhi's murder, and not worthy of enquiry or action. If the administration's refusal to uphold the majesty of the law was astonishing, Parliament's inaction was stranger still. It passed no resolution condemning the wholesale killings, nor condoled with the victims. No suggestion on these lines was made by any section of the House.

When the intent to appoint a commission was eventually announced, *almost six months after the events* (Justice Ranganath Misra, a judge of India's Supreme Court, was nominated to the job), it took another two and a half months for the commission to start proceedings. These were leisurely and unhurried. The first hearing was held on July 29, and the second not till September 11. A year would pass before the commission got to work in earnest, and another ten months before it submitted its report in August 1986! Another six months were taken by the government to place the report before Parliament in February 1987.

The report itself was astounding, not just for those Sikhs who had still hoped for decency and justice to be restored to public life in India, but for fair-minded and impartial citizens of all communities across the nation. In an excellent and extensive commentary on the report, Harji Malik, writing in the prestigious *Economic and Political Weekly*, observed:

> Justice Misra, while admitting that the Delhi killings are "one of the darkest tragedies in Independent India's history," has failed to identify the guilty, has failed to condemn the government for not having brought to book even one killer responsible for even one of the nearly 4,000 deaths in Delhi alone. His report has furthered the cause of the Sikh terrorists who have always claimed that Sikhs can expect no justice from the present regime in India. Perhaps even more important is the blow to the credibility of the Indian state in the eyes of citizens who believe in justice and the rule of law...Only an honest, fearless, unbiassed, complete investigation to expose the true facts of the violence, could have helped to mitigate the nation's shame. In accepting the assignment Justice Misra assumed the role of the national conscience, the responsibility of restoring the credibility of the state itself...it [the Commission] embodied the hopes of hundreds of traumatised Indian citizens including a huge number of widows who saw in the commission their one recourse to justice. So what went wrong.?[20]

A great many things went wrong.

1. To start with, Justice Misra decided to hold the hearings *in camera*: he barred the press and the public from attending them. He drew a shroud of secrecy over a matter of vital public interest, and even the briefings of the press, after two sessions, were stopped.

2. Then, the continuance of the Citizens' Justice Commission (C.J.C.) was rendered impossible and it was left with no recourse but to withdraw, which it did on March 31, 1986. This suited the Misra Commission fine. A word about the C.J.C.: it was established to assist the commission to arrive at the truth and

---

20. Harji Malik, "Misra Commission Report: Salt on Raw Wounds," *Economic and Political Weekly*, April 25, 1987.

was headed by Justice S.M. Sikri, the former Chief Justice of the Supreme Court of India. It included among its members Justice R.S. Narula, former chief justice of the Punjab and Haryana High Court; Justice V.M. Tarkunde, former judge of the Bombay High Court; Soli Sorabji, former Solicitor General; Govind Mukhoty, civil-rights lawyer; and others, all men of enormous standing in the country. But, since the C.J.C. was making the commission very uncomfortable with its watchdog role, it had to go, and conditions to ensure it did so were accordingly created. In its memorandum to the commission, announcing its withdrawal, the C.J.C. observed that

> to wrap up the whole inquiry behind closed doors...is inconsistent with the right to information which is a part of the fundamental right of free speech and expression guaranteed under Article 19(1)(a) and is also subversive to the principle of open government especially in the matter of such public importance.[21]

3. The Commission, while allowing several hastily formed and blatantly partisan bodies to attend its *in camera* sessions, barred admission to organisations like the People's Union for Civil Liberties and the People's Union for Democratic Rights. The unique role of these bodies in the aftermath of the November killings had done more to counter Sikh anger—and restore to some extent Sikh faith in the country—than any action of the national government or the capital's administration. Yet Justice Misra refused them a role in his commission's hearings.

4. As a recent analysis of the Misra Commission Report pointed out,

> the procedures adopted by the Commission throughout the inquiry were highly questionable in nature. First, out of the 2,905 affidavits received, the Commission selected only 128 for recording evidence. The basis of such selection was never laid down and in effect it excluded a number of affidavits which would have contradicted the eventual findings of the Commission, especially in relation to the role of the Congress (I) party. Again the Commission's own Agency arbitrarily selected only 30 of the affidavits (v. 2, pp. 8-10) for investigation. The investigation itself was reduced to checking and cross-checking the affidavits without any independent inquiry worth the name. Secondly, the repeated request for relevant documents to be produced was disallowed. Eventually, when some select documents were summoned, they were not shown to all the participants. Further, while the Commission allowed them [participants] to put interrogatives to the officials, crucial questions were disallowed on the ground that they were "against the public interest" or that they were "irrelevant."[22]

5. The Commission exonerated of any wrongdoing several of the senior most ruling party Members of Parliament from Delhi, including a minister in the union cabinet who, despite the grave allegations levelled against him, still continues to hold a prestigious portfolio in the cabinet. The rationale provided by Justice Misra in the Misra Commission Report for exonerating this man was

---

21. Ibid.
22. "Justice Denied: A Critique of the Misra Commission Report on the Riots in November 1984." Published by the People's Union for Democratic Rights and People's Union for Civil Liberties (April, 1987), pp. 4, 5.

that being a sitting MP and minister he "was not likely to misbehave in the manner alleged."

And so on.

Is it any wonder that in the face of government's amazing unconcern with bringing to justice criminals responsible for the large-scale crimes against Sikhs in November 1984, outraged members of the community have taken it upon themselves to avenge the massacre of their kin? Since vengeance is also viewed as a form of justice, extremist actions will continue to haunt the country so long as the government delays or denies justice to the aggrieved or discriminates in its dispensation.

Sikhs are equally outraged at the increasing frequency with which they are singled out for search and interrogation all across the country and subjected to public humiliation. Many are led away for indefinite detention under laws which make a mockery of India's democratic pretension. Some of them, like the Terrorist and Disruptive Activities (Prevention) Act, Terrorist Affected Areas (Special Courts) Act, and the National Security Act (NSA), give the government limitless powers, including the arrest and detention of persons for up to two years without trial. These powers neither oblige the state to inform the accused of the crimes for which they are being apprehended, nor require the authorities to frame any charges. There are 370 Sikhs, including women, detained in Jodhpur jail under the NSA on charges of "waging war against the state" during Operation Bluestar. They have been there since June 1984, from the time of the assault on the Golden Temple. They were still awaiting trial at the start of 1987 though they had been in detention for over three years. There are numerous other instances of the abuse of such powers.

The observations of a recent Amnesty International report on Punjab place these detentions in their proper legal and human-rights perspective:

> Amnesty International believes there is a possibility that there may be prisoners of conscience among those now held without trial for well over two years, apparently under the National Security Act. There may be men and women among them who did not use or advocate violence and who were arrested simply as a result of having been present in the Golden Temple for religious or peaceful political purposes. Moreover, Amnesty International is concerned that, if tried under the Terrorist Affected Areas (Special Courts) Act, these detainees may not have a fair trial in accordance with internationally accepted human rights standards. Amnesty International believes they should now either be released, or if tried, be brought to justice under ordinary procedures of criminal law with customary safeguards. They should not be deprived of the minimum legal safeguards for a fair trial laid down in international human rights standards to which India is a party.[23]

Another reckless provocation in the existing already dangerously charged atmosphere, is the torture and deaths of Sikhs in police custody. Listing some of them in an article published last year, I pointed out in one particular case that:

> It is difficult to understand why the death of this young man in the prime of his life who had his whole future before him—he was due to be married—

---

23. Amnesty International, London, December 1, 1986.

should have evoked no sense of outrage and anger, no demand for putting on trial the inquisitors who ended his life in the torture cells of the national capital. Not one question was asked in Parliament, not one editorial was written in any of the six English newspapers published in Delhi every day. An increasing number of Sikhs no longer ask why this is so. Deep inside them they are convinced they can expect no justice.[24]

Clearly, the challenges that face the Sikhs cannot be considered in insolation from the actions of the Indian administration. New Delhi has to face the fact that some of its functionaries are criminals whose actions are undermining the foundations of the state. It is unreasonable, if not self-deluding, for it to expect the Sikhs to forget the indignities they have faced for close to three years, even as police and security agencies continue to harass and torture them indiscriminately. It should be plain to the government that the Sikhs cannot be put down by brute force, though this mesmerising belief appears to be held by some of the less than sane elements in and outside the corridors of power. On the contrary, because persecution breeds its own forms of brutality, a progressive deterioration in the day to day tenor of life will quickly make India a very troubled and unsettled society.

The challenge before the political leadership of India, thus, is to take the wiser course: of not duplicating its errors; of showing through political magnanimity its concern for the larger national purpose; of proving that persistence in error will not be allowed to become the policy of any government in a land which historically has contributed to the world much philosophic thought, spiritual direction and intellectual wisdom.

If those who are presently in power in India are able to see this as the only course open to them, and are able to break the dangerous impasse by rejecting preconceived notions and the existing obsession with narrow electoral goals and communal politics, the Sikhs too will respond. Since they have the fibre with which to face the challenges, they will with zest, face up to the most rewarding one of them all: the challenge of overcoming their alienation and merging themselves once more into the national mainstream.

---

24. Patwant Singh, "Needed: Salves for the Sikhs' Wounds," *Sunday Mail*, March 30 - April 5, 1986.

Sikhs at the Turn
of the New Century

Amrik Singh

Two comparatively recent related developments have created a new situation for the future of the Sikhs. One is the partition of India in 1947; the other, the consequent dispersion of the Sikhs. As a result, the Punjab ceased to be the only region where large concentrations of Sikhs are to be found.

Till 1947, only individual Sikhs had moved outside the Punjab. As a community they originated in the Punjab, and that is the region to which they continued to belong. It was mainly in pursuit of employment that they moved outside. Except for a very small number in Bihar and in Maharashtra (seats of Takht Patna Saheb and Takht Hazoor Saheb respectively), there was no appreciable settlement of Sikhs in India outside the Punjab. There was some migration to other countries, but the numbers were not particularly large. Kenya was in a somewhat separate category, as quite a large number of Sikhs did settle there and established themselves more or less as a community. To some extent the same phenomenon took place in respect of the United Kingdom and the west coast of Canada and the United States. But the phenomenon did not assume the proportions of a major social development.

I

After 1947 there were marked changes in the demographic situation. Virtually every Sikh left (Pakistani) West Punjab and moved over to India. While the majority of them settled in the Punjab, a substantial number settled down in Delhi or moved over to other urban centres in India. Bombay and Calcutta, which had small numbers of Sikhs before 1947, developed into important centres of Sikh population, Bombay today having almost 100,000 Sikhs. Other towns like Kanpur, Indore, Jabalpur, Ranchi and Ahmedabad also attracted a substantial Sikh population. Towns like Lucknow, Jaipur, Varanasi, Meerut, Daltonganj (Bihar), Baroda, even Coimbatore, were not far behind. Quite a large number went to Assam and other northeastern states. Sikhs constitute over 6% and less than 1% of the Haryana and Himachal population

[Joseph T. O'Connell, Milton Israel, Willard G. Oxtoby, eds., with W.H. McLeod and J.S. Grewal, visiting eds., *Sikh History and Religion in the Twentieth Century* (S. Asian Studies Papers, 3) (Toronto: S. Asian Studies, Univ. of Toronto, 1988)]

respectively. In sum, by the time of the 1981 census the number of Sikhs outside Punjab was more than three million, i.e., more than 20% of the total Sikh population.

Two related developments may also be noted. As a result of migration from West Punjab, there was pressure on land in East Punjab. Some of the peasants found that the Tarai region of Uttar Pradesh, which was being colonised at that time, offered them good opportunities. Hard-working and adventurous, they did not hesitate after 1947 to open up this virgin territory. Approximately 300,000 Sikhs are now to be found in that region.

Similarly Ganganagar, a district of Rajasthan that borders Punjab, received something like 300,000 settlers, an overwhelming majority of them being landowners and cultivators who bought up land there and settled. Outside the Punjab and Haryana, these are the two states in which agricultural communities of Sikhs have settled down. For the rest, the Sikhs outside Punjab are to be found mainly in business or in professions, with transport following close behind. Till the November 1984 carnage, for instance, Delhi had a population of more than 600,000 Sikhs. (Over 50,000 of them have moved to the Punjab since then.) This is the picture as far as India is concerned.

Almost a million have migrated abroad. While the Southeast Asian countries always had a small number of Sikhs, especially Malaya, they received a fresh accession of strength after 1947. Though entry is tightly controlled in Singapore, their presence even there is several thousand strong. The bulk of overseas migration, however, took place to the United Kingdom. Of over 1.5 million Indians in the United Kingdom, Sikhs constitute approximately one-third. Similarly, many have settled in Canada. Toronto contains more Sikhs than any other metropolitan city in North America. The western province, British Columbia, has many more than any other province of Canada. In the United States, Sikhs are dispersed throughout, especially in New York and California.

II

This historically recent dispersion of the Sikhs has a number of important consequences. The most obvious is the concentration of Sikhs in the now considerably shrunken (Indian) state of Punjab. In the pre-1947 period, Sikhs constituted only 13% of the total Punjab population. In today's Punjab state they are roughly 60%. The way the boundaries were organised in 1966 indicated an attempt by the Central government was well as the Akalis (for their respective reasons, which in basic assumptions were at odds with each other) to ensure that the percentage of Sikhs was as high in the newly established state as possible. The case of Kangra is interesting from this point of view.

Kangra is essentially Punjabi-speaking. Punjabi and Pahadi are so akin to each other that it is difficult to distinguish between the two. It is the linguists more than anyone else who can establish the distinction; ordinary people cannot. Had Kangra continued to be a part of the Punjab, from the linguistic point of view there could have been little to say. But Kangra is more than 95% Hindu. It was decided therefore to detach it from the Punjab and make it part of Himachal Pradesh. Even two decades after Himachal was established, there is political rivalry between Kangra and the rest of Himachal.

The important thing to note here is that while the decision to reorganise Punjab was taken in 1966 the logic of that decision was not fully accepted. It is not out of place to mention here that the decision to reorganise Punjab came two decades after 1947. Those two decades had witnessed jockeying for power between Hindus and Sikhs, marked by acrimony and political horse-trading. Eventually, however, when the decision to reorganise Punjab was taken, not all outstanding issues were clearly identified or properly resolved. Some of the issues, for instance the territorial disputes and the dispute about water between Punjab and Haryana, arose as results of the reorganisation of 1966. Had the reorganisation been planned properly and executed systematically, the results might have been different.

The Akalis were so delighted at the Punjabi Suba having been conceded that Sant Fateh Singh, who had led the fight, travelled to the United Kingdom after the announcement and spent several weeks there. During this period, the Ministry of Home Affairs facilitated the passage of the Punjab Reorganisation Act, leaving all these unresolved problems to bedevil the situation. The logic of the reorganisation of the Punjab two decades after 1947 implied conceding political power to the Akalis, who had led the struggle for it. But the variety of stratagems adopted by the ruling party (accentuated by persistent infighting among the Akalis) led to a situation where, except for brief spells of power, the Akalis have not been able to exercise power in the reorganised state.

One important aspect of this reorganisation, however, needs to be noted. While the Jats constitute approximately two-thirds of the total Sikh population, they had been divided into two political segments until 1947. A substantial number of them were to be found in the princely states. Soon after partition these states were consolidated into what was called P.E.P.S.U. (Patiala and East Punjab States Union). It was in 1956 that Punjab and P.E.P.S.U. were merged. Once that happened, the Sikh Jats, who had so far been divided into two distinct political entities, were consolidated into one political entity.

Two important consequences ensued. One was a shift in the leadership of the Akalis. Since the late 1950's the leadership of this party has come mainly from the Malwa region of Punjab which lies to the east of the river Sutlej. This is the area which before 1947 was for the most part under the control of the princes. Secondly, because of the combined weight of the Sikh Jats, their drive for political power, which had been deflected and held back for a long time, came to the fore. Much of what has been happening in the Punjab during recent decades can be traced to this historical development.

When one advances this point of view, one encounters people who question its validity as well as the motives of those who project it. They refer to Jats in Haryana, Rajasthan, Uttar Pradesh and other parts of India as people who come from the same ethnic stock, and on that ground regard this argument as a pseudo-explanation. Without going into unnecessary details, we should recognise the historical experience of the last three centuries of the Sikh Jats. It is the Sikh Jats, more than any other section of the population, who fought the Mughals, drove out the Afghans, carried out raids as far as Delhi, Aligarh and Saharanpur and established a sovereign kingdom under Ranjit Singh. These inter-linked events were in marked contrast to the passivity with which people living in northern India had all these centuries reacted to repeated invasions during the pre-Mughal and the Mughal days. In complete reversal of the earlier trend, the Sikh Jats carried the offensive right up to the Khyber and established a regime there which left a deep imprint on the minds of people settled in that region.

It must, however, be added that the collapse of this regime and the establishment of British rule in the Punjab led to widespread demoralisation. A number of factors, including the British policy of preferential recruitment of the Sikhs into the army on a large scale, resulted in a change of outlook and ethos. What basically transformed the situation, however, was the Gurdwara Reform movement of 1920-25. This movement, as has been noted by a number of scholars, was at one level a revolt against the British and at another level an assertion of Sikh identity. The historical memory of the eighteenth century, which had been submerged to some extent after the British occupation of the Punjab, was revived. So much of what has been happening in recent years could not have happened but for the baptism of fire and sacrifice through which the Sikhs passed during this agitation.

While the contribution of every other section of the community was substantial, the burden of the struggle basically fell upon the Jats. One explanation for it was obvious: they constitute approximately two-thirds of the total Sikh population. Equally obvious should be the fact that the struggle was waged both in British India and princely India. This bond of common struggle united them in a manner that nothing else could have done. When, after 1956, the artificial political barrier dividing the Punjab and P.E.P.S.U. disappeared, a new bond of unity developed. The cementing factor was urgency to exercise political power. Various related factors have accentuated this urge, but at the root of it lies the ethnic factor of Sikh Jats' having come together in one geographic unit which was demarcated at the time of the 1966 reorganisation. Most people, even in Punjab, have failed to grasp the significance of this historical development.

The outlines of what finally emerged could be seen even in 1947-48. With millions of people migrating from Pakistan, the question arose as to where to settle them. Instead of allowing them to settle down wherever they pleased, some kind of broad policy framework had to be followed. The decision taken was that those who came from canal colonies should go back to the villages from which they had originally come. They had family links and it seemed reasonable for them to settle down there.

But there were others who had no links in East Punjab. In most cases *ad hoc* decisions were taken; but it was recognised that the existing bonds of social solidarity need not be disturbed. For instance, almost everyone who came from Kasur in Lahore district was given land in Zira in Ferozepur district, and so on. Then there was delay in certain cases in being evacuated. For instance, those who came from Multan and Jhang came somewhat later and were settled in Rohtak district, which too had been evacuated somewhat late.

Altogether a pattern began to emerge as the districts which now constitute Punjab came to have a high concentration of Sikh population. The then governor of Punjab, C.L. Trivedi, is said to have observed that these demographic changes were going to have long-range political implications. These became apparent within a few years. The rise of Partap Singh Kairon was evidence of the changes that had taken place. It is not necessary, however, to go into the other question of how sustained conflict with the Akalis became the cornerstone of his political strategy, which in turn led to prolonged agitations by the Akalis and a gap of almost twenty years between the partition of the country and the eventual formation of the reorganised Punjab.

III

I dilate upon these matters because the present stalemate in the Punjab is rooted in them. And upon the outcome of the stalemate will depend to a great extent the future of the Sikhs as they enter the next century. Since the early 1980's, the Punjab has been in a state of turmoil. Three events stand out as marking the process of deterioration that has been at work. First was the post-1980 phase of the dominance of Bhindranwale, which culminated in Operation Bluestar in 1984. This was followed by the assassination of the Prime Minister and the killing and carnage that took place as a sequel to that. The third milestone was the Rajiv-Longowal accord and the subsequent developments including Sant Longowal's assassination and various political developments.

In their aggregate, these events have two important consequences; in fact, one of them could be described more as a cause than as a consequence. One is the dire need of the Congress party to keep the cauldron boiling. This statement would be challenged by many people, but the way things have developed, there seems to be no other explanation for what has been happening. The other is the alienation of the Sikhs from the mainstream of political life.

After the consolidation of the Sikh Jats into one territorial division (the reorganised Punjab) the Jat drive for domination and political power was the logical, indeed the inevitable, next step in the political life of the state. While a small number of Jats were to be found in the Congress Party, the majority of them were organised behind the Akali Party. Sooner or later this gross disproportion of political and ethnic power was bound to have its effect. The Congress Party, with substantial help from the Hindu population as well as the Harijans in the state, was able to establish a kind of coalition, which could endure for some time but not indefinitely. Sooner or later it was bound to be challenged and that happened in the early 1980's.

The rise of Bhindranwale and the manner in which he conducted his activities fired the Sikhs with a new fervour. Before long he had outdistanced both the official Akali Dal and the other political groups and forces in the state in terms of mass appeal and militancy. In this process he received indirect support from the then Prime Minister, for reasons which cannot bear too close a scrutiny. Her most compelling reason was the need for political survival. She had won the 1980 election on the transitory issue of the poor performance of the Janata Party. That ceased to be an issue as soon as she returned to power.

After she had won the general election in 1980, an important question before Indira Gandhi was how to remain in power. With her extraordinary instinct for things political, she could see that what was unfolding in Punjab could be put to political use. No wonder she allowed the Bhindranwale brand of politics to gather strength, even at the cost of destroying the state apparatus and the credibility of her own party. But she knew that eventually she would call the tune, and this happened in June 1984. As a skillful strategist, she allowed the situation to deteriorate to such an extent that when she sent the army into the Golden Temple she was hailed by a large number of people as a saviour of the nation.

While it is too early to strike a balance sheet of those events, some of the obvious implications cannot be overlooked. Not only did the Sikhs get a heightened sense of identity, but so also did the Hindus. How could it be otherwise? In the process of attacks and counter-attacks everyone's identity became redefined—either as a Hindu or as a Sikh. This is what communalism is all about. If anyone chooses to pretend otherwise or wishes to quibble about it, in my view he is not being fair to the facts and is most likely trying to mislead others. Not to recognise the events of 1980-84 as the starting point of all subsequent complications is to fail to acknowledge that while organised deception can be practised as a fine art, it cannot be elevated into an acceptable political strategy—least of all, when the stakes are as high as the future of the country.

Over the decades the Congress Party, which had been consistently in power since 1947, except for a brief interval, had not fully and honestly grappled with the problems of social and economic development that faced the country. There was always more rhetoric than action. Expectations had been aroused, but not fulfilled. Despite this negative feature, the ruling party at the Centre did enjoy, without question, mass support in several parts of the country, but it was based more on rosy promises than on actual performance. When somebody could play the same game better, as, for instance, N.T. Rama Rao did in Andhra Pradesh, it led to a massive shift against the Congress Party.

It was a dilemma which it was not easy to solve. But solved it had to be and, in a sense, Telugu Desam had shown the way. It had shown how economic and political problems could be given a back seat and the spotlight could be put on other issues, provided those were related to one's national or ethnic identity. An important plank of N.T. Rama Rao's hurricane campaign through the Andhra countryside was that Andhra dignity had to be restored. Here was a first-rate political strategy which someone with Mrs. Indira Gandhi's political shrewdness could understand.

It was clear that a new strategy had to be evolved. The Punjab situation provided the occasion and the take-off point. In fact, the strategy had already been evolved. The elections in Delhi, in early 1983, showed how it was to be implemented. What happened in Jammu and Kashmir a couple of months later confirmed further the efficacy of the strategy. In both these elections, the Bharatiya Janata Party had the galling experience of having its slogans used against it.

What was overlooked was the fact that while the ruling party at the Centre would return to power, as, indeed, it triumphantly did, this strategy would unleash forces that it would be difficult to curb or control. This in turn would change the whole complexion of the Indian polity. Now, the issues of social and economic development were no longer at the centre of things. Instead the issue became the unity and integrity of the country. An issue it certainly is, and an important one at that, but to treat it as the central issue of the Indian polity, as was done, meant relegating the issue of development to the background.

IV

Now what of the future? It is difficult to speculate in any precise way, but one can attempt to assess the strength and direction of some of the forces at work. This may in turn provide a clue to what might happen tomorrow. In this connexion two aspects of the situation may be noted. One is the continuing need of the Congress Party to get the support of the Hindi heartland in order to stay in power, and the second is the political fallout of the failure to implement the Rajiv-Longowal accord. When an attempt was made to implement the Accord, the biggest road-block was the compulsion not to alienate public opinion in Haryana; an election to the state assembly was due to take place in the near future. A reverse in Haryana, it was argued, would be a prelude to reverses in the Hindi heartland at a later stage. This in turn, it was further argued, would lead to the defeat of the ruling party in the next general election. The prospect of such a defeat drained the ruling party of all inclination to implement the Accord in spirit and substance. The subsequent distortions in regard to various commissions and so on can be traced mainly to that compelling consideration.

This compulsion has by no means diminished with the passage of time; it is as strong as it was at the end of 1985. The Hindi heartland argument is likely to become stronger with every day that passes. A general election is to take place in another few years, and the probability of the ruling party's being able to perform even adequately is not particularly high. The problem of management of the party itself is also getting more and more serious.

On occasion it is even argued that a snap general election might be held much earlier than it is due so as to be able to sidestep the problems of poor performance. Yet another suggestion is that the country should switch over to the presidential system instead of adhering to the parliamentary system. The very fact that these alternatives are discussed indicates the continuing uncertainty in regard to the results of the next general election.

As of this moment, while the ruling party would like to avoid aggravating the communal situation, it would not like to abandon this particular strategy altogether. That would amount to renouncing a weapon which, in the existing unfavourable situation, can always be resurrected and put to use again. In case this point of view be regarded as an overstatement, and some people are likely to think that way, the positive feature of this particular strategy deserves to be noted. The Hindi heartland is regarded as the special preserve of the ruling party. In certain other parts of India, the opposition may have done well for itself or at least it may have made an impact. But the Hindi heartland should remain, as though untouched by infection from other political forces; this appears to be the dominant philosophy of the ruling party.

In this situation, what are the chances of a settlement in the Punjab? Not particularly high, it may be said. The most feasible framework for such a settlement was provided by the terms of the Rajiv-Longowal accord. That was the utmost that any responsible Sikh leader could accept. Even then some of his important associates, particularly Badal and Tohra, were reluctant to go along with Sant Longowal. Soon after he was assassinated, they chose to strike a different note.

This difference of perception and approach needs to be understood, for it throws considerable light on the psyche of the Sikhs today. Most of them distrust the Centre. Their experience over the last couple of decades has led them to believe that the Centre deliberately promotes factionalism amongst them and is able to corrupt them in a variety of ways. In consequence they have a whole litany of complaints concerning the manner in which they claim to have been consistently deceived and outmanœuvred. While this perception is not without some factual basis, it fails to acknowledge the unabashed factionalism in which the Akalis indulge themselves.

Sant Longowal's calculations were slightly different. For one thing, he genuinely believed in the unity and integrity of the country. For another, he was deeply touched by the fraternal help extended to the Sikhs during the riots in Delhi. According to his way of thinking, therefore, if a way could be found to settle some of the other outstanding issues, a settlement could be reached. During the negotiations, when terms which he regarded as favourable were offered to him, he agreed to sign the Accord despite the obvious risks.

He recognised his personal danger, and the fact that he was eventually assassinated makes clear that the risk was real. But he was prepared for it; he was that kind of man. The second risk which he ran was that the terms agreed upon might not be implemented faithfully and honestly. Though he knew that his associates would not go with him all the way, he was confident of being able to carry them with him far enough. His death and the failure of the Accord have changed the situation in a qualitative way.

The basic significance of the Rajiv-Longowal accord was to put an end to all that has been described above. To put it another way, the intention was to inaugurate a new chapter of peace and harmony in the state. But what has happened is the exact opposite. This is not the occasion to go into the details of why and how the Accord has not been implemented. But two obvious implications of non-implementation must be noted: those like Badal and Tohra have been vindicated; and there has been a near-total loss of credibility by the Centre and by anyone who chooses to talk on its behalf. In addition, no Akali leader with any standing is now likely to enter into a formal arrangement with the Centre. Informal understanding there can be, but a formal arrangement would not be feasible. Anyone who chooses to do so would be risking his own political career.

In consequence, we have now a situation that is distinctly worse than before. The communal identity of each community has been aroused. None of the participants, particularly the ruling party at the Centre, is therefore able to dismount the tiger of communalism. Who is responsible for what, is a matter of detail and is best left to the judgement of history. But meanwhile the country has to live with the consequences of deliberate, self-serving political calculations of electoral victory and defeat.

The Punjab situation has become hopelessly tangled. It causes anxiety to everyone, particularly when people are singled out and killed for no reason other than that they are not Sikhs. That some terrorism can be lived with seems to be the ruling philosophy of the Centre. The Centre, it seems, would not mind living with terrorism almost indefinitely, only if this were not to happen too often! This whole approach is based on the assumption that a political settlement is not feasible and only administrative measures can be taken. A kind of stalemate has developed which is occasionally disturbed by ghastly murders and other unacceptable acts, such as attacks on the children of policemen.

V

Those who believe that sustained terrorism and individual killings would solve the Punjab problems are utterly mistaken. Terrorism is destructive. It can both intimidate and infuriate, but it is no substitute for political action. On the contrary, it is a sign of desperation, if not of weakness. It would be wrong, however, to assume that better policing alone can take care of the problems. Serious attention must be given to the social and economic factors that have contributed to the origin and growth of terrorism. Casual statements suggesting that the country would have to live with terrorism for a long time might make good copy but do not help us to understand the problem, let alone resolve it.

Terrorism is born of the peculiar social and economic problems of Punjab, but what gives it continuing vitality is the feeling of injustice from which the

Sikhs suffer. Not only has this feeling not been combatted; on the contrary, it has been strengthened by the failure of the Rajiv-Longowal accord. It is all a question of sympathies; those who sympathise with the Sikhs (and they are not too many) see the tension under which they are living; those who do not, regard them as a nuisance and worse and would perhaps like to see them liquidated. Some people would regard this statement as outrageous. It is outrageous without question. But there are people around, and some of them with access to those in corridors of power, who speak in this idiom. They are not taken seriously. The existence of such a lunatic fringe demonstrates, however, the extent to which the rot in our body politic has gone.

In order to remove the feeling of injustice the Centre would have to act against its own perceived interests, and that it is not prepared to do. Hence the stalemate. How can the stalemate be overcome? There is no ready-made solution, nor can there be any shortcuts. Political processes do not ordinarily lend themselves to instant solutions. The Congress Party, though built on foundations of sand, so to speak, is not about to fold up or crumble because of the weight of its contradictions. As to the opposition, the less said the better. Both through its failures of omission and commission, it ends up by helping the ruling party. The prospect is grim. To say, therefore, that it is going to be a long haul for the Sikhs would not be an overstatement.

Though communalism is riding high throughout the country (and it receives considerable reinforcement from unabated terrorism in the Punjab), the prospect need not be all that dark. For one thing, more and more people are beginning to see through the game. The rout of the Congress in Haryana is a pointer in that direction. The process of disenchantment with communal policies has begun, but it will be a long time before it gathers strength. Meanwhile, much more repression than one has encountered so far is likely to take place. The Sikhs already have had a foretaste of it. In the next phase of Indian politics many more are likely to taste it. Despite these onslaughts, people are beginning to see for themselves that the deliberate communalisation of Indian polity was not an accident; the unstated part of it was how to stay in power.

In addition, the Sikhs have an almost unlimited capacity for fighting such a battle of attrition. Their history is a testimony to it. Weariness, even exhaustion, eventually can set in. There are no signs of it yet, but there would be nothing surprising if this were to come to pass in the near future. If and when that happens, it would certainly mean a decline in terrorism. But that would not be the end of the matter. In geopolitical terms, the Punjab is so important to the rest of the country that no serious student of strategy can write off the state.

As of today, the situation is favourable for India. Because of the Russian occupation of Afghanistan, Pakistan has been under pressure. That has not, however, discouraged it from fishing in troubled Punjab waters. But things keep on changing. Nobody knows what will happen tomorrow or the day after that. Whatever might happen, the Punjab will always be a factor in India's security, and the Sikhs, being astride that border, will always be a factor to be reckoned with. In plain words, the Sikhs may be treated harshly and even unjustly, as has been happening for some years; but they can neither be crushed nor written off as a group of no significance.

How long will the Sikhs continue to be a political football in the game for power? It is difficult to say. Whether the present stalemate is overcome in the near future or gets extended even into the twenty-first century is anybody's guess. The latter development need not happen, but one can never rule it out.

Whichever way it works out, two interrelated consequences cannot be avoided. One is that because of what has been happening, the Sikhs will enter the twenty-first century partly with a sense of grievance and partly with a sense of heightened consciousness. For a couple of decades in the twenty-first century, therefore, there would be a sense of being beleaguered. All this harks back to the earlier history of persecution and the saga of sacrifices that go with the imperative of survival. But the question to ask is: once this pressure is relaxed, what will be the state of the Sikh psyche and Sikh morale? In my judgement, two crucial factors will have a direct bearing upon the situation and each one of them requires discussion in some detail.

One factor is the pattern of management of gurdwaras. Gurdwaras play a crucial role in the life of the Sikh community. For the size of the community the sheer number of gurdwaras is remarkable. There are historic gurdwaras and there are other gurdwaras. The historic gurdwaras are those which are connected with incidents and events in the lives of the Sikh Gurus and various other historic personages. In view of the fact that there were ten Gurus and there was a period of almost two centuries during which they interacted with their followers, a large number of places came to be associated with their lives and activities. These shrines are held in special reverence and are looked upon as treasure houses of religious sanctity.

In addition, wherever the Sikhs go and settle down they establish gurdwaras. Once established, these become centres of social activity and organisation as well as sites of worship. To some extent parallels occur in other communities also, but as far as the Sikhs are concerned the gurdwaras appear to be more central to their social organisation than are parallel institutions in other communities. It may be affirmed without any fear of contradiction that how they manage the gurdwaras is a matter which is likely to have an enormous and continuing impact upon the religious and social life of the Sikhs.

Control of the historic gurdwaras was the central issue of the Gurdwara Reform movement of 1920-25, not control of the non-historic ones. One outcome of the 1920-25 struggle, however, was the establishment of the Shiromani Gurdwara Prabandhak Committee (S.G.P.C.), followed by its step-by-step centralisation of control over the whole range of gurdwaras, historic and non-historic as well. Its historic role has not yet been exhausted.[1]

---

1. See the chapters by Mohinder Singh and Attar Singh in this volume for more on the S.G.P.C.
—Editors' note.

In this connexion, the experience of the last sixty years needs to be analysed. It was only after 1947 that the local gurdwara committees were divested of their powers, which were then transferred to the S.G.P.C. Around this time the Akalis and the Congress Party were locked into a conflict that was essentially political in character but also had other overtones. It is only in the post-1947 period that some of these gurdwaras, notably the Golden Temple, became the theatre of a political tug-of-war. All this has seriously diluted the strictly religious character of the gurdwaras, clearly an issue that will be at the centre of things for many years to come.

It will be a bold man who would say that the gurdwaras have been managed as they ought to have been managed. Master Tara Singh, who came to prominence at the time of the Gurdwara Reform movement, is on record as having said that while the Sikhs had been successful in getting rid of the traditional *mahants*, it would not be easy to get rid of the new *mahants* that were now climbing into power. History has proved him right, and the situation in regard to the management of gurdwaras today is much more unsatisfactory and characterised by more corruption than is usually acknowledged.

One role that the S.G.P.C. has signally failed to perform is to undertake missionary work on a systematic or organised scale. This is not the occasion to seek to analyse why Sikhism did not spread beyond the Punjab. All kinds of historical and other factors had a good deal to do with it. But there should be no doubt that one crucial weakness of the Sikh mode of organisation related to the near absence of a strong missionary tradition. Almost every world religion that has spread to other countries had at its disposal a strong missionary cadre and a well-organised system of spreading the faith. This has been as true of Christianity as of Islam. Buddhism too conformed to this pattern, though there were marked variations in its spread from country to country. Political power had a good deal to do with the manner in which these religions spread, but not less integral to the thrust and spread of those religions was the commitment of extraordinarily gifted and committed bands of missionaries. They went into new territories, indigenised themselves in a creative way, made use of the local languages and cultures and spread the gospels in alien lands.

This tradition is almost entirely missing among Sikhs. It would be too much to expect that a tradition that does not have any historical sanction behind it can now be created out of nowhere. But what could still happen is the development of a whole new system of missionary activity on a scientific basis. It should not be necessary to go into further details here except to say that a high priority for the management of gurdwaras should be to devise a strategy for spreading the Sikh gospel. This statement, however, needs to be qualified.

In today's world, most people do not renounce their inherited religion and adopt another; those days of mass conversion are gone. The basic missionary role in the modern world is mainly to facilitate the spread of literature and knowledge about the gospel and, no less important, to keep up the morale and solidarity of the community. This can be done through a sense of pride in one's heritage and the capacity to come to terms with problems as they arise from day to day. In the case of a community like the Sikhs there are some special problems. The fact that until half a century ago they were exclusively Punjabi speaking and were more or less confined to one geographically defined area makes the task of continuing solidarity a matter of both considerable importance and some urgency.

Fundamental to this entire approach is an unwavering commitment to education and to contemporary knowledge. The Sikh community has been so negligent in this regard that the best that can be said about it is that it has not lagged behind other communities. The need of the hour, however, is to move ahead of others in regard to both the diffusion and the creation of knowledge. Diffusion of knowledge has been taking place to some extent, but creation of knowledge in the sense of research, new interpretations and fresh discoveries has been totally neglected.

A pre-condition for the creation of new knowledge is that knowledge be valued both for the strength it gives to the members of the community and for its own sake. In other words, disinterested pursuit of knowledge is as important as the pursuit of knowledge as a vehicle for social mobility. If these be the objectives, it requires no effort to show that as a whole the Sikh community has so far not concerned itself seriously with the pursuit of knowledge and the gains that follow from a belief in and commitment to the primacy of knowledge. The Sikhs have hardly established any worthwhile research institutions or laboratories in any part of the world. Nor have the universities and other institutions which they dominate given much evidence of being committed to the pursuit of knowledge, whether fundamental or applied.

All this discussion needs to be understood in the wider context of modernising the economy and society of the Punjab. Broadly speaking, the Punjab is divided into three social , cultural and economic zones: Majha, Doaba and Malwa. While the geographical boundaries are well-defined, in social and economic terms the boundaries are somewhat flexible and represent different stages of development. It should not be necessary to go into further details except to discuss the problem from the point of view of education.

Majha and Doaba have had a longer and more pervasive tradition of education, whereas Malwa, which consisted largely of princely states before 1947, has been comparatively backward. In the princely states, there was hardly any tradition of voluntary effort in the field of education. Almost the entire initiative came from the government. This in turn meant the establishment of quite a few schools and colleges, which in their ethos of working generated a certain kind of social and political momentum. The feel of life was and still continues to be different in Malwa as compared to Majha and Doaba.

The establishment of Punjabi University in Patiala represented an attempt to help that part of the state to draw abreast of the others. That has not happened beyond a certain point, and in educational terms Malwa still continues to lag behind. The level of elementary and secondary schooling in particular is exceptionally poor. In consequence, the hinterland that is to prepare students for admission to the university and professional colleges fails to perform as effectively as in the other two regions. There is a widespread fallacy in contemporary India that in order to register educational progress it is important to establish universities and the like. What happens at the lower levels is not given adequate attention.

The issue also needs to be understood in the context of the dominant rural character of the region, with overtones of tribal structure still lingering on. Once this begins to undergo a change, and that process is already under way, a new kind of culture has to develop, and the role of the school is particularly important. But it is school education, more than any other level of education, that has been given a raw deal. In consequence the process of evolving a new culture remains both weak and anaemic. The establishment of universities alone cannot take care of the problem. It should not be necessary to dilate upon this theme further; the experience of developed countries in this regard does not leave any room for doubt or ambiguity.

The role even of the S.G.P.C. in regard to the spread of education has on the whole been one of benign neglect, or almost so. This is not to suggest that nothing has been done, but it has not been as vigorous and all-pervasive as it should have been. There is no reason, for instance, why even with the limited objective of spreading knowledge about Sikh religion, it should not have made use of the network of gurdwaras in the villages. In addition to spreading literacy, there is also the intermediate network of libraries and other means of cultural dissemination. In respect of each one of them the situation is singularly unsatisfactory. As has been commented upon critically by several sympathetic observers, the only way the village youth know how to spend their leisure time is to drink. Even the use of drugs is not all that uncommon. Clearly what is required is some kind of policy regarding both education and culture; any talk of education must be in a framework where culture is included as its encompassing context.

VII

At this stage it is pertinent to recall what was stated in the beginning. With more than 20% of the Sikhs living outside the Punjab and about 5% to 6% of them living outside India, the issue of linkages and interaction between those located in Punjab and those beyond its borders cannot be overlooked. The issue is crucial to the future of the community and needs to be looked at closely as well as realistically.

In India those who are living outside Punjab are obliged to come to terms with the language and culture of the people in whose midst they live. Those who belong to the first generation outside Punjab speak Punjabi and have close social and family links with the state of their origin. The next generation, which is now growing up, does not fit into this description except partially. Quite a number of them do not know Punjabi. They do speak it in most cases, but they are unable to read or write it. This undermines their ability to read the scriptures and so many other things that go with the knowledge of the language of their forefathers. In the course of time this trend is likely to become stronger, as has been the experience of migrants all over the world.

When it comes to those settled in countries other than India, the problem becomes even more complex. Those living within India can travel to the Punjab, visit the holy places and renew their contacts in a variety of ways. Those living in other countries find it more difficult. The current disturbances in the Punjab have created all kinds of artificial barriers, and even those who would like to make the trip for personal and family reasons find it difficult.

The barrier of language is one of the problems and is in a class by itself. No less unsettling is the problem of children growing up in the new environment, strongly influenced by the social forces operating on them. The different social and cultural context makes it difficult for them to remain heirs of their legacy and at the same time come to terms with the society in which they live. In some foreign countries there are hundreds and thousands of young boys and girls who at best have a smattering of their mother tongue, and that is all. For the rest, they are completely overwhelmed by the linguistic, social and cultural influences that surround them.

By the beginning of the twenty-first century this process of alienation from their roots will have been at work for almost half a century, for almost two generations. This single fact is going to create new strains for the Sikhs in social and cultural terms. To what extent Sikhism can survive in these alien surroundings, is a difficult question to answer. So much will depend upon the adaptability of the individuals concerned and their ability to evolve a new identity for themselves.

As should be evident, what happens to the community in the state of its origin as well as in the rest of India will influence, and maybe determine, what happens to the community in these foreign countries. Without question it will depend upon the two factors referred to already: the status of the Sikhs within India generally as well as in the state of Punjab; and their skills in managing the gurdwaras, which are a source of power as well as a focus of collective action. Management of gurdwaras, and the contribution they can make both for good and ill, are subjects requiring detailed analysis and cannot be dealt with here. One thing should be clear, however. Whatever might have happened in the past, the real burning question today is: what is going to happen tomorrow?

It should not be inferred from what has been stated above that the communities in these foreign countries are only at the receiving end and have no contributions to make. In foreign countries the situation in regard to Sikh education and identity and gurdwara administration can undergo a complete and fundamental change. Within a generation a whole group of people can arise who can show commitment to both religious and secular knowledge. In terms of secular knowledge, quite a few of them are beginning to do well. There will be much more evidence of this phenomenon forthcoming in the next decade or two.

By the time we enter the twenty-first century the communities settled in these various countries will have given considerable evidence of a high degree of achievement in higher and professional education.

The same thing can also happen in respect of religious scholarship. Within India something is being done in this field, but it is more notional than real. The fact of the matter is that standards of scholarship are neither exact nor rigorous. In consequence what is being done in these institutions does not add much to the sum of knowledge. When the same job is undertaken in some of these foreign countries, the outcome may be qualitatively better. Learning from the environment of scholarship in those countries, those who are engaged in the study of Sikhism may bring to bear a new level of competence and sophistication upon their understanding of the problem. Should that come to pass, and I feel sanguine about it, it would be an instance of the community outside India setting a model for the community in India. And that would be a step in the right direction.

VIII

Meanwhile, how is one to forget the hurt and the humiliation of the trap in which the community is caught? Terrorism is no answer to the continuing agony. In order to understand why, one has to understand the nature and the limits of terrorism. In the Punjab it is composed of several elements. Fundamentalism is one, and the corruption of political life is another. Smuggling and criminal activities add yet another dimension to it. Undergirding everything, however, is the sense of injustice from which the community suffers. Had the Rajiv-Longowal accord been implemented, the sense of injustice would have been overcome to a large extent. That not having happened, it is all the keener and has added to the bitterness people have felt for several years.

To repeat: can terrorism solve the problem with which the Sikhs are confronted? The answer is in the negative, mainly for two reasons. One, it cannot succeed. It has not succeeded anywhere. Guerrilla fighting does succeed, and a number of instances in support of such precedents can be quoted. But terrorism is something else. Its source of propulsion is creating fear in the minds of everyone. The distinction between the guilty and the innocent does not exist for the terrorists, and sooner or later it creates revulsion in the minds of most people. To say that the country would have to live with it for a long, long time is correct only as a statement of fact. When it is also implied—and the implication is not absent from the statements made by people who either cannot or will not apply their minds to the problem—that administrative measures alone are the answer, one cannot but reject this line of approach.

Secondly, the only thing that can succeed is a political strategy in terms of which the policies now being implemented by the ruling party are reversed. This in turn implies an alternative political line wherein the Sikhs are no longer treated as a plaything of Indian politics and there is straightforward political activity. The political position that succeeds must be one that does not use the communal or the ethnic card but treats the need and the urgency for development as its base. As anyone can see, this is a tall order. Such a state of consummation may not come about for quite some time and the picture will therefore remain murky and confused as at present. Implicit in this whole argument is the signal failure of the opposition parties in evolving an alternative strategy of political life.

Nothing illustrates political ineptitude more decisively than failure to see that the kind of repressive measures being adopted to curb terrorism will lead to more and more extinction of civil liberties and democratic rights. In fact, it is a real dilemma. Were terrorism to succeed, that would lead to tyranny but of another kind. To permit the present strategies of the government in power to succeed would equally lead to approximately the same consequences. How to solve this dilemma is the central political problem that confronts the country today.

It is difficult to see as of this moment how this problem is going to be solved. And as long as it is not solved, the Sikhs will continue to be the victims of injustices that are being perpetrated upon them. Not only that, a few years more of such disturbed conditions and continued repression can lead to a state of mind within the community which may not be so easily turned back. This aspect of the situation is no less disquieting than the continued sway of terrorism.

IX

Two other aspects of the situation also need to be noted. One is the rise of fundamentalism during recent years. This is not the occasion to go into the details of how it arose, what social and religious forces propelled it and the extent of power that it wields today. Important as these details are, they are not particularly relevant to the issue in hand. The salient point to make is that fundamentalism is a fact of life and is beginning to exercise a certain degree of influence upon the thinking of young people in particular. Its influence may be greater in some parts, but the influence is unmistakable. The only safe statement that one can therefore make in regard to the next decade or two is that fundamentalism (whatever the term may include or exclude) will continue to be a force and to shape the thinking of a substantial number of people, particularly in the younger age group.

There is a tendency to equate fundamentalism with terrorism. There is no necessary connexion between the two, though in certain cases it might become possible to establish some links. The origins and growth of terrorism are traceable to a range of factors, and fundamentalism is not always one of them. The two have got mixed up with each other, but, as far as one can judge, the connexion was accidental and transitory and not part of an integral pattern.

More to the point is the social and economic situation that arose in the wake of the "Green Revolution." While it brought unprecedented prosperity to the state, it also led to a shift of economic power. Increasing use of machinery, import of labour from other states and the reluctance of the youth to adapt themselves to the changing situation are some of its more noticeable features. In any case the avenues of employment become increasingly limited. Growth of industry did not keep pace with the growth of income in the rural sector and the corresponding social and economic changes that were taking place. Due to the inability of the state government to evolve a plan of development and the insensitivity of the central government to such pleas as were made, a situation has arisen where a large number of semi-educated young men do not know what to do with themselves. It is in this context that smuggling and crime, which had been growing for a number of years, unsettled the situation further.

It should not be necessary to go into further details except to underline one point: smuggling and crime, particularly in the border districts, have become so extensive and so well-organised that both administration and political life have been infected. This is not a phenomenon unique to the state of Punjab; it has occurred in other states as well. But it has penetrated Punjab administration and political life much more decisively than in other states. Oddly enough, sometimes there is conflict between fundamentalism and these developments and sometimes there is collusion. In either case any attempt at reform comes up against the phenomenon of all-pervasive corruption and crime.

This phase of corruption and crime and their interpenetration with administration and political life is likely to continue for some time. Its decline is linked up with a number of factors including the state of political health in the country as a whole, developments in other states and above all a resolution of the Punjab-Centre problem. This last aspect is much more important than any other aspect. Should some kind of Punjab-Centre resolution be achieved, it would give rise to new trends and tendencies. One of them will have to be a definite arresting of the process of corruption and crime that has been growing apace in the state.

Should such a happy consummation take place, both the factors referred to above—the management of the gurdwaras and the growth and spread of education—would have very important roles to play. In large measure, therefore, what happens in these two spheres of activities may shape and determine constructively the future of the Sikhs at the dawn of a new century.

Postscript: The View from Toronto

Joseph T. O'Connell

July 12, 1988

Patwant Singh and Amrik Singh have commented from Sikh perspectives on recent (and not quite so recent) events affecting Sikhs in India. A comment on recent events in Canada from a non-Sikh is perhaps in order. My comments are, by comparison, very brief. They focus on incidents and developments occurring since the February 1987 Sikh conference. The issues raised, however, are of ongoing significance to the Sikhs of Canada as a minority ethnic group in relation to the wider Canadian population.

Canada is officially a bilingual and multicultural country. But between official ideal and actual practice there is, as in all human societies, some distance. And what multiculturalism means in Toronto's urban "ethnic" neighbourhoods differs appreciably from its meaning in some rural areas whose immigration and settlement by northern Europeans took place a long time ago. Multiculturalism is not something fixed and given, but is constantly being forged in the crucible of events.

It is as engagements in the challenging venture of creating multicultural structures in Canada that I view the several incidents and developments mentioned in this postscript. Despite the controversial and in some cases profoundly painful nature of certain of these, I think they point to a fundamentally stable and constructive underlying process. To paraphrase the late John Courtney Murray, S.J., "Civility is being locked in argument." There is much of argument in this Canada on its way toward multicultural structures. That is as it should be. We should recognize and rejoice in the underlying civility that keeps us hanging in, to argue, to resolve, to move beyond impasse.

Enough of preliminaries to what is but a postscript. Let me touch briefly upon several of the more sensitive points of articulation of Sikhs and the wider Canadian population, which of course includes other Canadians of Indian, but not Sikh, background. These are my personal observations, not those of the editors as a team. Having been quite close personally and professionally to Sikhs and non-Sikhs of Indian background for my twenty years in Canada (as

[Joseph T. O'Connell, Milton Israel, Willard G. Oxtoby, eds., with W.H. McLeod and J.S. Grewal, visiting eds., *Sikh History and Religion in the Twentieth Century* (S. Asian Studies Papers, 3) (Toronto: S. Asian Studies, Univ. of Toronto, 1988)]

well as before then), and having been immersed in, if not preoccupied with, Sikh-related issues for the last two years, I think I have some warrant for making what observations I do, though I claim no expertise in Canadian Sikh affairs. I have tried to address sensitive matters sensitively and sensibly, but to the extent my attempt may fall short, I rely on the basic civility of any who may be offended or may disagree in substance.

We may begin by mentioning the extradition treaty between Canada and India that was signed just prior to the Toronto conference and about which Canada's Minister of External Affairs, the Honourable Joe Clark, spoke on February 14, 1987, to those who had assembled for the conference. The reactions expressed to the Minister (mostly by observers rather than by the scholars, it may be noted) were generally critical of the treaty and of the Government of Canada for entering into it. The Minister stood his ground, of course. It was a spirited debate, but well within the bounds of civility. Since the treaty has been in force, no Canadian, Sikh or other, has been extradited to India under its provisions. Nor has there been anyone extradited from India to Canada.

As of this writing there is an extradition case in process, this one in England. It relates to a bomb explosion at the Narita airport near Tokyo, which resulted in loss of life. There is general agreement that explosives had been placed aboard a trans-Pacific Air India flight before it left Canada; and there is speculation linking that explosion to the almost simultaneous crash of an Air India trans-Atlantic flight, also originating in Canada, involving terrible loss of life. In India the cause of the latter crash has officially been judged a bomb explosion, although the finding is not without its critics. In Canada, the Air India crash (with the unresolved issues of cause and responsibility) remains after three years a corrosive factor at the edge of the consciousness of Canadians generally. But to many whose kin or friends died in the tragedy, it remains centrally and agonizingly present. These persons, and many who sympathize with them, are tormented by the thought that this tragedy was, or may have been, a deliberate act of sabotage and mass murder. They clamour for a definitive judgment and, should it prove to have been such an act, for the identification and bringing to justice of those responsible.

There has been for some time in the public domain a welter of hearsay and circumstantial evidence emanating from officials, news media, and certain popular books. It is probably no exaggeration to say that on the basis of impressions arising from this welter of unconfirmed evidence the majority of Canadians tend to suspect or presume the Air India crash to have been the result of a bomb arranged by a fanatic cell of Sikhs based in Canada. There is also a counter-suspicion widely held among Sikhs, which some but probably not many others take seriously, that there indeed was a bomb aboard the trans-Atlantic flight, but one arranged by forces inimical to the Sikhs in hope of defaming the community and bringing about reprisals. Till now, three years after the event, there has been no definitive confirmation or disconfirmation of these suspicions.

Until such time as there is a credible resolution of the cause of the crash, there will likely remain a pall of doubt and suspicion--to say nothing of pain and misdirected anger--hanging over many issues involving Sikhs and Canada. It has been repeatedly pointed out that no one has yet been found responsible for either of the Air India-related tragic events. And it is obvious that Sikhs in general (or any other ethnic group) would not condone and should not be held responsible for such an atrocity, should it be proven to have been the deed of one or more individuals. But no matter how many times these observations are repeated, the pall of suspicion still hangs there, poisoning the atmosphere of mutual respect between Sikhs and other Canadians of Indian origin, and subtly permeating the vague stereotypes by which many Canadians relate to Sikhs in particular and other immigrants of Indian origin generally.

It is crucial for the sake of truth and a sense of reality that, if at all possible, a credible resolution be reached, so that the corrosion of trust, respect and candour that this unresolved tragedy has bequeathed may be dissipated. Wherever the truth may lie, the matter is far too weighty to be shelved, to be made a partisan issue, to be used to denigrate a whole community, or to be in any way shielded from legitimate investigation and public scrutiny.

Regrettably, there have been several criminal cases affecting Sikhs in Canada in which investigating or prosecuting officials have been found to have compromised the integrity and credibility of their work. As a result, evidence improperly gathered or lacking in authenticity has been disallowed in court, and charges dismissed. This repeated violation of the normal legal guidelines in the case of Sikh defendants has alienated many Sikhs and undermined public confidence in Canadian investigative and judicial agencies that deal with minorities. There must be a restoration of a climate of integrity, trust and co-operation in which Canadians will be willing to co-operate where appropriate with legitimate law-enforcement officers and where the latter will resolutely abide by the same high legal and moral standards in dealing with persons of all ethnic orientations in this country.

An important area where Canadian Sikhs may find themselves in common cause with several other sectors of the Canadian public, including non-Sikhs of Indian background, is opposition to proposed new immigration legislation. The proposed legislation is supposed to curtail alleged abuse of the status of refugee, which when granted allows a person entry to Canada without the usual restrictions and delays. Elements of the legislation have come under fire from churches, human-rights advocates, and ethnic groups, among other critics. Oft-criticized provisions in the proposed legislation include: the requirement that the refugee have in his or her possession official emigration or other documents issued by the very government he or she is fleeing; provision for turning back refugees on the seas without the opportunity to present their case to Canadian authorities; and penalizing individuals and organizations who might aid such refugee claimants deemed technically to have entered Canada illegally.

The refugee immigration issue had been building up for some years, fueled especially by refugees from Central America. But ironically, it came to dramatic public attention when a boatload of would-be immigrants claiming refugee status landed suddenly and secretively on the east coast of Canada, in July 1987. Most were Sikhs who had been for some time in Europe. This was the second such dramatic boatload, an earlier one of Tamils arriving from Sri Lanka via Europe having been warmly received by Canadian authorities. This time the reception was vastly different. An extraordinary barrage of media publicity covered the event, as Canadian authorities held the new arrivals under conditions of para-military security. Much ink and adrenalin were poured out speculating on who among the bearded arrivals might be terrorists posing threats to Canadian security. Eventually all the individuals were released on bond (often supplied by one or another supportive gurdwara) to await the normal processing of their claims. But in the first two weeks or so, a near-hysteria was stirred up over this initially mysterious boatload of immigrants who at some risk to themselves had ingeniously attempted a way, albeit not a legal one, around the normally protracted immigration process. The Government of Canada, whether by design or coincidence, was positioned to take advantage of the media blitz over the boatload of "mysterious," possibly "dangerous" bearded Sikhs. It simultaneously pushed forward, though not to final passage, its controversial immigration bills.

It may readily be granted that it can be difficult to identify and confirm refugee claimants and also a sensitive matter to establish and apply guidelines marking that degree of risk or oppression that would justify granting refugee status, and to assess the "innocence" of the applicant. Presumably there is room for immigrant-community advice as well as for professional advice to government officials in devising and applying guidelines. But blanket exclusions and unreasonable impediments are not the answer. Nor is automatic acceptance of anyone bold enough to lodge a refugee claim an answer (nor is acquiescence to intensive lobbying by those with influence). But even less acceptable is exploiting sensationalistic media coverage and xenophobic stereotypes to secure backing for legislation or policy that would be difficult to justify on its own merits.

Immigration policy and legislation constitute an area where very different priorities and values are bound to come into conflict, however well-intentioned individuals may be and however soundly conceived be the multicultural structures that are shaping up in Canada. Sikhs are by far the largest ethnic group of South Asian background in Canada and are steadily becoming more mature organizationally and more effective in civil debates on many levels of Canadian life. They can be expected to have a major ongoing role in this area on their own behalf and on that of other related groups.

Sikhs in Canada continue to be engaged in discussions and negotiations, and occasionally litigation, with public Canadian institutions and private business organizations. The issues are diverse, but include saliently the wearing of the insignia of Khalsa initiation, especially unshorn hair (*kesh*) with turban, and the steel blade (*kirpan*). Results vary from one constituency to the next. The Metropolitan Toronto Police, for instance, now welcome wearing of the hair with turban as part of the standard uniform. The Canadian Armed Forces have not gone all the way. They allow wearing of hair and turban but still require that a protective helmet be worn in certain situations deemed especially dangerous (for which reason a serviceman was discharged not long ago).

Wearing of beard, hair and turban has long been a focus of negotiation with private employers, sometimes involving intervention of human-rights authorities. Results generally have favoured wearing of hair and turban, though in a few cases technicalities have resulted in negative decisions. Wearing of *kirpan* has been supported in principle under the Charter of Rights, but here again technicalities have gone against the Sikh in some specific cases. In a recent case a lower Ontario court has asked that the Supreme Court of Ontario determine whether a board of education may prevent a Sikh teenager from wearing *kirpan* to class. But in some other cases where the issue has arisen, schools are reported to have quietly allowed the practice as long as there occurs no misuse of *kirpan* (nor, presumably, use of it in athletics or other situations where it could pose a safety hazard). And so it goes. While some of these cases may be disappointing and frustrating to many Sikhs, the overall process of face-to-face discussion and negotiation is a positive process and may be expected gradually to lead to better understanding and mutual forbearance. And in the main, both the principle and the specific decisions have been favourable to wearing of the "five k's."

The past year and a half since our conference seems to have been a time of consolidation and stabilization for Sikhs in Canada, at least in the Toronto area. There has been little or no news of serious factional disturbances within the local community, as had in the past been reported from time to time. Nor have public demonstrations turned ugly, though there have been very well-attended and high-spirited gatherings. Nor do we hear of harassment of officials of the Government of India. Conversely, Sikh participation in public affairs has been more visible, and more sophisticated relations with the news media seem to have been emerging.

As we move toward the last year of the 1980's there is ground for hope that, for all the tempests and torment that have affected Sikh life in India and abroad in this troubled decade, there may be a certain calming process in the making, at least in this corner of the Sikh diaspora. I call to mind the frontispiece or cover of this volume, from Will Oxtoby's early-morning photo of the Harmandir Sahib surrounded by the waters of the Amritsar, the Lake of Nectar of Immortality. A profound calm and peace is there. It may be the symbol of a quality of life we seek in the world today.

Glossary of Punjabi Terms

Where more than one spelling is provided, the first form is the spelling generally followed throughout this book. Forms given in parentheses depart from the transliteration system followed here, and are therefore included without diacritical marks.

Ādi Granth   ਆਦਿ ਗ੍ਰੰਥ
The "first book," i.e., the Sikh scripture as compiled by Guru Arjan, consisting of his own and preceding Gurus' compositions and selected hymns of *bhagats* or saints.

Akāl Purakh   ਅਕਾਲ ਪੁਰਖ
"The Timeless Being," Guru Nanak's concept of the divine Being; analogous to "God."

(Akal Takht) Akāl Takhat   ਅਕਾਲ ਤਖਤ
"Throne of the Timeless"; seat of temporal authority of the Gurū (especially Gurū-Panth) located on the premises of the Harmandir or Golden Temple at Amritsar.

Akālī   ਅਕਾਲੀ
"a devotee of Akāl (the Timeless One)." During the eighteenth and early nineteenth centuries the title designated Sikh warriors noted for their bravery. Today it signifies a member of the Akālī Dal.

Akālī Dal   ਅਕਾਲੀ ਦਲ
"a unified army of the Akalis"; the prominent political party of the Sikhs. It came into being early in the twentieth century when Sikhs were agitating for freedom of the gurdwaras from private, hereditary control.

akhaṇḍ pāṭh   ਅਖੰਡ ਪਾਠ
"unbroken reading," an uninterrupted recitation of the entire Guru Granth Sahib by a team of readers.

(*amrit bani*)   ਅੰਮ੍ਰਿਤ ਬਾਣੀ
ammrit bāṇī
"Immortal utterance," the nectar-like, immortal divine Word.

(*amrit pahul*)   ਅੰਮ੍ਰਿਤ ਪਾਹੁਲ
ammrit pāhul
"nectar," the water used in the initiation ceremony of the Khālsā; the initiation itself.

(*amrit sanskar*)   ਅੰਮ੍ਰਿਤ ਸੰਸਕਾਰ
ammrit sanskār
the initiation ceremony into the Khālsā of Guru Gobind Singh; *amrit pāhul.*

anand kāraj   ਅਨੰਦ ਕਾਰਜ
"bliss" + "ceremony," often referred to simply as *anand.* A distinctly Sikh marriage ritual devoid of Hindu or Brahmanic influence.

(*anbhav prakash*)   ਅਨੁਭਵ ਪ੍ਰਕਾਸ਼
anubhav prakāsh
"enlightened experience."

ardās   ਅਰਦਾਸ
"petition," the daily Sikh congregational prayer.

āshram   ਆਸ਼ਰਮ
spiritual commune.

bābā   ਬਾਬਾ
"father" or "grandfather," a term of affection and respect, often used of religious figures (including the Ādi Granth) as well as within the family.

[Joseph T. O'Connell, Milton Israel, Willard G. Oxtoby, eds., with W.H. McLeod and J.S. Grewal, visiting eds., *Sikh History and Religion in the Twentieth Century* (S. Asian Studies Papers, 3) (Toronto: S. Asian Studies, Univ. of Toronto, 1988)]

Babbar Akālī ਬੱਬਰ ਅਕਾਲੀ
"Lion" among the Akālīs; a radical early twentieth-century variant of Sikh militants.

Bābar bāṇī ਬਾਬਰ ਬਾਣੀ
hymns of Guru Nānak containing references to the Emperor Babur.

bairāg ਬੈਰਾਗ
detachment (from worldly affairs); intensification of the desire (for the divine) into yearning.

bāṇā ਬਾਣਾ
uniform of the Khālsā: tight-fitting trousers, long outer shirt, sash, *kirpān* with belt diagonally over the right shoulder.

bāṇī ਬਾਣੀ
the utterances of the Gurus and *bhagats* recorded in the Adi Granth. For *Gurū bāṇī* the simplified form *gurbāṇī* is commonly used.

benatī ਬੇਨਤੀ
"request" or "appeal," an appeal to the Sikhs worldwide for a particular cause.

bhagat bāṇī ਭਗਤ ਬਾਣੀ
the utterances of the poet-saints of *bhakti, sant* and Sūfī origins, which (along with the compositions of the Sikh Gurūs) are recorded in the Guru Granth Sāhib.

bhāī ਭਾਈ
"brother," a title applied to Sikhs of acknowledged learning and piety, or any Sikh congregational leader.

(*bhakti*) *bhagatī* ਭਗਤੀ
"devotion"; a tradition of ardent worship based on an attitude of loving devotion.

bhāshā ਭਾਸ਼ਾ
language; sometimes specifically vernacular language

bhūt ਭੂਤ
the spirit of the dead male person.

birādarī (*baradarī*) ਬਿਰਾਦਰੀ
maximal lineages; brotherhood, community.

buddhī ਬੁੱਧੀ
intelligence, thought; *nirmal buddhī* is pure thought.

(*Chabian da morcha*) ਚਾਬੀਆਂ ਦਾ ਮੋਰਚਾ
cābiān dā morcā
the Sikh agitation over the Keys affair in the 1920's.

(*chalit-bhasha*) ਚਲਿਤ-ਭਾਸ਼ਾ
calit-bhāshā
simple, everyday spoken and written language; contrasted with formal Sanskritized vernacular language called *sādhu-bhāshā.*

(Chamar) Camār ਚਮਾਰ
the caste of leather-workers; the Chamars are ranked low, as a "scheduled" caste.

(*charan pahul*) ਚਰਨ ਪਾਹੁਲ
caraṇ pāhul
the pre-Khālsā form of ritual for initiation, performed by administering water sanctified with the touch of the toe of the right foot of a holy figure, a Gurū or a member of a Gurū lineage such as the Bedis, Bhallas and Sodhis.

(Churah) Cūhṛā ਚੂਹੜਾ
the sweeper caste; the Churahs are ranked low, as a "scheduled" caste.

(*churel*) *curel* ਚੁੜੇਲ
the spirit of the dead female person.

dalit ਦਲਿਤ
"oppressed"; the Indian "scheduled castes" or lower classes have taken up the use of the term as a self-description.

Dal Khālsā ਦਲ ਖਾਲਸਾ
"Khālsā horde," esp. the combined forces of the Khālsā *misls* during the eighteenth century.

darbār ਦਰਬਾਰ
royal court; formal assembly.

Dasam Granth ਦਸਮ ਗ੍ਰੰਥ
the sacred writings attributed to the Dasam ("tenth") Gurū, Gobind Singh.

ḍerā (*dehra*) ਡੇਰਾ
a camp; a temporary or permanent residential establishment.

dhāḍī ਢਾਡੀ
minstrel.

dharā ਧੜਾ
faction.

dharam (dharm) ਧਰਮ
appropriate moral and religious obligations.

dharamsālā (dharmsala) ਧਰਮ ਸਾਲਾ
in early Sikh usage, a room or building used for devotional singing and
prayer, i.e., gurdwara.

dharam yuddh ਧਰਮ ਯੁੱਧ
(*dharam yudh, dharm yudh*)
"a war fought in defense of dharam";
may be used of political struggle with
religious overtones.

(*diwan*) *dīvān* ਦੀਵਾਨ
keeper of treasury; a responsible committee or association.

(Doaba) *Duābā* ਦੁਆਬਾ
the plains of central Punjab bounded
by the Beas and Sutlej rivers.

dubidhā ਦੁਬਿਧਾ
duality or polarity, such as between
pleasure and pain or between spirituality and materiality.

(*ekadasi*) *ekādashi* ਏਕਾਦਸੀ
eleventh day of the lunar fortnight,
observed especially among Vaiṣṇava
Hindus.

ghar ਘਰ
house; household.

giānī (gyani) ਗਿਆਨੀ
a learned person, esp. one versed in
Sikh scriptures.

gorā ਗੋਰਾ
"white," especially a white male.

gorī ਗੋਰੀ
a white female.

got ਗੋਤ
"clan," exogamous grouping within
the endogamous group or *zat.*

Granth ਗ੍ਰੰਥ
book, religious scripture, esp. the
Gurū Granth Sāhib, or Ādi Granth,
the scripture venerated by Sikhs.

granthī ਗ੍ਰੰਥੀ
a "reader" of the Gurū Granth Sāhib;
the functionary in charge of a gurdwara.

Gurbāṇī kīrtan ਗੁਰਬਾਣੀ ਕੀਰਤਨ
devotional singing (*kīrtan*) of the
Gurū's word (*bāṇī*)

gur-celā (gur-chela) ਗੁਰ-ਚੇਲਾ
at once the master (Gurū) and the disciple (*celā*); or the relationship between master and disciple.

gurdarshan ਗੁਰਦਰਸ਼ਨ
the visual emanations of the Gurū; a
glimpse of the Gurū.

gurduārā ਗੁਰਦੁਆਰਾ
(gurdwara, gurudwara)
"the Gurū's door" or "by means of the
Gurū's grace"; the Sikh place of worship, i.e., the temple or room in which
is kept the Gurū Granth Sāhib.

gurmaryāda ਗੁਰਮਰਯਾਦਾ
the prescriptions of life-cycle rituals
according to the Gurū's teaching.

(*gurmat*) *gurmati* ਗੁਰਮਤਿ
"the view of the Gurū," the sum total
of the Gurū's teachings; the doctrines
referred to as "Sikhism."

(*gurmata*) *gurmattā* ਗੁਰਮਤਾ
"the intention of the Gurū," the will of
the eternal Gurū expressed in a formal
decision made by a representative assembly of Sikhs; a resolution of the
Sarbat Khālsā.

gurmukh ਗੁਰਮੁਖ
"one who faces toward the Gurū"; a
follower of the divine, of the Gurū.

Gurmukhī ਗੁਰਮੁਖੀ
"from the mouth of the Gurū"; the
script in which the compositions of
the Gurūs were first written. It has
become the script in which Punjabi is
written by most Sikhs, and by some
others. Sometimes used to designate
Punjabi language as used by Sikhs.

(*gurpurb*) *gurpurab* ਗੁਰ ਪੁਰਬ
celebration of the birth or death anniversary of one of the ten Sikh Gurūs.

Gurū   ਗੁਰੂ
Master, teacher; the mode of the divine (Akāl Purakh) as teacher and guide, manifested in the form of divine word in the human heart, in the form of ten human *gurūs*, and in the form of the Gurū Granth (scriptural guidance) and Gurū Panth (the community's authority).

(*Guru-bhakti*)   ਗੁਰੂ-ਭਗਤੀ
Gurū-bhagatī
devotion to God as Gurū.

Gurū Granth Sāhib   ਗੁਰੂ ਗ੍ਰੰਥ ਸਾਹਿਬ
Honorific title of the Granth, or Ādi Granth.

Gurū kā Shabad   ਗੁਰੂ ਕਾ ਸਮਬਦ
Gurū's word, esp. that which is recorded in hymns of the Gurūs in the Gurū Granth Sāhib.

Gurū-Panth   ਗੁਰੂ-ਪੰਥ
the Panth (community) of the Gurū, and the Panth as the Gurū; the latter refers to the doctrine of the authoritative presence of the eternal Gurū in an assembly of his followers.

Gurū-Panth kā dās   ਗੁਰੂ ਪੰਥ ਕਾ ਦਾਸ
"the slave of the *Guru-Panth*"; the President of the Akālī Party generally refers to himself as such.

Gurū Shabad   ਗੁਰੂ ਸਮਬਦ
(*Gur Shabad*)
Gurū's Word; Word as the Gurū.

hane hane mīrī   ਹੰਨੇ ਹੰਨੇ ਮੀਰੀ
"a king on every saddle"; the phrase became current at the time of Sikh warrior groups (*misls*) in the eighteenth century.

haumai   ਹਉਮੈ
"I-ness, my-ness," self-centredness, the powerful impulse to succumb to personal gratification.

hukam (hukum, hukm)   ਹੁਕਮ
"order," the divine command governing the entire universe, an order that is synonymous with harmony; a more specific command by a Sikh authority.

(*hukumnama, hukmnama*)   ਹੁਕਮਨਾਮਾ
hukam-nāmā
"decree," esp. the decree issued by *pañj piāre* from the Akal Takht, considered authoritative and binding on the entire Panth.

izzat   ਇੱਜਤ
prestige.

jāgīrdār   ਜਾਗੀਰਦਾਰ
landlord, grantee.

jajmānī   ਜਜਮਾਨੀ
gift or stipend for services paid by a patron, on which customary exchange Brahmins, barbers and others have a traditional claim.

janam-sākhī   ਜਨਮ-ਸਾਖੀ
"birth anecdote," traditional hagiographic narrative, especially of Gurū Nānak.

(*janeo*) *janeū*   ਜਨੇਉ
sacred thread, worn by Hindu males of the three upper castes.

jap   ਜਪ
devout repetition of a passage from scripture, a divine name, etc.

Jāp   ਜਾਪ
a prayer composed by Gurū Gobind Singh.

Japji   ਜਪੁਜੀ
a fundamental Sikh prayer composed by Gurū Nānak and recited daily.

Jat   ਜੱਟ
a member of the particular landholding caste group that is dominant in the Punjab and comprises the majority of Sikhs. Not to be confused with *zāt*, Sanskrit *jāti*, a generic term for caste.

jathā   ਜਥਾ
"military detachment"; organized group of Sikhs with a particular mission of preaching and reform or religio-political agitation. Each territorial unit of the Akālī party (the

dominant political party of the Sikhs) is so designated.

jathedār   ਜਥੇਦਾਰ
"commander," the title of a leader of a Sikh band, esp. as applied to a custodian of one of the five historic *takhats* (thrones).

jhatkā   ਝਟਕਾ
meat prepared by killing the animal with one "jerk" or stroke; only *jhatkā* meat is approved by Sikhs.

(kach) kachh   ਕੱਛ
more fully, *kachhaira*: pair of shorts required to be worn by members of the Khālsā.

kāl   ਕਾਲ
"time"; mortality; the negative force in life.

kal yug   ਕਲਜੁਗ
"the era of strife," the fourth and last of the cosmic ages, the age of degeneracy.

Kalāl   ਕਲਾਲ
the caste of brewers and distillers.

kanghā   ਕੰਘਾ
hair comb, one of the "five k's" required to be worn by a Sikh of the Khālsā.

karā   ਕੜਾ
steel bracelet worn on the wrist as a sign of initiation into the Khālsā, and also by many non-Khālsā Sikhs.

(karah parshad)   ਕੜਾਹ ਪ੍ਰਸਾਦ
karāh prashād
sacramental food dispensed in gurdwaras, made of flour, sugar and ghee in an iron bowl (*karāh*).

karam (karm)   ਕਰਮ
"activity," the principle of cause and effect that holds a person firmly within the cycle of *sansār*; any activity; grace.

kārdār   ਕਾਰਦਾਰ
agent, worker; used esp. of administrators at the *ta'alluqa* or *pargana* level during Sikh rule.

Kartār   ਕਰਤਾਰ
"Creator," another term of Gurū Nānak's for divine Being.

kathā   ਕਥਾ
an exposition of the scriptures, or the narrating of an incident from the lives of the Gurūs or from later Sikh history.

Kaur   ਕੌਰ
"princess"; used as a name by female members of the Khālsā.

(kesh) kes   ਕੇਸ
hair, esp. the unshorn hair kept as symbol of dedication to the Gurū via the Khālsā.

(keshdhari) kesdhārī   ਕੇਸਧਾਰੀ
"hair-bearing," the term used for the Sikhs who keep their hair intact, generally Sikhs of the Khālsā.

keskī   ਕੇਸਕੀ
a small turban worn by Sikh women belonging to the Akhand Kīrtanī Jathā under their traditional *chunnis* (scarves).

khalīfā   ਖਲੀਫਾ
"succession," the position of supreme religious-cum-political authority among the Muslims.

Khālistān   ਖਾਲਿਸਤਾਨ
"the Land of the Pure," the proposed name for an independent Sikh state or other form of Sikh homeland.

Khālsā   ਖਾਲਸਾ
Gurū's "own" community; specifically, those Sikhs answering Gurū Gobind Singh's call to dedicate themselves thoroughly to the Gurū; also thought of as the community of the "pure."

khān   ਖਾਨ
a title used for nobles of Pathan descent. Not to be confused with the names Kahan and Kahn, which are variants of "Krishna."

khaṇḍe dā·pāhul ਖੰਡੇ ਦਾ ਪਾਹੁਲ
the baptism of the double-edged sword, i.e., Khālsā initiation.

Khatrī ਖਤਰੀ
the cluster of merchant caste groups including Bedīs, Sodhīs and Bhallās, from whom have come the Sikh Gurūs.

kirpān ਕਿਰਪਾਨ
sword or dagger of steel worn by a Sikh of the Khālsā, a symbol of dedication.

kīrtan ਕੀਰਤਨ
devotional hymn-singing.

kūkā ਕੂਕਾ
"crier"; the Kuka Sikhs, a nineteenth-century millenarian revivalist movement, were so called because they gave out loud shrieks at the time of devotional chanting.

(*kutha*) *kuṭṭhā* ਕੁੱਠਾ
meat slaughtered in a gradual process painful to the animal, opposite of *jhatka*.

lāgī ਲਾਗੀ
a go-between, one who opens negotiations between two households that could lead to an eventual marriage.

lambardār ਲੰਬਰਦਾਰ / ਨੰਬਰਦਾਰ
(*nambardar*)
village headman.

laṅgar ਲੰਗਰ
the community kitchen attached to every gurdwara, from which food is served to all regardless of caste or creed.

liv ਲਿਵ
constant remembrance, awareness of the divine.

(*ma-bap*) *mān-bāp* ਮਾ ਬਾਪ
"mother-father," characterization of the government or other authority as the parental source of justice and patronage.

Mahalā (Mahalla) ਮਹੱਲਾ
literally, "body"; a code-word used to distinguish works by different Gurūs in the Ādi Granth. Gurū Nānak, as

first Gurū, is designated Mahalā 1 or simply M.1; the works by Gurū Angad, Gurū Amardas, Gurū Ramdas, Gurū Arjan and Gurū Teg Bahadur are designated M.2, M.3, M.4, M.5 and M.9 respectively.

mahant ਮਹੰਤ
a custodian of the Sikh gurdwaras; the position tended to be hereditary before the Gurdwaras act of 1925.

Mājhā ਮਾਝਾ
"middle," the area of central Punjab between the Beas and Ravi rivers.

(Malwa) Mālvā ਮਾਲਵਾ
the plains extending south and southeast of the Sutlej river, particularly the area occupied by Ferozepur, Ludhiana and Patiala districts.

manmat ਮਨਮਤ
instruction based on one's ego.

manmukhtā ਮਨਮੁਖਤਾ
a stage of false ego-identification in which one seeks worldly objects, possessiveness and achievement, through one's own self-centred impulses rather than the guidance of the Gurū.

māṇṇ ਮਾਣ
prestige, the communal evaluation of a family.

(*masand*) *massand* ਮਸੰਦ
authorized leader of a local assembly of Sikhs.

melā ਮੇਲਾ
festival, usually associated with a religious occasion but embracing a wider range of activities.

mīṇā ਮੀਣਾ
"the dissembling scoundrels," followers of Prithi Chand, eldest son of Guru Ramdās, an unsuccessful claimant to the succession conferred on his younger brother Gurū Arjan.

mīrī-pīrī ਮੀਰੀ-ਪੀਰੀ
the assumption of temporal (*mīrī*) as well as spiritual (*pīrī*) authority; the doctrine goes back go Gurū Hargobind, who symbolically donned two

swords, one for each type of authority.

misl   ਮਿਸਲ
"equal"; Sikh military band of the eighteenth century; also a Sikh principality in that century.

moksha   ਮੋਕਸ਼
"liberation" or "redemption"; the liberation for Sikhs tends to be through pious involvement in worldly activities, not through disengagement from mundane matters.

(*morcha*) *morcā*   ਮੋਰਚਾ
"facing the enemy," an organized political campaign with religious overtones.

muklāvā   ਮੁਕਲਾਵਾ
ceremony of a Hindu type marking the consummation of a marriage; it may follow several years after the marriage of a young bride.

mūlmantra   ਮੂਲਮੰਤਰ
"the seed formula," the basic theological statement with which the Gurū Granth Sāhib opens. Its text: "There is one Supreme Being, the Eternal Reality. He is the Creator, without fear and devoid of enmity. He is immortal, never incarnated, self-existent, known by grace through the Gurū."

(*nahar roko*)   ਨਹਿਰ ਰੋਕੋ
nahir roko
"canal" + "stop," Akālī agitation to block work on the Yamuna-Sutlej link canal in 1982.

nām   ਨਾਮ
"name"; the "name" or total expression of all that Akāl Purakh (the divine) is.

nām-simaran   ਨਾਮ ਸਿਮਰਨ
"remembering the Name," a discipline ranging from simple repetition of an appropriate word through the devout singing of hymns (*kīrtan*), to sophisticated meditation.

Nānak-panth   ਨਾਨਕ-ਪੰਥ
the "way" or community of Gurū Nānak; his followers were known as Nānak-panthīs.

Niraṅkār   ਨਿਰੰਕਾਰ
the Formless One, a designation of the divine, Akāl Purakh.

nirbhaitā   ਨਿਰਭੈਤਾ
"fearlessness," freedom from the anxieties of life.

(*nirguna bhakti*)   ਨਿਰਗੁਣ ਭਗਤੀ
nirguṇa bhagatī
"devotion to formless" but loving God.

nirmal buddhī   ਨਿਰਮਲ ਬੁੱਧੀ
pure thought.

nishān sāhib   ਨਿਸ਼ਾਨ ਸਾਹਿਬ
Sikh flag flown over a gurdwara.

paṅgat   ਪੰਗਤ
communal dining hall where all Sikhs sit in rows regardless of caste or creed to share a common repast.

pañj kakke   ਪੰਜ ਕੱਕੇ / ਕਕਾਰ
(*panj kakkar*)
the "five k's"; the five items, each of whose name begins with the letter "k," that a Khālsā Sikh should wear: the *kes* (unshorn hair), *kanghā* (wooden comb), *kirpān* (sword), *karā* (steel bracelet), and *kachh* (undershorts).

pañj piāre   ਪੰਜ ਪਿਆਰੇ
(*panj pyare*)
the exalted "beloved five" leaders who constitute the authority in the Sikh Panth; the designation recalls the five who offered their lives for Gurū Gobind Singh.

Panth   ਪੰਥ
"path," "way"; the Sikh community. The Sikh doctrine of *Gurū-Panth* ascribes religious authority after the last of the ten human Gurūs to the corporate assembly.

patit   ਪਤਿਤ
"fallen"; one who, once having accepted the *amrit*, no longer follows the Khālsā *rahit*.

paṭṭīdārī   ਪੱਤੀਦਾਰੀ
"shareholder in conquered territory."

454   Glossary of Punjabi Terms

pauṛī   ਪਉੜੀ
"staircase," "stanza"; name of a category of hymns in the Gurū Granth Sāhib.

pherā   ਫੇਰਾ / ਲਾਵ
"circling": of the fire in a Hindu marriage ceremony, and (also called *lāvān*) of the Gurū Granth Sāhib in an *anand* Sikh marriage.

phul   ਫੁਲ
bones remaining unburnt after cremation.

piṇḍa   ਪਿੰਡ
five balls of rice and flour placed on the corpse at cremation in some funeral ceremonies.

piṇḍa dān   ਪਿੰਡ ਦਾਨ
balls of rice, ghee and sugar, either fed to a crow or thrown into a river in post-cremation rituals of Hindu type.

pitar   ਪਿਤਰ
"father," a venerable male ancestor.

(prachar) pracār   ਪ੍ਰਚਾਰ
"preaching," the Sikh missionary activity

pret   ਪ੍ਰੇਤ
the disembodied ghost. On death the soul of the deceased is thought to leave the body as a spirit dangerous both to itself and to the living.

pūjārī   ਪੁਜਾਰੀ
a Hindu village priest or temple specialist.

purohit   ਪੁਰੋਹਿਤ
the family priest; among Hindus, usually a Brahmin.

qaum   ਕੌਮ
etymologically in Arabic, "a people who stand together"; hence an ethnic group, or even a nation.

qaumī zabān   ਕੌਮੀ ਜ਼ਬਾਨ
national language (of Pakistan).

rāgī   ਰਾਗੀ
a Sikh musician who sings the hymns in the gurdwara.

rahit (rehat, reht)   ਰਹਿਤ
the Khālsā code of conduct.

rahit maryādā   ਰਹਿਤ ਮਰਯਾਦਾ
(rehat maryada)
the code of discipline of the Khālsā; a specific text on this subject.

rahit-nāmā   ਰਹਿਤਨਾਮਾ
one of a category of Sikh manuals of conduct.

raīs   ਰਈਸ
a socially eminent and affluent person.

rājā   ਰਾਜਾ
a king or sovereign.

rāj karegā khālsā   ਰਾਜ ਕਰੇਗਾ ਖ਼ਾਲਸਾ
"the Khālsā shall rule." The phrase became current in the eighteenth century as part of the Sikh aspirations for sovereign rule. It has become a part of the prayer-anthem of the Sikhs.

rāshtra-bhāshā   ਰਾਸ਼ਟਰ ਭਾਸ਼ਾ
national language (of India)

sadā vigās   ਸਦਾ ਵਿਗਾਸ
"spiritual gaiety," the continual flowering of the spirit.

sahaj   ਸਹਜ
"simple," "spontaneous," "natural"; the ultimate condition of blissful union with the divine, achieved when the spirit ascends to *sach khaṇḍ*, the "realm of truth."

sahajdhārī   ਸਹਜਧਾਰੀ
(sehjdhari, sehajdhari)
designates persons who affirm allegiance to the teachings of Gurū Nānak and his successors (particularly to the doctrine and practice of *nām-simaran*) but who decline to accept Khālsā initiation.

salwār kamīz   ਸਲਵਾਰ ਕਮੀਜ਼
the Punjabi female dress, consisting of trousers (*salwār*) and a long blouse (*kamīz*).

samānā, samāṇā   ਸਮਾਨਾ / ਸਮਾਣਾ
"merging," spontaneous, egoless union with the divine.

sanskāras, samskāras   ਸੰਸਕਾਰ
the life-cycle rituals.

saṅgat   ਸੰਗਤ
assembly, religious congregation, holy fellowship.

sansār   ਸੰਸਾਰ
the cycle of birth and death.

sant   ਸੰਤ
spiritual person, saint, holy man; one who realizes Truth (*sat*); a devotional tradition of North India

sant-sipāhī   ਸੰਤ - ਸਿਪਾਹੀ
one who combines the spirituality of the devout believer (*sant*) with the bravery and obedience of the true soldier (*sipāhī*).

sarbat Khālsā   ਸਰਬੰਤ ਖ਼ਾਲਸਾ
the entire body of the Sikhs of the Khālsā.

sardār   ਸਰਦਾਰ
chieftain; leader of a *misl*. *Sardār* is now a title of address for all Sikh males. The corresponding title for a Sikh woman is *Sardārnī*.

sarpañch   ਸਰਪੰਚ
head of the village council

(Sat Sri Akal)
Sati Sri Akāl   ਸਤਿ ਸ੍ਰੀ ਅਕਾਲ
"Truth is Timeless (or immortal)"; the Sikh greeting, war-cry.

satī   ਸਤੀ
a virtuous woman; also used in the Ādi Granth to describe a widow's act of self-immolation on her husband's funeral pyre.

satsaṅg   ਸਤਸੰਗ
"spiritual fellowship," a congregation of pious Sikhs.

satyāgraha   ਸਤਿਆਗ੍ਰਹਿ
"non-violent holding fast to Truth"; agitation for what is right; Mahatma Gandhi's strategy in India's freedom struggle.

sevā (sewa)   ਸੇਵਾ
"service" to a gurdwara. In a broader sense, service is to assist a community or alleviate individual suffering. *Sevā* and *simaran* are regarded as the two pillars of Sikh faith.

shabad (shabd)   ਸਬਦ
literally, "word"; both the divine Word received from God, and the expression of that Word in a hymn or song of praise in the Gurū Granth Sāhib.

shahīd   ਸਹੀਦ
originally in Arabic, "witness," thence "martyr." A *shahīd* group among the Sikhs was the suicide squad in 1920 prepared to liberate the Raqab Ganj gurdwara (Delhi) and rebuild its wall.

shahīdī dīvān   ਸਹੀਦੀ ਦੀਵਾਨ
congregational service to honour the martyrs.

shiqdār   ਸਿਕਦਾਰ
a noble in the royal court; a revenue collector.

shalok (shlok, shloka)   ਸਲੋਕ
a couplet from a religious text.

shrāddh   ਸਰਾਧ
a Hindu-type post-cremation ritual, often repeated on each death anniversary. Not to be confused with *shraddhā*, "trust" or "faith."

shuddhī   ਸੁੱਧੀ
the reclamation or "purifying" ceremony used by the Arya Samaj movement to bring Hindu converts to Islam and their descendants, and lower-caste Sikhs, into the Hindu fold.

shuddhī sabhā   ਸੁੱਧੀ ਸਭਾ
"purifying gathering": to counter the Arya Samaj *shuddhī* campaign, Sikhs had their own *shuddhī sabhās*.

Sikh   ਸਿੱਖ
a "learner" or "disciple"; applied to the disciples of Gurū Nānak and his nine spiritual successors.

(sikhi) sikkhī   ਸਿੱਖੀ
"discipleship"; "Sikh-ness," referring to the characteristics of Sikh identity broadly conceived. Cf. *siṅghī*.

Siṅgh   ਸਿੰਘ
"lion," used as a name by male members of the Khālsā.

Siṅgh Sabhā ਸਿੰਘ ਸਭਾ
"the Siṅgh Society," a movement based on several local societies and eventually co-ordinated by the Chief Khalsa Diwan, dedicated to religious and educational reform among Sikhs. It accentuated the sense of Sikh identity as fundamentally different from being Hindu. It flourished in the late nineteenth and early twentieth centuries.

siṅghī ਸਿੰਘੀ
Sikh identity more strictly conceived in the Khālsā form. Cf. *sikkhī.*

sukh ਸੁਖ
happiness.

surat shabad yoga ਸੁਰਤ ਸਬਦ ਯੋਗ
meditative discipline representing spiritual harmony acoustically, seeking to merge the soul with the flow of sound of divine hymns.

(swaraj) svarāj ਸਵਰਾਜ
"self-rule," rallying cry of the Indian nationalist movement.

(takht) takhat ਤਖਤ
throne; one of five major seats of authority among Sikhs, e.g., at Amritsar, Patna, Nander, Anandpur, Damdama.

Tarkhān, Tarkhāṇ ਤਰਖਾਣ
the carpenter caste.

Tat Khālsā ਤੱਤ ਖਾਲਸਾ
the more rigorous, "reformed" mode of being Sikh advocated by the Singh Sabha movement.

ṭhānedār ਠਾਣੇਦਾਰ
the officer in charge of a police station; a police sub-inspector.

tilak ਤਿਲਕ
a sect mark made on the forehead, especially among Hindus.

toshākhānā ਤੋਸ਼ਾਖਾਨ
"storehouse," a treasury for precious articles at the Golden Temple, Amritsar.

umarā ਉਮਰਾ
a courtier.

updeshak ਉਪਦੇਸ਼ਕ
"preacher," a Sikh functionary who instructs, advises and motivates the faithful.

Vāhigurū ਵਾਹਿਗੁਰੂ
(Vahguru, Wahguru, Waheguru)
"Wonderful Gurū"; commonly used in the Sikh tradition to refer to Ultimate Reality.

vanjāra ਵੰਜਾਰਾ
"itinerant merchant," a symbol of soul, human being and God in Sikh usage.

varṇa ਵਰਨ / ਵਰਣ
one of four classifications by reference to which Hindu endogamous groupings (jātis) are ranked according to brahmanic standards of ritual purity: Brahmin (priest), Kshatriya (warrior), Vaishya (farmer and merchant), Shudra (labourer, servant).

vedī ਵੇਦੀ
in marriage rituals, a place marked off with four upright stakes joined by cross-pieces of wood at the top and interior and covered with a red cloth.

(vikalpa) vikalp ਵਿਕਲਪ
"mental construction"; analytical as contrasted with intuitive processes of thought.

(vikara) vikār ਵਿਕਾਰ
deformation, deviation; esp. passion and attachment.

vismād ਵਿਸਮਾਦ
immense awe; ecstasy engendered by awe; a response of wonder to omnipotent Reality.

(vivek) bibek ਵਿਵੇਕ / ਵਿਬੇਕ
"discriminate awareness," discerning judgment in spiritual matters.

zaildār ਜ਼ੈਲਦਾਰ
the headman of a *zail,* consisting of one or several villages.

zāt ਜ਼ਾਤ
endogamous caste grouping; cf. Sanskrit *jāti.*

Bibliography

This bibliography of English-language publications is divided into six sections, the first being in the form of an introductory essay (1. General). The remaining sections,

2. Guru Period (c. 1500-1708)
3. Post-Guru Period to Annexation (1708-1849)
4. Colonial Period (1849-1947)
5. India since Independence (1947 to the present)
6. The Sikh Diaspora

are listed alphabetically by author and are divided into books and articles. Names with an element following Singh or Kaur are alphabetized under that element; names ending in Singh or Kaur are alphabetized under the element preceding.

For additional references to primary and secondary sources in English, Punjabi and other languages, consult the notes to the respective chapters of this volume.

1. General

Readers new to the study of the Sikhs and their tradition may wish to begin with articles on the Sikhs in the *Encyclopædia Britannica* (1974 or 1985 editions) and the *Encyclopedia of Religion* (New York: Macmillan, 1987), both by Khushwant Singh; or with the remarkably incisive short piece by Christopher Shackle, *The Sikhs* (London: Minority Rights Group, revised edition 1986). A very readable book-length introduction (with glossary, reading lists and other useful aids) is W. Owen Cole and Piara Singh Sambhi, *The Sikhs: Their Religious Beliefs and Practices* (London: Routledge and Kegan Paul, 1978). Cole's *The Guru in Sikhism* (London: Darton, Longman & Todd, 1982) offers another effective *entrée* into the religious perspective of the Sikhs. Providing well-translated textual passages with concise explanatory comments is W.H. McLeod, *Textual Sources for the Study of Sikhism* (Manchester: Manchester University Press, 1984). For children in the pre-teen years, W.H. McLeod's attractively printed *The Way of the Sikh* (Amersham: Hulton, new edition 1986) may be recommended.

Classical accounts of the Sikhs in English include Joseph Davey Cunningham, *A History of the Sikhs from the Origin of the Nation to the Battle of the Sutlej* (London: John Murray, 1849), which is long since dated, and the still influential, though also dated, Max Arthur Macauliffe, *The Sikh Religion*, 6 vols. (Oxford: Clarendon Press, 1909; reprinted in 3 vols. in 1963), and John

Clark Archer, *The Sikhs in Relation to Hindus, Moslems, Christians and Ahmadiyas: A Study in Comparative Religion* (Princeton: Princeton University Press, 1946). Standard modern historical surveys of the Sikhs include Khushwant Singh, *A History of the Sikhs*, 2 vols. (Princeton: Princeton University Press, 1963-66; Delhi: Oxford University Press, 1977), and H.R. Gupta's multi-volume *History of the Sikhs* (New Delhi: Munshiram Manoharlal, 1978 and continuing). A recently reissued volume conveying the *élan* of participation in the Sikh tradition is Harbans Singh, *The Heritage of the Sikhs* (Columbia, Missouri: South Asia Books, revised edition 1973). There will soon be a one-volume survey by J.S. Grewal, *The Sikhs of the Punjab*, in the *New Cambridge History of India* (Cambridge: Cambridge University Press, forthcoming).

Among important volumes of collected papers on Sikh topics there are *Sikhism and Indian Society*, vol. 4 of *Transactions of the Indian Institute of Advanced Study* (Simla: Rashtrapati Nivas, 1967) and Mark Juergensmeyer and N. Gerald Barrier, eds., *Sikh Studies: Comparative Perspectives on a Changing Tradition* (Berkeley: Berkeley Religious Studies Series, Graduate Theological Union, 1979). Some important recent scholarship on the Sikhs in relation to the religious milieu at their origins may be found in Karine Schomer and W.H. McLeod, eds., *The Sants: A Devotional Tradition of India* (Berkeley: Berkeley Religious Studies Series and New Delhi: Motilal Banarsidass, 1986). Two volumes by W.H. McLeod soon to be published will be of interest to Sikhs and non-Sikhs alike: *Who Is a Sikh? The Problem of Sikh Identity* (Oxford: Clarendon Press, forthcoming) and *The Sikhs: History, Religion and Society* (New York: Columbia University Press, forthcoming).

Early translations of the Sikh scripture, the Guru Granth Sahib, include the tendentious, incomplete version by Ernest Trumpp, *The Adi Granth or the Holy Scriptures of the Sikhs* (London: Allen and Unwin, 1877) and the more sympathetic (and better received) translated excerpts contained in Macauliffe's *The Sikh Religion*. For more recent complete translations see Manmohan Singh, tr., *Adi Granth*, 6 vols. (Amritsar: Shiromani Gurdwara Prabandhak Committee, 1969), which includes text, explanatory lexicon and translation. Other complete translations include Gopal Singh, tr., *Sri Guru Granth Sahib*, 4 vols. (New Delhi: World Sikh Center, international edition 1984; earlier edition 1962) and Gurbachan Singh Talib in conjunction with Bhai Jodh Singh, *Sri Guru Granth Sahib*, 2 vols. (Patiala: Punjabi University, 1984). A number of scholars and writers combined to produce for UNESCO a selection of passages, *The Sacred Writings of the Sikhs* (London: Allen and Unwin, 1960), and G.S. Mansukhani has provided an anthology, *Hymns from the Holy Granth* (New Delhi: Hemkunt Press, 1975). Khushwant Singh has brought out his own translations of the first Guru's compositions, *Hymns of Guru Nanak* (New Delhi: Orient Longmans, 1969). (A French translation of the entire Guru Granth Sahib is in progress, the work of Jarnail Singh of Toronto.)

For Sikh theology as rooted in the teachings of Guru Nanak see W.H. McLeod, *Guru Nanak and the Sikh Religion* (Oxford: Clarendon Press, 1969) and G.S. Talib, *Guru Nanak: His Personality and Vision* (Delhi: Gur Das Kapur & Sons, 1969). For Sikh ethics see Avtar Singh, *Ethics of the Sikhs* (Patiala: Punjabi University, 1970); and for philosophy see Sher Singh, *Philosophy of Sikhism* (Delhi: Stirling Publishers, 1966) and S.S. Kohli, *Outline of Sikh Thought* (New Delhi: Punjabi Prakashak, 1966) and his *Philosophy of Guru Nanak* (Chandigarh: Panjab University, 1969).

A major reference project for Sikh studies is the *Encyclopedia of Sikhism* currently in preparation under the editorship of Harbans Singh. Major academic journals regularly publishing articles on the Sikhs and their tradition include *Panjab Past and Present* (Patiala), *Journal of Sikh Studies* (Amritsar) and *Studies in Sikhism and Comparative Religion* (Delhi). Other relevant periodicals include *The Sikh Review* (Calcutta), *Sikh Bulletin* (Chichester), *The Sikh Courier* (London), *Spokesman* (Delhi) and *Journal of Comparative Sociology and Religion* (Ottawa).

For further suggestions for reading, consult the interesting bibliographic essay by Khushwant Singh, "The Sikhs," in Charles J. Adams, ed., *A Reader's Guide to the Great Religions* (New York: The Free Press, 2nd ed. 1977; avoid the first edition as it has no chapter on the Sikhs). Jane Singh, co-ordinating editor, and collaborators have recently brought out *South Asians in North America: An Annotated and Selected Bibliography* (Occasional Papers Series, 14; Berkeley: Center for South and Southeast Asia Studies, University of California, 1988). Additional bibliographies on Sikhs in India or overseas are listed in the sections following in this bibliography: e.g., Ganda Singh (1966) in Section 3; N. Gerald Barrier in Section 4; Darshan Singh Tatla and Eleanor M. Nesbitt (1987), Norman Buchignani (1977) and Joseph T. O'Connell (1986) in Section 6.

2. Guru Period (c. 1500-1708)

Books

Ahluwalia, Jasbir Singh. *The Sovereignty of the Sikh Doctrine*. New Delhi: Bahri Publications Pvt. Ltd., 1983.

Archer, John Clark. *The Sikhs, in Relation to Hindus, Moslems, Christians and Ahmadiyas: A Study in Comparative Religion*. Princeton: Princeton University Press, 1946.

Athar Ali, M. *The Mughal Nobility Under Aurangzeb*. Bombay: Asia Publishing House, 1970. (Reprint, first published 1968.)

Banerjee, Anil Chandra. *Guru Nanak and His Times*, Patiala: Punjabi University, 1971.

Banerjee, Indubhushan. *Evolution of the Khalsa*, 2 Vols. Calcutta: A. Mukherjee & Co., 1962 (2nd ed).

de Bary, William Theodore, general ed. *Sources of Indian Tradition*, ed. and revised by Ainslee T. Embree and Stephen Hay, 2 vols. New York: Columbia University Press, 1988.

Bhandari, Sujan Rai. *Khulasatu-t-Tawarikh*, tr. Ranjit Singh Gill and ed. Fauja Singh. Patiala: Punjabi University, 1972.

460   Bibliography

Beveridge, Annette Susanah. *Babur-Nama (Memoirs of Babur of Zahiru'ddin Muhammad Babur Padsah Ghazi*, 2 vols. New Delhi: Oriental Books Reprint Corporation, 1970 (reprint, first published 1922).

Beveridge, H., tr. *The Akbar Nama of Abu-l-Fazl*, 3 vols. Delhi: Ess Ess Publications, reprint 1977.).

Chandher, Gurmukh Singh. *A Brief History of the Golden Temple, Amritsar.* Lahore: the author, 1892.

Cole, W. Owen. *Sikhism and its Indian Context 1469-1708.* New Delhi: D.K. Agencies, 1984.

Farquhar, J.N. *Modern Religious Movements in India.* London: Macmillan & Co., 1919 and reprinted.

Fauja Singh. *Hukamnamas Shri Guru Tegh Bahadur Sahib.* Patiala: Punjabi University, 1976.

Fauja Singh and Gurbachan Singh Talib. *Guru Tegh Bahadur: Martyr and Teacher.* Patiala: Punjabi University, 1975.

Fauja Singh and L.M. Joshi, eds. *History of the Punjab From Pre-Historic Times to the Age of Asoka.* Patiala: Punjabi University, 1977.

Ganda Singh, ed. *Hukam-name* (in Punjabi). Patiala: Punjabi University, 1967.

Giani Gian Singh. *Sri Guru Panth Parkash*, ed. Giani Kirpal Singh, 5 vols. Amritsar, 1974.

Gopal Singh. *A History of the Sikh People, 1469-1978.* New Delhi: World Sikh University Press, 1979.

Grewal, J.S. *From Guru Nanak to Maharaja Ranjit Singh: Essays in Sikh History.* Amritsar: Guru Nanak Dev University, 1972.

———. *Guru Nanak in History.* Chandigarh: Panjab University, 1969.

———. *Guru Tegh Bahadur and the Persian Chroniclers.* Amritsar: Guru Nanak Dev University, 1976.

Guru Gobind Singh. *Zafarnama* (in Punjabi). Patiala: Punjab Languages Department, 1964.

Habib, Irfan. *The Agrarian System of Mughal India (1526-1707.* Bombay: Asia Publishing House, 1963.

Harbans Singh. *Guru Gobind Singh.* New Delhi: Sterling Publishers, 1979.

———. *Guru Nanak and Origins of the Sikh Faith.* Bombay: Asia Publishing House, 1969.

———. *Guru Tegh Bahadur.* New Delhi: Sterling Publishers Private Ltd., 1982.

Ibn Hasan. *The Central Structure of the Mughal Empire and Its Practical Working up to the Year 1657.* New Delhi: Munshiram Manoharlal, reprinted 1970. First published in 1936.

Kapur Singh. *Contributions of Guru Nanak.* Chandigarh: Panjab University, 1975-76.

———. *Parasharprasna or the Baisakhi of Guru Gobind Singh.* Jullundur: Hind Publishers Ltd., 1959.

Khan, Ahsan Raza. *Position of Chieftains in the Mughal Empire During Akbar's Reign.* Simla: Indian Institute of Advanced Study, 1977.

Khan, Mustaad. *Maasiri Alamgiri*, tr. Darshan Singh, ed. Fauja Singh. Patiala: Punjabi University, 1977.

Kohli, Surinder Singh. *Philosophy of Guru Nanak.* Chandigarh: Panjab University, 1969.

Loehlin, Clinton H. *The Granth of Guru Gobind Singh and the Khalsa Brotherhood.* Lucknow: Lucknow Publishing House, 1971.

———. *The Sikhs and Their Scriptures.* Lucknow: Lucknow Publishing House, 1968.

Macauliffe, Max Arthur. *The Sikh Religion, Its Gurus, Sacred Writings and Authors*, 6 vols. New Delhi: S. Chand & Company, 2nd ed. 1978. Original edition 1909.

Madanjit Kaur. *The Golden Temple: Past and Present.* Amritsar: Guru Nanak Dev University, 1983.

McLeod, W.H. *Early Sikh Tradition: A Study of the Janam-Sakhis.* Oxford: Clarendon Press, 1980.

———. *The B40 Janam-Sakhi.* Amritsar: Guru Nanak Dev University, 1980.

———. *The Evolution of the Sikh Community: Five Essays.* Delhi: Oxford University Press, 1975; Oxford: Clarendon Press, 1976.

———. *Guru Nanak and the Sikh Religion.* Oxford: Clarendon Press, 1968.

———. *The Sikhs of the Punjab.* Ludhiana: Lyall Book Depot, 1969.

McMullen, Clarence O., ed. *The Nature of Guruship.* Delhi: I.S.P.C.K., 1976.

Moreland, W.H. *India at the Death of Akbar: An Economic Study.* Delhi: Atma Ram & Sons, 1962.

———. *The Agrarian System of Moslem India: A Historical Essay with Appendices.* First published in 1929. Delhi: Oriental Books Reprint Corporation, 2nd ed., 1968.

Narang, Gokal Chand. *Transformation of Sikhism.* New Delhi: New Book Society of India, 4th ed., 1956.

Nisami, Khaliq Ahmad. *The Life and Times of Shaikh Farid-u'd-Din Ganj-i-Shakar.* Aligarh: Aligarh Muslim University, 1955.

Nural Hasan, Saiyid. *Thoughts on Agrarian Relations in Mughal India.* New Delhi: People's Publishing House, 1973.

Qureshi, I.H. *The Administration of the Delhi Sultanate.* Lahore: 1944.

Ray, Niharranjan. *The Sikh Gurus and the Sikh Society: A Study in Social Analysis.* Patiala: Punjabi University, 1970.

Rizvi, Saiyid Athar Abbas. *Muslim Revivalist Movements in Northern India in the Sixteenth and Seventeenth Centuries.* Agra, 1965.

Sachan, Edward C., ed. *Alberuni's India,* 2 vols. New Delhi: S. Chand & Co. (reprint).

Sainapati. *Sri Guru Sabha,* ed. Ganda Singh. Patiala: Punjabi University, 1967. Cf. Senapat.

Sardul Singh Kavishar. *Sikh Studies.* Lahore: The National Publications, 1937.

Senapat. *Sri Guru Sobha,* ed. Shamsher Singh ("Ashok"). Amritsar: Shiromani Gurdwara Prabandhak Committee, 1967.

Sewa Singh Sewak, ed. *Prachin Janam Sakhi (Sri Guru Nanak Dev Ji).* Jullundur: New Book Company, 1969.

Talib, Gurbachan Singh. *Baba Sheikh Farid.* New Delhi: National Book Trust, India, 1974.

———. *Bani of Sri Guru Amar Das.* A Guru Amar Das Quincentenary Memorial Volume. New Delhi: Sterling Publishers, 1979.

———. *Guru Nanak: His Personality and Vision.* Delhi: Guru Das Kapur & Sons, 1969.

———. *Japuji: The Immortal Prayer-Chant.* New Delhi: Munshiram Manoharlal, 1977.

Teja Singh. *Guru Nanak and His Mission.* Amritsar: Shiromani Gurdwara Prabandhak Committee, 6th ed., 1984.

———. *Sikhism: Its Ideals and Institutions.* Bombay: Green & Co., 1937.

Teja Singh and Ganda Singh. *A Short History of the Sikhs,* v. 1. Bombay: Orient Longmans, 1950.

Trilochan Singh. *Guru Tegh Bahadur: Prophet and Martyr (A Biography).* Delhi: Gurdwara Prabandhak Committee, 1967.

Trumpp, Ernest, tr. *The Adi Granth or The Holy Scriptures of the Sikhs.* First published 1877. New Delhi: Munshiram Manoharlal, 2nd ed., 1970.

Uberoi, Mohan Singh. *Sikh Mysticism: The Sevenfold Yoga of Sikhism.* Amritsar: the author, 1964.

Wazir Singh. *Aspects of Guru Nanak's Philosophy.* Lahore: Lahore Book Shop, 1969.

Articles

Chetan Singh. "Riverine Transport in Punjab and the Decline of Trade in Multan during the Second half of the 17th Century." *Proceedings, Punjab History Conference*, Patiala, 1982, pp. 80-86.

Goswamy, B.N. "The Context of Painting in the Sikh Punjab." *Journal of Regional History* 2 (1981), 85-105.

Grewal, J.S. "The Sikh Movement: A Historical Note," *Dissent Protest and Reform in Indian Civilization*, ed. S.C. Malik. Simla: Indian Institute of Advanced Study, 1977, pp. 159-66.

———. "The Sikh Panth 1500-1850." *Religious Change and Cultural Domination*, ed. David N. Lorenzen. Mexico City: El Colegio de Mexico, 1981, pp. 193-98.

Hambye, E.R. "A Contemporary Jesuit Document on Guru Arjun Dev's Martyrdom." *Punjab Past and Present: Essays in Honour of Dr. Ganda Singh*, ed. N. Gerald Barrier and Harbans Singh. Patiala: Punjabi University, 1976, pp. 113-18.

Habib, Irfan. "Evidence for Sixteenth-Century Agrarian Conditions in the Guru Granth Sahib." *Indian Economic and Social History Review* 1:3 (1964), 64-72.

———. "Jatts of Punjab and Sind." *Punjab Past and Present: Essays in Honour of Dr. Ganda Singh*, ed. N. Gerald Barrier and Harbans Singh. Patiala: Punjabi University, 1976, pp. 92-103.

Hans, Surjit. "Social Transformation and Early Sikh Literature," *Journal of Regional History* 3 (1982), 1-14.

Kang, Kanwarjit. "Sikh Gurus in the Murals of the 19th Century Punjab." *Punjab Murals on Sikh Gurus*, Patiala: Punjabi University, n.d.

———. "Tradition of Mural Painting in Punjab." *Punjab Murals on Sikh Gurus*, Patiala: Punjabi University, n.d.

Leech, R. "Notes on the Religion of the Sikhs, being a notice of their Prayer, Holidays and Shrines." *Journal of the Asiatic Society of Bengal*, no. 162, 1845.

Madanjit Kaur. "A Documentary Evidence of the Sikh Reaction at Trumpp's Translation of the Adi Granth." *Proceedings, Punjab History Conference*, Patiala, 1980, pp. 219-24.

McLeod, W.H. "Trade and Investment in Sixteenth and Seventeenth Century Punjab: The Testimony of the Sikh Devotional Literature." *Punjab Past and Present: Essays in Honour of Dr. Ganda Singh*, ed. N. Gerald Barrier and Harbans Singh. Patiala: Punjabi University, 1976, pp. 81-91.

Naqvi, Hamida Khatoon. "Urban Growth in the Punjab (11th to 17th centuries." *Studies in Urban History*, ed. J.S. Grewal and Indu Banga. Amritsar: Guru Nanak Dev University, pp. 61-69.

Nural Hasan. "Medieval Punjab." *Punjab Past and Present: Essays in Honour of Dr. Ganda Singh*, ed. N. Gerald Barrier and Harbans Singh. Patiala: Punjabi University, 1976, pp. 73-80.

McLeod, W.H. "Kabir, Nanak and the early Sikh Panth." *Religious Change and Cultural Domination*, ed. David N. Lorenzen. Mexico City: El Colegio de Mexico, 1981.

3. Post-Guru Period to Annexation (1708 to 1849)

Books

Bal, S.S. *British Administration in the Punjab and Its Aftermath*. Amritsar: Guru Nanak Dev University, 1986.

Banga, Indu. *Agrarian System of the Sikhs*. New Delhi: Manohar Publications, 1978.

Bell, Evans. *The Annexation of the Punjab, and the Maharaja Duleep Singh.* Patiala: Punjab Languages Department, 2nd ed., 1970.

Bhangu, Ratan Singh. *Prachin Panth Parkash* (in Punjabi). Amritsar: Khalsa Samachar, 5th ed., 1972. First published in 1914.

Burnes, Alexander. *Travels into Bukhara.* London: John Murray, 1834.

Chopra, Barkat Rai. *Kingdom of the Punjab, 1839-45.* Hoshiarpur: Vishveshvaranand Institute, 1969.

Chopra, Gulshanlal. *The Punjab as a Sovereign State.* Lahore: Utter Chand Kapur and Sons, 1928.

Cunningham, Joseph Davy. *A History of the Sikhs, From The Origin of the Nation to the Battle of the Sutlej.* London: John Murray, 1849.

Despatches and General Orders announcing the Victories achieved by the Army of the Sutlej over the Sikh Army at Moodkee, Ferozeshah, Aliwal and Sobraon in December 1845 and January and February, 1846. Patiala: Punjab Languages Department, 1970 (reprint).

Diwan Ajudhia Parshal. *Waqai Jang-i-Sikhan,* tr. and ed. V.S. Suri. Chandigarh: Punjab Itihas Prakashan, 1975.

Fauja Singh. *After Ranjit Singh.* New Delhi: Master Publishers, 1982.

———. *Military System of the Sikhs.* Delhi: Motilal Banarsidass, 1964.

Ganda Singh. *A Bibliography of the Punjab.* Patiala: Punjabi University, 1966.

———. *Ahmad Shah Durrani.* Bombay: Asia Publishing House, 1959.

———. *Baba Banda Singh Bahadur: His Life and Achievements and the Place of his Execution.* Sirhind: Sirhind Historical Research Society, 1976.

———, ed. *Early European Accounts of the Sikhs.* Calcutta: Indian Studies, Past and Present, reprint 1962.

———. *Life of Banda Singh Bahadur.* Amritsar: Khalsa College, 1935.

———, ed. *The Punjab in 1839-40: Selections from Punjab Akhbars, Punjab Intelligence.* Patiala: Sikh History Society, 1952.

Garrett, H.L.O., tr. and ed. *The Punjab a Hundred Years Ago, as Described by V. Jacquomant and A. Soltykoff.* Patiala: Punjab Government Record Office, Monograph No.18, Punjab Languages Department, 1911.

Garrett, H.L.O. and G.L. Chopra, tr. and ed. *Events at the Court of Ranjit Singh 1810-1817).* Patiala: Punjab Government Record Office Publications, Monograph No. 17, Punjab Languages Department, reprint 1970.

Gibbon, F.P. *The Lawrences of the Punjab.* London: J.M. Dent, 1908.

Goswamy, B.N. and J.S. Grewal. *The Mughal and Sikh Rulers and the Vaishnavas of Pindori (A Historical Interpretation of 52 Persian Documents).* Simla: Indian Institute of Advanced Study, 1959.

Gough, Charles; and Arthur D. Innes. *The Sikhs and the Sikh Wars: The Rise, Conquest, and Annexation of the Punjab State.* Patiala: Punjab Languages Department, 1970 (reprint).

Grewal, J.S. *The City of the Golden Temple.* Amritsar: Guru Nanak Dev University, 1986.

———. *Historian's Punjab: Miscellaneous Articles.* Amritsar: Guru Nanak Dev University, 1974.

———. *In the By-Lanes of History: Some Persian Documents from a Punjab Town.* Simla: Indian Institute of Advanced Studies, 1975.

———. *Maharaja Ranjit Singh.* Amritsar: Guru Nanak Dev University, 1982.

———. *The Mughals and the Jogis of Jakhbar (some Madad-i-Ma'ash and Other Documents).* Simla: Indian Institute of Advanced Studies, 1967.

———. *The Reign of Maharaja Ranjit Singh: Structure of Power, Economy and Society.* Sita Ram Kohli Memorial Lectures, 1981. Patiala: Punjabi University, 1981.

Grewal, J.S.; and Indu Banga, tr. and ed. *Early Nineteenth Century Panjab* (a part of Ganesh Das' *Char Bagh-i-Panjab*). Amritsar: Guru Nanak Dev University, 1975.

Griffin, Lepel. *The Panjab Chiefs: Historical and Biographical Notices of the Principal Families in the Lahore.* Lahore: McGarthy Press, 1865.

———. *The Rajas of the Punjab.* Lahore: The Punjab Printing, 1870.

Gupta, H.R. *History of the Sikhs, 1739-68,* 7 vols. New Delhi: Munshiram Manoharlal, 1978 and continuing.

———. *Panjab on the Eve of the First Sikh War.* Chandigarh: Panjab University, 2nd ed., 1975.

———. *Studies in Later Mughal History of the Panjab.* Lahore: Minerva Bookshop, 1944.

Hans, Surjit Singh. "Historical Analysis of Sikh Literature (A.D. 1500-1850)." Ph.D. dissertation, Guru Nanak Dev University, Amritsar, 1980.

Hasrat, Bikrama Jit. *Ango-Sikh Relations 1799-1849.* Hoshiarpur: V.V. Research Institute Press, 1968.

———. *The Punjab Papers.* Hoshiarpur: V.V. Research Institute Book Agency, 1970.

Hugel, Charles. *Travels in Cashmeer and the Panjab,* tr. T.B. Jervis. London: John Petheram, 1845.

Hutchison, J.; and J. Ph. Vogel. *History of the Panjab Hill States,* 2 vols. Lahore: Government Printing Panjab, 1933.

Joginder Kaur, ed. *Ram Sukh Rao's Fateh Singh Partap Prabhakar (A History of the Early Nineteenth Century Punjab).* Patiala: the editor, 1980.

Johal, Daljinder Singh. "Society and Culture as Reflected in Punjabi Drama (1750-1850)." Ph.D. dissertation, Guru Nanak Dev University, Amritsar, 1985.

Khushwant Singh. *A History of the Sikhs, 1469-1839,* vol. 1. Princeton: Princeton University Press, 1963; reprinted Delhi: Oxford University Press, 1977.

———. *Ranjit Singh: Maharaja of the Punjab.* London: George Allen & Unwin Ltd., 1962.

Kirpal Singh. *A Short Lifesketch of Maharaja Ala Singh.* Amritsar, 1953.

Kohli, Sita Ram. *Catalogue of the Khalsa Darbar Records,* 2 vols. Lahore: Government Printing Punjab, 1919 and 1927.

———. *Sunset of the Sikh Empire.* New Delhi: Orient Longmans, 1967.

———. *Trial of Diwan Mul Raj (Governor of Multan).* Lahore: Punjab Government Records Office, Monograph no. 14, 1933.

Malik, Zahir Uddain. *The Reign of Muhammad Shah 1719-1748.* Bombay: Asia Publishing House, 1977.

M'Gregor, W.L. *The History of the Sikhs.* 2 vols. London: James Maden, 1846.

McLeod, W.H. *The Chaupa Singh Rahit-nama.* Dunedin: University of Otago Press, 1987.

The Minor Phulkian Families. Patiala: Punjab Languages Department, 2nd ed., 1970.

Moorcraft, W.; and G. Frebeck. *Travels in the Himalayan Provinces of Hindostan and the Punjab, in Ladakh and Kashmir, in the Peshawar, Kabul and Kunduz and Bokhara from 1819 to 1825.* London: John Murray, 1837.

Osborne, W.F. *The Court and Camp of Ranjeet Singh.* London, 1840.

Pearse, Hugh. *Memories of Alexander Gardner (Colonel of Artillery in the Service of Maharaja Ranjit Singh).* Patiala: Punjab Languages Department, reprinted 1970. First published 1848.

Prinsep, Henry T. *Origin of the Sikh Power and Political Life of Maharaja Ranjit Singh with an Account of Religion, Laws and Customs of the Sikhs.* Patiala: Punjab Languages Department, 1970 (reprint).

Rao, Ram Sukh. "Jassa Singh Binod." MS, M/772. Patiala: Punjab State Archives.

Sachdeva, Veena. "Polity and Economy in the Late Eighteenth-Century Punjab." Ph.D. dissertation, Guru Nanak Dev University, Amritsar, 1987.

Satish Chandra. *Parties and Politics at the Mughal Court 1707-1740.* New Delhi: People's Publishing House, 2nd ed., 1972.

Shahamat Ali. *The Sikhs and Afghans.* Patiala: Punjab Languages Department (reprint, first published 1883).

Siddiqi, Naman Ahmad. *Land Revenue Administration Under the Mughals (1700-1750).* Bombay: Asia Publishing House, 1970.

Sinha, N.K. *Impact of Events in the Punjab (1756-1827) on British India and Historical Data from Missionary Writings: Punjab in the Second Half of the Nineteenth Century.* Sita Ram Kohli Memorial Lecture. Patiala: Punjabi University, 1966.

————. *Ranjit Singh.* Calcutta: A. Mukherjee & Co., 1968.

————. *Rise of the Sikh Power.* Calcutta: A. Mukherjee & Co., 1973 (reprint, first published 1936).

Smith, Wilfred Cantwell. *The Crystallization of Religious Communities in Mughal India. Yad-name-ye-Irani-ye Minorsky,* ed. Mojtaba Minovi and Iraj Afshar (Ganjine-ye Tahqiqat-e Irani, no. 57; Publications of Tehran University, no. 1241). Tehran: Intisharat Daneshgah, 1969, pp. 197-220.

Steinbach, H. *The Punjaub,* intro. by W.H. McLeod. Karachi: Oxford University Press, 1976. First published 1846.

Sulakhan Singh. "Udasis Under the Sikh Rule (1750-1850)." Ph.D. dissertation, Guru Nanak Dev University, Amritsar, 1985.

Suri, Sohan La. *Umdat-ut-Tawarikh* tr. V.S. Suri), Daftars II and IV. New Delhi: S. Chand & Co., 1961 and 1972.

Tahmas Beg Khan. *Tahmas Nameh,* ed. Muhammad Aslam. Lahore: University of the Punjab, 1986.

Thackwell, Edward Joseph. *Narrative of the Second Sikh War in 1848-49, with a Detailed Account of the Battles of Ramnagger, the Passage of the Chenab, Chillanwallah, Goojerat, etc.* Patiala: Punjab Languages Department (reprint). First published 1851.

Vigne, G.T. *A Personal Narrative of a Visit to Ghazni, Cabul and Afghanistan and of a Residence at the Court of Dost Mohammad with Notices of Ranjit Singh, Khiva and Russian Expedition.* London: Whittaker & Co., 1840.

Vogel, J.Ph. *Catalogue of Bhuri Singh Museum at Chamba.* Calcutta: 1909.

Wadhera, Ganesh Das. *Char Bagh-i-Punjab,* ed. Kirpal Singh. Amritsar: Sikh History Research Department, 1965.

Waheeduddin. *The Real Ranjit Singh.* Karachi: Lion Art Press (Karachi), 4th ed., 1965.

Webster, John C.B. *The Christian Community and Change in Nineteenth Century North India.* Delhi: The Macmillan Company of India Ltd., 1976.

Wilson, H.H. *A Glossary of Judicial and Revenue Terms.* Delhi: Munshiram Manohar Lal, 1968.

Articles

Bal, S.S. "Dalhousie and Annexation of the Punjab." *Proceedings, Punjab History Conference,* Patiala, 1971, 204-27.

Banga, Indu. "Ala Singh: The Founder of Patiala State." *Punjab Past and Present: Essays in Honour of Dr. Ganda Singh,* ed. N. Gerald Barrier and Harbans Singh. Patiala: Punjabi University, 1976, pp. 150-60.

————. "Landed Rights in Medieval Punjab." *Journal of Regional History* 4 (1983), 43-55.

————. "The Maharaja Orders: A Study of 462 Paowanas." *Journal of Regional History* 2 (1981), 106-28.

————. "Polity, Economy and Urbanization in the Upper Bari Doab (1700-1947)." *Studies in Urban History,* ed. J.S. Grewal and Indu Banga. Amritsar: Guru Nanak Dev University, pp. 192-205.

————. "The Ruling Class in the Kingdom of Lahore." *Journal of Regional History* 3 (1982), 15-24.

————. "The Sikh Polity During the Eighteenth Century." *Proceedings, Punjab History Conference*, Patiala: 1982, pp. 105-10.

————. "Sikh Revenue Administration: The Framework." *Studies in Local and Regional History*. Amritsar: Guru Nanak Dev University, 1974, pp. 55-85.

————. "State Formation Under Sikh Rule." *Journal of Regional History*, 1 (1980), 15-35.

Bhagat Singh. "Giani Gian Singh." *Proceedings, Punjab History Conference*, 1975, pp. 180-94.

Gauba, A. "Amritsar in the 1840s." *Journal of Regional History* 1 (1980), 36-50.

Grewal, J.S.   "Historical Geography of the Punjab", *Journal of Regional History* 1 (1980), 1-14.

————. "Literary Evidence: The Case of Hir Waris." *Journal of Regional History* 4 (1983), 1-6.

————. "The Prem Sumarg: A Theory of Sikh Social Order." *Proceedings, Punjab History Conference*, Patiala: 1965, pp. 100-11.

————. "Ramdaspur to Amritsar: From a Town to a City." *Studies in Urban History*, ed. J.S. Grewal and Indu Banga. Amritsar: Guru Nanak Dev University, pp. 115-22.

————. "The World of Waris." *Social Transformation and Creative Imagination*, ed. Sudhir Chandra. New Delhi: Allied Publishers, pp. 107-25.

Grewal, Reeta. "Polity, Economy and Urbanization." *Journal of Regional History* 4 (1983), 56-72.

Gupta, Jugal Kishore. "Maharaja Ranjit Singh: Commercial Relations with Seth Mirza Mal Podda of Chura." *Proceedings Punjab History Conference*, Patiala: 1982, pp. 128-32.

Habib, Irfan.   "The Social Distribution of Landed Property in Pre-British India (A Historical Survey)," *Indian Society: Historical Probings, In Memory of D.D. Kosambi*, ed. R.S. Sharma and Vivekanand Jha. New Delhi: People's Publishing House, 1974, pp. 264-316.

Hans, Surjit. "Polity Before and After the Annexation of the Punjab." *Punjab Journal of Politics* 9:1 (1985), 49-66.

————. "The Gurbilas in the Early Nineteenth Century." *Journal of Regional History* 2 (1981), 43-56.

Johal, Daljinder Singh. "Evidence on Religion in Punjabi Literature: Late 18th and Early 19th Century." *Journal of Regional History* 5 (1984), 27-39.

————. "Heroic Literature in Punjabi (1800-1850)." *Journal of Regional History* 2 (1981), 57-84.

————. "Literary Evidence on Social Institutions during the Sikh Rule." *Proceedings Punjab History Conference*, PatialaL 1982, pp. 162-70.

————. "Literary Evidence on Social Structure in the Punjab (1750-1850)." *Journal of Regional History*, 1 (1980), 51-69.

————. "Punjabi Literature: Late 18th - Early 19th Century." *Journal of Regional History* 4 (1983), 20-42.

Kohli, Sita Ram. "Land Revenue Administration under Maharaja Ranjit Singh." *Journal of Punjab Historical Studies* 7 (1918), 74-90.

Leech, R. "Report on the Commerce of Multan." *Indian Government Papers*, Section 3, pp. 79-88.

Manhinder. "European Travellers to the Punjab." *Journal of Regional History*, 5 (1984), 41-67.

Ramgarhia, Sunder Singh. "Annals of the Ramgarhia Sardars." *Panjab Past and Present* 8:2 (1974), 115-43.

Ramusack, Barbara N. "Punjab States: Maharajas and Gurdwaras: Patiala and the Sikh Community." *People, Princes and Paramount Power: Society and Politics in the Indian Princely States.* Delhi: Oxford University Press, 1978, pp. 170-204.

Rodgers, C.J. "On the Coins of the Sikhs." *Journal of the Asiatic Society of Bengal,* 1:1 (1881), 71-93.

Roseberry, J. Royal III. "Place and Wealth and Power, Elite Group Rivalries as a Decisive Factor in the Conquest oif Multan 1848-49." *Panjab Past and Present,* 19:2 (1985), 401-21.

Sachdeva, Veena. "Administration Under the Bhangi Chiefs." *Proceedings Punjab History Conference,* Patiala: 1981, pp. 94-104.

———. "Jagirdari System in the Punjab." *Journal of Regional History* 5 (1984), 1-13.

———. "The Non-Sikh Chiefs of the Punjab Plains and Maharaja Ranjit Singh." *Journal of Regional History* 2 (1981), 1-11.

Sharma, Radha. "State Policy and Agrarian Classes in the Punjab." *Journal of Regional History* 5 (1984), 15-25.

———. "The Peasant-Proprietors in the Core Region of the Dominions of Maharaja Ranjit Singh." *Journal of Regional History* 2 (1981), 21-34.

Sulakhan Singh. "Udasi Beliefs and Practices." *Journal of Regional History* 4 (1983), 73-98.

———. "Udasi Establishments Under Sikh Rule." *Journal of Regional History* 1 (1980), 70-87.

———. "The Udasis in the Early Nineteenth Century." *Journal of Regional History* 2 (1981), 35-42.

Wadhwa, Asha. "Vaishnava Establishments in the Punjab." *Journal of Regional History* 3 (1982), 25-32.

4. Colonial Period (1849 to 1947)

Books

Adhikari, G. *Sikh Homeland through Hindu-Muslim Sikh Unity.* Bombay: People's Publishing House, 1944.

Ahluwalia, M.L. *Sant Nihal Singh, Alias Bhai Maharaj Singh, A Saint Revolutionary of the 19th Century Punjab.* Patiala: Punjabi University, 1972.

Ahluwalia, M.S.; and Kirpal Singh. *The Punjab's Pioneer Freedom Fighters.* Bombay: Orient Longmans, 1963.

Amar Singh. *Memorandum of the Central Akali Dal.* Lahore: West End Press, 1946.

Attar Singh, ed. *Bhai Vir Singh: Life, Times and Works.* Chandigarh: Panjab University, 1973.

Attar Singh (Sardar, Chief of Bhadaur), *Sakhee Book.* Benares: The Medical Hall Press, 1873.

Banerjee, Himadri. *Agrarian Society of the Punjab (1849-1901.* New Delhi: Manohar, 1982.

Barrier, N. Gerald. *Banned Controversial Literature and Political Control in British India 1907-1947.* New Delhi: Manohar, 1976.

———. *Punjab History in Printed British Documents.* Columbia, Missouri: University of Missouri Press, 1969.

———. *The Punjab Alienation of Land Bill of 1900.* Monograph and Occasional Papers Series, no. 2. Durham: Duke University Program in Comparative Studies on Southern Asia, 1966.

———. *The Punjab in Nineteenth Century Tracts.* East Lansing: Asia Studies Center, Michigan State University, 1969.

———. *The Sikhs and Their Literature (A Guide to Tracts, Books and Periodicals 1849-1919).* Delhi: Manohar Book Service, 1970.

Barrier, N. Gerald; and Paul Wallace. *The Punjab Press, 1880-1905*. East Lansing: Asia Studies Center, 1970.

Beaumont, Roger. *Sword of the Raj: The British Army in India 1747-1947*. Indianapolis: Bobbs-Merrill, 1977.

Brecher, Michael. *Nehru: A Political Biography*. London: Oxford University Press, reprint 1969. First published 1959.

Calvert, H. *The Wealth and Welfare of the Punjab: Being Some Studies in Punjab Rural Economics*. Lahore, 1922.

Chaddha, T.R. *A Study of the Communist Movement in the Punjab*. Ghaziabad: Jyoti Brakashan, 1954.

Chandra, Bipin. *Nationalism and Colonialism in Modern India*. New Delhi: Orient Longmans, 1979.

————. *The Rise and Growth of Economic Nationalism*. New Delhi: People's Publishing House, 1966.

Clark, Robert. *A Brief Account of Thirty Years of Missionary Work of the Church Missionary Society in the Punjab and Sindh, 1852 to 1882*. Lahore: Albert Press, 1883.

Collins, Larry; and Dominique Lapierre. *Mountbatten and the Partition of India, March 22–August 15, 1947*, vol. 1. New Delhi: Vikas Publishing, 1982.

Congress Punjab Inquiry Report 1919-1920. Bombay: Karnatak Printing Press, 1920.

Darling, Malcolm Lyall. *Apprentice to Power: India 1904-1908*. London, 1966.

————. *At Freedom's Door*. London, 1949.

————. (Rusticus Loquitur, pseud.). *The Old Light and the New in the Punjab Village*. Oxford: Oxford University Press, 1930.

————. *The Punjab Peasant in Prosperity and Debt*. London: Oxford University Press, 1928.

———— (Rusticus Loquitur, pseud.). *Wisdom and Waste in the Punjab Village*. London: Oxford University Press, 1934.

Datta, V.N. *Jallianwalla Bagh*. Ludhiana: Lyall Book Depot, 1969.

Davis, Emmet. *Press and Politics in British Western Punjab 1836-1947*. Delhi: Academic Publications, 1983.

Deol, G.S. *Shahid Ajit Singh*. Patiala: Punjabi Unviersity, 1973.

————. *Shahid Bhagat Singh*. Patiala: Punjabi University, 1973.

Desai, A.R. *Social Background of Indian Nationalism*. Bombay: Popular Book Depot, 1954.

Deva Singh. *Colonisation in the Rachna Doab*. Lahore: Punjab Government Record Office, 1929.

Douis, James. *The Punjab, North Western Province and Kashmir*. Cambridge: University Press, 1916.

Draper, Alfred. *Amritsar: The Massacre That Ended the Raj*. Delhi: Macmillan India Limited, 1981.

Dungen, P.H.M. Van den. *The Punjab Tradition*. London: George Allen and Unwin Ltd., 1972.

Durlab Singh. *Sikh Leadership*. Delhi: Sikh Literature Distributors, 1950.

————. *The Valiant Fighter: A Biographical Study of Master Tara Singh*. Lahore.

Elsmie, G.R. *Thirty-Five Years in the Punjab 1858-1893*. Edinburgh, 1908.

Fauja Singh. *Eminent Freedom Fighters of Punjab*. Patiala: Punjabi University, 1972.

————. *Kuka Movement: An Important Phase in Punjab's Role in India's Struggle for Freedom*. Delhi: Motilal Banarsidass, 1965.

————, ed. *Who's Who: Punjab Freedom Fighters*. Patiala: Punjabi University, 1972.

Fox, Richard G. *Lions of the Punjab: Culture in the Making*. Berkeley: University of California Press, 1985.

Ganda Singh, ed. "Bhagat Lakshman Singh: An Autobiography." Ms. in Private Collection of Ganda Singh, Patiala.

————, ed. *Some Confidential Papers of the Akali Movement.* Amritsar: Shiromani Gurdwara Prabandhak Committee, 1965.

Ganda Singh and L.S. Giani. *The Idea of the Sikh State.* Lahore: Lahore Bookshop, 1946.

Gajrani, S. *Peasant Movement in Punjab.* Patiala: Madaan Publishers, 1986.

————. *Peasants and Prices: Agrarian Unrest in the East Punjab States 1920-48.* Patiala: Madaan Publishers, 1986.

Grewal, J.S.; and H.K. Puri. *Letters of Udham Singh.* Amritsar: Guru Nanak Dev University, 1974.

Griffin, Lepel; and C.F. Massy. *Chiefs and Families of Note in the Punjab.* Lahore: Government Printing, 1909.

————. *Appendix: Revised Pedigree-Tables of the Families Mentioned in the Revised Edition of Chiefs and Families of Note in the Punjab.* Lahore: Government Printing, 1940.

Gulab Singh. *Under the Shadow of Gallows.* Delhi: Rup Chand, 2nd ed., 1964.

Gulati, Kailash Chander. *The Akalis: Past and Present.* New Delhi: Ashajanak Publications, 1974.

Gurjit Singh, Baba. *Voyage of Komagata Maru or India's Slavery Abroad.* Ptd.

Guru Nanak Dev Mission. *Sikhism and the Nirankari Movement.* Patiala, Punjab: the author, n.d.

Gustafason, W. Eric; and Kenneth W. Jones. *Sources on Punjab History.*   Delhi: Manohar Book Service, 1975.

Handa, R.L. *A History of the Development of the Judiciary in the Punjab, 1846.* Lahore: Punjab Government Record Office, 1927.

Hardy, P. *The Muslims of British India.* Cambridge: Cambridge University Press, 1972.

Husain, A. *Fazl-i-Husain: A Political Biography.* Bombay: Orient Longmans, 1946.

Ibbetson, Denzil C. *Punjab Castes.* Patiala: Punjab Languages Department, reprint. First published in the Report on the Census of the Panjab, 1883).

————. *Report on the Census of the Punjab of 1881.* Lahore: Government Printing, 1882.

Jalal, Ayesha. *The Sole Spokesman: Jinnah, the Muslim League and the Demand for Pakistan.* Cambridge: Cambridge University Press, 1985.

Johnston, Hugh. *The Voyage of the Komagata Maru: The Sikh Challenge to Canada's Colour Bar.* Delhi: Oxford University Press, 1979.

Jones, Kenneth W. *Arya Dharm: Hindu Consciousness in 19th Century Punjab.* Berkeley: University of California Press, 1976.

Josh, Bhagwan. *Communist Movement in Punjab (1926-47).* Delhi: Anupama Publications, 1979.

Josh, Sohan Singh. *Hindustan Gadar Party: A Short History.* New Delhi: People's Publishing House, 1977.

Joshi, Vijaya Chandra, ed. *Lala Lajpat Rai: Writing and Speeches,* 2 vols.   Delhi: University Publishers, 1966.

Kalia, Barkat Ram. *A History of the Development of the Police in the Punjab 1849-1905.* Lahore: Punjab Government Records Office, 1929.

Khullar, K.K. *Shaheed Bhagat Singh.* New Delhi: Hem Publishers Pvt. Ltd., 1981.

Khushwant Singh. *A History of the Sikhs, 1839-1974,* vol. 2. Princeton: Princeton University Press, 1966; reprint Delhi: Oxford University Press, 1977.

Kirpal Singh. *Sardar Sham Singh Attariwala.* Patiala: Punjabi University, 1969.

————. *The Partition of the Punjab.* Patiala: Punjabi University, 1972.

[Kukas.] *Parliamentary Paper No. 356 on the Kuka Outbreak* (reply to an address in the House of Commons, July 22, 1872).

Kurin, Richard. "Sect Formation and Definition in the Indian Context: The Sikh Case." M.A. thesis, Anthropology, University of Chicago, 1974.

Lavan, Spencer. *The Ahmadiyah Movement: A History and Perspective.* New Delhi: Manohar Book Service, 1974.

Leigh, M.S. *The Panjab and the War.* Lahore: Government Printing, 1922.

Leitner, G.W. *Indigenous Education in the Punjab Since Annexation and in 1882.* Patiala: Punjab Languages Department, reprint 1970.

Login, E. Dalhousie. *Lady Login's Recollections: Couert Life and Camp Life 1820-1904.* Patiala: Punjab Languages Department, reprint 1970.

Loquitur, Rusticus (pseud.). Cf. Malcolm L. Darling.

Macauliffe, M.; H.H. Wilson; Frederic Pincott; John Malcolm; and Sardar Kahan Singh. *The Sikh Religion: A Symposium.* Calcutta: Susil Gupta, 1958.

Macmunn, G. *The Armies of India, Gian.* Delhi, 1980. First published 1911.

Malik, Ikram Ali. *Punjab Muslim Press and the Muslim World 1888-1911.* Lahore: South Asian Institute, 1974.

Marenco, Ethne K. *The Transformation of Sikh Society.* New Delhi: Heritage Publishers, 1976.

Mathur, Y.B. *British Administration of Punjab (1849-75).* Delhi: Surjeet Book Depot.

Mehta, H.R. *A History of the Growth and Development of Western Education in the Punjab 1846-1884.* Patiala: Punjab Government Record Office, Monograph no. 5, Punjab Languages Department, reprint 1971. First published 1929.

Menon, V.P. *Transfer of Power in India.* New Delhi: Sangam Books, reprint 1979. First published 1957.

Mohan, Kamlesh. *Militant Nationalism in the Punjab 1919-1935.* New Delhi: Manohar Publication, 1988.

Mohinder Singh. *The Akali Movement.* Delhi: The Macmillan Company of India Limited, 1978.

————. *The Akali Struggle: A Retrospect.* New Delhi: Atlantic, 1988.

Moon, P. *Divide and Quit.* London: Chatto & Windus, 1961.

Nahar Singh. *Documents Relating to Bhai Maharaj Singh.* Ludhiana: The Sikh History Source Material Search Association, 1968.

Nath, Amar. *The Development of Local Self Government in the Punjab 1849-1900.* Lahore: Punjab Government Records Office, 1929.

Oberai, A.S.; and H.K. Manmohan Singh. *Causes and Consequences of Internal Migration: A Study in the Indian Punjab.* Delhi: Oxford University Press, 1983.

Oxen, Stephen. *The Sikhs and the Punjab Politics 1921-1947.* Vancouver: University of British Columbia, 1964.

Petrie, Sir David. *Developments in Sikh Politics (1900-1911),* Report, Chief Khalsa Diwan. Amritsar, 1911.

Prakash Singh. *Changing Social Structure in Rural Punjab.* New Delhi: Sterling Publishers, 1974.

Prior, L.F. Loveday. *Punjab Prelude.* London: John Murray, 1952.

Punjab Land Administration Acts and Rules Having the Force of Law Thereunder, vol. 1, Acts. Lahore: Government Printing, 1933.

Puri, Harish K. *Ghadar Movement: Ideology, Organisation and Strategy.* Amritsar: Guru Nanak Dev University, 1983.

Rai, Lajpat. *The Agony of the Punjab.* Madras: Tagore & Co., 1920.

————. *The Study of my Life by Lala Lajpat Rai: An Unknown Fragment,* ed. Joginder Singh Dhanki. New Delhi: Gitanjali Prakashan, 1978.

Rai, Satya M. *Legislative Politics and the Freedom Struggle in the Panjab 1897-1947.* New Delhi: Indian Council of Historical Research, 1984.

Raja, Ram. *The Jallianwala Bagh Massacre: A Premeditated Plan.* Chandigarh: Panjab University, 2nd ed., 1978.

Rose, H.A. *A Glossary of the Tribes and Castes of the Punjab and North-West Frontier Province*, 3 Vols. Patiala: Punjab Languages Department (reprint).

Rusticus Loquitur (pseud.) Cf. Malcolm L. Darling.

Sahni, Ruchi Ram. *Struggle for Freedom in Sikh Shrines*, ed. Ganda Singh. Amritsar: Sikh Itihas Research Board, Shiromani Gurdwara Prabandhak Committee, n.d.

Sarkar, Sumit. *Modern India 1885-1947*. Delhi: Macmillan India Limited, 1983.

Sen, S.P. *Dictionary of National Biography*, 4 Vols. Calcutta: Institute of Historical Studies, 1974.

Sethi, G.R. *Sikh Struggle for Gurdwara Reform*. Amritsar: Union Press, 1927.

Sexena, K.M.L. *The Military System of India*. New Delhi, Sterling, 1974.

Sharma, Sri Ram. *Panjab in Ferment*. Delhi: S. Chand & Co., 1971.

Spear, Percival. *India: A Modern History*. Ann Arbor: University of Michigan Press, 1972.

Sadhu Swarup Singh. *The Sikhs Demand Their Home Land*. Lahore: Sikh University Press, 1946.

Swinson, Arthur. *Six Minutes to Sunset*. London: Peter Davies, 1964.

Tandon, Prakash. *Punjabi Century*. New Delhi: Orient Paperbacks, 1961.

Teja Singh. *Gurdwara Reform Movement and the Sikh Awakening*. Jullundur: Desh Sewak Book Agency, 1922-23.

Teja Singh and Ganda Singh. *Gurdwara Reform Movement and Sikh Awakening*. Jullundur: Desh Bhagat Yadgar Committee, 1922.

Thakur, Gopal. *Bhagat Singh: The Man and His Ideas*. New Delhi: People's Publishing House, 1965.

Thorburn, S.S. *Musalmans and Money-lenders in the Punjab*. Delhi: Mittal Publications, 1983.

————. *The Punjab in Peace and War*. Patiala: Punjab Languages Department, reprint 1970. First published 1883.

Trevaskis, H.K. *Punjab of Today, An Economic Survey of the Punjab in Recent Years 1890-1925*, 2 vols. 1931.

————. *The Land of the Five Rivers: An Economic History of the Punjab from the Earliest Times to the Year of Grace 1890*. Oxford: Oxford University Press, 1928.

Tuteja, K.L. *Sikh Politics 1920-1940*. Kurukshetra: Vishal Publications, 1984.

Uprethy, P.R. *Religion and Politics in Punjab in the 1920's*. New Delhi: Sterling Publishers, 1980.

Walia, Ramesh. *Praja Mandal Movement in East Punjab States*. Patiala: Punjabi University, 1972.

Webster, John C.B. *The Nirankari Sikhs*. Delhi: The Macmillan Company of India Limited, 1979.

Yadav, Kripal C. *Elections in Punjab 1920-1947*. New Delhi: Manohar Publications, 1987.

Articles

Ahluwalia, M.L. "Maharaja Dalip Singh's Mission in Russia, 1887-1888." *Proceedings, Punjab History Conference*, Patiala, 1965, pp. 165-74.

Arora, A.C. "British Interference with Internal Administration of the Punjab States, 1895-1905," *Proceedings, Punjab History Conference*. Patiala, 1973, pp. 115-31.

————. "British Policy Regarding Appointments of Europeans in the Native States of the Punjab, 1858-1905," *Proceedings, Punjab History Conference*, Patiala, 1979, pp. 168-74.

————. "British Policy Regarding Famines in Punjab States 1858-1905." *Proceedings, Punjab History Conference*, Patiala, 1978, pp. 154-64.

————. "British Policy Regarding Railways in the Punjab States 1870-1900." *Proceedings, Punjab History Conference*, Patiala, 1982, pp. 249-59.

472   Bibliography

Bajaj, S.K. "Indianization of Indian Civil Service." *Panjab Past and Present* 5:1 (1971), 211-26.

Bajaj, Y.P.; and Sunil Jain. "Congress Politics 1900-1906, The Punjab Response." *Proceedings, Punjab History Conference*, Patiala, 1985, pp. 349-54.

Bajaj, Y.P.; and Naresh Inder Singh. "Congress Politics on the Eve of 1936-37 General Elections to the Punjab Legislative Assembly." *Proceedings, Punjab History Conference*, Patiala, 1985, pp. 426-31.

Bal, Sukhmani. "The Central Sikh League and the Non-Cooperation Movement." *Proceedings, Punjab History Conference*, Patiala, 1982, pp. 323-32.

Bal, S.S. "National Movement in the Punjab." *Punjab Journal of Politics* 9 (1985), 1-13.

Banerjee, Himadri. "Growth of Commercial Agriculture in the Punjab During the Second half of the Nineteenth Century." *Panjab Past and Present* 12:1 (1978), 221-56.

Barrier, N. Gerald. "The Arya Samaj and Congress Politics in the Punjab, 1849-1908." *Journal of Asian Studies* 26:3 (1967), 363-79.

———. "The British and Controversial Publications in Punjab." *Panjab Past and Present* 8:1 (1974), 32-60.

———. "The Formulation and Enactment of the Punjab Alienation of Land Bill." *The Indian Economic and Social History Review* 2:2 (1965), 145-65.

———. "Hindi, Urdu and Punjabi Tracts on Nineteenth Century Punjab." *Panjab Past and Present* 4:1 (1970), 156-87.

———. "How to Rule India: Two Documents on the I.C.S. and the Politics of Administration." *Panjab Past and Present* 5:2 (1971), 276-97.

———. "Mass Politics and the Punjab Congress in the Pre-Gandhian Era." *Panjab Past and Present* 9:1 (1975), 349-59.

———. "Muslim Politics in the Punjab 1870-1890." *Panjab Past and Present* 5:1 (1971), 84-127.

———. "The Punjab Disturbances of 1907: The Response of the British Government in India to Agrarian Unrest." *Modern Asian Studies* 1:4 (1967), 353-83.

———. "The Punjab Government and Communal Politics, 1870-1908." *Journal of Asian Studies* 27 (1968), 523-40.

Baxter, Craig, ed. "The 1937 Election and the Sikandar-Jinnah Pact." *Panjab Past and Present* 10:2 (1976), 356-85.

Bhagat Singh. "Bhai Vir Singh's Interest in the Punjab History." *Panjab Past and Present* 6:2 (1972), 297-302.

"Bhai Ram Singh Kooka." *Panjab Past and Present* 7 (1968), 142-43.

"Bhai Vir Singh and His Associates as Seen by British Indian Police in 1911" (extracts from Secret C.I.D. Memorandum on Recent Developments in Sikh Politics by D. Petrie, Assistant Director, Criminal Intelligence, Government of India). *Panjab Past and Present* 6:2 (1972), 337-42.

Bhatia, Shyamala. "Military Recruitment and Revival of Sikhism." *Proceedings, Punjab History Conference*, Patiala, 1982, pp. 294-97.

Billings, Martin H.; and Arjan Singh. "Labour and Green Revolution: An Experience in Punjab." *Economic and Political Weekly*, Review of Agriculture, v. 4A, 221-24.

Brown, Emily C. "The Ideology of Har Dayal." *Political Dynamics of Punjab*, ed. Paul Wallace and Surendra Chopra. Amritsar: Guru Nanak Dev University, 1981, pp. 345-69.

Caveeshar, Sardul Singh. "The Sikgh Kanya Mahavidyala." *Panjab Past and Present*, 7:1 (1973), 97-109.

"Census of the Punjab, 1868, and of India, 1871-72 (extracts)." *Panjab Past and Present* 8:2 (1974), 346-50.

Chawla, A.S.; and B.S. Bhatia. "Banking History of Punjab." *Proceedings, Punjab History Conference*, Patiala, 1985, pp. 359-63.

Choudhry, Devendra K. "Initiative, Entrepreneurship and Occupational Mobility in an Indian Caste: A Study of the Khatris of Punjab (1881-1914)." *Proceedings, Punjab History Conference*, Patiala, 1982, pp. 272-77.

Choudhary, Prem. "Sir Chhotu Ram: An Evaluation of His Role in Punjab Politics, 1924-45." *Journal of Politics* 7:2 (1983), 126-50.

Chief Khalsa Diwan—Fifty Years of Service (1902-1951).} *Panjab Past and Present* 7:1 (1973), 59-67.

Churchill, Edward D., Jr. "The Muslim Societies of the Punjab, 1860-1890." *Panjab Past and Present* 8:1 (1974), 69-91.

———. "The Muhammadan Educational Conference and the Aligarh Movement, 1886-1900." *Panjab Past and Present* 8:2 (1974), 266-81.

Datar, Kiran. "Traders as Administrators: The Khatris of Punjab." *Proceedings, Punjab History Conference*, Patiala, 1985, pp. 320-28.

Darshan Singh. "Western Research on Punjab Economy." *Journal of Regional History* 3 (1982), 17-22.

Dewan, D.L. "Degeneration of Village Communal Character in the Jullundur Doab under the British Rule." *Proceedings, Punjab History Conference*, Patiala, 1970, pp. 208-19.

Dhami, M.S. "Praja Mandal Movement in East Punjab States: Notes on the Elite Political Culture." *Punjab Journal of Politics* 7:2 (1983), 99-112.

Dhanki, Joginder Singh. "Sardar Ajit Singh, an Early Indian Revolutionary." *Proceedings, Punjab History Conference*, Patiala, 1982, pp. 275-84.

Dolers Domin. "Some Aspects of British Land Policy in Punjab After its Annexation in 1849." *Panjab Past and Present* 8:1 (1974), 12-31.

Farquhar, J.N. "The Arya Samaj." *Panjab Past and Present* 8:1 (1973), 206-32.

Fauja Singh. "Akalis and the Indian National Congress (1920-1947)." *Panjab Past and Present* 15:2 (1981), 453-70.

———. "The Effects of Land Transfers on Rural Economy During the Latter Half of the 19th Century." *Proceedings, Punjab History Conference*, Patiala, 1979, pp. 258-69.

Fox, Richard G. "Urban Class and Communal Consciousness in Colonial Punjab: The Genesis of India's Intermediate Regime." *Modern Asian Studies* 18 (1984), 459-89.

G.B. Singh. "Sikh Relics in Eastern Bengal." *Panjab Past and Present* 9:1 (1975), 82-102.

Gajrani, S.D. "Peasant Movement in Some Parts of the Punjab (1931-1939)." *Proceedings, Punjab History Conference*, Patiala, 1985, pp. 421-25.

Ganda Singh. "Bhai Vir Singh and the History of the Sikhs." *Panjab Past and Present* 6:2 (1972), 477-81.

———. "Sikh Educational Conference." *Panjab Past and Present* 8:1 (1973), 68-70.

———. "Was the Kuka (Namdhari) Movement a Rebellion Against the British Government?" *Panjab Past and Present* 8:2 (1974), 326-41.

———. "The Indian Mutiny of 1857 and the Sikhs." *Panjab Past and Present* 12:1 (1978), 103-20.

Gauba, Anand. "Demographic Study of a British India City: Amritsar (1849-1947)." *Studies in Urban History*, ed. J.S. Grewal and Indu Banga. Amritsar: Guru Nanak Dev University, pp. 135-49.

Ghose, L.N. "Sindar Attar Singh of Bhadaur." *Panjab Past and Present* 6:1 (1972), 227-30.

Gill, Kamaljit. "Role of the Vernacular Press during the Gurdwara Reform Movement." *Proceedings, Indian History Congress*, Burdwan, 1983, pp. 463-70.

Gobinder Singh. "The Gurdwara Reform Movement: A Study in Participation and Appropriation." *Punjab Journal of Politics* 7:2 (1983), 63-76.

Grewal, J.S. "Business Communities of Punjab." *Business Communities of India*, ed. Dwijendra Tripathi. New Delhi: Manohar Publications, 1984, pp. 209-24.

————. "The Emergence of Punjabi Drama: A Cultural Response to Colonial Rule." *Journal of Regional History* 5 (1984), 115-55.

Grewal, Reeta. "The Pattern of Urbanization in the Punjab under Colonial Rule." *Journal of Regional History* 5 (1984), 69-81.

————. "Urban Pattern in the Punjab (1881-1931)." *Proceedings, Indian History Congress*, Burdwan, 1983, pp. 513-21.

Gulcharan Singh. "The Labanas." *Quarterly Review of Historical Studies* 14 (1979-80), 51-55.

Gurdarshan Singh. "Origin and Development of the Singh Sabha Movement." *Panjab Past and Present* 7 (1973), 45-58.

Gurdial Singh. "Sardar Thakur Singh Sindhanwalia." *Panjab Past and Present* 2:2 (1968), 364-65.

Gurmukh Nihal Singh. "Sikhism in the Age of Science and Socialism." *Panjab Past and Present* 11:1 (1977), 142-48.

Gursharan Singh. "Maharaja Bhupinder Singh and the Akali Movement." *Proceedings, Punjab History Conference*, Patiala, 1982, pp. 341-53.

Harbans Singh. "The Bakapur Diwan and Babu Teja Singh of Bhadaur." *Panjab Past and Present* 9:2 (1985), 322-32.

————. "Beginnings of Modern Sikh Education." *Panjab Past and Present* 8:1 (1974), 127-44.

————. "Bhai Vir Singh—His Life and Works." *Panjab Past and Present* 6:2 (1972), 291-96.

————. "Origins of the Singh Sabha." *Punjab Past and Present: Essays in Honour of Dr. Ganda Singh*, ed. N. Gerald Barrier and Harbans Singh. Patiala: Punjabi University, 1976, pp. 273-82.

————. "Polemic over the Electrification of Golden Temple." *Panjab Past and Present* 14:1 (1980), 59-62.

Hardy, P. "Wahabis in the Punjab." *Panjab Past and Present* 15:2 (1981), 428-32.

"Jawahar Lal Nehru, K. Santanam and A.T. Gidwani's Arrest at Jaito (Nabha)" (extracts from *An Autobiography of Jawahar Lal Nehru*). *Panjab Past and Present* 8:1 (1974), 183-204.

Joginder Singh. "Socio-Political Beliefs and Attitudes of the Sikh Elites in the Last Quarter of Nineteenth Century." *Panjab Journal of Politics* 7:2 (1983), 1-11.

————. "The Foundings of Singh Sabha" (summary). *Proceedings, Punjab History Conference*, Patiala, 1979, p. 190.

Jones, Kenneth W. "Communalism in the Punjab, the Arya Samaj Contribution." *Journal of Asian Studies* 28:1 (1968).

————. "Ham-Hindu Nahin: The Arya Sikh Relations, 1877-1905." *Panjab Past and Present* 11:2 (1977), 330-55.

————. "The Bengali Elite in Post-Annexation Punjab: An Example of Inter-Regional Influence in Nineteenth Century India." *The Punjab Past and Present: Essays in Honour of Dr. Ganda Singh*, ed. N.G. Barrier and Harbans Singh. Patiala: Punjabi University, 1976, pp. 243-51.

Josh, Bhagwan Singh. "Organization and Politicisation of the Peasantry in the Punjab 1925-45." *Punjab Journal of Politics* 2 (1978), 64-95.

Kabul Singh. "Lahore Session of the Congress, 1900." *Proceedings, Punjab History Conference*, Patiala, 1985, pp. 345-48.

Kansal, M.R. "Educational Services in Punjab." *Proceedings, Punjab History Conference*, Patiala, 1982, pp. 225-33.

Kanal, S.P. "The Dev Samaj." *Panjab Past and Present* 7:1 (1973), 233-44.

Kashmir Singh. "Managing Committee of Khalsa College, Amritsar: Its Relations with British Government." *Proceedings, Punjab History Conference*, Patiala, 1983, pp. 221-24.

Kerr, Ian J. "The British and the Administration of the Golden Temple in 1859." *Panjab Past and Present* 10:2 (1976), 306-21.

———. "Urbanization and Colonial Rule in 19th Century India: Lahore and Amritsar, 1849-1881." *Panjab Past and Present* 14:1 (1980), 210-24.

Khosla, G.S. "The Growth of the Railway System in the Punjab." *Punjab Past and Present: Essays in Honour of Dr. Ganda Singh*, ed. N. Gerald Barrier and Harbans Singh. Patiala: Punjabi University, 1976, pp. 283-90.

Kirpal Singh. "A Hindu-Muslim Riot in the Punjab: 1881." *Proceedings, Punjab History Conference*, Patiala, 1971, pp. 288-95.

———. "Bhai Vir Singh's Portrayal in History." *Proceedings, Punjab History Conference*, Patiala, 1972, pp. 233-45.

———. "Genesis of the Partition of the Punjab 1947." *Panjab Past and Present* 5:2 (1971), 391-408.

———. "Historical Significance of Sundari, Bijay Singh and Satwant Kaur." *Panjab Past and Present* 6:2 (1972), 313-20.

Komma. "The Sikh Situation in the Punjab (1907-1922)." *Panjab Past and Present* 12:2 (1978), 425-38.

Kumar, Davinder. "The Brahmo Samaj." *Panjab Past and Present* 7 (1973), 200-5.

Lavan, Spencer. "Communalism in the Punjab: The Ahmadiyah Versus the Arya Samaj During the Lifetime of Mirza Ghulam Ahmad." *Panjab Past and Present* 5:2 (1971), 320-42.

———. "Polemics and Conflict in Ahmadiyah History: The Missionaries, the Ulama and the British." *Punjab Past and Present: Essays in Honour of Dr. Ganda Singh*, ed. N. Gerald Barrier and Harbans Singh. Patiala: Punjabi University, 1976, pp. 454-74.

Madan, J.C. "Police Reforms in the Punjab, 1849-1862." *Proceedings, Punjab History Conference*, Patiala, 1973, pp, 105-14.

———. "The Growth and the Development of Police Administration in the Punjab 1862-1902." *Proceedings, Punjab History Conference*, Patiala, 1975, pp. 168-79.

Mahajan, Ganeshi. "Punjabi Participation in the Indian National Conference 1885-1905." *Proceedings, Punjab History Conference*, Patiala, 1980, pp. 209-18.

Mahajan, Sucheta. "Anti British Agitation in 1907 Punjab." *Proceedings, Punjab History Conference*, Patiala, 1982, pp. 290-309.

Malik, Ikram Ali. "Muslim Anjumans in the Punjab." *Journal of Regional History* 5 (1984), 97-113.

Mathur, L.P. "University of the Punjab Lahore, Its Origin and Objects." *Panjab Past and Present* 2:1 (1968), 137-41.

Maynard, John. "The Sikh Problem in the Punjab 1920-23." *Panjab Past and Present* 15:1 (1977), 129-41.

McLeod, W.H. "Ahluwalias and Ramgarhias: Two Sikh Castes." *South Asia: Journal of South Asian Studies* 4 (1974), 78-90.

———. "The Kukas: A Millenarian Sect of the Punjab." *Panjab Past and Present* 14:1 (1977), 129-41.

Mishra, Satish Chandra. "Commercialization, Peasant Differentiation and Merchant Capital in Late Nineteenth Century Bombay and Punjab." *Journal of Peasant Studies* 10 (1982), 9.

Mohan, Kamlesh. "The Babbar Akalis: An Experience in Terrorism." *Journal of Regional History* 1 (1980), 142-74.

Mohinder Singh. "Akali Involvement in the Nabha Affair." *Panjab Past and Present* 5:1 (1971), 368-90.

Mukherjee, Mridula. "Communists and Peasants in Punjab: A Focus on the Muzara Movement in Patiala: 1937-53." *Studies in History* 3:1-2 (1981), 401-46.

———. "Peasant Movement in a Princely State: Patiala 1937-48." *Proceedings, Punjab History Conference*, Patiala, 1982, pp. 310-22.

Narang, Surjit Singh. "Chief Khalsa Diwan: An Analytical Study of Its Perspectives." *Punjab Journal of Politics* 5:1 (1981), 67-81.

———. ."Elections and the Shiromani Dal: A Socio-Psychological Approach." *Punjab Journal of Politics* 5:2 (1981), 19-31.

———. "Sikh Aristocracy and Punjab Politics (1849-1900)." *Punjab Journal of Politics* 9:2 (1985), 55-71.

Nazer Singh. "Act XX of 1863 and the Management of Socio-Religious Institutions Under the British: A Case Study (Tomb of Maharaja Ranjit Singh and Kharak Singh)." *Proceedings, Punjab History Conference*, Patiala, 1982, pp. 196-207.

———. "An Introduction to Some Newspapers in the Punjab (1850-80)." *Proceedings, Punjab History Conference*, Patiala, 1985, pp. 271-76.

Nazer Singh and Palwinder Kaur, "Panchayati Raj Leadership in Punjab: A Case Study." *Punjab Journal of Politics* 1:1 (1977), 187-206.

Puri, Harish K. "Ghadar Movement: An Experiment in New Patterns of Socialisation." *Journal of Regional History* (1980), 120-41.

———. "Revolutionary Organization: A Study of the Ghadr Movement." *Social Scientist* 9 (1980), 54-55.

———. "Singh Sabha and Ghadar Movement: Contending Political Orientations." *Punjab Journal of Politics* 7:2 (1983), 12-26.

Puri, Nina. "Sardar Dyal Singh Majithia 1849-1898." *Proceedings, Punjab History Conference*, Patiala, 1982, pp. 242-48.

Qureshi, Waheed. "A Survey of Punjabi Language and Literature." *Panjab Past and Present* 14:1 (1980), 98-120.

Ramusack, Barbara N. "The Incident at Nabha." *Journal of Asian Studies* 28:3 (1969).

———. "The Patiala and East Punjab States Union (PEPSU)." *The Encyclopaedia of Sikhism*, forthcoming.

Roseberry, J. Royal, II. "Multan During the 1857 Revolt." *Panjab Past and Present* 12:2 (1978), 315-33.

Roy, P.C. "Gurcharan Singh's Mission in Central Asia." *Panjab Past and Present* 8:1 (1974), 205-10.

Setton-Kaur, W.S. "Administration of Lord Dalhousie." *The Panjab Past and Present* 12:2 (1978), 288-309.

Sharma, Harish Chander. "A Note on Urban Artisans of the British Punjab." *Proceedings, Indian History Congress*, Bardwan, 1983, pp. 506-12.

———. "Artisans in the Punjab (11849-1947): Occupational Change and New Social Revlations." *Journal of Regional History* 1 (1980), 107-19.

———. "Politicization of the Punjabi Chamars: Early 20th Century." *Journal of Regional History* 4 (1983), 128-38.

Sharma, Inderjit. "Punjab Famines and the British Policy in the 19th Century." *Proceedings, Punjab History Conference*, Patiala, 1979, pp. 128-89.

Smith, Wilfred Cantwell. "The Ahmadiyah Movement." *Panjab Past and Present* 7:1 (1973), 250-54.

Sohal, S.S. "British Policies and Moneylenders in the Agrarian Economy of the Punjab." *Journal of Regional History* 4 (1983), 115-27.

———. "Middle Classes and Communalism in the Colonial Punjab." *Journal of Regional History* 5 (1984), 83-95.

———. "Moneylenders and the Agrarian Economy of the Punjab," *Panjab Past and Present* 19:2 (1983), 420-37.

———. "Political Economy of Communalism: Late Nineteenth Century Colonial Punjab." *Man and Development* 9:2 (1987), 12-20.

————. "Professional Middle Classes in the Punjab." *Journal of Regional History* 3 (1982), 72-86.

Sukhwant Singh. "Agricultural Development in the Punjab." *Journal of Regional History* 1 (1980), 88-106.

————. "Agricultural Transformation in the Punjab, 1849-1947." *Proceedings, Punjab History Conference*, Punjabi University, Patiala, 1982, pp. 204-12.

————. "Agricultural Technology in the Punjab Under the British Rule." *Proceedings, Indian History Congress*, Kurukshetra University, Kurukshetra, 1982, pp. 479-86.

————. "Effects of the British Agrarian Policies in the Punjab During the Late Nineteenth Century." *Proceedings, Punjab History Conference*, Patiala, 1985, pp. 320-39.

————. "Government Policy and Agricultural Development in Punjab, 1849-1901." *Proceedings, Punjab History Conference*, Patiala, 1979, pp. 156-66.

————. "The Peasant Proprietor in the Punjab, 1849-1901." *Proceedings, Punjab History Conference*, Patiala 1980, pp. 185-96.

Surinder Kaur. "British Policy Towards High Education in Punjab" (summary). *Proceedings, Punjab History Conference*, Patiala, 1985, p. 280.

Talwar, R.S. "Anand Marriage Act." *Panjab Past and Present* 2:2 (1968), 400-10.

Teja Singh. "Khalsa College Amritsar." *Panjab Past and Present* 7:1 (1973), 76-83.

————. "The Singh Sabha Movement." *Panjab Past and Present*, 7:1 (1973), 31-44.

"The Akali Dal and Shiromani Gurdwara Parbandhak Committee 1921-22" (A Confidential Memorandum prepared by the Punjab Government in the Criminal Investigation Department [Political] for the information of the Government of India and of the Secretary of State for India in London). *Panjab Past and Present* 1:2 (1967), 252-311.

Thomas, Antony. "Communalism and the Unionist Minister in Punjab 1937-39." *Proceedings, Punjab History Conference*, Patiala, 1982, pp. 354-62.

Tuteja, K.L. "Sikhs and the Congress: 1930-1940." *Political Dynamics of Punjab*, ed. Paul Wallace and Surendra Chopra. Amritsar: Guru Nanak Dev University, 1981, pp. 95-112.

Uberoi, J.P. Singh. "On Being Unshorn," in *Sikhism and Indian Society* (Transactions of the IIAS, 4). Simla: Indian Institute of Advanced Study, 1967, pp. 87-100.

Uprety, Prem. "The Sikh Disturbances of 1922-25: The Response of British Government in India to a Religious Unrest." *Panjab Past and Present* 12:2 (1978), 359-369.

Virinder Singh. "Working of Dyarchy in Punjab: A Case Study of Political Parties and Groups in the Legislative Council (1921-37)" (summary). *Proceedings, Punjab History Conference*, Patiala, 1985, p. 399.

Wallace, Paul. "Communalism, Factionalism and National Integration in the Pre-Independence Punjab." *Punjab Past and Present: Essays in Honour of Dr. Ganda Singh*, ed. N. Gerald Barrier and Harbans Singh. Patiala: Punjabi University, 1978, pp. 389-406.

Wasti, S. Razi. "The Punjab Colonization Act and Sir Mian Muhemmad Shafi." *Panjab Past and Present* 10:1 (1976), 120-290.

Webster, John C.B. "Competing Systems of Western Education in the Punjab, 1858-1882," *Proceedings, Punjab History Conference*, 1966, pp. 187-92.

5. India since Independence (1947 to the Present)

Books

Aggarwal, Partap C. *The Green Revolutiona and Rural Labour.* New Delhi: Shri Ram Centre for Industrial Relations and Human Resources, 1973.

Ajit Singh Sarhadi. *Punjabi Suba: The Story of the Struggle.* Delhi: K.C. Kapur & Sons, 1970.

Amrik Singh, ed. *Punjab in Indian Politics: Issues and Trends.* Delhi: Ajanta Publications, 1985.

Attar Singh. *Secularism and the Sikh Faith.* Amritsar: Guru Nanak Dev University, 1973.

Brass, Paul R. *Language, Religion and Politics in North India.* London: Cambridge University Press, 1974.

———. *Factional Politics in an Indian State.* Berkeley: University of California Press, 1965.

Chakravarti, Uma; and Nandita Haksar. *The Delhi Riots: Three Days in the Life of a Nation.* New Delhi: Lancer International, 1987.

Chopra, V.D.; R.K. Mishra; and Nirmal Singh, eds. *Agony of the Punjab.* New Delhi: Patriot Publishers, 1984.

Das, S.R. *Commission Report on Grievances of the Sikhs,* Delhi: Government of India Press, 1962.

Dhami, M.S. *Minority Leaders Image of the Indian Political System: An Exploratory Study of the Attitudes of Akali Leaders.* New Delhi: Sterling Publishers Pvt. Ltd., 1975.

Dhar, A.G. *Misery of the Punjab.* New Delhi, 1963.

Discrimination Against the Sikh Backward Castes. Amritsar: S.G.P.C., 1953.

Gargi, Balwant. *Nirankari Baba.* Delhi: Thomson Press (India) Ltd., 1973.

Gobinder Singh. *Religion and Politics in the Punjab.* New Delhi: Deep & Deep Publications, 1986.

Gur Rattan Pal Singh. *The Illustrated History of the Sikhs (1947-78.* Chandigarh: published by the author, 1979.

Gurnam Singh. *A Unilingual Punjabi State and the Sikh Unrest.* New Delhi: Super Press, 1960.

Harbans Singh. *Khalistan Sarabpakhi Adhiyan.* New Delhi: Punjabi Writers Co-operative, 1982.

Hukam Singh. *The Sikh Problem and Its Solution.* Amritsar: Shiromani Akali Dal, 1951.

Iqbal Singh. *Punjab under Siege: A Critical Analysis.* New York, London, Toronto, Sydney: Allen, McMillan and Enderson, 1986.

Jeffre, Robin. *What's Happening to India? Punjab Ednhic Conflict, Mrs Gandhi's Death and the Test for Federalism.* London: Macmillan, 1986.

Joshi, Chand. *Bhindranwala Myth and Reality.* New Delhi: Vikas Publishing House, 1984.

Juergensmeyer, Mark. *Religion as Social Vision: The Movement against Untouchability in 20th Century Punjab.* Berkeley: University of California Press, 1982. Revised version titled *Religious Rebels in the Punjab: The Social Vision of Untouchables.* Delhi: Ajanta Press, 1988.

Kapur, Anup Chand. *The Punjab Crisis: An Analytical Study.* New Delhi: S. Chand & Company Ltd., 1985.

Kapur, Rajiv A. *Sikh Separatism: The Politics of the Faith.* London: Allen & Unwin, 1986.

Keller, Stephen L. *Uprooting and Social Change: The Role of Refugees in Development.* Delhi: Manohar Book Service, 1975.
Maini, Darshan Singh. *Cry, the Beloved Punjab.* Siddharth, 1986.
Narang, A.S. *Storm Over the Sutlej: The Akali Politics.* New Delhi: Gitanjali Publishing House, 1983.
Nayar, Baldev Raj. *Minority Politics in the Punjab.* Princeton: Princeton University Press, 1966.
Nayar, Kuldip; and Khushwant Singh. *Tragedy of Punjab: Operation Bluestar and After.* New Delhi: Vision Books, 1984.
Kumar, Parmod; Manmohan Sharma, Atul Sood and Ashwani Handa. *Punjab Crisis: Context and Trends.* Chandigarh: Centre for Research in Rural and Industrial Development, 1984.
Pettigrew, Joyce. *Robber Noblemen: A Study of the Political System of the Sikh Jats.* Boston: Routledge and Kegal Paul, 1975.
Rai, Satya M. *Punjab Since Partition.* Delhi: Durga Publications, 1986.
Randhawa, M.S. *Green Revolution.* Ludhiana: Punjab Agricultural University, 1947.
Saberwal, Satish. *Mobile Men: Limits to Social Change in Urban Punjab.* New Delhi: Vikas, 1976.
Shiromani Akali Dal. *Facts About Punjabi Suba Agitation: A Collection of Memorandums Presented Before the Das Commission.* Amritsar, Shiromani Gurdwara Prabandhak Committee, 1965.
White Paper on the Punjab Agitation. New Delhi: Government of India, July 10, 1948.

Articles

Attar Singh. "Punjabi Literature." In Srinivas Ayenger, ed., *Indian Literature since Independence.* New Delhi: Sahitya Akademi, 1973.
————. "Secularism and Modern Punjabi Literature." In Arabinda Poddar, ed., *Indian Literature.* Simla: Indian Institute of Advanced Studies, 1972.
Aulakh, H.S.; and P.S. Raikhy. "Linkages Between Agriculture and Industry and Punjab Economy." *PSE Economic Analyst* 2 (1980), 154-62.
Azad, N.S. "Agrarian Production Relations in Punjab." *Mainstream* 19:35 (1981), 15-20.
Ballard, Roger. "The Bitter Dream of the Sikhs." *New Society* 68, No. 1126, June, 1984, pp. 464-66.
Barrier, N. Gerald. "The Role of Ideology and Institution-Building in Modern Sikhism." In Mark Juergensmeyer and N. Gerald Barrier, eds., *Sikh Studies: Comparative Perspectives on a Changing Tradition.* Berkeley: Graduate Theological Union, 1979, pp. 41-51.
Bhalla, G.S. "Political Economy of Indian Development Since Independence." *On Aspects of Planned Development: Discussion Series 2,* Centre for Research in Rural and Industrial Development. Chandigarh, 1985, pp. 67-80.
Bipan, Chandra. "Communalism—The Way Out." *Many Faces of Communalism,* ed. Khushwant Singh and Bipan Chandra. Chandigarh: Centre for Research in Rural and Industrial Development, 1985, pp. 41-73.
Bombwall, K.R. "The Nation State and Ethno-Nationalism: A Note on the Akali Demand for a Self-Determined Political Status for Sikhs." *Punjab Journal of Politics* 9:2 (1983), 166-83.
Chhabra, Aseem. "Thousands of Sikhs Protest." *India Today,* 14:37 (1984), pp. 1, 14.
Dang, Satya Pal. "The Punjabi Suba Movement." *Punjab Journal of Politics* 7:2 (1983), 151-65.
Dhami, M.S. "Caste, Class and Politics in the Rural Punjab: A Study of Two Villages in Sangrur District." *Political Dynamics of Punjab,* ed. Paul Wallace and Surendra Chopra. Amritsar: Guru Nanak Dev University, 1981, pp. 292-317.

————. "Changing Support Base of the Congress Party in Punjab, 1952-80." *Punjab Journal of Politics* 8:1 (1984), 65-97.

————. "Communalism in Punjab: A Socio-Historical Analysis." *Punjab Journal of Politics* 9:1 (1985), 1-30.

————. "March-1977, Parliamentary Elections in the Punjab State." *Punjab Journal of Politics*, vol. I, No. 1, 1977, 123-86.

————. "The Punjab Assembly Elections, June 1977: A Micro-Study of Three Assembly Constituencies." *Punjab Journal of Politics*, vol. 2, 1978, 1-45.

Jagjit Singh. "Egalitarian Society," in *The Sikh Revolution.* New Delhi: Vikas, 1981, pp. 115-35.

Jasmail Singh. "Socio-Economic Background of the CPI Leadership in Punjab." *Political Dynamics of Punjab*, ed. Paul Wallace and Surendra Chopra. Amritsar: Guru Nanak Dev University, 1981, 333-44.

Juergensmeyer, Mark. "Political Origins of a Punjabi Lower Caste Religion." *Political Dynamics of Punjab*, ed. Paul Wallace and Surendra Chopra. Amritsar: Guru Nanak Dev University, 1981, 209-230.

Khushwant Singh. "Dangers of Communalism in Contemporary India." *Many Faces of Communalism*, ed. Khushwant Singh and Bipan Chandra. Chandigarh: Centre for Research in Rural and Industrial Development, 1985, pp. 23-40.

————. "Separatist Tendencies in Sikh History." *Many Faces of Communalism*, ed. Khushwant Singh and Bipan Chandra. Chandigarh: Centre for Research in Rural and Industrial Development, 1985, pp. 1-22.

Mehra, Arun. "Akali-Janata Coalition: An Analysis." *Punjab Journal of Politics* 9:1 (1985), 67-85.

Mishra, R.K. "Army Action in Punjab." *Agony of Punjab.* New Delhi: Patriot Publishers, 1984, pp. 13-38.

Mustafa, Seema. "Bhindranwala: Not for Peace but for Power." *Secular Democracy*, 1983, pp. 12-14.

Narang, A.S. "Punjab Elections: Retrospect and Prospect." *Punjab Journal of Politics* 9:2 (1985), 99-110.

Narula, D.D. "Socio-Economic Development of Punjab: Problems and Prospects." *On Aspects of Manned Development: Discussion Series 2.* Chandigarh: Centre for Research in Rural and Industrial Development, 1985, pp. 81-96.

Nirmal Singh. "Sikh Fundamentalism and Ist Support Structure." *Agony of Punjab.* New Delhi: Patriot Publishers, 1984, pp. 133-51.

Petrie, D. "Secret CID Memorandum on Recent Development in Sikh Police, 1971." *Panjab Past and Present* 4:2 (1970), 302-79.

Puri, Harish K. "Akali Politics: Emerging Compulsions." *Political Dynamics of Punjab*, ed. Paul Wallace and Surendra Chopra. Amritsar: Guru Nanak Dev University, 1981, pp. 33-41.

Rai, Satya M. "The Structure of Regional Politics in the Punjab." *Political Dynamics of the Punjab*, ed. Paul Wallace and Surendra Chopra. Amritsar: Guru Nanak Dev University, 1981, pp. 113-31.

Sen, B. "Capital Inputs in Punjab Agriculture, 1950-51 to 1964-65." *Economic and Political Weekly, Review of Agriculture* 5A (1970), 163-68.

Sharma, A.C. "Employment and Wage Structure of a Farm Labourer in Punjab." *Manpower Journal* 2:4 (1967), 75-90.

Sharma, T.R. "Political Implications of the Green Revolution." *Political Dynamics of Punjab*, ed. Paul Wallace and Surendra Chopra. Amritsar: Guru Nanak Dev University, 1981, pp. 265-91.

Tuteja, K.L. "The Sikhs and the Nehru Report." *Political Dynamics of Punjab*, ed. Paul Wallace and Surendra Chopra. Amritsar: Guru Nanak Dev University, 1981, pp. 82-94.

Wallace, Paul. "Religious and Secular Politics in Punjab: The Sikh Dilemma in Competing Political Systems." *Political Dynamics of Punjab*, ed. Paul Wallace and Surendra Chopra. Amritsar: Guru Nanak Dev University, 1981, pp. 1-32.

Wallace, Paul. "The Sikhs as a 'Minority' in a Sikh Majority State." *Asian Survey*, 26: 3 (1986), 363-77.

6. The Sikh Diaspora

Books

Anwar, M. *Between Two Cultures: A Study of Relationships between Generations in the Asian Community*. London: Community Relations Commission, 1976.

Aurora, Gurdip Singh. "Indian Workers in England: A Socio-historical Survey of Indian Workers in England." M.Sc. thesis, Economics, University of London, 1960.

——. *The New Frontiersmen: A Sociological Study of Indian Immigrants in the U.K.* Bombay: Popular Prakashan, 1967.

Barrier, N. Gerald; and Verne A. Dusenbery, eds. *The Sikh Diaspora: Migration and the Experience beyond Punjab*. Delhi: Manohar, forthcoming 1988.

Beetham, D. *Transport and Turbans: A Comparative Study in Local Politics*. Oxford: Oxford University Press, for the Institute of Race Relations, 1970.

Bhachu, P.K. "Marriage and Dowry Among Selected East African Sikh Families in the United Kingdom." Ph.D. dissertation, University of London, 1981.

——. *Twice Migrants: East African Sikh Settlers in Britain*. London: Tavistock, 1985.

Bradfield, Helen. "The East Indians of Yuba City: A Study in Acculturation." M.A. thesis, Anthropology, Sacramento State College, 1971.

Brass, Paul. *Ethnic Groups and the State*. London: Croom Helm, 1985.

Brooks, D. *Race and Labour in London Transport*. London: Oxford University Press, for the Institute of Race Relations, 1975.

Buchignani, Norman; and Doreen Indra, with Ram Srivast[a]va. *Continuous Journey: A Social History of South Asians in Canada*. Toronto: McClelland and Stewart, 1985.

Chadney, James G. "The Vancouver Sikhs: An Ethnic Community in Canada." Ph.D. dissertation, Michigan State University, 1976.

——. *The Sikhs of Vancouver*. New York: AMS Press, 1984.

Chakravorty, Robindra. "The Sikhs of El Centro: A Study in Social Integration." Ph.D. dissertation, Anthropology, University of Minnesota, 1968.

Das, Rajani Kant. *Hindustanee Workers on the Pacific Coast*. Berlin: Walter de Gruyter, 1923.

Deol, G.S. *The Role of the Ghadar Party in the National Movement*. Delhi: Sterling.

Desai, Rashmi. *Indian Immigrants in Britain*. London: Oxford University Press, 1963.

DeWitt, John, Jr. *Indian Workers Associations in Britain*. London: Oxford University Press, 1969.

Dusenbery, Verne A. "'Why Would Anybody Join...?' A Study of Recruitment and the Healthy, Happy, Holy Organization." B.A. honors essay, Anthropology, Stanford University, 1973.

——. "Sikh Persons and Practices: A Comparative Ethnosociology." Ph.D. dissertation, University of Chicago.

——. "Straight→freak→yogi→Sikh: A 'Search for Meaning' in Contemporary American Culture." M.A. thesis, Anthropology, University of Chicago, 1975.

Gupta, Santosh P. "The Acculturation of Asians in Central Pennsylvania." Ph.D. dissertation, Pennsylvania State University, 1969.

Helweg, Arthur W. "A Punjab Community in an English Town: A Study in Migrant Adaptation." Ph.D. dissertation, Michigan State University, 1977.

————. *Sikhs in England: The Development of a Migrant Community*. Delhi: Oxford University Press, 2nd ed., 1986.

Jacoby, Harold S. "East Indians in the United States: The First Half-Century." Unpublished manuscript, 1978.

James, A. *Sikh Children in Britain*. London: Oxford University Press for the Institute of Race Relations, 1976.

Johnston, Hugh. *The Voyage of the Komagata Maru: The Sikh Challenge to Canada's Colour Bar*. Delhi: Oxford University Press, 1979.

Kalra, S.S. *Daughters of Traditions: Adolescent Sikh Girls and Their Accommodation to Life in British Society*. Birmingham: Diane Balbir Publications, 1980.

Keupper, W.B.; G.L. Lackey; and E.N. Swinerton. *Ugandan Asians in Britain: Forced Migration and Social Absorption*. London: Croom Helm, 1975.

King, W.L. Mackenzie. *Report of the Royal Commission into the Methods by which Oriental Labourers Have Been Induced to Come to Canada*. Ottawa: King's Printer, 1908.

Klug, Francesca; and Paul Gordon. *Different Worlds: Racism and Discrimination in Britain*. London: The Runnymede Trust, 1983.

LaBrack, Bruce. *The Sikhs of Northern California: 1904-1986*. New York: American Migration Series Press, forthcoming 1988.

Lal, B. "East Indians in British Columbia (1904-1914): A Historical Study in Growth and Integration." M.A. thesis, History, University of British Columbia, 1976.

de Lepervanche, Marie M. "A Boat Load of Grandfathers." Ph.D. dissertation, University of Sydney, 1974.

————. *Indians in a White Australia: An Account of Race, Class and Indian Immigration to Eastern Australia*. Sydney, London, Boston: George Allen & Unwin, 1984.

Mathur, Laxman P. *Indian Revolutionary Movement in the United States of America*. Delhi: S. Chand, 1970.

McLeod, W.H. *Punjabis in New Zealand*. Amritsar: Guru Nanak Dev University, 1986.

Melendy, Brett H. *Asians in America*. New York: Hippocrene Books, 1981.

Remmer, Malcolm. *Race and Industrial Conflict: A Study on a Group of Midland Foundries*. London, 1972.

Rose, E.J.B. *Colour and Citizenship: A Report on British Race Relations*. London: Oxford University Press, 1969.

Scanlon, T. Joseph. *The Sikhs of Vancouver: A Case Study of the Role of the Media in Ethnic Relations*. Carleton University: Mimeo, 1975.

Tatla, Darshan Singh; and Eleanor M. Nesbitt. *Sikhs in Britain: An Annotated Bibliography*. Coventry: Center for Research in Ethnic Relations, University of Warwick, 1987.

Thompson, M. "A Study of Generational Difference in Immigrant Groups, with Particular Reference to the Sikhs." M.Phil. thesis, University of London, 1970.

Tinker, Hugh. *The Banyan Tree: Overseas Emigrants from India, Pakistan and Bangladesh*. New York, Delhi, Karachi: Oxford University Press, 1977.

————. *A New System of Slavery: The Export of Indian Labour Overseas 1830-1920*. Bombay: Oxford University Press, 1974.

Trilochan Singh. *Sikhism and Tantric Yoga* [on 3HO]. Ludhiana: the author, 1977.

Wood, Ann. "East Indians in California: A Study of Their Organizations, 1900-1947." M.A. thesis, Anthropology, University of Wisconsin, 1966.

Articles

Ballard, C. "Arranged Marriages in the British Context." *New Community* 6 (1978), 181-96.

_____. "Family Organization among the Sikhs in Britain." *New Community* 2 (1973), 12-24.

_____. "Family Organization in a Wider Context: Jullunder and Mirpur Compared." *New Community* 11 (1983), 1-2.

Ballard, Roger; and Catherine Ballard. "The Development of South Asian Settlements in Britain." *Between Two Cultures; Migrants and Minorities in Britain*, ed. James L. Watson. Oxford: Basil Blackwell, 1977, pp. 21-56.

Barber, John. "A Troubled Community." *Macleans* XCI:X (1986), pp. 19-23.

Barrier, N. Gerald. "Sikh Immigrants and Their Homeland: The Transmission of Information, Resources, and Values in the Early Twentieth Century." *The Sikh Diaspora: Migration and the Experience beyond Punjab*, ed. N. Gerald Barrier and Verne A. Dusenbery. Delhi: Manohar, forthcoming.

Bhachu, P.K. "East African Sikhs in Britain: Experienced Settlers with Traditionalistic Values." *Immigrants and Minorities* 3:3 (1984), 276-95.

Bharati, Agehananda. "Indian Expatriates in North America and Neo-Hindu Movements." *The Communication of Ideas*, ed. J.S. Yadava and V. Gautam. New Delhi: Concept Publishing, 1980, pp. 245-55.

Brooks, D.; and K. Singh. "Ethnic Commitment Versus Structural Reality: South Asian Immigrant Workers in Britain." *New Community* 7:1 (1978).

Bryce-Laporte, Roy Simon, ed. *Sourcebook on the New Immigration: Implications for the United States and the International Community.* New Brunswick, N.J.: Transaction Books, 1980.

Buchignani, Norman. "Accommodation, Adaptation and Policy: Aspects of the South Asian Experience in Canada." *Proceedings of the Second Colloquium on Asians in Canada*, ed. K.V. Ujimoto and G. Hirabayashi. Guelph: University of Guelph, 1978, pp. 30-71.

_____. "Accommodation, Adaptation and Policy: Dimensions of the South Asian Experience in Canada." *Visible Minorities and Multiculturalism: Asians in Canada.* Toronto: Butterworths, 1980, pp. 121-50.

_____. "Anthropological Approaches to the Study of Ethnicity." *Occasional Papers on Ethnic and Immigration Studies* 82-13. Toronto: Multicultural History Society of Ontario, 1982.

_____. "Canadian-Sikh Ethnic and Race Relations, and Their Implications for the Study of the Sikh Diaspora." *The Sikh Diaspora: Migration and the Experience beyond Punjab*, ed. N. Gerald Barrier and Verne A. Dusenbery. Delhi: Manohar, forthcoming.

_____. "Ethnic Phenomena and Contemporary Social Theory: Their Implications for Archaeology." *Conference Proceedings, 18th Annual Chacmool Conference.* Calgary: University of Calgary, 1988.

_____. "A Review of the Historical and Sociological Literature on East Indians in Canada." *Canadian Ethnic Studies* 9:1 (1977), 86-108.

_____. "The Social and Self Identities of Fijian Indians in Vancouver." *Urban Anthropology* 9:1 (1981), 75-98.

_____. "Social Science Research on South Asians and Canada: Retrospect and Prospect." *The South Asian Diaspora in Canada: Six Essays*, ed. Milton Israel. Toronto: Multicultural History Society of Ontario and Center for South Asian Studies, University of Toronto, 1987, pp. 113-41.

_____. "South Asians and the Ethnic Mosaic: An Overview." *Canadian Ethnic Studies* 11:1 (1980), 48-68.

Buchignani, Norman; and Doreen Indra.   "Inter-Group Conflict and Community Solidarity: Sikhs and South Asian Fijians in Vancouver." *Canadian Journal of Anthropology* 1:2 (1981)[a], 149-57.

————. "The Political Organization of South Asians in Canada." *Ethnicity, Power and Politics in Canada*, ed. J. Dahlie and T. Fernando. Toronto: Methuen, 1981, pp. 202-32.

Buddle, V. "Sikhism at 'A' Level." *Sikh Bulletin* 3 (1987).

Chan, Sucheng. "Overseas Sikhs in the Context of International Migrations." *Sikh Studies: Comparative Perspectives on a Changing Tradition*, ed. Mark Juergensmeyer and N. Gerald Barrier. Berkeley: Graduate Theological Union, 1979, pp. 191-206.

Chandran, Ramesh. "United Kingdom: Tackling Terrorism." *India Today* 10:22 (1985), pp.28-29.

Chaudri, J.J.M. "The Emigration of Sikh Jats from Punjab to England." *Social Science Research Council Report*, ed. A. Mayer. Project HR 331-1, 1973. London.

Cole, W. Owen. "Sikhism at GCSE." {Sikh Bulletin} 3 (1987).

Dadabhay, Yusuf. "Circuitous Assimilation among Rural Hindustanis in California." *Social Forces* 33 (1954), 138-41.

Dahya, B. "Pakistanis in Britain, Transients or Settlers?" *Race* 14:3 (1973).

Dusenbery, Verne A. "Canadian Ideology and Public Policy: The Impact on Vancouver Sikh Ethnic and Religious Adaptation." *Canadian Ethnic Studies* 8:3 (1981), 101-20.

————. "On the Moral Sensitivities of Sikhs in North America." *Consuming Passions: Emotion and Feeling in Indian Culture*, ed. O. Lynch and P. Kolenda. Forthcoming.

————. "The Sikh Person, the Khalsa Panth and Western Sikh Converts." *Religious Movements and Social Identity: Conflict and Change in India*, ed. Bardwell L. Smith. Leiden: E.J. Brill, forthcoming.

Fleuret, Anne K. "Incorporation into Networks among Sikhs in Los Angeles." *Urban Anthropology* 3 (1974), 27-33.

Ghuman, P. "Bhattra Sikhs in Cardiff: Family and Kinship Organization." *New Community* 8:3 (1980).

Gmelch, George. "Return Migration." *Annual Review of Anthropology* (Palo Alto) 9 (1980).

Gonzales, Juan L.   "Asian Indian Immigration Patterns: The Origins of the Sikh Community in California." *International Migration Review* 20:1 (1986), 40-54.

Graves, Nancy B.; and Theodore Graves. "Return Migration." *Annual Review of Anthropology* (Palo Alto) 3 (1974).

Grewal, Balwant Singh. "Growth of the Sikh Missionary Society UK and Development of Its Work." *Sikh Bulletin* no. 3 (1987).

Helweg, Arthur W. "Emigrant Remittances: Their Nature and Impact on a Punjabi Village." *New Community* 10:3 (1983).

————. "Indians in England: A Study of the Interactional Relationships of Sending, Receiving and Migrant Societies." *Studies in Migration: Internal and International Migration in India*, ed. M.S.A. Rao. Delhi: Manohar, 1986.

————. "India's Sikhs: Problems and Prospects." *Journal of Contemporary Asia* 17:2 (1987), 140-59.

————. "Punjabi Farmers: Twenty Years in England." *India International Center Quarterly* 5:1 (1978).

————. "Why Leave India for America? A Case Study Approach to Understanding Migrant Behaviour." *International Migration* 25:2 (1987), 165-78.

Hiro, Dilip. "Indians in Britain." *India International Center Quarterly* 6:3 (1979).

Indra, Doreen. "The Portrayal of South Asians in the Vancouver Press, 1905-76." *Ethnic and Racial Studies* 2:2 (1979), 164-87.

Jacoby, Harold S. "More Thind Against than Sinning." *The Pacific Historian* 11:4 (1958), 1-2, 8.

Joy, Annamma. "Work and Ethnicity: The Case of the Sikhs in the Okanagan Valley of British Columbia." *South Asians in the Canadian Mosaic*, ed. Rabindra Kanungo. Montreal: Kala Bharati, 1984.

Juergensmeyer, Mark. "The Ghadar Syndrome: Immigrant Sikhs and Nationalist Pride." *Sikh Studies: Comparative Perspectives on a Changing Tradition*, ed. M. Juergensmeyer and N.G. Barrier. Berkeley: Graduate Theological Union, 1979, pp. 173-90.

Khalsa, Shakti Parwha Kaur; and Gurubanda Singh Khalsa. "The Siri Singh Sahib." *The Man Called the Siri Singh Sahib*, ed. S.P.K. Khalsa and S.K.K. Khalsa. Los Angeles: Sikh Dharma, 1979, pp. 117-31.

LaBrack, Bruce. "The New Patrons: Sikhs Overseas." *The Sikh Diaspora: Migration and the Experience beyond Punjab*, ed. N. Gerald Barrier and Verne A. Dusenbery. New Delhi: Manohar, forthcoming 1988.

――――. "The Reconstitution of Sikh Society in Rural California." *Overseas Indians: A Study in Adaptation*, ed. G. Kurian and R. Srivastava. New Delhi: Vikas, 1983, pp. 215-40.

――――. "Sants and the Sant Tradition in the Context of Overseas Indian Communities." *The Sants: A Devotional Tradition of India*, ed. Karine Schomer and W.H. McLeod. Berkeley: Berkeley Religious Studies Series, Graduate Theological Union; and New Delhi: Motilal Banarsidass, 1987.

――――. "Sikhs Real and Ideal: A Discussion of Text and Context in the Description of Overseas Sikh Communities." *Sikh Studies: Comparative Perspectives on a Changing Tradition*, ed. Mark Juergensmeyer and N. Gerald Barrier. Berkeley: Graduate Theological Union, 1979, pp. 127-42.

――――. LaBrack, Bruce; and Karen Leonard. "Conflict and Compatibility in Punjabi-Mexican Immigrant Families in Rural California, 1915-1965." *Journal of Marriage and the Family* 64:3 (1984), 527-37.

Leonard, Karen. "Marriage and Family Life Among Early Asian Indian Immigrants." *Population Review* 25:1-2 (1982), 67-75.

――――. "Immigrant Punjabis in Early 20th-Century California: A Life History." *Intersections: Studies in Ethnicity, Gender, and Inequality*, ed. Sucheng Chan. Forthcoming.

――――. "A Note on Given Names and Chicano Intermarriage." *La Red* 52 (1982), 4-5.

――――. "The Pahkar Singh Murders: A Punjabi Response to California's Alien Land Law." *Amerasia Journal* 11:1 (1984), 75-87.

――――. "Pioneer Voices from California: Reflections on Race, Religion, and Ethnicity." *The Sikh Diaspora: Migration and the Experience beyond Punjab*, ed. N. Gerald Barrier and Verne A. Dusenbery. Delhi: Manohar, forthcoming 1988.

――――. "Punjabi Farmers and California's Alien Land Law." *Agricultural History* 59:4 (1985), 549-62.

Lesser, Jeff H. "Always 'Outsiders': Asians, Naturalization, and the Supreme Court." *Amerasia* 12:1 (1985-86), 83-100.

McLeod, W.H. "The Punjabi Community in New Zealand." *Indians in New Zealand: Studies in a Sub-culture*, ed. Kapil N. Tiwari. Wellington: Price Milburn, 1980.

――――. "The Sikhs of the South Pacific." *Sikh Studies: Comparative Perspectives on a Changing Tradition*, ed. Mark Juergensmeyer and N. Gerald Barrier. Berkeley: Graduate Theological Union, 1979, pp. 143-58.

Oberai, A.S.; and H.K. Manmohan Singh. "Migration, Remittances and Rural Development: Findings of a Case Study in the Indian Punjab." *International Labour Review* 109:2 (1980).

O'Connell, Joseph T. "Sikh Studies and Studies of Sikhs in Canada." *Studies in Sikhism and Comparative Religion* 5 (October 1986), 154-73.

Papademetrios, Demetrios G. "Effects of Emigration on the Sending Countries: Some Thoughts and Parallels between the American and Recent European Experiences with 'Labor Emigration.'" *Sourcebook on the New Immigration: Implications for the United States and the International Community*, ed. Roy Simon Bryce-Laporte. New Brunswick, N.J.: Transaction Books, 1980.

Porter, John. "Ethnic Pluralism in Canadian Perspective." *Ethnicity: Theory and Experience*, ed. Nathan Glazer and Daniel P. Moynihan. Cambridge, Mass.: Harvard University Press, 1975.

Premka Kaur, Sardarni. "Listen, O 'Patit' and Learn." *Gurdwara Gazette* 46:4 (1975), 4-13.

———. "Rejoinder." *The Sikh Review* 21 (232), (1973), 52-56.

Ray, Shantanu. "Militant Chief Admits Canada Ties." *Indian Abroad* 16:49 (1986), 1, 5.

Robinson, V. "Asians in Britain: A Study in Encapsulation and Marginality." *Geography and Ethnic Pluralism*, ed. C. Clarke, D. Ley and C. Peach. London: Allen and Unwin, 1972.

Uberoi, Narindar. "Sikh Women In Southall." *Race* 6:1 (1964), 34-40.

United States Senate, Immigration Commission. "Report of the Immigration Commission: Immigrants in Industries, Part 25: Japanese and Other Immigrant Races in the Pacific Coast and Rocky Mountain States." Washington, D.C.: Government Printing Office, 1911.

Vatuk, Sylvia; and Ved P. Vatuk. "Protest Songs of East Indians on the West Coast, U.S.A." *Thieves in My House: Four Studies in Indian Folklore of Protest and Change*, ed. Ved Vatuk. Benares: Vishwavidyalaya Prakashan, 1969, pp. 63-80.

Wenzel, Lawrence. "The Rural Punjabis of California: A Religio-Ethnic Group." *Phylon* 60:29 (1968), 245-56.

Wood, John R. "East Indians and Canada's New Immigration Policy." *Overseas Indians: A Study in Adaptation*, ed. G. Kurian and R. Srivastava. New Delhi: Vikas, 1983, pp. 3-29.

"Yogi Bhajan's Synthetic Sikhism: The Leader of 3HO Inspires Devotion and Hostility." *Time*, September 5, 1977, pp. 70-71.

Chronological Table

The Ten Sikh Gurus

		Birth	Guruship	Death
1.	Guru Nanak	1469	1469-1539	1539
2.	Guru Angad	1504	1539-1552	1552
3.	Guru Amardas	1479	1552-1574	1574
4.	Guru Ramdas	1534	1574-1581	1581
5.	Guru Arjan	1563	1581-1606	1606
6.	Guru Hargobind	1595	1606-1644	1644
7.	Guru Har Rai	1630	1644-1661	1661
8.	Guru Har Krishan	1656	1661-1664	1664
9.	Guru Tegh Bahadur	1621	1664-1675	1675
10.	Guru Gobind Singh	1666	1675-1708	1708

The Five Takhats

(seats of authority)

1.	Sri Akal Takhat	Amritsar, Punjab
2.	Takhat Sri Harimandir Ji	Patna, Bihar
3.	Takhat Sri Keshgarh Sahib	Anandpur, Punjab
4.	Takhat Sri Damdama Sahib	Talvandi Sabo Ki, Bhatinda, Punjab
5.	Takhat Sri Hazur Sahib	Nander, Maharashtra

Institutional and Individual Donors
to the Conference and Volume
on Sikh History and Religion in the Twentieth Century

Gursikh Sabha Canada
Ontario Khalsa Darbar
Sri Guru Singh Sabha

Kishori Allagh
Amrik Singh
Dr. Gurcharan Singh Attariwala
Gurmeze Singh Bains
Suresh Pal Singh Bhalla
Mrs. Nicket Bhasin
Savinder Singh Bhasin
Baljit Singh Chadha
Baljinder Chahal
Manoj Chaman
Inderpaul S. Chandhoke
Kuldeep Chhatwal
Daljit Singh
M.S. Dhaliwal
Surinder Dhaliwal
S.K. Dhanoya
Balbir S. Dhillon
Harjit S. Dhillon
Inderjit Singh Dhillon
Harbanse (Herb) S. Doman
Shami Dugal
David Fleet, M.P.P.
Baljit Gill
Hardial Singh Gill
Dr. Pam Gill
Gill International Travel
Gurdass (Gary) Singh
Jasdev S. Grewal
Dr. K.S. Grewal
Paul Grewal

Toni Ianno
Jasbir Kaur Singh
Gursaran Singh Jhandu
Brig. D.S. Jind
Ambi Kalra
Kamaljit Kang
N.S. Khalon
Dr. Kuldip Kular
Surinder Singh Latti
Lember Singh
Harvinder Luthra
Dr. Birinder Malhotra
Deshpal Malhotra
Gurdish S. Mangat
Mrs. S.K. Mangat
Mohinder Singh
Parminder S. Parma
Pavitar Singh
Raj Phalpher
Prabh Singh
Punjab Poultry Farms
Mr. and Mrs. Sham Singh Rai
Surjit and Mary S. Rajpal
Ajit Singh Sahota
Harjeet S. Sandhu
Baljinder Sangha
Sarbjit Singh
Bupinder S. Sarkaria
Ted Schwartz
Gurpas Sidhu (deceased)
Dr. Jagmeet Soin

Invited Speakers and Respondents

at the Conference "Sikh History and Religion in the Twentieth Century"
Toronto, February 13-15, 1987

Speakers

Prof. Amrik Singh
    Centre for Policy Research, New Delhi

Prof. Attar Singh
    Medieval Indian Literature, Panjab University, Chandigarh

Dr. Himadri Banerjee
    Reader, Department of History, Rabindra Bharati University, Calcutta

Prof. Indu Banga
    Department of History, Guru Nanak Dev University, Amritsar

Prof. N. Gerald Barrier
    Department of History, University of Missouri, Columbia, Missouri

Prof. Norman Buchignani
    Department of Anthropology, University of Lethbridge, Alberta

Dr. Owen Cole
    Head, Department of Religious Studies, West Sussex Institution of Higher
        Education, Chichester

Prof. J.S. Grewal
    Department of History, Guru Nanak Dev University, Amritsar
    and Indian Institute of Advanced Study, Simla

Prof. Hugh Johnston
    Department of History, Simon Fraser University, Burnaby, British
        Columbia

Prof. Mark Juergensmeyer
    Graduate Theological Union, Berkeley
    and Religious Studies Program, University of California, Berkeley

Prof. Ian J. Kerr
    Department of History, University of Manitoba, Winnipeg

Prof. Darshan Singh Maini
    Department of English, Punjabi University, Patiala

Prof. W.H. McLeod (paper read in his absence)
    Department of History, Otago University, Dunedin, New Zealand

Dr. Mohinder Singh
    Director, Guru Nanak Foundation, New Delhi

Prof. Harjot S. Oberoi
    Department of Asian Studies, University of British Columbia, Vancouver

Patwant Singh
   Editor, *Design*, New Delhi
Prof. Amarjit Singh Sethi
   Faculty of Administration, University of Ottawa
Prof. Paul Wallace
   Department of Political Science, University of Missouri, Columbia,
   Missouri

Respondents

Prof. Nanda Choudhry
   Department of Economics, University of Toronto
Prof. Arthur W. Helweg
   College of General Studies, Western Michigan University, Kalamazoo
Prof. Milton Israel
   Centre for South Asian Studies, University of Toronto
Prof. Bruce LaBrack
   Department of Sociology, University of the Pacific, Stockton, California
Mr. S. Gurinder Singh Mann
   Department of Religious Studies, Columbia University, New York, N.Y.
Clarence McMullen
   Director, Christian Institute of Sikh Studies, Batala, Punjab
Prof. Ronald Neufeldt
   Department of Religious Studies, University of Calgary, Alberta
Prof. Joseph T. O'Connell
   Department of Religious Studies, St. Michael's College, University of
   Toronto
Prof. Willard G. Oxtoby
   Department of Religious Studies, Trinity College, University of Toronto
Dr. Sunita Puri
   Lady Sriram College, Delhi
Prof. Arthur G. Rubinoff
   Department of Political Science, University of Toronto
Prof. B.S. Saini
   Department of Economics, Concordia University, Montreal
Prof. Christopher Shackle
   School of Oriental and African Studies, University of London
Prof. Avtar Singh
   Department of Philosophy, Punjabi University, Patiala
Ms. Jane Singh
   Center for South and Southeast Asia Studies, University of California,
   Berkeley
Dr. Jarnail Singh
   Government of Ontario, Toronto

Mr. Pashaura Singh
  Department of Religious Studies, University of Toronto
Prof. Wilfred Cantwell Smith
  (Harvard University, emeritus) Toronto
Prof. John Thursby
  Department of Religion, University of Florida, Gainesville, Florida
Prof. Douglas Verney
  Department of Political Science, York University, Toronto
Prof. Narendra K. Wagle
  Department of History, University of Toronto
Mr. William Warden
  Department of External Affairs, Government of Canada
  and Centre for International Education and Business, University of Calgary
Dr. John C.B. Webster
  Presbyterian Church, Waterford, Connecticut

Institutionally Affiliated Observers

General Jagjit Singh Aurora
  Member of Lok Sabha (Parliament), India
Mr. Prem Shankar Jha
  Editor, *Hindustan Times*, Delhi
Paul McCrossan
  Member of Parliament, Canada
Aideen Nicholson
  Member of Parliament, Canada
Mr. Gar Pardy
  Department of External Affairs, Government of Canada
Mr. Keith Richardson
  Office of the Secretary of State, Government of Canada
Virendra P. Singh
  Consul General of India, Toronto

At the request of the Department of External Affairs, Government of Canada, arrangements were made for the Minister of External Affairs, the Honourable Joe Clark, to meet with the participants in the conference for an exchange of views. Following the Friday afternoon session of the conference (February 14, 1987), many of the speakers, respondents and observers met with the Minister in University College. The main topic of discussion was the recently concluded extradition treaty between Canada and India.

Bio-bibliographical Notes
on Contributors and Editors

Amrik Singh

Visiting Professor, Centre for Policy Research, New Delhi, senior educationist and former Vice-Chancellor (Punjabi University, Patiala), has edited and contributed to a major volume of analysis and background of the recent Punjab-Centre crisis: *Punjab in Indian Politics: Issues and Trends* (Delhi: Ajanta, 1985). His other publications include: *Higher Learning in India,* with Philip Altbach (Delhi: Vikas, 1974) and *Asking for Trouble: What It Means to Be a Vice-Chancellor Today* (Delhi: Vikas, 1984).

Attar Singh

Professor, Sheikh Baba Farid Chair in Medieval Indian Literature, Panjab University (Chandigarh), has written voluminously (in Punjabi and English) on Punjabi language and literature. Among his English-language works are: *Secularism and Sikh Faith* (Amritsar: Guru Nanak Dev University, 1973); the edited volume *Bhai Vir Singh: Life, Times and Works*; and *History of Punjabi Literature* (New Delhi: Sahitya Akademi, forthcoming, to be translated into other Indian languages).

Himadri Banerjee

Reader in History, Rabindra Bharati University, Calcutta, specializes in economic history of the Punjab under British rule, Sikh history and Bengali perceptions of the Sikhs. His publications include *History of the Sikhs and Sikhism in Bengal* (New Delhi: Manohar, forthcoming), introductions to editions of S.S. Thorburn's works on the Punjab and numerous articles on Sikhs and the Punjab.

Indu Banga

Professor of History, Guru Nanak Dev University, Amritsar, has done extensive research in economic and political history of the Sikhs especially in the pre-colonial period, and also in the years just prior to Indian independence. Her publications include: *Agrarian System of the Sikhs* (New Delhi: Manohar, 1978); an edition and translation, jointly with J.S. Grewal, *Early Nineteenth Century Punjab* (from Ganesh Das, *Char Bhag i Panjab*; Amritsar: Guru Nanak Dev University); and "State Formation under Sikh Rule," *Journal of Regional History* 1 (1980).

N. Gerald Barrier

Professor of History, University of Missouri (Columbia), concentrates his research on the Punjab and on Sikh history, and directs the publishing firm South Asia Books. Among his publications are: *India and America: American Publications on India, 1930-1985* (Columbia, Missouri: South Asia Books, 1986); *The Sikh Diaspora: Migration and the Experience beyond Punjab,* eo-edited with Verne A. Dusenbery (New Delhi: Manohar, 1988); and *Banned: Political Control and Controversial Literature in British India, 1907-47* (Columbia: University of Missouri Press, 1975; Indian reprint, 1976).

Norman Buchignani

Associate Professor of Anthropology, University of Lethbridge, Alberta, is an expert in Canadian ethnic studies with specialization on South Asian immigrants in Canada. He is the author, with Doreen Indra and Ram Srivastava, of *Continuous Journey: A Social History of South Asians in Canada* (Toronto: McClelland and Stewart, 1985), of *Anthropological Approaches to Ethnicity* (Toronto: Multicultural History Society of Ontario, Occasional Paper 82-13, 1982), of "A Review of the Historical and Sociological Literature on East Indians in Canada," *Canadian Ethnic Studies* 9:1 (1977), and other articles.

Owen Cole

Head of Religious Studies, West Sussex Institution of Higher Education, Chichester, writes extensively on Sikh studies and religious education. His books include: *The Sikhs: Their Religious Beliefs and Practices*, written jointly with Piara Singh Sambhi (London: Routledge and Kegan Paul, 1976, 1986); *Sikhism and Its Indian Context* (London: Darton, Longman & Todd, 1983); and, jointly with Piara Singh Sambhi *A Dictionary of Sikhism* (London: Curzon Press, forthcoming).

Verne A. Dusenbery

teaches in the Department of Sociology and Anthropology, Carleton College, Northfield, Minnesota. He is the co-editor, with N. Gerald Barrier, of *The Sikh Diaspora: Migration and the Experience beyond Punjab* (Delhi: Manohar, forthcoming 1988), and author of articles including "Canadian Ideology and Public Policy: The Impact on Vancouver Sikh Ethnic and Religious Adaptation," *Canadian Ethnic Studies* 8:3 (1981), and "The Sikh Person, the Khalsa Panth and Western Sikh Converts," in Bardwell L. Smith, ed., *Religious Movements and Social Identity: Continuity and Change* (Leiden: E.J. Brill, forthcoming).

J.S. Grewal

Fellow of the Indian Institute of Advanced Study, Simla; formerly Professor and Head of History and Vice-Chancellor of Guru Nanak Dev University, Amritsar, and visiting professor of Sikh history and religion, University of Toronto, 1988; has conducted and directed extensive research in Sikh, Punjab and Mughal history. Among his books are: *The Sikhs of the Punjab* (Cambridge: Cambridge University Press, forthcoming), *Guru Nanak in History* (Chandigarh: Publications Bureau, Panjab University, 1969), and *The Reign of Maharaja Ranjit Singh: Structure of Power, Economy and Society* (Patiala: Punjabi University, 1981).

Surjit Hans

Professor and Head of History, Guru Nanak Dev University, Amritsar, is author of *A Reconstruction of Sikh History from Sikh Literature* (Jullundur: ABS Publications, forthcoming), *B-40 Janamsakhi Guru Baba Nanak Paintings* (Amritsar: Guru Nanak Dev University Press, 1987) and *Sikh Ki Karn?* (Amritsar: Balraj Sahni Yadgar, 1985).

Arthur W. Helweg

Professor of General Studies, Western Michigan University, Kalamazoo, does anthropological research regarding development in India and Pakistan and research on Indians in the diaspora, especially Sikhs in Britain. His publications include: *Sikhs in England: The Development of a Migrant Community* (Delhi: Oxford Universiy Press, 2nd ed. 1986); "India's Sikhs: Problems and Prospects," *Journal of Contemporary Asia* 17:2 (1987),and "Why Leave India for America? A Case Study Approach to Understanding Migrant Behaviour," *International Migration* 25:2 (1987).

Milton Israel

Associate Professor of History, and Director of the Centre for South Asian Studies, University of Toronto, also served as President and Resident Director of the Shastri Indo-Canadian Institute in New Delhi in 1980-81. He specializes in Indian history in the period of the British Raj. He has published *Pax Britannica* (London: Oliver and Boyd, 1968), and edited *National Unity: The South Asian Experience* (New Delhi: Promilla, 1983) and *The South Asian Diaspora in Canada: Six Essays* (Toronto: Multicultural History Society of Ontario, 1987), and co-edited with Narendra K. Wagle *Islamic Culture and Society: Essays in Honour of Professor Aziz Ahmad* (New Delhi: Manohar, 1983).

Hugh Johnston

Professor of History, Simon Fraser University, Burnaby, British Columbia, does research in Canadian immigration history and especially the history of Sikhs in Canada. He has authored, among other works, *The Voyage of the Komagata Maru: The Sikh Challenge to Canada's Colour Bar* (Delhi: Oxford University Press, 1979), *The East Indians in Canada* (Ottawa: Canadian Historical Association Ethnic Booklets, 1984) and "The Surveillance of Indian Nationalists in North America, 1908-19," *B.C. Studies*, forthcoming.

Mark Juergensmeyer

Professor of Ethics and the Phenomenology of Religions, Graduate Theological Union, Berkeley, and Co-ordinator, Religious Studies Program, University of Californi, Berkeley, has published widely in comparative religion and in religion and society in South Asia, and has organized Sikh studies conferences at Berkeley in 1976 and 1987. Recent books include: *Religious Rebels in the Punjab: The Social Vision of Untouchables* (Delhi: Ajanta Press, 1988), *Fighting Fair: Nonviolent Strategy for Resolving Everyday Conflicts* (San Francisco: Harper & Row, 1986); and, co-translated with John Stratton Hawley, *Songs of the Saints of India* (New York: Oxford University Press, 1988).

Ian J. Kerr

Associate Professor of History, University of Manitoba, Winnipeg. His researches on railways in India and colonial rule in the Punjab are recorded in: "Constructing Railways in India—An Estimate of the Numbers Employed, 1850-80," *Indian Economic and Social History Review* 20:3 (July-September 1983);"British Relationships with the Golden Temple, 1849-1890," *Indian Economic and Social History Review* 21:2 (April-June 1984);and "Working Class Protest in 19th Century India: Example of Railway Workers," *Economic and Political Weekly* 20:4 (January 26, 1985).

Karen Leonard

Professor of Anthropology, School of Social Sciences, University of California, Irvine. Her areas of scholarship are family, caste and social history of India and comparative Asian-American experience. Her Sikh-related publications include: "Pioneer Voices from California: Reflections on Race, Religion and Ethnicity," in N. Gerald Barrier and Verne A. Dusenbery, eds., *The Sikh Diaspora: Migration and the Experience beyond Punjab* (New Delhi: Manohar, forthcoming 1988); "The Pahkar Singh Murders: A Punjabi Response to California's Alien Land Law," *Amerasia Journal* 11:1 (spring-summer 1984); and "Punjabi Farmers and California's Alien Land Law," *Agricultural History,* 59:4 (Octaober 1985).

Darshan Singh Maini

Professor and Head of English (retired), Punjabi University, Patiala, is well versed in both English and Punjabi literature and an authority on American authors, especially Henry James and Walt Whitman. His books include *Henry James: The*

Indirect Vision (Bombay: Tata Press; and New York: McGraw-Hill, 1973), *Studies in Punjabi Poetry* (New Delhi: Vikas, 1979), *Cry, the Beloved Punjab* (Bombay: Siddarth, 1986), *The Portrait of a Lady: An Assessment*, and, as editor, *Sikhism* and *Guru Gobind Singh.*

W.H. McLeod

Professor of History, University of Otago, Dunedin, New Zealand, and Visiting Professor of Sikh History and Religion, University of Toronto, 1988, has published extensively in the field. Recent work includes: *The Chaupa Singh Rahit-nama* (Dunedin: University of Otago Press, 1987), *The Sikhs: History, Religion and Society* (New York: Columbia University Press, forthcoming), and *Who Is a Sikh? The Problem of Sikh Identity* (Oxford: Clarendon Press, forthcoming). His *Guru Nanak and the Sikh Religion* (Oxford: Clarendon Press, 1968) and *The Evolution of the Sikh Community* (London: Oxford University Press, 1975) are standard works.

Mohinder Singh

Director, Guru Nanak Foundation, New Delhi, and editor of the journal *Studies in Sikhism and Comparative Religion*, has done his main research on the Akali movemet in the early twentieth century. He has two books on the topic, *The Akali Movement* (Delhi: Macmillan, 1978) and *The Akali Struggle: A Retrospect* (New Delhi: Atlantic, 1988), as well as articles on a wider range of Sikh and other religious and historical topics.

Eleanor M. Nesbitt

Research Fellow in the Department of Arts Education, University of Warwick, Coventry, specializes in Sikhism in Britain and the transmission of Hindu culture in Britain. Her publications include "Sikhism" in R.C. Zaehner, ed., *The Hutchinson Encyclopedia of Living Faiths* (London: Hutchinson, 4th ed. 1988), entries on Sikhism in John Bowker, ed., *Oxford Companion to Religions of the World* (London: Oxford University Press, forthcoming), and, with Darshan Singh Tatla, *Sikhs in Britain: An Annotated Bibliography* (Coventry: Centre for Research in Ethnic Relations, Unviersity of Warwick, 1987).

Harjot S. Oberoi

occupies the Chair of Sikh and Punjabi Studies, University of British Columbia, Vancouver. His research in the social history of religious discourse in modern South Asia is reflected in "A World Reconstructed: Religion, Ritual and Community among the Sikhs, 1850-1909," Ph.D. dissertation, Australian National University, Canberra, 1987, and many published articles, including "A Historiographical Reconstruction of the Singh Sabha in Nineteenth Century Punjab," *Journal of Sikh Studies* 10 (1983).

Joseph T. O'Connell

Associate Professor of Religious Studies, St. Michael's College, University of Toronto, teaches and writes on the history of religion in South Asia, with special interest in its sixteenth- to twentieth-century devotional traditions, Hindu, Sikh, and Muslim. He was program chairman of the 1987 conference in Toronto from which this book derives. He has published "Bengali Religions," *Encyclopedia of Religion* (New York: Free Press, 1987), has edited *Bengal Vaiṣṇavism, Orientalism, Society and the Arts* (East Lansing: Asian Studies Center, Michigan State University, 1985), and compiled "Sikh Studies and Studies of Sikhs in Canada," *Studies in Sikhism and Comparative Religion* 5 (October 1986), and produced a number of articles and translations on religion in Bengal.

Willard G. Oxtoby

Professor of Religious Studies, Trinity College, University of Toronto, studies the historical interaction and present-day comparison of religious traditions. In a non-technical book, *The Meaning of Other Faiths* (Philadelphia: Westminster Press, 1983; also published in translation in Germany and Taiwan), he urges Christian readers to openness toward others in interfaith relations. His historical studies in Middle Eastern religions extend to India via Zoroastrianism; see his articles "Zoroastrians" and "Parsis" in *Abingdon Dictionary of Living Religions* (Nashville: Abingdon, 1981), and "Parsis," *Encyclopedia of Religion* (New York: Free Press, 1987).

Patwant Singh

Editor of *Design* (leading architectural magazine in India), founder of Kabliji Hospital near Delhi, and analyst of political and international affairs. He has authored *India and the Future of Asia* (New York: Knopf, 1966), *The Struggle for Power in Asia* (London: Hutchinson, 1971), and *A Plague o' Both Your Houses* (forthcoming), and has edited with Harji Malik *Punjab: The Fatal Miscalculation* (New Delhi: the editors, 1986).

Amarjit Singh Sethi

Associate Professor of Health Administration, University of Ottawa, edits the *Journal of Comparative Sociology and Religion* and is author of *Universal Sikhism* (Delhi: Vikas, 1972) and *Meditation as an Intervention in Stress Reactivity* (New York: AMS Press, forthcoming), and has edited, with D. Caro and H.J. Schuler *Strategic Management of Technostress in an Information Society* (Toronto: Hogrefe International, 1985). His work with the Ottawa Sikh Studies Circle has led to a number of papers on theoretical and practical aspects of Sikh spiritual exercises.

Christopher Shackle

Professor of Modern Languages of South Asia, School of Oriental and African Studies, University of London, is a scholar in Punjabi language and literature, classical Sikh studies, Urdu and Islam in South Asia. His publications include: *A Guru Nanak Glossary* (London: S.O.A.S.; and Vancouver: University of British Columbia, 1981), *An Introduction to the Sacred Language of the Sikhs* (London: S.O.A.S., 1983) and *The Sikhs* (London: Minority Rights Group, revised edition 1986).

Paul Wallace

Professor of Political Science, University of Missouri (Columbia), concentrates on South Asian studies, especially federalism and state politics, of Punjab in particular. He has edited *Region and Nation in India* (Oxford and Indian Book House, 1985), and, with Surendra Chopra, *Political Dynamics of Punjab* (Amritsar: Guru Nanak Dev University Press, 1981) and *Political Dynamics and Crisis in Punjab* (Amritsar: Guru Nanak Dev University Press, 1988).